THE SPORT AMERICANA®

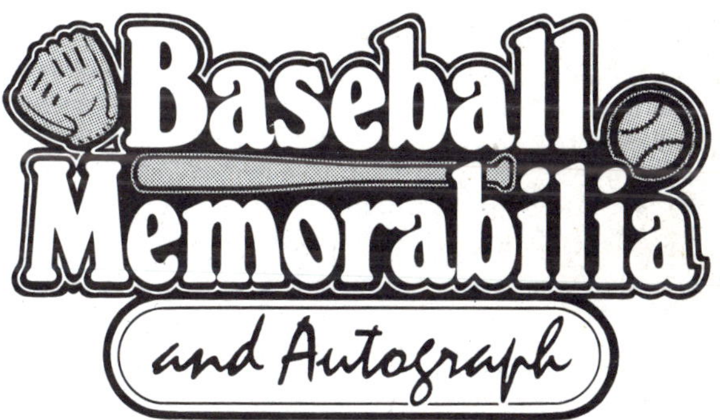

PRICE GUIDE

NO. 1

By
Dr. James Beckett
and Dennis W. Eckes

 Printed in the U.S.A., 1982. Co-published by Den's Collectors Den, P.O. Box 606, Laurel, Maryland 20707; and Edgewater Book Company, Inc., Box 586, Lakewood, Ohio 44107.

ISBN 0-937424-08-0

ACKNOWLEDGEMENTS

Because so many different collectibles are presented in this volume, we have relied heavily on the collectors whose individual specialties are elements of this book. With great pleasure we should like to thank, in alphabetical order, the following collectors who have provided major input to this book: Chris Benjamin, Rich Binder, Tom Collier, Mike Cramer, Bill & Diane Dodge, Herb Elk (posthumously), Gervise Ford, John Greenwald (cover art), Mike & Howie Gordon, Bill Haber, Barry Halper, Don Hazelwood, Lew Lipset, Don McPherson, Ray Medeiros, Jeff Morey (The Autograph Review), Jim Nicewander, Dick Perez & Frank Steele, Paul (Jack) Pollard, Tom Reid, Dick Reuss, Gavin Riley, Elwood Scharf, Jack Smalling, Howard (Smitty) Smith, John Spalding, Tom Wiley, Bill Zekus.

In addition, many other collectors have contributed to this effort with illustrative material, checklist verification and price input. We thank the following for their contributions: Ron Adelson, Mimi Alongi, Mike Anderson, Mike Aronstein, Buck Barker, Frank & Vivian Barning, Bob Bartosz, Jim & Geri Borgen, Jim Buchanan, Hal Bussey, Tony Carrafiell & family, Dwight Chapin, Norm Cohen, Steve Cooper, Pete D'Amico, Patricia Denny, Mike Dieguez, Dick Dobbins, Bill Dod, Bruce Dorskind, John Douglas, Mike Dyer, Dennis William Eckes, Nick Edson, Rich Egan, Dan Even, Doak Ewing, Bob Flynne, Joe Gerson, George Girsch, Larry Gladstone, Goody Goldfadden, Jeff Goldstein, Peter Golenboch, Dick Gordon, Bill Gradzewicz, Buz Grauer, Wayne Grove, Bill Hall, Hall's Nostalgia, Gary Hoover, Jim Horne, George Husby, Dave & Rosie Jones, Frank Keetz, Larry Kelley, Tom Koppa, Joe Kunigonis, Don Lepore, Irv Lerner, Robert Lifson, George Lyons, Dan Marcella, Paul Marchant, Jim McAllister, Tony McLaughlin, David McNaughton, Bob McVay, Joe Mulka, B.A. Murry, Ralph Nozaki, Bob Parker, David Paxson, Neal Payne, Joel & Deborah Perdelwitz, Tom Pfirrman, Andrew Pywowarczuk, Pat Quinn, Owen Ricker, Dave Ring, Randall Root, Herb Ross, Gordon Ruiter, John Rumierz, Dave Rumsey, John Scott, Joe Sencay, Mort Shanerman, Nick Shoff, Geoff Sindelar, Scott Snyder, Don Steinbach, Jerry Stone, Neal Sussman, Jerry (Fish) Taylor, Bob Thing, Wayne Varner, Sal Visali, John D. Wagner, Richard West, Bob Wilke, Doug Wood, Bill Zimpleman.

In any first edition, particularly one which contains a large amount of numerical and illustrative material, rather than simple text, the clerical and typographical requirements of the work are immense. We have had the good fortune of having competent and qualified clerical and typographic help throughout the preparation of this manuscript: Frank Darley, Denise Delss, "Slick" Phillips, Gary Parkman, Carollyn Roach, Margaret Schultz.

A special thank you to Patti Beckett for her moral support, patience and assistance in many of the time consuming functions associated with this book.

THE SPORT AMERICANA BASEBALL MEMORABILIA & AUTOGRAPH PRICE GUIDE

TABLE OF CONTENTS

INTRODUCTION

Baseball memorabilia is the general classification for all items related to the game of base from its inception to the present. It entails the plentiful and the unique, the old and the new, the costly and the inexpensive, the elaborate and the simple. It is impossible even to list all the types of baseball memorabilia that have been saved and treasured by baseball buffs for the last hundred or more years. What we shall attempt to accomplish in this volume is to list, describe and appraise those items of baseball memorabilia which are currently collected by a widespread portion of the sports collectibles hobby. Unfortunately, time and space requirements have precluded the inclusion of many collected items of baseball memorabilia. We apologize if your own specialty is not, in your opinion, given its just deserts in this first edition.

The memorabilia and autograph price guide is an outgrowth of the successful Sport Americana Baseball Card Price Guide, now in its fourth edition. One of the shortcomings of the baseball card price guide is that its covers but one portion, albeit by far the largest portion, of the sports collectibles hobby. We hope with this book to fill the information need of collectors of items other than popular baseball cards. The format of the baseball price guide had been maintained whenever possible for those items that lend themselves to it. Unfortunately, many popular items of baseball memorabilia are not consistent with the baseball card format. In these cases, a different format has been developed for each item—a format which is explained in the introduction to the section in which this item is contained.

The second major theme of this book, as the title implies, is autographs. Always a collectible by a small group of hobbyists, this phase of the hobby has grown by leaps and bounds over the past few years. While general price structures for baseball player autographs have been presented before (The Sport Americana Baseball Card Price Guide had a page on Hall of Famer autographs in its first three editions), never has a list so complete and covering so many items been presented. With the information in this volume and The Sport Americana Baseball Address List (1982 version to be released soon), which lists mailing addresses and obituary data of almost all players, an autograph collector has all he needs for a firm foundation in this hobby pursuit.

The material in this price guide has been presented in sections of various length, each containing items of a similar nature. In addition to descriptions and price data, the guide contains interesting data on the game of baseball itself. Team rosters of the most significant teams since the turn of the century are presented in the team autographed ball section. The World Series and All-star memorabilia section contains team, game, location and divisional championship information along with price data for associated memorabilia.

The authors would be interested in your comments concerning this work—what you liked, disliked; what you believe needs to be added, removed; if you found it easy from which to extract information, or if you found the format confusing. Time constraints prevent the authors from replying to your comments; however, all are read and considered.

Sincerely,
Jim Beckett
Denny Eckes

PACIFIC TRADING CARDS, INC. ★ SPORTS COLLECTORS STORE

NEW
Complete Set of Topps 1982 Baseball Cards
This year's set contains (792) Major League player's cards
Complete set
$18.50
(sets available late March)

NEW
Complete Set of Fleer 1982 Baseball Cards
The new Fleer set will contain (660) Major League player cards.
$14.50
(sets available in late February)

NEW
Complete Set 1982 Donruss Baseball Cards
Donruss will have (660) Major League player cards in their 1982 edition.
$14.50
(Sets available in February)
FREE! 63 piece puzzle card set with above purchase.

BASEBALL legends

60 card set features All-time Greats
Series I **$2.95** (30 cards)
Series II **$2.95** (30 cards)

1981 Topps Football
Complete set of 528 cards
$13.50

BASEBALL CARD CHECKLIST BOOK
Each copy contains checklists, information, and complete set value for: **$3.50**

- All Bowman Issues 1948-1955
- All Leaf Gum Issues 1948-1960
- All Fleer Issues 1959-61, 1963 and 1981-82
- All Topps Regular Issues 1951-1982
- All Kelloggs 3-D Issues 1970-1980
- All Post Cereal Issues 1961-1963
- Donruss 1981-82

1981-82 Topps Hockey or Basketball
198 Cards in each set
Each set $7.50

1980 TOPPS SUPERSTARS
Beautiful Full Color 5"x7" Photos
60 Card Set (Gray Backs)
$8.50

BASEBALL FEVER T-SHIRTS
All 26 teams available plus the Baseball Fever logo.
Youth Sizes S-M-L-XL
Adult Sizes S-M-L-XL
State your team and size.
Youth $7.95 Adult $8.95 ***CATCH IT!***

TOPPS FOOTBALL CARD SETS SPECIAL
1980, 1979, 1978
All 3 years only $34.95

10 DIFFERENT TOPPS CARDS
OUR CHOICE

1960	3.00	1963	2.50	1966	2.40
1961	2.80	1964	2.50	1967	2.40
1962	2.80	1965	2.50	1968	2.25

UNOPENED CASES
Ever thought of selling cards yourself? We offer the below unopened cases to get you started.
1981 Topps Football - 8,000 cards - $65.00 ppd
1980 Topps Football - 8,000 cards - $70.00 ppd
1981 Topps Basketball - 7,000 cards - $55.00 ppd
1978 Topps Basketball - 8,000 cards - $75.00 ppd

1981 TOPPS BASEBALL CREDIT CARDS
32 Major League Stars
Look and feel just like credit cards
Rose, Brett, Jackson, Lynn, etc.
$32.95

OTHER CARD SETS AVAILABLE

BASEBALL SETS

1981 Topps (726)	$20.50
1980 Topps (726)	26.50
1978 Topps (726)	37.50
1977 Topps All-Star Patches (73)	32.95
1979 Topps Bazooka Test Comics (33)	7.50
1978 O-Pee Chee Major League (242)	16.50
1981 Topps Premium 5x7 Photos (15) Brett, Rose, etc.	6.95
1981 Topps 5x7 Super Star Photos (18) LA Dodgers & Angels	2.95
1982 Donruss 63-piece Puzzle Set	3.95
1981 Donruss First Issue ever (605)	22.50
1981 Fleer First Issue ever (660)	22.50
1981 Topps/Coke Stars - scarce set (132)	14.95
1980 Baseball Immortals (173)	12.95
1974 Kelloggs 3-D Baseball (54)	32.50
1980 300-400-500 Home Run Club (30)	3.95
1977 Pacific Coast League (96)	14.50
1978 Pacific Coast League (120)	16.50
1975 KOMO Tacoma Twins (21) Special	1.95
1976 Motorola Old-Timers (11)	4.95
1976 Coke Phoenix Giants (24) color	3.95
1977 7UP Hawaii Islanders (24) Color	3.95

FOOTBALL SETS

1980 Topps (528)	14.50
1979 Topps (528)	15.50
1978 Topps (528)	15.50
1980 Topps 5x7 SuperStars	8.50
1979 Fleer Action Cards (69)	5.50
1980 Fleer Action Cards (70)	4.50
1970 Kelloggs 3-D Stars (60)	19.50
1976 Wonder Bread NFL Stars (24)	3.95
1976 Crane Chip NFL Discs (30)	3.95

BASKETBALL SETS

1980-81 Topps (264)	5.50
1979-80 Topps (132)	6.50
1978-79 Topps (132)	8.50
1977-78 Topps (132)	10.50
1976-77 Topps (132)	12.50

HOCKEY SETS

1980-81 Topps (264)	6.50
1979-80 Topps (264)	8.50
1978-79 Topps (264)	10.50
1977-78 Topps (264)	12.00
1978-79 O-Pee Chee NHL (396)	14.00
1977-78 O-Pee Chee WHA (66)	5.25
1977-78 O-Pee Chee Photos (22)	1.95
1977-78 McDonald's Pitts Penguins (18) Special	1.95

1979 or 1981 O-Pee Chee Canadian Baseball

374 Major League Players — Educational Set.
Backs are French and English Language.
Many different poses from the Topps set.
Each set $12.50

1977 TOPPS STAR WARS "The Set of the Decade" All 330 cards
$14.95

1981 Drakes Big Hitters
Beautiful 33 card set - all the best hitters in the American League and National League.
Complete set $11.95

VINYL SHEETS AND ALBUMS
Protect your cards. 6 sizes to choose from.
S-9 Pocket - holds 1957 to present, Topps, Fleer, etc.
S-8 Pocket - holds 1952-57 Topps & Bowmans
S-4 Pocket - holds postcards
S-2 Pocket - holds 5x7 photos
S-10 Pocket - holds 8x10 photos
Y-1 Pocket - 9x11 Yearbook cover
Great for legal size papers.

YOUR CHOICE OF SIZES

10-24	20¢ each
25-49	19¢ each
50-249	18¢ each
250-499	16¢ each
500-1000	15¢ each

Dealer inquiries invited on larger quantities
SPECIAL - 100 S-8 or S-9 sheets
$16.00

1981 Topps Scratch-offs
108 players in the set, 3 players per card.
You can play baseball with this unique set.
Complete set $3.95

Official Major League Souvenir Helmets

All Major League teams available
State your team(s)
$3.50 Each

ALBUMS
Brown vinyl lettered in gold
Your choice of lettering
☐ Baseball Card Album
☐ Card Album
☐ Sports Card Album
☐ Football Card Album
☐ Blank - no lettering
☐ Star Wars collection
Each $4.50
4 for $15.95

SPECIALS
1 Album (your choice) and 50 S-9 Vinyl Sheets **$11.95**
2 or more specials $10.95 each

BASEBALL DISCS
1976 ROUND BASEBALL CARDS
70 cards in set, all Major League stars.
Includes Jackson, Bench, Rose, Carew, Sutton, many more. COMPLETE SET
SPECIAL **$7.50**

BASEBALL HOLDER
$2.50 Each
2 for $4.00

PRO-SPORTS PENNANTS
Major League Baseball – all teams in stock
NFL Football – all teams in stock
NBA Basketball – all teams in stock
NHL Hockey – all teams in stock
NASL Soccer – all teams in stock
"10 different your choice
$14.95
State your sport and team.
$2.00 Each

REPLICA MAJOR LEAGUE BASEBALL UNIFORM TOPS
All Teams Available
List your team and size
Youth Sizes – S-M-L-XL **$9.95**
Adult Sizes – S-M-L-XL **$11.95**

"THE TRADING CARD VENDOR"
Price list and Hobby Magazine issued 4 times a year
$1.00 or FREE with any order

Store Hours: Mon.-Sat. 9 to 8 p.m.

SEND TO:
Pacific Trading Cards, Inc.
7505 Olympic View Dr. Dept. MPG
Edmonds, WA 98020
Phone (206) 774-8473

Check or money order only. Washington residents add 6.3% sales tax. Canadian and overseas orders add 25% to total. U.S. FUNDS ONLY. Prices subject to change without notice. All orders add shipping as follows:

$.01 to $6.00 add $1.50	$19.01 to $29.00 add $2.50
$6.01 to $19.00 add $2.00	$29.01 and over add $3.00

Master Card and VISA accepted

ABOUT THIS PRICE GUIDE

Over the past 10 years, there have been several attempts to present baseball memorabilia — descriptions, prices and illustrative material —in a coherent and usable form. John Douglas' "Sport Memoribilia," issued in 1975, is a well-written, well-presented, and well-illustrated work through that time period; however, many baseball memorabilia items are omitted, pricing data is absent, and the format of the book makes specific information somewhat difficult to extract. Bert Sugar's "Sports Collectors Bible" is an excellent volume which provides similar material to that contained in this book. To be sure, until this volume, the Sports Collectors Bible was the best source of information on baseball memorabilia in existence. Unfortunately, the book suffers from lack of illustrative material, sketchy pricing data, and cumbersomeness. Many other pamphlets and catalogues have been issued on one or two items of baseball memorabilia. Tom Collier issued excellent handbooks on baseball pins and baseball player postcards, both of which have formed the basis for sections in this volume. Elwood Scharf's work on exhibits, which has appeared in several of the hobby papers over the past few years, is also an example of excellent work in a particular area. Chris Benjamin's "Illustrated Wrapper Checklist" provides much of the data in this book but omits the prices. Other examples of item-specific work can be found.

When the authors decided to develop a baseball memorabilia price guide, we thought the project would require a duration of no more than three or four months. Unfortunately, this proved not to be the case. After over a year working on this volume, a year which included many alterations, deletions, additions, and changes in concepts, we believe this volume provides an excellent base for most popular and collected baseball memorabilia items. The initial theme of baseball memorabilia has been expanded to include autographs because player signatures have become one of the most popular and collected items of baseball memorabilia. This first edition is not all-inclusive. To attempt such an endeavor which would result in an encyclopedic volume which because of sheer size, would probably not be released for years. Subsequent editions will, of course, include more material.

If you read the table of contents, you can see that information in about 15 major categories of baseball memorabilia is provided in this book. Autographs are highlighted in the Autographs section, the Team Autograph Ball section, and the Baseball Commemorative Envelope part of the Recent Memorabilia section. Hall of Fame players and superstars are highlighted in all of the autograph sections as autographs of these players are those most sought after and popular. The Coins and Pins section is intended to provide information on the most popular of these issues. Coins and pins are one of the areas that data has been requested by a large number of readers of The Sport Americana Baseball Card Price Guide. The Exhibits section relies heavily on the exploratory work of Elwood Scharf and illustrative material provided by Jack Pollard.

In the four editions of the baseball price guide, many sets have been omitted because (a) they are not popular or widely collected or (b) they feature non-major league subjects. Several of these obscure and/or minor league card sets have been included here. Illustrations and set descriptions for the two largest minor league T card issues, Old Mills and Obaks, have been included; however, becuase of space availability, complete checklists have been omitted and only general price information has been provided. The Postcard section relies heavily on Tom Collier's "Postcard Handbook," which Tom was generous enough to update for us, and features baseball player postcards only. Stadium postcards and team issue postcards have not been included because of sheer volume and incomplete checklist data. The baseball card premiums and other large baseball player cards, originally appearing in the baseball card price guide, have been "moved" to this volume because of both space limitations in the baseball card price guide and because that these cards are not standard-sized baseball cards. The Publications section of this book presents guides, magazines, and annuals from the mid-1800's through 1981.

The authors do not believe that such a volume as this would be complete without the inclusion of some of the recent work done in the baseball memorabilia area, work which doubtlessly will be the collected material of the future. We have selected from the large amount of material available five items which the authors believe both well done and significant. The Gateway Stamp Company baseball commemorative envelope series has been listed in its entirety, thanks to data provided by Tom Wiley of Gateway. These issues fit well into the autograph theme of this book as the addition of player autographs to these envelopes enhances their appearance, desirability and value. The Perez-Steele Galleries Hall of Fame postcard series has been included not because it has been sanctioned by the Hall of Fame, not because it is in a postcard format, but for one reason only—it is well done; very, very well done. Two quasi-collector baseball card sets have been included. The Sport Americana Diamond Stars set and the TCMA 1952 Bowman Extension set are both original sets produced from artwork of the 1930's and 1950's respectively. The TCMA 1960's Series II set, which rounds out the Recent Memorabilia section, is included as an example of the work of TCMA, who has been one of the innovators, and perhaps, the most quality conscious of the collector card issuers over the past 10 years. TCMA reprints most of their material; hence, prices will seldom increase on their sets. However, price stability should not detract from the quality of their issues.

The Team Autograph Ball section not only provides an interesting value structure for autographs, but provides an immense amount of information in the form of rosters, injury data, and trade data on most of the successful baseball teams of this century. Topps paper inserts, stamps, and test issues have been included because of their popularity and because they do not logically belong in the baseball card price guide, although many were issued as inserts with baseball cards. The authors have made an attempt to omit Topps insert issues which are so obscure and limited in distribution as to provide novelty but not collectibility characteristics. We thank Mike Gordon for providing much of the information in this section. Resident Sport Americana wrapper expert Chris Benjamin provided most of the pricing material and the article on wrappers. We have no doubt that this is the most complete and descriptive work ever provided on baseball wrappers.

The Yearbook, Program, World Series and All-Star section provides, by year, information on yearbooks, programs, and memorabilia associated with the two most significant yearly baseball events. Press pins, commemorative bat, and ticket stub information is presented in this section.

Over four years ago, the authors developed the standard Sport Americana format to provide the collector with an easy-to-use method of describing, illustrating, and pricing baseball cards. This format has also proved to be quite flexible in describing other items of memorabilia. When possible, the standard Sport Americana format, described below, is used in this volume. Unfortunately, flexible though it be, the standard Sport Americana format does not lend itself to all baseball memorabilia. We direct your attention to the introductory material for the particular sections in this book when format compatable with the standard Sport Americana format is lacking and another format had to be developed.

STANDARD SPORT AMERICANA FORMAT

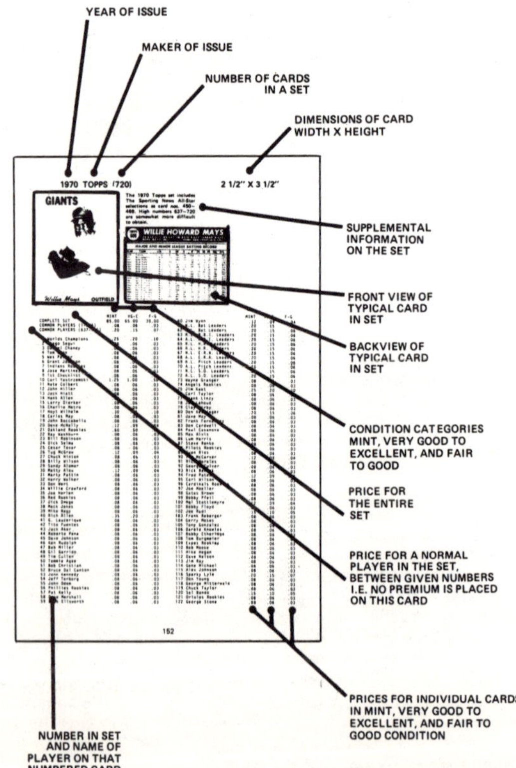

AUTOGRAPHS

The alphabetical list below presents autograph values for all members of the Baseball Hall of Fame and most of the other thousands of major league baseball players of the 20th century. The base value given is the value of the player's signature on a 3" X 5" card; signatures on other media would be valued higher or lower, e.g., cut signatures would be worth less and signed photos, gum cards, and personal letters would be worth more. Other value considerations include: (1) value given is for a clear ink signature, pencil would be worth 25% to 50% less depending on the propensity of the pencil to smear or fade; (2) smearing or fading also lessens the value of ink signatures; (3) personalized signatures are less desirable than non-personalized signatures, except to the original recipient; (4) autographs purchased in quantity (such as in an autograph book) can usually be obtained with a substantial discount on the total sum of the individual autograph values; (5) for popular players (not necessarily difficult autographs), the incremental value of the player's autograph on a Topps card is also given, a value which could also serve as the value of an autographed photo, snapshot, or postcard of the player; (6) autographed ball prices for Hall of Famers refer to balls for which that player is the ONLY player on the ball.

The reasons why every autograph in the list below is not ".15" are not complex. Autograph values increase because of the following factors: (1) death, for an obvious reason, the supply is cut off; (2) popularity, i.e., demand for the autograph; (3) difficulty in obtaining the signature based on the player's prerogative to sign or not to sign (which more and more current players are exercising in the negative because of the frequent rudeness of many autograph seekers); (4) players with unknown addresses; the very best source of major league player mailing addresses is the Smalling and Eckes Sport Americana Baseball Address List (the 1982 edition of which is due to be released on the heels of this book); in most cases, if Jack Smalling does not list an ex-player's address, then the player's autograph value goes up as the many collectors using Smalling's book no longer have accessibilty to that ex-player's autograph.

Players are listed in alphabetical order for easy reference. Where ambiguities exist in the identity of the player, clarification is given in the form of (a) middle names, initials, or nicknames, (b) dates (years) that the player played in the major leagues, and finally, (c) the player's deceased date if applicable.

As much autograph collector activity centers around signatures of Hall of Fame members, these players are indicated on the list by the following designation "**** h * o * f ****." In addition, the Hall of Fame sanctioned postcards of the Perez-Steele Galleries (see recent memorabilia section) have been featured for every Hall of Famer inductee through 1981.

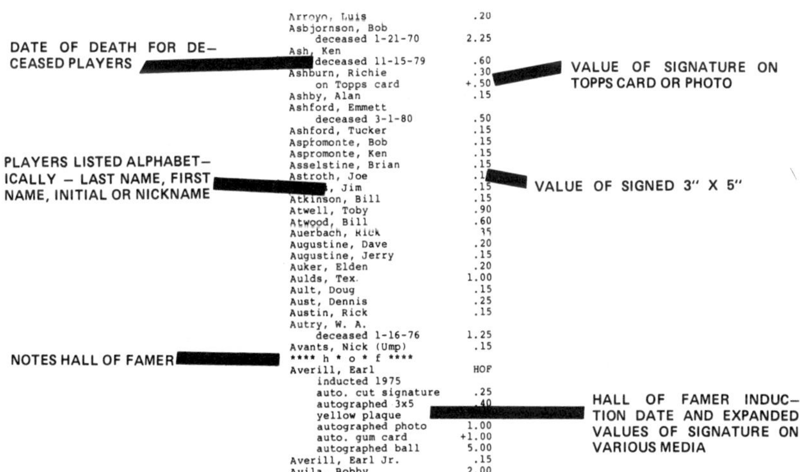

Name	Price
**** h * o * f ****	
Aaron, Hank	HOF
inducted 1982	
"Best Wishes" stamp	.15
autographed cut	2.00
signed 3x5	6.00
signed photo	8.00
on Topps card	+10.00
autographed ball	15.00
Aaron, Tommie	.15
Aase, Don	.15
Abbott, Glenn	.15
Aber, Al	.15
Abernathie, Bill	.15
Abernathy, Ted	.25
Abernathy, Virgil Woodrow	.15
Aberson, Cliff (47-49)	
deceased 6-23-73	2.00
Abrams, Cal	.15
Abrams, George	.15
Abreu, Joe	.60
Acker, Tom	.15
Acosta, Cy	.35
Acosta, Ed	.35
Adair, Bill	.15
Adair, Jimmie	.25
Adair, Kenneth Jerry	.15
Adams, Ace T.	.15
Adams, Bobby H. (46-59)	.15
Adams, C.B. "Babe"	
deceased 7-27-68	2.50
Adams, C.D. "Red"	.15
Adams, Earl J. "Sparky"	.30
Adams, Elvin C. "Buster"	3.00
Adams, Glenn	.15
Adams, Herb	.30
Adams, Rich L.	.35
Adams, Robert A.	
deceased 3-6-70	2.00
Adams, Spencer	
deceased 11-25-70	2.00
Adamson, Mike	.50
Adcock, Joe	.20
Addis, Bob	.15
Adkins, Dewey	1.50
Agee, Tommie	.75
Agganis, Harry (54)	
deceased 6-27-55	25.00
on '55 Topps card	+100.00
Agler, Joe	
deceased 4-26-71	2.00
Aguirre, Hank	.25
Aikens, Willie Mays	.20
on Topps card	+.30
Ainge, Danny	.20
on gum card	+.30
Ainsmith, Ed W. (10-24)	.50
Aiton, George Wilson	
deceased 8-16-76	1.25
Aker, Jack	.15
Albanese, Joseph F.	.25
Albosta, Ed	1.75
Albright, John H.	.25
Albury, Vic	.15
Alcock, John Forbes	
deceased 1-30-73	1.50
Alderson, Dale	.15
Aldridge, Vic	
deceased 4-17-73	1.50
Aleno, Chuck	.15
Alexander, D. Dale (29-33)	
deceased 3-2-79	.65
Alexander, Doyle	.30
stamped signature	.03
Alexander, Gary	.15
**** h * o * f ****	
Alexander, Grover C.	HOF
deceased 11-4-50	
inducted 1938	
auto. cut signature	35.00
autographed 3x5	60.00
b & w plaque	90.00
autographed photo	90.00
auto. gum card	+80.00
autographed ball •	90.00
Alexander, Hugh	.15
Alexander, Matt	.20
Allard, Brian	.15
Allen, Bernie	.15
Allen, Bob	.25
Allen, Dick	2.50
on Topps card	+4.00
Allen, Ethan	.30
Allen, Hank (66-73)	.25
Allen, H.T. "Pug"	.15
Allen, J.M.	
deceased 9-24-67	3.50
Allen, John T. (32-44)	
deceased 3-29-59	8.00
Allen, Lloyd	.15
Allen, Neil	.20
Allenson, Gary	.15
Alley, Len "Gene"	.15
Allietta, Bob	.15
Allison, Bob	.20
Almada, Mike	1.00
Almon, Bill	.15
Aloma, Luis	3.00
Alomar, Sandy	.35
Alou, Felipe	.50
Alou, Jesus	.35
Alou, Matty	.90
Alston, Dell	.15
Alston, Walt	.20
Altenburg, Jesse H.	
deceased 3-12-73	1.50
Altman, George	.45
Altobelli, Joe	.15
Alusik, George	.15
Alvarado, Luis	.25
Alvarez, Ossie	1.50
Alvis, Roy M. "Max"	.15
Alyea, Brant	.15
Amalfitano, Joe	.15
Amaro, Ruben	.15
Amoros, Sandy	1.25
Anderson, Alf	.15
Anderson, Andy	.45
Anderson, Arnold	
deceased 8-7-72	1.75
Anderson, Bob	.20
Anderson, Craig	.15
Anderson, Dwain	.15
Anderson, Ferrell J.	
deceased 3-12-78	.90
Anderson, George (Sparky)	.25
Anderson, Hal	
deceased 5-1-74	1.25
Anderson, Harry W.	.15
Anderson, Jim	.15
Anderson, Larry	.15
Anderson, Mike	.15
Anderson, Walter C. (17,19)	.40
Andre, John E.	
deceased 11-25-76	2.00
Andres, Ernie	.35
Andrew, Kim	.15
Andrews, Elbert	.15
Andrews, Herb	.15
Andrews, Hub	.50
Andrews, Ivy Paul (31-38)	
deceased 11-23-70	2.00
Andrews, Mike	.15
Andrews, Nathan	.15
Andrews, Rob	.15
Andrews, Stanley J.	.25
Andrews, William M.	.15
Angelini, Norm	.15
Ankenman, Fred N.	.30

Name	Price
**** h * o * f ****	
Anson, Cap	HOF
deceased 4-14-22	
inducted 1939	
auto. cut signature	200.00
autographed 3x5	300.00
autographed photo	400.00
auto. card	+300.00
autographed ball	500.00

Name	Price
Anthony, Merlyn (Ump)	.15
Antonelli, John A. (48-61)	.15
Antonelli, John L. (44-45)	.15
Antonello, Bill	.15
Aparicio, Luis	1.50
on Topps card	+3.00
Apodaca, Bob	.15
Appleton, Peter W.	
deceased 1-18-74	1.25
**** h * o * f ****	
Appling, Luke	HOF
inducted 1964	
auto. cut signature	.25
autographed 3x5	.40
yellow plaque	1.50
autographed photo	1.00
auto. gum card	+1.00
autographed ball	5.00

Name	Price
Aragon, Angel	.20
Archer, Jim	.15
Archie, George	.15
Arcia, Jose	3.00
Arft, Hank	.20
Arlin, Steve	.15
Armas, Tony	.20
on Topps card	+.30
Armbrister, Ed	.15
Armstrong, George	.50
Arnold, Chris	.15

Arnovich, Morris (36-46)	
deceased 7-20-59	8.00
Arroyo, Fernando	.15
Arroyo, Luis	.20
Asbjornson, Bob	
deceased 1-21-70	2.25
Ash, Ken	
deceased 11-15-79	.60
Ashburn, Richie	.30
on Topps card	+.50
Ashby, Alan	.15
Ashford, Emmett	
deceased 3-1-80	.50
Ashford, Tucker	.15
Aspromonte, Bob	.15
Aspromonte, Ken	.15
Asselstine, Brian	.15
Astroth, Joe	.15
Atkins, Jim	.15
Atkinson, Bill	.15
Atwell, Toby	.90
Atwood, Bill	.60
Auerbach, Rick	.35
Augustine, Dave	.20
Augustine, Jerry	.15
Auker, Elden	.20
Aulds, Tex	1.00
Ault, Doug	.15
Aust, Dennis	.25
Austin, Rick	.15
Autry, W. A.	
deceased 1-16-76	1.25
Avants, Nick (Ump)	.15
**** h * o * f ****	
Averill, Earl	HOF
inducted 1975	
auto. cut signature	.25
autographed 3x5	.40
yellow plaque	2.00
autographed photo	1.00
auto. gum card	+1.00
autographed ball	5.00

Averill, Earl Jr.	.15
Avila, Bobby	2.00
Avrea, Jim	1.00
Ayers, Bill	1.50
Aylward, Dick	.15
Azcue, Joe	.20

Babcock, Bob	.15
Babe, Loren	.15
Babich, John	.20
Backman, Lester	
deceased 11-8-75	1.10
Bacsik, Mike	.15
Baczewski, Fred J.	
deceased 11-14-76	2.25
Bader, King	
deceased 6-2-73	1.50
Badgro, Johnny	.15
Bagby, Jim Sr.	
deceased 7-28-54	10.00
Bagby, Jim Jr.	.20
Bagwell, William	
deceased 10-5-76	1.00
Bahnsen, Stan	.15
Bailey, A. E. "Gene"	
deceased 11-14-73	1.50
Bailey, Bob	.45
Bailey, Ed	.15
Bailey, Steve	.15
Bailor, Bob	.15
Bain, Loren	.15
Baines, Harold	.25
on gum card	+.35
Bair, Doug	.15
Baird, Al	
deceased 11-27-76	1.00
Baker, Bill	.15
Baker, Chuck	.15
Baker, Delmar David	
deceased 9-11-73	1.50
Baker, Dusty	.30
on Topps card	+.50
Baker, Floyd	.20
Baker, Frank J. (69)	.20
Baker, Frank W. (70-74)	.35
Baker, Gene	.30
**** h * o * f ****	
Baker, Home Run	HOF
inducted 1957	
deceased 6-28-63	
auto. cut signature	15.00
autographed 3x5	25.00
b & w plaque	30.00
autographed photo	30.00
auto. gum card	+20.00
autographed ball	35.00

Baker, Neal	.15
Balas, Mitchell	.15
Balaz, John	.15
Balcena, Bobby	.15
Baldschun, Jack	.15
Baldwin, Dave	.15
Baldwin, Reggie	.15
Baldwin, Rick	.15
Bales, Lee	.15
Ballanfant, Lee (Ump)	.25
Balsamo, Tony	.15
Bamberger, George	.20
**** h * o * f ****	
Bancroft, Dave	HOF
inducted 1971	
deceased 10-9-72	
auto. cut signature	1.00
autographed 3x5	3.00
yellow plaque	10.00
autographed photo	5.00
auto. gum card	+5.00
autographed ball	15.00
Bando, Sal	.30
on Topps card	+.50
Bane, Eddie	.15
Bankhead, Dan	
deceased 5-2-76	5.00
**** h * o * f ****	
Banks, Ernie	HOF
inducted 1977	
auto. cut signature	.75
autographed 3x5	1.50
yellow plaque	3.00
autographed photo	3.00
auto. gum card	+4.00
autographed ball	10.00
Bankston, W.E.	
deceased 2-26-70	2.00
Bannister, Alan	.15
Bannister, Floyd	.15
Banta, Jack	.15
Barbeau, Wm. J.	
deceased 9-10-69	2.50
Barbee, Dave	.60
Barber, Steve	.40
Barber, Turner	
deceased 10-20-68	3.00
Barbieri, Jim	.15
Barclay, Curt	.15
Bare, Ray	.15
Barker, Len	.20
on gum card	+.30
Barker, Ray	.15
Barlick, Al (Ump)	.15
Barlow, Mike	.15
Barmes, Bruce	.15
Barna, Babe	
deceased 5-18-72	1.50
Barnabe, Charles	
deceased 8-16-77	1.00
Barnes, John F.	.15
Barnes, Robert	.15
Barnes, Sammy	
deceased 2-19-81	.50
Barnett, Larry (Ump)	.15
Barney, Rex	1.50
Barnhart, Clyde	
deceased 1-21-80	.60
Barnhart, Edgar	.15
Barnhart, Rex	1.50
Barnicle, Barn	1.00
Barone, Dick	.15
Barr, Jim	.15
Barr, Steve	.15
Barragon, Cuno	.15
Barrett, Charles "Red"	.20
Barrett, John	
deceased 8-17-74	1.25
Barron, Dave	.50

**** h * o * f ****	
Barrow, Ed	HOF
inducted 1953	
deceased 12-15-53	
auto. cut signature	20.00
autographed 3x5	30.00
autographed photo	40.00
auto. gum card	+50.00
autographed ball	50.00

Barry, Hardin	
deceased 11-5-69	2.25
Bartell, Dick	.65
Bartirome, Tony	.15
Bartley, Boyd	1.00
Bartling, Irving	
deceased 6-12-73	1.50
Barton, Bob	.15
Bartosch, Dave	.60
Basgall, Monte	.15
Bashore, Walt	.45
Basinski, Eddie	.20
Bass, Norm	.25
Bassler, John	
deceased 6-29-79	.65
Batchelder, Joseph	.15
Bates, Buddy	.15
Bates, Charlie	1.50
Bates, Del	.20
Bateman, John	.20
Batten, George	
deceased 8-4-72	1.50
Batts, Matt	.15
Bauer, Hank	.25
on Topps card	+.35
Baumer, Jim	.45
Baumann, Frank	.15
Baumgartner, Ross	.15
Baumholtz, Frank	.15
Bavasi, Buzzie (Exec.)	.25
Baxes, D.S. "Jim"	.15
Baxes, Mike	.35
Baylor, Don	.40
on Topps card	+.75
Bayne, Bill	.15
Beall, Bob	.15
Beamon, Charles Jr.	.35
Bean, Bel	.20
Beard, Mike	.15
Beard, Ralph	.15
Beard, Ted	.15
Bearden, Gene	1.00
Beare, Gary	.15
Bearnarth, Larry	.15
Beauchamp, Jim	.15
Beazley, Johnny	.15
Beck, Rich	.25
Beck, Walter	.25
Beck, Zinn B.	.50
Becker, Heinz	.15
Becker, Joe	.15
Beckert, Glenn	.20
**** h * o * f ****	
Beckley, Jake	HOF
deceased 6-25-18	
inducted 1971	
auto. cut signature	200.00
autographed 3x5	300.00
autographed photo	400.00
auto. gum card	+300.00
autographed ball	500.00

Beckman, James	.25
Becquer, Julio	.40
Bedell, Howie	.15
Beeler, Jodie	1.50
Beene, Fred	.15
Beers, Clarence	.50
Beggs, Joe	.15
Behrman, Hank	7.00
Bejma, Ollie	.35
Belanger, Mark	.20
Belardi, Wayne	.50
Belinski, Bo	.25
on Topps card	+.35
Bell, Buddy	.30
on Topps card	+.50
Bell, Gary	.25
Bell, Gus	2.50
**** h * o * f ****	
Bell, James "Cool Papa"	HOF
inducted 1974	
auto. cut signature	1.00
autographed 3x5	2.00
yellow plaque	3.00
autographed photo	3.00
auto. gum card	+2.00
autographed ball	10.00

Bell, Jerry	.15
Bell, Kevin	.15
Bell, Les	.30
Bell, Roy C. "Beau"	
deceased 9-14-77	1.00
Belloir, Rob	.15
Bench, Johnny	
stamped	.10
signed 3x5	3.50
on Topps card	+7.00

**** h * o * f ****	
Bender, Chief	HOF
inducted 1953	
deceased 5-22-54	
auto. cut signature	25.00
autographed 3x5	40.00
autographed photo	50.00
auto. gum card	+50.00
autographed ball	75.00

Benedict, Bruce	.15
Benes, Joe	.15
Benge, Ray	.15
Bengough, Bennie	
deceased 12-22-68	3.25
Beniquez, Juan	.30
Benjamin, Stan	.20
Bennett, Dave	.15
Bennett, Dennis	.15
Bennett, Joe	.15
Benson, Allen	.45
Benson, Vern	.15
Benton, J. Al	
deceased 4-14-68	5.00
Berardino, John (sic)	.60
Beradino, John	.20
Berberet, Lou	.15
Berenger, Carroll	.15
Berenyi, Bruce	.15
Berg, Morris (23-39)	
deceased 5-29-72	7.50
Bergamo, Augie	
deceased 8-19-74	1.25
Berger, Louis "Boze"	.15
Berger, Wally	.20
Bergman, Dave	.15
Berly, John	
deceased 6-26-77	1.00
Berman, Robert	.15
Bernier, Carlos	5.00
Bero, Johnny	.50
Berra, Dale	.45

Name	Value
**** h * o * f ****	
Berra, Yogi	HOF
inducted 1972	
auto. cut signature	.50
autographed 3x5	1.50
yellow plaque	3.00
autographed photo	2.50
auto. gum card	+2.50
autographed ball	10.00
Berres, Ray	.15
Berry, Bill	.20
Berry, Charles	
deceased 9-6-72	1.60
Berry, Claude	
deceased 2-1-74	1.40
Berry, J. Howard Jr.	
deceased 4-29-76	1.10
Berry, Ken	.15
Berry, Neil	.50
Bertaina, Frank	.25
Bertell, Dick	.15
Bertoia, Reno	.30
Bertrand, R.	.35
Besana, Fred	.15
Bessent, Don	.50
Betcher, Frank	.15
Betcher, Ralph (Ump)	.15
Bethea, Bill	.35
Bethke, Jim	.35
Bettencourt, Larry	
deceased 9-15-78	.90
Betts, Huck	.15
Bevacqua, Kurt	.15
Bevan, Harold Joseph	
deceased 10-5-68	6.00
Bevans, Bill	.25
Biasetti, Hank	.75
Bibby, Jim	.20
Bickford, Vern	
deceased 5-8-60	10.00
Bickman, Ed	.15
Bicknell, Charles	.50
Bigbee, Carson Lee	
deceased 10-17-64	6.00
Biittner, Larry	.15
Bilbrey, Jim	.60
Bildilli, Emil (37-41)	
deceased 9-16-46	15.00
Bilko, Stephen Thomas	
deceased 3-7-78	2.00
Billingham, Jack	.15
Billings, John A.	.30
Billings, Rich	.15
Binks, George	.15
Bird, Doug	.15
Bird, James E.	
deceased 3-23-72	1.75
Birkhofer, Ralph	
deceased 3-16-71	2.25
Birrer, Babe	.15
Bishop, Charlie	.15
Bishop, Lloyd	
deceased 6-17-68	3.00
Bishop, Max	
deceased 2-4-62	8.00
Bisland, R. M.	
deceased 1-11-73	1.50
Bissonette, Del	
deceased 6-9-72	1.60
Bivin, Jim	.60
Black, Joe	.35
on Topps card	+.75
Blackaby, Ethan	.15
Blackburn, Ron	.15
Blackburn, Wayne	.15
Blackburne, Russell A.	
deceased 2-29-68	3.00
Blackerby, George	.50
Blackwell, Ewell	.25
Blackwell, Tim	.15
Blades, F. Ray	
deceased 5-18-79	.70
Bladt, Rich	.15
Blaeholder, George F.	
deceased 12-29-47	15.00
Blair, Clarence	.15
Blair, Dennis	.15
Blair, Louis N. "Buddy"	.15
Blair, Paul	.25
on Topps card	+.40
Blake, Eddie	.15
Blake, Fred	.15
Blakely, Linc	
deceased 9-28-76	1.00
Blanchard, John	.40
on Topps card	+.80

Name	Value
Blanco, Gilbert H.	.30
Blanco, Ossie	2.00
Blandford, Fred	.15
Blankenship, Homer	
deceased 6-22-74	1.30
Blanks, Larvell	.20
Blanton, Darrell	
deceased 9-13-45	15.00
Blasingame, Don	.20
Blass, Steve	.15
Blateric, Steve	.15
Blatnik, Johnny	.15
Blattner, Bud	.15
Blaylock, Gary	.15
Blaylock, Marv	1.00
Blefary, Curt	.50
Blemker, Ray	.15
Blethen, C. W.	
deceased 4-11-73	1.50
Block, Cy	.15
Blomberg, Ron	.20
Bloodworth, Jimmy	.15
Bloomfield, Jack	.15
Blue, Vida	.30
on Topps card	+.60
Blue, Lu (21-33)	
deceased 7-28-58	9.00
Bluege, Ossie	.15
Bluege, Otto	
deceased 6-28-77	1.10
Blyleven, Bert	.30
on Topps card	+.50
Boccabella, John	.15
Bocek, Milt	.15
Bochte, Bruce	.15
Bochy, Bruce	.15
Bockman, Eddie	.15
Bodle, W.F.	.15
Boehmer, Len	.15
Boerner, Larry	
deceased 10-16-69	2.25
Bogart, John	.15
Boggs, Tommy	.15
Bohne, Sam	
deceased 5-23-77	1.00
Boisclair, Bruce	.15
Boken, Bob	.15
Bokins, Joe	.15
Bokleman, Dick	.15
Bolger, Jim	.15
Bolin, Bob	.15
Bolling, Frank	.15
Bolling, John "Jack"	1.00
Bolling, Milt	.15
Bollo, Greg	.20
Bollweg, Don	.15
Bolton, Cliff	
deceased 4-21-79	1.50
Bond, Walt	
deceased 9-14-67	8.00
Bonds, Bobby	.50
on Topps card	+1.00
Bongiovani, Nino	.15
Bonham, Bill	.15
Bonnell, Barry	.15
Bonura, Zeke	.20
Bool, Albert	1.00
Boone, Bob	.20
Boone, Lute J.	.30
Boone, Ray	.15
Boozer, John	.15
Borbon, Pedro	.50
Bordagaray, Stan	.15
Bordi, Dick	.15
Bordley, Bill	.20
Borgmann, Glenn	.15
Bork, Frank	.15
Borkowski, Bob	.15
Borland, Tom	.15
Borom, Red	.15
Boros, Steve	.15
Borowy, Hank	.15
Bosch, Don	.15
Bosetti, Rick	.15
Bosley, Thad	.15
Bosman, Dick	.15
Bostock, Lyman	
deceased 9-24-78	3.50
on Topps card	+5.00
on '78 Topps card	+10.00
Boswell, Dave	.15
Boswell, Ken	.15
**** h * o * f ****	
Bottomley, Jim	HOF
deceased 12-11-59	
inducted 1974	

Name	Value
auto. cut signature	25.00
autographed 3x5	40.00
auto. gum card	+35.00
autographed ball	75.00

Name	Value
Botz, Bob	.15
Bouchee, Ed	.25
Boucher, Al	
deceased 6-23-74	1.25
**** h * o * f ****	
Boudreau, Lou	HOF
inducted 1970	
auto. cut signature	.35
autographed 3x5	.75
yellow plaque	2.00
autographed photo	2.00
auto. gum card	+1.50
autographed ball	7.50

Name	Value
Bouldin, Carl	.15
Bourque, Pat	.15
Bouton, Jim	.30
on Topps card	+.50
Bowa, Larry	.35
on Topps card	+.60
Bowen, Sam (77-)	.15
Bowens, Sam (63-69)	.15
Bowers, Doc	.15
Bowles, Charles	10.00
Bowman, Bob J.	
deceased 9-4-72	1.50
Bowman, Bob L.	.15
Bowman, Elmer	.15
Bowman, Joe	.15
Bowman, Roger	.15
Bowsfield, Ed O. "Ted"	.15
Boyd, Bob	.60
Boyd, Gary	.15
Boyer, Clete	1.00
Boyer, Cloyd	.15
Boyer, Ken	.50
on Topps card	+1.00

Boyland, Dorian .15
Boyle, Jack
deceased 4-3-71 2.00
Boyle, Ralph "Buzz"
deceased 11-12-78 1.00
Boyles, Harry .15
Brabender, Gene .15
Brack, Gilbert Herman
deceased 1-20-60 8.00
Bradey, Don .15
Bradford, Buddy .15
Bradford, Larry .15
Bradford, William D. .15
Bradley, Fred .50
Bradley, George .15
Bradley, Tom .15
Brady, Bob .50
Brady, Cliff
deceased 9-25-74 1.30
Brady, Jim .15
Bragan, Bobby .15
Bragan, Jimmy .15
Bramhall, Cart .15
Branca, Ralph .25
Brancato, Al .15
Branch, Roy .15
Brand, Ron .15
Brandon, D.G. .15
Brandon, Darrell .15
Brandt, Edward A. (28-)
deceased 11-1-44 17.00
Brandt, John G. .25
Branom, "Dud" Edgar
deceased 2-4-80 .65
Bratcher, Joe .15
Braun, Steve .15
Bray, Clarence .15
Brazill, Frank
deceased 11-3-76 1.00
Brazle, Alpha E.
deceased 10-24-73 2.50
Breazeale, Jim .15
Brecheen, Harry .40
Breeden, Dan .15
Breeden, Hal .15
Breeding, Marv .15
Bremer, Hank
deceased 11-28-79 .70
Bremigan, Nick (Ump) .15
Brenneman, Jim .15
Brenner, Del
deceased 4-11-71 2.00
Brenzel, Bill
deceased 6-12-79 .80
**** h * o * f ****
Bresnahan, Roger HOF
deceased 12-4-44
inducted 1945
auto. cut signature 75.00
autographed 3x5 150.00
autographed photo 150.00
auto. gum card +100.00
autographed ball 250.00

Bressler, Ray
deceased 11-7-76 1.00
Bressoud, Eddie .15
Breton, J. F.
deceased 5-30-73 1.50

Brett, George 1.00
on Topps card +2.00
Brett, Ken .15
Breuer, Marvin .15
Brewer, Jack .50
Brewer, Jim .25
Brewer, Tom .25
Brewster, Charlie .15
Brice, Al .15
Brickell, Fritz
deceased 10-15-65 9.00
Brickner, Ralph .15
Brideweser, Jim .15
Bridges, Marshall .15
Bridges, Rocky .15
Bridges, Thomas J.D.
deceased 4-19-69 3.25
Bridwell, Al
deceased 1-24-69 2.75
Briggs, Dan .15
Briggs, John E. .15
Briggs, John T. (56-60) .15
Bright, Harry .15
Briles, Nelson .15
Brillheart, J. B.
deceased 9-2-72 1.50
Brinkman, Chuck .15
Brinkman, Ed .15
Brinkman, Joe (Ump) .15
Brinkopf, Leon .15
Brissie, Lou .75
Bristol, Dave .15
Brittain, Gus
deceased 2-16-74 1.25
Brittin, John .15
Britton, Gilbert .15
Britton, Jim .15
Britton, Stephen G. .30
Broberg, Pete .15
Brock, Lou .75
on Topps card +1.50
Brodowski, Dick .35
Broglio, Ernie .15
Brohamer, Jack .15
Brookens, Ed .15
Brookens, Tom .15
Brooks, Hubie .30
on Topps card +.50
Broskie, Sigmund
deceased 5-17-75 1.25
Brosnan, Jim .20
Brosseau, Frank .15
Brouhard, Mark .15
**** h * o * f ****
Brouthers, Dan HOF
deceased 8-3-32
inducted 1945
auto. cut signature 200.00
autographed 3x5 300.00
autographed photo 300.00
auto. gum card +200.00
autographed ball 500.00

Brovia, Joe .15
Brown, Al .15
Brown, Barney .20
Brown, Bobby (46-54) .15
Brown, Bob Murray (30-36) .75
Brown, Carroll
deceased 2-8-77 1.00

Brown, Curt .15
Brown, Dick E.
deceased 4-12-70 5.00
Brown, Hal .15
Brown, Isaac "Ike" .15
Brown, Jackie .15
Brown, Jesse
deceased 5-25-80 .50
Brown, Jimmy R. (37-46)
deceased 12-29-77 .80
Brown, Larry .15
Brown, Leon .15
Brown, Lloyd
deceased 1-14-74 1.25
Brown, Mace .15
**** h * o * f ****
Brown, Mordecai HOF
deceased 2-14-48
inducted 1949
auto. cut signature 40.00
autographed 3x5 75.00
autographed photo 80.00
auto. gum card +60.00
autographed ball 110.00

Brown, Myrl Lincoln
deceased 2-20-81 .75
Brown, Norman .50
Brown, Ollie .25
Brown, Oscar .15
Brown, Paul .15
Brown, Tom .15
Brown, Walter I. (47) 1.00
Brown, Walter G.
deceased 10-2-66 3.75
Brown, Willard J. (47) 1.00
Brown, William J. "Gates" .20
Browne, Byron .20
Browne, Earl .15
Brubaker, Bill
deceased 4-2-78 .75
Bruce, Bob .35
Brucker, Earle F. .50
Bruckmiller, Andy
deceased 1-12-70 2.25
Brumley, Mike .20
Bruner, Jack 1.00
Brunet, George .25
Bruno, Tom .15
Brunsberg, Arlo .15
Brusstar, Warren .15
Bruton, Bill .60
Bryan, Bill .15
Bryant, Clay .15
Bryant, Derek .15
Bryant, Don .15
Bryant, Ron .20
Brye, Steve .15
Bucha, Johnny .15
Buchek, Jerry .15
Bucher, Jimmy .25
Buck, Jack (Media) .20
Buckeye, Garland
deceased 11-14-75 1.00
Buckles, Jess
deceased 8-2-75 1.00
Buckner, Bill .30
on Topps card +.50
Buddin, Don .15

Name	Price
Budnick, Mike	.15
Buford, Don	.65
Buggs, Ray	.15
Buhl, Bob	.45
Buker, Cy	.15
**** h * o * f ****	
Bulkeley, Morgan	HOF
deceased 11-6-22	
inducted 1937	
auto. cut signature	125.00
autographed 3x5	200.00
autographed photo	300.00
auto. gum card	+300.00
autographed ball	500.00

Name	Price
Bulling, Terry (Bud)	.15
Bumbry, Al	.20
Bunker, Wally	.15
Bunning, Jim	.25
on Topps card	+.40
Burbach, Bill	.15
Burbrink, Nelson	.15
Burchart, Larry	.15
Burda, Ed R.	.15
Burdette, Lou	1.25
on Topps card	+2.00
Burgess, Smokey	.30
on Topps card	+.45
Burgess, Tom	.15
Burgmeier, Tom	.15
Burgo, Bill	.50
Burke, Bob	
deceased 2-8-71	2.00
Burke, Joe (Exec.)	.15
Burke, Leo	.15
Burke, Les	
deceased 5-6-75	1.25
**** h * o * f ****	
Burkett, Jesse	HOF
inducted 1946	
deceased 5-27-53	
auto. cut signature	50.00
autographed 3x5	90.00
b & w plaque	90.00
autographed photo	90.00
auto. gum card	+100.00
autographed ball	150.00

Name	Price
Burkhart, Ken	.15
Burleson, Rick	.35
on Topps card	+.70
Burnette, Wally	.15
Burns, Britt	.20
Burns, George	
deceased 1-7-78	.90
Burns, Joe F. (10,13)	.15
Burns, Joe J.	
deceased 6-24-74	1.30
Burns, John Irving	
deceased 4-18-75	1.25
Burnside, Pete	.15
Burnside, Sheldon	.15
Burpo, George	.50
Burright, Larry	.15
Burris, M.L. (Dick)	
deceased 12-2-72	1.60
Burris, Ray	.25
Burroughs, Jeff	.30
Burrows, John	2.00
Burton, Ellis	.50
Burton, Jim	.15
Burtschy, Ed	.15
Burwell, Bill	
deceased 6-11-73	1.50
Busby, Jim	.15
Busby, Paul	.50
Busby, Steve	.15
Bush, Owen "Donie"	
deceased 3-28-72	2.00
Bush, Guy	.25
Bush, Leslie Ambrose	
deceased 11-1-74	1.25
Buskey, Tom	.15
Butcher, Hank	
deceased 12-28-79	.60
Butcher, John	.15
Butcher, Max	
deceased 9-15-57	7.00
Butera, Sal	.15
Butland, Bill	.15
Butler, Bill	.15
Butters, Tom	.15
Buxton, Ralph	.65
Buzas, Joe	.65
Buzhardt, John	.15
Byerly, Bud	.15
Byrd, Harry	.15
Byrd, Sam	
deceased 5-11-81	.50
Byrne, Tommy	.40
Byrnes, Milt	
deceased 1-1-79	1.00
Bystrom, Marty	.15

Name	Price
Caballero, Ralph	.15
Cabell, Enos	.15
Cadore, Leon Joseph	
deceased 3-16-58	9.00
Cady, Forrest Leroy (12-)	
deceased 3-3-46	14.00
Cain, Bob	.15
Cain, Les	.40
Cain, Merritt (Sugar)	
deceased 4-3-75	1.25
Calderone, Sam	.15
Caldwell, Earl	.15
Caldwell, Mike	.15
Caldwell, Ralph	
deceased 8-5-69	2.50
Caliguerri, Fred	.15
Callaghan, Marty	
deceased 6-24-75	1.25
Callaway, Frank	.15
Callison, Johnny	.25
on Topps card	+.35
Calmus, Dick	.15
Calvert, Paul	1.00
Camacho, Ernie	.15
Camacho, Joe	.15
Camelli, Hank	.15
Camilli, Dolph	.15
Camilli, Doug	.15
**** h * o * f ****	
Campanella, Roy	HOF
accident in 1958	
inducted 1969	
(stamped)	.10
auto. cut signature	30.00
autographed 3x5	45.00
autographed photo	40.00
auto. gum card	+50.00
autographed ball	75.00

Name	Price
Campaneris, Bert	.40
on Topps card	+.75
Campanis, Al	.15
Campanis, Jim	.25
Campbell, Bill	.25
Campbell, Bruce	.15
Campbell, Dave A. (77-78)	.15
Campbell, Dave W. (67-74)	.15
Campbell, Jim R.	.15
Campbell, Paul	.15
Campbell, Ron	.15
Campbell, William Gilthorpe	
deceased 2-21-73	2.00
Camper, Cardell	.15
Campisi, Sal	.15
Candelaria, John	.25
Candini, Milo	.15
Cannizzaro, Chris	.15
Cantwell, Benjamin C.	
deceased 12-4-62	7.00
Capilla, Doug	.20
Capra, Buzz	.15
Capron, Ralph E.	
deceased 9-0-80	.50
Caray, Harry (Media)	.25
Carbo, Bernie	.40
Cardenal, Jose	.40
on Topps card	+.80
Cardenas, Leo "Chico"	1.50
Cardwell, Don	.15
Carew, Rod	1.00
on Topps card	+2.00
Carey, Andy	.35
**** h * o * f ****	
Carey, Max	HOF
inducted 1961	
deceased 5-30-76	
auto. cut signature	.75
autographed 3x5	2.00
yellow plaque	4.50
b & w plaque	12.00
autographed photo	4.00
auto. gum card	+3.00
autographed ball	12.50

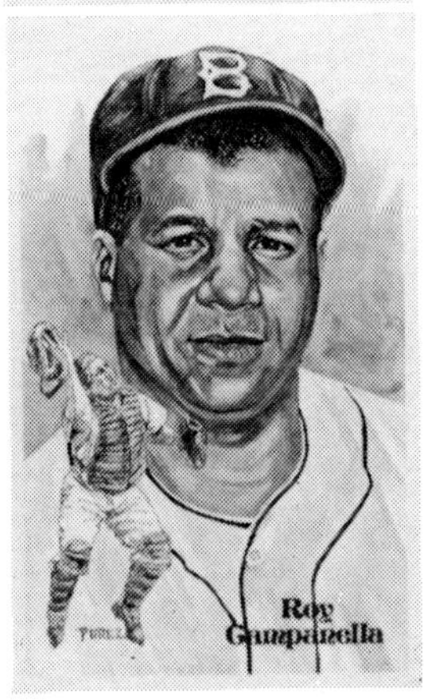

Name	Price
Carey, Thomas F.A.	
deceased 2-21-70	2.50
Carisch, Fred	
deceased 4-19-77	1.00
Carleton, Tex	
deceased 1-11-77	1.00
Carlin, Jim	.15
Carlos, Cisco	.15
Carlsen, Don	.40
Carlton, Steve	1.50
on Topps card	+3.00
Carmel, Duke	.25
Carnett, Eddie	.15
Carnevale, Dan	.15
Carpenter, Bob	.15
Carpin, Frank	.15
Carrasquel, Chico	2.50
Carreon, Camilo	.35
Carrigan, Bill	
deceased 7-8-69	2.50
Carrithers, Don	.15
Carroll, Clay	.25
Carroll, Dorsey	.15
Carroll, Owen	
deceased 6-8-75	1.25
Carroll, Tom M. (74-75)	.15
Carson, Walter	.15
Carswell, Frank	.15
Carter, Arnie	.50
Carter, Gary	.35
on Topps card	+.60
Carter, Paul	.15
Carter, S.M.	.15
**** h * o * f *******	
Cartwright, Alexander	HOF
deceased 7-12-92	
inducted 1938	
auto. cut signature	150.00
autographed 3x5	300.00
autographed photo	300.00
auto. gum card	+500.00
autographed ball	750.00

Name	Price
Carty, Rico	.35
on Topps card	+.70
Casale, Jerry	.15
Casanova, Paul	.35
Cascarella, Joe	.50
Case, George	.20
Casey, Hugh Thomas (35-)	
deceased 7-3-51	15.00
Cash, Dave	.50
Cash, Norm	.75
on Topps card	+1.50
Cash, Ron	.15
Cashen, Frank (Exec.)	.15
Castiglia, James	.15
Castiglione, Pete	.15
Castillo, Bobby	.25
Castino, John	.15
Castleman, Clyde	.15
Castleman, Foster	5.00
Castro, Bill	.15
Cater, Danny	.15
Cathey, Hardin	1.25
Caulfield, John	1.50
Causey, Wayne	.15
Cavaretta, Phil	.20
Ceccarelli, Art	.15
Cedeno, Cesar	.50
on Topps card	+1.00
Center, Marvin E.	.20
Center, Pete	.15
Cepeda, Orlando	1.50
on Topps card	+3.00
Cerone, Rick	.20
Cerv, Bob	.15
Cey, Ron	.30
on Topps card	+.50
**** h * o * f *******	
Chadwick, Henry	HOF
deceased 4-20-08	
inducted 1938	
auto. cut signature	200.00
autographed 3x5	300.00
autographed photo	300.00
auto. gum card	+300.00
autographed ball	600.00

Name	Price
Chakales, Bob	.15
Chalk, Dave	.15
Chamberlain, Bill	.30
Chamberlain, Chris	.15
Chambers, Cliff	.15
Chambliss, Chris	.35
Champion, Bill	.15
Champion, Mike	.15
Chance, Dean	.30
**** h * o * f *******	
Chance, Frank	HOF
deceased 9-15-24	
inducted 1946	
auto. cut signature	125.00
autographed 3x5	200.00
autographed photo	175.00
auto. gum card	+150.00
autographed ball	300.00

Name	Price
**** h * o * f *******	
Chandler, A.B. (Happy)	HOF
inducted 1982	
auto. cut signature	.40
autographed 3x5	.80
autographed photo	2.00
auto. gum card	+2.00
autographed ball	12.00
Chandler, Ed	1.00
Chandler, Spud	.15
Chaney, Darrel	.15
Chant, Charles	.15
Chaplin, B.E.	
deceased 8-15-78	.90
Chapman, Cal	.15
Chapman, Ed	.15
Chapman, Fred	.45
Chapman, Glenn	.15
Chapman, Raymond J. (12-20)	
deceased 8-17-20	100.00
Chapman, Sam	.15
Chapman, W.B. "Ben"	.15
Chappas, Harry Perry	.20
Charbonneau, Joe	.30
Charles, Ed D.	.15
**** h * o * f *******	
Charleston, Oscar	HOF
deceased 11-6-31	
inducted 1976	
auto. cut signature	75.00
autographed 3x5	150.00
autographed photo	150.00
auto. gum card	+150.00
autographed ball	225.00

Name	Price
Charton, Pete	.15
Chase, Ken	.15
Chatham, Buster	
deceased 12-15-75	1.00
Chelini, Italo	
deceased 8-25-72	1.50
Chervinko, Paul	
deceased 6-3-76	1.00

THE PICTURES USED IN THIS SECTION ARE FROM THE PEREZ-STEELE HALL OF FAME POSTCARD SET (SEE RECENT MEMORABILIA SECTION OF THIS BOOK). FOR INFORMATION ON THIS SET WRITE PEREZ-STEELE GALLERIES, DEPT. MPG, BOX 1776, FORT WASHINGTON, PA 19034.

**** h * o * f *******
Chesbro, Jack HOF
deceased 11-6-31
inducted 1946
auto. cut signature 125.00
autographed 3x5 200.00
autographed photo 150.00
auto. gum card +150.00
autographed ball 300.00

Chesnes, Bob 1.00
Chiozza, Dino
deceased 4-23-72 1.75
Chiozza, Louis Peo (34-39)
deceased 2-28-71 2.00
Chipman, Bob
deceased 11-8-73 1.40
Chipple, Walter .15
Chiti, Harry .30
Chittum, Nelson .15
Chozen, Harry .15
Chrisley, Neil .15
Christenson, Larry .15
Christian, Bob C. (68-)
deceased 2-20-74 7.00
Christman, Mark
deceased 10-9-76 1.00
Christopher, Lloyd .15
Church, Bubba .15
Church, Leonard .15
Churn, C.N. "Chuck" .15
Churry, John
deceased 2-8-70 2.00
Chylak, Nestor (Ump)
deceased 2-17-82 .40
Cicero, Joe .60
Cicotte, Al .35
Cicotte, Eddie
deceased 5-5-69 4.00
Cieslak, Ted .50
Cihocki, Al .50
Cihocki, Eddie .15
Cimoli, Gino .50
Cimino, Pete .15
Ciola, Lou .60
Cisar, George .15
Cisco, Galen .15
Cissell, Chalmer William
deceased 3-15-49 13.00
Clabaugh, Moose .15
Clancy, Jim .15
Clancy, John (Bud)
deceased 9-26-68 3.00
Clark, Allie .50
Clark, Jack .25
Clark, Jim 1.00
Clark, Mel .15
Clark, Mike .15
Clark, Otey .15
Clark, Phil .15
Clark, W. Watson
deceased 3-4-72 1.75
**** h * o * f ****
Clarke, Fred HOF
inducted 1945
deceased 8-14-60
auto. cut signature 12.50
autographed 3x5 20.00
autographed photo 20.00
auto. gum card +20.00
autographed ball 40.00

Clarke, Horace .15
Clarke, Richard C. .15
Clarke, Rufus .15
**** h * o * f ****
Clarkson, John HOF
deceased 2-4-09
inducted 1963
auto. cut signature 150.00
autographed 3x5 250.00
autographed photo 250.00
auto. gum card +200.00
autographed ball 500.00

Clary, Ellis .15
Claset, Gowell "Lefty"
deceased 3-8-81 .45
Clay, Dain .40
Clay, Ken .15
Clear, Bob .15
Clemens, Chet .50
Clemens, Douglas .15
**** h * o * f ****
Clemente, Roberto HOF
deceased 12-31-72
inducted 1973
auto. cut signature 15.00
autographed 3x5 25.00
autographed photo 35.00
auto. gum card +45.00
autographed ball 60.00
Clemons, Doug .15
Clemons, Lance .15
Clendennon, Donn .35
Cleveland, Reggie .15
Clift, Harland .15
Clifton, Herman "Flea" .15
Cline, Ty .35
Clines, Gene .15
Clinton, Lou .15
Cloninger, Tony .15
Closter, Alan E. .20
Cluck, Bob .15
Clyde, David .15
Clyde, Tom .50
Coan, Gil .45
Coates, Jim .15
**** h * o * f ****
Cobb, Ty HOF
inducted 1936
deceased 7-17-61
auto. cut signature 15.00
autographed 3x5 30.00
b & w plaque 50.00
autographed photo 50.00
auto. gum card +60.00
autographed ball 75.00

**** h * o * f ****	
Cochrane, Gordon "Mickey"	HOF
inducted 1947	
deceased 6-2-62	
auto. cut signature	15.00
autographed 3x5	25.00
b & w plaque	35.00
autographed photo	30.00
auto. gum card	+30.00
autographed ball	50.00

Coffman, Dick	
deceased 3-24-72	1.70
Coggins, Rich	.15
Cohen, Albert	.50
Cohen, Alfred (Ump)	.15
Cohen, Andy	.15
Cohen, Syd	.25
Coker, Jim	.15
Colavito, Rocky	.35
on Topps card	+.60
Colbert, Nate	.25
Colbert, Vince	.15
Colborn, Jim	.15
Cole, Bert	
deceased 5-30-75	1.25
Cole, Dave	.15
Cole, Dick	.15
Cole, Ed	.15
Coleman, Curtis	
deceased 7-1-80	.60
Coleman, Gordy	.20
Coleman, Jerry	.20
Coleman, Joe Jr.	.15
Coleman, Joe Sr.	.15
Coleman, Ken (Media)	.25
Coleman, Ray	.35
Coles, Charles E.	.15
Collard, Earl	
deceased 7-14-68	3.00
Collins, Dave	.20
Collins, Eddie T. Jr.	.15
**** h * o * f ****	
Collins, Eddie T. Sr.	HOF
inducted 1939	
deceased 3-25-51	
auto. cut signature	20.00
autographed 3x5	35.00
b & w plaque	60.00
autographed photo	40.00
auto. gum card	+40.00
autographed ball	75.00
Collins, James (Rip)	
deceased 4-16-70	2.50
**** h * o * f ****	
Collins, Jimmy	HOF
deceased 3-6-43	
inducted 1945	
auto. cut signature	150.00
autographed 3x5	250.00
autographed photo	250.00
auto. gum card	+200.00
autographed ball	400.00
Collins, Joe	.25
Collins, Kevin	.15
Collins, Ray W.	
deceased 1-9-70	2.25
Collum, Jack	.45
Colman, Frank	.70

Colosi, Nick (Ump)	.15
Colson, Lloyd	.15
Colton, Larry	.15
Coluccio, Bobby	.15
**** h * o * f ****	
Combs, Earle	HOF
inducted 1970	
deceased 7-21-76	
auto. cut signature	1.00
autographed 3x5	2.50
yellow plaque	5.00
autographed photo	3.00
auto. gum card	+3.00
autographed ball	10.00

Combs, Merrill	.15
Comellas, Jorge	3.00
Comer, Harry	.15
Comer, Steve	.15
Comer, Wayne	.15
**** h * o * f ****	
Comiskey, Charles	HOF
deceased 10-26-31	
inducted 1939	
auto. cut signature	50.00
autographed 3x5	100.00
autographed photo	90.00
auto. gum card	+100.00
autographed ball	150.00

Comorsky, Adam Anthony	
deceased 3-2-51	11.00
Compton, Anna (Pete)	
deceased 2-3-78	.90
Compton, Mike	.15
Conatser, Clint	.50
Concepcion, Dave	.50
on Topps card	+1.00
Concepcion, Onix	.20
Conger, Dick	
deceased 2-16-70	2.00
Conigliaro, Billy	.50
Conigliaro, Tony	.50
on Topps card	+1.00
**** h * o * f ****	
Conlan, Jocko	HOF
inducted 1974	
auto. cut signature	.75
autographed 3x5	1.50
yellow plaque	3.00
autographed photo	2.50
auto. gum card	+2.50
autographed ball	8.00

Conley, Gene .20
Conley, Robert B. .25
Connally, George (Sarge)
deceased 1-27-78 1.00
Connatser, Bruce
deceased 1-27-71 2.00
Connell, Joe
deceased 9-21-77 1.25
Connelly, Bill
deceased 11-27-80 1.00
Connolly, Ed .15
**** h * o * f ****
Connolly, Tom HOF
inducted 1953
deceased 4-28-61
auto. cut signature 25.00
autographed 3x5 35.00
autographed photo 25.00
auto. gum card +30.00
autographed ball 50.00

**** h * o * f ****
Connor, Roger HOF
deceased 1-4-31
inducted 1976
auto. cut signature 150.00
autographed 3x5 250.00
autographed photo 200.00
auto. gum card +200.00
autographed ball 500.00

Connors, Bill .15
Connors, Chuck 1.50
Connors, Merv J. .15
Conroy, Bill .15
Consolo, Bill .50
Constable, Jim .15
Consuegra, Sandy 1.00
Conway, C.C.
deceased 9-12-68 2.75
Conway, Jack 2.00
Coogan, Dale .50

Cook, Cliff 1.00
Cook, Luther
deceased 6-30-73 1.50
Cook, Rollin E.
deceased 8-11-75 1.15
Cook, Ron .35
Cooke, Dusty
signed 3x5 1.00
stamped .03
Coombs, Bobby .15
Coombs, Danny .15
Cooney, James .15
Cooney, Johnny .30
Cooney, Terry (Ump) .15
Cooper, Cal .50
Cooper, Cecil .30
on Topps card +.50
Cooper, Claude
deceased 1-24-74 1.50
Cooper, Gary .15
Cooper, Morton Cecil
deceased 11-17-58 10.00
Cooper, Pat .15
Cooper, Walker .15
Cooper, Wilbur
deceased 8-7-73 1.50
Corbett, Doug .20
Corbett, Gene .15
Corbin, Ray .15
Corcoran, Tim .15
Corey, Mark .15
Corrales, Pat .15
Correll, Vic .15
Corriden, John .50
Corriden, John M. Sr. (10-)
deceased 9-28-59 8.00
Corwin, Elmer N. .20
Coscarart, Pete .15
Cosgrove, Mike .15
Cosman, Jim .15
Cote, Warren .60
Cotes, Eugenio .20
Cottier, Chuck .15
Couch, Johnny
deceased 12-8-75 1.25
Coumbe, Fred
deceased 3-21-78 1.00
Coulter, Tom .15
Courtney, Clint
deceased 6-16-75 2.50
Cousins, Derryl (Ump) .15
**** h * o * f ****
Covaleskie, Stan HOF
inducted 1969
auto. cut signature .35
autographed 3x5 1.00
yellow plaque 2.00
autographed photo 1.50
auto. gum card +1.50
autographed ball 9.00

Covington, Wes 1.00
Cowan, Billy .15
Cowens, Al .35
Cox, Bob .15
Cox, Casey .15
Cox, Ernest
deceased 4-29-74 1.25
Cox, George .15

Cox, Jim .15
Cox, Larry .15
Cox, Ted .15
Cox, William Richard
deceased 3-30-78 1.75
Cozart, Charles .15
Crabtree, Estel
deceased 1-4-67 3.75
Craddock, Walt
deceased 7-6-80 .75
Craft, Harry .15
Craig, Pete .15
Craig, Roger .15
Cram, Jerry .15
Cramer, Roger "Doc" .15
Crandall, Del .15
Crawford, Gerry (Ump) .15
Crawford, Jim .15
Crawford, Pat .15
**** h * o * f ****
Crawford, Sam HOF
inducted 1957
deceased 6-15-68
auto. cut signature 7.50
autographed 3x5 15.00
yellow plaque 15.00
b & w plaque 25.00
autographed photo 20.00
auto. gum card +15.00
autographed ball 30.00

Crawford, Shag (Ump) .20
Crawford, Willie 1.00
Creel, Jack 1.00
Creger, Bernard O. .20
Cremins, Robert .15
Crespi, Frank .15
Cress, Walker .50
Cresse, Mark .15
Crider, Jerry .15
Critz, Hugh
deceased 1-13-80 .50
Cromartie, Warren .25
Crone, Ray .15
Cronin, Jim .25
**** h * o * f ****
Cronin, Joe HOF
inducted 1956
auto. cut signature .40
autographed 3x5 .80
yellow plaque 2.00
b & w plaque 5.00
autographed photo 2.00
auto. gum card +2.00
autographed ball 9.00
Crosby, Ed .15
Crosetti, Frank .20
Cross, Joff .15
Crouch, Bill .40
Crowder, General
deceased 4-3-72 1.50
Crowe, George .20
Crowley, Terry .15
Cruise, Walton E.
deceased 1-9-75 1.25
Crumling, Gene .15
Crump, Buddy
deceased 9-7-76 1.50
Cruthers, Charles P.
deceased 12-17-76 2.00

Cruz, Hector .25
Cruz, Henry .35
Cruz, Jose .25
Cruz, Julio .20
Cruz, Todd .15
Cruz, Victor .30
Cubbage, Mike .15
Cuccinello, Al .15
Cuccinello, Tony .15
Cuccurullo, Art 1.00
Cuellar, Charles .50
Cuellar, Mike .75
Culberson, Leon .45
Cullen, John P. .15
Cullen, Tim .15
Cullenbine, Roy .40
Cullop, Henry (Nick)
deceased 12-8-78 .90
Culloton, Bud
deceased 11-9-76 1.00
Culp, Benny .15
Culp, Ray .15
Culp, Wm. E.
deceased 9-3-69 2.25
Culver, George .15
Cumberland, John .50
**** h * o * f ****
Cummings, Candy HOF
deceased 5-17-24
inducted 1939
auto. cut signature 200.00
autographed 3x5 300.00
autographed photo 250.00
auto. gum card +250.00
autographed ball 500.00

Cunningham, George
deceased 3-10-72 1.50
Cunningham, Joe .15
Currence, Delancy .15
Currin, Perry .50
Curry, Tony .25
Curtis, Jack P. (61-63) .15
Curtis, John D. (70-) .15
Curtis, Vernon .15
Curtright, Guy .15
Cutshaw, George W.
deceased 8-22-73 1.40
**** h * o * f ****
Cuyler, Kiki HOF
deceased 2-11-50
inducted 1968
auto. cut signature 25.00
autographed 3x5 50.00
autographed photo 45.00
auto. gum card +45.00
autographed ball 75.00

Cvengros, Michael J. (22-)
deceased 8-2-70 2.50
Cypert, Albert
deceased 1-9-73 1.50

D'Acquisto, John .15
Dade, Paul .15
Dagenhard, John .15
Dahlgren, Babe .15
Dahlke, Jerry .15
Dailey, Bill .15
Dal Canton, Bruce .15
Dale, Jerry (Ump) .15
Daley, Bud .15
Daley, John F. .30
Daley, Pete .15
Dallessandro, Dominic .15
Dalrymple, Clay .15
Dalton, Harry (Exec.) .20
Danforth, Dave
deceased 9-19-70 2.00
Daniels, Bennie .25
Daniels, Fred .50
Daniels, Jack .15
Danning, Harry .45
Danning, Ike .50
Dantonio, John 1.00
Dapper, Cliff .65
Darcy, Pat .15
Daringer, Cliff
deceased 12-12-71 1.50
Dark, Alvin .30
Darr, Mike .15
Darwin, Bobby .25
Darwin, Danny .15
Dascoli, Frank (Ump) .15
Dasso, Frank .50
Daugherty, Doc .15
Dauer, Rich .20
Dauss, George
deceased 7-27-63 6.50
Davanon, Jerry .15
Davenport, Jim .30
Davidson, Satch (Ump) .20
Davidson, Ted .15
Davie, Jerry .25
Davilillo, Vic 1.00
Davis, Bill .15
Davis, Bob B. (52-53) .15
Davis, Bob E. (58,60) .15
Davis, Bob J. E. (73-) .15
Davis, Brandy .15
Davis, Brock .15
Davis, Curtis Benton
deceased 10-12-65 6.00
Davis, Dick .15
Davis, George A.
deceased 6-4-61 9.00
Davis, George W. (26-38) .15
Davis, Harry 2.00
Davis, Jim .15
Davis, Lawrence .15
Davis, Peaches .15
Davis, Ray .15
Davis, Red .15
Davis, Ron .15
Davis, Thomas Todd
deceased 12-31-78 .90
Davis, Tommy .40
Davis, Virgil "Spud" .25
Davis, Willie 2.00
Davis, Woodrow .15
Dawson, Andre .35
on Topps card +.60
Day, Charles (Boots) .15
Day, Leon .20
Deal, Charlie
deceased 9-16-79 .55
Deal, Ellis "Cot" .15
Deal, Lindsay F.
deceased 4-18-79 .60
Dean, Alfred "Chubby"
deceased 12-21-70 2.00
**** h * o * f ****
Dean, Dizzy HOF
inducted 1953
deceased 7-17-74
auto. cut signature 2.00
autographed 3x5 4.00
yellow plaque 6.00
b & w plaque 15.00
autographed photo 5.00
auto. gum card +15.00
autographed ball 30.00

Dean, Tommy .15
Dear, Buddy 1.00
Debus, Adam
deceased 5-13-77 .90
DeBusschere, Dave .40
DeCinces, Doug .15
Dede, Arthur
deceased 9-6-71 1.75
Deegan, Bill (Ump) .15
Degerick, Mike A. .15
Deidel, Jim .15
DeJesus, Ivan .25
**** h * o * f ****
Delahanty, Ed HOF
deceased 7-2-03
inducted 1945
auto. cut signature 250.00
autographed 3x5 350.00
autographed photo 300.00
auto. gum card +300.00
autographed ball 750.00
De la Hoz, Mike 1.50
Delancey, William
deceased 11-28-46 15.00

Name	Price
Del Greco, Bob	.15
Delker, Ed	.20
DeLock, Ike	.15
Del Savio, Gar	.50
Delsing, Jim	.15
DeMaestri, Joe	.15
Demaree, Joseph Franklin	
deceased 8-30-58	8.50
DeMars, Billy	.15
DeMerit, John	.15
Demery, Larry	.75
Demeter, Don	.35
Demeter, Steve	.15
Demola, Don	.15
Dempsey, Con	.15
Dempsey, Rick	.15
Denehy, Bill	.15
Denkinger, Don (Ump)	.15
Dennis, Don	.15
Denny, John	.35
Dent, Bucky	.25
Dent, Elliott	
deceased 11-25-74	1.25
Dente, Sam	.15
DePhillips, Tony	.50
Derrick, Mike	.30
Derringer, Paul	2.00
Derrington, Charles J.	.15
Derry, Russ	.15
Desautels, Gene	.15
Deshong, Jim	.25
Detherage, Bob	.15
Detore, George	.15
Dettore, Tom	.15
Detweiler, Ducky	.15
Deutsch, Melvin	.15
Devens, Charlie	.15
Devine, Adrian	.15
Devine, Bing	.25
DeVivieros, Bernard	.15
Devormer, Albert E.	
deceased 8-29-66	5.00
Dezelan, Frank (Ump)	.15
Diaz, Bo	.15
Dicken, Paul	.15
Dickerman, Leo	.15
**** h * o * f ****	
Dickey, Bill	HOF
inducted 1954	
auto. cut signature	.50
autographed 3x5	1.50
yellow plaque	3.00
b & w plaque	10.00
autographed photo	3.00
auto. gum card	+3.00
autographed ball	10.00
Dickey, G.W. "Skeets"	
deceased 6-16-76	1.10
Dickman, Emerson	
deceased 4-27-81	.50
Dickshot, John	.15
Dickson, Jim E.	.15
Dickson, Murry	.15
Didier, Bob	.15
Diering, Chuck	.15
Dierker, Larry	.15
Dietrich, Bill	
deceased 6-20-78	1.00

Name	Price
Dietz, Dick	.15
Dietz, Lloyd	
deceased 10-29-72	1.50
Dietzel, Ray	.15
Difani, Jay	1.00
Diggs, Reese	2.00
**** h * o * f ****	
Dihigo, Martin	HOF
deceased 5-22-71	
inducted 1977	
auto. cut signature	75.00
autographed 3x5	150.00
autographed photo	150.00
autographed ball	300.00

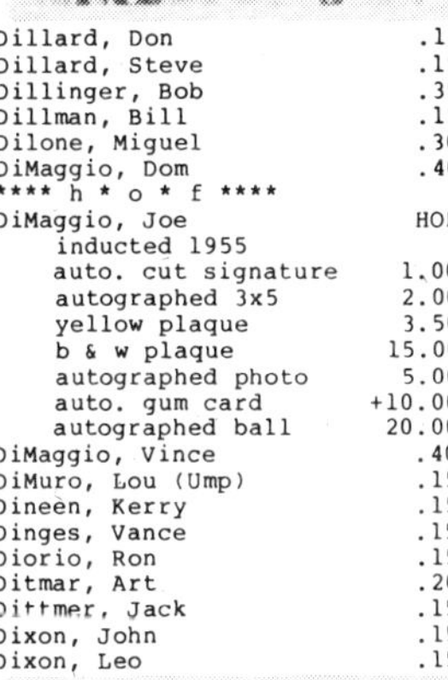

Name	Price
Dillard, Don	.15
Dillard, Steve	.15
Dillinger, Bob	.35
Dillman, Bill	.15
Dilone, Miguel	.30
DiMaggio, Dom	.40
**** h * o * f ****	
DiMaggio, Joe	HOF
inducted 1955	
auto. cut signature	1.00
autographed 3x5	2.00
yellow plaque	3.50
b & w plaque	15.00
autographed photo	5.00
auto. gum card	+10.00
autographed ball	20.00
DiMaggio, Vince	.40
DiMuro, Lou (Ump)	.15
Dineen, Kerry	.15
Dinges, Vance	.15
Diorio, Ron	.15
Ditmar, Art	.20
Dittmer, Jack	.15
Dixon, John	.15
Dixon, Leo	.15

Name	Price
Dixon, Thomas E.	.15
Dobb, John	.15
Dobbek, Dan	.15
Dobernic, Jess	.15
Dobson, Chuck	.15
Dobson, Joe	.15
Dobson, Pat	.20
Doby, Larry	.35
on Topps card	+.50
Dockins, George	.60
Doerr, Bobby	.15
Doherty, John	.15
Doljack, Frank Joseph	
deceased 1-23-48	14.00
Donald, Atley	2.00
Donaldson, John	.15
Donatelli, Augie	.25
Dondero, Leonard	.15
Donnelly, S.U. "Blix"	
deceased 6-20-76	1.25
Donnelly, Ed	.15
Donnelly, Rich	.15
Donohue, John	.50
Donohue, Pete	.15
Donohue, Tom	.15
Donovan, Bill	.15
Donovan, Dick	.15
Dorish, Harry	.15
Dorsett, Calvin Leavelle	
deceased 10-22-70	2.50
Dotter, Gary R.	.15
Dotterer, Dutch	.15
Douglas, Astyanax	
deceased 1-26-75	1.50
Douglas, John	.50
Douglas, Whammy	.20
Douthit, Taylor	.15
Dowd, John L.	
deceased 1-31-81	.50
Dowling, Dave	.25
Downing, Al	.15
Downing, Brian	.15
Doyle, Brian	.15
Doyle, Denny	.15
Doyle, Howard	.50
Doyle, Larry	
deceased 3-1-74	1.25
Doyle, Paul	.15

Name	Price
Dozier, Will	.50
Drabowsky, Moe	.25
Drago, Dick	.15
Drake, Larry	.50
Drake, Tom	.40
Dreesen, Bill	
deceased 11-9-71	2.00
Dreisewerd, Clem	.15
Dressen, Chuck	
deceased 8-10-66	4.00
on Topps card	+6.50
Dressler, Rob	.15
Drews, Frank	
deceased 4-22-72	2.50
Drews, Karl August	
deceased 8-15-63	6.50
Driessen, Dan	.40
Drill, Lewis	
deceased 7-4-69	2.50
Dropo, Walt	.15

Drott, Dick	.15
Drysdale, Don	.65
on Topps card	+1.00
Dubiel, Walt	
deceased 10-25-69	3.25
Duckworth, Jim R.	.15
Dudley, Clise	.50
Dues, Hal	.15
Duffalo, Jim	.25
Duffy, Frank	.15
**** h * o * f ****	
Duffy, Hugh	HOF
inducted 1945	
deceased 10-19-54	
auto. cut signature	30.00
autographed 3x5	60.00
b & w plaque	75.00
autographed photo	60.00
auto. gum card	+60.00
autographed ball	100.00

Duffy, Jim (Ump)	.15
Dugan, Joe	.25
Dugos, Jimmie	.15
Duliba, Bob	.15
Duncan, Dave	.15
Duncan, Taylor	.15
Dunegan, Jim	.15
Dunlap, Bill	.60
Dunlap, Grant	.15
Dunlop, George	
deceased 12-12-72	1.50
Dunlop, Harry	.15
Dunn, Ron	.15
Dunning, Steve	.15
Duran, Dan	.15
Duren, Ryne	.25
Durham, Donald G.	.15
Durham, Ed	
deceased 4-27-76	1.15
Durham, Joe	.20
Durham, Leon	.25
Durnbaugh, Robert	.15
Durocher, Leo	.35
Durham, Joe	.15
Durst, Cedric	
deceased 2-16-71	2.00
Dusak, Erv	.15
Dustal, Bob	.15
Dwyer, Jim	.15
Dwyer, Joe	.15
Dybzinski, Jerry	.15
Dyck, Jim	.15
Dyer, Duffy	.15
Dyer, Eddie	
deceased 4-20-64	5.00
Dykes, Jimmy	
deceased 6-15-76	1.50

Earley, Arnold	.15
Earley, Jake	.15
Earley, Tom	.15
Earnshaw, George L.	
deceased 12-1-76	2.00
Easler, Mike	.20
Eason, Mal	
deceased 4-16-70	2.00
East, Hugh	.15
Easter, Luke	
deceased	2.00
on gum card	+3.00
Easterly, Jamie	.15
Easton, John	.15
Eastwick, Rawly	.25
Eaton, Zeb	.45
Eckersley, Dennis	.30
Eddy, Don	.35
Edelman, John	.15
Eden, Mike	.15
Edington, Jake	
deceased 11-29-69	2.25
Edmondson, Paul M. (69)	
deceased 2-13-70	15.00
Edmonston, Sam	
deceased 4-12-79	.75
Edwards, Charles Bruce	
deceased 4-25-75	2.00
Edwards, Dave	.15
Edwards, Foster	
deceased 1-4-80	.50
Edwards, Hank	.30
Edwards, John	.15
Edwards, Mike	.15
Egan, Tom	.15
Eggert, Elmer	
deceased 4-9-71	1.75
Ehmke, Howard J.	
deceased 3-17-59	9.00
Eilers, Dave	.15
Eisenstat, Harry	.15
Elder, George	.50
Elia, Lee	.20
Ellerbe, Frank	.15
Ellingsen, Bruce	.15
Elliott, Allen (Ace)	
deceased 5-6-79	.65
Elliott, Eugene B.	
deceased 1-5-76	1.25
Elliott, H. Glenn	
deceased 7-27-69	2.50
Elliott, Harry	.15
Elliott, Lawrence (62)	.15
Elliott, Robert Irving	
deceased 5-4-66	6.00
Ellis, Bob	.15
Ellis, Dock	.65
on Topps card	+1.00
Ellis, John	.15
Ellis, Sam	.15
Ellsworth, Dick	.15
Elmore, Verdo	
deceased 8-5-69	2.25
Elston, Don	.15
Embree, Charles "Red"	.30
Emery, Cal W.	.15
Emery, Spoke	
deceased 6-2-75	1.50
Emmerich, Bill	.15
Endicott, Bill	.35
Engel, Bob (Ump)	.15
Engel, Joseph	
deceased 6-12-69	2.25
English, Charles	1.25
English, Gilbert R. (31)	.15
English, Woody	.25
Engmann, Johnny	.15
Ennis, Del	.35
Enyart, Terry	.15
Epperly, Al	.15
Epstein, Mike	.30
Erautt, Eddie	.15
Erautt, Joe	
deceased 10-6-76	1.00
Erickson, Dick	.15
Erickson, Don L.	.15
Erickson, Leif	.40
Erickson, Paul	.50
Ermer, Cal	.15
Erskine, Carl	.25
Espinosa, Nino	.20
Esposito, Sam	.15
Essegian, Chuck	.15
Essian, Jim	.15
Estelle, Dick	.15
Estock, George	.15
Estrada, Chuck	.15
Etchebarren, Andy	.15
Etchison, Buck	.15
Etten, Nick	.15
Evans, Bill L. (49,51)	.50

**** h * o * f ****	
Evans, Billy	HOF
deceased 1-23-56	
inducted 1973	
auto. cut signature	25.00
autographed 3x5	50.00
autographed photo	50.00
autographed ball	100.00

Evans, Darrell	.15
Evans, Dwight	.25
Evans, Jim (Ump)	.15
Evans, Red	.15
Evers, Hoot	.15
**** h * o * f ****	
Evers, Johnny	HOF
inducted 1946	
deceased 3-28-47	
auto. cut signature	60.00
autographed 3x5	120.00
autographed photo	125.00
auto. gum card	+125.00
autographed ball	225.00

**** h * o * f ****	
Ewing, Buck	HOF
deceased 10-20-06	
inducted 1939	
auto. cut signature	250.00
autographed 3x5	350.00
autographed photo	450.00
auto. gum card	+300.00
autographed ball	750.00
Ewing, Sam	.15
Ewoldt, Arthur	
deceased 12-8-77	.90
Eyrich, George	.45
Ezzell, Homer	
deceased 8-3-76	1.25

**** h * o * f ****	
Faber, Red	HOF
inducted 1964	
deceased 9-25-76	
auto. cut signature	.75
autographed 3x5	2.00
yellow plaque	4.00
autographed photo	3.00
auto. gum card	+3.00
autographed ball	10.00

Face, Roy	.20
Faeth, Tony	.20
Fagan, Everett	.15
Fahey, Bill	.15
Fahr, G. "Red"	.15
Fahrer, Clarence	
deceased 6-10-67	3.25
Fahey, Bill	.15
Fain, Ferris	.45
Fairey, Jim	.15
Fairly, Ron	.25
Falcone, Pete	.15
Falk, Bibb	.20
Fallon, George	.15
Falsey, Peter J.	
deceased 5-23-76	2.00
Fannin, Clifford Bryson	
deceased 12-11-66	5.00
Fanning, Jim	.15
Fanovich, Frank	.15
Fanzone, Carmen	.15
Farley, Bob	.15
Farmer, Ed	.40
Farmer, Floyd H. "Jack"	
deceased 5-21-70	2.00
Farrell, Kerby	
deceased 12-17-75	1.10
Farrell, Richard J. (56-)	
deceased 6-11-77	3.00
on Topps card	+5.00

Fast, Darcy	.15
Faszholz, Jack	.15
Faul, Bill	.15
Fazio, Ernie	.15
Federoff, Alfred	.20
Feeney, Charles (Exec.)	.25
Fehring, Dutch	.15
Feinberg, Ed	.65
Felderman, M.W.	2.00
**** h * o * f ****	
Feller, Bob	HOF
inducted 1962	
auto. cut signature	.50
autographed 3x5	1.00
yellow plaque	3.00
b & w plaque	12.50
autographed photo	3.00
auto. gum card	+3.00
autographed ball	10.00

Felske, John	.15
Felton, Terry	.15
Fenwick, Bob	.15
Ferens, Stan	.75
Ferguson, Joe	.25
Fernandez, H.P. "Chico"	.30
Fernandez, Frank	.25
Fernandez, Nan	1.00
Ferrara, Al	.30
Ferrarese, Don	.15
Ferraro, Mike	.15
Ferrell, Rick	.25
Ferrell, Wes	
deceased 12-9-76	1.50
Ferrick, Tom	.25
Ferriss, Dave "Boo"	.30
Fette, Lou	
deceased 1-3-81	.50
Fidrych, Mark "Bird"	.45
Fieber, Lefty	2.00
Figueroa, Ed	.25
Filipowicz, Steve	
deceased 2-21-75	1.25
Finch, Joel	.15
Fine, Tommy	.50
Fingers, Rollie	.60
on Topps card	+1.00
Finigan, Jim	
deceased 5-16-81	.60
Fink, Herman	
deceased 8-14-80	.75
Finley, Charles O. (Exec.)	.50
Finney, Hal	.15
Finney, Louis K.	
deceased 4-22-66	4.50
Fiore, Mike	.15
Fischer, Bill	.15
Fischer, Rube	.15
Fisher, Don	
deceased 7-29-73	1.50
Fisher, Eddie	.15
Fisher, George	.15
Fisher, Gus	
deceased 4-8-72	1.50
Fisher, Jack	.15
Fisher, Ray	.15
Fisher, Tom	
deceased 9-3-72	1.50
Fisher, Tom	.15

Fisk, Carlton	.40
on Topps card	+.60
Fittery, Paul	
deceased 1-28-74	1.50
Fitzgerald, Ed	.15
Fitzgerald, Ray	
deceased 9-6-77	1.00
Fitzmorris, Al	.15
Fitzpatrick, John	.15
Fitzpatrick, Mike (Ump)	.15
Fitzsimmons, Fred	
deceased 11-18-79	.70
Flack, Ray	
deceased 7-31-75	1.25
Flager, Wally	3.00
Flaherty, John (Ump)	.15
Flair, Al	.15
Flanagan, Mike	.35
on Toipps card	+.50
Flanigan, Ray	.50
Flannery, Mike	.15
Flannery, Tim	.15
Flaskamper, Ray	
deceased 2-3-78	1.00
Flavin, John	.15
Fleitas, Angel	.50
Fleming, Bill	1.00
Fleming, Les	
deceased 5-5-80	.50
Fletcher, Elbie	.15
Fletcher, Tom	.15
**** h * o * f ****	
Flick, Elmer	HOF
inducted 1963	
deceased 1-9-71	
auto. cut signature	2.00
autographed 3x5	4.00
yellow plaque	6.00
b & w plaque	25.00
autographed photo	6.00
auto. gum card	+6.00
autographed ball	15.00

Flick, Lew	.50
Flitcraft, Hildreth M.	.20
Flood, Curt	2.00
on Topps card	+3.00
Flores, Jess	.75
Flowers, Ben	.30
Flowers, Wes	.15
Floyd, Bob	.15
Floyd, L.R.	.50
Flynn, Doug	.15
Fodge, Gene	.15
Foiles, Hank	.15
Foli, Tim	.15
Folkers, Rich	.15
Fondy, Dee	.15
Fonseca, Lew	.20
Foor, Jim	.15
Foote, Barry	.15
Ford, Dale (Ump)	.15
Ford, Dan	.35
on Topps card	+.50
Ford, Horace	
deceased 1-29-77	.90
Ford, Wenty	
deceased 7-8-80	6.00

**** h * o * f ****
Ford, Whitey HOF
inducted 1974
auto. cut signature .75
autographed 3x5 1.50
yellow plaque 3.50
autographed photo 2.50
auto. gum card +2.50
autographed ball 10.00

Fornieles, Mike .15
Forsch, Bob .25
Forsch, Ken .15
Forster, Terry .20
Fosse, Ray .15
Foster, Alan .15
Foster, George .65
on Topps card +1.00
Foster, Larry L. .15
Foster, Leo .15
Foucault, Steve .15
Fowler, Art .15
Fowler, Dick
deceased 5-22-72 2.00
Fowler, J. Chester .20
Fox, Charlie .15
Fox, Ervin
deceased 7-5-66 5.00
Fox, Howard Francis
deceased 10-9-65 6.00
Fox, Nelson
deceased 12-1-75 2.50
on Topps card +4.00
Fox, Terry .15
**** h * o * f ****
Foxx, Jimmie HOF
inducted 1951
deceased 7-21-67
auto. cut signature 12.00
autographed 3x5 20.00
yellow plaque 30.00
b & w plaque 35.00
autographed photo 20.00
auto. gum card +20.00
autographed ball 50.00

Foy, Joe .20
Foytack, Paul .15
Frailing, Ken .15
Francis, Earl .15
Francona, Terry .15
Francona, Tito .15
Frankhouse, Fred .15
Franklin, Jack .50
Franklin, Murray
deceased 3-16-78 1.00
Franks, Herman .15
Frazier, George .15
Frazier, Joe .15
Frederick, John
deceased 6-18-77 1.00
Freed, Irwin .15
Freed, Roger .15
Freehan, Bill .30
on Topps card +.50
Freeman, Harvey
deceased 1-10-70 2.00
Freeman, Hersh .15
Freeman, Jim .15
Freeman, Mark .15
Freese, Gene .15
Freeze, C.A. .15
Fregosi, Jim .20
Freiburger, V. .60
Freisleben, Dave .15
Freitas, Tony .15
French, Jim .15
French, Larry .15
French, Ray
deceased 4-3-78 .90
French, Walter .15
Frey, Lonnie .15
Frey, Jim .15
Frias, Pepe .75
Fricano, Mario
deceased 5-18-76 3.00
*** h * o * f ****
Frick, Ford HOF
inducted 1970
deceased 4-8-78
auto. cut signature 1.00
autographed 3x5 2.50
yellow plaque 5.00
autographed photo 4.00
auto. gum card +5.00
autographed ball 12.50

Fridley, Jim .20
Friend, Bob .25
Friend, Owen .15
**** h * o * f ****
Frisch, Frankie HOF
inducted 1947
deceased 3-12-73
auto. cut signature 2.50
autographed 3x5 5.00
yellow plaque 8.00
b & w plaque 20.00
autographed photo 7.00
auto. gum card +7.00
autographed ball 25.00
Frisella, Dan
deceased 1-1-77 5.00
Froemming, Bruce (Ump) .15
Frost, Dave .15
Fryman, Woodie .15
Fuentes, Miguel (69)
deceased 1-29-70 15.00

Fuentes, Tito .30
Fuhr, Oscar
deceased 3-27-75 1.25
Fuller, Jim .15
Fuller, Vern .15
Fullis, Charles Philip
deceased 3-28-46 14.00
Funk, Frank .15
Furillo, Carl 2.00
on Topps card +3.00
Fusselman, Lester Leroy
deceased 5-21-70 3.50

Gabler, John .15
Gabler, William L. .15
Gabrielson, Len .30
Gaedel, Edward Carl (51)
deceased 6-19-61 50.00
Gaffke, Fabian .15
Gagliano, Phil .30
Gagliano, Ralph .15
Gaines, Joe .20
Gaines, Willard R.
deceased 1-28-79 .80
Galan, Augie .15
Galasso, Bob .15
Galatzer, Milt
deceased 1-29-76 1.00
Gale, Rich .15
Galehouse, Denny .15
Galla, Stan .15
Gallagher, Al .15
Gallagher, Bob .15
Gallagher, Doug .15
Gallagher, Joe .15
Gallia, Mel
deceased 3-19-76 1.00
Galloway, C.E. "Chick"
deceased 11-7-69 2.25

**** h * o * f ****
Galvin, Pud HOF
deceased 3-7-02
inducted 1965
auto. cut signature 250.00
autographed 3x5 350.00
autographed photo 300.00
auto. gum card +300.00
autographed ball 750.00

Gamble, Lee .15
Gamble, Oscar .25
Gandil, Charles Arnold
deceased 12-12-70 2.50
Gantenbein, J. .50
Gantner, Jim .15
Ganzel, Babe
deceased 2-6-78 1.00
Garagiola, Joe .40
Garbark, Bob .15
Garbark, Mike .50
Garber, Bob M. .15
Garber, Gene .15
Garcia, Dave .15
Garcia, Kiko .25
Garcia, Mike .20
Garcia, Pedro .25
Garcia, Rich (Ump) .20
Gardella, Al .15
Gardella, Dan .50
Gardner, Bill .15
Gardner, Larry
deceased 3-11-76 1.00
Gardner, Ray
deceased 5-3-68 3.00
Gardner, Richard F. (65) .20
Garibaldi, Bob .15
Garland, Wayne .25
Garman, Mike .15
Garms, Debs .15
Garner, Phil .60
on Topps card +1.00
Garr, Ralph .40
Garrett, Adrian .15
Garrett, C. R.
deceased 2-11-77 1.00
Garrett, Wayne .15
Garrison, Cliff 2.00
Garrison, Ford .15
Garver, Ned .15
Garvey, Steve .50
on Topps card +.75
Garvin, Jerry .15
Gaspar, Rod .15
Gassaway, Charles .50
Gaston, Alex
deceased 2-8-79 .70
Gaston, Cito .35
Gaston, Milt .15
Gatewood, Aubrey .15
Gaudet, Jim .15
Gautreau, Walt "Doc"
deceased 8-23-70 2.00
Gautreaux, Sid
deceased 4-19-80 .50
Gazella, Mike
deceased 9-11-78 .80
Geary, Eugene F.
deceased 3-0-81 .75

Geary, Robert
deceased 1-31-80 .60
Gebhard, Bob .15
Gebrian, Peter (47) .25
Gee, John .15
**** h * o * f ****
Gehrig, Lou HOF
inducted 1939
deceased 6-2-41
auto. cut signature 75.00
autographed 3x5 150.00
autographed photo 200.00
auto. gum card +200.00
autographed ball 250.00

**** h * o * f ****
Gehringer, Charlie HOF
inducted 1949
auto. cut signature .50
autographed 3x5 1.00
yellow plaque 2.00
b & w plaque 9.00
autographed photo 2.50
auto. gum card +4.00
autographed ball 10.00

Gehrman, Paul .15
Geiger, Gary .15
Geishert, Vern .15
Gelbert, Charley
deceased 1-13-67 3.50
Gelnar, John .15
Genewich, Joe .15
Genovese, Chick
deceased 2-12-81 .90
Gentile, Jim .20
Gentile, Sam .50
Gentry, Gary .20
Gentry, James .15
George, Charles .15
Gerhardt, Al .15
Gerhauser, Al (Lefty)
deceased 5-28-72 1.50

Gerken, George
deceased 10-23-77 .90
Gerlach, John 1.00
Gernert, Dick .15
Geronimo, Cesar .45
Gettel, Allen .15
Getz, Gus
deceased 5-28-69 2.50
Gibbon, Joe .20
Gibbs, Jake .35
**** h * o * f ****
Gibson, Bob HOF
inducted 1981
auto. cut signature 1.00
autographed 3x5 2.00
autographed photo 3.00
auto. gum card +6.00
autographed ball 8.00

**** h * o * f ****
Gibson, Josh HOF
deceased 1-20-47
inducted 1972
auto. cut signature 100.00
autographed 3x5 200.00
autographed photo 200.00
autographed ball 300.00

Gibson, Russ .15
Gibson, Sam 1.25
Gideon, Jim .20
Giebel, Joseph H.
deceased 3-17-81 .50
Giebell, Floyd .15
Giel, Paul .15
Gigon, Norm .15
Gilbert, Andy .15
Gilbert, Buddy .15
Gilbert, Charles .30
Gilbreath, Bill .15
Gilbreath, Rod .15
Giles, George .20

**** h * o * f ****
Giles, Warren HOF
deceased 2-7-79
inducted 1979
auto. cut signature 1.00
autographed 3x5 3.00
autographed photo 4.00
auto. gum card +6.00
autographed ball 12.00

Gilhooley, Frank Patrick
deceased 7-11-59 8.00
Gill, John .30
Gillenwater, Claral
deceased 2-26-78 1.00
Gillespie, Bob .15
Gilliam, James W.
deceased 10-8-78 2.50
on Topps card +4.00
Gilliford, Paul .15
Gilligan, John .15
Gilmore, Len .50
Ginsberg, Joe .35
Gionfriddo, Al .20
Giordano, Tom .15
Giuliani, Angelo .15
Giusti, Dave .15
Gladd, Jim .50
Gladding, Fred .15
Gladu, Roland .50
Glaviano, Tom .15
Glazner, Whitey .15
Gleason, Jim .15
Gleason, Roy .50
Gleaton, Jerry Don .15
Gleeson, Jim .15
Glenn, Joe .15
Gliatto, Sal .15
Glossop, Al 1.00
Glynn, Bill .15
Glynn, Ed .15
Goetz, Russ (Ump) .15
Goggin, Chuck .15
Gogolewski, Bill .15
Goldman, Jonah
deceased 8-17-80 .65
Goldsberry, Gordon .15
Goldsmith, Harold .15
Goldstein, Les .50
Goldstein, "Spud" (Exec.) .25
Goldy, Purnell .25
Goletz, Stan .15
Goliat, Mike .15
Golden, Jim .15
Goldsberry, Gordon .15
Goltz, Dave .15
**** h * o * f ****
Gomez, Lefty HOF
inducted 1972
auto. cut signature .75
autographed 3x5 1.50
yellow plaque 3.00
autographed photo 3.00
auto. gum card +3.00
autographed ball 10.00
Gomez, Luis .15
Gomez, Preston .15
Gonder, Jesse .15
Gonzales, Joe .15
Gonzales, Tony .60
Gonzalez, Fernando .25
Gonzalez, Julio .25
Gonzalez, Mike
deceased 2-19-77 1.00
Gooch, Charles .75
Gooch, Johnny
deceased 5-15-75 1.50
Goodman, Billy .15
Goodman, Ival .25
Goodson, Ed .15
Goodwin, Claire
deceased 2-15-72 1.75
Goodwin, Danny .15
Goodwin, Jim .50
Goossen, Greg .15
Gorbous, Glen .15
Gordon, Joe
deceased 4-14-78 2.00
Gordon, Sid
deceased 6-17-75 2.50
Gore, Artie (Ump) .20
Gorinski, Bob .15
Gorman, H.P. "Lefty" .15
Gorman, Tom A. .15
Gornicki, Hank .65
Gorsica, Johnny .15
Goryl, John .15
Gosger, Jim .15
**** h * o * f ****
Goslin, Goose HOF
inducted 1968
deceased 5-15-71
auto. cut signature 2.50
autographed 3x5 5.00
yellow plaque 8.00
autographed photo 6.00
auto. gum card +6.00
autographed ball 15.00

Goss, Howie .15
Gossage, Rich "Goose" .25
on Topps card +.40
Goulish, Nick .50
Govin, Charlie .15
Gowdy, Harry
deceased 8-1-66 4.00
Grabarkewitz, Billy .15
Grace, Earl
deceased 11-22-80 .50
Grace, Joe
deceased 9-18-69 2.50

Graff, Milt .15
Graham, Bill .15
Graham, Dan .15
Graham, Jack B. (46,49) .15
Gramley, Tom .50
Grammas, Alex .25
Grampp, Henry .50
Granger, Wayne .15
Grant, James C. "Jimmy"
deceased 7-8-70 2.00
Grant, Jim (Mudcat) .60
Grantham, George Farley
deceased 3-16-54 10.00
Grasmick, Lou .50
Grasso, Newton Michael
deceased 10-15-75 2.00
Grate, Don 2.00
Graves, Joe
deceased 12-22-80 .50
Graves, Sid .15
Gray, Dick B. .35
Gray, John .15
Gray, Pete 8.00
Gray, Ted .15
Grba, Eli 4.00
on Topps card +6.00
Greason, Bill .15
Green, Dallas .20
Green, Dick .15
Green, Fred A. .15
Green, Gene L. .15
Green, Lenny .15
Green, Pumpsie 1.00
**** h * o * f ****
Greenberg, Hank HOF
inducted 1956
auto. cut signature .75
autographed 3x5 1.50
yellow plaque 4.00
b & w plaque 12.00
autographed photo 4.00
auto. gum card +4.00
autographed ball 12.00

Greenfield, Kent
deceased 3-14-78 1.00
Greengrass, Jim .15
Greenwood, Bob .15
Greer, Brian .15
Greif, Bill .15
Gregg, Hal .70
Gregory, Howard
deceased 5-30-70 2.00
Gregory, Paul .15
Gremp, Buddy .15
Grich, Bobby .35
on Topps card +.50

Grieve, Bill (Ump)	
deceased 8-17-79	.80
Grieve, Tom	.15
Griffey, Ken	.35
on Topps card	+.50
Griffin, Alfredo	.20
Griffin, Doug	.15
Griffin, Tom	.15
Griffith, Cal (Exec)	.35
**** h * o * f ****	
Griffith, Clark	HOF
inducted 1946	
deceased 10-27-55	
auto. cut signature	15.00
autographed 3x5	25.00
b & w plaque	30.00
autographed photo	20.00
auto. gum card	+25.00
autographed ball	50.00

Griffith, Derrel	.15
Griffith, Lee	.50
Grigsby, Denver	
deceased 11-10-73	1.50
Grilli, Steve	.15
Grim, Bob	.15
**** h * o * f ****	
Grimes, Burleigh	HOF
inducted 1964	
auto. cut signature	.50
autographed 3x5	1.00
yellow plaque	3.00
autographed photo	2.00
auto. gum card	+2.00
autographed ball	10.00

Grimes, Ed	
deceased 10-4-74	1.25
Grimes, Oscar	.65
Grimes, Oscar Ray Sr.	
deceased 5-25-53	10.00
Grimes, Roy Austin	
deceased 9-13-54	10.00

Grimm, Charlie	.20
Grimsley, John (Ump)	.15
Grimsley, Ross	.15
Grissom, Lee	.25
Grissom, Marv	.15
Groat, Dick	.75
Grob, Conrad G.	.15
Grodzicki, John	.15
Groh, Henry Knight	
deceased 8-22-68	4.00
Groh, Lewis Carl	
deceased 10-20-60	8.00
Gromek, Steve	.15
Gross, Don	1.00
Gross, Greg	.15
Gross, Wayne	.15
Grosskloss, Howard H.	.20
Grossman, Harley	.15
Grote, Jerry	1.00
on Topps card	+2.00
Groth, Johnny	.15
**** h * o * f ****	
Grove, Lefty	HOF
inducted 1947	
deceased 5-22-75	
auto. cut signature	2.00
autographed 3x5	4.00
yellow plaque	6.00
b & w plaque	12.00
autographed photo	5.00
auto. gum card	+5.00
autographed ball	15.00

Grove, Orval	.15
Grover, Roy A.	
deceased 2-7-78	1.00
Grubb, John	.15
Grubbs, Thomas	.15
Grube, Franklin Thomas	
deceased 7-2-45	15.00
Grunwald, Al	.15
Grygiel, George (Ump)	.15
Gryska, Sigmund	.15
Grzenda, Joe	.25
Guerrero, Mario	.25
Guerrero, Pedro	.25
Guglielmo, Angie (Ump)	.15
Guidry, Ron	.35
on Topps card	+.50
Guindon, Bob	.15
Guinn, Skip	.50
Guintini, Ben	1.50
Gullett, Don	.35
on Topps card	+.50
Gullie, Ted	.15
Gumbert, Harry	.15
Gumpert, Randy	.15
Gunning, Hyland	
deceased 3-28-75	1.25
Gura, Larry	.20
Gustine, Frank	.15
Gutteridge, Don	.15
Gyselman, Dick	.15

Haas, Bert	.15
Haas, Moose	.20
Haas, Mule	
deceased 6-30-74	1.25

Habenicht, Bob	
deceased 12-24-80	.50
Hack, Stan	
deceased 12-15-79	.80
Hacker, Dick	.15
Hacker, Warren	.15
Haddix, Harvey	.15
Hadley, Irving Darius	
deceased 2-15-63	7.00
Hadley, Kent	.15
Haeffner, Bill	.15
Haefner, Mickey	.15
**** h * o * f ****	
Hafey, Chick	HOF
inducted 1971	
deceased 7-2-73	
auto. cut signature	1.50
autographed 3x5	4.00
yellow plaque	7.00
autographed photo	6.00
auto. gum card	+6.00
autographed ball	15.00

Hafey, Daniel "Bud"	.15
Hafey, Tom	.15
Hague, Joe	.20
Hahn, Dick	3.00
Hahn, Don	.15
Haines, Hinkey	
deceased 1-9-79	.80
**** h * o * f ****	
Haines, Jesse	HOF
inducted 1970	
deceased 8-5-78	
auto. cut signature	1.00
autographed 3x5	2.00
yellow plaque	4.00
autographed photo	3.00
auto. gum card	+5.00
autographed ball	10.00

Name	Price
Hairston, Jerry	.15
Hairston, Sam	.15
Hajduk, Chet	.15
Halas, George	.60
Hale, Bob	.30
Hale, John	.15
Hale, Odell	.30
Hale, Sam	
deceased 9-6-74	1.25
Haley, Ray T. "Pat"	
deceased 10-8-73	1.50
Halicki, Ed	.15
Hall, Bob	.15
Hall, Dick W.	.15
Hall, Irv	1.00
Hall, John S. (48)	.75
Hall, Tom	.20
Hallahan, Bill	.15
Haller, Bill (Ump)	.15
Haller, Tom	.15
Hallett, Jack	.15
Halt, Al	
deceased 1-22-73	1.50
Hamby, Sanford	1.25
**** h * o * f ****	
Hamilton, Billy	HOF
deceased 12-16-40	
inducted 1961	
auto. cut signature	100.00
autographed 3x5	200.00
autographed photo	150.00
auto. gum card	+150.00
autographed ball	300.00

Name	Price
Hamilton, Dave	.15
Hamilton, Steve	.15
Hamilton, Tom	
deceased 11-29-73	1.50
Hamlin, Ken	.15
Hamlin, Luke	
deceased 2-18-78	1.00
Hamm, Pete	.45
Hamner, Granville	1.50
Hamner, Ralph	.50
Hamner, Wes	2.50
Hampton, Isaac B.	.25
Hamrick, Ray	.60
Hancken, Buddy	.15
Hancock, Fred	.15
Hancock, Gary	.15
Hand, Rich	.15
Handley, Gene	.15
Handley, Lee	
deceased 4-8-70	2.00
Hands, Bill	.15
Hanebrink, Harry	.15
Haney, Fred	
deceased 11-9-77	1.25
Haney, Larry	.15
Hanna, Preston	.15
Hannah, J. H. "Truck"	.15
Hannan, Jim	.15
Hanning, Loy	1.25
Hansen, Andy	.60
Hansen, Bob	.15
Hansen, Ron	.15
Hankins, Jay	.15
Hanyzewski, Eddie	.15

Name	Price
Harder, Mel	.20
Hardin, W.E. "Bud"	.15
Hardin, Jim	.15
Harding, Charles	
deceased 10-30-71	1.50
Hardy, Carroll	.25
Hardy, Larry	.15
Hardy, Red	.15
Hargan, Steve	.15
Hargreaves, Charlie	
deceased 5-9-79	.65
Hargrove, Mike	.15
Harkness, Tim	.15
Harlow, Larry	.15
Harmon, Bill	1.25
Harmon, Chuck	.15
Harmon, Terry	.15
Harper, George	
deceased 8-18-78	.80
Harper, Tommy	.75
on Topps card	1.50
Harrah, Toby	.15
Harrell, Bill	.40
Harrell, John	.15
Harrell, Ray	.60
Harrelson, Bill	.15
Harrelson, Bud	.15
Harrelson, Ken	.45
**** h * o * f ****	
Harridge, Will	HOF
deceased 4-9-71	
inducted 1972	
auto. cut signature	7.50
autographed 3x5	15.00
autographed photo	20.00
auto. gum card	+20.00
autographed ball	30.00

Name	Price
Harrington, Andy	
deceased 1-26-79	.80
Harrington, C.M.	.15
Harris, Billy	.15
Harris, Bob (38-42)	.15
**** h * o * f ****	
Harris, Bucky	HOF
inducted 1975	
deceased 11-8-77	
auto. cut signature	.75
autographed 3x5	1.50
yellow plaque	4.50
autographed photo	2.50
auto. gum card	+3.50
autographed ball	10.00
Harris, Charlie	.50
Harris, David S.	
deceased 9-18-73	1.25
Harris, Gail	.50
Harris, Jim	.15
Harris, Luman	.15
Harris, Robert N.	
deceased 12-18-76	1.00
Harris, Spencer	.15
Harris, Vic	.15
Harris, W.F. "Buddy"	.15
Harrison, Chuck	.15
Harrison, Roric	.15
Harrist, Earl	.60
Harshany, Sam	.15
Harshman, Jack	.15

Name	Price
Harstad, Oscar	.15
Hart, Jim Ray	.75
Hartenstein, Chuck	.15
Hartman, Bob	.20
Hartman, J. C.	.20
**** h * o * f ****	
Hartnett, Gabby	HOF
inducted 1955	
deceased 12-20-72	
auto. cut signature	2.00
autographed 3x5	4.00
yellow plaque	6.00
b & w plaque	12.00
autographed photo	5.00
auto. gum card	+5.00
autographed ball	15.00

Name	Price
Harts, Greg	.35
Hartsfield, Roy	.15
Hartung, Clint	.15
Hartzell, Paul	.15
Harvel, Red	.15
Harvey, Doug (Ump)	.15
Hasbrook, Robert	
deceased 2-9-76	1.25
Hasenmayer, Don	.15
Hash, Herb	.15
Hassett, Bud	.25
Hassey, Ron	.15
Hassler, Andy	.15
Hassler, Joe	
deceased 9-4-71	1.50
Hasson, Charles	.25
Hasty, Robert	
deceased 5-28-72	1.50
Hatcher, Mickey	.15
Hatfield, Fred	.15
Hathaway, Roy	.15
Hatten, Joe	.15
Hatton, Grady	.15
Haughey, Chris	.50

Name	Price
Haugstad, Phil	1.00
Hauser, Joe	.15
Hausman, Tom	.15
Hausmann, George	.40
Hawes, Roy	.15
Hawkins, Wynn	.25
Hawks, Chick	
deceased 5-26-73	1.50
Haydel, Hal	.15
Hayes, Minter C. (27)	.25
Haynes, Joe	
deceased 1-6-67	3.50
Haywood, Bill	.35
Hayworth, Myron "Red"	.15
Hayworth, Ray	.15
Hazle, Bob	.20
Head, Ed	
deceased 1-31-80	.50
Healey,Thomas F. (15-)	
deceased 1-15-74	2.00
Healy, Tom	.15
Hearn, Jim	.15
Heath, Bill	.35
Heath, Jeff	
deceased 12-9-75	1.75
Heath, Mike	.15
Heath, Minor	.15
Heath, Tommy	
deceased 2-26-67	3.50
Heaverlo, Dave	.15
Hebart, Wally	.15
Hebner, Richie	.30
Hedlund, Mike	.15
Heffner, Bob	.15
Heffner, Don	.15
Heflin, Randy	.15
Hegan, Jim	.15
Hegan, Mike	.15
Heidemann, Jack	.15
**** h * o * f ****	
Heilmann, Harry	HOF
deceased 7-9-51	
inducted 1952	
auto. cut signature	35.00
autographed 3x5	70.00
autographed photo	70.00
auto. gum card	+70.00
autographed ball	120.00

Name	Price
Heim, Val	.15
Heimach, Fred	
deceased 6-1-73	1.50
Heine, William	
deceased 9-2-76	1.00
Heintzelman, Ken	.15
Heintzelman, Tom	.15
Heise, Bob	.15
Heise, Clarence	.15
Heise, Jim	.15
Heist, Al	.15
Heitmann, Henry Anton	
deceased 12-15-58	8.00
Held, Mel	.15
Held, Woodie	.15
Helf, Hank	.15
Helms, Tommy	.20
Heltzel, W.W.	2.00
Heman, Russ	.15
Hemshaw, Roy	2.00
Hemsley, Rollie	
deceased 7-31-72	2.00
Hemus, Solly	.15
Henderson, Joe	.25
Henderson, Ken	.15
Hendley, Bob	.15
Hendrick, George	1.50
on Topps card	+2.50
Hendrick, Harvey Lee	
deceased 10-29-41	18.00
Hendricks, Ellie	.20
Hendrix, Claude Raymond	
deceased 3-22-44	15.00
Hendry, Ted (Ump)	.15
Henley, Gail	.15
Henline, Walter John	
deceased 10-9-57	8.00
Hennessey, G.	.15
Hennigan, Phil	.15
Henninger, Rich	.15
Henrich, Bob	.15
Henrich, Tommy	.20
Henry, Bill F. (66)	.45
Henry, Bill R. (52-69)	.15
Henry, Earl	.35
Henry, Fred M.	.15
Henry, Jim	
deceased 8-15-76	1.25
Hepler, Bill	.15
Herbel, Ron	.15
Herbert, Ernie	
deceased 1-13-68	3.00
Herbert, Ray	.20
Herman, Albert D.	
deceased 8-21-80	.50
Herman, Babe	.25
**** h * o * f ****	
Herman, Billy	HOF
inducted 1975	
auto. cut signature	.35
autographed 3x5	.75
yellow plaque	2.50
autographed photo	2.00
auto. gum card	+2.00
autographed ball	7.50

Name	Price
Hermann, Al	.15
Hermanski, Gene	.15
Hermoso, Angel	2.00
Hernaiz, Jesus	.15
Hernandez, Enzo	.25
Hernandez, G. Evelio	.75
Hernandez, Jackie (65-73)	.50
Hernandez, Keith	.40
on Topps card	+.75
Hernandez, Ramon (67-77)	3.00
Hernandez, Rodolfo "Rudy"	.30
Hernandez, Rudy (60-61)	.25
Hernandez, S. R. "Chico"	7.00
Hernandez, Willie	.35
Herndon, Larry	.25
Herr, Tom	.15
Herrara, Mike	
deceased 2-3-78	2.50
Herrera, Pancho	.75
Herriage, T.	.20
Herring, Art	.15
Herrmann, Ed	.15
Herrmann, Leroy	
deceased 7-3-72	1.50

Name	Price
Herrnstein, John	.15
Herrscher, Rick	1.00
Hersch, Earl W.	.15
Hershberger, Mike	.15
Hershberger, Will. (38-40)	
deceased 8-3-40	50.00
Hertweck, Neal	.25
Hertz, Steve	.15
Herzog, Whitey	.15
Hesselbacher, George	
deceased 2-18-80	1.00
Hetki, John	.15
Heving, Joe	
deceased 4-11-70	2.00
Heving, John	
deceased 12-24-68	3.00
Heydeman, Greg	.15
Hiatt, Jack	.15
Hibbs, Jim	.15
Hickey, Jim	.15
Hickman, Jesse	.15
Hickman, Jim	.15
Hicks, Buddy	.50
Hicks, Jim	.35
Hicks, Joe	.15
Higbe, Kirby	.15
Higdon, Bill	.40
Higgins, Denny	.15
Higgins, M.F. "Pinky"	
deceased 3-21-69	3.00
High, Andy	
deceased 2-22-81	.45
Hildebrand, Oral	
deceased 9-8-77	1.00
Hilgendorf, Tom	.15
Hill, Carmen	.15
Hill, Dave B.	.15
Hill, Garry	.15
Hill, Jess	.15
Hill, John C.	
deceased 9-20-70	2.00
Hill, Marc	.15
Hillebrand, Homer	
deceased 1-23-74	2.00
Hiller, Chuck	.15
Hiller, Frank	.40
Hiller, John	.20
Hillman, Dave	1.50
Hilton, David	.15
Himsl, Vedi	.15
Hinds, Sam	.15
Hinkle, Gordon	
deceased 3-19-72	1.50
Hinrichs, Bill	
deceased 8-18-72	1.50
Hinrichs, Paul	.15
Hinsley, Jerry	1.00
Hinton, Chuck	.20
Hinton, Rich	.15
Hippauf, Herb	.30
Hiser, Gene	.15
Hisle, Larry	.30
on Topps card	+.45
Hisner, Harley	.15
Hitchcock, Billy	.15
Hittle, Lloyd	.15
Hoag, Myril	
deceased 7-28-71	1.50
Hoak, Donald Albert	
deceased 10-9-69	6.00
Hobaugh, Ed	.15
Hobbie, Glen	.15
Hobson, Butch	.35
Hockenberg, C.	.20
Hockette, George	.25
Hodapp, Johnny	
deceased 6-14-80	.60
Hoderlein, Mel	.15
Hodge, Clarence	
deceased 12-31-67	3.50
Hodge, Gomer	.15
Hodges, Gilbert Raymond	
deceased 4-2-72	5.00
Hodges, Ron	.15
Hodgin, Ralph	.45
Hodkey, Al	.15
Hoeft, Bill	.15
Hoerner, Joe	.15
Hoerst, Frank	.15
Hoff, Chester	.15
Hofferth, Stew	.40
Hoffman, Bill J. (39)	2.00
Hoffman, Glenn	.15
Hoffman, Guy	.15
Hoffman, John	.15
Hoffman, Ray L. (42)	2.00

Name	Price
Hofman, Bobby	.15
Hogan, Ken	
deceased 1-2-80	.75
Hogsett, Chief	.15
Hogue, Bobby	.15
Hogue, Cal	.40
Holborow, Wally	.40
Holbrook, Sam	.15
Holcombe, Ken	.40
Holden, Joe	.15
Holdsworth, Fred	.15
Holland, Al	.15
Holley, Edgar	2.00
Hollingsworth, Al	.15
Hollingsworth, John B.	.15
Hollison, John	
deceased 8-19-69	2.50
Hollmig, Stan	.15
Holloman, Bobo	.30
Holloway, Jim	.15
Holly, Jeff	.40
Holm, Bill	.15
Holman, Gary	.35
Holmes, Tommy	.25
Holshouser, H.	.25
Holt, Gordy	.15
Holt, Jim	.15
Holtgrave, Vern	.15
Holtzman, Ken	.25
Honeycutt, Rick	.25
Honochick, Jim (Ump)	.25
Hood, Don	.15
Hood, Wally	.15
Hook, Jay	.15
Hooks, Alex	.15
Hooper, Bob	
deceased 3-17-80	1.50
**** h * o * f ****	
Hooper, Harry	HOF
inducted 1971	
deceased 12-18-74	
auto. cut signature	1.25
autographed 3x5	2.50
yellow plaque	4.50
autographed photo	3.00
auto. gum card	+3.00
autographed ball	10.00

Name	Price
Hooten, Leon	.15
Hooton, Burt	.25
Hoover, Dick	
deceased 4-13-81	.60
Hopkins, Don	.30
Hopkins, Gail	.15
Hopkins, Paul	.15
Hopp, Johnny	.15
Horlen, Joel	.15
Horne, Berlyn	.25
Horner, Bob	.75
on gum card	+1.50
**** h * o * f ****	
Hornsby, Roger	HOF
inducted 1942	
deceased 1-5-63	
auto. cut signature	12.50
autographed 3x5	25.00
b & w plaque	40.00
autographed photo	35.00
auto. gum card	+25.00
autographed ball	50.00

Name	Price
Horstman, Oscar	
deceased 5-11-77	1.00
Horton, Tony	.50
Horton, Willie	1.00
Hoscheit, Vern	.15
Hoskins, Dave	
deceased 4-2-70	9.00
Hosley, Tim	.15
Host, Gene	.35
Hostetler, Charles	
deceased 2-18-71	2.00
Hottman, Ken	.15
Houck, Byron	
deceased 6-17-69	2.50
Hough, Charlie	.15
Houk, Ralph	.25
House, Frank	.35
House, Pat	.20
House, Tom	.15
Householder, Paul	.15
Houtteman, Art	.25
Hovley, Steve	.15
Howard, Bruce	.15
Howard, Doug	.15
Howard, Elston	
deceased 12-14-80	2.00
on Topps card	+3.00
Howard, Frank	.50
Howard, Fred	.15
Howard, Larry	.40
Howard, Lee	.40
Howard, Wilbur	.15
Howarth, Jimmy	.15
Howe, Art	.15
Howe, Cal	.15
Howe, Lester C.	
deceased 7-16-76	1.00
Howe, Steve	.25
Howell, H.E. "Dixie"(47-56)	.25
Howell, M.F."Dixie" (40,49)	
deceased 3-18-60	8.00
Howell, Roy	.15
Howerton, Bill	.35
Howser, Dick	.15
**** h * o * f ****	
Hoyt, Waite	HOF
inducted 1969	
auto. cut signature	.35
autographed 3x5	.75
yellow plaque	2.00
autographed photo	1.50
auto. gum card	+1.50
autographed ball	10.00
Hrabosky, Al	.45
Hriniak, Walt	.15
**** h * o * f ****	
Hubbard, Cal	HOF
inducted 1976	
deceased 10-16-77	
auto. cut signature	2.00
autographed 3x5	6.00
yellow plaque	12.00
autographed photo	7.50
auto. gum card	+7.50
autographed ball	20.00
Hubbard, Glenn	.15

Name	Price
**** h * o * f ****	
Hubbell, Carl	HOF
inducted 1947	
auto. cut signature	.50
autographed 3x5	1.00
yellow plaque	2.50
b & w plaque	10.00
autographed photo	2.50
auto. gum card	+2.50
autographed ball	10.00

Hubbs, Ken (61-63)	
deceased 2-15-64	20.00
on Topps card	+30.00
Huber, Otto	.50
Hudlin, Willis	.15
Hudson, Charlie	.15
Hudson, John	
deceased 11-7-70	2.00
Hudson, Sid	.15
Huenke, Albert	
deceased 9-20-74	1.25
Huffman, Bennie	.15
Huffman, Phil	.15
**** h * o * f ****	
Huggins, Miller	HOF
deceased 9-25-29	
inducted 1964	
auto. cut signature	125.00
autographed 3x5	200.00
autographed photo	175.00
auto. gum card	+175.00
autographed ball	300.00

Hughes, Dick	.15
Hughes, Jim R. (52-57)	.15
Hughes, Jim M. (74-77)	.15
Hughes, Roy	.15
Hughes, Terry	.45
Hughes, Tom E.	.40
Hughes, Tommy F. (30)	.15
Hughson, Tex	.15
Hume, Tom	.15
Humphrey, Byron	.15
Humphrey, Terry	.15
Humphreys, Bob	.15
Hunnefield, Bill	
deceased 8-28-76	1.25
Hunnicutt, Rick	.20
Hunt, Joel	
deceased 7-24-78	1.00
Hunt, Ken	.15
Hunt, Ron	.25
Hunter, Bill M. (62,64)	.15
Hunter, Buddy	.15
Hunter, Gordon "Billy"	.15
Hunter, Jim "Catfish"	.35
on Topps card	+.50
Huntz, Steve	.15
Huntzinger, Walter	.15
Hurd, Tom	.15
Hurdle, Clint	.20
Hurley, Ed (Ump)	
deceased 11-12-69	2.00
Huston, Harry	
deceased 10-13-69	2.25
Hutchinson, Fred	
deceased 11-12-64	8.00
Hutchinson, Ira	
deceased 8-21-73	1.50
Hutton, Tom	.15
Hyde, Dick	.15

Ingram, Melvin	
deceased 10-28-79	.60
Iorg, Dane	.15
Iorg, Garth	.15
Iott, Clarence "Hooks"	
deceased 8-17-80	.50
**** h * o * f ****	
Irvin, Monte	HOF
inducted 1973	
auto. cut signature	.35
autographed 3x5	.75
yellow plaque	2.00
autographed photo	2.00
auto. gum card	+2.00
autographed ball	7.50

Irwin, Walter K.	
deceased 8-18-76	1.00
Ivie, Mike	.20
Izquierdo, Hank	.25

Jablonski, Ray	.20
Jackman, Bob	.15
Jackowski, Bill (Ump)	.15
Jackson, Al	.15
Jackson, Darrell	.15
Jackson, George	
deceased 11-25-72	1.50
Jackson, Grant	.35
Jackson, Larry	.15
Jackson, Louis Clarence	
deceased 5-27-69	6.00
Jackson, Norman "Jelly"	
deceased 2-13-80	1.00
Jackson, Randy	.15
Jackson, Reggie	5.00
signed "Reggie"	2.00
Jackson, Ron H. (54-60)	.15
Jackson, Ron (75-)	.15
Jackson, Roy	.15
Jackson, R.T. "Sonny"	.20
**** h * o * f ****	
Jackson, Travis	HOF
inducted 1982	
auto. cut signature	.35
autographed 3x5	.80
autographed photo	2.00
auto. gum card	+2.00
autographed ball	10.00
Jacobs, Forrest (Spook)	.15
Jacobs, Jake	.15
Jacobs, Newton	.15
Jacobs, Tony	
deceased 12-21-80	.65
Jacobson, W.C. (Baby Doll)	
deceased 1-16-77	1.00
Jacobson, Merwin	
deceased 1-13-78	.90
Jakucki, Sig	
deceased 5-28-79	.75
James, Byrne	.15
James, Charlie	.15
James, Cleo	.15
James, Phil	.15
James, W.L. (Bill)	
deceased 3-10-71	2.00
Janowicz, Vic	.30
Jansen, Larry	.15
Jarvis, Bob	.15
Jarvis, Leroy	1.00
Jarvis, Pat	.15
Jarvis, Ray	.15
Jaster, Larry	.15
Javery, Al	
deceased 9-13-77	1.50

Javier, Julian	1.00
Jay, Joey	.80
Jeffcoat, Hal	.25
Jefferson, Jesse	.25
Jeffries, Irv	2.00
Jelincich, Frank	.15
Jenkins, Fergie	.50
on Topps card	+1.00
Jennings, Bill	.15
**** h * o * f ****	
Jennings, Hughey	HOF
deceased 2-1-28	
inducted 1945	
auto. cut signature	100.00
autographed 3x5	175.00
autographed photo	125.00
auto. gum card	+125.00
autographed ball	300.00

Jensen, Forrest "Woody"	.15
Jensen, Jackie	.35
on Topps card	+.75
Jessee, Dan	
deceased 4-30-70	2.25
Jestadt, Gary	.15
Jester, Virgil	.15
Jeter, John	1.00
Jethroe, Sam	5.00
John, Tommy	.35
on Topps card	+.75
Johns, A. F. "Lefty"	
deceased 9-12-75	1.25
Johnson, A. Rankin Jr.	.15
Johnson, A. Rankin Sr.	
deceased 7-2-72	1.50
Johnson, Alex	.30
on Topps card	+.50
Johnson, Art	.15
**** h * o * f ****	
Johnson, Ban	HOF
deceased 3-28-31	
inducted 1937	
auto. cut signature	75.00
autographed 3x5	150.00
autographed photo	100.00
auto. gum card	+150.00
autographed ball	200.00

Johnson, Bart	.15
Johnson, Billy R. (43)	.20
Johnson, Bob D. (69-77)	.30
Johnson, Bob L. (33-45)	.15
Johnson, Bob W. (60-70)	.15
Johnson, Chet	.50
Johnson, Cliff (stamped)	.03
Johnson, Connie	.15
Johnson, Darrell	.15
Johnson, Dave A. (65-78)	.20
Johnson, Dave C. (72-78)	.15
Johnson, Deron	.15
Johnson, Dick A.	.15
Johnson, Don R. (47-58)	.35
Johnson, Don S. (43-48)	.35
Johnson, Earl	.15
Johnson, Ed	
deceased 7-3-75	1.50
Johnson, Ernie	.15
Johnson, Frank	.20
Johnson, Hank	.15
Johnson, Jerry	.50
Johnson, John Henry	.15
Johnson, John "Swede" (44)	7.00
**** h * o * f ****	
Johnson, Judy	HOF
inducted 1975	
auto. cut signature	.50
autographed 3x5	1.00
yellow plaque	3.00
autographed photo	2.00
autographed ball	8.00

Johnson, Ken C. (47-52)	.35
Johnson, Ken T. (58-70)	.15
Johnson, Lamar	.15
Johnson, Larry	.15
Johnson, Lou	3.00
Johnson, Roy	.15
Johnson, Si	.15
Johnson, Stan	.15
Johnson, Syl	.15
Johnson, Tim	.15
Johnson, Tom R. (74-78)	.15
Johnson, Victor O.	.15
**** h * o * f ****	
Johnson, Walter	HOF
inducted 1936	
deceased 12-10-46	
auto. cut signature	40.00
autographed 3x5	80.00
autographed photo	65.00
auto. gum card	+65.00
autographed ball	100.00
Johnston, Rex	.15
Johnstone, Jay	.25
Joiner, Roy M.	.15
Jok, Stan	
deceased 3-6-72	3.00
Jolley, Smead	.15
Jolly, David	
deceased 5-27-63	10.00
Jones, Art	.15
Jones, Bob	.15
Jones, Cleon	1.00
Jones, Dale E. "Nubs"	
deceased 11-8-80	.60
Jones, Dalton	.15
Jones, David J.	
deceased 3-30-72	1.50

Jones, Decatur	.15
Jones, Earl	.15
Jones, Gordon	.15
Jones, Jesse	
deceased 9-7-77	1.25
Jones, Lynn	.15
Jones, Mack	.25
Jones, Nippy	.15
Jones, Odell	.15
Jones, Randy	.30
Jones, Red (Ump)	.15
Jones, Rick	.15
Jones, Samuel (51-)	
deceased 11-5-71	6.50
Jones, Samuel Pond (14-)	
deceased 7-6-66	4.50
Jones, Steve	.15
Jones, Willie	6.00
Jonnard, Clarence "Bubba"	
deceased 8-23-77	1.00
Joost, Eddie	.15
Jordan, Baxter "Buck"	.15
Jordan, Niles	.15
Jordan, Tom	.45
Jorgens, Art	
deceased 3-17-80	.50
Jorgenson, Carl	.15
Jorgensen, John "Spider"	.15
Jorgensen, Mike	.35
Joseph, Ricardo Emelino	
deceased 1979	3.00
Josephson, Duane	.15
Joshua, Von	.25
**** h * o * f ****	
Joss, Addie	HOF
deceased 4-14-11	
inducted 1978	
auto. cut signature	200.00
autographed 3x5	325.00
autographed photo	300.00
auto. gum card	+300.00
autographed ball	500.00

Joyce, Bob	.15
Joyce, Dick	.15
Judd, Oscar	2.00
Judge, Joseph Ignatius	
deceased 3-11-63	6.50
Judnich, Walter Franklin	
deceased 7-12-71	2.00
Judson, Howie	.15
Judy, Lyle	2.00
Jumonville, George	.65
Jungels, Ken	
deceased 9-9-75	1.25
Jurewicz, Mike	.15
Jurges, Bill	.15
Jurisich, Al	.25
Just, Joe	.40
Jutze, Skip	.15

Kaat, Jim	.25
Kahle, Bob	.15
Kahn, Lou	.15
Kaiser, Alfred	
deceased 4-11-69	2.50
Kaiser, Bob	.15
Kaiser, Don	.15
Kaiser, Ken (Ump)	.15
Kalin, Frank	
deceased 1-12-75	1.25
**** h * o * f ****	
Kaline, Al	HOF
inducted 1980	
auto. cut signature	.50
autographed 3x5	1.00
autographed photo	3.00
auto. gum card	+3.00
autographed ball	9.00

Kallia, Rudy	
deceased 4-6-79	.65
Kalloway, Dan	.15
Kamm, Willie	.15
Kampouris, Alex	.75
Kane, Thomas	
deceased 11-26-73	1.50
Kanehl, Rod	.15
Karl, Andy	.15
Karow, Marty	.15
Karpel, Hal	.50
Karr, Ben	
deceased 12-8-68	2.75
Kasko, Eddie	.15
Katt, Ray	.15
Kaufmann, Tony	.15
Kazak, Ed	.15
Kazanski, Ted	.15
Kealey, Steve	.15
Keane, Johnny	
deceased 1-6-67	5.00
Keck, Fred	
deceased 2-6-81	.50
Keefe, Dave	
deceased 2-4-78	1.00

THE PICTURES USED IN THIS SECTION ARE FROM THE PEREZ-STEELE HALL OF FAME POSTCARD SET (SEE RECENT MEMORABILIA SECTION OF THIS BOOK). FOR INFORMATION ON THIS SET WRITE PEREZ-STEELE GALLERIES, DEPT. MPG, BOX 1776, FORT WASHINGTON, PA 19034.

**** h * o * f ****
Keefe, Tim HOF
deceased 4-23-33
inducted 1964
auto. cut signature 125.00
autographed 3x5 250.00
autographed photo 200.00
auto. gum card +200.00
autographed ball 500.00

Keegan, Bob .15
**** h * o * f ****
Keeler, Willie HOF
deceased 1-1-23
inducted 1939
auto. cut signature 125.00
autographed 3x5 250.00
autographed photo 200.00
auto. gum card +200.00
autographed ball 500.00

Keely, Bob .15
Keen, Vic
deceased 12-10-76 1.00
Kehn, Chet 1.00
Kekich, Mike .15
Kell, Everett .15
Kell, George .25
Kelleher, Frank
deceased 4-13-79 1.00
Kelleher, Mick .15
Keller, Charlie .20
Keller, Hal .15
Keller, Ron .15
Kellert, Frank
deceased 11-19-76 2.00
Kelley, Dick .15
**** h * o * f ****
Kelley, Joe HOF
deceased 8-14-43
inducted 1971
auto. cut signature 100.00
autographed 3x5 175.00
autographed photo 150.00
auto. gum card +150.00
autographed ball 300.00

Kelley, Tom .15
Kellner, Alex .15
Kellner, Walt .15
**** h * o * f ****
Kelly, George L. HOF
inducted 1973
auto. cut signature .50
autographed 3x5 1.00
yellow plaque 2.00
autographed photo 1.50
auto. gum card +2.50
autographed ball 7.50

**** h * o * f ****
Kelly, King HOF
deceased 11-8-94
inducted 1945
auto. cut signature 250.00
autographed 3x5 400.00
autographed photo 400.00
auto. gum card +400.00
autographed ball 750.00
Kelly, Pat .15
Kelly, J. Thomas .15
Kelly, Van .15
Kelso, Bill .15
Keltner, Ken .20
Kemmerer, Russ .25
Kemner, Dutch .60
Kemp, Steve .35
on Topps card +.50
Kendall, Fred .15
Kenna, Eddie
deceased 8-21-72 1.50
Kennedy, Arthur .15
Kennedy, Bill 1.50
Kennedy, Bob .15

Kennedy, John .15
Kennedy, Junior .15
Kennedy, Monte 2.50
Kennedy, Terry .20
Kennedy, Vernon .15
Kenney, Jerry .15
Kenworthy, Dick .15
Keough, Joe .45
Keough, Marty .35
Keough, Matt .15
Kerlin, Orie
deceased 10-29-74 1.25
Kern, Jim .25
Kern, William G. .15
Kernek, George .15
Kerns, Russ .15
Kerr, J.M. .15
Kerr, John Joseph "Buddy" .50
Kerr, Johnny .15
Kerr, Richard Henry
deceased 5-4-63 6.50
Kessinger, Don .20
stamped .03
Kester, Rick .35
Khames, John .15
Kibbie, Hod
deceased 10-19-75 1.30
Kibble, John
deceased 12-13-69 2.50
Kibler, John (Ump) .15
Kiely, Leo .15
Kilkenny, Mike .20
Killebrew, Harmon .60
on Topps card +1.00
Kimball, Newell .15
Kimm, Bruce .15
Kimmick, Walter .15

Kindall, Jerry .15
Kinder, Ellis Raymond
deceased 10-16-68 6.00
**** h * o * f ****
Kiner, Ralph HOF
inducted 1975
auto. cut signature .50
autographed 3x5 1.00
yellow plaque 2.00
autographed photo 2.00
auto. gum card +2.00
autographed ball 7.50
King, Chick .15
King, Clyde .15
King, Jim .15
King, Lynn
deceased 5-11-72 1.50
King, Nellie .15
Kingdon, Wes
deceased 4-19-75 1.50
Kingman, Dave 1.00
on Topps card +2.00
Kinnamon, Bill (Ump) .15
Kinney, Dennis .15
Kinsella, Ed
deceased 1-17-76 1.25
Kinzy, Harry .15
Kipp, Fred .15
Kipper, Thornton .15
Kirby, Clay .15
Kirby, Jim .15

Name	Price
Kirk, Bill	.15
Kirkland, Willie	.25
Kirkpatrick, Ed	.20
Kirkwood, Don	.15
Kirrene, Joe	.15
Kish, Ernie	.15
Kison, Bruce	.20
Kissell, George	.15
Kittle, Hub	.15
Klaerner, Hugo	.15
Klages, Fred	.15
Klaus, Bill	.15
Klaus, Bob	.15
Klee, Ollie	
deceased 2-9-77	1.00
**** h * o * f ****	
Klein, Chuck	HOF
deceased 3-28-58	
inducted 1980	
auto. cut signature	25.00
autographed 3x5	50.00
autographed photo	35.00
auto. gum card	+35.00
autographed ball	75.00

Name	Price
Klein, Lou	
deceased 6-20-76	1.00
Kleinhans, Ted	.15
**** h * o * f ****	
Klem, Bill	HOF
deceased 9-16-51	
inducted 1953	
auto. cut signature	40.00
autographed 3x5	80.00
autographed photo	80.00
autographed ball	100.00
Klieman, Ed	
deceased 11-15-79	.70
Klimchock, Lou	.15
Klimkowski, Ron	.15
Kline, Bob	.15
Kline, Ron	.15
Kline, Steve	.15
Klinger, Bob	
deceased 8-9-77	.90
Klippstein, Johnny	.15
Klopp, Stan	
deceased 3-11-80	.50
Kluszewski, Ted	.35
on Topps card	+.50
Klutts, Mickey	.15
Kluttz, Clyde	
deceased 5-12-79	.75
Knapp, Chris	.15
Knepper, Bob	.15
Knetzer, Elmer	
deceased 10-3-75	1.25
Knicely, Alan	.15
Knickerbocker, A.	.15
Knickerbocker, William Hart	
deceased 9-8-63	6.50
Knight, Ray	.35
Knoop, Bobby	.15
Knott, Jack	.25
Knowles, Darold	.15
Knox, Cliff	
deceased 9-24-65	4.00
Knox, John	.15
Kobel, Kevin	.15
Koecher, Dick	1.00
Koenig, Fred	.30
Koenig, Mark	.15
Kokos, Dick	.15
Kolb, Gary	.15
Kolloway, Don	.45
Kolstad, Hal	.20
Konieczny, Doug	.15
Konopka, Bruce	.75
Konstanty, Jim	
deceased 6-11-76	2.00
Koonce, Cal	.15
Koosman, Jerry	.35
Kopf, Larry	.15
Koplitz, Howie	.15
Koppe, Joe	.50
Korcheck, Steve	.15
Kores, Artie	
deceased 3-26-74	1.25
Kosco, Andy	.15
Koshorek, Clem	.15
Koski, Bill	.15
Koslo, Dave	
deceased 12-1-75	1.50
Kosman, Mike	.60
Kostro, Frank	.15
**** h * o * f ****	
Koufax, Sandy	HOF
inducted 1972	
auto. cut signature	.50
autographed 3x5	1.00
yellow plaque	3.00
autographed photo	3.00
auto. gum card	+3.00
autographed ball	10.00
Koy, Ernie	.15
Krakauskas, Joseph V. L.	
deceased 12-8-60	7.50
Kralick, Jack	.15
Kramer, Jack	.15

Name	Price
Kranepool, Ed	.15
Krausse, Lew Jr.	.15
Krausse, Lew Sr.	.15
Kravec, Ken	.15
Kravitz, Danny	.15
Kreevich, Mike	.15
Kreitner, Mickey	.45
Kremer, Remy Peter	
deceased 2-8-65	5.00
Kremmel, Jim	.15
Kress, Charlie	.15
Kress, Ralph	
deceased 11-29-62	6.50
Kretlow, Lou	.35
Kreutzer, Frank	.15
Krieger, Kurt	
deceased 8-16-70	2.25
Krist, Howard	.15
Kroc, Ray (Exec.)	.30
Kroll, Jack	.15
Kroner, John Harold	
deceased 8-26-68	3.00
Krsnich, Mike	.15
Krsnich, Rocky	1.50
Krueger, Ernie	
deceased 4-22-76	1.00
Krueger, Rich	.15
Krug, Chris	.15
Krukow, Mike	.15
Kryhoski, Dick	.15
Kubek, Tony	.35
on Topps card	+.50
Kubiak, Ted	.15
Kubiszyn, Jack	.15
Kucab, Johnny	
deceased 5-26-77	1.00
Kucek, Jack	.15
Kucks, Johnny	.15
Kuczek, Stan	.15
Kuczynski, Burt	.15
Kuehl, Karl	.15
Kuenn, Harvey	.25
Kuhel, Joe	.15
Kuhn, Bowie (Exec.)	.20
Kuiper, Duane	.15
Kunkel, Bill	.15
Kurowski, Whitey	.15
Kush, Emil	
deceased 11-26-69	2.25
Kusick, Craig	.15
Kusnyer, Art	.15
Kutyna, Marty	.15
Kuzava, Bob	.15

Name	Price
Laabs, Chet	.15
Labine, Clem	.15
Laboy, Jose	.20
Lacey, Bob	.15
Lachemann, Marcel	.15
Lachemann, Rene	.15
LaCock, Pete	.20
LaCorte, Frank	.15
LaCoss, Mike	.20
Lacy, Lee	.25
LaFata, Joe	.15
Lafitte, Ed	
deceased 4-12-71	2.00
Lagger, Edwin	2.00
LaGrow, Lerrin	.15
Lahoud, Joe	.15

Lajeskie, Dick	
deceased 8-15-76	1.50
**** h * o * f ****	
Lajoie, Napoleon	HOF
inducted 1937	
deceased 2-7-59	
auto. cut signature	20.00
autographed 3x5	30.00
b & w plaque	40.00
autographed photo	25.00
auto. gum card	+25.00
autographed ball	50.00

Lakeman, Al	
deceased 5-25-76	1.25
Lamabe, Jack	.15
LaMacchia, Al	.15
Lamanna, Frank	
deceased 9-11-80	1.00
Lamanno, Roy	.15
LaMaster, Wayne	.15
Lamb, Ray	.15
Lambert, Clay	.50
Lambert, Gene	.15
Lamont, Gene	.15
Lamp, Dennis	.15
Lampard, Keith	.15
Lanahan, Dick	
deceased 3-12-75	1.25
Lance, Gary	.15
Landestoy, Rafael	.20
Landis, Bill	.15
Landis, Jim	.15
**** h * o * f ****	
Landis, Kenesaw M.	HOF
inducted 1944	
deceased 11-25-44	
auto. cut signature	25.00
autographed 3x5	60.00
autographed photo	25.00
auto. gum card	+25.00
autographed ball	55.00

Landreaux, Ken	.25
Landrith, Hobie	.15
Landrum, Don	.35
Landrum, Joe	.15
Landrum, Terry	.15
Lane, Jerry	.15
Lanford, L.G.	
deceased 9-14-70	2.25
Lanfranconi, W.O.	2.00
Lang, Bob	.15
Lang, Don	.15
Lange, Dick	.15
Lange, Erv	
deceased 4-24-71	2.00
Langford, Rick	.15
Langford, Sam	1.50
Lanier, Hal	.15
Lanier, Max	.15
Lanning, John	.15
Lansford, Carney	.35
on gum card	+.60
LaPalme, Paul	.15
Lapihuska, Andy	1.50
Larker, Norm	.15
Larkin, Stephen Patrick	
deceased 5-2-69	2.50
LaRoche, Dave	.15
LaRose, Vic	.50
LaRoss, Harry	
deceased 3-22-54	8.00
Larsen, Don	.30
Larson, Dan	.15
LaRussa, Tony	.15
Lary, Al	.15
Lary, Frank	.25
Lary, Lyn	
deceased 1-9-73	1.50
Lasley, Bill	.15
Lasorda, Tom	.20
Lathers, Chick	
deceased 7-26-71	2.00
Latman, Barry	.50
Lau, Charley	.15
Lauzerique, George	.85
Lavagetto, Cookie	.25
Lavelle, Gary	.15
Law, Rudy	.25
Law, Vance	.15
Law, Vernon	.35
Lawing, Butch	1.00
Lawrence, Brooks	.35
Lawson, A. V. "Roxie"	
deceased 4-9-77	1.00
Lawson, Steve	.15
Laxton, Bill	.15
Laydon, Pete	.50
Layne, Herman	
deceased 8-27-73	1.50
Layne, Hillis	.15
Layton, Les	.50
Lazar, Dan	.15
Lazor, John	.15
Lazzeri, Anthony Michael	
deceased 8-6-46	25.00
Lea, Charlie	.15
Leach, Fred	.15
Leach, Tommy	
deceased 9-29-69	2.50
Leal, Luis	.20
Lear, Charles	
deceased 10-31-76	1.25
Leathers, Hal	
deceased 4-12-77	1.25
Ledbetter, Slats	
deceased 2-1-69	2.50
Lee, Bill C. (34-47)	
deceased 6-15-77	1.00
Lee, Bill F. (69-)	.20
Lee, Bob	.15
Lee, Clifford	
deceased 8-25-80	.50
Lee, Don E.	.15
Lee, Dudley	
deceased 1-7-71	2.25
Lee, Hal	.15
Lee, Leron	.25
Lee, Mike	.15
Lee, Roy	.25
Lee, Thornton	.15
Leek, Gene	.15
Lefebvre, Jim	.20
Lefebvre, Joe	.15
Lefebvre, Wilfred	.15
Lefler, Wade	.15
LeFlore, Ron	.65
on Topps card	+1.00

Legett, Louis	.15
Lehman, Ken	.15
Lehner, Paul Eugene	
deceased 12-27-67	5.00
Leiber, Hank	.15
Leibrandt, Charles	.15
Leifield, A.P. "Lefty"	
deceased 10-10-70	2.25
Leinhauser, W. C.	
deceased 4-14-78	.90
Leip, Eddie	.15
LeJohn, Don	.15
Lemanczyk, Dave	.15
Lemaster, Denny	.15
Lemaster, Johnnie	.15
Lemay, Dick	.15
**** h * o * f ****	
Lemon, Bob	HOF
inducted 1976	
auto. cut signature	.35
autographed 3x5	.75
yellow plaque	2.50
autographed photo	1.50
auto. gum card	+2.00
autographed ball	8.00

Lemon, Chet	.50
on Topps card	+.75
Lemon, Jim	.25
Lemonds, Dave	.15
Lemongello, Mark	.15
Lenhardt, Don	.15
Lennon, Robert	.25
Leon, Eddie	.15
Leon, Max	.15
**** h * o * f ****	
Leonard, Buck	HOF
inducted 1972	
auto. cut signature	.50
autographed 3x5	1.00
yellow plaque	2.00
autographed photo	1.50
auto. gum card	+1.50
autographed ball	7.50

Leonard, Dennis .25
on Topps card +.40
Leonard, Elmer "Tiny"
deceased 5-27-81 .50
Leonard, Emil "Dutch" .15
Leonhard, Dave .15
Lepcio, Ted .15
Leppert, Don .15
Lerch, Randy .15
Lerchen, George .15
Leshnock, Don .15
Leslie, Roy
deceased 4-9-72 1.50
Leslie, Sam
deceased 1-21-79 .80
Letchas, Charlie .15
Levan, Jesse 7.50
Levey, Jimmy
deceased 3-14-70 2.25
Levsen, Emil "Dutch"
deceased 3-12-72 1.50
Levy, Lenny .15
Lewallyn, Dennis .15
Lewis, Allan 1.50
Lewis, Buddy .15
Lewis, G. E. "Duffy"
deceased 6-17-79 .80
Lewis, Johnny .15
Lewis, William A. "Buddy"
deceased 10-24-77 1.00
Lezcano, Carlos .20
Lezcano, Sixto .40
Libke, Al .15
Libran, Francisco .20
Liddle, Don .15
Lieb, Fred (bb writer)
deceased 6-3-80 .25
Lillard, Bill .15
Lillard, Gene .15
Lillis, Bob .15
Limmer, Lou .15
Lind, Jack .15
Lindbeck, Emerick .15
Lindblad, Paul .25
Lindell, John .15
Linden, Walt .15
Lindquist, Carl .15
**** h * o * f ****
Lindstrom, Fred HOF
inducted 1976
deceased 10-4-81
auto. cut signature .50
autographed 3x5 1.00
yellow plaque 3.00
autographed photo 2.00
auto. gum card +2.50
autographed ball 9.00

Linke, Ed .15
Lintz, Larry 1.00
Linz, Phil 1.50
Linzy, Frank .15
Lipietri, M.A. .15
Lipon, Johnny .15
Lipscomb, Jerry
deceased 2-27-78 1.00
Lipski, Bob .15
Lis, Joe .15
Lisenbee, Hod 1.50
Littell, Mark .15
Little, Jim .15
Littlefield, Dick .15
Littlefield, John .15
Littlejohn, Dennis .15
Litwhiler, Danny .25
Lively, Bud .15
Lively, Jack
deceased 12-5-67 3.00
Livingood, Wes .15
Livingston, M. .50
Livingston, Paddy
deceased 9-19-77 1.00
**** h * o * f ****
Lloyd, John Henry HOF
deceased 3-19-64
inducted 1977
auto. cut signature 75.00
autographed 3x5 150.00
autographed photo 150.00
autographed ball 250.00

Loane, Bob 1.25
Lobert, Hans
deceased 9-14-68 3.00
Locke, Bobby .15
Locke, Charles .15
Locker, Bob .15
Locklear, Gene .15
Lockman, Whitey .15
Lockwood, Claude "Skip" .15
Lodigiani, Dario .15
Loes, Billy 2.00
Lofato, Joe .15
Logan, Bob (Lefty)
deceased 5-20-78 1.00
Logan, Johnny .15
Lohr, Howard
deceased 6-9-77 1.00
Lohrke, Jack .50
Lohrman, Bill .25
Lolich, Mickey .65
on Topps card +1.00
Lollar, Sherm
deceased 9-24-77 2.00
on Topps card +3.00
Lollar, Tim .15
Lombardi, Ernie
deceased 9-26-77 1.50
Lombardi, Vic .65
Lonborg, Jim .20
Long, Dale .25
Long, James
deceased 9-14-70 2.25
Long, J.K. "Jeoff" .15
Long, Thomas A.
deceased 6-15-72 1.50
Lonnett, Joe .15
Look, Bruce .15
Lopat, Ed .25
Lopata, Stan .15
Lopatka, Art .15
Lopes, Dave .50
**** h * o * f ****
Lopez, Al HOF
inducted 1977
auto. cut signature .35
autographed 3x5 .75
yellow plaque 2.00
autographed photo 1.50
auto. gum card +1.50
autographed ball 7.50

Lopez, Aurelio .25
Lopez, Hector .50
Lotz, Joe
deceased 10-9-69 2.50
Loucks, Scott .15
Loun, Don .15
Lovelace, Tom
deceased 7-12-79 .90
Lovett, Merritt .15
Lovitto, Joe .25
Lovrich, Pete .15
Low, Fletcher
deceased 6-6-73 1.50
Lowdermilk, Louis
deceased 12-27-75 1.00
Lowenstein, John .15
Lown, Turk .15
Lowrey, Peanuts .15
Lowry, Sam .75
Lucadello, John .15
Lucas, C.F. "Red" .15
Lucas, Fred .15
Lucas, Gary .15
Lucas, John
deceased 10-31-70 2.25
Lucas, Ray
deceased 10-9-69 2.50
Lucchesi, Frank .15
Lucey, Joseph
deceased 7-30-80 .50
Luciano, Ron (Ump) .25
Lucier, Lou .15
Luebbe, Ray .15
Luebber, Steve .15
Luebke, Dick
deceased 12-4-74 2.50
Luhrsen, W. F.
deceased 8-15-73 1.50
Lukon, Eddie .15
Lum, Mike .15
Lumenti, Ralph .15
Lumpe, Jerry .25
Luna, Memo 10.00
Lund, Don .15
Lund, Gordon .15
Lundgren, Delmar .15
Lupien, Tony .15
Luplow, Al .15
Luque, Adolfo
deceased 7-3-57 8.00
Lutz, Louie .15
Lutz, Joe .15
Luzinski, Greg 1.00
on Topps card +2.00
Lyle, Sparky .50
on Topps card +.80
Lynch, Jerry .15
Lynch, Walter
deceased 12-21-76 1.00
Lynn, Fred 1.00
on Topps card +2.00
Lynn, J.M. (Red)
deceased 10-27-77 1.00
Lyons, Eddie .50
Lyons, George
deceased 1981 .60

Lyons, Herschell .15
Lyon, Russ .25
**** h * o * f ****
Lyons, Ted HOF
inducted 1955
auto. cut signature .75
autographed 3x5 1.50
yellow plaque 3.00
b & w plaque 10.00
autographed photo 3.00
auto. gum card +3.00
autographed ball 10.00

Lyttle, Jim .15

Maas, Duke
deceased 12-7-76 3.00
MacDonald, Bill .50
MacDonald, Webster .20
MacFayden, Danny
deceased 8-26-72 1.50
**** h * o * f ****
Mack, Connie HOF
inducted 1937
deceased 2-8-56
auto. cut signature 15.00
autographed 3x5 25.00
b & w plaque 25.00
autographed photo 20.00
auto. gum card +20.00
autographed ball 35.00

Mack, Earle
deceased 2-4-67 3.50
Mack, Joe 1.00
Mack, Raymond James
deceased 5-7-69 2.50
Mackanin, Pete .15
Mackenzie, H.G. .15
Mackenzie, Ken .15

Mackiewicz, Felix .15
Macko, Steve
deceased 11-15-81 1.00
MacLeod, Ralph .15
MacLeod, William D. .15
Macon, Max .15
**** h * o * f ****
MacPhail, Larry HOF
deceased 10-1-75
inducted 1978
auto. cut signature 10.00
autographed 3x5 20.00
autographed photo 20.00
autographed ball 30.00

MacPhail, Lee (Exec.) .20
MacPherson, Harry .50
MacWhorter, Keith .15
Maddern, Clarence .50
Maddox, Elliott .15
Maddox, Garry .50
Madlock, Bill .40
Maestri, H.A. .15
Maggert, Harl 3.00
Maglie, Sal .40
Magnuson, Jim .15
Magrini, P.A. .15
Maguire, Jack .15
Mahaffey, Lee Roy
deceased 7-23-69 3.00
Mahan, Art .15
Mahlberg, Greg .15
Mahler, Mickey .15
Mahoney, Bob .15
Mahoney, Jim .15
Maier, Bob 1.00
Mails, Walter
deceased 7-5-74 1.25
Maisel, George
deceased 11-20-68 2.75
Majeski, Hank .15
Makosky, Frank .15
Malkmus, Bobby .15
Mallette, Mal .15
Mallon, Les .15
Mallonee, H. B.
deceased 6-11-79 .90
Mallory, Jim .15
Malmberg, Harry
deceased 10-29-76 1.00
Malone, Eddie .50
Malone, Lew
deceased 7-5-74 1.25
Malone, Perce Leigh
deceased 5-13-43 15.00
Maloney, George (Ump) .15
Maloney, Jim .20
Maloy, Paul
deceased 3-18-76 1.00
Maltzberger, Gordon
deceased 12-11-74 1.00
Malzone, Frank .15
Mamaux, Albert Leon
deceased 1-2-63 6.50
Mancuso, Frank .15
Mancuso, Gus .15
Manders, Hal .15
Mangan, Jim .15
Mangual, Angel .70

Manion, Clyde
deceased 9-4-67 3.25
Mankowski, Phil .15
Mann, Garth 1.50
Mann, Johnny
deceased 3-31-77 1.00
Manning, Ernest "Ed"
deceased 4-28-73 1.25
Manning, Rick .15
Manno, Don .15
Mantilla, Felix .60
**** h * o * f ****
Mantle, Mickey HOF
inducted 1974
auto. cut signature 5.00
autographed 3x5 10.00
yellow plaque 10.00
autographed photo 12.00
auto. gum card +12.00
autographed ball 40.00

Manuel, Chuck .15
**** h * o * f ****
Manush, Heine HOF
inducted 1964
deceased 5-12-71
auto. cut signature 2.00
autographed 3x5 4.00
yellow plaque 6.00
autographed photo 4.00
auto. gum card +5.00
autographed ball 15.00

Mapes, Cliff .15
Maple, Howard
deceased 11-9-70 2.00
Maranda, Georges .25

**** h * o * f ****
Maranville, Rabbit HOF
deceased 1-5-54
inducted 1954
auto. cut signature 20.00
autographed 3x5 45.00
autographed photo 55.00
auto. gum card +55.00
autographed ball 75.00

Marberry, Fred
deceased 6-30-76 1.25
Marcum, John .25
Marentette, Leo .15
Marichal, Juan 1.00
on Topps card +2.00
Marion, Marty .20
Marion, Red
deceased 3-13-75 1.50
Maris, Roger .60
on Topps card +1.00
Markell, Duke .15
Markland, Gene .15
Marlowe, Richard Burton
deceased 12-30-68 4.00
Marone, Lou .60
**** h * o * f ****
Marquard, Rube HOF
inducted 1971
deceased 6-1-80
(stamped) .05
auto. cut signature .80
autographed 3x5 2.00
yellow plaque 3.00
autographed photo 2.50
auto. gum card +2.50
autographed ball 10.00

Marquez, Luis .25
Marquis, Bob .20
Marquis, Roger .20
Marrero, Connie 1.00
Marsh, Fred .15
Marshall, Bill
deceased 5-5-77 1.00
Marshall, Charlie .25
Marshall, Dave .40
Marshall, Edward .15
Marshall, Jim R. .15
Marshall, Keith .15
Marshall, Max 2.00
Marshall, Mike 10.00
Marshall, Roy D. "Cy"
deceased 6-11-80 .60
Marshall, Willard W. .15
Martin, Alfred "Billy" 1.00
on Topps card +2.00
Martin, Babe .50
Martin, Fred
deceased 6-11-79 .75
Martin, Herschel
deceased 11-17-80 .50
Martin, Jack
deceased 7-4-80 .60
Martin, Joe .15
Martin, John L. "Pepper"
deceased 3-5-65 6.00
Martin, Morris .50
Martin, Ray .50
Martin, Stu .15
Martinez, Buck .15
Martinez, Jose .25
Martinez, Marty .20
Martinez, Orlando O. .20
Martinez, Ted .20
Martinez, Tippy .25
Marty, Joe .15
Martyn, Bob .15
Martz, Randy .15
Mashore, Clyde .15
Masi, Phil .15
Mason, Don .15
Mason, Jim .15
Masters, Walt .15
Masterson, P.N. "Lefty" .15
Masterson, Walt .15
Matarazzo, Len .15
Matchick, Tom .65
Mathes, Joe
deceased 12-21-78 .90
**** h * o * f ****
Mathews, Eddie HOF
inducted 1978
auto. cut signature .50
autographed 3x5 1.00
yellow plaque 2.50
autographed photo 2.00
auto. gum card +2.00
autographed ball 9.00

Mathews, Nelson .15
**** h * o * f ****
Mathewson, Christy HOF
deceased 10-7-25
inducted 1936
auto. cut signature 100.00
autographed 3x5 175.00
autographed photo 175.00
auto. gum card +150.00
autographed ball 300.00
Mathewson, Dale .50
Mathias, Carl .15
Matlack, Jon .20
Matthews, Gary .45
Mattick, Bobby .15
Mattox, Cloy .60
Mattox, Jim
deceased 10-12-73 1.50
Matula, Rick .15
Matuzak, Harry A.
deceased 11-26-78 .90
Mauch, Gene .20
Mauldin, Marshall .70
Mauney, Dick
deceased 2-6-70 2.25
Mauro, Carmen 1.50
Mavis, Bob .15
Maxie, Larry .15
Maxvill, Dal .15
Maxwell, Charlie .15
May, Dave .25
May, Frank S. (Jake)
deceased 6-3-70 2.00
May, Jerry .25
May, Lee .45
May, Merrill "Pinky" .15
May, Milt .15
May, Rudy .15
Mayberry, John .35
on Topps card +.50
Maye, Lee .40
Mayo, Jack .15
Mays, Carl William
deceased 4-4-71 2.50
**** h * o * f ****
Mays, Willie HOF
inducted 1979
auto. cut signature 1.00
autographed 3x5 3.00
yellow plaque 6.00
autographed photo 6.00
auto. gum card +6.00
autographed ball 15.00

FIRST BASE
A SPORTS MEMORABILIA STORE
c/o GERVISE FORD
9916 VISTADALE
DALLAS, TEXAS 75238
(214) 327-9581 (STORE)
SAT & SUN ONLY

Our store is located in Dallas at the corner of Garland Road and Jupiter Road in the Lockwood Mall. It is the most complete sports nostalgia shop in the Southwest. We have been in business since June 1980 and have already sold tens of thousands of cards and other items to hundreds of satisfied customers. Just send a self-addressed stamped envelope for our price list of cards for sale. Special bonus for Texas residents: free Ranger or Astro card included with our price list. Our well-stocked inventory of over a million items roughly consists of the following:

(1) 800,000 baseball cards from 1910 to the present including Topps, Bowman, Post, Play Ball, Goudey, Fleer, Red Man, etc., including complete sets from most of the years between 1952 and 1980.

(2) 150,000 football, basketball, hockey, non-sport, etc., cards including many complete sets.

(3) 2,000 hardbound and paperback sports books (old and new).

(4) Thousands of sports magazines and programs covering all sports.

(5) 13,000 autographs, primarily on Topps cards.

(6) A full line of price guides, albums, plastic sheets, ball holders, card lockers, and other hobby supplies.

(7) Over 500 cigarette baseball cards from early 1900's.

(8) Special section devoted to Cowboys, Rangers, Astros, and Oilers containing over 6,500 cards from these Texas teams.

(9) Numerous other one-of-a-kind baseball and football collectible items.

BUYING

We are interested in buying collections and accumulations of cards and autographs either for resale or for our own collections. We especially need pre-1942 cards.

FOR SALE–BASEBALL

OFFER 1: Select one of the following years or year combinations and receive $25 worth for $20 or $50 worth for $40 or $100 worth for $75:

a. 1955 Topps, b. 1956 Topps, c. 1957 Topps, d. 1958 Topps, e. 1959 Topps, f. 1960 Topps, g. 1961 Topps, h. 1962 Topps, i. 1963-1965 Topps, j. 1966-1969 Topps, k. 1970-1976 Topps, l. 1955 Bowman, m. 1961-1963 Post, n. 1960-1961 Fleer.

OFFER 2: You tell us the name of your favorite team or teams and we'll send you $100 worth of cards for $80 (Yankees $90) or $50 worth for $40. Cards will be Topps and Bowman from 1952-1972 from only the team(s) you designate.

OFFER 3: Selling autographed Topps cards 1960-1979: 30 different for $10, 70 different for $20, 200 different for $50, or 500 assorted for $100.

Note that cards in all offers are our choice, although included are specials, stars, and superstars. Selling price has been established at 75% to 90% of the retail value established in this Price Guide. You may include your personal want list with your order, but final selection and choice is ours. All lots are at least 95% vg-mint. Add $1.00 postage to your total order.

Come by and visit us. We're open Saturday and Sunday afternoons and by appointment. When you come in, show us this ad for a 10% discount on a purchase of your choice.

Sincerely,
Gervise Ford

Mazeroski, Bill	.35
Mazzera, Mel	.35
Mazzilli, Lee	.35
on gum card	+.50
McAnally, Ernie	.15
McArthur, Oland	.15
McAuliffe, Dick	.15
McAvoy, J. E.	
deceased 7-5-73	1.50
McAvoy, Tom	.15
McBride, Bake	.75
on Topps card	+1.50
McBride, Geo	
deceased 7-2-73	1.50
McBride, Ken	.15
McBride, Tom	.15
McCabe, Joe	.15
McCabe, Tim	
deceased 4-12-77	1.00
McCahan, Bill	.15
McCalahan, Pete	.15
McCall, Alex	.15
McCall, Bob	.50
McCall, John "Windy"	.15
McCarren, Bill	.15
McCarthy, Alex	
deceased 3-12-78	1.00
**** h * o * f ****	
McCarthy, Joe	HOF
inducted 1957	
deceased 1-13-78	
auto. cut signature	.75
autographed 3x5	1.50
yellow plaque	4.00
b & w plaque	12.00
autographed photo	3.00
auto. gum card	+3.00
autographed ball	15.00

McCarthy, Johnnie	
deceased 9-13-73	1.25
**** h * o * f ****	
McCarthy, Tommy	HOF
deceased 8-5-22	
inducted 1946	
auto. cut signature	200.00
autographed 3x5	325.00
autographed photo	350.00
auto. gum card	+300.00
autographed ball	600.00
McCarver, Tim	.35
McCalin, Eugene "Jeep"	.20
McClain, Joe	.15
McClure, Bob	.15
McCool, Bill	.20
McCormick, Frank	.15
McCormick, Mike F. (56-71)	.15
McCormick, Myron (40-51)	
deceased 4-14-76	1.20
McCorry, Bill	
deceased 3-22-73	1.50
McCosky, Barney	.15
McCovey, Willie	1.00
on Topps card	+2.00
McCoy, Benny	.15
McCoy, Larry (Ump)	.15
McCrabb, Les	.15
McCraw, Tom	.25
McCullough, Clyde	.15

McCullough, Philip L.	1.00
McDaniel, Lindy	.15
McDaniel, Von	.20
McDevitt, Danny	.15
McDonald, Dave	.15
McDonald, Henry	.15
McDonald, Joe	.15
McDonnell, Jim	1.00
McDonnell, Maje	.15
McDougald, Gil	.15
McDowell, Sam	.35
McElyea, Frank	.35
McEnany, Will	.20
McGaha, Mel	.15
McGarr, James	.15
McGee, Bill	.15
McGhee, Bill	.15
McGhee, Ed	.35
McGillen, John	.50
McGinn, Dan	.15
**** h * o * f ****	
McGinnity, Joe	HOF
deceased 11-14-29	
inducted 1946	
auto. cut signature	200.00
autographed 3x5	300.00
autographed photo	350.00
auto. gum card	+300.00
autographed ball	600.00

McGlothen, Lynn	.20
McGlothin, James Milton	
deceased 12-23-75	4.00
McGowan, Earl	.50
McGowan, Jack	.15
McGraw, Bob	
deceased 6-2-78	.90

**** h * o * f ****	
McGraw, John	HOF
deceased 2-25-34	
inducted 1937	
auto. cut signature	60.00
autographed 3x5	125.00
autographed photo	100.00
auto. gum card	+100.00
autographed ball	200.00

McGraw, Tug	.35
on Topps card	+.50
McGregor, Scott	.20
McHale, John	.35
McHale, Marty	
deceased 5-7-79	.80
McIlwain, William Stover	
deceased 1-15-66	9.00
McIntosh, Joe	.15
McKain, Archie	.15
McKay, Dave	.15
**** h * o * f ****	
McKechnie, Bill	HOF
inducted 1962	
deceased 10-29-65	
auto. cut signature	10.00
autographed 3x5	20.00
b & w plaque	35.00
autographed photo	20.00
auto. gum card	+20.00
autographed ball	30.00

McKee, Roger	.15
McKeon, Jack	.15
McKinley, Bill (Ump)	
deceased 8-1-80	.50
McKinney, Rich	.15
McLain, Denny	2.00
on Topps card	+3.00
McLarry, Howard Z. "Polly"	
deceased 11-4-71	2.00
McLaughlin, Bo	.15

Name	Value
McLaughlin, Byron	.35
McLaughlin, Joey	.15
McLeland, Wayne	.15
McLeod, S. James	.15
McLish, Cal	.15
McMahan, Jack	.15
McMahon, Don	.15
McManus, Martin Joseph	
deceased 2-18-66	3.50
McMillan, Norman	
deceased 9-28-69	2.25
McMillan, Roy	.15
McMillan, Tom	.15
McMullen, Ken	.25
McNabb, Carl	.15
McNair, Donald Erie	
deceased 3-11-49	13.00
McNally, Michael Joseph	
deceased 5-29-65	5.00
McNamara, John	.15
McNamara, Thomas	
deceased 5-5-74	1.25
McNamara, Tim	.15
McNamars, Bob	.50
McNertney, Gerry	.15
McNulty, Bill	.50
McQuaig, Gerald	.60
McQueen, Mel	.15
McQueen, Mike	.15
McQuillen, Red	.15
McQuinn, George	
deceased 12-24-78	.85
McRae, Hal	.75
McSherry, John (Ump)	.15
McWilliams, Larry	.15
Mead, Charlie	.50
Meadows, Henry Lee	
deceased 1-29-63	6.50
Medlinger, Irv	
deceased 9-3-75	1.25
**** h * o * f ****	
Medwick, Joe	HOF
inducted 1968	
deceased 3-21-75	
auto. cut signature	1.25
autographed 3x5	2.50
yellow plaque	5.00
autographed photo	3.50
auto. gum card	+3.50
autographed ball	10.00

Name	Value
Meeks, Sammy	.15
Meine, Heine	
deceased 3-18-68	3.00
Meixell, M. M.	.15
Mele, Al "Dutch	
deceased 2-12-75	1.25
Mele, Sam	.15
Melillo, Oscar Donald	
deceased 11-14-63	6.00
Melton, Bill	.15
Melton, Dave	.15
Mendoza, Mario	.25
Menke, Denis	.15
Menze, Ted	
deceased 12-23-69	2.25
Meola, Mike	
deceased 9-1-76	1.00
Meoli, Rudy	.20
Merchant, Jim	.15
Merena, John	
deceased 3-8-77	1.00
Merrill, Durwood (Ump)	.15
Merriman, Lloyd	.15
Merritt, Jim	.15
Merritt, Lloyd	.15
Merson, John	.15
Mertz, Jim	.60
Merullo, Lennie	.15
Mesner, Steve	
deceased 4-6-81	.50
Messenger, Andy	
deceased 11-4-71	1.75
Messersmith, Andy	.35
Metcalf, Tom	.15
Metha, Frank	1.25
Metheny, Bud	.15
Metkovich, George	.15
Metro, Charlie	.15
Metzger, Butch	.20
Metzger, Roger	.15
Metzig, Bill	2.00
Metzler, Alex	
deceased 11-30-73	1.50
Meusel, Bob	
deceased 11-28-77	1.00
Meusel, Emil Frederick	
deceased 3-1-63	6.50
Meusel, Robert William	
deceased 11-28-77	1.25
Meyer, Benny	
deceased 2-6-74	1.50
Meyer, Bob	.15
Meyer, Dan	.15
Meyer, Dutch	.15
Meyer, John Robert	
deceased 3-9-67	9.00
Meyer, Russ	.15
Michael, Gene	.15
Michaels, Cass	.15
Michaels, Johnny	.15
Michaels, Ralph	.15
Mickelson, Ed	.15
Mickens, Glenn	.15
Middleton, James B.	
deceased 1-12-74	1.50
Mierkowicz, Ed	.50
Miggins, Larry	.15
Mihalic, John	.60
Mikkelson, Pete	.15
Miksis, Ed	.35
Milan, Horace Robert	
deceased 6-29-55	10.00
Miles, Carl	.15
Miley, Michael W. (75-76)	
deceased 1-6-77	7.00
on 1976 Topps card	25.00
Miljus, John	
deceased 2-11-76	1.00
Millan, Felix	.25
Miller, Bill	.25
Miller, Bob G. (53-62)	.15
Miller, Bob J. (49-58)	.15
Miller, Bruce	.15
Miller, Dyar	.15
Miller, Ed L. (77-)	.15
Miller, Eddie R. (36-50)	.30
Miller, Edmund "Bing"	
deceased 5-7-66	4.00
Miller, Edwin E. (12-18)	.15
Miller, George	.15
Miller, John A. "Ox"	.15
Miller, John E.	.15
Miller, Leo	
deceased 10-20-73	1.50
Miller, Norm	.15
Miller, Ralph D.	
deceased 5-8-73	1.25
Miller, Ray	.15
Miller, Rick	.15
Miller, Roger	.15
Miller, Rudy	.15
Miller, Stu	.15
Miller, Thomas R.	
deceased 8-13-80	1.00
Miller, Walter J.	
deceased 8-20-75	1.25
Millies, Walt	.15
Milligan, John	
deceased 5-15-72	1.50
Milliken, Bob	.25
Mills, Art	
deceased 7-23-75	1.25
Mills, Bus	.15
Mills, Frank	.15

Name	Value
Mills, Howard R. (34-40)	.70
Milnar, Al	.15
Milnar, Walt	.15
Milne, Art	.15
Milner, John	.15
Milstead, George	
deceased 8-9-77	1.00
Minarcin, Rudy	.15
Mincher, Don	.15
Minetto, Craig	.15
Mingori, Steve	.15
Minner, Paul	.35
Minnick, Don	.15
Minoso, Minnie	.50
on Topps card	+1.00
Minton, Greg	.15
Mirabella, Paul	.15
Miranda, Willie	.25
Mitchell, Dale	.15
Mitchell, Fred	
deceased 10-13-70	2.00
Mitchell, Monroe	
deceased 9-4-76	1.00
Mitchell, Paul	.15
Mitchell, Willie	
deceased 11-23-73	1.25
Mitterwald, George	.15
**** h * o * f ****	
Mize, Johnny	HOF
inducted 1981	
auto. cut signature	.35
autographed 3x5	.75
autographed photo	1.50
auto. gum card	+1.50
autographed ball	9.00

Name	Value
Mizell, Vinegar Bend	.15
Mizeur, Bill	
deceased 8-27-76	1.00
Moates, Dave	.15
Moeller, Joe	.15
Moeller, Ron R.	.15
Moffitt, Randy	.20
Mogridge, George Anthony	
deceased 3-4-62	7.00
Moisan, Bill	.15
Mokan, John	.15
Molinaro, Bob	.15
Molitor, Paul	.35
on gum card	+.50
Moloney, Richie	.15
Monaco, Blas	.15
Monahan, Ed	.15
Monbouquette, Bill	.15
Monchak, Al	.15
Monday, Rick	.65
on Topps card	+1.00
Money, Don	.25
Monge, Sid	.15
Monroe, Larry	.15
Montague, Ed (Ump)	.15
Montague, Eddie	.15
Montague, John	.15
Montanez, Willie	.45
Montefusco, John "Count"	.35
on Topps card	+.50
Montemayor, F.	3.00
Montgomery, Bob	.15
Monzant, Ray	.50

Name	Price
Monzon, Dan	.15
Moock, Joe	.15
Moon, Wally	.20
on Topps card	+.30
Mooney, Jim	
deceased 4-27-79	.75
Moore, Al	
deceased 11-29-74	1.25
Moore, Alvin	.15
Moore, Anse	.50
Moore, Balor	.15
Moore, Charlie	.15
Moore, Dee	.80
Moore, Donnie	.15
Moore, Euel	.25
Moore, G. Eddie	
deceased 2-10-76	1.00
Moore, Gene	
deceased 3-12-78	1.00
Moore, Jackie	.15
Moore, James	.15
Moore, Joe	.25
Moore, Johnny	.15
Moore, Junior	.15
Moore, Randy	.15
Moore, Terry	.20
Moore, Tom	.15
Moore, Tony	.15
Moore, Whitey	.15
Moose, Robert Ralph	
deceased 10-9-76	5.00
Mooty, Jake	
deceased 4-20-70	2.25
Mora, Andres	7.00
Morales, Jerry	.15
Morales, Jose	.25
Morales, Rich	.15
Moran, Billy	.15
Morehart, Ray	.15
Morehead, Dave	.15
Morehead, Seth	.15
Moreno, Omar	.65
on Topps card	+1.00
Moret, Roger	.60
Morgan, Bobby	.35
Morgan, Chester	.15
Morgan, Eddie	
deceased 4-9-80	.50
Morgan, Joe L.	.40
on Topps card	+.60
Morgan, Joe M. (59-64)	.15
Morgan, Tom	.15
Morgan, Vern T.	
deceased 11-8-75	2.50
Morgenweck, Henry (Ump)	.15
Morhardt, Moe	.15
Morlan, John	.15
Morris, Doyt	2.00
Morris, Jack (77-)	.20
on Topps card	+.30
Morris, John W. (66-74)	.15
Morrison, Jim	.30
Morrissey, Joseph Anselm	
deceased 5-2-50	16.00
Morse, Newell	.15
Morton, Carl	.15
Morton, Guy Jr.	.15
Moryn, Walt	.15
Moseby, Lloyd	.15
Moser, Arnie	1.50
Moses, Jerry	.15
Moses, Wally	.15
Moskau, Paul	.15
Moss, C. Malcolm	.15
Moss, Howie	.15
Moss, Les	.15
Moss, Ray	.35
Mossi, Don	.15
Mostil, Johnny	
deceased 12-10-70	2.00
Mota, Manny	.25
on Topps card	+.40
Mott, Bitsy	.15
Motton, Curt	.15
Moulder, Glen	1.00
Mowry, Joe	.15
Mueller, Bill	.50
Mueller, Don	.65
Mueller, Emmett "Heinie"	.15
Mueller, Gordon	.15
Mueller, Heine (20-35)	
deceased 1-23-75	1.25
Mueller, Les	.15
Mueller, Ray	.15
Mueller, Walter J.	
deceased 8-16-71	1.75
Muffett, Billy	.15
Muir, Joseph H.	
deceased 6-25-80	.60
Mulcahy, Hugh	.15
Mulleavy, Gregory Thomas	
deceased 2-1-80	.60
Mullen, Ford	.15
Mullen, Wm. J.	
deceased 5-4-71	2.00
Muller, Freddie	
deceased 10-20-76	1.25
Mulligan, Eddie	.15
Mulligan, Joe	.15
Mullin, Pat	.15
Mullinicks, Rance	.15
Mumphrey, Jerry	.15
Muncrief, Bob	.15
Munger, George "Red"	.65
Mungo, Van Lingle	.20
Munninghoff, Scott	.15
Munson, Joe	.15
Munson, Thurman	
deceased 8-2-79	20.00
on Topps card	+25.00
on '79 Topps card	+50.00
Mura, Steve	.15
Murakami, Masanori	7.50
on Topps card	+25.00
Murcer, Bobby	.35
on Topps card	+.50
Murff, John R. "Red"	.15
Murphy, Dale	.20
on Topps card	+.30
Murphy, Danny	.15
Murphy, Dwane	.20
Murphy, John	
deceased 1-14-70	2.00
Murphy, Tom	.15
Murray, Anthony	
deceased 3-19-74	1.25
Murray, Dale	.15
Murray, Ed	
deceased 11-8-70	2.25
Murray, Eddie	.45
on Topps card	+.75
Murray, Larry	.15
Murray, Ray	.15
Murray, Tony	
deceased 3-19-74	1.50
Murrell, Ivan	.25
Murtaugh, Danny	
deceased 12-2-76	2.00
Muser, Tony	.15
Musgraves, Dennis	.15
**** h * o * f ****	
Musial, Stan	HOF
inducted 1969	
auto. cut signature	.50
autographed 3x5	1.00
yellow plaque	3.00
autographed photo	3.00
auto. gum card	+3.00
autographed ball	10.00

Name	Price
Musser, Paul	
deceased 7-7-73	1.50
Mustaikis, Alex	
deceased 1-17-70	2.50
Myatt, George	.15
Myatt, Glenn Calvin (20-)	
deceased 8-9-69	2.50
Myer, C.S. "Buddy"	
deceased 10-31-74	1.50
Myers, Bill	.15
Myers, Elmer G.	
deceased 7-29-76	1.00
Myers, Richard	.15
Myrick, Bob	.15
Nagel, Bill	9.00
Nagelson, Louis Marcellus	
deceased 10-22-65	5.00
Nagelson, Russ	.15
Nagle, Walter	
deceased 5-27-71	2.00
Nagy, Mike	.15
Nahem, Sam	2.00
Nahorodny, Bill	.15
Naples, Al	.15
Napoleon, Dan	.15
Napp, Larry (Ump)	.15
Naragon, Hal	.15
Narleski, Ray	.15
Narleski, Steve	.15
Narron, Jerry	.15
Narron, Sam	.15
Narum, Buster	.15
Nash, Cotton	.15
Nash, Ken	
deceased 2-16-77	1.00
Navarro, Julio	.35
Naylor, Earl	.50
Naymick, Mike	.15
Neal, Charlie	1.50
Neale, A. Earle	
deceased 11-2-73	3.00
Necciai, Ron	.15
Negray, Ron	.15
Nehf, Arthur Neukom	
deceased 12-18-60	7.50
Neibauer, Gary	.15
Neiger, Al	.15
Neill, Tom	1.50
Neis, Bernie	
deceased 11-29-72	1.50
Nekola, Bats	.15
Nelson, Bob	.15
Nelson, Dave	.15
Nelson, Dick (Ump)	.15
Nelson, Luther	.15
Nelson, Lynn Bernard	
deceased 2-15-55	10.00
Nelson, Mel	.15
Nelson, Rocky	.15
Nelson, Roger	.15
Nelson, Tom C. (45)	
deceased 9-24-73	1.50
Nen, Dick	.15
Nettles, Graig	.35
on gum card	+.50
Nettles, Jim	.15
Nettles, Morris	.15
Neudecker, Jerry (Ump)	.15
Neun, Johnny	.15
Nevel, Ernie	.15
Nevers, Ernie	
deceased 5-3-76	4.00
Newcombe, Don	.25
on Topps card	+.40
Newhouser, Hal	.20
Newlin, Maurice	.15
Newman, Fred	.15
Newman, Jeff	.15
Newsome, Lamar	.15
Niarhos, Gus	.15
Nichols, Chet Jr.	.15
Nichols, Chet Sr.	.15
Nichols, Dolan	.15
**** h * o * f ****	
Nichols, Kid	HOF
inducted 1949	
deceased 4-11-53	
auto. cut signature	15.00
autographed 3x5	30.00
b & w plaque	50.00
autographed photo	30.00
auto. gum card	+30.00
autographed ball	50.00
Nichols, Reid	.15
Nichols, Roy	.50
Nicholson, Bill	.15
Nicholson, Dave	.35
Nicholson, Frank C.	
deceased 11-11-72	1.50

Nicholson, Ovid
deceased 3-24-68 3.00
Niebergall, Charles .15
Niehoff, Bert
deceased 12-8-74 1.25
Niekro, Joe .20
Niekro, Phil .30
on Topps card +.45
Nielsen, Milt .50
Nieman, Bob .15
Niemann, Randy .15
Nietzke, Ernie
deceased 4-22-77 1.00
Niggeling, John Arnold
deceased 9-16-63 7.00
Nippert, Merlin .15
Nischwitz, Ron .15
Nixon, Willard .15
Nolan, Gary .15
Nolan, Joe .15
Nonnenkamp, Leo .15
Nordbrook, Tim .15
Nordhagen, Wayne .15
Noren, Irv .15
Noriega, John .15
Norman, Dan .15
Norman, Fred .15
Norris, Jim .15
Norris, Mike .40
on Topps card +.60
North, Bill .65
on Topps card +1.00
North, Lou
deceased 5-16-74 1.25
Northey, Ronald James
deceased 4-16-71 3.00
Northrup, Jim .15
Norton, Tom .15
Norwood, Willie .20
Nossek, Joe .15
Nottebart, Don .15
Novikoff, Lou
deceased 9-30-70 2.50
Nuxhall, Joe .15
Nye, Rich .15
Nyman, Jerry .15
Nyman, Nyls .15

Oana, Prince
deceased 6-19-76 2.00
Oates, Johnny .15
Oberkfell, Ken .20
O'Bradovich, Jim .15
O'Brien, Eddie .35
O'Brien, Frank
deceased 11-4-71 2.00
O'Brien, Johnny .35
O'Brien, Syd .15
Oceak, Frank .15
Ock, Whitey
deceased 3-18-75 1.25
O'Connell, Jimmy
deceased 11-11-76 1.00
O'Connell, Dan
deceased 10-2-69 4.00
O'Connor, Andy
deceased 9-26-80 .50

O'Dea, Ken .15
O'Dea, Paul
deceased 12-11-78 .70
O'Dell, Billy .35
Odom, Dave 1.00
Odom, Herm
deceased 8-31-70 2.00
Odom, Jim (Ump) .15
Odom, John "Blue Moon" .30
on Topps card +.45
O'Donnell, James M. (Ump) .15
O'Donoghue, John .15
O'Doul, Francis J. "Lefty"
deceased 12-7-69 4.00
Oertel, Charles F. .15
Oeschger, Joe .20
O'Farrell, Bob .15
Office, Rowland .20
Ogden, John M.
deceased 11-9-77 1.00
Ogden, Warren
deceased 8-6-64 5.00
Oglivie, Ben .25
on Topps card +.40
Ojeda, Bob .20
Oldis, Bob .15
Oliva, Tony .40
on Topps card +.75
Olivares, E.B. .25
Oliver, Al .65
on Topps card +1.00
Oliver, Bob .30
Oliver, David .15
Oliver, Gene .15
Oliver, Tom .25
Olivo, Diomedes Antonio
deceased 2-15-77 7.00
Olivo, Federico Emilio
deceased 2-3-77 7.00
Ollom, Jim .15
Olmo, Luis 1.00
Olsen, Al .50
Olsen, Barney
deceased 3-30-77 1.00
Olsen, Vern .15
Olson, Andy (Ump) .15
Olson, T.O. .15
O'Mara, Ollie .15
O'Neal, Skinny .15
O'Neil, Buck .15
O'Neil, Johnny .50
O'Neill, Emmett 1.00
O'Neill, James L.
deceased 9-5-76 1.10
O'Neill, Stephen Francis
deceased 1-26-62 7.00
Onslow, Eddie
deceased 5-8-81 .50
Ontiveros, Steve .35
Oravetz, Ernie .15
Orengo, Joe .15
O'Riley, Don .50
Orosco, Jesse .15
O'Rourke, Frank .25
**** h * o * f ****
O'Rourke, Jim HOF
deceased 1-18-19
inducted 1945
auto. cut signature 150.00
autographed 3x5 250.00
autographed photo 250.00
auto. gum card +200.00
autographed ball 500.00
Orrell, Joe .15
Orsatti, Ernest Ralph
deceased 9-4-68 3.50
Orsino, John .15
Orta, Jorge .40
Ortenzio, Frank .20
Ortiz, José 2.00
Orwoll, Ossie
deceased 5-8-67 3.50
Osborn, Danny .15
Osborn, Don
deceased 4-23-79 .80
Osborne, Larry .15
Osborne, Wayne .15
Osinski, Dan .20
Osteen, Claude .15
Ostermueller, Frederick R.
deceased 12-17-57 9.00
Ostrowski, Joe .15
Ostrowski, John .50
Otis, Amos .30
Otis, Harry G.
deceased 1-29-76 1.25

Otis, Paul .15
O'Toole, Dennis .15
O'Toole, Jim .15
Ott, Ed .15
**** h * o * f ****
Ott, Mel HOF
inducted 1951
deceased 11-21-58
auto. cut signature 15.00
autographed 3x5 25.00
b & w plaque 40.00
autographed photo 30.00
auto. gum card +30.00
autographed ball 50.00

Otten, Jim .15
Oulliber, Johnny .15
Outlaw, Jimmy .20
Overmire, Stubby
deceased 3-3-77 1.50
Owchinko, Bob .15
Owen, Arnold "Mickey" .20
Owen, Marv .25
Owens, Jim .15
Oyler, Andrew
deceased 10-24-70 2.25
Oyler, Ray
deceased 1-26-81 1.00
on Topps card +2.00
Ozark, Danny .15
Ozmer, Horace
deceased 12-28-70 2.25

Pacheco, Tony .15
Paciorek, Tom .20
Padgett, Don .15
Padden, Tom
deceased 6-11-73 1.50
Paepke, Dennis .15
Paepke, Jack .15

Pafko, Andy .15
Pagan, Dave .15
Pagan, Jose .30
Page, Al .15
Page, Joe
  deceased 4-21-80 1.50
Page, Mitchell .35
Page, Sam .50
Page, Vance Linwood
  deceased 7-14-51 16.00
Pagel, Karl .15
Pagliaroni, Jim .25
**** h * o * f ****
Paige, Satchel HOF
  inducted 1971
  auto. cut signature .75
  autographed 3x5 1.50
  yellow plaque 3.50
  autographed photo 3.00
  auto. gum card +3.50
  autographed ball 12.00

Paine, Phil
  deceased 2-19-78 2.50
Palagyi, Mike .15
Palermo, Steve (Ump) .15
Palica, Erv .15
Pallone, Dave (Ump) .15
Palm, Mike .50
Palmer, David .15
Palmer, Edwin .15
Palmer, Jim .60
  on Topps card +1.00
Palmer, Lowell .15
Palmquist, Ed .15
Palys, Stan .15
Panther, Jim .15
Papa, John .15
Paparella, Joe (Ump) .15
Pape, Ken .15
Papi, Stan .15
Pappas, Milt .25
Parent, Fred
  deceased 11-2-72 1.50
Parker, Ace .30
Parker, Billy .15
Parker, Clarence .15
Parker, Dave 1.50
  on Topps card +3.00
Parker, Douglas W. "Dixie"
  deceased 5-15-72 2.00
Parker, Harry .15
Parker, Salty .15
Parker, Wes .20
Parks, Dallas (Ump) .15
Parmalee, Roy .15
Parnell, Mel .15
Parrish, Lance .20
Parrish, Larry .15
Parrott, Mike .15
Parsons, Bill .15
Parsons, Dixie .30
Partee, Roy .15
Partenheimer, H. P.
  deceased 6-16-71 2.00
Partenheimer, S. .15
Partridge, Jay
  deceased 1-4-74 1.50
Pasarella, Art (Ump) .15

Paschal, Bill
  deceased 11-10-74 1.25
Pascual, Camilo .50
Pasek, John P.
  deceased 3-13-76 1.00
Passeau, Claude .15
Pastore, Frank .15
Patek, Fred .20
Pattee, Harry
  deceased 7-17-71 2.00
Patterson, Bill
  deceased 10-1-77 1.00
Patterson, Daryl .15
Pattin, Marty .15
Patton, Gene .15
Patton, Tom A. .15
Paul, Mike .15
Paulson, Paul .15
Pavletich, Don .15
Pawloski, Stan .15
Paxton, Mike .15
Pazik, Mike .15
Peacock, Johnny .15
Pearson, Albie .15
Pearson, Ike .25
Pearson, Monte
  deceased 1-27-78 1.00
Pechous, Charles
  deceased 9-13-80 .50
Peck, Hal .15
Peckinpaugh, Roger
  deceased 11-17-77 .90
Peden, Les .15
Peel, Homer .15
Peerson, Jack
  deceased 10-23-66 3.50
Peery, George .15
Peete, Charles (56)
  deceased 11-27-56 25.00
Pelekoudas, Chris (Ump) .15
Pellagrini, Eddie .25
Pena, Orlando .35
Pena, Tony .20
Pence, Russ W.
  deceased 8-11-71 2.00
Pendleton, Jim 3.50
*** h * o * f ****
Pennock, Herb HOF
  deceased 1-30-48
  inducted 1948
  auto. cut signature 25.00
  autographed 3x5 50.00
  autographed photo 50.00
  auto. gum card +40.00
  autographed ball 75.00

Pentz, Gene .15
Pepitone, Joe .35
  on Topps card +.50
Pepper, Don .15
Pepper, Ray .30
Perconte, Jack .15
Perdue, Hub
  deceased 10-31-68 2.75
Perez, Marty .15
Perez, Pascual .15
Perez, Tony .50
  on Topps card +1.00
Perkins, Broderick .15

Perkins, Cecil .50
Perlozzo, Sam .15
Perranoski, Ron .15
Perry, Bob .15
Perry, Boyd .75
Perry, Gaylord .50
  on Topps card +1.00
Perry, Jim .20
Pesky, Johnny .20
Peters, Gary .15
Peters, Russ .15
Peterson, Buddy .15
Peterson, Cap
  deceased 5-17-80 1.50
  on Topps card +3.00
Peterson, Fritz .25
Peterson, Harding "Pete" .15
Peterson, Jim
  deceased 4-8-75 1.25
Peterson, Kent .35
Peterson, Kurt .15
Peterson, Sid .15
Petosky, Fred .15
Petrocelli, Rico .35
Petry, Dan .15
Pettini, Joe .15
Pettit, Paul .15
Petty, Jesse Lee
  deceased 10-23-71 2.00
Pfeffer, E.J. "Jeff"
  deceased 8-15-72 1.50
Pfeil, Bob .15
Pfund, Lee .15
Phelps, Gordon .15
Phelps, Ray
  deceased 7-7-71 2.00
Philley, Dave .15
Phillips, Bubba .15
Phillips, Dave (Ump) .20
Phillips, Dee .50
Phillips, Dick .15
Phillips, Harold Ross
  deceased 6-12-72 3.00
Phillips, Jack .50
Phillips, Red .15
Phillips, Taylor .15
Phoebus, Tom .20
Picchota, Al .15
Picciolo, Rob .15
Piche, Ron .15
Picinich, Valentine John
  deceased 12-5-42 17.00
Pickrel, Clar .50
Pickup, Clarence
  deceased 8-2-74 1.25
Pierce, Billy .20
Pierce, Jack .15
Pierce, Tony .15
Pieretti, Marino
  deceased 1-30-81 1.00
Piersall, Jim .35
  on Topps card +.50
Piet, Tony .15
Pignatano, Joe .15
Pilarcik, Al .15
Pillette, Duane .30
Pillette, Herman Polycarp
  deceased 4-30-60 8.00
Pilney, Andy .15
Pinelli, Babe .25
Piniella, Lou .30
Pinkston, Alfred
  deceased 3-81 1.00
Pinson, Vada 1.00
  on Topps card +2.00
Pipgras, Edward John
  deceased 4-13-64 6.00
Pipgras, George .20
Pipp, Walter Charles
  deceased 1-11-65 6.00
Pitler, Jake
  deceased 2-3-68 3.00
Pittenger, Pinky
  deceased 11-4-77 .90
Pizarro, Juan .35
Pladson, Gordy .15
**** h * o * f ****
Plank, Eddie HOF
  deceased 2-24-26
  inducted 1946
  auto. cut signature 125.00
  autographed 3x5 250.00
  autographed photo 250.00
  auto. gum card +200.00
  autographed ball 400.00
Plarski, Don .15

Platt, Mizell George
deceased 7-27-70 3.00
Plaza, Ron .15
Pleis, Bill .15
Pless, Rance .15
Plews, Herb .15
Plummer, Bill .15
Poat, Ray .15
Pocoroba, Biff .15
Podgauhy, John
deceased 3-2-71 2.00
Podres, Johnny .25
on Topps card +.40
Poffenberger, Boots .15
Pofahl, Jim 1.00
Poholsky, Tom .15
Pointer, Aaron E. .15
Poland, Hugh .15
Pole, Dick .15
Pollett, Howard
deceased 8-8-74 2.50
Pomorski, John
deceased 12-6-77 1.00
Ponder, Elmer
deceased 4-29-74 1.25
Poole, Jim
deceased 1-2-75 1.50
Poole, Ray .75
Pope, Dave .25
Popovich, Paul .15
Popowski, Eddie .15
Poquette, Tom .15
Porter, Darrell .30
Porter, Dick
deceased 9-24-74 1.25
Porter, Irv
deceased 2-20 71 2.00
Porter, J.W. 1.00
Porterfield, Dick
deceased 1981 .80
on Topps card +2.00
Porto, Al .15
Posedel, Bill .15
Poser, Bob .15
Possehl, Lou .50
Post, Wally .20
Potter, Nelson .15
Powell, Alvin Jacob
deceased 11-4-48 16.00
Powell, Grover .15
Powell, Hosken .15
Powell, John "Boog" .65
on Topps card +1.25
Powell, Robert .15
Powell, William
deceased 9-28-67 3.00
Power, Vic .45
Powers, John .15
Powers, John Lloyd (27-)
deceased 12-22-68 3.00
Powers, Mike .15
Prall, Willie .15
Pramesa, John .65
Pratt, Derrell B.
deceased 9-30-77 1.00
Pratt, Frank
deceased 3-8-74 1.25
Preibisch, Mel
deceased 4-12-80 .50

Presko, Joe .15
Pressnell, Forest .15
Price, Jim .15
Priddy, Bob .15
Priddy, Jerry
deceased 3-3-80 1.50
Priest, John G.
deceased 11-4-79 .65
Pritchard, Bob .15
Pritchard, Bud .15
Proly, Mike .15
Prothro, Doc
deceased 10-14-71 2.00
Prudhomme, John .50
Pruess, Earl H.
deceased 8-28-79 .65
Pruett, James .50
Pruitt, Ron .15
Pryor, John "Paul" (Ump) .15
Pryor, Greg .15
Puckett, Troy L.
deceased 4-13-71 2.00
Puhl, Terry .20
Pujols, Luis .20
Pulli, Frank (Ump) .15
Purdin, John .15
Purkey, Bob .15
Putman, Ed .15
Putnam, Pat .15
Pyecha, John .15
Pyle, Lefty .15
Pytlak, Frank
deceased 5-8-77 1.20

Qualls, Jim .40
Qualters, Tom .15
Queen, Billy .15
Queen, Mel .15
Quilici, Frank .15
Quinn, Frank 1.50
Quirk, Art L. .15
Quirk, Jamie .15

Rachunok, Steve .75
Rackley, Marv .40
Radatz, Dick .15
Radcliff, Raymond Allen
deceased 5-23-62 7.00
Rader, Dave .15
Rader, Don .15
Rader, Doug .15
Rader, Drew
deceased 6-5-75 1.20
**** h * o * f ****
Radbourn, Old Hoss HOF
deceased 2-5-97
inducted 1939
auto. cut signature 175.00
autographed 3x5 300.00
autographed photo 300.00
auto. gum card +250.00
autographed ball 700.00

Radtke, Jack 2.00
Raffensberger, Ken .25
Raffo, Al .15
Ragland, Tom .15
Raich, Eric .15

Raines, Larry .50
Raines, Tim .35
on gum card +.50
Rainey, Chuck .15
Rajsich, Dave .15
Rakow, Ed .15
Ramazotti, Bob .25
Ramos, Pedro .60
Ramsdell, Willie
deceased 10-8-69 3.50
Ramsey, Bill 1.50
Randall, Bob .15
Randle, Len .15
Randolph, Willie .40
on Topps card +.60
Ranew, Merritt .15
Rapp, Earl .30
Rapp, Vern .15
Raschi, Vic .25
Rasmussen, Eric (Harry) .15
Rasmussen, Harry .30
Rath, Fred .15
Ratliff, Paul H. .15
Rau, Doug .15
Rautzhan, Lance .15
Rawley, Shane .15
Rawlings, John
deceased 10-16-72 1.50
Ray, Jim .15
Raymond, Claude .15
Raymond, Louis
deceased 5-29-79 .70
Reardon, Beans (Ump) .15
Rebel, Art 2.00
Reberger, Frank .15
Reder, Johnny .15
Redman, Glen .15
Reed, Howie .15
Reed, John B. .15
Reed, Ron 1.00
on Topps card +2.00
Reeder, Bill 1.50
Reese, Jimmie .20
Reese, Pee Wee .35
on Topps card +.75
Reese, Rich .15
Regalado, Rudy .15
Regan, Phil .15
Rego, Tony
deceased 1-6-78 2.00
Reich, Herm 1.00
Reichardt, Rick .50
Reid, Earl .50
Reid, Scott .50
Reinbach, Mike .15
Reinholz, Arthur
deceased 3-81 .60
Reis, Bob
deceased 5-1-73 1.50
Reis, Tom .45
Reiser, Pete
deceased 10-25-81 .50
Reitz, Ken .25
Remneas, Alex
deceased 8-27-75 1.25
Remy, Jerry .20
Renfroe, Marshall (59-)
deceased 12-10-70 9.00
Renick, Rick .15
Reniff, Hal .15
Reninger, Jim .60
Renko, Steve .15
Renna, Bill .15
Rennert, Dutch (Ump) .15
Repass, Bob .15
Repoz, Roger .15
Repulski, Rip .15
Rescigno, Xavier 9.00
Restelli, Dino .15
Rettenmund, Merv .15
Rettig, Adolph
deceased 6-16-77 1.00
Reusà, George "Tony" .15
Reuschel, Paul .15
Reuschel, Rick .20
Reuss, Jerry .35
on Topps card +.60
Revering, Dave .15
Reyes, Nap .50
Reynolds, Allie .30
Reynolds, Archie .15
Reynolds, Bob .15
Reynolds, Carl
deceased 5-29-78 1.00
Reynolds, Craig .20
Reynolds, Dan .15

Reynolds, Ken	.15
Reynolds, Tom	.35
Rhawn, Robert	.15
Rhem, Charles Flint	
deceased 7-30-69	2.50
Rhoden, Rick	.15
Rhodes, Dusty	.15
Ribant, Dennis	.15
Riccelli, Frank	.15
Rice, Del	.15
Rice, Hal	2.00
Rice, Harry	
deceased 1-1-71	2.25
Rice, Jim	1.50
on Topps card	+3.00
Rice, John (Ump)	.15
Rice, Len	.50
**** h * o * f ****	
Rice, Sam	HOF
inducted 1963	
deceased 10-13-74	
auto. cut signature	1.00
autographed 3x5	2.00
yellow plaque	5.00
b & w plaque	15.00
autographed photo	4.00
auto. gum card	+4.00
autographed ball	12.00

Rich, Woody	.60
Richard, J. R.	.40
on Topps card	+.75
Richard, Lee "Bee Bee"	.15
Richards, Duane	.15
Richards, Fred C.	.15
Richards, Gene	.20
Richards, Paul	.15
Richardson, Bobby	.30
Richardson, K.	.50
Richardt, Mike	.15
Richbourg, Lance	
deceased 9-10-75	1.00
Richert, Pete	.15
Richman, Beryl	.15
Richmond, Don	.15
Richter, Allen	.15
Rickard, Culley	.15
Ricketts, Dave	.15
Ricketts, Dick	.15
**** h * o * f ****	
Rickey, Branch	HOF
deceased 12-9-65	
inducted 1967	
auto. cut signature	15.00
autographed 3x5	25.00
autographed photo	25.00
auto. gum card	+25.00
autographed ball	35.00
Rico, Fred	2.00
Riddle, Elmer	.15
Riddle, John	.30
Riddleberger, Denny	.15
Riebe, Harv	.15
Riggert, Joe	
deceased 12-10-73	1.25
Riggs, Lew	
deceased 8-12-75	1.25
Rigney, Bill	.15
Rigney, John	.15

Rineer, Jeff	.15
Ring, James Joseph	
deceased 7-22-65	5.00
Ripken, Cal	.15
Ripley, Allen	.15
Ripley, Walt	.15
Ripple, Charlie	
deceased 5-6-79	.75
Ripple, James Albert	
deceased 7-16-59	8.00
Ripplemeyer, Ray	.15
Risberg, Charles August	
deceased 10-13-75	1.50
Ritchie, Jay	.15
Rivera, Jim	.25
Rivers, Mickey	.40
on Topps card	+.75
**** h * o * f ****	
Rixey, Eppa	HOF
deceased 2-28-63	
inducted 1963	
auto. cut signature	10.00
autographed 3x5	25.00
autographed photo	25.00
auto. gum card	+25.00
autographed ball	35.00

Rizzo, John	
deceased 12-4-77	1.00
Rizzuto, Phil	.50
on Topps card	+1.00
Roach, Mel	.15
Roarke, Mike	.15
Robbins, Bruce	.15
Robello, Tony	.75
Roberge, Bert	.15
Roberge, J. A. A. "Skip"	1.50
Roberts, Charles	.50
Roberts, Curtis Benjamin	
deceased 11-14-69	10.00
on Topps card	+25.00

Roberts, Dale	.15
Roberts, Dave A. (69-)	.15
Roberts, Dave W. (72-)	.15
Roberts, Leon	.15
**** h * o * f ****	
Roberts, Robin	HOF
inducted 1976	
auto. cut signature	.50
autographed 3x5	1.00
yellow plaque	2.50
autographed photo	2.50
auto. gum card	+2.50
autographed ball	9.00

Robertson, Bob	.25
Robertson, Daryl	.15
Robertson, Davis	
deceased 7-8-69	2.50
Robertson, Jerry	.35
Robertson, Jim	.15
Robertson, Sherry	
deceased 10-23-70	2.25
Robinson, Aaron Andrew	
deceased 3-9-66	5.00
Robinson, Bill	.25
Robinson, Brooks	.35
on Topps card	+1.00
Robinson, Craig	.15
Robinson, Dave	.15
Robinson, Don	.20
Robinson, Eddie	.15
Robinson, Floyd	.15
**** h * o * f ****	
Robinson, Frank	HOF
inducted 1982	
auto. cut signature	.75
autographed 3x5	2.00
autographed photo	3.00
on Topps card	+3.00
autographed ball	10.00

THE PICTURES USED IN THIS SECTION ARE FROM THE PEREZ-STEELE HALL OF FAME POSTCARD SET (SEE RECENT MEMORABILIA SECTION OF THIS BOOK). FOR INFORMATION ON THIS SET WRITE PEREZ-STEELE GALLERIES, DEPT. MPG, BOX 1776, FORT WASHINGTON, PA 19034.

**** h * o * f ****	
Robinson, Jackie	HOF
inducted 1962	
deceased 10-24-72	
auto. cut signature	6.00
autographed 3x5	12.00
yellow plaque	15.00
b & w plaque	35.00
autographed photo	20.00
auto. gum card	+25.00
autographed ball	50.00

Robinson, John A.	.45
Robinson, Sheriff	.15
**** h * o * f ****	
Robinson, Wilbert	HOF
deceased 8-8-34	
inducted 1945	
auto. cut signature	100.00
autographed 3x5	150.00
autographed photo	150.00
auto. gum card	+125.00
autographed ball	250.00

Robson, Tom	.15
Rocco, Mickey	.15
Rochefort, Ben	.15
Rochelli, Lou	.15
Rock, Les	.50
Rockett, Pat	.15
Rodgers, Andre	.75
Rodgers, Bill	1.00
Rodgers, Bob	.15
Rodin, Eric	.15
Rodriguez, Armando (Ump)	.15
Rodriguez, Aurelio	.25
Rodriguez, Ed	.15
Rodriguez, Ellie	.15
Roe, Preacher	.35
Roebuck, Ed	.25
Roenicke, Gary	.15
Roettger, Oscar	.15
Rogell, Bill	.15
Rogers, Lee "Porky"	.25
Rogers, Stan	.15
Rogers, Steve	.20
Roggenburk, Garry	.15
Rogodzinski, Mike	.15
Rogovin, Saul	1.50
Rohr, Bill	.15
Rohr, Les	.50
Rojas, Cookie	.35
Rojek, Stan	.25
Roland, Jim	.15
Rolfe, Red	
deceased 7-8-69	2.50
Rollings, William Russell	
deceased 12-31-64	5.50
Rollins, Rich	.15
Romano, Jim	.15
Romano, John	.15
Rommel, Ed	
deceased 8-26-70	2.25
Romonosky, John	.15
Roof, Phil	.15
Rooker, Jim	.15
Root, Charles Henry	
deceased 11-5-70	2.50
Rosar, Warren "Buddy"	.25
Rose, Pete	4.00
on Topps card	+7.50
Roseboro, John	.35
Roselli, Bob	.15
Rosello, Dave	.15
Rosen, Al	.30
on Topps card	+.50
Rosenbaum, Glenn	.15
Rosenthal, Larry	.25
Rosenthal, Si	
deceased 4-7-69	2.50
Roser, Steve	1.25
Ross, Bob	.15
Ross, Chet	1.00
Ross, Gary	.15
Ross, Lee	.15
Rosso, Francis	.50
Rotblatt, Marv	.50
Rothel, Bob	.50
Rothrock, Jack	
deceased 2-2-80	.60
Rounsaville, Gene	.15
**** h * o * f ****	
Roush, Edd	HOF
inducted 1962	
auto. cut signature	.50
autographed 3x5	1.00
yellow plaque	2.00
b & w plaque	15.00
autographed photo	2.00
auto. gum card	+2.00
autographed ball	7.50

Rowe, Harland	
deceased 5-26-69	2.50
Rowe, Lynwood Thomas	
deceased 1-8-61	8.00
Rowe, Ralph	.15
Rowell, Carvel	.15
Rower, Ray	.15
Rowland, Charlie	.15
Rowland, Pants	
deceased 5-17-69	2.50

Roy, Emile	1.50
Royster, Jerry	.20
Rozek, Dick	.15
Rozema, Dave	.20
Roznovsky, Vic	.15
Rubeling, Al	.15
Ruberto, Sonny	.15
Ruble, Art	.20
Rucker, John	.15
Rudi, Joe	.35
on Topps card	+.60
Rudolph, Ernie Jr.	.15
Rudolph, Frederick Donald	
deceased 9-12-68	8.00
Rudolph, Ken	.15
Rue, Joe (Ump)	.15
Ruel, Herold Dominic	
deceased 11-13-63	6.00
Ruether, Walter Henry	
deceased 5-16-70	2.50
Rufer, Rudy	.15
**** h * o * f ****	
Ruffing, Red	HOF
inducted 1967	
auto. cut signature	.75
autographed 3x5	1.50
yellow plaque	3.00
autographed photo	2.00
auto. gum card	+3.00
autographed ball	9.00

Ruhle, Vern	.15
Ruiz, "Chico" H. S.	
deceased 2-9-72	6.50
Runge, Ed (Ump)	.20
Runge, Paul (Ump)	.15
Runnels, Pete	.15
Rush, Bob	.15
**** h * o * f ****	
Rusie, Amos W.	HOF
deceased 12-6-42	
inducted 1977	
auto. cut signature	200.00
autographed 3x5	300.00
autographed photo	250.00
auto. gum card	+300.00
autographed ball	600.00

Name	Price
Russell, Albert E. (Reb)	
deceased 9-30-73	1.50
Russell, Bill	.15
Russell, Glen "Rip"	
deceased 9-26-76	1.00
Russell, Jack	.25
Russell, Jimmy	.15
Russo, Marius	.40
Rusteck, Rich	.15
Ruszkowski, Hank	.15
**** h * o * f ****	
Ruth, Babe	HOF
inducted 1936	
deceased 8-16-48	
auto. cut signature	90.00
autographed 3x5	135.00
b & w plaque	200.00
autographed photo	200.00
auto. gum card	+200.00
autographed ball	250.00

Name	Price
Rutherford, Jim	.15
Rutherford, John	.15
Ruthven, Dick	1.00
Ryan, Connie	.15
Ryan, Mike	.15
Ryan, Nolan	.50
on Topps card	+1.00
Ryan, Rosie	
deceased 12-10-80	.50
Ryan, Walter (Ump)	.15
Ryba, Mike	
deceased 12-13-71	1.75
Ryerson, Gary	.15

Name	Price
Sabo, Al	.15
Sadecki, Ray	.15
Sadek, Mike	.15
Sadowski, Bob	.15
Sadowski, Ed	.15
Sadowski, Jim	.15
Sadowski, Ted	.15
Saffell, Tom	.15
Saier, Victor Sylvester	
deceased 5-14-67	3.50
Sain, Johnny	.35
St. Clair, Ebba	.15
St. Clair, Ed	.35
Salazar, Luis	.20
Salerno, Alex (Ump)	.15
Salkeld, Bill	
deceased 4-22-67	4.00
Salmon, Chico	.20
Saltsgaver, Otto "Jack"	
deceased 2-1-78	1.00
Salveson, Jack	
deceased 12-28-74	1.25
Salvo, Manuel	.15
Sambito, Joe	.15
Samford, Ron	.25
Sample, Billy	.15
Samuels, Joe	.35
Sanchez, Celerino	.15
Sanders, Ken	.15
Sanders, Ray	.15
Sanders, Reggie	.15
Sanderson, Scott	.15
Sandlock, Mike	.15

Name	Price
Sands, Charlie	.50
Sanford, Freddie	.15
Sanford, Jack D. (40-46)	1.00
Sanford, Jack S. (56-67)	.25
Sanguillen, Manny	1.00
"Sangy"	.25
Sanichi, Ed	.15
Santo, Ron	.65
on Topps card	+1.00
Santorini, Al	.15
Satriano, Tom	.15
Saucier, Frank	.15
Saucier, Kevin	.15
Sauer, Ed	.50
Sauer, Hank	.20
Saul, Jim	.15
Savage, Bob	.15
Savage, Ted	.45
Saverine, Bob	.15
Sawatski, Carl	.15
Sawyer, Eddie	.15
Sawyer, Rich	.15
Sax, Ollie	.15
Sayles, Bill	.15
Scanlon, Pat	.15
Scarberry, Randy	.15
Scarborough, Ray	.25
Scarce, Mac	.15
Scarsella, Leslie George	
deceased 12-16-58	8.00
Schaal, Paul	.15
Schacht, Al	.20
Schacker, Hal	.50
Schaeffer, Harry	.15
Schaffer, Jim	.15
Schaffernoth, Joe	.15
**** h * o * f ****	
Schalk, Ray	HOF
inducted 1955	
deceased 5-19-70	
auto. cut signature	1.50
autographed 3x5	3.00
yellow plaque	6.00
b & w plaque	15.00
autographed photo	5.00
auto. gum card	+5.00
autographed ball	15.00

Name	Price
Schallock, Art	.15
Schang, Walter Henry	
deceased 3-6-65	5.00
Schanz, Charlie	.45
Scharein, Art	
deceased 7-3-69	2.50
Scharein, George	1.50
Schatzeder, Dan	.15
Scheer, Heinie	
deceased 3-21-76	1.00
Scheetz, Owen	.15
Scheffing, Bob	.15
Scheib, Carl	.15
Scheinblum, Richie	.15
Schell, Clyde Daniel	
deceased 5-11-72	3.50
Schemer, Michael	.15
Schenz, Henry	.15
Scherbarth, Bob	.15
Scherger, George	.15
Scherman, Fred	.15

Name	Price
Schick, Maurice	.15
Schilling, Chuck	.15
Schindler, William G.	.15
Schlesinger, Bill	.15
Schliebner, Dutch	
deceased 4-15-75	1.50
Schlueter, Jay	.15
Schlueter, Norm	.15
Schmelz, Al	.50
Schmidt, Bob	.15
Schmidt, Fred	.15
Schmidt, Mike	1.00
on Topps card	+2.00
Schmidt, Walter	
deceased 7-4-73	1.50
Schmidt, Willard	.35
Schmitz, Johnny	.25
Schneck, Dave	.15
Schneider, Dan	.15
Schoendienst, Red	.25
Schofield, Dick	.15
Schott, Gene	.15
Schreiber, Hank	
deceased 2-23-68	3.00
Schreiber, Paul	.15
Schreiber, Ted H.	.15
Schuble, Heine	.75
Schueler, Ron	.25
Schulmerich, Wes	.15
Schult, Art	.15
Schulte, Fred	.15
Schulte, Herman J.	.15
Schulte, John	
deceased 6-28-78	.90
Schulte, Len	.50
Schultz, Barney	.15
Schultz, Buddy	.15
Schultz, Howie	1.25
Schultz, Joe	.15
Schultz, Webb	.15
Schumacher, Hal	.15
Schupp, Ferdinand M.	
deceased 12-16-71	2.00
Schuster, Bill	.60
Schwall, Don	.15
Schwamb, Ralph	5.00
Schwartz, Randy	.15
Scioscia, Mike	.15
Scoffie, Louis	.15
Score, Herb	.20
Scott, George	.35
Scott, John	.20
Scott, LeGrant	.80
Scott, Mickey	.15
Scott, Rodney	.35
Scott, Tony	.25
Scrivener, Chuck	.15
Scurry, Rod	.15
Seale, Johnnie	.15
Seats, Tom	.55
Seaver, Tom	.50
on Topps card	+1.00
Seay, Richard "Dick"	
deceased 4-6-81	1.00
Secory, Frank	.15
Secrist, Don	.15
Seeds, Bob	.15
Seelbach, Chuck	.15
Seerey, Pat	.15
Segui, Diego	.35
Seibold, Harry	
deceased 9-21-65	5.00
Selkirk, George	.20
Sells, Dave	.15
Selma, Dick	.15
Selph, Carey	
deceased 2-24-76	1.25
Sembera, Andy	.15
Seminick, Andy	.15
Semproch, Ray	.15
Senerchia, S.	.15
Septowski, Ted	.15
Serena, Bill	.15
Serum, Gary	.15
Sessi, Walt	.15
Settlemine, Lefty	.15
Sevcik, John	.15
Severeid, Hank	
deceased 12-17-68	2.50
Severinsen, Al	.35
Seward, Frank	.50

**** h * o * f ****

Sewell, Joe	HOF
inducted 1977	
auto. cut signature	.40
autographed 3x5	.80
autographed photo	1.50
auto. gum card	+2.00
autographed ball	7.50

Sewell, Luke	.30
Sewell, Rip	.15
Sexton, Jimmy	.15
Seyfried, Gordon	.15
Shamsky, Art	.15
Shannon, Mike	.15
Shannon, Wally	.15
Shantz, Billy	.15
Shantz, Bobby	.20
Sharp, Bill	.15
Shaute, Joe	
deceased 2-21-70	2.25
Shaw, Al	
deceased 12-30-74	1.25
Shaw, Bob	.25
Shaw, Don	.15
Shaw, Royal "Hunky"	
deceased 7-3-69	2.50
Shawkey, Bob	
deceased 12-31-80	.55
Shea, Frank	.15
Shearer, Ray	.15
Shears, George	
deceased 11-12-78	.75
Sheehan, Jack	.15
Sheehan, Tom	.15
Sheldon, Bob	.15
Sheldon, Rollie	.35
Shellenback, Frank	
deceased 8-17-69	2.50
Shellenback, Jim	.15
Shelley, Hub	
deceased 5-16-78	.80
Shemo, Steve	1.00
Shepard, Bert	.15
Shepard, Jack	.15
Shepard, Larry	.15
Shepardson, Ray	
deceased 11-8-75	1.25
Sherdel, Bill	
deceased 11-14-68	2.75
Sherid, Roy	.60
Sheridan, Gene	
deceased 11-25-75	1.25
Sheridan, Neill	.50
Sherlock, John	.15
Sherman, Joel	.15
Sherry, Fred P.	
deceased 7-27-75	1.25
Sherry, Larry	.20
Sherry, Norm	.15
Shetrone, Barry	.15
Shields, Ben	.15
Shifflett, Garland	.15
Shillock, Jack	.15
Shipley, Joe	.35
Shirley, Bart	.15
Shirley, Bob	.15
Shirley, Tex	.15
Shockley, John Costen	3.00
Shoemaker, Charles	.15
Shoffner, Milt	
deceased 1-19-78	1.00
Shofner, Strick	1.50
Shokes, Eddie	.15
Shook, Ray	
deceased 9-16-70	2.00
Shoop, Ron	.15
Shopay, Tom	.15
Shore, Ernie	
deceased 9-24-80	.60
Shore, Ray	.15
Shores, Bill	1.00
Short, Bill	.15
Short, Chris	.15
Short, Paul	.50
Shoun, Clyde Mitchell	
deceased 3-20-68	3.00
Shriver, Harry	
deceased 1-21-70	2.25
Shuba, George	.15
Sicking, Eddie	
deceased 8-30-78	.90
Siebern, Norm	.25
Siebert, Dick	
deceased 12-9-78	.80
Siebert, Paul	.15
Siebert, Sonny	.50
Siebler, Dwight L.	.15
Sievers, Roy	.15
Sigafoss, Frank L.	
deceased 4-12-68	3.00
Silber, Ed	.75
Silva, Dan	
deceased 4-4-74	1.25
Silvera, Al	.15
Silvera, Charlie	.15
Silvestri, Ken	.15
Sima, Al	3.00

**** h * o * f ****

Simmons, Al	HOF
inducted 1953	
deceased 5-26-56	
auto. cut signature	20.00
autographed 3x5	35.00
b & w plaque	50.00
autographed photo	30.00
auto. gum card	+30.00
autographed ball	50.00

Simmons, Curt	.25
Simmons, Ted	.35
on Topps card	+.50
Simons, Mel	
deceased 10-11-74	1.25
Simpson, Harry	
deceased 4-3-79	1.00
Simpson, Joe	.15
Simpson, Wayne	.25
Sims, Duke	.15
Singer, Bill	.15
Singleton, Elmer	.50
Singleton, Ken	.35
Sington, Fred	.25
Sipek, Dick	.15
Sisk, Tom	.15
Sisler, Dave	.35
Sisler, Dick	.25

**** h * o * f ****

Sisler, George	HOF
inducted 1939	
deceased 3-26-73	
auto. cut signature	1.50
autographed 3x5	3.00
yellow plaque	6.00
b & w plaque	15.00
autographed photo	6.00
auto. gum card	+6.00
autographed ball	15.00

Sisti, Sibbi	.20
Sizemore, Ted	.15
Skaff, Frank	.15
Skaggs, Dave	.15
Skaugstad, Dave	.15
Sketchley, Harry	
deceased 1979	2.00
Skidmore, Roe	.15
Skiff, Bill	
deceased 12-25-76	1.00
Skinner, Bob	.15
Skizas, Lou	.15
Skowron, Bill "Moose"	.25
on Topps card	+.40
Slade, Gordon	
deceased 1-2-74	1.50
Slapnicka, Cy	
deceased 10-20-79	.70
Slaton, Jim	.15
Slaughter, Enos	.30
on Topps card	+.50
Slayton, Steve	.15
Sleater, Lou	.15
Sloan, Bruce	
deceased 9-24-73	2.00
Sloat, Dwain	.30
Small, Jim	.15
Small, Lefty	.15
Smalley, Roy Jr.	.35
Smalley, Roy Sr.	.15
Smaza, Joe	.50
Smith, Al (Ump)	.15
Smith, Alfred J. (34-45)	
deceased 4-28-77	1.00
Smith, Art	.15
Smith, Bernie	.15
Smith, Bill G. (58-62)	1.50
Smith, Billy (75-79)	.15
Smith, Bob E. (23-37)	.15
Smith, Bob G. (55-59)	.15
Smith, Charles	.15
Smith, Dave M. (38-39)	.15
Smith, Dave S. (80-)	.15
Smith, Dick K. (69)	.75
Smith, Eddie	.15
Smith, Edgar	.35
Smith, Elmer J.	.15
Smith, Frank T. (50-56)	.15
Smith, George S. (26-30)	2.50
Smith, Hal R. (56-65)	.20
Smith, Hal W. (55-64)	.15
Smith, Harold L. (32-35)	.15
Smith, Jack H.	.15
Smith, Jimmy L.	
deceased 1-1-74	1.50
Smith, Lawrence	.15
Smith, Lonnie	.25

Smith, Mayo
deceased 11-24-77 1.00
on Topps card +2.00
Smith, Ozzie .20
Smith, Paul .15
Smith, Peter L. .15
Smith, Reggie .75
on Topps card +1.50
Smith, Richard "Red"
deceased 3-8-78 1.00
Smith, Rufus .60
Smith, Tommy (73-77) .15
Smith, Vincent Ambrose
deceased 12-14-79 .65
Smith, Willie .20
Snell, Charles A. .15
Snell, Walter
deceased 7-23-80 .50
**** h * o * f ****
Snider, Duke HOF
inducted 1980
auto. cut signature .50
autographed 3x5 1.00
autographed photo 3.00
auto. gum card +3.00
autographed ball 9.00

Snodgrass, Fred
deceased 4-5-74 1.50
Snyder, Bernie 1.00
Snyder, Gene .15
Snyder, Jerry .15
Snyder, Jim .15
Snyder, Russ .15
Soar, Hank (Ump) .15
Soderholm, Eric .15
Solaita, Tony .30
Solomon, Buddy .15
Solomon, Eddie .15
Solters, Julius "Moose"
deceased 9-28-75 1.50
Sommers, Donny .15
Sorensen, Lary .15
Sorrell, Victor
deceased 5-4-72 1.50
Sorrells, Joe 2.00
Sosa, Elias .45
Sothern, Denny
deceased 12-1-77 1.00
Souchock, Steve .15
Southworth, Bill F. (64) .15
Southworth, Bill H.
deceased 11-15-69 2.50
**** h * o * f ****
Spahn, Warren HOF
inducted 1973
auto. cut signature .40
autographed 3x5 .80
yellow plaque 2.00
autographed photo 2.00
auto. gum card +2.00
autographed ball 9.00
**** h * o * f ****
Spalding, Albert HOF
deceased 9-9-15
inducted 1939
auto. cut signature 100.00
autographed 3x5 175.00
autographed photo 200.00
auto. gum card +200.00
autographed ball 300.00

Spangler, Al .15
Spanswick, Bill .15
Sparks, Joe .15
Sparma, Joe .15
Speake, Bob .15
**** h * o * f ****
Speaker, Tris HOF
inducted 1937
deceased 12-8-58
auto. cut signature 15.00
autographed 3x5 30.00
b & w plaque 40.00
autographed photo 35.00
auto. gum card +30.00
autographed ball 50.00

Speece, Byron
deceased 9-29-74 1.25
Speed, Horace .50
Speier, Chris .15
Spence, Bob .15
Spence, Stan .15
Spencer, Daryl .15
Spencer, George .15
Spencer, Glenn Edward
deceased 12-30-58 8.00
Spencer, Jim .25
Spencer, Roy
deceased 2-8-73 1.50
Spencer, Tom .15
Sperber, Ed
deceased 1-5-76 1.25
Sperring, Rob .15
Spicer, Bob .15
Spiezio, Ed .15
Spikes, Charlie .25
Spillner, Dan .15
Spilman, Harry .15
Spindel, Hal 1.25
Spinks, Scipio .50
on Topps card +1.00
Splittorff, Paul .15
Spohrer, Al
deceased 7-21-72 1.50
Sprague, Ed .15
Spring, Jack .15
Spring, Joe .15
Springstead, Marty (Ump) .15
Sprinz, Joe .15
Sproull, Charles
deceased 1-13-80 .65
Spurgeon, Fred
deceased 11-5-70 2.25
Squires, Mike .15
Staehle, Marv .15
Stafford, Bill .15
Stafford, Harry
deceased 1-29-72 1.75
Staggs, Steve .15
Stahl, Larry .15
Staiger, Roy .15
Stainback, Tuck .25
Staley, Jerry .15
Stallard, Tracy .15
Stallcup, Virgil .15
Staller, George .15
Stanek, Al .15
Stange, Lee .15
Stanhouse, Don .15
Stanka, Joe .15
Stanky, Eddie .35
on Topps card +.60
Stanley, Bob .15
Stanley, Fred .25
Stanley, Mickey .40
Stanton, George .60
Stanton, Lee .25
Stapleton, Dave .25
Stargell, Willie 1.50
on Topps card +3.00
Starr, Bill .15
Starr, Dick .15
Starr, Raymond Francis
deceased 2-9-63 6.00
Starrette, Herm .15
Statz, Arnold "Jigger" .25
Staub, Rusty .75
on Topps card 1.50
Stearns, John .20
Steevens, Morris .15
Stegman, Dave .15
Stein, Bill .15
Stein, Irvin .15
Steinbacher, Hank
deceased 4-3-77 1.00
Steiner, Ben 1.00
Steiner, Jim 1.00
Steiner, Mel (Ump) .15
Steinke, Bill .15
Stello, Dick (Ump) .15
Stelmaszek, Rich .15
**** h * o * f ****
Stengel, Casey HOF
inducted 1966
deceased 9-29-75
auto. cut signature 1.50
autographed 3x5 3.00
yellow plaque 7.00
autographed photo 8.00
auto. gum card +8.00
autographed ball 20.00
Stenhouse, Dave .15

Name	Price
Stennett, Rennie	.50
on Topps card	+1.00
Stephen, Buzz	.15
Stephen, Lou	.15
Stephens, Bryan	1.50
Stephens, Gene	.15
Stephens, Paul E. "Jake"	
deceased 2-5-81	1.00
Stephens, Vernon D.	
deceased 11-4-68	4.00
Stephenson, Bob	.15
Stephenson, Jerry	.15
Stephenson, John	.15
Stephenson, Riggs	.20
Stephenson, Walt	.15
Steven, Bob	.15
Stevens, Chuck	.15
Stevens, Ed	.15
Stevens, Johnny (Ump)	.15
Stevens, R.C.	.15
Stewart, Bob (Ump)	.15
Stewart, Ed	.15
Stewart, Frank	.50
Stewart, Glen	.15
Stewart, Jim (63-73)	.15
Stewart, John	.15
Stewart, Sammy	.15
Stewart, Walter	
deceased 9-26-74	1.25
Stigman, Dick	.15
Stiles, Rolland M.	.15
Stillman, Royle	.15
Stillwell, Ron	.15
Stimac, Craig	.15
Stine, Lee	.55
Stinson, Bob	.25
autographed SSPC card	25.00
Stirnweiss, George Henry	
deceased 9-15-58	12.00
Stobbs, Chuck	.30
Stock, Milt	
deceased 7-16-77	1.00
Stock, Wes	.15
Stoddard, Tim	.15
Stokes, Al	.60
Stone, Dean	.30
Stone, Dwight E.	
deceased 7-3-76	1.00
Stone, George	.15
Stone, Harry	.15
Stone, Ron	15
Stone, Steve	.35
on Topps card	+.50
Stoneman, Bill	.15
Storti, Lindo I.	.15
Stottlemyre, Mel	.20
Stout, Allyn M.	
deceased 12-22-74	1.25
Stoviak, Ray	1.00
Stowe, Hal	.15
Strahler, Mike	.15
Strahs, Dick	.15
Strain, Joe	.15
Strampe, Bob	.15
Strand, Paul	
deceased 7-2-74	1.50
Strange, Alan	.15
Stratton, Monte	.20

Name	Price
Strickland, George	.15
Strickland, Jim	.15
Striker, Jake	.15
Strincevich, Nick	.15
Stringer, Lou	.15
Stripp, Joe	.15
Strohmayer, John	.15
Strom, Brent	.15
Stromme, Floyd	.15
Strunk, Amos A.	
deceased 7-22-79	.60
Struss, Clarence	1.25
Stuart, Dick	2.50
on Topps card	+4.00
Stuart, John	
deceased 5-13-70	2.25
Stuart, Marlin	.50
Stuffel, Paul	.15
Stump, Jim G.	.15
Stumpf, George	.15
Sturgeon, Bob	.15
Sturm, Johnny	.15
Suarez, Ken	.15
Such, Dick	.15
Suche, Charley	.15
Suchecki, Jim	1.50
Sudakis, Bill	.20
Suder, Pete	.15
Sudol, Ed (Ump)	.20
Suhr, Gus	.15
Sukeforth, Clyde	.15
Sukla, Ed	.15
Sullivan, Bill Jr.	.15
Sullivan, Frank	.15
Sullivan, Haywood	.20
Sullivan, Jack	1.25
Sullivan, Joe	.15
Sullivan, John P. (63-68)	.15
Sullivan, Russ	.15
Summers, Champ	.15
Sumner, Carl	.50
Sundberg, Jim	.25
Sundra, Stephen Richard	
deceased 3-23-52	13.00
Sunkel, Thomas	.15
Surkont, Max	.60
Susce, George C.M. Sr.	.15
Susko, Pete	
deceased 5-22-78	.90
Sutcliffe, Butch	.15
Sutherland, Darrel	.15
Sutherland, Gary	.15
Sutherland, Harv	
deceased 5-11-72	1.50
Sutter, Bruce	.35
on Topps card	+.50
Sutton, Don	.35
on Topps card	+.50
Sutton, Johnny	.15
Swan, Craig	.20
Swanson, Art	.15
Swanson, Evar	
deceased 7-17-73	1.50
Swanson, Karl	.50
Swanson, Red	.15
Swanson, Stan	.15
Swartz, Monroe	.15
Sweet, Rick	.15
Sweetland, Les	
deceased 3-4-74	1.25
Swetonic, Stephen Albert	
deceased 4-22-74	1.25
Swift, Bob	
deceased 10-17-66	4.00
Swift, William Vincent	
deceased 2-23-69	2.75
Swigart, Oadis	.15
Swigler, Adam	
deceased 2-28-75	1.25
Swindell, Josh	
deceased 3-19-69	2.50
Swisher, Steve	.15
Swoboda, Ron	.25
Sykes, Bob	.15
Szotkiewicz, Ken	.15

Name	Price
Tabacchi, Frank (Ump)	.15
Tabor, James R.	
deceased 8-22-53	12.00
Talbot, Bob	.15
Talbot, Fred	.15
Talcott, Roy	.50
Tamargo, John	.15
Tamulis, Vito	
deceased 5-5-74	1.25
Tanana, Frank	.35
on Topps card	+.50
Tanner, Chuck	.15
Tappe, El	.15
Tartabull, Jose	.35
Tasby, Willie	1.50
Tata, Terry (Ump)	.15
Tate, Al	.50
Tate, Benny	
deceased 10-27-73	1.25
Tate, Lee	.15
Tate, Randy	.15
Tatum, Ken	.15
Tatum, Tom	3.00
Tauscher, Walter	.15
Taussig, Don	.15
Taveras, Frank	.35
Taylor, A.S. "Tony"	.25
Taylor, Bill	.15
Taylor, Bob D.	.15
Taylor, Bob L. "Hawk" (57-)	.15
Taylor, C. L.	
deceased 7-7-80	.50
Taylor, Carl	.20
Taylor, Chuck	.15
Taylor, Dan	
deceased 10-11-72	1.50
Taylor, Eddie	.15
Taylor, Fred	.15
Taylor, Gary	.35
Taylor, Harry	1.00
Taylor, Joe	.15
Taylor, Ron	.15
Taylor, Sammy	.15
Taylor, J.W. "Zack"	
deceased 9-19-74	1.40
Teachout, Bud	1.25
Tebbetts, Birdie	.15
Teed, Dick	.15
Temple, Johnny	2.00
Templeton, Garry	3.00
on Topps card	+5.00
Tenace, Gene	.25
Tepedino, Frank	.15
Tepsic, Joe	1.00
Terpko, Jeff	.15
Terrell, Jerry	.15
**** h * o * f ****	
Terry, Bill	HOF
inducted 1954	
auto. cut signature	.40
autographed 3x5	.80
yellow plaque	2.00
b & w plaque	10.00
autographed photo	2.00
auto. gum card	+2.00
autographed ball	10.00

Name	Price
Terry, Ralph	.15
Terry, Zeb A.	.15
Terwilliger, Wayne	.15
Testa, Nick	.15
Thacker, Moe	.15
Theodore, George	.15
Thevenow, Thomas Joseph	
deceased 7-28-57	9.00
Thiel, Bert	.15
Thies, Dave R.	.15
Thies, Jake	.15

Name	Price
Thoenen, Dick	2.00
Thomas, Bobby	.15
Thomas, John "Bud" (51)	.15
Thomas, Danny	
deceased 6-12-80	5.00
Thomas, Derrel	.20
Thomas, Frank	.15
Thomas, George E.	.15
Thomas, Gorman	.40
on Topps card	+.75
Thomas, Jim L.	.15
Thomas, Keith	.15
Thomas, Lee	.15
Thomas, Ray	1.00
Thomas, Roy	.15
Thomas, Stan	.15
Thomas, Tommy	.15
Thomasson, Gary	.15
Thompson, Bobby	.15
Thompson, C. T.	.15
Thompson, Danny	
deceased 12-10-76	4.00
on Topps card	+7.50
Thompson, David Forrest	
deceased 2-26-79	1.00
Thompson, Don	.50
Thompson, Fresco	
deceased 11-20-68	2.75
Thompson, Fuller	
deceased 2-19-72	1.50
Thompson, Gene	.15
Thompson, Henry Curtis	
deceased 9-30-69	7.50
on Topps card	+15.00
Thompson, James A.	.15
Thompson, Jason	.40
Thompson, Jocko	.15
Thompson, L. Fresco (25-)	
deceased 11-20-68	3.00
**** h * o * f ****	
Thompson, Sam	HOF
deceased 11-7-22	
inducted 1974	
auto. cut signature	200.00
autographed 3x5	350.00
autographed photo	250.00
auto. gum card	+200.00
autographed ball	500.00

Name	Price
Thompson, Scot	.15
Thompson, Tommy	.15
Thomson, Bobby	.25
Thonan, Louis	.15
Thormodsgard, Paul	.15
Thornton, Andre	.15
Thorpe, Bob	.15
Thorpe, James Francis	
deceased 3-28-53	50.00
Thorpe, Robert J. (55-)	
deceased 3-17-60	15.00
Throneberry, Faye	.15
Throneberry, Marv	.75
on Topps card	+1.50
Throop, George	.15
Thurman, Bob	.25
Thurston, Hollis	
deceased 9-14-73	1.25
Tiant, Luis	.35
on Topps card	+.50
Tidrow, Dick	.15
Tiefenauer, Bob	.15
Tietje, Les	.15
Tighe, Jack	.15
Tillman, Bob	.15
Tillotson, Thad	.15
Timberlake, Gary	.15
Timmerman, Tom	.15
Tincup, Ben	
deceased 7-5-80	.60
**** h * o * f ****	
Tinker, Joe	HOF
inducted 1946	
deceased 7-27-48	
auto. cut signature	65.00
autographed 3x5	125.00
autographed photo	125.00
auto. gum card	+100.00
autographed ball	150.00

Name	Price
Tinning, Lyle Forrest	
deceased 1-17-61	7.00
Tipton, Eric	.15
Tipton, Joe	.15
Tischinski, Tom	.15
Tobik, Dave	.15
Tobin, John M. (32)	1.00
Tobin, John P. (45)	.70
Tobin, John T. (14-27)	
deceased 12-10-69	2.50
Tobin, M. B. "Pat"	
deceased 1-21-75	1.25
Todd, Al	.15
Todd, Jackson	.15
Todd, Jim	.15
Todt, Phil	
deceased 11-15-73	1.25
Toenes, Hal	.50
Tolan, Bob	.50
on Topps card	+1.00
Tomanek, Dick	.15
Tomlin, Dave	.15
Tompkins, Ron	.15
Toms, Tom	.15
Toney, Frederick Arthur	
deceased 3-11-53	10.00
Tooley, Bert	
deceased 8-17-76	1.00
Torborg, Jeff	.15
Torgesen, Earl	.15
Torporcer, George	.15
Torre, Frank	.35
Torre, Joe	.35
on Topps card	+.50
Torres, Gil (40-46)	5.00
Torres, Hector	.25
Torres, Rusty	.15
Torrez, Mike	.35
on Topps card	+.50
Tovar, Cesar	.25
Townsend, Leo	
deceased 12-3-76	1.00
Tracewski, Dick	.15
Tramback, Red	.15
Trammell, Alan	.20
Travers, Bill	.15
Travis. Cecil	.15

Name	Price
**** h * o * f ****	
Traynor, Pie	HOF
inducted 1948	
deceased 3-16-72	
auto. cut signature	2.00
autographed 3x5	6.00
yellow plaque	9.00
b & w plaque	20.00
autographed photo	10.00
auto. gum card	+10.00
autographed ball	20.00

Name	Price
Treadway, Red	.50
Tremark, Nick	.15
Tremblay, Rich (Ump)	.15
Tremel, Bill	.15
Tresh, Mike	
deceased 10-1-66	3.75
Tresh, Tom	.20
Triandos, Gus	.65
on Topps card	+1.00
Trillo, Manny	.25
Trimble, Joe	.15
Trinkle, Ken	.50
Triplett, Coak	3.00
Troedson, Rich	.15
Trosky, Hal Sr.	
deceased 6-18-79	.75
Trosky, Hal Jr.	.15
Trotter, Bill	.15
Trout, Paul "Dizzy"	
deceased 2-28-72	1.50
Trout, Steve	.15
Trowbridge, Bob	
deceased 4-3-80	1.00
on Topps card	+2.00
Trucks, Virgil	.20
Tsitouris, John	.15
Tucker, Thurman	.15
Turbeville, George	2.00
Turchin, Edward	.35
Turgeon, Pete	
deceased 1-24-77	1.00
Turk, Lucas	.15
Turley, Bob	.20
Turner, Jerry	.15
Turner, Jim	.15
Turner, Tom	.50
Tuttle, Bill	.15
Tutweiler, Elmer	
deceased 5-3-76	1.00
Twining, Howard	
deceased 6-14-73	1.50
Twitchell, Wayne	.15
Tyler, John	
deceased 7-11-72	1.50
Tyrone, Jim	.15
Tyson, Cecil	.50
Tyson, Mike	.75

Name	Price
Uecker, Bob	.25
Uhalt, Bernie	.15
Uhlaender, Ted	.15
Uhle, Bob	.15
Uhle, George	.15
Ulisney, Mike	.15
Umbarger, Jim	.15

Umbricht, James (59-)	
deceased 4-8-64	12.50
on Topps card	+25.00
Umont, Frank (Ump)	.15
Underhill, Vern	
deceased 10-26-70	2.25
Underwood, Pat	.15
Underwood, Tom	.15
Unser, Al	.35
Unser, Del	.15
Upham, John	1.00
Upright, Dixie	.15
Upshaw, Cecil	.15
Upton, Tom	.15
Urban, Jack	.15
Urban, Louis J.	
deceased 12-7-80	.60
Urban, Luke	.15
Urbanski, Bill	
deceased 7-12-73	1.50
Urrea, John	.15
Usher, Bob	1.00

Vail, Mike	.15
Valdespino, Sandy	.35
Valdivielso, Jose	2.00
Valentine, Bill (Ump)	.15
Valentine, Bob	.25
Valentine, Corky	.15
Valentine, Ellis	.60
on Topps card	+1.00
Valentine, Fred	.15
Valentinetti, Vito	.35
Valenzuela, Fernando	1.00
Valo, Elmer	.15
Van Atta, Russ	.15
Van Camp, Albert	
deceased 2-3-81	.50
**** h * o * f ****	
Vance, Dazzy	HOF
inducted 1955	
deceased 2-16-61	
auto. cut signature	15.00
autographed 3x5	25.00
b & w plaque	40.00
autographed photo	30.00
auto. gum card	+25.00
autographed ball	50.00

Vance, Joe	
deceased 7-4-78	1.00
Vance, Sandy	.15
Van Cuyk, Chris	.15
Van Cuyk, John	1.50
Vandenberg, Hy	.15
VanderMeer, Johnny	.25
Van Dusen, Fred	.15
VanGilder, Elam	
deceased 4-30-77	1.00
Vargo, Ed (Ump)	.20
Vargus, Bill	
deceased 2-12-79	.80
Varney, Pete	.15
Vaughan, Charlie	.15
Vaughan, Glenn	.15
Vaughan, Joseph Floyd	
deceased 8-30-52	16.00
Vaughn, Porter	.15

Veach, Robert Henry	
deceased 8-7-45	15.00
Veal, Coot	.15
Veale, Bob	.35
Veeck, Bill (Exec)	.35
Veigel, Al	.60
Velazquez, Fred	2.00
Velez, Otto	.30
Veltman, Arthur	
deceased 8-1-80	.60
Verban, Emil	.15
Verdi, Frank	.15
Vergez, John	.15
Verhoeven, John	.15
Vernon, Mickey	.25
Versailles, Zoilo	.65
on Topps card	+1.00
Veryzer, Tom	.15
Vick, Ernie	
deceased 7-18-80	.50
Vick, Sam B.	.15
Vico, George	.15
Vincent, Al	.15
Vineyard, Dave	.15
Vinson, Chuck	.15
Viox, Jim	
deceased 1-6-69	2.50
Virdon, Bill	.25
Virgil, Ozzie Jr.	.15
Virgil, Ozzie Sr.	.15
Vitt, Oscar Joseph	
deceased 1-31-63	7.00
Vogel, Henry	
deceased 7-19-69	2.50
Voigt, Ole	
deceased 4-7-70	2.25
Voiselle, Bill	.15
Vollmer, Clyde	.15
Von Hoff, Bruce	.15
Vosmick, Joseph Franklin	
deceased 1-27-62	7.50
Voss, Bill	.15
Vukovich, George	.15
Vukovich, John	.15

**** h * o * f ****	
Waddel, Rube	HOF
deceased 4-1-14	
inducted 1946	
auto. cut signature	200.00
autographed 3x5	350.00
autographed photo	300.00
auto. gum card	+250.00
autographed ball	750.00

Waddey, Frank	.15
Wade, Ben	.15
Wagner, Charlie	.15
Wagner, Gary	.15
Wagner, Hal	
deceased 8-7-79	.65
**** h * o * f ****	
Wagner, Honus	HOF
inducted 1936	
deceased 12-6-55	
auto. cut signature	20.00
autographed 3x5	35.00
b & w plaque	60.00

autographed photo	40.00
auto. gum card	+35.00
autographed ball	75.00

Wagner, Mark	.15
Wahl, Kermit	.45
Waitkus, Edward Stephen	
deceased 9-15-72	3.00
Waits, Rick	.15
Wakefield, Bill	.15
Wakefield, Dick	.15
Walberg, George	
deceased 10-27-78	.90
Walezak, Eddie	.15
Walk, Bob	.15
Walker, Bob	.15
Walker, Dixie	.15
Walker, Frank	
deceased 9-16-74	1.25
Walker, Gerald "Gee"	
deceased 3-20-81	.50
Walker, Harry	.15
Walker, Hub	.15
Walker, Jerry	.15
Walker, Johnny M.	
deceased 8-19-76	1.25
Walker, Luke	.20
Walker, Rube	.15
Walker, Tom	.15
Walkup, James	.15
Wall, Murray	
deceased 10-8-71	3.50
**** h * o * f ****	
Wallace, Bobby	HOF
inducted 1953	
deceased 11-3-60	
auto. cut signature	17.50
autographed 3x5	35.00
b & w plaque	50.00
autographed photo	60.00
auto. gum card	+50.00
autographed ball	75.00

Wallace, Don	.15
Wallace, F. R.	
deceased 12-31-64	5.00
Wallace, Jim	.15
Wallace, Mike	.15
Wallach, Tim	.15
Wallaesa, Jack	.15
Walling, Denny	.15
Wallis, Joe	.15
Walls, Lee	.45
Walsh, Augie	1.00
**** h * o * f ****	
Walsh, Ed	HOF
inducted 1946	
deceased 5-26-59	
auto. cut signature	17.50
autographed 3x5	35.00
b & w plaque	50.00
autographed photo	45.00
auto. gum card	+40.00
autographed ball	60.00

Walsh, Jim	.15
Walter, Bernard	.15
Walters, Bucky	.15
Walters, Charlie	.45
Walters, Ken	.15
Walton, Danny	.15
Walton, Jim	.15
Wambsganss, Bill	
deceased	.60
**** h * o * f ****	
Waner, Lloyd	HOF
inducted 1967	
auto. cut signature	.40
autographed 3x5	.80
yellow plaque	2.00
autographed photo	2.00
auto. gum card	+2.00
autographed ball	9.00

**** h * o * f ****	
Waner, Paul	HOF
inducted 1952	
deceased 8-29-65	
auto. cut signature	7.50
autographed 3x5	20.00
b & w plaque	30.00
autographed photo	25.00
auto. gum card	+20.00
autographed ball	35.00

Wanninger, Paul	.15
Wantz, Richard C. (65)	
deceased 5-13-65	25.00
Ward, Chris	.15
Ward, Chuck	
deceased 4-4-69	2.50
Ward, Pete T.	.15
Ward, Preston	.70
**** h * o * f ****	
Ward, John Montgomery	HOF
deceased 3-4-25	
inducted 1964	
auto. cut signature	125.00
autographed 3x5	250.00
autographed photo	250.00
auto. gum card	+200.00
autographed ball	500.00

Ward, Pete	.15
Warden, Jon	.15
Wares, Buzzy	
deceased 5-26-64	5.00
Warneke, Lon	
deceased 6-3-76	1.25
Warner, Harry	.15
Warner, Jack D. (62-65)	.15
Warner, Jack J. (66)	.15
Warner, John R.	.15
Warren, Ben	.15
Warstler, Harold Burton	
deceased 5-31-64	6.00

Warthen, Dan	.15
Warwick, Carl	.15
Warwick, Firman	.15
Wasdell, Jimmy	.15
Washburn, George	
deceased 1-5-79	.75
Washburn, Greg	.15
Washburn, Ray	.15
Washington, Claudell	.65
on Topps card	+1.00
Washington, Larue	.15
Waslewski, Gary	.15
Waters, Fred	
deceased 2-1-80	.50
Wathan, John	.15
Watkins, Dave	.15
Watlington, Neal	.15
Watson, Bob	.35
on Topps card	+.50
Watt, Albert	
deceased 3-15-68	3.00
Watt, Ed	.15
Watwood, John C.	
deceased 3-1-80	.60
Waugh, Jim	.15
Way, Bobby	
deceased 6-20-74	1.50
Weafer, Hal (Ump)	.15
Weatherly, Roy	.45
Weaver, Earl	.25
Weaver, D. Floyd	.15
Weaver, Monte	.15
Weaver, Jim	.15
Webb, Hank	.15
Webb, Sam	.50
Webb, Skeeter	.15
Webber, Les	1.50
Webster, Ramon	2.00
Webster, Ray	.15
Weekly, John	
deceased 11-24-74	6.00
on Topps card	+12.00
Wegener, Mike	.35
Wehde, Wilbur	
deceased 9-21-70	2.25
Wehmeier, Herman Ralph	
deceased 5-21-73	4.00
Wehrmeister, Dave	.15
Weigel, Ralph	.50
Weik, Dick	1.25
Weiland, Bob	.15
Weinert, Phil	
deceased 4-17-73	1.50
Weingartner, D.	.50
Weintraub, Phil	.15
Weir, Bill	.15
Weis, Art	.15
**** h * o * f ****	
Weiss, George	HOF
inducted 1971	
deceased 8-13-72	
auto. cut signature	8.00
autographed 3x5	15.00
autographed photo	15.00
autographed ball	25.00

Welaj, John	.15
Welch, Bob	.20

**** h * o * f ****
Welch, Mickey HOF
deceased 7-30-41
inducted 1973
auto. cut signature 150.00
autographed 3x5 250.00
autographed photo 250.00
auto. gum card +200.00
autographed ball 500.00

Welch, Milt .50
Wellman, Bob .50
Wells, Eddie .15
Wells, Fred .50
Wells, Les .50
Welteroth, Dick 1.00
Wendlesteadt, Harry .15
Wensloff, Charles .50
Wentzel, Stan .50
Wenz, Fred .15
Wera, Julian
deceased 12-12-75 1.50
Werber, Bill .15
Werhas, John .15
Werle, Bill .15
Werner, Don .15
Wert, Don .15
Wertz, Vic .15
West, Dick .15
West, Max .15
West, Sam .15
West, Weldon .50
Westlake, Jim .15
Westlake, Wally .15
Weston, Al 1.25
Westrum, Wes .15
Weyer, Lee (Ump) .15
Wheat, Lee .15
Wheat, McKinley D.
deceased 8-14-79 .75
**** h * o * f ****
Wheat, Zach HOF
inducted 1959
deceased 3-11-72
auto. cut signature 1.50
autographed 3x5 4.00
yellow plaque 7.00
b & w plaque 15.00
autographed photo 7.00
auto. gum card +6.00
autographed ball 15.00
Wheeler, Don 1.00
Wheelock, Gary .15
Whisenant, Pete .15
Whitaker, Lou .20
Whitby, Bill .15
Whitcher, Bob .15
White, Adel 2.00
White, Al "Fuzzy" .15
White, Bill D. (56-) .20
White, Don 1.00
White, Ed .15
White, Ernie
deceased 5-22-74 2.00
White, Frank .15
White, Guy
deceased 2-17-69 2.50
White, Hal .15
White, Jerry .15
White, Jo Jo .15
White, Mike .15
White, Roy .20
White, Sammy .15
White, Stephen
deceased 1-29-75 1.25
White, William B. (45-) .50
Whitehead, John
deceased 10-20-64 5.00
Whitehead, Whitey .15
Whitehill, Earl Oliver
deceased 10-22-54 9.50
Whitfield, Fred .15
Whitfield, Terry .25
Whitman, Dick .15
Whitney, Pinky .15
Whitson, Eddie .25
Whitt, Ernie .15
Wicker, Floyd .15
Wicker, Kemp
deceased 6-11-73 1.50
Wickersham, Dave .15
Widmar, Al .15
Wieand, Ted .15
Wiesler, Bob .15
Wietelman, Whitey .15
Wight, Bill .15
Wilber, Del .15
Wilborn, Ted .15
Wilcox, Milt .15
Wiley, Mark .15
Wilfong, Rob .15
Wilhelm, J. Hoyt .50
on Topps card +.75
Wilhelm, Spider .15
Wilkie, Aldon .50
Wilkins, Bob .50
Wilkins, Eric .15
Wilks, Ted .75
Will, Bob .15
Willhite, Nick .15
Williams, Al E.
deceased 7-19-69 2.50
Williams, Bernie .15
Williams, Billy .40
on Topps card +.75
Williams, Billy (Ump) .15
Williams, Charley .15
Williams, Dave .15
Williams, Dewey .35
Williams, Dib .15
Williams, Dick .25
Williams, Don .15
Williams, Earl .50
Williams, Fred "Cy"
deceased 4-23-74 1.25
Williams, George .15
Williams, Jim .15
Williams, Jimmy (Coach) .15
Williams, Kenneth Roy
deceased 1-22-59 10.00
Williams, Rees G.
deceased 6-29-79 .75
Williams, Rick .15
Williams, Robert F.(40,46) 1.00
Williams, Stan .15

**** h * o * f ****
Williams, Ted HOF
inducted 1966
stamped .10
auto. cut signature 3.00
autographed 3x5 6.00
yellow plaque 10.00
autographed photo 12.00
auto. gum card +10.00
autographed ball 25.00

Williams, Walt .15
Williams, Woodrow .15
Williamson, Al .15
Willingham, H. .60
Willis, Les 1.50
Willis, Mike .15
Willoughby, C.
deceased 8-14-73 1.50
Wills, Bump .25
Wills, Maury .75
on Topps card +1.50
Wilson, Archie .15
Wilson, Bill H. (69-73) .30
Wilson, Bob .15
Wilson, Don
deceased 1-5-75 6.00
Wilson, Earl .55
Wilson, Frank E.
deceased 11-25-74 1.25
**** h * o * f ****
Wilson, Hack HOF
deceased 11-23-48
inducted 1979
auto. cut signature 40.00
autographed 3x5 80.00
autographed photo 100.00
auto. gum card +90.00
autographed ball 150.00

Wilson, Jim A. (45-58) .15
Wilson, Roy
deceased 12-3-69 2.25

Name	Price
Wilson, S. M. "Mike"	
deceased 5-16-78	1.00
Wilson, Walt	.35
Wilson, Willie	.75
on gum card	+1.50
Wiltse, Harold	.15
Wine, Bobby	.15
Wineapple, Ed	.60
Winegard, Ernie	
deceased 1-17-77	1.00
Windhorn, Gordon	.15
Winegarner, Ralph	.15
Winfield, Dave	.75
on Topps card	+1.50
Wingfield, Fred	
deceased 6-11-73	1.25
Winkles, Bob	.15
Winn, George	
deceased 11-1-69	2.25
Winsett, John	1.00
Winsett, Tom	.15
Wise, Archie	
deceased 2-2-78	1.00
Wise, Ogden	.50
Wise, Rick	.15
Wisner, Jack	.15
Wistert, Whitey	.15
Withrow, Ray W.	.15
Witek, Mickey	.15
Witt, Whitey	.15
Witte, Jerry	.15
Wittig, John	.15
Wockenfuss, John	.15
Woehr, Andy	.15
Wohlford, Jim	.15
Wojcik, John	.15
Wolf, Wally	.15
Wolf, Walter	
deceased 9-25-71	2.00
Wolfe, Ed	.15
Wolfe, Larry	.15
Wolff, Roger	.15
Womack, Dooley	.15
Wood, C. S. "Doc"	
deceased 11-3-74	1.25
Wood, Jake	.25
Wood, Joe	.25
Wood, Joe F. (44)	.15
Wood, Ken	.60
Wood, Roy	
deceased 4-6-74	1.25
Wood, Wilbur	.35
Woodeschick, Hal	.15
Woodling, Gene	.15
Woods, Al	.15
Woods, George	.50
Woods, Jim	.15
Woods, Ron	.50
Woodson, Dick	.15
Woodward, Wm. F. "Woody"	.15
Wooten, Earl	.50
Wortham, Rich	.15
Worthington, Al	.15
Wright, Al	.75
Wright, Bill	.15
Wright, Clyde	.25
Wright, Ed	.15
**** h * o * f ****	
Wright, George	HOF
inducted 1937	
deceased 8-31-37	
auto. cut signature	75.00
autographed 3x5	150.00
autographed photo	200.00
auto. gum card	+200.00
autographed ball	350.00
Wright, Glenn	.15
**** h * o * f ****	
Wright, Harry	HOF
deceased 10-3-95	
inducted 1953	
auto. cut signature	75.00
autographed 3x5	150.00
autographed photo	200.00
auto. gum card	+200.00
autographed ball	350.00
Wright, Jim	.15
Wright, Mel	.15
Wright, R. C.	.15
Wright, Roy E.	.15
Wright, Taft	.15
Wright, Tom	.15
Wrightstone, Russell Guy	
deceased 3-1-69	2.50
Wuestling, George "Yats"	
deceased 4-26-70	2.00

Name	Price
Wyatt, Joe	
deceased 12-5-70	2.50
Wyatt, Loral	
deceased 12-5-70	2.00
Wyatt, Whitlow	.15
Wynegar, Butch	.15
**** h * o * f ****	
Wynn, Early	HOF
inducted 1972	
auto. cut signature	.75
autographed 3x5	2.00
yellow plaque	6.00
autographed photo	3.00
auto. gum card	+4.00
autographed ball	10.00

Name	Price
Wynn, Jim	.65
on Topps card	+1.00
Wynne, Bill	.15
Wyrostek, Johnny	.15
Wyse, Hank	.35
Yancy, Hugh	.15
Yankowski, George	.50
Yarrison, Byron	
deceased 4-22-77	1.50
Yastrzemski, Carl	3.00
on Topps card	+5.00
"Yaz"	1.00
**** h * o * f ****	
Yawkey, Tom	HOF
deceased	
inducted 1980	
auto. cut signature	10.00
autographed 3x5	20.00
autographed photo	25.00
autographed ball	30.00

Name	Price
Yeager, Steve	.15
Yelle, Archie	.15
Yerkes, Steve	
deceased 1-31-71	2.00
Yewcic, Tom J.	.15
Yochim, Lenny	.15
Yochim, Ray	1.25
York, Jim	.15
York, Rudy	
deceased 2-5-70	2.50
York, Tony	
deceased 4-18-70	2.00
Yost, Ed Jr.	.15
Yost, Ed Sr.	.15
Yoter, Elmer	
deceased 7-26-66	4.00
Young, Babe	5.00
Young, Del	2.50
**** h * o * f ****	
Young, Denton T. "Cy"	HOF
inducted 1937	
deceased 11-4-55	
auto. cut signature	20.00
autographed 3x5	30.00
b & w plaque	40.00
autographed photo	30.00
auto. gum card	+30.00
autographed ball	50.00
Young, Kip	.15
Young, Lem. "Pep" (33-45)	
deceased 1-14-62	6.50
Youngblood, Joel	.15
**** h * o * f ****	
Youngs, Ross	HOF
deceased 10-22-27	
inducted 1972	
auto. cut signature	150.00
autographed 3x5	225.00
autographed photo	250.00
auto. gum card	+200.00
autographed ball	500.00
Yount, Eddie	
deceased 10-26-73	1.50
Yount, Robin	.35
on Topps card	+.50
Yowell, Carl	.15
Yvars, Sal	.35

THE PICTURES USED IN THIS SECTION ARE FROM THE PEREZ-STEELE HALL OF FAME POSTCARD SET (SEE RECENT MEMORABILIA SECTION OF THIS BOOK). FOR INFORMATION ON THIS SET WRITE PEREZ-STEELE GALLERIES, DEPT. MPG, BOX 1776, FORT WASHINGTON, PA 19034.

Zabala, Adrian	.15
Zabel, George deceased 5-31-70	2.25
Zachary, A.M. "Chink"	1.00
Zachary, Bill C. "Chris"	.15
Zachary, Tom deceased 1-24-69	2.50
Zachry, Pat	.15
Zahn, Geoff	.15
Zak, Frankie deceased 2-6-72	1.50
Zamora, Oscar	.15
Zanni, Dom	.15
Zarilla, Al	.15
Zauchin, Norm	.15
Zdeb, Joe	.15
Zeber, George	.15
Zeider, Rollie Hubert deceased 9-12-67	3.50
Zepp, Bill	.15
Zernial, Gus	.15
Zientra, Ben	.15
Zimmer, Don	.15
Zimmerman, Jerry	.15
Zimmerman, Roy	1.00
Zinn, James E.	.15
Zinser, Bill	.15
Zipfel, Marion "Bud"	.15
Zisk, Richie	.65
on Topps card	+1.00
Zitzmann, Bill	.15
Zoldak, Samuel Walter deceased 8-25-66	5.00
Zuber, Bill	.15
Zuverink, George	.15
Zwilling, E. H. deceased 3-27-78	1.00

1951-52 FISCHER BAKING (32) 2 3/4" X 2 3/4"

One of the popular "Bread For Energy" end-label sets, these labels are found with blue, red and yellow backgrounds. They were distributed mainly in the northeast section of the country and there may be an album associated with the set. The SCB designation is D290-3.

	MINT	VG-E	F-G
COMPLETE SET	1000.00	650.00	300.00
COMMON PLAYER(1-32)	30.00	20.00	8.00
1 Bickford-Braves	30.00	20.00	8.00
2 Branca-Dodgers	35.00	24.00	10.00
3 Brecheen-Cards	35.00	24.00	10.00
4 Carrasquel-White Sox	30.00	20.00	8.00
5 Chambers-Pirates	30.00	20.00	8.00
6 Evers-Tigers	30.00	20.00	8.00
7 Garver-Browns	30.00	20.00	8.00
8 Goodman-Red Sox	30.00	20.00	8.00
9 Hodges-Dodgers	45.00	30.00	12.00
10 Jansen-Giants	30.00	20.00	8.00
11 Jones-Phils	30.00	20.00	8.00
12 Joost-A's	30.00	20.00	8.00
13 Kell-Tigers	35.00	24.00	10.00
14 Kellner-A's	30.00	20.00	8.00
15 Kluszewski-Reds	40.00	26.00	11.00
16 Konstanty-Phils	35.00	24.00	10.00
17 Lemon-Indians	45.00	30.00	12.00
18 Michaels-Senators	30.00	20.00	8.00
19 Mize-Yanks	45.00	30.00	12.00
20 Noren-Senators	30.00	20.00	8.00
21 Page-Yanks	35.00	24.00	10.00
22 Pafko-Cubs	30.00	20.00	8.00
23 Parnell-Red Sox	30.00	20.00	8.00
24 Sain-Braves	35.00	24.00	10.00
25 Schoendienst-Cards	35.00	24.00	10.00
26 Sievers-Browns	30.00	20.00	8.00
27 Smalley-Cubs	30.00	20.00	8.00
28 Wehmeier-Reds	30.00	20.00	8.00
29 Werle-Pirates	30.00	20.00	8.00
30 Westrum-Giants	30.00	20.00	8.00
31 Wynn-Indians	35.00	24.00	10.00
32 Zernial-White Sox	30.00	20.00	8.00

1952 TIP TOP (48)

2 3/4" X 2 1/2"

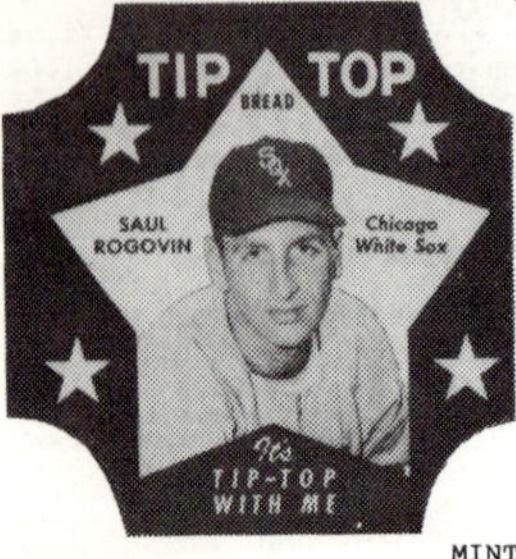

This set of 48 bread end-labels was issued by Tip Top in 1952. An album distributed with the labels names 47 ball-players and has one blank slot with advertising. A second pose of Rizzuto—which appears "cropped" from the first photo—suggests either a last minute substitution for another player, or simply his popularity in the market area. The ACC designation is D290-1.

	MINT	VG-E	F-G
COMPLETE SET	2100.00	1400.00	600.00
COMMON PLAYER(1-48)	30.00	20.00	8.00
1 Bauer-Yanks	35.00	24.00	10.00
2 Berra-Yanks	75.00	50.00	20.00
3 Branca-Dodgers	35.00	24.00	10.00
4 Brissie-Indians	30.00	20.00	8.00
5 Campanella-Dodgers	75.00	50.00	20.00
6 Cavaretta-Cubs	35.00	24.00	10.00
7 Dickson-Pirates	30.00	20.00	8.00
8 Fain-A's	30.00	20.00	8.00
9 Furillo-Dodgers	35.00	24.00	10.00
10 Garver-Brown	30.00	20.00	8.00
11 Gordon-Braves	30.00	20.00	8.00
12 Groth-Tigers	30.00	20.00	8.00
13 Hamner-Phils	30.00	20.00	8.00
14 Hearn-Giants	30.00	20.00	8.00
15 Hermanski-Cubs	30.00	20.00	8.00
16 Hodges-Dodgers	45.00	30.00	12.00
17 Jansen-Giants	30.00	20.00	8.00
18 Joost-A's	30.00	20.00	8.00
19 Kell-Tigers	35.00	24.00	10.00
20 Leonard-Cubs	30.00	20.00	8.00
21 Lockman-Giants	30.00	20.00	8.00
22 Lopat-Yanks	35.00	24.00	10.00
23 Maglie-Giants	30.00	20.00	8.00
24 Mantle-Yanks	400.00	300.00	125.00
25 McDougald-Yanks	35.00	24.00	10.00
26 Mitchell-Indians	30.00	20.00	8.00
27 Mueller-Giants	30.00	20.00	8.00
28 Pafko-Dodgers	30.00	20.00	8.00
29 Porterfield-Senators	30.00	20.00	8.00
30 Raffensberger-Reds	30.00	20.00	8.00
31 Reynolds-Yanks	35.00	24.00	10.00
32 Rizzuto-Yanks (large)	45.00	30.00	12.00
33 Rizzuto-Yanks (small)	45.00	30.00	12.00
34 Roberts-Phil	45.00	30.00	12.00
35 Rogovin-White Sox	30.00	20.00	8.00
36 Scarborough-Red Sox	30.00	20.00	8.00
37 Schoendienst-Cards	35.00	24.00	10.00
38 Sisler-Reds	30.00	20.00	8.00
39 Slaughter-Cards	40.00	26.00	11.00
40 Snider-Dodgers	75.00	50.00	20.00
41 Spahn-Braves	55.00	35.00	14.00
42 Stephens-Red Sox	30.00	20.00	8.00
43 Torgeson-Braves	30.00	20.00	8.00
44 Vernon-Senators	35.00	24.00	10.00
45 Waitkus-Phils	30.00	20.00	8.00
46 Westrum-Giants	30.00	20.00	8.00
47 Yost-Senators	30.00	20.00	8.00
48 Zarilla-White Sox	30.00	20.00	8.00

1952 NATIONAL TEA (48?)

2 3/4" X 2 11/16"

The bread labels in this set are often called "Red Borders" because of their distinctive trim. Issued with the bakery products of the National Tea Company, there are thought to be 48 different labels in the set, although only 39 have been cataloged to date. The labels are also known as the "Bread For Health" set and may have included an album. The SCB designation is D290-2.

	MINT	VG-E	F-G
COMPLETE SET	1200.00	800.00	350.00
COMMON PLAYER(1-48)	30.00	20.00	8.00
1 Bearden-Senators	30.00	20.00	8.00
2 Berra-Yankees	75.00	50.00	20.00
3 Brissie,Lou-A's	30.00	20.00	8.00
4 Chapman-A's	30.00	20.00	8.00
5 Diering-Cards	30.00	20.00	8.00
6 DiMaggio-Red Sox	40.00	26.00	11.00
7 Edwards-Dodgers	30.00	20.00	8.00
8 Ennis-Phils	30.00	20.00	8.00
9 Fain-A's	30.00	20.00	8.00
10 Gordon-Braves	30.00	20.00	8.00
11 Groth-Tigers	30.00	20.00	8.00
12 Hamner-Phils	30.00	20.00	8.00
13 Jones-Giants	30.00	20.00	8.00
14 Judson-White Sox	30.00	20.00	8.00
15 Lollar-Browns	30.00	20.00	8.00
16 Marshall,C-Browns	30.00	20.00	8.00
17 Mueller-Giants	30.00	20.00	8.00
18 Murtaugh-Pirates	30.00	20.00	8.00
19 Philley-White Sox	30.00	20.00	8.00
20 Priddy,Jerry-Tigers	30.00	20.00	8.00
21 Rigney,Bill-Giants	30.00	20.00	8.00
22 Roberts,Robin Phils	45.00	30.00	12.00
23 Robinson,Eddie-W S	30.00	20.00	8.00
24 Roe-Dodgers	35.00	24.00	10.00
25 Rojek-Pirates	30.00	20.00	8.00
26 Rosen-Indians	40.00	26.00	11.00
27 Rush-Cubs	30.00	20.00	8.00
28 Sauer-Cubs	30.00	20.00	8.00
29 Schmitz-Cubs	30.00	20.00	8.00
30 Slaughter-Cards	40.00	26.00	11.00
31 Snider-Dodgers	75.00	50.00	20.00
32 Spahn-Braves	55.00	35.00	14.00
33 Staley-Cards	30.00	20.00	8.00
34 Stallcup-Reds	30.00	20.00	8.00
35 Torgeson-Braves	30.00	20.00	8.00
36 Trout-Tigers	30.00	20.00	8.00
37 Vernon-Senators	35.00	24.00	10.00
38 Westlake-Pirates	30.00	20.00	8.00
39 Wyrostek-Reds	30.00	20.00	8.00
40 Yost-Senators	30.00	20.00	8.00

1953 NORTHLAND BREAD (32) 2 11/16" X 2 11/16"

This 32 label set features two players from each major league team and is one of the popular "Bread For Energy" sets. Although the labels are printed in black and white, the 1953 Northland Bread set includes a "Baseball Stars" album which provides additional information concerning "Baseball Immortals" and "Baseball Tips." The amended SCB designation is D290-3A.

	MINT	VG-E	F-G
COMPLETE SET	1000.00	650.00	300.00
COMMON PLAYER(1-32)	30.00	20.00	8.00
1 Abrams-Pirates	30.00	20.00	8.00
2 Ashburn-Phils	40.00	26.00	11.00
3 Bell-Reds	30.00	20.00	8.00
4 Busby-Nationals	30.00	20.00	8.00
5 Courtney-Browns	30.00	20.00	8.00
6 Cox-Dodgers	30.00	20.00	8.00
7 Dyck-Browns	30.00	20.00	8.00
8 Fox-White Sox	40.00	26.00	11.00
9 Gordon-Braves	30.00	20.00	8.00
10 Hacker-Cubs	30.00	20.00	8.00
11 Hearn-Giants	30.00	20.00	8.00
12 Hutchinson-Tigers	35.00	24.00	10.00
13 Irvin-Giants	45.00	30.00	12.00
14 Jensen-Nationals	35.00	24.00	10.00
15 Kluszewski-Reds	40.00	26.00	11.00
16 Lemon-Indians	45.00	30.00	12.00
17 McDermott-Red Sox	30.00	20.00	8.00
18 Minoso-White Sox	35.00	24.00	10.00
19 Mize-Yanks	45.00	30.00	12.00
20 Parnell-Red Sox	30.00	20.00	8.00
21 Pollet-Pirates	30.00	20.00	8.00
22 Priddy-Tigers	30.00	20.00	8.00
23 Reynolds-Yanks	35.00	24.00	10.00
24 Roe-Dodgers	35.00	24.00	10.00
25 Rosen-Indians	40.00	26.00	11.00
26 Ryan-Phillies	30.00	20.00	8.00
27 Sauer-Cubs	30.00	20.00	8.00
28 Schoendienst-Cards	35.00	24.00	10.00
29 Schantz-A's	30.00	20.00	8.00
30 Slaughter-Cards	40.00	26.00	11.00
31 Spahn-Braves	55.00	35.00	14.00
32 Zernial-A's	30.00	20.00	8.00

1955 ARMOUR FRANKS COINS (24) 1 1/2" D

The front of each of the plastic baseball "coins" in this set contains a raised profile of a ballplayer. Although similar in design to the 1959 and 1960 issues by Armour, the 1955 set is distinguished by a number of details: the full team name under the profile, the listing of birthplace and date and batting and throwing preferences on the back and, of course, the 1954 batting or won-lost record located on the reverse. The coins are not numbered and come in colors of black, blue, blue-green, green, orange, red, and yellow. Mantle and Kuenn exist in two variations each.

	MINT	VG-E	F-G
COMPLETE SET	150.00	100.00	40.00
COMMON PLAYER	2.50	1.70	.70
1 Antonelli	2.50	1.70	.70
2 Berra	8.00	5.50	2.25
3 Crandall	2.50	1.70	.70
4 Doby	2.50	1.70	.70
5 Finigan	2.50	1.70	.70
6 Ford	7.00	4.75	2.00
7 Gilliam	4.00	2.75	1.10
8 Haddix	2.50	1.70	.70
9 Jackson	2.50	1.70	.70
10 Jensen	2.50	1.70	.70
11 Kluszewski	2.50	1.70	.70
12a Kuenn (reg.)	2.50	1.70	.70
12b Kuenn (cond.)	15.00	10.00	4.00
13a Mantel (incor.)	15.00	10.00	4.00
13b Mantle (corr.)	75.00	50.00	20.00
14 Mueller	2.50	1.70	.70
15 Reese	6.00	4.00	1.60
16 Reynolds	2.50	1.70	.70
17 Rosen	2.50	1.70	.70
18 Simmons	2.50	1.70	.70
19 Snider	8.00	5.50	2.25
20 Spahn	8.00	5.50	2.25
21 Thomas	2.50	1.70	.70
22 Trucks	2.50	1.70	.70
23 Turley	2.50	1.70	.70
24 Vernon	2.50	1.70	.70

1959 ARMOUR FRANKS COINS (20) 1 1/2" D

There are 20 coins in the 1959 Armour set, 10 from each league. In contrast to the 1955 set produced by this company, the raised profiles are not as finely detailed and the lettering is larger. In addition, the team "nickname" (for example, "Redlegs") is listed below the profile, and the reverse does not record birth date and place or batting and throwing preferences. The coins are not numbered and are found in colors of dark and pale blue, dark and pale green, orange, red, and pale yellow.

	MINT	VG-E	F-G
COMPLETE SET	50.00	35.00	14.00
COMMON PLAYER	1.50	1.00	.40
1 Aaron	10.00	6.50	3.00
2 Antonelli	1.50	1.00	.40
3 Ashburn	3.00	2.00	.80
4 Banks	6.00	4.00	1.60
5 Blasingame	1.50	1.00	.40
6 Cerv	1.50	1.00	.40
7 Crandall	1.50	1.00	.40
8 Ford	6.00	4.00	1.60
9 Fox	3.00	2.00	.80
10 Jensen	3.00	2.00	.80
11 Kuenn	3.00	2.00	.80
12 Malzone	1.50	1.00	.40
13 Podres	3.00	2.00	.80
14 Frank Robinson	5.00	3.50	1.40
15 Sievers	1.50	1.00	.40
16 Skinner	1.50	1.00	.40
17 Thomas	1.50	1.00	.40
18 Triandos	1.50	1.00	.40
19 Turley	1.50	1.00	.40
20 Vernon	1.50	1.00	.40

1960 ARMOUR FRANKS COINS (20) 1 1/2" D

Although the 20 plastic baseball player coins produced by Armour Franks in 1960 were identical in style to those of the 1959 set, there was quite a turnover in personnel. Thirteen new subjects were depicted, with Aaron, Banks, Crandall, Ford, Fox, Malzone, and Triandos the only returnees. The reverse of these unnumbered coins lists the 1959 record for each individual. They are found in the following colors: two shades of blue, two shades of green, orange, red, salmon, tan, and yellow.

	MINT	VG-E	F-G
COMPLETE SET	90.00	60.00	25.00
COMMON PLAYER	1.50	1.00	.40
1 Aaron	10.00	6.50	3.00
2 Allison	1.50	1.00	.40
3 Banks	6.00	4.00	1.60
4 Boyer	3.00	2.00	.80
5 Colavito	3.00	2.00	.80
6 Conley	1.50	1.00	.40
7 Crandall	1.50	1.00	.40
8 Daley	1.50	1.00	.40
9 Drysdale	5.00	3.50	1.40
10 Ford	5.00	3.50	1.40
11 Fox	1.50	1.00	.40
12 Kaline	6.00	4.00	1.60
13 Malzone	1.50	1.00	.40
14 Mantle	15.00	10.00	4.00
15 Mathews	5.00	3.50	1.40
16 Mays	10.00	6.50	3.00
17 Pinson	1.50	1.00	.40
18 Stuart	1.50	1.00	.40
19 Triandos	1.50	1.00	.40
20 Wynn	5.00	3.50	1.40

1969 CITGO (20) — 1" D

This set of metal coins was distributed at Citgo stations in 1969 to commemorate the 100th anniversary of professional baseball. Although the coins are not numbered, they are arranged in the checklist below according to numbers found on a display card (which could be obtained from the company via mail). Each coin depicts a ballplayer in a raised portrait; the brass-like metal plating is often found discolored due to oxidation.

		MINT	VG-E	F-G
	COMPLETE SET	30.00	20.00	7.00
	COMMON PLAYER	.50	.35	.15
1	McLain	.75	.50	.20
2	McNally	.50	.35	.15
3	Lonborg	.50	.35	.15
4	Killebrew	2.25	1.50	.65
5	Stottlemyre	.50	.35	.15
6	Willie Horton	.75	.50	.20
7	Fregosi	.75	.50	.20
8	Petrocelli	.50	.35	.15
9	Bahnsen	.50	.35	.15
10	Frank Howard	.75	.50	.20
11	Torre	.75	.50	.20
12	Koosman	.50	.35	.15
13	Santo	.75	.50	.20
14	Rose	8.00	5.50	2.25
15	Staub	.75	.50	.20
16	Aaron	7.50	5.00	2.00
17	Allen	.75	.50	.20
18	Swoboda	.50	.35	.15
19	McCovey	3.00	2.00	.80
20	Bunning	.75	.50	.20

1965 OLD LONDON (40) — 1 1/2" D

The Old London set of metal baseball coins was distributed in that company's snack products in 1965. The coin was produced for Old London by Space Magic, Ltd., a Canadian firm which manufactured similar sets for Topps in 1964 and 1971. The silver-colored backs contain the company logo and a short biographical sketch of the player. Each team is represented by two ballplayers, except for the Mets (1) and the Cardinals (3)—Stallard traded from the former to the latter.

		MINT	VG-E	F-G
	COMPLETE SET	200.00	130.00	55.00
	COMMON PLAYER	2.00	1.30	.55
1	Aaron	20.00	13.00	5.50
2	Allen	4.00	2.75	1.10
3	Banks	11.00	7.00	3.00
4	Boyer	4.00	2.75	1.10
5	Bunning	2.00	1.30	.55
6	Cepeda	4.00	2.75	1.10
7	Davis	2.00	1.30	.55
8	Fairly	2.00	1.30	.55
9	Farrell	2.00	1.30	.55
10	Friend	2.00	1.30	.55
11	Groat	3.00	2.00	.80
12	Hunt	2.00	1.30	.55
13	Ken Johnson	2.00	1.30	.55
14	Mays	20.00	13.00	5.50
15	Mazeroski	3.00	2.00	.80
16	Pinson	3.00	2.00	.80
17	F. Robinson	11.00	7.00	3.00
18	Stallard	2.00	1.30	.55
19	Torre	4.00	2.75	1.10
20	Billy Williams	4.00	2.75	1.10
21	Allison	2.00	1.30	.55
22	Chance	2.00	1.30	.55
23	Colavito	4.00	2.75	1.10
24	Davalillo	2.00	1.30	.55
25	Fregosi	2.00	1.30	.55
26	Hinton	2.00	1.30	.55
27	Kaline	11.00	7.00	3.00
28	Killebrew	7.50	5.00	2.00
29	Lock	2.00	1.30	.55
30	Mantle	30.00	20.00	8.00
31	Maris	7.50	5.00	2.00
32	Peters	2.00	1.30	.55
33	Powell	4.00	2.75	1.10
34	Radatz	2.00	1.30	.55
35	B. Robinson	11.00	7.00	3.00
36	Wagner	2.00	1.30	.55
37	Ward	2.00	1.30	.55
38	Wickersham	2.00	1.30	.55
39	Wyatt	2.00	1.30	.55
40	Yastrzemski	20.00	13.00	5.50

1962 SALADA TEA PLASTIC COINS (221) — 1 3/8" D

There are 221 different players in the 1962 plastic baseball coins marketed in Salada Tea and Junket pudding mixes. The initial production run consisted of 10 representatives from each of the 18 major league teams. A subsequent run added 20 players from the Mets and the Colt 45's and also dropped 21 of the original subjects, who were replaced by 21 new players assigned higher numbers. The "coin" itself is made of one-color plastic (light or dark blue, black, orange, red, or white) which has a color portrait printed on paper inserted into the obverse surface. A 10-coin, shield-like holder was available for each team.

		MINT	VG-E	F-G
	COMPLETE SET	900.00	600.00	250.00
	COMMON PLAYER	1.00	.65	.30
1	Gentile	1.00	.65	.30
2	Pierce	50.00	35.00	15.00
3	Fernandez	1.00	.65	.30
4	Brewer	5.00	3.50	1.40
5	Held	1.00	.65	.30
6	Herbert	5.00	3.50	1.40
7a	Aspromonte, Angels	5.00	3.50	1.40
7b	Aspromonte, Cleve.	3.00	2.00	.80
8	Ford	13.50	9.00	4.00
9a	Lemon, red buttons	5.00	3.50	1.40
9b	Lemon, white but	2.00	1.30	.55
10	Klaus	1.00	.65	.30
11	Barber	5.00	3.50	1.40
12	Fox	5.00	3.50	1.40
13	Bunning	3.00	2.00	.80
14	Malzone	2.00	1.30	.55
15	Francona	1.00	.65	.30
16	Del Greco	1.00	.65	.30
17a	Bilko, red but	5.00	3.50	1.40
17b	Bilko, white but	2.00	1.30	.55
18	Kubek	11.00	7.00	3.00
19	Battey	1.00	.65	.30
20	Cottier	1.00	.65	.30
21	Tasby	1.00	.65	.30
22	Allison	2.00	1.30	.55
23	Maris	11.00	7.00	3.00
24	Averill, red but	5.00	3.50	1.40
24	Averill, white but	2.00	1.30	.55
25	Lumpe	1.00	.65	.30
26	Grant	9.00	6.00	2.50
27	Yastrzemski	20.00	13.00	5.50
28	Colavito	2.00	1.30	.55
29	Smith, A.	1.00	.65	.30
30	Busby	5.00	3.50	1.40

PX11 1962 Salada Baseball Coins

31 Howser	1.00	.65	.30
32 Perry	3.00	2.00	.80
33 Berra	11.00	7.00	3.00
34a Hamlin, red but	5.00	3.50	1.40
34b Hamlin, white but	2.00	1.30	.55
35 Long	1.00	.65	.30
36 Killebrew	9.00	6.00	2.50
37 Brown	1.00	.65	.30
38 Geiger	1.00	.65	.30
39a Minoso, White Sox	15.00	10.00	4.00
39b Minoso, Cardinals	11.00	7.00	3.00
40 Robinson, B.	20.00	13.00	5.50
41 Mantle, Mickey	40.00	26.00	11.00
42 Daniels	1.00	.65	.30
43 Martin	3.00	2.00	.80
44 Power	1.00	.65	.30
45 Pignatano	1.00	.65	.30
46a Duren, red but	5.00	3.50	1.40
46b Duren, white but	2.00	1.30	.55
47a Runnels, 2nd base	5.00	3.50	1.40
47b Runnels, 1st base	3.00	2.00	.80
48a Williams,D,name rt	15.00	10.00	4.00
48b Williams,D,name lf	3.00	2.00	.80
49 Landis	2.00	1.30	.55
50 Boros	1.00	.65	.30
51a Versalles, red but	5.00	3.50	1.40
51b Versalles, wh. but	2.00	1.30	.55
52 Temple, Indians	5.00	3.50	1.40
52 Temple, Orioles	3.00	2.00	.80
53a Brandt, Oriole	2.00	1.30	.55
53b Brandt, Orioles	15.00	10.00	4.00
54 McLain	1.00	.65	.30
55 Lollar	1.00	.65	.30
56 Stephens	1.00	.65	.30
57a Wagner, red but.	5.00	3.50	1.40
57b Wagner, white but.	2.00	1.30	.55
58 Lary	1.00	.65	.30
59 Skowron	2.00	1.30	.55
60 Wertz	5.00	3.50	1.40
61 Kirkland	1.00	.65	.30
62 Posada	1.00	.65	.30
63a Pearson, red but.	3.00	2.00	.80
63b Pearson, white but	1.00	.65	.30
64 Richardson	5.00	3.50	1.40
65a Breeding, SS	3.00	2.00	.80
65b Breeding, 2nd B	2.00	1.30	.55
66 Sievers	15.00	10.00	4.00
67 Kaline	15.00	10.00	4.00
68a Buddin, Red Sox	3.00	2.00	.80
68b Buddin, 45's	2.00	1.30	.55
69a Green, L.,red but.	3.00	2.00	.80
69b Green, L.,wh. but.	1.00	.65	.30
70 Green, G.	5.00	3.50	1.40
71 Aparicio	3.00	2.00	.80
72 Cash	2.00	1.30	.55
73 Jensen	5.00	3.50	1.40
74 Phillips	1.00	.65	.30
75 Archer	1.00	.65	.30
76a Hunt, red but.	3.00	2.00	.80
76b Hunt, white but.	1.00	.65	.30
77 Terry	3.00	2.00	.80
78 Pascual	1.00	.65	.30
79 Keough	5.00	3.50	1.40
80 Boyer, C.	3.00	2.00	.80
81 Pagliaroni	1.00	.65	.30
82a Leek, red but.	3.00	2.00	.80
82b Leek, white but.	1.00	.65	.30
83 Wood	1.00	.65	.30
84 Veal	5.00	3.50	1.40
85 Siebern	1.00	.65	.30
86a Carey, White Sox	5.00	3.50	1.40
86b Carey, Phillies	2.00	1.30	.55
87a Tuttle, red but.	3.00	2.00	.80
87b Tuttle, white but.	1.00	.65	.30
88a Piersall, Indians	3.00	2.00	.80
88b Piersall, Senators	2.00	1.30	.55
89 Hansen	3.00	2.00	.80
90a Stobbs, red buttons	3.00	2.00	.80
90b Stobbs, white but.	1.00	.65	.30
91a McBride, red but.	3.00	2.00	.80
91b McBride, white but	1.00	.65	.30
92 Bruton	1.00	.65	.30
93 Triandos	1.00	.65	.30
94 Romano	1.00	.65	.30
95 Howard	1.00	.65	.30
96 Woodling	.1.00	.65	.30
97a Wynn, pitching	15.00	10.00	4.00
97b Wynn, portrait	9.00	6.00	2.50
98 Pappas	1.00	.65	.30
99 Monboquette	1.00	.65	.30
100 Causey	1.00	.65	.30
101 Elston	1.00	.65	.30
102a Neal, Dodgers	3.00	2.00	.80
102b Neal, Mets	2.00	1.30	.55
103 Blasingame	1.00	.65	.30
104 Thomas	5.00	3.50	1.40
105 Covington	1.00	.65	.30
106 Hiller	1.00	.65	.30
107 Hoak	1.00	.65	.30
108a Lillis, Cardinals	3.00	2.00	.80
108b Lillis, 45's	2.00	1.30	.55
109 Koufax	15.00	10.00	4.00
110 Coleman	1.00	.65	.30
111 Matthews (Mathews)	9.00	6.00	2.50
112 Mahaffey	1.00	.65	.30
113a Bailey, red but.	5.00	3.50	1.40
113b Bailey, white but.	1.00	.65	.30
114 Burgess	1.00	.65	.30
115 White	1.00	.65	.30
116 Bouchee	5.00	3.50	1.40
117 Buhl	1.00	.65	.30
118 Pinson	2.00	1.30	.55
119 Sawatski	1.00	.65	.30
120 Stuart	1.00	.65	.30
121 Kuenn	5.00	3.50	1.40
122 Herrera	1.00	.65	.30
123a Zimmer, Cubs	5.00	3.50	1.40
123b Zimmer, Mets	2.00	1.30	.55
124 Moon	1.00	.65	.30
125 Adcock	1.00	.65	.30
126 Jay	1.00	.65	.30
127a Wills, blue #3	6.00	4.00	1.60
127b Wills, red #3	6.00	4.00	1.60
128 Altman	1.00	.65	.30
129a Buzhardt, Phillies	5.00	3.50	1.40
129b Buzhardt, Wh.Sox	2.00	1.30	.55
130 Alou	1.00	.65	.30
131 Mazeroski	1.00	.65	.30
132 Broglio	1.00	.65	.30
133 Roseboro	1.00	.65	.30
134 McCormick	1.00	.65	.30
135a Smith, C., Phil.	5.00	3.50	1.40
135b Smith, C., Wh.Sox	2.00	1.30	.55
136 Santo	3.00	2.00	.80
137 Freese	1.00	.65	.30
138 Groat	3.00	2.00	.80
139 Flood	3.00	2.00	.80
140 Bolling	1.00	.65	.30
141 Dalrymple	1.00	.65	.30
142 McCovey	9.00	6.00	2.50
143 Skinner	1.00	.65	.30
144 McDaniel	1.00	.65	.30
145 Hobbie	1.00	.65	.30
146a Hodges, Dodgers	13.50	9.00	4.00
146b Hodges, Mets	6.00	4.00	1.60
147 Kasko	1.00	.65	.30
148 Cimoli	11.00	7.00	3.00
149 Mays	30.00	20.00	8.00
150 Clemente	20.00	13.00	5.50
151 Schoendienst	3.00	2.00	.80
152 Torre	3.00	2.00	.80
153 Purkey	1.00	.65	.30
154a Davis, T., OF	3.00	2.00	.80
154b Davis, T., 3rd B	2.00	1.30	.55
155a Rodgers, SS	3.00	2.00	.80
155b Rodgers, 1st B	2.00	1.30	.55
156 Taylor, T.	1.00	.65	.30
157 Friend	1.00	.65	.30
158a Bell, Gus, Reds	3.00	2.00	.80
158b Bell, Gus, Mets	2.00	1.30	.55
159 McMillan	1.00	.65	.30
160 Warwick	1.00	.65	.30
161 Davis, W.	1.00	.65	.30
162 Jones	5.00	3.50	1.40
163 Amaro	1.00	.65	.30
164 Taylor, S.	1.00	.65	.30
165 Robinson, Fr.	9.00	6.00	2.50
166 Burdette	2.00	1.30	.55
167 Boyer, K.	2.00	1.30	.55
168 Virdon	2.00	1.30	.55
169 Davenport	1.00	.65	.30
170 Demeter	1.00	.65	.30
171 Ashburn	9.00	6.00	2.50
172 Podres	2.00	1.30	.55
173a Cunningham, Cards	15.00	10.00	4.00
173b Cunningham, Wh.Sox	9.00	6.00	2.50
174 Face	1.00	.65	.30
175 Cepeda	2.00	1.30	.55
176a Smith, B.G., Phil	5.00	3.50	1.40
176b Smith, B.G., Mets	2.00	1.30	.55
177a Banks, OF	15.00	10.00	4.00
177b Banks, SS	11.00	7.00	3.00
178a Spencer, 3rd B	5.00	3.50	1.40
178b Spencer, 1st B	2.00	1.30	.55
179 Schmidt	5.00	3.50	1.40
180 Aaron	30.00	20.00	8.00
181 Landrith	2.00	1.30	.55
182a Broussard (Bressoud)	30.00	20.00	8.00
182b Bressoud	9.00	6.00	2.50
183 Mantilla	2.00	1.30	.55
184 Farrell	2.00	1.30	.55

PX11 1962 Salada Baseball

No.	Player	MINT	VG-E	F-G
185	Miller, B.	2.00	1.30	.55
186	Taussig	2.00	1.30	.55
187	Green, P.	2.00	1.30	.55
188	Shantz	3.00	2.00	.80
189	Craig	2.00	1.30	.55
190	Smith, H.	2.00	1.30	.55
191	Edwards	2.00	1.30	.55
192	DeMerit	2.00	1.30	.55
193	Amalfitano	2.00	1.30	.55
194	Larker	3.00	2.00	.80
195	Heist	2.00	1.30	.55
196	Spangler	3.00	2.00	.80
197	Grammas	3.00	2.00	.80
198	Lynch	2.00	1.30	.55
199	McKnight	2.00	1.30	.55
200	Pagen (Pagan)	3.00	2.00	.80
201	Gilliam	9.00	6.00	2.50
202	Ditmar	2.00	1.30	.55
203	Daley	2.00	1.30	.55
204	Callison	3.00	2.00	.80
205	Miller, S.	2.00	1.30	.55
206	Snyder	2.00	1.30	.55
207	Williams, B.	9.00	6.00	2.50
208	Bond	2.00	1.30	.55
209	Koppe	2.00	1.30	.55
210	Schwall	2.00	1.30	.55
211	Gardner	3.00	2.00	.80
212	Estrada	3.00	2.00	.80
213	Bell, Gary	2.00	1.30	.55
214	Robinson, Fl.	2.00	1.30	.55
215	Snider	15.00	10.00	4.00
216	Maye	2.00	1.30	.55
217	Bedell	2.00	1.30	.55
218	Will	2.00	1.30	.55
219	Green, D.	5.00	3.50	1.40
220	Hardy	2.00	1.30	.55
221	O'Connell	2.00	1.30	.55

1963 SALADA TEA METAL COINS (63) 1 1/2" D

The 1963 baseball coin set distributed by Salada Tea and Junket Pudding marked a drastic change from the set of the previous year. The coins were made of metal, rather than plastic, with conspicuous red rims for National League players and blue rims for their American League counterparts. The subject's portrait was printed in color on the front, with his name, position, team and 1962 statistics listed on the back. Also on the reverse is located the coin number and the line "Save and Trade 63 All Star Baseball Coins."

	MINT	VG-E	F-G
COMPLETE SET	275.00	180.00	75.00
COMMON PLAYER	1.50	1.00	.40

No.	Player	MINT	VG-E	F-G
1	Drysdale	7.50	5.00	2.00
2	Farrell	1.50	1.00	.40
3	Gibson	12.00	8.00	3.50
4	Koufax	15.00	10.00	4.00
5	Marichal	5.00	3.50	1.40
6	Purkey	1.50	1.00	.40
7	Shaw	1.50	1.00	.40
8	Spahn	12.00	8.00	3.50
9	Podres	1.50	1.00	.40
10	Mahaffey	1.50	1.00	.40
11	Crandall	1.50	1.00	.40
12	Roseboro	1.50	1.00	.40
13	Cepeda	3.00	2.00	.80
14	Mazeroski	3.00	2.00	.80
15	Boyer	5.00	3.50	1.40
16	Groat	3.00	2.00	.80
17	Banks	15.00	10.00	4.00
18	Bolling	1.50	1.00	.40
19	Davenport	1.50	1.00	.40
20	Wills	5.00	3.50	1.40
21	Davis	1.50	1.00	.40
22	Mays	25.00	17.00	7.00
23	Clemente	20.00	13.00	5.50
24	Aaron	25.00	17.00	7.00
25	Alou	1.50	1.00	.40
26	Callison	1.50	1.00	.40
27	Ashburn	5.00	3.50	1.40
28	Mathews	12.00	8.00	3.50
29	Robinson, F.	15.00	10.00	4.00
30	Williams	12.00	8.00	3.50
31	Altman	1.50	1.00	.40
32	Aguirre	3.00	2.00	.80
33	Bunning	1.50	1.00	.40
34	Donovan	1.50	1.00	.40
35	Monbouquette	1.50	1.00	.40
36	Pascual	1.50	1.00	.40
37	Stenhouse	1.50	1.00	.40
38	Terry	3.00	2.00	.80
39	Wilhelm	3.00	2.00	.80
40	Kaat	3.00	2.00	.80
41	McBride	1.50	1.00	.40
42	Herbert	1.50	1.00	.40
43	Pappas	1.50	1.00	.40
44	Battey	1.50	1.00	.40
45	Howard	3.00	2.00	.80
46	Romano	1.50	1.00	.40
47	Gentile	1.50	1.00	.40
48	Moran	1.50	1.00	.40
49	Rollins	1.50	1.00	.40
50	Aparicio	5.00	3.50	1.40
51	Siebern	1.50	1.00	.40
52	Richardson	7.50	5.00	2.00
53	Robinson, B.	15.00	10.00	4.00
54	Tresh	3.00	2.00	.80
55	Wagner	1.50	1.00	.40
56	Mantle	35.00	24.00	10.00
57	Maris	15.00	10.00	4.00
58	Colavito	5.00	3.50	1.40
59	Thomas	1.50	1.00	.40
60	Landis	1.50	1.00	.40
61	Runnels	1.50	1.00	.40
62	Berra	15.00	10.00	4.00
63	Kaline	15.00	10.00	4.00

1964 TOPPS COINS (164) 1 1/2" D

This set of 164 numbered coins issued in 1964 is sometimes divided into two sets—the regular series (1-120) and the all-star series (121-164). The regular series features gold and silver coins with a full color photo of the player, including the background of the photo. The player's name, team and position are delineated on the coin front. The back includes the line "Collect the entire set of 120 all-stars." The all-star series contains a full color cutout photo of the player on a solid background. The fronts feature the line "1964 All-stars" along with the name only of the player. The backs contain the line "Collect all 44 special stars." Mantle, Causey, and Hinton appear in two variations each.

	MINT	VG-E	F-G
COMPLETE SET	270.00	180.00	75.00
COMMON PLAYER	.60	.40	.15

No.	Player	MINT	VG-E	F-G
1	Zimmer	1.00	.65	.30
2	Wynn	.60	.40	.15
3	Orsino	.60	.40	.15
4	Bouton	1.00	.65	.30
5	Groat	1.00	.65	.30
6	Wagner	.60	.40	.15
7	Malzone	.60	.40	.15
8	Barber	.60	.40	.15
9	Romano	.60	.40	.15
10	Tresh	.60	.40	.15

1964 Topps Coins

11 Alou	.60	.40	.15
12 Stuart	1.00	.65	.30
13 Osteen	.60	.40	.15
14 Pizarro	.60	.40	.15
15 Clendenon	.60	.40	.15
16 Hall	.60	.40	.15
17 Jackson	.60	.40	.15
18 B. Robinson	5.00	3.50	1.40
19 Allison	1.50	1.00	.40
20 Roebuck	.60	.40	.15
21 Ward	.60	.40	.15
22 McCovey	5.00	3.50	1.40
23 E. Howard	2.00	1.30	.55
24 Segui	.60	.40	.15
25 Boyer	2.00	1.30	.55
26 Yastrzemski	10.00	6.50	3.00
27 Mazeroski	1.00	.65	.30
28 Lumpe	.60	.40	.15
29 Held	.60	.40	.15
30 Radatz	.60	.40	.15
31 Aparicio	2.00	1.30	.55
32 Nicholson	.60	.40	.15
33 Mathews	5.00	3.50	1.40
34 Drysdale	5.00	3.50	1.40
35 Culp	.60	.40	.15
36 Marichal	2.00	1.30	.55
37 Fr. Robinson	5.00	3.50	1.40
38 Hinton	.60	.40	.15
39 Fl. Robinson	1.50	1.00	.40
40 Harper	.60	.40	.15
41 Hansen	.60	.40	.15
42 Banks	8.00	5.50	2.25
43 Gonder	.60	.40	.15
44 Williams	2.00	1.30	.55
45 Pinson	1.00	.65	.30
46 Colavito	1.50	1.00	.40
47 Monbouquette	.60	.40	.15
48 Alvis	.60	.40	.15
49 Siebern	.60	.40	.15
50 Callison	.60	.40	.15
51 Rollins	.60	.40	.15
52 McBride	.60	.40	.15
53 Lock	.60	.40	.15
54 Fairly	.60	.40	.15
55 Clemente	10.00	6.50	3.00
56 Ellsworth	.60	.40	.15
57 Tommy Davis	1.00	.65	.30
58 Gonzalez	.60	.40	.15
59 Gibson	5.00	3.50	1.40
60 Maloney	.60	.40	.15
61 F. Howard	1.50	1.00	.40
62 Pagliaroni	.60	.40	.15
63 Cepeda	1.50	1.00	.40
64 Perranoski	.60	.40	.15
65 Flood	1.50	1.00	.40
66 McBean	.60	.40	.15
67 Chance	.60	.40	.15
68 Santo	1.00	.65	.30
69 Baldschun	.60	.40	.15
70 Pappas	.60	.40	.15
71 Peters	.60	.40	.15
72 Richardson	2.00	1.30	.55
73 Thomas	.60	.40	.15
74 Aguirre	.60	.40	.15
75 Willey	.60	.40	.15
76 Pascual	.60	.40	.15
77 Bob Friend	.60	.40	.15
78 White	1.50	1.00	.40
79 Cash	.60	.40	.15
80 Mays	10.00	6.50	3.00
81 Carmel	.60	.40	.15
82 Rose	15.00	10.00	4.00
83 Aaron	10.00	6.50	3.00
84 Aspromonte	.60	.40	.15
85 O'Toole	.60	.40	.15
86 Davalillo	.60	.40	.15
87 Freehan	.60	.40	.15
88 Spahn	7.00	4.75	2.00
89 Hunt	.60	.40	.15
90 Menke	.60	.40	.15
91 Farrell	.60	.40	.15
92 Hickman	.60	.40	.15
93 Bunning	1.00	.65	.30
94 Hendley	.60	.40	.15
95 Broglio	.60	.40	.15
96 Staub	1.00	.65	.30
97 Brock	5.00	3.50	1.40
98 Fregosi	2.00	1.30	.55
99 Grant	1.50	1.00	.40
100 Kaline	7.00	4.75	2.00
101 Battey	.60	.40	.15
102 Causey	.60	.40	.15
103 Schilling	.60	.40	.15
104 Powell	1.00	.65	.30
105 Wickersham	.60	.40	.15
106 Koufax	8.00	5.50	2.25
107 Bateman	.60	.40	.15
108 Brinkman	.60	.40	.15
109 Downing	.60	.40	.15
110 Azcue	.60	.40	.15
111 Pearson	1.50	1.00	.40
112 Killebrew	5.00	3.50	1.40
113 Taylor	.60	.40	.15
114 Jackson	.60	.40	.15
115 O'Dell	.60	.40	.15
116 Demeter	.60	.40	.15
117 Charles	.60	.40	.15
118 Torre	2.00	1.30	.55
119 Nottebart	.60	.40	.15
120 Mantle	20.00	13.00	5.50
121 Pepitone	.60	.40	.15
122 Stuart	.60	.40	.15
123 Richardson	2.00	1.30	.55
124 Lumpe	.60	.40	.15
125 B. Robinson	5.00	3.50	1.40
126 Malzone	.60	.40	.15
127 Aparicio	1.00	.65	.30
128 Fregosi	1.00	.65	.30
129 Kaline	5.00	3.50	1.40
130 Wagner	.60	.40	.15
131a Mantle, RH	15.00	10.00	4.00
131b Mantle, LH	15.00	10.00	4.00
132 Pearson	.60	.40	.15
133 Killebrew	2.00	1.30	.55
134 Yastrzemski	10.00	6.50	3.00
135 Howard	1.00	.65	.30
136 Battey	.60	.40	.15
137 Pascual	.60	.40	.15
138 Bouton	.60	.40	.15
139 Ford	5.00	3.50	1.40
140 Peters	.60	.40	.15
141 White	.60	.40	.15
142 Cepeda	1.00	.65	.30
143 Mazeroski	1.00	.65	.30
144 Taylor	.60	.40	.15
145 Boyer	1.50	1.00	.40
146 Santo	1.00	.65	.30
147 Groat	1.00	.65	.30
148 McMillan	.60	.40	.15
149 Aaron	10.00	6.50	3.00
150 Clemente	8.00	5.50	2.25
151 Mays	10.00	6.50	3.00
152 Pinson	1.00	.65	.30
153 Davis	.60	.40	.15
154 F. Robinson	5.00	3.50	1.40
155 Torre	2.00	1.30	.55
156 McCarver	1.50	1.00	.40
157 Marichal	2.00	1.30	.55
158 Maloney	.60	.40	.15
159 Koufax	6.00	4.00	1.60
160 Spahn	6.00	4.00	1.60
161a Causey, NL	10.00	6.50	3.00
161b Causey, AL	.60	.40	.15
162a Hinton, NL	10.00	6.50	3.00
162b Hinton, AL	.60	.40	.15
163 Aspromonte	.60	.40	.15
164 Hunt	.60	.40	.15

SALADA COINS PACKAGE

1971 TOPPS COINS (153)

1 1/2" D

This full color set of 153 coins contains the photo of the player surrounded by a colored band, which contains the player's name, his team, his position and several stars. The backs contain the coin number, short biographical data, and the line "Collect the entire set of 153 coins."

		MINT	VG-E	F-G
COMPLETE SET		135.00	90.00	40.00
COMMON PLAYER		.35	.24	.09
1	Gaston	.35	.24	.09
2	Dave Johnson	.35	.24	.09
3	Bunning	.35	.24	.09
4	Spencer	.35	.24	.09
5	Millan	.35	.24	.09
6	Moses	.35	.24	.09
7	Jenkins	.60	.40	.15
8	F. Alou	.60	.40	.15
9	McGlothlin	.35	.24	.09
10	McAuliffe	.35	.24	.09
11	Torre	1.00	.65	.30
12	J. Perry	1.00	.65	.30
13	Bonds	.60	.40	.15
14	Cater	.35	.24	.09
15	Mazeroski	.60	.40	.15
16	Aparicio	1.00	.65	.30
17	Rader	.35	.24	.09
18	Pinson	.60	.40	.15
19	Bateman	.35	.24	.09
20	Krausse	.35	.24	.09
21	Grabarkewitz	.35	.24	.09
22	Howard	.60	.40	.15
23	Koosman	.60	.40	.15
24	Carew	5.00	3.50	1.40
25	Ferrara	.35	.24	.09
26	McNally	.60	.40	.15
27	Hickman	.35	.24	.09
28	Alomar	.35	.24	.09
29	L. May	.35	.24	.09
30	Petrocelli	.35	.24	.09
31	Money	.35	.24	.09
32	Rooker	.35	.24	.09
33	Dietz	.35	.24	.09
34	White	.60	.40	.15
35	Morton	.35	.24	.09
36	W. Williams	.35	.24	.09
37	Niekro	.60	.40	.15
38	Freehan	.35	.24	.09
39	Javier	.35	.24	.09
40	Monday	.35	.24	.09
41	Wilson	.35	.24	.09
42	Fosse	.35	.24	.09
43	Shamsky	.35	.24	.09
44	Savage	.35	.24	.09
45	Osteen	.35	.24	.09
46	Brinkman	.35	.24	.09
47	M. Alou	.35	.24	.09
48	Oliver	.35	.24	.09
49	Coombs	.35	.24	.09
50	F. Robinson	3.00	2.00	.80
51	Hundley	.35	.24	.09
52	Tovar	.35	.24	.09
53	Simpson	.35	.24	.09
54	Murcer	1.00	.65	.30
55	Taylor	.35	.24	.09
56	John	1.50	1.00	.40
57	McCovey	3.00	2.00	.80
58	Yastrzemski	6.00	4.00	1.60
59	Bailey	.35	.24	.09
60	Wright	.35	.24	.09
61	Cepeda	1.00	.65	.30
62	Kaline	5.00	3.50	1.40
63	Gibson	4.00	2.75	1.10
64	Campaneris	.60	.40	.15
65	Sizemore	.35	.24	.09
66	Sims	.35	.24	.09
67	Harrelson	.60	.40	.15
68	McNertney	.35	.24	.09
69	Wynn	.60	.40	.15
70	Bosman	.35	.24	.09
71	Clemente	6.00	4.00	1.60
72	Reese	.35	.24	.09
73	G. Perry	1.50	1.00	.40
74	Powell	1.00	.65	.30
75	B. Williams	1.50	1.00	.40
76	Melton	1.00	.65	.30
77	Colbert	.35	.24	.09
78	Smith	.35	.24	.09
79	Deron Johnson	.35	.24	.09
80	Hunter	1.50	1.00	.40
81	Tolan	.35	.24	.09
82	Northrup	.35	.24	.09
83	Fairly	.60	.40	.15
84	A. Johnson	.35	.24	.09
85	Jarvis	.35	.24	.09
86	McDowell	.35	.24	.09
87	Brock	4.00	2.75	1.10
88	Walton	.35	.24	.09
89	Menke	.60	.40	.15
90	Palmer	3.00	2.00	.80
91	Agee	.60	.40	.15
92	Josephson	.60	.40	.15
93	Davis	.60	.40	.15
94	Stottlemyre	.60	.40	.15
95	Santo	1.00	.65	.30
96	Otis	.60	.40	.15
97	Henderson	.35	.24	.09
98	Scott	.60	.40	.15
99	Ellis	.60	.40	.15
100	Killebrew	3.00	2.00	.80
101	Rose	8.00	5.50	2.25
102	Reichardt	.60	.40	.15
103	C. Jones	.35	.24	.09
104	Perranoski	.35	.24	.09
105	Perez	.60	.40	.15
106	Lolich	.60	.40	.15
107	McCarver	.60	.40	.15
108	Jackson	5.00	3.50	1.40
109	Cannizzaro	.35	.24	.09
110	Hargan	.35	.24	.09
111	Staub	.60	.40	.15
112	Messersmith	.60	.40	.15
113	Carty	.60	.40	.15
114	B. Robinson	4.00	2.75	1.10
115	Carlton	4.00	2.75	1.10
116	Hegan	.35	.24	.09
117	Morgan	1.50	1.00	.40
118	Munson	4.00	2.75	1.10
119	Kessinger	.60	.40	.15
120	Horlen	.35	.24	.09
121	Parker	.35	.24	.09
122	Siebert	.35	.24	.09
123	Stargell	2.00	1.30	.55
124	Rodriguez	.35	.24	.09
125	Marichal	1.50	1.00	.40
126	Epstein	.35	.24	.09
127	Seaver	5.00	3.50	1.40
128	Oliva	1.00	.65	.30
129	Merritt	.35	.24	.09
130	Horton	.60	.40	.15
131	Wise	.35	.24	.09
132	Bando	1.00	.65	.30
133	Brown	.35	.24	.09
134	Harrelson	.60	.40	.15
135	M. Jones	.35	.24	.09
136	Fregosi	.60	.40	.15
137	Aaron	6.00	4.00	1.60
138	Peterson	.35	.24	.09
139	Hague	.35	.24	.09
140	Harper	.35	.24	.09
141	Dierker	.35	.24	.09
142	Conigliaro	.35	.24	.09
143	Beckert	.35	.24	.09
144	C. May	.35	.24	.09
145	Sutton	1.00	.65	.30
146	Casanova	.35	.24	.09
147	Moose	.35	.24	.09
148	Cardenas	.35	.24	.09
149	Bench	4.00	2.75	1.10
150	Cuellar	.60	.40	.15
151	Clendenon	.35	.24	.09
152	Piniella	1.00	.65	.30
153	Mays	6.00	4.00	1.60

1969 MLBPA PINS (60) 7/8" D

This 1969 pin set was issued by the Major League Baseball Player's Association. The 60-pin set contains 30 pins each of National League players and American League players. The outer bands of the pins are red for American League players and blue for National League players. The pictures on the pins are black & white, head only photos. The line "c 1969 MLBPA MFG. R.R. Winona, Minn." appears at the bottom of each pin.

	MINT	VG-E	F-G
COMPLETE SET	45.00	30.00	12.00
COMMON PLAYER	.45	.30	.12
1 Max Alvis-Indians	.45	.30	.12
2 Luis Aparicio-W.Sox	.60	.40	.15
3 George Brunet-Angels	.45	.30	.12
4 Rod Carew-Twins	1.50	1.00	.45
5 Dean Chance-Twins	.45	.30	.12
6 Bill Freehan-Tigers	.60	.40	.15
7 Jim Fregosi-Angels	.60	.40	.15
8 Ken Harrelson-R.Sox	.60	.40	.15
9 Joel Horlen-W.Sox	.45	.30	.12
10 Tony Horton-Indians	.60	.40	.15
11 Willie Horton-Tigers	.60	.40	.15
12 Frank Howard-Sen.	.60	.40	.15
13 Al Kaline-Tigers	1.50	1.00	.45
14 H.Killebrew-Twins	.90	.60	.25
15 Mickey Lolich-Tigers	.60	.40	.15
16 Jim Lonborg-Red Sox	.45	.30	.12
17 Sam McDowell-Indians	.60	.40	.15
18 Denny McLain-Tigers	.60	.40	.15
19 Rick Monday-Athlet.	.60	.40	.15
20 Tony Oliva-Twins	.60	.40	.15
21 Joe Pepitone-Yankees	.45	.30	.12
22 Boog Powell-Orioles	.60	.40	.15
23 R.Reichardt-Angels	.45	.30	.12
24 Pete Richert-Sen.	.45	.30	.12
25 B.Robinsin-Orioles	1.50	1.00	.45
26 F.Robinson-Orioles	1.50	1.00	.45
27 M.Stottlemyre-Yanks	.60	.40	.15
28 Luis Tiant-Indians	.60	.40	.15
29 Pete Ward-White Sox	.45	.30	.12
30 C.Yastrzemski-R.Sox	2.00	1.30	.55
31 Hank Aaron-Braves	2.00	1.30	.55
32 Felipe Alou-Braves	.60	.40	.15
33 Richie Allen-Phil.	.60	.40	.15
34 Ernie Banks-Cubs	1.50	1.00	.45
35 Johnny Bench-Reds	1.50	1.00	.45
36 Lou Brock-Cardinals	1.50	1.00	.45
37 J.Callison-Phillies	.45	.30	.12
38 O.Cepeda-Braves	.60	.40	.15
39 R.Clemente-Pirates	1.50	1.00	.45
40 Willie Davis-Dodgers	.60	.40	.15
41 Don Drysdale-Dodgers	.90	.60	.25
42 Ron Fairly-Dodgers	.45	.30	.12
43 Curt Flood-Cardinals	.60	.40	.15
44 Bob Gibson-Cardinals	.90	.60	.25
45 Bud Harrelson-Mets	.45	.30	.12
46 Jim Hart-Giants	.45	.30	.12
47 Tommy Helms-Reds	.45	.30	.12
48 Don Kessinger-Cubs	.60	.40	.15
49 Jerry Koosman-Mets	.60	.40	.15
50 Jim Maloney-Reds	.45	.30	.12
51 Juan Marichal-Giants	.90	.60	.25
52 Willie Mays-Giants	1.50	1.00	.45
53 T.McCarver-Cardinals	.45	.30	.12
54 W.McCovey-Giants	.90	.60	.25
55 Pete Rose-Reds	2.00	1.30	.55
56 Ron Santo-Cubs	.60	.40	.15
57 Ron Swoboda-Mets	.45	.30	.12
58 Joe Torre-Cardinals	.60	.40	.15
59 Billy Williams-Cubs	.60	.40	.15
60 Jim Wynn-Astros	.45	.30	.12

1956 TOPPS PINS (60) 1 3/16" D

This set of 60 full-color pins was Topps first and only baseball player pin set. Although the set was advertised to contain 90 pins, only 60 were issued. The checklist below lists the players in alphabetical order. Diering and Stobbs are more difficult to obtain than other pins the set.

	MINT	VG–E	F–G
COMPLETE SET	330.00	220.00	90.00
COMMON PLAYER	4.50	3.00	1.25
1 Aaron, Hank OF	12.50	8.50	3.50
2 Amoros, Sandy OF	4.50	3.00	1.25
3 Arroyo, Luis P	4.50	3.00	1.25
4 Banks, Ernie SS	7.50	5.00	2.00
5 Berra, Yogi C	9.00	6.00	2.50
6 Black, Joe P	6.00	4.00	1.60
7 Boone, Ray 3B	4.50	3.00	1.25
8 Boyer, Ken 3B	6.00	4.00	1.60
9 Collins, Joe 1B	4.50	3.00	1.25
10 Conley, Gene P	4.50	3.00	1.25
11 Diering, Chuck OF	12.50	8.50	3.50
12 Donovan, Dick P	4.50	3.00	1.25
13 Finigan, Jim 2B	4.50	3.00	1.25
14 Fowler, Art P	4.50	3.00	1.25
15 Gomez, Ruben P	4.50	3.00	1.25
16 Groat, Dick SS	4.50	3.00	1.25
17 Haddix, Harvey P	4.50	3.00	1.25
18 Harshman, Jack P	4.50	3.00	1.25
19 Hatton, Grady 3B	4.50	3.00	1.25
20 Hegan, Jim C	4.50	3.00	1.25
21 Hodges, Gil 1B	7.50	5.00	2.00
22 Hofman, Bobby LF	4.50	3.00	1.25
23 House, Frank C	4.50	3.00	1.25
24 Jensen, Jackie OF	6.00	4.00	1.60
25 Kaline, Al OF	9.00	6.00	2.50
26 Kennedy, Bob 3B	4.50	3.00	1.25
27 Kluszewski, Ted 1B	6.00	4.00	1.60
28 Long, Dale 1B	4.50	3.00	1.25
29 Lopez, Hector 3B	4.50	3.00	1.25
30 Mathews, Ed 3B	7.50	5.00	2.00
31 Mays, Willie OF	12.50	8.50	3.50
32 McMillan, Roy SS	4.50	3.00	1.25
33 Miranda, Willie SS	4.50	3.00	1.25
34 Moon, Wally OF	4.50	3.00	1.25
35 Mossi, Don P	4.50	3.00	1.25
36 Negray, Ron P	4.50	3.00	1.25
37 O'Brien, Johnny 2B	4.50	3.00	1.25
38 Paula, Carlos OF	4.50	3.00	1.25
39 Power, Vic 1B	4.50	3.00	1.25
40 Rivera, Jim OF	4.50	3.00	1.25
41 Rizzuto, Phil SS	7.50	5.00	2.00
42 Robinson, Jackie 3B	12.50	8.50	3.50
43 Rosen, Al 3B	6.00	4.00	1.60
44 Sauer, Hank OF	4.50	3.00	1.25
45 Sievers, Roy OF	4.50	3.00	1.25
46 Skowron, Bill 1B	6.00	4.00	1.60
47 Smith, Al OF	4.50	3.00	1.25
48 Smith, Hal C	4.50	3.00	1.25
49 Smith, Mayo Mgr.	4.50	3.00	1.25
50 Snider, Duke OF	9.00	6.00	2.50
51 Spahn, Warren P	6.00	4.00	1.50
52 Spooner, Karl P	4.50	3.00	1.25
53 Stobbs, Chuck P	12.50	8.50	3.50
54 Sullivan, Frank P	4.50	3.00	1.25
55 Tremel, Bill P	4.50	3.00	1.25
56 Triandos, Gus 1B	4.50	3.00	1.25
57 Turley, Bob P	4.50	3.00	1.25
58 Wehmeier, Herman P	4.50	3.00	1.25
59 Williams, Ted OF	12.50	8.50	3.50
60 Zernial, Gus OF	4.50	3.00	1.25

45 Card Set of All Superstars

- NO commons
- NO stiffs
- NO benchwarmers
- NO has-beens
- NO have-nots
- NO reprint set

4 different poses of
- Mickey Mantle
- Willie Mays
- Hank Aaron
- Ted Williams
- Joe Dimaggio
- Babe Ruth
- Lou Gehrig
- Sandy Koufax
- Bob Clemente

$3.50

GOUDEY I (Stamped reprint) A limited supply of this first reprint of the Goudey series 32 cards including Ruth, 2 Gehrig, Hornsby . . . $ 25.00

GOUDEY II (Laminated for a forever mint appearance) Includes 3 Ruths, Gehrig, Cobb— 32 cards. . . . . . $ 8.00

GOUDEY III – 32 cards including Williams, DiMaggio, Ruth . . . . $ 5.00

PLAY BALL I – 42 reprints of the 1941 series . . . . $ 5.00

PLAYBALL II – 42 more reprints including 10 tinted cards from 1940 . . . . . $ 5.00

ADD POSTAGE AND HANDLING (P & H)

REPRINTS

BALL HOLDERS
$ 2.50 plus postage & handling

House your favorite baseball or that special autographed ball in this attractive and functional gold-based holder.

POSTAGE & HANDLING SCHEDULE (P & H)
$ .01 to $ 20.00 add $ 2.00
$ 20.01 to $ 30.00 add $ 2.50
Over $ 30.00 add $ 3.00

MARYLAND RESIDENTS ADD 5% TAX
CANADIAN ORDERS – BOOKS ONLY
CANADIAN BOOK ORDERS ADD 25% postage
Orders outside contiguous U.S.A. add 25% more
U.S. FUNDS ONLY

SEND $ 1.00 for DEN'S BIG 48-PAGE CATALOGUE

CATALOGUE WILL BE SENT FREE WITH ORDER

DEN'S COLLECTORS DEN

MPG
P.O. BOX 606, LAUREL, MD 20707

EXHIBIT (Hall of Famers)
$ 4.00 plus postage & handling

This 32 card set features all Hall of Fame players. Issued in late 1980, this is the second set released by the new owners of the Exhibit Supply Co., who have been issuing cards since the 1920's. Included are Ruth, Cobb, Mantle, DiMaggio, Williams, Foxx and 26 more.

DEN'S COLLECTORS DEN

1981 DALLAS COWBOY CHEERLEADERS
$ 6.00 plus postage and handling

The card above is number 11 in the set of 30. Would you really rather look at Mickey Mantle or George Brett than what is above? The cards are actual 5 x 7 photos of high quality – similar to the Superstar Photo series of baseball and football players issued by Topps over the last two years.

COMPLETE MINT CARD SETS
number of cards in set= ( )

BASEBALL

1982 TOPPS (792) . . . . $ 21.00
1982 FLEER (660). . . . . $ 15.00
1982 DONRUSS (660) . . . . . . $ 15.00
1981 TOPPS (726) . . . . $ 22.00
1981 FLEER (660). . . . . $ 18.00
1981 DONRUSS (605) . . . . . . $ 18.00
1981 COKE (132). . . . . $ 15.00
1981 Topps Home Team- 5x7 Photos
Dodgers—Angels (18) . . . $ 5.00
White Sox—Cubs (18) . . . $ 5.00
Yankees—Mets (18). . . . . $ 5,00
Rangers—Astros (12). . . . $ 3.50
1981 Topps National Superstar Photos – 5x7 Photos. . . . $ 5.00
1981 Topps Scratch-offs (108) . $ 8.00
1981 Topps Stickers (262) . . . $ 25.00
1980 TOPPS (726) . . . . $ 24.00
1980 Topps 5x7 Photos (60). . $ 12.00
1978 TOPPS (726) . . . . $ 30.00
1977 Topps Cloth (73) . . . . . . $ 25.00
1976 KELLOGG (54 of 57) . . . $ 7.00
1975 HOSTESS (6 panels of 3) . $ 7.50
1973 KELLOGG 2-D (54). . . . $ 40.00

FOOTBALL

1981 TOPPS (528) . . . . $ 17.00
1980 TOPPS (528) . . . . $ 19.00
1980 Topps 5x7 Photos (30). . . $ 6.00
1975 FLEER Hall of Fame (84) $ 7.50
1970 KELLOGG (60) . . . . $ 16.00

ADD POSTAGE AND HANDLING (P & H) TO ALL ITEMS

1982 BASEBALL
COLLECTOR'S EDITION

A BASEBALL CARD ALBUM, SPECIALLY DESIGNED FOR 1982, WITH YOUR OWN NAME IN GOLD LETTERS ON THE FRONT, HIGHLIGHTS THIS COLLECTORS EDITION COMBINATION. ALSO INCLUDED ARE A COMPLETE SET OF 792 TOPPS 1982 BASEBALL CARDS AND 44 CLEAR PLASTIC CARD HOLDER SHEETS, WHICH ARE ENOUGH FOR THE ENTIRE SET.

ONLY $ 36.00

____ COMBINATION ALBUM/TOPPS BASEBALL CARD SET/SET OF 44 STYLE 9 PLASTIC SHEETS . . . . $ 36.00 PPD
____ PERSONALIZED ALBUM . . . . $ 8.00 PPD
____ TOPPS 1982 BASEBALL CARD SET . . . . $ 21.00 PPD
____ SET OF 44 STYLE 9 PLASTIC SHEETS . . . . $ 11.00 PPD

PERSONALIZE THE ALBUM(S) WITH THE NAME(S): ....

YOUR NAME (PLEASE PRINT) ....

ADDRESS ....

MAKE CHECK OR MONEY ORDER PAYABLE TO:
DEN'S COLLECTORS DEN
MPG
P.O.BOX 606, LAUREL, MD 20707

U.S. FUNDS ONLY

TOPPS

MD RESIDENTS ADD 5% SALES TAX

ADD POSTAGE AND HANDLING (P & H) TO ALL ITEMS NOT MARKED POSTPAID

1921-1924 EXHIBITS (155) 3 3/8" X 5 3/8"

Although the Exhibit Supply Company issued 64 cards in 1921 and 128 cards in each of the following three years, the category 1921-24 was created because of the large number of pictures found repeated in all four years. The cards of 1921 are characterized by ornate hand-lettered names while the cards of 1922-24 have players' names hand-written in a plainer style. Also for 1921 cards, the abbreviation used for the junior circuit is "Am.L." In contrast, cards of the 1922-24 period have the American League abbreviated "A.L." All the cards in the 1921-24 category are black and white and have blank backs; some have white borders measuring approximately 3/16" in width. There is some mislabeling of pictures, incorrect assignment of proper names, and many misspellings.

	MINT	VG-E	F-G
COMPLETE SET	1500.00	1000.00	400.00
COMMON PLAYER	6.00	4.00	1.50
1 Chas. B. Adams	6.00	4.00	1.50
2 Grover C. Alexander	12.00	8.00	3.50
3 James Bagby	6.00	4.00	1.50
4 J. Frank Baker	9.00	6.00	2.50
5 David Bancroft	9.00	6.00	2.50
6 Walter Barbare	6.00	4.00	1.50
7 Turner Barber	6.00	4.00	1.50
8 Clyde Barnhart	6.00	4.00	1.50
9 John Bassler	6.00	4.00	1.50
10 Carlson L. Bigbee	6.00	4.00	1.50
11 Ray Blades	6.00	4.00	1.50
12 Sam Bohne	6.00	4.00	1.50
13 James Bottomley	9.00	6.00	2.50
14 Geo. Burns (Cinn) portrait	6.00	4.00	1.50
15 Geo. J. Burns (NY NL)	6.00	4.00	1.50
16 George Burns (Bos AL)	6.00	4.00	1.50
17 George Burns (Cleveland)	6.00	4.00	1.50
18 Joe Bush	6.00	4.00	1.50
19 Owen Bush	6.00	4.00	1.50
20 Leon Cadore	6.00	4.00	1.50
21 Max G. Carey	9.00	6.00	2.50
22 Jim Caveney	6.00	4.00	1.50
23 Dan Clark	6.00	4.00	1.50
24 Ty R. Cobb	35.00	25.00	10.00
25 Eddie T. Collins	9.00	6.00	2.50
26 John Collins	6.00	4.00	1.50
27 Wilbur Cooper	6.00	4.00	1.50
28 Stanley Coveleskie	9.00	6.00	2.50
29 Walton E. Cruise	6.00	4.00	1.50
30 George Cutshaw	6.00	4.00	1.50
31 Dave Danforth	6.00	4.00	1.50
32 Jacob E. Daubert	6.00	4.00	1.50
33 George Dauss	6.00	4.00	1.50
34 Charles A. Deal	6.00	4.00	1.50
35 Bill Doak (Brook)	6.00	4.00	1.50
36 Bill Doak (St.Louis NL)	6.00	4.00	1.50
37 Joe Dugan (Bos AL)	6.00	4.00	1.50
38 Joe A. Dugan (New York AL)	6.00	4.00	1.50
39 Joe A. Dugan (Phila. AL)	6.00	4.00	1.50

No.	Player			
40	Pat Duncan	6.00	4.00	1.50
41	James Dykes	6.00	4.00	1.50
42	Howard J. Ehmke (Boston AL)	6.00	4.00	1.50
43	Howard Ehmke (Detroit) (with border)	6.00	4.00	1.50
44	Wm. Evans	9.00	6.00	2.50
45	U.C. "Red" Faber	9.00	6.00	2.50
46	Bib Falk	6.00	4.00	1.50
47	Dana Fillingim	6.00	4.00	1.50
48	Ira Flagstead (Boston AL)	6.00	4.00	1.50
49	A. Fletcher	6.00	4.00	1.50
50	J.F. Fournier (Brooklyn)	6.00	4.00	1.50
51	J.F. Fournier (St.L. NL)	6.00	4.00	1.50
52	Howard Freigau	6.00	4.00	1.50
53	Frank F. Frisch	12.00	8.00	3.50
54	C.E. Galloway	6.00	4.00	1.50
55	W.L. Gardner (Cleveland)	6.00	4.00	1.50
56	Joe Genewich	6.00	4.00	1.50
57	Wally Gerber	6.00	4.00	1.50
58	Mike Gonzales	6.00	4.00	1.50
59	H.M. "Hank" Gowdy (Boston NL)	6.00	4.00	1.50
60	H.M. "Hank" Gowdy (New York NL)	6.00	4.00	1.50
61	Burleigh A. Grimes	9.00	6.00	2.50
62	Ray Grimes	6.00	4.00	1.50
63	Charles Grimm	6.00	4.00	1.50
64	Heinie Groh (Cinn)	6.00	4.00	1.50
65	Heinie Groh (NY NL)	6.00	4.00	1.50
66	Jesse Haines	9.00	6.00	2.50
67	Chas. L. Hartnett	9.00	6.00	2.50
68	George Harper	6.00	4.00	1.50
69	Sam Harris	6.00	4.00	1.50
70	Slim Harris	6.00	4.00	1.50
71	Clifton Heathcote	6.00	4.00	1.50
72	Harry Heilmann	9.00	6.00	2.50
73	Andy High	6.00	4.00	1.50
74	Umpire Hildebrand	6.00	4.00	1.50
75	Walter L. Holke (Boston NL)	6.00	4.00	1.50
76	Walter L. Holke (Phila. NL)	6.00	4.00	1.50
77	Chas. J. Hollocher	6.00	4.00	1.50
78	Rogers Hornsby	15.00	10.00	4.50
79	Wilbert Hubbell	6.00	4.00	1.50
80	Bill Jacobson	6.00	4.00	1.50
81	Charles D. Jamieson	6.00	4.00	1.50
82	E.R. Johnson	6.00	4.00	1.50
83	James H. Johnson	6.00	4.00	1.50
84	Walter P. Johnson	15.00	10.00	4.50
85	Sam P. Jones	6.00	4.00	1.50
86	Joe Judge	6.00	4.00	1.50
87	Willie Kamm	6.00	4.00	1.50
88	Tony Kaufman	6.00	4.00	1.50
89	Geo. L. Kelly	9.00	6.00	2.50
90	Dick Kerr	6.00	4.00	1.50
91	William L. Killefer	6.00	4.00	1.50
92	Bill Klem	9.00	6.00	2.50
93	Ed Konetchy	6.00	4.00	1.50
94	John "Doc" Lavan	6.00	4.00	1.50
95	Dudley Lee	6.00	4.00	1.50
96	Harry Liebold (Boston AL)	6.00	4.00	1.50
97	Harry Liebold (Washington) (with border)	6.00	4.00	1.50
98	Adolph Luque	6.00	4.00	1.50
99	Walter Mails	6.00	4.00	1.50
100	Geo. Maisel	6.00	4.00	1.50
101	Walt. J. Maranville	9.00	6.00	2.50
102	W.C.(Wid) Matthews	6.00	4.00	1.50
103	Carl W. Mays	6.00	4.00	1.50
104	John McGraw	12.00	8.00	3.50
105	J. "Stuffy" McInnis (Boston AL)	6.00	4.00	1.50
106	J. "Stuffy" McInnis (Boston NL)	6.00	4.00	1.50
107	Lee Meadows	6.00	4.00	1.50
108	Clyde Milan	6.00	4.00	1.50
109	Ed (Bing) Miller	6.00	4.00	1.50
110	Hack Miller	6.00	4.00	1.50
111	Umpire Moriarty	6.00	4.00	1.50
112	Johnny Morrison	6.00	4.00	1.50
113	John A. Mostil	6.00	4.00	1.50
114	Robert Meusel	6.00	4.00	1.50
115	Harry Myers	6.00	4.00	1.50
116	Rollie C. Naylor	6.00	4.00	1.50
117	A. Earl Neale	6.00	4.00	1.50
118	Arthur Nehf	6.00	4.00	1.50
119	Joe Oeschger	6.00	4.00	1.50
120	Ivan M. Olson	6.00	4.00	1.50
121	Geo. O'Neil	6.00	4.00	1.50
122	S.F. "Steve" O'Neil	6.00	4.00	1.50
123	J.F. O'Neill	6.00	4.00	1.50
124	Ernest Padgett	6.00	4.00	1.50
125	Roger Peckinpaugh (New York AL) (with border)	6.00	4.00	1.50
126	Peckinpaugh (Wash)	6.00	4.00	1.50
127	Ralph "Cy" Perkins	6.00	4.00	1.50
128	Val Picinich (Boston AL)	6.00	4.00	1.50
129	Val Picinich (Wash)	6.00	4.00	1.50
130	Bill Piercy (Light Backgr'd)	6.00	4.00	1.50
131	Bill Piercy (Dark Backgr'd)	6.00	4.00	1.50
132	Herman Pillett	6.00	4.00	1.50
133	Wally Pipp	6.00	4.00	1.50
134	Raymond R. Powell (Light Backgr'd)	6.00	4.00	1.50
135	Raymond R. Powell (Dark Backgr'd)	6.00	4.00	1.50
136	Del Pratt (Det)	6.00	4.00	1.50
137	Derrill Pratt (Boston AL)	6.00	4.00	1.50
138	Joe "Goldie" Rapp	6.00	4.00	1.50
139	Walter Reuther	6.00	4.00	1.50
140	Edgar S. Rice	9.00	6.00	2.50
141	Umpire Rigler	6.00	4.00	1.50
142	E. E. Rigney	6.00	4.00	1.50
143	Jimmy Ring	6.00	4.00	1.50
144	Eppa Rixey	9.00	6.00	2.50
145	Chas. Robertson	6.00	4.00	1.50
146	Eddie Rommel	6.00	4.00	1.50
147	Muddy Ruel	6.00	4.00	1.50
148	Geo.H. "Babe" Ruth	50.00	35.00	15.00
149	Geo.H. "Babe" Ruth (with border)	50.00	35.00	15.00
150	J. H. Sand	6.00	4.00	1.50
151	Ray W. Schalk	9.00	6.00	2.50
152	Wallie Schang	6.00	4.00	1.50
153	Everett Scott (Boston AL)	6.00	4.00	1.50
154	Everett Scott (New York AL)	6.00	4.00	1.50
155	Harry Severeid	6.00	4.00	1.50
156	Joseph Sewell	9.00	6.00	2.50
157	H.S. Shanks	6.00	4.00	1.50
158	Earl Sheely	6.00	4.00	1.50
159	Urban Shocker	6.00	4.00	1.50
160	Al Simmons	12.00	8.00	3.50
161	Geo. H. Sisler	12.00	8.00	3.50
162	Earl Smith (NY NL) (with border)	6.00	4.00	1.50
163	Earl Smith (NY NL) (2/3 shot)	6.00	4.00	1.50
164	Elmer Smith (Boston AL)	6.00	4.00	1.50
165	Jack Smith	6.00	4.00	1.50
166	R.E. Smith	6.00	4.00	1.50
167	Sherrod Smith (Brooklyn)	6.00	4.00	1.50
168	Sherrod Smith (Cleveland)	6.00	4.00	1.50
169	Frank Snyder	6.00	4.00	1.50
170	Allan Sothoron	6.00	4.00	1.50
171	Tris Speaker	12.00	8.00	3.50
172	Arnold Statz	6.00	4.00	1.50
173	Casey Stengel	15.00	10.00	4.50
174	J.R. Stevenson	6.00	4.00	1.50
175	Milton Stock	6.00	4.00	1.50
176	James Tierney (Boston NL)	6.00	4.00	1.50
177	James Tierney (Pittsburgh)	6.00	4.00	1.50
178	John Tobin	6.00	4.00	1.50
179	George Toporcer	6.00	4.00	1.50
180	Robert Veach	6.00	4.00	1.50
181	Clarence (Tillie) Walker	6.00	4.00	1.50
182	Curtis Walker	6.00	4.00	1.50
183	Aaron Ward	6.00	4.00	1.50
184	Zack D. Wheat	9.00	6.00	2.50
185	Geo. B. Whitted	6.00	4.00	1.50
186	Cy Williams	6.00	4.00	1.50
187	Kenneth R. Williams	6.00	4.00	1.50
188	Ivy B. Wingo	6.00	4.00	1.50
189	Joe Wood	6.00	4.00	1.50
190	L. Woodall	6.00	4.00	1.50
191	Russell G. Wrightstone	6.00	4.00	1.50
192	Moses Yellowhorse	6.00	4.00	1.50
193	Ross Youngs	9.00	6.00	2.50

1925 EXHIBITS (128)　　3 3/8" X 5 3/8"

The most dramatic change in the 1925 series from that of the preceding group was the printed legend which appeared for the first time in this printing. The subject's name, position, team, and the line "(Made in U.S.A.)" appear on four separate lines in a bottom corner, enclosed in a small white box. The name of the player is printed in large capitals while the other lines are of a smaller type size. The cards are black and white, have plain backs, and are unnumbered. There are 128 cards in the set and numerous misspellings exist. Note: the card marked "Robert Veach" does not picture that player, but is thought to contain a photo of Ernest Vache.

	MINT	VG-E	F-G
COMPLETE SET	900.00	600.00	250.00
COMMON PLAYER	6.00	4.00	1.50
1 David Bancroft	9.00	6.00	2.50
2 Jesse Barnes	6.00	4.00	1.50
3 Lawrence Benton	6.00	4.00	1.50
4 Maurice Burrus	6.00	4.00	1.50
5 Joseph Genewich	6.00	4.00	1.50
6 Frank Gibson	6.00	4.00	1.50
7 David Harris	6.00	4.00	1.50
8 George O'Neil	6.00	4.00	1.50
9 John H. Deberry	6.00	4.00	1.50
10 Decatur	6.00	4.00	1.50
11 Jacques F. Fournier	6.00	4.00	1.50
12 Burleigh A. Grimes	9.00	6.00	2.50
13 James H. Johnson (Johnston)	6.00	4.00	1.50
14 Milton J. Stock	6.00	4.00	1.50
15 A.C. "Dazzy" Vance	9.00	6.00	2.50
16 Zack Wheat	9.00	6.00	2.50
17 Sparky Adams	6.00	4.00	1.50
18 Grover C. Alexander	12.00	8.00	3.50
19 John Brooks	6.00	4.00	1.50
20 Howard Freigau	6.00	4.00	1.50
21 Charles Grimm	6.00	4.00	1.50
22 Leo Hartnett	9.00	6.00	2.50
23 Walter Maranville	9.00	6.00	2.50
24 A.J. Weis	6.00	4.00	1.50
25 Raymond Bressler	6.00	4.00	1.50
26 Hugh M. Critz	6.00	4.00	1.50
27 Peter Donohue	6.00	4.00	1.50
28 Charles Dressen	6.00	4.00	1.50
29 John (Stuffy) McInnes (McInnis)	6.00	4.00	1.50
30 Eppa Rixey	9.00	6.00	2.50
31 Ed. Roush	9.00	6.00	2.50
32 Ivy Wingo	6.00	4.00	1.50
33 Frank Frisch	12.00	8.00	3.50
34 Heine Groh	6.00	4.00	1.50
35 Travis C. Jackson	6.00	4.00	1.50
36 Emil Meusel	6.00	4.00	1.50
37 Arthur Nehf	6.00	4.00	1.50
38 Frank Snyder	6.00	4.00	1.50
39 Wm. H. Southworth	6.00	4.00	1.50
40 William Terry	12.00	8.00	3.50
41 George Harper	6.00	4.00	1.50
42 Nelson Hawks	6.00	4.00	1.50
43 Walter Henline	6.00	4.00	1.50
44 Walter Holke	6.00	4.00	1.50
45 Wilbur Hubbell	6.00	4.00	1.50
46 John Mokan	6.00	4.00	1.50
47 John Sand	6.00	4.00	1.50
48 Fred Williams	6.00	4.00	1.50
49 Carson Bigbee	6.00	4.00	1.50
50 Max Carey	9.00	6.00	2.50
51 Hazen Cuyler	9.00	6.00	2.50
52 George Grantham	6.00	4.00	1.50
53 Ray Kremer	6.00	4.00	1.50
54 Earl Smith	6.00	4.00	1.50
55 Harold Traynor	9.00	6.00	2.50
56 Glenn Wright	6.00	4.00	1.50
57 Lester Bell (horiz)	6.00	4.00	1.50
58 Raymond Blates (Blades)	6.00	4.00	1.50
59 James Bottomly (Bottomley)	9.00	6.00	2.50
60 Max Flack	6.00	4.00	1.50
61 Rogers Hornsby	15.00	10.00	4.50
62 Clarence Mueller	6.00	4.00	1.50
63 William Sherdell	6.00	4.00	1.50
64 George Toporcer	6.00	4.00	1.50
65 Howard Ehmke	6.00	4.00	1.50
66 Ira Flagstead	6.00	4.00	1.50
67 I. Valentine Picinich	6.00	4.00	1.50
68 John Quinn	6.00	4.00	1.50
69 Charles Ruffing	9.00	6.00	2.50
70 Philip Todt	6.00	4.00	1.50
71 Robert Veach	6.00	4.00	1.50
72 William Wambsganss	6.00	4.00	1.50
73 Eddie Collins	9.00	6.00	2.50
74 Bib Falk	6.00	4.00	1.50
75 Harry Hooper	9.00	6.00	2.50
76 Willie Kamm	6.00	4.00	1.50
77 I.M. Davis	6.00	4.00	1.50
78 Ray Shalk (Schalk)	9.00	6.00	2.50
79 Earl Sheely	6.00	4.00	1.50
80 Hollis Thurston	6.00	4.00	1.50
81 Wilson Fewster	6.00	4.00	1.50
82 Charles Jamieson	6.00	4.00	1.50
83 Walter Lutzke	6.00	4.00	1.50
84 Glenn Myatt	6.00	4.00	1.50
85 Joseph Sewell	9.00	6.00	2.50
86 Sherrod Smith	6.00	4.00	1.50
87 Tristram Speaker	12.00	8.00	3.50
88 Homer Summa	6.00	4.00	1.50
89 John Bassler	6.00	4.00	1.50
90 Tyrus Cobb	35.00	25.00	10.00
91 George Dauss	6.00	4.00	1.50
92 Harry Heilmann	9.00	6.00	2.50
93 Frank O'Rourke	6.00	4.00	1.50
94 Emory Rigney	6.00	4.00	1.50
95 Al Wings (Wingo) (horiz)	6.00	4.00	1.50
96 Larry Woodall	6.00	4.00	1.50
97 Henry L. Gehrig	45.00	32.00	13.00
98 Robert W. Muesel (Meusel)	6.00	4.00	1.50
99 Walter C. Pipp	6.00	4.00	1.50
100 Geo.H. "Babe" Ruth	50.00	35.00	15.00
101 Walter H. Shang (Schang)	6.00	4.00	1.50

1925 Exhibits

102 J.R. Shawkey	6.00	4.00	1.50
103 Urban J. Shocker	6.00	4.00	1.50
104 Aaron Ward	6.00	4.00	1.50
105 Max Bishop	6.00	4.00	1.50
106 James J. Dykes	6.00	4.00	1.50
107 Samuel Gray	6.00	4.00	1.50
108 Samuel Hale	6.00	4.00	1.50
109 Edmund (Bind) Miller (Bing)	6.00	4.00	1.50
110 Ralph Perkins	6.00	4.00	1.50
111 Edwin Rommel	6.00	4.00	1.50
112 Frank Welch	6.00	4.00	1.50
113 Walter Gerber	6.00	4.00	1.50
114 William Jacobson	6.00	4.00	1.50
115 Martin McManus	6.00	4.00	1.50
116 Henry Severid (Severeid)	6.00	4.00	1.50
117 George Sissler (Sisler)	12.00	8.00	3.50
118 John Tobin	6.00	4.00	1.50
119 Kenneth Williams	6.00	4.00	1.50
120 Ernest Wingard	6.00	4.00	1.50
121 Oswald Bluege	6.00	4.00	1.50
122 Stanley Coveleski	9.00	6.00	2.50
123 Leon Goslin	9.00	6.00	2.50
124 Stanley Harris	9.00	6.00	2.50
125 Walter Johnson	15.00	10.00	4.50
126 Joseph Judge	6.00	4.00	1.50
127 Earl McNeely	6.00	4.00	1.50
128 Harold Ruel	6.00	4.00	1.50

1926 EXHIBITS (128) 3 3/8" X 5 3/8"

The year 1926 marked the last of the 128-card sets produced by Exhibit Supply. Of this number, 70 cards are identical to those issued in 1925 but are easily identified because of the new blue-gray color introduced in 1926. Another 21 cards use 1925 pictures but contain the line "Ex. Sup. Co.,U.S.A." rather than "Made in U.S.A." The 37 photos new to this set have an unboxed legend and carry the new company line. Bischoff is incorrectly placed with Boston, N.L. (should be A.L.); the picture of Galloway is reversed; the photos of Hunnefield and Thomas are erroneously exchanged.

	MINT	VG-E	F-G
COMPLETE SET	900.00	600.00	250.00
COMMON PLAYER	6.00	4.00	1.50
1 Lawrence Benton (B)	6.00	4.00	1.50
2 Andrew High (B)	6.00	4.00	1.50
3 Maurice Burrus (B)	6.00	4.00	1.50
4 David Bancroft (B)	9.00	6.00	2.50
5 Joseph Genewich (B)	6.00	4.00	1.50
6 Bernie F. Neis (B)	6.00	4.00	1.50
7 Edward Taylor	6.00	4.00	1.50
8 J. Taylor (B)	6.00	4.00	1.50
9 John Butler (B)	6.00	4.00	1.50
10 Jacques F. Furnier (B) (Fournier)	6.00	4.00	1.50
11 Burleigh A.Grimes(B)	9.00	6.00	2.50
12 Wilson Fewster (B)	6.00	4.00	1.50
13 Douglas McWeeny (B)	6.00	4.00	1.50
14 George O'Neil (B)	6.00	4.00	1.50
15 Walter Maranville(B)	9.00	6.00	2.50
16 Zach Wheat (B)	9.00	6.00	2.50
17 Sparky Adams	6.00	4.00	1.50
18 J. Fred Blake (B)	6.00	4.00	1.50
19 James E. Cooney (B)	6.00	4.00	1.50
20 Howard Freigau	6.00	4.00	1.50
21 Charles Grimm	6.00	4.00	1.50
22 Leo Hartnett	9.00	6.00	2.50
23 C.E. Heathcote (B)	6.00	4.00	1.50
24 Joseph M. Munson (B)	6.00	4.00	1.50
25 Raymond Bressler	6.00	4.00	1.50
26 Hugh M. Critz	6.00	4.00	1.50
27 Peter Donohue	6.00	4.00	1.50
28 Charles Dressen	6.00	4.00	1.50
29 Walter C. Pipp (B)	6.00	4.00	1.50
30 Eppa Rixey	9.00	6.00	2.50
31 Ed. Roush	9.00	6.00	2.50
32 Ivy Wingo	6.00	4.00	1.50
33 Edward S.Farrell(B)	6.00	4.00	1.50
34 Frank Frisch (B)	15.00	10.00	4.50
35 Frank Snyder (B)	6.00	4.00	1.50
36 Fredrick Lindstrom (B) (Frederick)	9.00	6.00	2.50
37 Hugh A.McQuillan(B)	6.00	4.00	1.50
38 Emil Musel (B) (Meusel)	6.00	4.00	1.50
39 James J. Ring (B)	6.00	4.00	1.50
40 William Terry (B)	15.00	10.00	4.50
41 John M. Bentley (B)	6.00	4.00	1.50
42 Bernard Friberg (B)	6.00	4.00	1.50
43 George Harper	6.00	4.00	1.50
44 Walter Henline (B)	6.00	4.00	1.50
45 Clarence Huber (B)	6.00	4.00	1.50
46 John Makan (B) (Mokan)	6.00	4.00	1.50
47 John Sand (B)	6.00	4.00	1.50
48 Russell Wrigtstone (B)(Wrightstone)	6.00	4.00	1.50
49 Carson Bigbee	6.00	4.00	1.50
50 Max Carey	9.00	6.00	2.50
51 Hazen Cuyler	9.00	6.00	2.50
52 George Grantham	6.00	4.00	1.50
53 Ray Kremer	6.00	4.00	1.50
54 Earl Smith	6.00	4.00	1.50
55 Harold Traynor	9.00	6.00	2.50
56 Glen Wright	6.00	4.00	1.50
57 Lester Bell (H)	6.00	4.00	1.50
58 Raymond Blates (Blades)	6.00	4.00	1.50
59 James Bottomly (Bottomley)	9.00	6.00	2.50
60 Rogers Hornsby	15.00	10.00	4.50
61 Clarence Mueller	6.00	4.00	1.50
62 Robert O'Farrell(B)	6.00	4.00	1.50
63 William Sherdell	6.00	4.00	1.50
64 George Torporcer	6.00	4.00	1.50
65 Ira Flagstead	6.00	4.00	1.50
66 Fred Haney (B)	6.00	4.00	1.50
67 Ramon Herrera (B)	6.00	4.00	1.50
68 John Quinn	6.00	4.00	1.50
69 Emory Rigney (B)	6.00	4.00	1.50
70 Charles Ruffing	9.00	6.00	2.50
71 Philip Todt	6.00	4.00	1.50
72 Fred Wingfield (B)	6.00	4.00	1.50
73 Ted Blankenship (B)	6.00	4.00	1.50
74 Eddie Collins	9.00	6.00	2.50
75 Bib Falk	6.00	4.00	1.50
76 Wm. Hunnefield (B) (Tommy Thomas)	6.00	4.00	1.50
77 Willie Kamm	6.00	4.00	1.50
78 Ray Shalk (Schalk)	9.00	6.00	2.50
79 Earl Sheely	6.00	4.00	1.50
80 Hollis Thurston	6.00	4.00	1.50
81 Geo. H. Burns (B) (horiz)	6.00	4.00	1.50
82 Walter Lutzke	6.00	4.00	1.50
83 Glenn Myatt	6.00	4.00	1.50
84 Joseph Sewell	9.00	6.00	2.50
85 Sherrod Smith	6.00	4.00	1.50
86 Tristram Speaker	12.00	8.00	3.50
87 Fred Spurgeon (B)	6.00	4.00	1.50
88 Homer Summa	6.00	4.00	1.50
89 John Bassler	6.00	4.00	1.50
90 Lucerne Blue (B) (Luzerne)	6.00	4.00	1.50
91 Tyrus Cobb	35.00	25.00	10.00
92 George Dauss	6.00	4.00	1.50

1926 Exhibits

No.	Player			
93	Harry Heilmann	9.00	6.00	2.50
94	Frank O'Rourke	6.00	4.00	1.50
95	Charles Gehringer (B)	12.00	8.00	3.50
96	John Warner (B)	6.00	4.00	1.50
97	Patrick T.Collins(B)	6.00	4.00	1.50
98	Earl B. Combs (B)	9.00	6.00	2.50
99	Henry L. Gehrig	45.00	32.00	13.00
100	Anthony Lazzeri (B)	6.00	4.00	1.50
101	Robert W. Muesel (Meusel)	6.00	4.00	1.50
102	Geo.H. "Babe" Ruth	50.00	35.00	15.00
103	J. R. Shawkey	6.00	4.00	1.50
104	Urban J. Shocker	6.00	4.00	1.50
105	Max Bishop	6.00	4.00	1.50
106	Joseph Galloway (B)	6.00	4.00	1.50
107	James J. Dykes	6.00	4.00	1.50
108	Joseph Hauser (B)	6.00	4.00	1.50
109	Edmund (Bind) Miller (Bing)	6.00	4.00	1.50
110	Ralph Perkins	6.00	4.00	1.50
111	Edwin Rommel	6.00	4.00	1.50
112	Wm. Wambsganss (B)	6.00	4.00	1.50
113	Wm. Hargrave (B)	6.00	4.00	1.50
114	William Jacobson	6.00	4.00	1.50
115	Martin McManus	6.00	4.00	1.50
116	Oscar Melillo (B)	6.00	4.00	1.50
117	Walter Gerber	6.00	4.00	1.50
118	George Sissler (Sisler)	12.00	8.00	3.50
119	Kenneth Williams	6.00	4.00	1.50
120	Ernest Wingard	6.00	4.00	1.50
121	Oswald Bluege	6.00	4.00	1.50
122	Stanley Coveleski	9.00	6.00	2.50
123	Leon Goslin	9.00	6.00	2.50
124	Stanley Harris	9.00	6.00	2.50
125	Walter Johnson	15.00	10.00	4.50
126	Joseph Judge	6.00	4.00	1.50
127	Earl McNeely	6.00	4.00	1.50
128	Harold Ruel	6.00	4.00	1.50

1927 EXHIBITS (64)

3 3/8" X 5 3/8"

Two innovations characterize the 64-card set produced by Exhibit Supply for 1927. The first was a radical departure from the color scheme of previous sets marked by this year's light green hue. The second was the installation of the divided legend, whereby the player's name (all caps) and team were set in one corner, and the lines "Ex. Sup. Co., Chgo." and "Made in U.S.A." were set in the other. All the photos employed in this set were taken from the previous issues in 1925 and 1926, although 13 players appear with new teams. The usual misspellings and incorrect labeling of names and initials occurs throughout the set. Note: Genewich and Hunnefield have a different style of print, and Myatt is missing the right side of the legend.

No.	Player	MINT	VG-E	F-G
	COMPLETE SET	450.00	300.00	125.00
	COMMON PLAYER	6.50	4.50	1.75
1	David Bancroft	9.50	6.50	2.75
2	Joseph Genewich	6.50	4.50	1.75
3	Andrew High	6.50	4.50	1.75
4	J. Taylor	6.50	4.50	1.75
5	John Buttler (Butler)	6.50	4.50	1.75
6	Wilson Fewster	6.50	4.50	1.75
7	Burleigh A. Grimes	9.50	6.50	2.75
8	Walter Henline	6.50	4.50	1.75
9	Sparky Adams	6.50	4.50	1.75
10	Charles Grimm	6.50	4.50	1.75
11	Leo Hartnett	9.50	6.50	2.75
12	Clifton Heathcote	6.50	4.50	1.75
13	Raymond Bressler	6.50	4.50	1.75
14	Walter C. Pipp	6.50	4.50	1.75
15	Eppa Rixey	9.50	6.50	2.75
16	Ivy Wingo	6.50	4.50	1.75
17	John M. Bentley	6.50	4.50	1.75
18	George Harper	6.50	4.50	1.75
19	Rogers Hornsby	15.00	10.00	4.50
20	Fredrick Lindstrom	9.50	6.50	2.75
21	A. R. Decatur	6.50	4.50	1.75
22	John "Stuffy" McInnes (McInnis)	6.50	4.50	1.75
23	John Mokan	6.50	4.50	1.75
24	Russell Wrightstone	6.50	4.50	1.75
25	Hazen Cuyler	9.50	6.50	2.75
26	Ray Kremer	6.50	4.50	1.75
27	Earl Smith	6.50	4.50	1.75
28	Harold Traynor	9.50	6.50	2.75
29	Grover C. Alexander	13.00	9.00	4.00
30	James Bottomly (Bottomley)	13.00	9.00	4.00
31	Robert O'Farrell	6.50	4.50	1.75
32	Wm. H. Southworth	6.50	4.50	1.75
33	Ira Flagstead	6.50	4.50	1.75
34	Fred Haney	6.50	4.50	1.75
35	Philip Todt	6.50	4.50	1.75
36	Fred Wingfield	6.50	4.50	1.75
37	Fred·Blankenship (Ted)	6.50	4.50	1.75
38	Wm. Hunnefield (Tommy Thomas)	6.50	4.50	1.75
39	Willie Kamm	6.50	4.50	1.75
40	Ray Schalk	9.50	6.50	2.75
41	Geo. H. Burns (horiz)	6.50	4.50	1.75
42	Walter Lutzke	6.50	4.50	1.75
43	Glenn Myatt	6.50	4.50	1.75
44	Bernie Neis	6.50	4.50	1.75
45	John Bassler	6.50	4.50	1.75
46	George Daus (*Dauss)	6.50	4.50	1.75
47	Charles Gehringer	9.50	6.50	2.75
48	Harry Heilman (Heilmann)	9.50	6.50	2.75
49	Henry L. Gehrig	50.00	35.00	15.00
50	Anthony Lazzeri	6.50	4.50	1.75
51	Robert W. Muesel (Meusel)	6.50	4.50	1.75
52	Geo.H. "Babe" Ruth	60.00	40.00	16.00
53	Tyrus Cobb	40.00	26.00	11.00
54	Eddie Collins	9.50	6.50	2.75
55	William Wambsganns (Wambsganss)	6.50	4.50	1.75
56	Zach Wheat	9.50	6.50	2.75
57	Wm. Hargrave	6.50	4.50	1.75
58	Kenneth Williams	6.50	4.50	1.75
59	George Sissler (Sisler)	13.00	9.00	4.00
60	Ernest Wingard	6.50	4.50	1.75
61	Leon Goslin	9.50	6.50	2.75
62	Walter Johnson	15.00	10.00	4.50
63	Harold Ruel	6.50	4.50	1.75
64	Tristam Speaker (Tristram)	15.00	10.00	4.50

1928 EXHIBITS (64) 3 3/8" X 5 3/8"

In contrast to the green color of the preceding year, the 64 Exhibit cards of 1928 are blue in color. They may be found with blank backs, or postcard backs containing a small premium-offer clip-off in one corner. The use of the divided legend was continued, with the Roush card being unique in the set as it also cites his position. Of the 64 players in the set, 24 appear for the first time, while 12 of the holdovers show new poses. In addition, four players are shown with new team affiliations. The remaining 24 cards are identical to those issued in 1927 except for color. Once again, there is at least one mistaken identity and many misspellings and wrong names.

	MINT	VG-E	F-G
COMPLETE SET	450.00	300.00	125.00
COMMON PLAYER	6.00	4.00	1.50
1 Edward Brown	6.00	4.00	1.50
2 Rogers Hornsby (horiz)	15.00	10.00	4.50
3 Robert Smith	6.00	4.00	1.50
4 J. Taylor	6.00	4.00	1.50
5 David Bancroft	9.00	6.00	2.50
6 Max G. Carey	9.00	6.00	2.50
7 Charles R. Hargraves	6.00	4.00	1.50
8 Arthur "Dazzy" Vance	9.00	6.00	2.50
9 E. English	6.00	4.00	1.50
10 Leo Hartnett	9.00	6.00	2.50
11 A. C. Root	6.00	4.00	1.50
12 L. R. (Hack) Wilson	9.00	6.00	2.50
13 Hugh M. Critz	6.00	4.00	1.50
14 Eugene Hargrave	6.00	4.00	1.50
15 Adolph Luque	6.00	4.00	1.50
16 William A. Zitzmann	6.00	4.00	1.50
17 Virgil Barnes	6.00	4.00	1.50
18 J. Francis Hogan	6.00	4.00	1.50
19 Fredrick Lindstrom (Frederick)	9.00	6.00	2.50
20 Edd. Roush, Outfield	9.00	6.00	2.50
21 Fred Leach	6.00	4.00	1.50
22 James Ring	6.00	4.00	1.50
23 Henry Sand (H)	6.00	4.00	1.50
24 Fred Williams	6.00	4.00	1.50
25 Ray Kremer	6.00	4.00	1.50
26 Earl Smith	6.00	4.00	1.50
27 Paul Waner	9.00	6.00	2.50
28 Glenn Wright	6.00	4.00	1.50
29 Grover C. Alexander (no emblem)	12.00	8.00	3.50
30 Francis R. Blades	6.00	4.00	1.50
31 Frank Frisch	12.00	8.00	3.50
32 James Wilson	6.00	4.00	1.50
33 Ira Flagstead	6.00	4.00	1.50
34 Bryan "Slim" Harriss	6.00	4.00	1.50
35 Fred Hoffman	6.00	4.00	1.50
36 Philip Todt	6.00	4.00	1.50
37 Chalmer W. Cissell (horiz)	6.00	4.00	1.50
38 Bib Falk	6.00	4.00	1.50
39 Theodore Lyons	9.00	6.00	2.50
40 Harry McCurdy	6.00	4.00	1.50
41 Chas. Jamieson	6.00	4.00	1.50
42 Glenn Myatt	6.00	4.00	1.50
43 Joseph Sewell	9.00	6.00	2.50
44 Geo. Uhle	6.00	4.00	1.50
45 Robert Fothergill	6.00	4.00	1.50
46 Jack Tavener (horiz)	6.00	4.00	1.50
47 Earl G. Whitehill	6.00	4.00	1.50
48 Lawrence Woodall	6.00	4.00	1.50
49 Pat Collins	6.00	4.00	1.50
50 Lou Gehrig	40.00	30.00	12.00
51 Geo.H. "Babe" Ruth	50.00	35.00	15.00
52 Urban J. Shocker	6.00	4.00	1.50
53 Gordon S. Cochrane	12.00	8.00	3.50
54 Howard Ehmke	6.00	4.00	1.50
55 Joseph Hauser	6.00	4.00	1.50
56 Al. Simmons	9.00	6.00	2.50
57 L.A. Blue	6.00	4.00	1.50
58 John Ogden (Warren Ogden)	6.00	4.00	1.50
59 Walter Shang (Schang)	6.00	4.00	1.50
60 Fred Schulte	6.00	4.00	1.50
61 Leon Goslin	9.00	6.00	2.50
62 Stanley Harris	9.00	6.00	2.50
63 Sam Jones	6.00	4.00	1.50
64 Harold Ruel	6.00	4.00	1.50

W463-1 1929-1930 FOUR-IN-ONE (32) EXHIBITS 3 3/8" X 5 3/8"

The years 1929-30 marked the initial appearance of the Exhibit Company's famous "Four-In-One" design. Each of the 32 cards depict four players from one team, with a total of 128 players shown (eight from each of 16 major league teams). The player's names and teams are located under each picture in dark blue or white print. All the reverses are post card style with the premium clip-off across one corner. There are 11 color combinations known for the fronts. The backs may be uncolored, red (black/red front), or yellow (blue/yellow front). The card labeled "Babe Herman" actually depicts Jesse Petty.

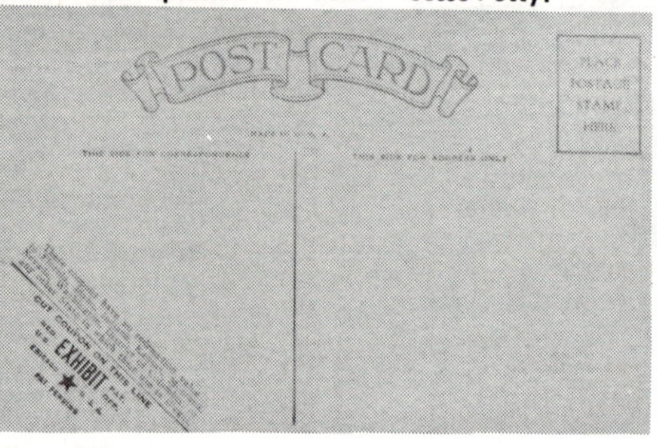

		MINT	VG-E	F-G
	COMPLETE SET	400.00	275.00	110.00
	COMMON PLAYER	12.00	8.00	3.50
1	Pat Collins	12.00	8.00	3.50
	Joe Dugan			
	Edward Farrel (Farrell)			
	George Sisler			
2	Lance Richbourg	12.00	8.00	3.50
	Fred Maguire			
	Robert Smith			
	George Harper			
3	D'Arcy Flowers	12.00	8.00	3.50
	Arthur "Dazzy" Vance			
	Nick Cullop			
	Harvey Hendrick			
4	Floyd C. Herman	12.00	8.00	3.50
	David Bancroft			
	John H. Deberry			
	Del L. Bisonette (Bissonette)			
5	Leo Hartnett	20.00	14.00	6.00
	C. E. Beck			
	L. R. (Hack) Wilson			
	Rogers Hornsby			
6	C. H. Root	12.00	8.00	3.50
	Hazen Cuyler			
	E. English			
	C.J. Grimm			
7	H.M. Critz	12.00	8.00	3.50
	W.C. Walker			
	G.L. Kelly			
	V.J. Picinich			
8	E.V. Purdy	12.00	8.00	3.50
	C.A. Pittenger			
	C.F. Lucas			
	H.E. Ford			
9	L. Benton	20.00	14.00	6.00
	Melvin Ott			
	William Terry			
	Andrew Reese			
10	J.F. Hogan	12.00	8.00	3.50
	T.C. Jackson			
	J.D. Welsh			
	Fred Lindstrom			
11	Frank O'Doul	12.00	8.00	3.50
	Bernard Friberg			
	Fresco Thompson			
	Donald Hurst			
12	Cy Williams	12.00	8.00	3.50
	A. C. Whitney			
	Ray Benge			
	Lester L. Sweetland			
13	Earl J. Adams	12.00	8.00	3.50
	R. Bartell			
	Harold Traynor			
	Earl Sheely			
14	Lloyd Waner	15.00	10.00	4.50
	Charles R. Hargreaves			
	Ray Kremer			
	Paul Waner			
15	Grover C. Alexander	25.00	17.00	7.00
	James Wilson			
	Frank Frisch			
	James Bottomly (Bottomley)			
16	Fred G. Haney	12.00	8.00	3.50
	Chas. J. Hafey			
	Taylor Douthit			
	Chas. M. Gilbert (Gelbert)			
17	J.A. Heving	12.00	8.00	3.50
	J. Rothrock			
	C.H. Ruffing			
	R.R. Reeves (R.E.)			
18	P.J. Todt	12.00	8.00	3.50
	H. Rhyne			
	W.W. Regan			
	D. Taitt			
19	Chalmer W. Cissell	12.00	8.00	3.50
	John W. Clancy			
	John L. Kerr			
	Willie Kamm			
20	Alex Metzler	12.00	8.00	3.50
	Alphonse Thomas			
	Carl Reynolds			
	Martin G. Autrey (Autry)			
21	L.A. Fonseca	12.00	8.00	3.50
	J. Sewell			
	Carl Lind			
	J. Tavener			
22	K. Holloway	12.00	8.00	3.50
	B. A. Falk			
	L. Sewell			
	Earl Averill			
23	Dale Alexander	12.00	8.00	3.50
	G. F. McManus			
	H. F. Rice			
	C. Gehringer			
24	M. J. Shea	12.00	8.00	3.50
	G. E. Uhle			
	H. E. Heilman (Heilmann)			
	C. N. Richardson			
25	Waite Hoyt	15.00	10.00	4.50
	Anthony Lazzeri			
	Benny Bengough			
	Earl B. Coombs (Combs)			

W463-1 1929-30 Four-in-One

No.	Players			
26	Mark Koenig	100.00	65.00	30.00
	Geo. H. "Babe" Ruth			
	Leo Durocher			
	Henry L. Gehrig			
27	Jimmy Foxx	35.00	24.00	10.00
	Gordon S. Cochrane			
	Robert M. Grove			
	George Haas			
28	Homer Summa	12.00	8.00	3.50
	James Dykes			
	Samuel Hale			
	Max Bishop			
29	H. Manush	12.00	8.00	3.50
	W.H. Shang (Schang)			
	S. Gray			
	R. Kress			
30	O. Melillo	12.00	8.00	3.50
	F.O. Rourke (O'Rourke)			
	L.A. Blue			
	F. Schulte			
31	Leon Goslin	12.00	8.00	3.50
	Oswald Bluege			
	Harold Ruel			
	Joseph Judge			
32	Sam Rice	12.00	8.00	3.50
	Jack Hayes			
	Sam P. Jones			
	Chas. M. Myer			

W463-2 1931-1932 FOUR-IN-ONE (32) 3 3/8" X 5 3/8" EXHIBITS

SAVE YOUR COUPONS and get these FREE PRIZES

SEND 50 COUPONS For any one of these Prizes

Noisy Nose Blower, Imp Bottle, Buffalo Kazoo, Rice Bead Necklace, Aeroplane Flyer, Cowboy Watch Fob, Celluloid Teeth, Trick Pencil, Jumping Frog, Ball Clapper Rattle, Chinese Puzzle, Magic Ball and Vase, Cowboy Hankerchief, Tom Mix Photo (7x10), Football Rule Book, Lucky Pocket Piece of Babe Ruth, Tom Mix, or Lindbergh

SEND 100 COUPONS For any one of these Prizes

Charlie Chaplin Squirter, Noisy Whirler, Rubber Dagger, Hunting Knife, En-Ess Top, Trick Cigar, Mouth-Organ, Wrist Band, Pocket Cat Cry, Snake Pistol, Cloth Purse, Referee's Whistle

INSTRUCTIONS

EXHIBIT SUPPLY COMPANY
Est. 1901
4222 WEST LAKE STREET
CHICAGO, ILL.

The collector should refer to the checklists when trying to determine the year of issue of any "Four-In-One" set because the checklist (showing the players as they are, appear in groups of four) and the card color will ultimately provide the right clues. Some of the colors of the previous issue—black on green, orange, red, or yellow, and blue on white—are repeated in this series, but the 1931-32 cards are distinguishable by the combinations of players which appear. The backs contain a description of attainable "FREE PRIZES" for coupons. The backs also contain the clip-off premium coupon. There are numerous misspellings, as usual, in the set.

	MINT	VG-E	F-G
COMPLETE SET	400.00	275.00	110.00
COMMON PLAYER	12.00	8.00	3.50

No.	Players	MINT	VG-E	F-G
1	Walter Maranville	12.00	8.00	3.50
	J.T. Zachary			
	Alfred Spohrer			
	Randolph Moore			
2	Lance Richbourg	12.00	8.00	3.50
	Fred Maguire			
	Earl Sheely			
	Walter Berger			
3	D'Arcy Flowers	12.00	8.00	3.50
	Arthur "Dazzy" Vance			
	Frank O'Doul			
	Fresco Thompson			
4	Floyd C. Herman	12.00	8.00	3.50
	Glenh Wright			
	Jack Quinn			
	Del L. Bisonette			
5	Leo Hartnett	20.00	14.00	6.00
	J.R. Stevenson (Stephenson)			
	L.R. (Hack) Wilson			
	Rogers Hornsby			
6	C.H. Root	15.00	10.00	4.50
	Hazen Cuyler			
	E. English			
	C.J. Grimm			
7	Les Durocher (Leo)	15.00	10.00	4.50
	W.C. Walker			
	Harry Heilmann			
	Nick Cullop			
8	W. Roettger	12.00	8.00	3.50
	Gooch			
	C.F. Lucas			
	H.E. Ford			
9	J.F. Hogan	12.00	8.00	3.50
	T.C. Jackson			
	H.M. Critz			
	Fred Lindstrom			
10	Robert O'Farrell	20.00	14.00	6.00
	Melvin Ott			
	William Terry			
	Fred Fitsimmons			
11	Chuck Klein	12.00	8.00	3.50
	A.C. Whitney			
	Ray Benge			
	Buzz Arlett			
12	Harry McCurdy	12.00	8.00	3.50
	Bernard Friberg			
	Richard Bartell			
	Donald Hurst			
13	Adam Comcrosky	12.00	8.00	3.50
	Gus Suhr			
	Harold Traynor			
	T.J. Thevenow			
14	Lloyd Waner	15.00	10.00	4.50
	George Grantham			
	Ray Kremer			
	Paul Waner			
15	Darl J. Adams	20.00	14.00	6.00
	James Wilson			
	Frank Frisch			
	James Bottomly (Bottomley)			
16	Bill Hallahan	12.00	8.00	3.50
	Chas. J. Hafey			
	Taylor Douthit			
	Chas. M. Gilbert (Gelbert)			
17	Chas. Berry	12.00	8.00	3.50
	J. Rothrock			
	Robt. Reeves			
	R.R. Reeves(R.E.)			
18	E.W. Webb	12.00	8.00	3.50
	H. Rhyne			
	Bill Sweeney			
	D. Mac Fayden			

W463-2 1931-32 Four-in-One

No.	Players	MINT	VG-E	F-G
19	L.L. Appling Ted Lyons Chalmer W. Cissell Willie Kamm	15.00	10.00	4.50
20	Smead Jolley L.A. Blue Carl Reynolds Henry Tate	12.00	8.00	3.50
21	Hunnefield J. Goldman Ed Morgan W. Ferrell	12.00	8.00	3.50
22	L.A. Fonseca B.A. Falk L. Sewell Earl Averill	15.00	10.00	4.50
23	Dale Alexander G.F. McManus G.E. Uhle C. Gehringer	15.00	10.00	4.50
24	Wallie Schang E. Funk Mark Koenig W. Hoyt	12.00	8.00	3.50
25	W. Dickey Anthony Lazzeri H. Pennock Earl B. Coombs (Combs)	30.00	20.00	8.00
26	Lyn Lary Geo. H. "Babe" Ruth James Reese Henry L. Gehrig	100.00	65.00	30.00
27	John Boley James Dykes E.J. Miller Al Simmons	15.00	10.00	4.50
28	Jimmy Foxx Gordon S. Cochrane Robert M. Grove George Haas	35.00	24.00	10.00
29	O. Melillo F.O. Rourke (O'Rourke) Leon Goslin F. Schulte	12.00	8.00	3.50
30	W. Stewart Richard Farrell (Ferrell) S. Gray R. Kress	12.00	8.00	3.50
31	Roy Spencer H. Manush Joe Cronin F. Marberry	20.00	14.00	6.00
32	O. Bluege J. Judge S. Rice C. Myer	12.00	8.00	3.50

W463-3 1933 FOUR-IN-ONE (16) EXHIBITS 3 3/8" X 5 3/8"

The physical dimensions of the cardboard sheet used by the Exhibit Supply Company in printing their card sets over the years allows the following correlation to be made when one establishes that 32 of the standard-size cards (3 3/8 X 5 3/8") are printed per sheet. Sets of 128 cards are equal to four sheets, 64 cards to two sheets, 32 cards to one sheet, and 16 cards to one-half sheet. Whether it was cost economics, the Depression, or simplicity of operation which caused the company to change their set totals in a descending order since 1922, in 1933. The first of a series of 16-card sets was released. The fronts of these cards are black on green, orange, red, or yellow; the backs are blank.

		MINT	VG-E	F-G
COMPLETE SET		250.00	170.00	70.00
COMMON PLAYER		12.00	8.00	3.50
1	Lance Richbourg Fred Maguire Earl Sheely Walter Berger	12.00	8.00	3.50
2	Vincent Lopez (Al) Glenn Wright Arthur "Dazzy" Vance Frank O'Doul	15.00	10.00	4.50
3	J.R. Stephenson C.J. Grimm E. English C.H. Root	15.00	10.00	4.50
4	Taylor Douthit George Grantham G. F. Lucas Chas. Hafey	12.00	8.00	3.50
5	Fred Fitzsimmons H. M. Critz Fred Lindstrom Robert O'Farrell	12.00	8.00	3.50
6	Chuck Klein Ray Benge Richard Bartell Donald Hurst	12.00	8.00	3.50
7	T. J. Thevenow Paul Waner Gus Suhr Lloyd Waner	15.00	10.00	4.50
8	Earl J. Adams Frank Frisch Bill Halloran Chas. Gelbert	15.00	10.00	4.50
9	D. MacFayden E. W. Webb H. Rhyne Chas. Berry	12.00	8.00	3.50
10	Charles Berry Bob Seeds C. A. Blue Ted Lyons	12.00	8.00	3.50
11	W. Ferrell L. Sewell Ed Morgan Earl Averill	15.00	10.00	4.50
12	"Muddy" Ruel G. E. Uhle Jonathon Stone C. Gehringer	15.00	10.00	4.50
13	George H. "Babe" Ruth H. Pennock Anthony Lazzeri W. Dickey	90.00	60.00	25.00
14	Mickey Cochrane Jimmy Foxx Al Simmons Robert M. Grove	50.00	35.00	15.00
15	Richard Farrell O. Melillo Leon Goslin S. Grey	12.00	8.00	3.50
16	H. Manush F. Marberry J. Judge Roy Spencer	12.00	8.00	3.50

W463-4 1934 FOUR-IN-ONE (16) EXHIBITS   3 3/8" X 5 3/8"

The emergence of the bubble gum card producers in 1933-34 may have motivated Exhibit Supply to make a special effort to provide a "quality" set for 1934. The new 16-card series was printed in colors of blue, brown, olive green and violet—all in softer tones than used in previous years. No less than 25 players appeared on cards for the first time, and another 16 were given entirely new poses. For the first time in the history of the Exhibit baseball series, there were no spelling errors. However, perfection is rarely attained in any endeavor, and the "bugaboo" of 1934 was the labeling of Al Lopez as Vincent Lopez (famous band leader and prognosticator). The cards have plain backs.

	MINT	VG-E	F-G
COMPLETE SET	300.00	200.00	80.00
COMMON PLAYER	12.00	8.00	3.50
1 Bill Urbansky Ed Brandt Walter Berger Frank Hogan	12.00	8.00	3.50
2 Vincent Lopez (Al) Glenn Wright Sam Leslie Leonard Koenecke	12.00	8.00	3.50
3 Chas. Klein C. J. Grimm E. English Lon Warneke	15.00	10.00	4.50
4 Botchi Lombardi Tony Piet Jimmy Bottomley Chas. J. Hafey	15.00	10.00	4.50
5 Blondy Ryan Bill Terry Carl Hubbell Mel Ott	30.00	20.00	8.00
6 Jimmy Wilson Wesley Schulmerich Richard Bartell Donald Hurst	12.00	8.00	3.50
7 T. J. Thevenow Paul Waner Pie Traynor Lloyd Waner	20.00	14.00	6.00
8 Pepper Martin Frank Frisch Bill Hallahan John Rothrock	15.00	10.00	4.50
9 Lefty Grove Roy Johnson Bill Cissell Dick Ferrell	15.00	10.00	4.50
10 Luke Appling Al Simmons Evar Swanson George Earnshaw	20.00	14.00	6.00
11 W. Ferrell Frank Pytlak Willie Kamm Earl Averill	15.00	10.00	4.50
12 Mickey Cochrane Goose Goslin Fred Marberry C. Gehringer	30.00	20.00	8.00
13 Geo.H."Babe" Ruth Vernon Gomez Lou Gehrig W. Dickey	150.00	100.00	40.00
14 Mickey Cochrane Jimmy Foxx Al Simmons Robert M. Grove	50.00	35.00	15.00
15 Irving Burns O. Melillo Irving Hadley Rollie Hemsley	12.00	8.00	3.50
16 H. Manush Alvin Crowder Joe Cronin Joe Kuhel	15.00	10.00	4.50

W463-5 1935 FOUR-IN-ONE (16)   3 3/8" X 5 3/8"

The year 1935 marked the return of the 16-card Exhibit series to a simple slate blue color. Babe Ruth appears with Boston, N.L., the last time his card would be made while he was playing, after being included in every Exhibit series since 1921. Of the 64 players pictured, 17 are shown for the first time, while 11 of the returnees are graced with new poses. The infamous "Vincent Lopez" card returns with this set, and the photo purportedly showing Tony Cuccinello is really that of George Puccinelli. The cards have plain backs.

	MINT	VG-E	F-G
COMPLETE SET	250.00	170.00	70.00
COMMON PLAYER	12.00	8.00	3.50
1 "Babe" Ruth Frank Hogan Walter Berger Ed Brandt	75.00	50.00	20.00
2 Van Mungo Vincent Lopez (Al) Dan Taylor Tony Cuccinello	12.00	8.00	3.50
3 Chas. Klein C. J. Grimm Lon Warneke Gabby Hartnett	20.00	14.00	6.00
4 Botchí Lombardi Paul Derringer Jimmy Bottomley Chas. J. Hafey	20.00	14.00	6.00
5 Hughie Critz Bill Terry Carl Hubbell Mel Ott	30.00	20.00	8.00
6 Jimmy Wilson Phil Collins John "Blondy" Ryan Geo. Watkins	12.00	8.00	3.50

W463-5 1935 Four-in-one

No.	Players			
7	Paul Waner Pie Traynor Gy Bush Floyd Vaughn	20.00	14.00	6.00
8	Pepper Martin Frank Frisch Jerome "Dizzy" Dean Paul Dean	50.00	35.00	15.00
9	Lefty Grove Billy Werber Joe Cronin Dick Ferrell	20.00	14.00	6.00
10	Al Simmons Jimmy Dykes Ted Lyons Henry Bonura	20.00	14.00	6.00
11	Mel Harder Hal Trosky Willie Kamm Earl Averill	12.00	8.00	3.50
12	Mickey Cochrane Goose Goslin Linwood Rowe (Lynwood) C. Gehringer	30.00	20.00	8.00
13	Tony Lazzeri Vernon Gomez Lou Gehrig W. Dickey	75.00	50.00	20.00
14	Slug Mahaffey Jimmy Foxx George Cramer Bob Johnson	20.00	14.00	6.00
15	Irving Burns O. Melillo L. N. Newson Rollie Hemsley	12.00	8.00	3.50
16	Buddy Meyer (Myer) Earl Whitehill H. Manush Fred Schulte	12.00	8.00	3.50

W463-6 1936 FOUR-IN-ONE (16) EXHIBITS 3 3/8" X 5 3/8"

In 1936, the 16-card Exhibit set retained the "slate," or blue-gray color of the preceding year, but also added an olive green hue to the set. The cards are blank-backed, but for the first time since the "Four-In-One" design was introduced in 1929, a line reading "Ptd in U.S.A." was placed in the bottom border on the obverse. The set contains 16 players making their debut in Exhibit cards, while nine holdovers have new poses. The photo of George Puccinelli was correctly identified and placed with Philadelphia, A.L.

		MINT	VG-E	F-G
	COMPLETE SET	250.00	170.00	70.00
	COMMON PLAYER	12.00	8.00	3.50
1	Bill Urbanski Pinky Whitney Walter Berger Danny MacFayden	12.00	8.00	3.50
2	Van Mungo Stan Bordagaray Fred Lindstrom Dutch Brandt	12.00	8.00	3.50
3	Billy Herman Augie Galan Lon Warneke Gabby Hartnett	16.00	11.00	4.50
4	Botchie Lombardi Paul Derringer Babe Herman Alex Kampouris	12.00	8.00	3.50
5	Gus. Mancuso Bill Terry Carl Hubbell Mel Ott	30.00	20.00	8.00
6	Jimmy Wilson Curt Davis Dolph Camilli Johnny Moore	12.00	8.00	3.50
7	Paul Waner Pie Traynor Guy Bush Floyd Vaughn	21.00	14.00	6.00
8	Joe "Ducky" Medwick Frank Frisch Jerome "Dizzy" Dean Paul Dean	50.00	35.00	15.00
9	Lefty Grove Jimmy Foxx Joe Cronin Dick Ferrell	40.00	26.00	10.00
10	Luke Appling Jimmy Dykes Ted Lyons Henry Bonura	21.00	14.00	6.00
11	Mel Harder Hal Trosky Joe Vosmik Earl Averill	12.00	8.00	3.50
12	Mickey Cochrane Goose Goslin Linwood Rowe (Lynwood) C. Gehringer	30.00	20.00	8.00
13	Tony Lazzeri Vernon Gomez Lou Gehrig Red Ruffing	75.00	50.00	20.00
14	Charles Berry Puccinelli Frank Higgins Bob Johnson	12.00	8.00	3.50
15	Harland Clift Sammy West Paul Andrews Rollie Hemsley	12.00	8.00	3.50
16	Buddy Meyer (Myer) Earl Whitehill Ossie Bluege L. N. Newsom	12.00	8.00	3.50

W463-7 1937 FOUR-IN-ONE (16) EXHIBITS

3 3/8" X 5 3/8"

It would appear that Exhibit Supply was merely "flip-flopping" color schemes during the three-year period 1935-37. In '35, the cards were blue-gray; in '36, the cards were either blue-gray or green; now, in '37, the cards appear in green only. As with the previous set, the name and team of each player is printed in two or three lines under his picture, the "Ptd in U.S.A." line appears in the bottom border (missing on some cards), and the backs are blank.

		MINT	VG-E	F-G
	COMPLETE SET	300.00	200.00	80.00
	COMMON PLAYER	12.00	8.00	3.50
1	Bill Urbanski Alfonso Lopez Walter Berger Danny MacFayden	12.00	8.00	3.50
2	Van Mungo E. English Johnny Moore(Phil-NL) Gordon Phelps	12.00	8.00	3.50
3	Billy Herman Augie Galan Bill Lee Gabby Hartnett	16.00	11.00	4.50
4	Botchi Lombardi Paul Derringer Lew Riggs Phil Weintraub	12.00	8.00	3.50
5	Gus Mancuso Sam Leslie Carl Hubbell Mel Ott	30.00	20.00	8.00
6	Pinky Whitney Wm. Walters Dolph Camilli Johnny Moore	12.00	8.00	3.50
7	Paul Waner Gus Suhr Cy Blanton Floyd Vaughn	12.00	8.00	3.50
8	Joe "Duck" Medwick Lon Warneke Jerome "Dizzy" Dean Stuart Martin	45.00	30.00	12.00
9	Lefty Grove Jimmy Foxx Joe Cronin Dick Ferrell	45.00	30.00	12.00
10	Luke Appling Jimmy Dykes Vernon Kennedy Henry Bonura	12.00	8.00	3.50
11	Bob Feller Hal Trosky Frank Pytlak Earl Averill	30.00	20.00	8.00
12	Mickey Cochrane Goose Goslin Linwood Rowe C. Gehringer	30.00	20.00	8.00
13	Tony Lazzeri Vernon Gomez Lou Gehrig Joe DiMaggio	125.00	85.00	35.00
14	Billy Weber (Werber) Harry Kelly (Kelley) Wallace Moses Bob Johnson	12.00	8.00	3.50
15	Harland Clift Sammy West Orval Hildebrand Rollie Hemsley	12.00	8.00	3.50
16	Buddy Meyer (Myer) Jonathan Stone Joe Kuhel L. N. Newsom	12.00	8.00	3.50

W463-8 1938 FOUR-IN-ONE (16)

3 3 /8" X 5 3/8"

The 1938 set of 16 cards demonstrates the fact that the one consistent "quality" of Exhibit Supply sets is their inconsistency. For example, the card of Tony Cuccinello once again contains the photo of George Puccinelli, a mistake first made in 1935, corrected in 1936, and now made again in 1938. The set is also rife with name and spelling errors. Of the 64 players depicted, 12 are new arrivals and three are returnees with new poses. Another ten retained their 1937 photos but were designated new team affiliations. The cards have blank backs. This set was the last to employ the "Four-In-One" format.

		MINT	VG-E	F-G
	COMPLETE SET	300.00	200.00	80.00
	COMMON PLAYER	12.00	8.00	3.50
1	Tony Cuccinello (Geo. Puccinelli) Roy Johnson Vince DiMaggio Danny MacFayden	12.00	8.00	3.50
2	Van Mungo Leo Durocher Dolph Camilli Gordon Phelps	12.00	8.00	3.50
3	Billy Herman Augie Galan Jerome "Dizzy" Dean Gabby Hartnett	50.00	35.00	14.00
4	Dutch Lombardi Paul Derringer Lew Riggs Ival Goodman	12.00	8.00	3.50
5	Hank Leiber Jim Ripple Carl Hubbell Mel Ott	30.00	20.00	8.00
6	Pinky Whitney Wm. Walters Chas. Klein Morris Arnovich	12.00	8.00	3.50

W463-8 1938 Four-in-one

No.	Players			
7	Paul Waner Gus Suhr Cy Blanton Floyd Vaughn	12.00	8.00	3.50
8	Joe "Ducky" Medwick Lon Warneke John Mize Stuart Martin	16.00	11.00	4.50
9	Lefty Grove Jimmy Foxx Joe Cronin Joe Vosmik	45.00	30.00	12.00
10	Luke Appling L. Sewell Mike Kreevich Ted Lyons	16.00	11.00	4.50
11	Bob Feller Hal Trosky Odel Hale Earl Averill	30.00	20.00	8.00
12	Hank Greenberg Rudy York Tom Bridges C. Gehringer	21.00	14.00	6.00
13	W. Dickey Vernon Gomez Lou Gehrig Joe DiMaggio	125.00	85.00	35.00
14	Billy Weber (Werber) Harry Kelly (Kelley) Wallace Moses Bob Johnson	12.00	8.00	3.50
15	Harland Clift Sammy West Beau Bell L. N. Newsom	12.00	8.00	3.50
16	Buddy Meyer (Myer) Jonathan Stone W. Ferrell Rick Ferrell	12.00	8.00	3.50

W465 1928 PCL EXHIBITS (32) 3 3/8" X 5 3/8"

Exhibit card collectors speculate that this 32-card set, produced in 1928, was distributed regionally, in California only, in conjunction with the Exhibit Company's regular series of major league players. The cards are blue in color (as are the major league cards) and contain pictures of ball players from the six California teams of the PCL. There are no cards known for Portland and Seattle (and given that 32 cards is the exact length of a one-half sheet printing, none can be expected to appear). The cards have plain backs and carry a divided legend (two lines on each side) on the front. Several names are misspelled, several more are wrongly assigned ("Carl" instead of "Walter" Berger), and the Hollywood team name should read "Sheiks."

	MINT	VG-E	F-G
COMPLETE SET	900.00	600.00	250.00
COMMON PLAYER	30.00	20.00	8.00
1 "Buzz Arlett	30.00	20.00	8.00
2 Earl Averill	50.00	35.00	14.00
3 Carl Berger (Walter, sic)	40.00	25.00	10.00
4 "Ping" Bodie	30.00	20.00	8.00
5 Carl Dittmar (H)	30.00	20.00	8.00
6 Jack Penton	30.00	20.00	8.00
7 Neal "Mickey" Finn (Cornelius, sic)	30.00	20.00	8.00
8 Tony Governor	30.00	20.00	8.00
9 Truck Hannah (H)	30.00	20.00	8.00
10 Mickey Heath (H)	30.00	20.00	8.00
11 Wally Hood	30.00	20.00	8.00
12 "Fuzzy" Hufft	30.00	20.00	8.00
13 Snead Jolly (Smead Jolley, sic)	30.00	20.00	8.00
14 Bobby "Ducky" Jones	30.00	20.00	8.00
15 Rudy Kallio	30.00	20.00	8.00
16 Johnny Kerr (H)	30.00	20.00	8.00
17 Harry Krause	30.00	20.00	8.00
18 Lynford H. Larry (Lary, sic)	30.00	20.00	8.00
19 Dudley Lee	30.00	20.00	8.00
20 Walter "Duster" Mails	30.00	20.00	8.00
21 Jimmy Reese	40.00	25.00	10.00
22 "Dusty" Rhodes	30.00	20.00	8.00
23 Hal Rhyne	30.00	20.00	8.00
24 "Hank" Severied (Severeid, sic)	30.00	20.00	8.00
25 Earl Sheely	30.00	20.00	8.00
26 Frank Shellenback	30.00	20.00	8.00
27 Gordon Slade	30.00	20.00	8.00
28 Hollis Thurston	30.00	20.00	8.00
29 "Babe" Twombly	30.00	20.00	8.00
30 Earl "Tex" Weathersby	30.00	20.00	8.00
31 Ray French	30.00	20.00	8.00
32 Ray Keating	30.00	20.00	8.00

1939-1946 SALUTATION EXHIBITS (80) 3 3/8" X 5 3/8"

This collection of 80 exhibit cards shares a common style: the "personal greeting" or "salutation". The specific greeting varies from card to card—"Yours truly, Best wishes, etc."—as does the location of the exhibit identification (lower left or lower right). Some players appear with different teams and there are occasional misspellings.

		MINT	VG-E	F-G
	COMPLETE SET	750.00	500.00	200.00
	COMMON PLAYER	1.35	.90	.40
1	Luke Appling (LL) Sincerely Yours	2.50	1.70	.70
2	Luke Appling (LR) Sincerely Yours	1.80	1.20	.50
3	Earl Averill Very Best Wishes	45.00	30.00	12.00
4	Charles"Red" Barrett Yours Truly	1.35	.90	.40
5	Henry "Hank" Borowy Sincerely Yours	1.35	.90	.40
6	Lou Boudreau Sincerely	1.80	1.20	.50
7	Adolf Camilli Very Truly Yours	4.50	3.00	1.20
8	Phil Caveretta Cordially Yours	1.35	.90	.40
9	Tony Cuccinello Very Best Wishes	7.50	5.00	2.00
10	Dizzy Dean Sincerely	12.00	8.00	3.50
11	Paul Derringer Yours Truly	1.35	.90	.40
12	Bill Dickey (LR) Cordially Yours	7.50	5.00	2.00
13	Bill Dickey (LL) Cordially Yours	7.50	5.00	2.00
14	Joe DiMaggio Cordially	7.50	5.00	2.00
15	Bob Elliott Truly Yours	1.35	.90	.40
16	Bob Feller Best Wishes	15.00	10.00	4.00
17	Bob Feller Yours Truly	4.50	3.00	1.20
18	Dave Ferriss Best of Luck	1.35	.90	.40
19	Jimmy Foxx Sincerely	21.00	14.00	6.00
20	Lou Gehrig Sincerely	90.00	60.00	25.00
21	Charlie Gehringer Yours Truly	12.00	8.00	3.50
22	Vernon Gomez Sincerely Yours	30.00	20.00	8.00
23	Joe Gordon (Cleve) Sincerely	7.50	5.00	2.00
24	Joe Gordon (NY) Sincerely	1.35	.90	.40
25	Hank Greenberg Truly Yours	4.50	3.00	1.20
26	Henry Greenberg Very Truly Yours	21.00	14.00	6.00
27	Robert Grove Cordially Yours	15.00	10.00	4.00
28	Gabby Hartnett Cordially	45.00	30.00	12.00
29	Buddy Hassett Yours Truly	4.50	3.00	1.20
30	Jeff Heath Best Wishes	4.50	3.00	1.20
31	Jeff Heath (Small Pic) Best Wishes	1.35	.90	.40
32	Kirby Higbe Sincerely	4.50	3.00	1.20
33	Tommy Holmes Yours Truly	1.35	.90	.40
34	Tommy Holmes Sincerely Yours	30.00	20.00	8.00
35	Carl Hubbell Best Wishes	7.50	5.00	2.00
36	Bob Johnson Yours Truly	4.50	3.00	1.20
37	Charles Keller Best Wishes	1.35	.90	.40
38	Ken Keltner Sincerly (sic)	7.50	5.00	2.00
39	Chuck Klein Yours Truly	30.00	20.00	8.00
40	Mike Kreevich Sincerely	21.00	14.00	6.00
41	Joe Kuhel Truly Yours	4.50	3.00	1.20
42	Bill Lee Cordially Yours	4.50	3.00	1.20
43	Ernie Lombardi(1/2 B) Cordially	21.00	14.00	6.00
44	Ernie Lombardi Cordially Yours	1.35	.90	.40
45	Marty Marion Best Wishes	1.35	.90	.40
46	Merrill May Best Wishes	4.50	3.00	1.20
47	Frank McCormick (LL) Sincerely	4.50	3.00	1.20
48	Frank McCormick (LR) Sincerely	1.35	.90	.40
49	George McQuinn (LL) Yours Truly	4.50	3.00	1.20
50	George McQuinn (LR) Yours Truly	2.50	1.70	.70
51	Joe Medwick Very Best Wishes	7.50	5.00	2.00
52	Johnny Mize (LL) Yours Truly	4.50	3.00	1.20
53	Johnny MIze (LR) Yours Truly	2.50	1.70	.70
54	Hugh Mulcahy Cordially	21.00	14.00	6.00
55	Hal Newhouser Best Wishes	1.35	.90	.40

56 Louis (Buck) Newsom Sincerely	1.35	.90	.40
57 Buck Newson (sic) Very Best Wishes	30.00	20.00	8.00
58 Mel Ott (LL) Sincerely Yours	12.00	8.00	3.50
59 Mel Ott (LR) Sincerely Yours	7.50	5.00	2.00
60 Andy Pafko Sincerely Yours	1.35	.90	.40
61 Andy Pafko Yours Truly	1.35	.90	.40
62 Claude Passeau Sincerely	1.35	.90	.40
63 Howard Pollett (LL) Best Wishes	4.50	3.00	1.20
64 Howard Pollett (LR) Best Wishes	1.35	.90	.40
65 Pete Reiser (LL) Truly Yours	21.00	14.00	6.00
66 Pete Reiser (LR) Truly Yours	1.35	.90	.40
67 Johnny Rizzo Sincerely Yours	21.00	14.00	6.00
68 Glen Russell Sincerely	21.00	14.00	6.00
69 George Stirnweiss Yours Truly	1.35	.90	.40
70 Cecil Travis Best Wishes	4.50	3.00	1.20
71 Paul Trout Truly Yours	1.35	.90	.40
72 Johnny Vander Meer Cordially Yours	7.50	5.00	2.00
73 Arky Vaughn Best Wishes	4.50	3.00	1.20
74 Fred "Dixie" Walker "D" on Hat Yours Truly	1.35	.90	.40
75 Fred "Dixie" Walker Cap blanked out Yours Truly	12.00	8.00	3.50
76 Bucky Walters Sincerely Yours	1.35	.90	.40
77 Lon Warneke Very Truly Yours	4.50	3.00	1.20
78 Ted Williams (#9) Sincerely	60.00	40.00	16.00
79 Ted Williams Sincerely Yours	7.50	5.00	2.00
80 Rudy York Cordially	1.35	.90	.40

1948 HALL OF FAME EXHIBITS (33) 3 3/8" X 5 3/8"

This exhibit set, entitled "Baseball's Great Hall of Fame," consists of black & white photos on gray background. The pictures are framed on the sides by Greek columns and a short biography is printed at the bottom. The cards are blank back. Twenty-four of the cards were reissued in 1974 on extremely white stock.

	MINT	VG-E	F-G
COMPLETE SET	120.00	80.00	30.00
COMMON PLAYER	1.75	1.25	.50
1 G.C. Alexander	3.00	2.00	.80
2 Roger Bresnahan	1.75	1.25	.50
3 Frank Chance	2.25	1.50	.60
4 Jack Chesbro	1.75	1.25	.50
5 Fred Clarke	1.75	1.25	.50
6 Ty Cobb	6.00	4.00	1.50
7 Mickey Cochrane	2.25	1.50	.60
8 Eddie Collins	1.75	1.25	.50
9 Hugh Duffy	1.75	1.25	.50
10 Johnny Evers	1.75	1.25	.50
11 Frankie Frisch	2.25	1.50	.60
12 Lou Gehrig	6.00	4.00	1.50
13 Clark Griffith	1.75	1.25	.50
14 Robert "Lefty" Grove	2.25	1.50	.60
15 Rogers Hornsby	3.00	2.00	.80
16 Carl Hubbell	2.25	1.50	.60
17 Hughie Jennings	1.75	1.25	.50
18 Walter Johnson	3.00	2.00	.80
19 Willie Keeler	2.25	1.50	.60
20 Nap Lajoie	2.25	1.50	.60
21 Connie Mack	2.25	1.50	.60
22 Christy Mathewson	3.00	2.00	.80
23 John McGraw	2.25	1.50	.60
24 Eddie Plank	1.75	1.25	.50
25A Babe Ruth(swinging)	9.00	6.00	2.50
25B Babe Ruth(bats in front) 10 bats	45.00	30.00	12.00
26 George Sisler	2.25	1.50	.60
27 Tris Speaker	3.00	2.00	.80
28 Joe Tinker	1.75	1.25	.50
29 Rube Waddell	1.75	1.25	.50
30 Honus Wagner	3.00	2.00	.80
31 Ed Walsh	1.75	1.25	.50
32 Cy Young	2.25	1.50	.60

1947-1966 EXHIBITS (319) 3 3/8" X 5 3/8"

This grouping encompasses a wide time span but displays a common design. The following players have been illegally reprinted in mass quantities on a thinner-than-original cardboard which is also characterized by a dark gray back: Aaron, Ford, Fox, Hodges, Elston Howard, Mantle, Mays, Musial, Newcombe, Reese, Spahn, and Ted Williams.

	MINT	VG-E	F-G
COMPLETE SET	450.00	300.00	120.00
COMMON PLAYER	.45	.30	.12
1 Hank Aaron	4.50	3.00	1.20
2A Joe Adcock(script)	.90	.60	.25
2B Joe Adcock(sign.)	.45	.30	.12
3 Max Alvis	.45	.30	.12
4A Johnny Antonelli (Brave)	.90	.60	.25
4B Johnny Antonelli (Giants)	.90	.60	.25
5A Luis Aparicio (portrait)	.90	.60	.25
5B Luis Aparicio (batting)	3.50	2.40	1.00
6 Luke Appling	1.80	1.20	.50
7A Richie Ashburn (Phillies)	.90	.60	.25
7B Richie Ashburn (Cubs)	1.80	1.20	.50
8 Bob Aspromonte	.45	.30	.12
9 Toby Atwell	.90	.60	.25
10A Ed Bailey (Cinn. cap)	.90	.60	.25
10B Ed Bailey(no cap)	.90	.60	.25
11 Gene Baker	.90	.60	.25
12A Ernie Banks(script)	4.50	3.00	1.20
12B Ernie Banks(sign.)	2.25	1.50	.65
12C Ernie Banks(port.)	2.25	1.50	.65
13 Steve Barber	.45	.30	.12
14 Earl Battey	.45	.30	.12
15 Matt Batts	.90	.60	.25
16A Hank Bauer(NY cap)	.90	.60	.25
16B Hank Bauer (plain cap)	1.80	1.20	.50
17 Frank Baumholtz	.90	.60	.25
18 Gene Bearden	.90	.60	.25
19 Joe Beggs	3.50	2.40	1.00
20A Yogi Berra	3.50	2.40	1.00
20B Larry "Yogi" Berra	2.70	1.80	.80
21 Steve Bilko	.90	.60	.25
22A Ewell Blackwell (foot up)	.90	.60	.25
22B Ewell Blackwell (portrait)	.90	.60	.25
23A Don Blasingame (St.L. cap)	.45	.30	.12
23B Don Blasingame (plain cap)	.45	.30	.12
24 Ken Boyer	.90	.60	.25
25 Ralph Branca	.90	.60	.25
26 Jackie Brandt	.45	.30	.12
27 Harry Brecheen	.90	.60	.25
28 Tom Brewer	.45	.30	.12
29 Lou Brissie	.90	.60	.25
30 Bill Bruton	.45	.30	.12
31A Lew Burdette (side view)	.90	.60	.25
31B Lew Burdette (facing)	.45	.30	.12
32 Johnny Callison	.45	.30	.12
33 Roy Campanella	3.50	2.40	1.00
34A Chico Carrasquel (White Sox)	.90	.60	.25
34B Chico Carrasquel (plain cap)	.90	.60	.25
35 George Case	1.80	1.20	.50
36 Hugh Casey	.90	.60	.25
37 Norm Cash	.90	.60	.25
38A Orlando Cepeda (portrait)	.90	.60	.25
38B Orlando Cepeda (batting)	1.80	1.20	.50
39A Bob Cerv (A's uniform)	.90	.60	.25
39B Bob Cerv (plain unif.)	.45	.30	.12
40 Dean Chance	.45	.30	.12
41 Spud Chandler	.90	.60	.25
42 Tom Cheney	.45	.30	.12
43 Bubba Church	.90	.60	.25
44 Roberto Clemente	3.50	2.40	1.00
45A Rocky Colavito (port.)	.90	.60	.25
45B Rocky Colavito (batt.)	.90	.60	.25
46 Choo-Choo Coleman	.45	.30	.12
47 Gordy Coleman	.45	.30	.12
48 Jerry Coleman	.90	.60	.25
49 Mort Cooper	.90	.60	.25
50 Walker Cooper (2)	.90	.60	.25
51 Roger Craig	.45	.30	.12
52 Delmar Crandall	.45	.30	.12
53A Joe Cunningham (port.)	.45	.30	.12
53B Joe Cunningham (batting, Cards)	.45	.30	.12
54 Guy Curtright (sic)	.90	.60	.25
55 Bud Daley	.45	.30	.12
56A Alvin Dark (Boston cap)	.90	.60	.25
56B Alvin Dark(NY cap)	1.80	1.20	.50
56C Alvin Dark(Cubs)	.90	.60	.25
57 Murray Dickson	.90	.60	.25
58 Bob Dillinger	.90	.60	.25
59 Dom DiMaggio	2.70	1.80	.80
60 Joe Dobson	.90	.60	.25
61 Larry Doby	.90	.60	.25
62 Bobby Doerr	.90	.60	.25
63A Dick Donovan(Brave, plain cap)	.90	.60	.25
63B Dick Donovan (White Sox)	.45	.30	.12
64 Walter Dropo	.90	.60	.25
65A Don Drysdale(port.)	1.80	1.20	.50
65B Don Drysdale (port. 1/2)	2.70	1.80	.80

66 Luke Easter	.90	.60	.25
67 Bruce Edwards	.90	.60	.25
68 Del Ennis	.45	.30	.12
69 Al Evans	.90	.60	.25
70 Walter Evers	.90	.60	.25
71A Ferris Fain (batting)	.90	.60	.25
71B Ferris Fain(port.)	.90	.60	.25
72 Dick Farrell	.45	.30	.12
73A Whitey Ford (no glove, throwing)	2.25	1.50	.65
73B Whitey Ford(port.)	4.50	3.00	1.20
73C Whitey Ford (glove on shoulder, throwing)	2.25	1.50	.65
74 Dick Fowler	.90	.60	.25
75 Nelson Fox	.45	.30	.12
76 Tito Francona	.45	.30	.12
77 Bob Friend	.45	.30	.12
78 Carl Furillo	.90	.60	.25
79 Augie Galan	.90	.60	.25
80 Jim Gentile	.45	.30	.12
81 Tony Gonzalez	.45	.30	.12
82A Billy Goodman (W.S., 1952)	.90	.60	.25
82B Billy Goodman (batt.)	.45	.30	.12
83 Ted Greengrass	.90	.60	.25
84 Dick Groat	.45	.30	.12
85 Steve Gromek	.90	.60	.25
86 Johnny Groth	.90	.60	.25
87 Orval Grove	.90	.60	.25
88A Frank Gustine (Pirates)	.90	.60	.25
88B Frank Gustine(Cubs)	.90	.60	.25
89 Berthold Haas	1.80	1.20	.50
90 Grady Hatton	.90	.60	.25
91 Jim Hegan	.90	.60	.25
92 Tom Henrich	1.80	1.20	.50
93 Ray Herbert	.45	.30	.12
94 Gene Hermanski	.90	.60	.25
95 Whitey Herzog	.45	.30	.12
96 Kirby Higbe	.90	.60	.25
97 Chuck Hinton	.45	.30	.12
98 Don Hoak	.45	.30	.12
99A Gil Hodges(Braves cap)	2.25	1.50	.65
99B Gil Hodges(LA cap)	2.25	1.50	.65
100 Johnny Hopp	.90	.60	.25
101 Elston Howard	.90	.60	.25
102 Frank Howard	.90	.60	.25
103 Ken Hubbs	.45	.30	.12
104 Tex Hughson	.90	.60	.25
105 Fred Hutchinson	.90	.60	.25
106 Monte Irvin	1.80	1.20	.50
107 Joey Jay	.45	.30	.12
108 Jackie Jensen	2.70	1.80	.80
109 Sam Jethroe	.90	.60	.25
110 Bill Johnson	.90	.60	.25
111 Walter Judnich	.90	.60	.25
112A Al Kaline(kneeling)	4.50	3.00	1.20
112B Al Kaline(port.)	2.70	1.80	.80
113 George Kell	.90	.60	.25
114 Charley Keller	.90	.60	.25
115 Alex Kellner	.90	.60	.25
116 Kenn Keltner	.90	.60	.25
117A Harmon Killebrew (pinstripes, batting)	1.80	1.20	.50
117B Harmon Killebrew (portrait)	2.70	1.80	.80
117C Harmon Killebrew (throwing)	2.70	1.80	.80
118 Ellis Kinder	.90	.60	.25
119 Ralph Kiner	2.25	1.50	.65
120 Billy Klaus	.45	.30	.12
121A Ted Kluszewski (Reds)	1.80	1.20	.50
121B Ted Kluszewski (Pirates)	.90	.60	.25
121C Ted Kluszewski (plain uniform)	.90	.60	.25
122 Don Kolloway	.90	.60	.25
123 Jim Konstanty	.90	.60	.25
124 Sandy Koufax	3.50	2.40	1.00
125 Ed Kranepool	2.70	1.80	.80
126A Tony Kubek(dark background)	1.80	1.20	.50
126B Tony Kubek(light background)	.90	.60	.25
127A Harvey Kuenn (Detroit)	1.80	1.20	.50
127B Harvey Kuenn(plain uniform)	.90	.60	.25
127C Harvey Kuenn(S.F.)	.90	.60	.25
128 Kurowski	.90	.60	.25
129 Eddie Lake	.90	.60	.25
130 Jim Landis	.45	.30	.12
131 Don Larsen	.90	.60	.25
132A Bob Lemon(left arm not shown)	2.70	1.80	.80
132B Bob Lemon(left arm extended)	2.70	1.80	.80
133 Buddy Lewis	.90	.60	.25
134 Johnny Lindell	4.50	3.00	1.20
135 Phil Linz	.45	.30	.12
136 Don Lock	.45	.30	.12
137 Whitey Lockman	.90	.60	.25
138 Johnny Logan	.45	.30	.12
139A Dale Long(Pirates)	.90	.60	.25
139B Dale Long(Cubs)	.45	.30	.12
140 Ed Lopat	.90	.60	.25
141A Harry Lowery	.90	.60	.25
141B Harry Lowery (smaller)	.90	.60	.25
142 Sam Maglie	.90	.60	.25
143 Art Mahaffey	.45	.30	.12
144 Hank Majeski	.90	.60	.25
145 Frank Malzone	.45	.30	.12
146A Mickey Mantle (batting to waist)	9.00	6.00	2.50
146B Mickey Mantle (batting full)	7.50	5.00	2.00
146C Mickey Mantle (portrait)	12.00	8.00	3.50
147 Marty Marion	.90	.60	.25
148 Roger Maris	2.25	1.50	.65
149 Willard Marshall	.90	.60	.25
150A Eddie Mathews (script)	3.50	2.40	1.00
150B Eddie Mathews (sign.)	2.70	1.80	.80
150C Ed Mathews	2.70	1.80	.80
151 Ed Mayo	.90	.60	.25
152A Willie Mays(N.Y.)	6.00	4.00	1.60
152B Willie Mays(S.F.)	4.50	3.00	1.20
153A Bill Mazeroski (port.)	.90	.60	.25
153B Bill Mazeroski (batt.)	.90	.60	.25
154 Ken McBride	.45	.30	.12
155A Barney McCaskey (sic)	2.70	1.80	.80
155B Barney McCoskey	1.80	1.20	.50
156 Lindy McDaniel	.45	.30	.12
157 Gil McDougald	.45	.30	.12
158 Albert Mele	1.80	1.20	.50
159 Sam Mele	.90	.60	.25
160A Orestes Minoso (W.S.)	.90	.60	.25
160B Orestes Minoso (Cleve.)	.90	.60	.25
161 Dale Mitchell	.90	.60	.25
162 Wally Moon	.45	.30	.12
163 Don Mueller	.90	.60	.25
164A Stan Musial(3 bats, kneeling)	4.50	3.00	1.20
164B Stan Musial(batt.)	4.50	3.00	1.20
165 Charles Neal	.45	.30	.12
166A Don Newcombe(hands folded)	1.80	1.20	.50
166B Don Newcombe (Brooklyn cap)	.90	.60	.25
166C Don Newcombe (plain cap)	.90	.60	.25
167 Hal Newhouser	.90	.60	.25
168 Ron Northey	.90	.60	.25
169 Bill O'Dell	.45	.30	.12
170 Andy Pafko	.45	.30	.12
171 Joe Page	2.70	1.80	.80
172 Satchel Paige	3.50	2.40	1.00
173 Milt Pappas	.45	.30	.12
174 Camilo Pascual	.45	.30	.12
175 Albie Pearson	.45	.30	.12
176 Johnny Pesky	.90	.60	.25
177 Gary Peters	.45	.30	.12
178 Dave Philley	.90	.60	.25
179 Billy Pierce	.45	.30	.12
180 Jimmy Piersall	3.50	2.40	1.00
181 Vada Pinson	.45	.30	.12
182 Bob Porterfield	.90	.60	.25
183 John "Boog" Powell	.90	.60	.25
184 Vic Raschi	.90	.60	.25
185 Harold "Pee Wee" Reese	2.25	1.50	.65
186 Del Rice	.45	.30	.12
187 Bobby Richardson	3.50	2.40	1.00
188 Phil Rizzuto	2.25	1.50	.65
189A Robin Roberts (sign.)	1.80	1.20	.50
189B Robin Roberts (script)	2.70	1.80	.80
190 Brooks Robinson	2.70	1.80	.80
191A Eddie Robinson (port.)	.90	.60	.25

EXHIBITS (CONTINUED)

191B Eddie Robinson (run.)	.90	.60	.25
192 Floyd Robinson	.45	.30	.12
193 Frankie Robinson	3.50	2.40	1.00
194 Jackie Robinson	3.50	2.40	1.00
195 Preacher Roe	.90	.60	.25
196 Bob Rogers(sic)	.45	.30	.12
197 Richard Rollins	.45	.30	.12
198 Pete Runnels	.90	.60	.25
199 John Sain	.90	.60	.25
200 Ron Santo	.45	.30	.12
201 Henry Sauer	.90	.60	.25
202A Carl Sawatski (Milwaukee cap)	.45	.30	.12
202B Carl Sawatski (Phila. cap)	.45	.30	.12
202C Carl Sawatski (plain cap)	.45	.30	.12
203 Johnny Schmitz	.90	.60	.25
204A Red Schoendienst (one foot shown, catching)	.90	.60	.25
204B Red Schoendienst (small C version of above, catch.)	.90	.60	.25
204C Red Schoendienst (batting)	.90	.60	.25
205A Herb Score (Cleveland cap)	.90	.60	.25
205B Herb Score (plain cap)	.45	.30	.12
206 Andy Seminick	.90	.60	.25
207 Rip Sewell	.90	.60	.25
208 Norm Siebern	.45	.30	.12
209A Roy Sievers(Browns)	.90	.60	.25
209B Roy Sievers (Senators)	.45	.30	.12
209C Roy Sievers (plain uniform)	.45	.30	.12
210 Curt Simmons	.45	.30	.12
211 Dick Sisler	.90	.60	.25
212A Bill Skowron(N.Y.)	.45	.30	.12
212B Bill "Moose" Skowron (White Sox)	2.70	1.80	.80
213 Enos Slaughter	1.80	1.20	.50
214A Duke Snider (Brooklyn)	2.70	1.80	.80
214B Duke Snider(L.A.)	2.70	1.80	.80
215A Warren Spahn (Boston, ball)	2.25	1.50	.65
215B Warren Spahn(Milw.)	2.25	1.50	.65
216 Stanley Spence	1.80	1.20	.50
217A Ed Stanky(arms up)	.90	.60	.25
217B Ed Stanky(Giants)	.90	.60	.25
218A Vern Stephens (Browns)	.90	.60	.25
218B Vern Stephens (Red Sox)	.90	.60	.25
219 Ed Stewart	.90	.60	.25
220 Snuffy Stirnweiss	1.80	1.20	.50
221 George "Birdie Tebbets	.90	.60	.25
222A Frankie Thomas (batting) (Bob Skinner pict.)	4.50	3.00	1.20
222B Frank Thomas(Cubs)	.45	.30	.12
223 Lee Thomas	.45	.30	.12
224 Bobby Thomson	.90	.60	.25
225A Earl Torgeson (Braves)	.90	.60	.25
225B Earl Torgeson (plain uniform)	.45	.30	.12
226 Gus Triandos	.45	.30	.12
227 Virgil Trucks	.90	.60	.25
228 Johnny Vandermeer	1.80	1.20	.50
229 Emil Verban	.90	.60	.25
230A Mickey Vernon (throwing)	.90	.60	.25
230B Mickey Vernon (batting)	.90	.60	.25
231 Bill Voiselle	1.80	1.20	.50
232 Leon Wagner	.45	.30	.12
233A Eddie Waitkus(Cub uniform)	2.25	1.50	.65
233B Eddie Waitkus (plain uniform)	.90	.60	.25
233C Eddie Waitkus (Phillie uniform)	.90	.60	.25
234 Dick Wakefield	.90	.60	.25
235 Harry Walker	.90	.60	.25
236 Bucky Walters	.90	.60	.25
237 Pete Ward	2.70	1.80	.80
238 Skeeter Webb	.90	.60	.25
239 Herman Wehmeier	.90	.60	.25
240A Vic Wertz(Tigers)	.90	.60	.25
240B Vic Wertz(Red Sox)	.45	.30	.12
241 Wally Westlake	.90	.60	.25
242 Wes Westrum	.90	.60	.25
243 Billy Williams	.90	.60	.25
244 Maurice Wills	.90	.60	.25
245 Gene Woodling	.45	.30	.12
246 Taffy Wright	.90	.60	.25
247 Carl Yastrzemski	4.50	3.00	1.20
248 Al Zarilla	.90	.60	.25
249 Gus Zernial	.90	.60	.25

1948-1956 TEAM EXHIBITS (16) 3 3/8" X 5 3/8"

The cards found listed in this classification were not a separate issue from the individual player cards of the same period but have been assembled together in the Price Guide for emphasis. Each of these 1948-1956 Exhibit team cards was issued to honor the champions of the National and American Leagues, except for 1953, when none were printed. Reprints of these popular cards are known to exist.

	MINT	VG-E	F-G
COMPLETE SET	75.00	50.00	20.00
COMMON PLAYER	3.75	2.50	1.00
1 1948 Boston Braves	5.00	3.50	1.40
2 1948 Cleve. Indians	5.00	3.50	1.40
3 1949 Brooklyn Dodgers	6.00	4.00	1.60
4 1949 New York Yankees	7.00	4.75	2.00
5 1950 Phila. Phillies	6.00	4.00	1.60
6 1950 New York Yankees	6.00	4.00	1.60
7 1951 New York Giants	5.00	3.50	1.40
8 1951 New York Yankees	6.00	4.00	1.60
9 1952 Brooklyn Dodgers	5.00	3.50	1.40
10 1952 New York Yankees	6.00	4.00	1.60
11 1954 New York Giants	3.75	2.50	1.00
12 1954 Cleve. Indians	3.75	2.50	1.00
13 1955 Brooklyn Dodgers	5.00	3.50	1.40
14 1955 New York Yankees	6.00	4.00	1.60
15 1956 Brooklyn Dodgers	5.00	3.50	1.40
16 1956 New York Yankees	6.00	4.00	1.60

1962 EXHIBIT STAT BACK (32) 3 3/8" X 5 3/8"

The 32-card sheet was a standard production feature of the Exhibit Card Company, although generally more than one sheet comprised a set. The 32 card set issued in 1962 thus amounted to one-half a normal printing, and it is differentiated from other concurrent Exhibit issues by the inclusion of records, printed in black, on the reverse of each card.

MANTLE, MICKEY CHARLES, Outfielder, New York Yankees Throws: Right
Born: Spavinaw, Oklahoma, October 20, 1931 Ht: 6' Wt: 200 Bats: Both

YEAR	CLUB	LEA.	POS.	G	AB	R	H	2B	3B	HR	RBI	SB	AVG
1949	Independence	Kom	SS	89	323	54	101	15	7	7	63	20	.313
1950	Joplin	W.A.	SS	137	519	141	199	30	12	26	136	22	.383
1951	Kansas City	A.A.	OF	40	166	32	60	9	3	11	50	5	.361
1951	New York	A.A	OF	96	341	61	91	11	5	13	65	8	.267
1952	New York	A.L.	OF-3B	142	549	94	171	37	7	23	87	4	.311
1953	New York	A.L.	OF-SS	127	461	105	136	24	3	21	92	8	.295
1954	New York	A.L.	OF-2B	146	543	129	163	17	12	27	102	5	.300
1955	New York	A.L.	OF-SS	147	517	121	158	25	11	37	99	8	.306
1956	New York	A.L.	OF	150	533	132	188	22	5	52	130	10	.353
1957	New York	A.L.	OF	144	474	121	173	28	6	34	94	16	.365
1958	New York	A.L.	OF	150	519	127	158	21	1	42	97	18	.304
1959	New York	A.L.	OF	144	541	104	154	23	4	31	75	21	.285
1960	New York	A.L.	OF	153	527	119	145	17	6	40	94	14	.275
1961	New York	A.L.	OF	153	514	132	163	16	6	54	128	12	.317
MAJOR LEAGUE TOTALS				1552	5519	1245	1700	241	66	374	1063	124	.308

	MINT	VG-E	F-G
COMPLETE SET	45.00	32.00	14.00
COMMON PLAYER(1-32)	.60	.40	.15

		MINT	VG-E	F-G
1	Aaron,Hank	5.00	3.50	1.50
2	Aparicio,Luis	1.00	.70	.30
3	Banks,Ernie	2.50	1.75	.75
4	Berra,Larry "Yogi"	2.50	1.75	.75
5	Boyer,Ken	.80	.55	.20
6	Burdette,Lew	.80	.55	.20
7	Cash,Norm	.80	.55	.20
8	Cepeda,Orlando	.80	.55	.20
9	Clemente,Roberto	3.50	2.50	1.00
10	Colavito,Rocky	1.00	.70	.30
11	Ford,Ed "Whitey"	2.50	1.75	.75
12	Fox,Nelson	1.00	.70	.30
13	Francona,Tito	.60	.40	.15
14	Gentile,Jim	.60	.40	.15
15	Groat,Dick	.80	.55	.20
16	Hoak,Don	.60	.40	.15
17	Kaline,Al	2.50	1.75	.75
18	Killebrew,Harmon	1.50	1.00	.45
19	Koufax,Sandy	3.50	2.50	1.00
20	Landis,Jim	.60	.40	.15
21	Mahaffey,Art	.60	.40	.15
22	Malzone,Frank	.60	.40	.15
23	Mantle,Mickey	7.50	5.50	2.50
24	Maris,Roger	3.50	2.50	1.00
25	Mathews,Eddie	1.50	1.00	.45
26	Mays,Willie	5.00	3.50	1.50
27	Moon,Wally	.60	.40	.15
28	Musial,Stan	5.00	3.50	1.50
29	Pappas,Milt	.80	.55	.20
30	Pinson,Vada	.80	.55	.20
31	Siebern,Norm	.60	.40	.15
32	Spahn,Warren	1.50	1.00	.45

1963 EXHIBIT STAT BACK (64) 3 3/8" X 5 3/8"

This 1963 Exhibit issue features 64 cards with statistics printed in red on the backs.

MAYS, WILLIE HOWARD, Jr., Outfielder, San Francisco Giants Bats: Right
Born: Fairfield, Ala., May 6, 1931 Ht: 5'11" Wt: 180 Throws: Right

YEAR	CLUB	LEA.	POS.	G	AB	R	H	2B	3B	HR	RBI	SB	AVG
1950	Trenton	Int. St.	O.F.	81	306	50	108	20	8	4	55	7	.353
1951	Minneapolis	A.A.	O.F.	35	149	38	71	18	3	8	30	5	.477
1951	New York	N.L.	O.F.	121	464	59	127	22	5	20	68	7	.274
1952	New York	N.L.	O.F.	34	127	17	30	2	4	4	23	4	.236
1952-3					(IN MILITARY SERVICE)								
1954	New York	N.L.	O.F.	151	565	119	195	33	13	41	110	8	.345
1955	New York	N.L.	O.F.	152	580	123	185	18	13	51	127	24	.319
1956	New York	N.L.	O.F.	152	578	101	171	27	8	36	84	40	.296
1957	New York	N.L.	O.F.	152	585	112	195	26	20	35	97	38	.333
1958	San Francisco	N.L.	O.F.	152	600	121	208	33	11	29	96	31	.347
1959	San Francisco	N.L.	O.F.	151	575	125	180	43	5	34	104	27	.313
1960	San Francisco	N.L.	O.F.	153	595	107	190	29	12	29	103	25	.319
1961	San Francisco	N.L.	O.F.	154	572	129	176	32	3	40	123	18	.308
1962	San Francisco	N.L.	OF	162	621	130	189	36	8	49	141	18	.304
MAJOR LEAGUE TOTALS				1534	5862	1143	1846	301	102	368	1076	240	.314

	MINT	VG-E	F-G
COMPLETE SET	80.00	55.00	25.00
COMMON PLAYER(1-64)	.60	.40	.15

	MINT	VG-E	F-G
1 Aaron,Hank	5.00	3.50	1.50
2 Aparicio,Luis	1.00	.70	.30
3 Aspromonte,Bob	.60	.40	.15
4 Banks,Ernie	2.50	1.75	.75
5 Barber,Steve	.60	.40	.15
6 Battey,Earl	.60	.40	.15
7 Berra,Larry "Yogi"	2.50	1.75	.75
8 Boyer,Ken	.80	.55	.20
9 Burdette,Lew	.80	.55	.20
10 Callison,Johnny	.60	.40	.15
11 Cash,Norm	.80	.55	.20
12 Cepeda,Orlando	.80	.55	.20
13 Chance,Dean	.60	.40	.15
14 Cheney,Tom	.60	.40	.15
15 Clemente,Roberto	3.50	2.50	1.00
16 Colavito,Rocky	1.00	.70	.30
17 Coleman,Choo Choo	.60	.40	.15
18 Craig,Roger	.60	.40	.15
19 Cunningham,Joe	.60	.40	.15
20 Drysdale,Don	1.50	1.00	.45
21 Farrell,Dick	.60	.40	.15
22 Ford,Ed "Whitey"	2.50	1.75	.75
23 Fox,Nelson	1.00	.70	.30
24 Francona,Tito	.60	.40	.15
25 Gentile,Jim	.60	.40	.15
26 Gonzales,Tony	.60	.40	.15
27 Groat,Dick	.80	.55	.20
28 Herbert,Ray	.60	.40	.15
29 Hinton,Chuck	.60	.40	.15
30 Hoak,Don	.60	.40	.15
31 Howard,Frank	1.00	.70	.30
32 Hubbs,Ken	.80	.55	.20
33 Jay,Joey	.60	.40	.15
34 Kaline,Al	2.50	1.75	.75
35 Killebrew,Harmon	1.50	1.00	.45
36 Koufax,Sandy	3.50	2.50	1.00
37 Kuenn,Harvey	.80	.55	.20
38 Landis,Jim	.60	.40	.15
39 Mahaffey,Art	.60	.40	.15
40 Malzone,Frank	.60	.40	.15
41 Mantle,Mickey	7.50	5.50	2.50
42 Maris,Roger	1.50	1.00	.45
43 Mathews,Eddie	1.50	1.00	.45
44 Mays,Willie	5.00	3.50	1.50
45 Mazeroski,Bill	.80	.55	.20
46 McBride,Ken	.60	.40	.15
47 Moon,Wally	.60	.40	.15
48 Musial,Stan	5.00	3.50	1.50
49 Neal,Charlie	.60	.40	.15
50 O'Dell,Bill	.60	.40	.15
51 Pappas,Milt	.80	.55	.20
52 Pascual,Camilo	.60	.40	.15
53 Piersall,Jim	.80	.55	.20
54 Pinson,Vada	.80	.55	.20
55 Robinson,Brooks	2.50	1.75	.75
56 Robinson,Frankie	2.50	1.75	.75
57 Runnels,Pete	.60	.40	.15
58 Santo,Ron	.80	.55	.20
59 Siebern,Norm	.60	.40	.15
60 Spahn,Warren	1.50	1.00	.45
61 Thomas,Lee	.60	.40	.15
62 Wagner,Leon	.60	.40	.15
63 Williams,Billy	1.00	.70	.30
64 Wills,Maurice	1.00	.70	.30

D350-1 STANDARD BAKING

B18 BLANKETS (91)

5 1/4" X 5 1/4"

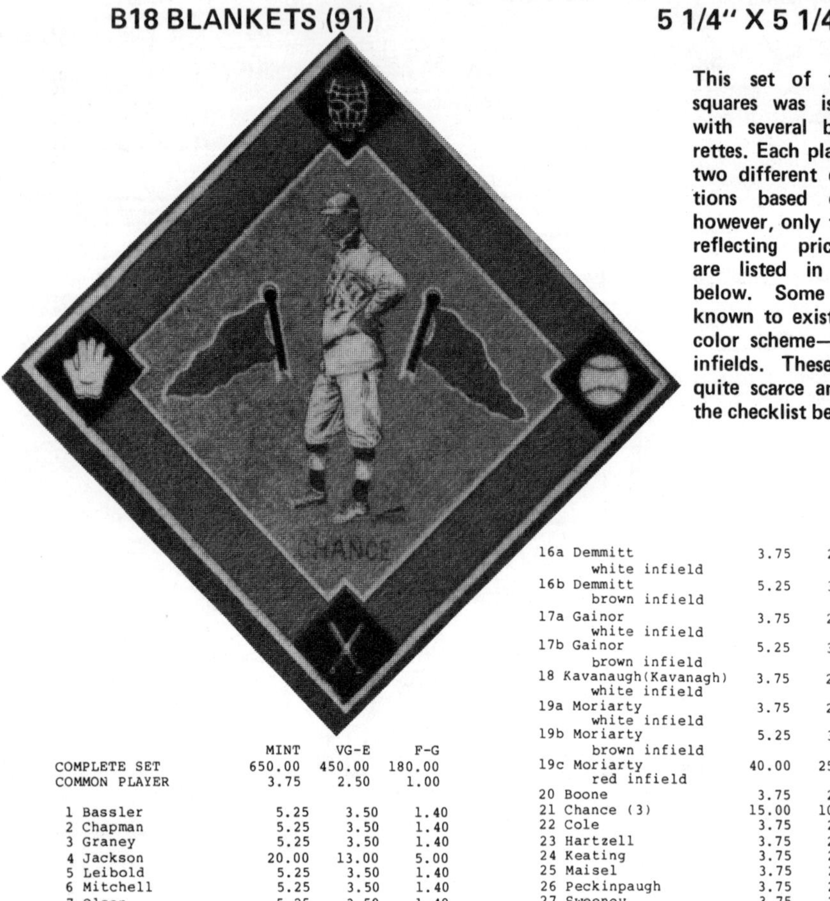

This set of felt-type cloth squares was issued in 1914 with several brands of cigarettes. Each player exists with two different color combinations based on his team; however, only those variations reflecting price differentials are listed in the checklist below. Some blankets are known to exist in a different color scheme—those with red infields. These blankets are quite scarce and are listed in the checklist below.

	MINT	VG-E	F-G
COMPLETE SET	650.00	450.00	180.00
COMMON PLAYER	3.75	2.50	1.00
1 Bassler	5.25	3.50	1.40
2 Chapman	5.25	3.50	1.40
3 Graney	5.25	3.50	1.40
4 Jackson	20.00	13.00	5.00
5 Leibold	5.25	3.50	1.40
6 Mitchell	5.25	3.50	1.40
7 Olson	5.25	3.50	1.40
8 O'Neil	5.25	3.50	1.40
9 Turner	5.25	3.50	1.40
10a Baker white infield	3.75	2.50	1.00
10b Baker brown infield	5.25	3.50	1.40
10c Baker** red infield	40.00	25.00	10.00
11a Bauman (Baumann) white infield	3.75	2.50	1.00
11b Bauman (Baumann) brown infield	5.25	3.50	1.40
11c Bauman (Baumann) red infield	40.00	25.00	10.00
12a Burns white infield	3.75	2.50	1.00
12b Burns brown infield	5.25	3.50	1.40
13a Cavanaugh(Kavanagh) white infield	3.75	2.50	1.00
13b Cavanaugh(Kavanagh) brown infield	5.25	3.50	1.40
13c Cavanaugh(Kavanagh) red infield	40.00	25.00	10.00
14a Cobb white infield	50.00	35.00	14.00
14b Cobb brown infield	60.00	40.00	16.00
14c Cobb red infield	90.00	60.00	25.00
15a H. Coveleski white infield	3.75	2.50	1.00
15b H. Coveleski brown infield	5.25	3.50	1.40
15c H. Coveleski red infield	40.00	25.00	10.00
16a Demmitt white infield	3.75	2.50	1.00
16b Demmitt brown infield	5.25	3.50	1.40
17a Gainor white infield	3.75	2.50	1.00
17b Gainor brown infield	5.25	3.50	1.40
18 Kavanaugh(Kavanagh) white infield	3.75	2.50	1.00
19a Moriarty white infield	3.75	2.50	1.00
19b Moriarty brown infield	5.25	3.50	1.40
19c Moriarty red infield	40.00	25.00	10.00
20 Boone	3.75	2.50	1.00
21 Chance (3)	15.00	10.00	4.00
22 Cole	3.75	2.50	1.00
23 Hartzell	3.75	2.50	1.00
24 Keating	3.75	2.50	1.00
25 Maisel	3.75	2.50	1.00
26 Peckinpaugh	3.75	2.50	1.00
27 Sweeney	3.75	2.50	1.00
28 Walsh	3.75	2.50	1.00
29 Agnew	5.25	3.50	1.40
30 Austin	5.25	3.50	1.40
31 Hamilton	5.25	3.50	1.40
32 McAllister (McAllester)	5.25	3.50	1.40
33 Pratt	5.25	3.50	1.40
34 Shotton	5.25	3.50	1.40
35 Wallace	7.50	5.00	2.00
36 Walsh	5.25	3.50	1.40
37 Williams	5.25	3.50	1.40
38 Ainsmith	3.75	2.50	1.00
39 Foster	3.75	2.50	1.00
40 Gandil	3.75	2.50	1.00
41 Johnson	20.00	13.00	5.00
42 McBride	3.75	2.50	1.00
43 Milan	3.75	2.50	1.00
44 Moeller	3.75	2.50	1.00
45 Morgan	3.75	2.50	1.00
46 Shanks	3.75	2.50	1.00
47a Connolly white infield	3.75	2.50	1.00
47b Connolly brown infield	5.25	3.50	1.40
48a Gowdy white infield	3.75	2.50	1.00
48b Gowdy brown infield	5.25	3.50	1.40
48c Gowdy red infield	40.00	25.00	10.00
49a Griffith white infield	3.75	2.50	1.00
49b Griffith brown infield	5.25	3.50	1.40
50a James white infield	3.75	2.50	1.00

B18 Blankets

50b James brown infield	5.25	3.50	1.40
51a Mann white infield	3.75	2.50	1.00
51b Mann brown infield	5.25	3.50	1.40
52a Maranville white infield	7.50	5.00	2.00
52b Maranville brown infield	9.00	6.00	2.50
52c Maranville red infield	45.00	30.00	12.00
53a Perdue white infield	3.75	2.50	1.00
53b Perdue brown infield	5.25	3.50	1.40
54a Tyler white infield	3.75	2.50	1.00
54b Tyler brown infield	5.25	3.50	1.40
54c Tyler red infield	40.00	25.00	10.00
55a Whaling white infield	3.75	2.50	1.00
55b Whaling brown infield	5.25	3.50	1.40
56 Cutshaw	3.75	2.50	1.00
57 Daubert	3.75	2.50	1.00
58 Hummel	3.75	2.50	1.00
59 Miller	3.75	2.50	1.00
60 Rucker	3.75	2.50	1.00
61 Smith	3.75	2.50	1.00
62 Stengel	15.00	10.00	4.00
63 Wagner	3.75	2.50	1.00
64 Wheat	7.50	5.00	2.00
65 Burns	3.75	2.50	1.00
66 Doyle	3.75	2.50	1.00
67 Fletcher	3.75	2.50	1.00
68 Grant	3.75	2.50	1.00
69 Meyers	3.75	2.50	1.00
70 Murray	3.75	2.50	1.00
71 Snodgrass	3.75	2.50	1.00
72 Tesreau	3.75	2.50	1.00
73 Wiltse	3.75	2.50	1.00
74 Adams	5.25	3.50	1.40
75 Carey	7.50	5.00	2.00
76 Gibson	5.25	3.50	1.40
77 Hyatt	5.25	3.50	1.40
78 Kelley (Kelly)	5.25	3.50	1.40
79 Konetchy	5.25	3.50	1.40
80 Mowrey	5.25	3.50	1.40
81 O'Toole	5.25	3.50	1.40
82 Viox	5.25	3.50	1.40
83 Doak	5.25	3.50	1.40
84 Dolan	5.25	3.50	1.40
85 Huggins	7.50	5.00	2.00
86 Miller	5.25	3.50	1.40
87 Robinson	5.25	3.50	1.40
88 Sallee	5.25	3.50	1.40
89 Steele	5.25	3.50	1.40
90 Whitted	5.25	3.50	1.40
91 Wilson	5.25	3.50	1.40

L1 BASEBALL LEATHER (25) 10" X 12"

This highly prized set of baseball player pictures on a piece of leather shaped to resemble the hide of a small animal was issued during the 1911 time period. While the pictures are those of the T3 Turkey Red card premium set, only the most popular players of the time are depicted. The cards are numbered at the bottom part of the leather away from the central image.

	MINT	VG-E	F-G
COMPLETE SET	10000.00	6000.00	2400.00
COMMON PLAYER	300.00	200.00	75.00

111 Marquard, NY NL	375.00	250.00	100.00
112 O'Toole, Pitt.	300.00	200.00	75.00
113 Rube Benton, Cinn.	300.00	200.00	75.00
114 Alexander, Phil. NL	450.00	300.00	120.00
115 Ford, NY AL	300.00	200.00	75.00
116 McGraw, NY NL	450.00	300.00	120.00
117 Rucker, Brooklyn	300.00	200.00	75.00
118 Mitchell, Cinn.	300.00	200.00	75.00
119 Bender, Phil. AL	375.00	250.00	100.00
120 Baker, Phil. AL	375.00	250.00	100.00
121 Lajoie, Cleve.	450.00	300.00	120.00
122 Tinker, Chicago NL	375.00	250.00	100.00
123 Magee, Phil. NL	300.00	200.00	75.00
124 Camnitz, Pitt.	300.00	200.00	75.00
125 Collins, Phil. AL	375.00	250.00	100.00
126 Dooin, Phil. NL	300.00	200.00	75.00
127 Cobb, Detroit	800.00	550.00	200.00
128 Jennings, Detroit	375.00	250.00	100.00
129 Bresnahan, St.L. NL	375.00	250.00	100.00
130 Stahl, Boston AL	300.00	200.00	75.00
131 Speaker, Boston AL	450.00	300.00	120.00
132 Welch, Chicago AL	300.00	200.00	75.00
133 Mathewson, NY NL	600.00	400.00	150.00
134 Evers, Chicago NL	375.00	250.00	100.00
135 Johnson, Washington	600.00	400.00	150.00

S74 BASEBALL SILKS (119)

2" X 3"
IMAGE 1 1/4" X 2 3/8"

Issued around 1911, these silk fabric collectibles have designs similar to the designs in the T205 Cigarette card set. The line work on the silks is in one color only, with colors of blue, red, brown, and several variations between red and brown known to exist. The field or stock color is known in white and several pastel tints. The cards are unnumbered but have been numbered and listed by team in alphabetical order in the checklist below. Turkey Red and Old Mill Cigarettes are among the issuers of these silks.

	MINT	VG-E	F-G
COMPLETE SET	1100.00	700.00	300.00
COMMON PLAYER	9.00	6.00	2.50
1 Carrigan-Boston	9.00	6.00	2.50
2 Cicotte-Boston	10.00	6.50	3.00
3 Speaker-Boston	15.00	10.00	4.00
4 Stahl-Boston	10.00	6.50	3.00
5 Duffy-Chicago	13.00	9.00	4.00
6 McConnelll-Chicago	9.00	6.00	2.50
7 Parent-Chicago	9.00	6.00	2.50
8 Payne-Chicago	9.00	6.00	2.50
9 Tannehill-Chicago	9.00	6.00	2.50
10 White-Chicago	9.00	6.00	2.50
11 Turner-Cleve	9.00	6.00	2.50
12 Young-Cleve	15.00	10.00	4.00
13 Cobb-Detroit	75.00	50.00	20.00
14 Delahanty-Detroit	9.00	6.00	2.50
15 Jones-Detroit	9.00	6.00	2.50
16 Moriarity-Detroit	9.00	6.00	2.50
17 Mullin-Detroit	9.00	6.00	2.50
18 Summers-Detroit	9.00	6.00	2.50
19 Willett-Detroit	9.00	6.00	2.50
20 Chase-NY	10.00	6.50	3.00
21 Ford-NY	9.00	6.00	2.50
22 Hemphill-NY	9.00	6.00	2.50
23 Knight-NY	9.00	6.00	2.50
24 Quinn-NY	9.00	6.00	2.50
25 Wolter-NY	9.00	6.00	2.50
26 Baker-Phil	13.00	9.00	4.00
27 Barry-Phil	9.00	6.00	2.50
28 Bender-Phil	13.00	9.00	4.00
29 Collins-Phil	13.00	9.00	4.00
30 Dygert-Phil	9.00	6.00	2.50
31 Hartsel-Phil	9.00	6.00	2.50
32 Krause-Phil	9.00	6.00	2.50
33 Murphy-Phil	9.00	6.00	2.50
34 Oldring-Phil	9.00	6.00	2.50
35 Pelty-StL	9.00	6.00	2.50
36 Stone-StL	9.00	6.00	2.50
37 Wallace-StL	11.00	7.00	3.25
38 Elberfeld-Wash	9.00	6.00	2.50
39 Johnson-Wash	22.50	15.00	6.00
40 Schaefer-Wash	9.00	6.00	2.50
41 Street-Wash	9.00	6.00	2.50
42 Beck-Boston	9.00	6.00	2.50
43 Graham-Boston•	9.00	6.00	2.50
44 Herzog-Boston	9.00	6.00	2.50
45 Mattern-Boston	9.00	6.00	2.50
46 Shean-Boston	9.00	6.00	2.50
47 Barger(2)-Brooklyn	9.00	6.00	2.50
48 Bell-Brooklyn	9.00	6.00	2.50
49 Bergen-Brooklyn	9.00	6.00	2.50
50 Dahlen-Brooklyn	9.00	6.00	2.50
51 Daubert-Brooklyn	10.00	6.50	3.00
52 Hummel-Brooklyn	9.00	6.00	2.50
53 Scanlon-Brooklyn	9.00	6.00	2.50
54 Smith-Brooklyn	9.00	6.00	2.50
55 Wheat-Brooklyn	13.00	9.00	4.00
56 Brown-Chicago	13.00	9.00	4.00
57 Chance-Chicago	13.00	9.00	4.00
58 Evers-Chicago	13.00	9.00	4.00
59 Foxen-Chicago	9.00	6.00	2.50
60 Graham-Chicago	9.00	6.00	2.50
61 Kling-Chicago	9.00	6.00	2.50
62 McIntire-Chicago	9.00	6.00	2.50
63 Needham-Chicago	9.00	6.00	2.50
64 Overall-Chicago	9.00	6.00	2.50
65 Reulbach-Chicago	9.00	6.00	2.50
66 Schulte-Chicago	9.00	6.00	2.50
67 Sheckard-Chicago	9.00	6.00	2.50
68 Steinfeldt-Chicago	10.00	6.50	3.00
69 Tinker-Chicago	13.00	9.00	4.00
70 Bescher-Cinn	9.00	6.00	2.50
71 Downey-Cinn	9.00	6.00	2.50
72 Fromme-Cinn	9.00	6.00	2.50
73 Grant-Cinn	9.00	6.00	2.50
74 Griffith	9.00	6.00	2.50
75 Hoblitzell	9.00	6.00	2.50
76 Ames-NY	9.00	6.00	2.50
77 Becker-NY	9.00	6.00	2.50
78 Bridwell-NY	9.00	6.00	2.50
79 Crandall-NY	9.00	6.00	2.50
80 Devlin-NY	9.00	6.00	2.50
81 Devore-NY	9.00	6.00	2.50
82 Doyle-NY	10.00	6.50	3.00
83 Fletcher-NY	9.00	6.00	2.50
84 Marquard-NY	13.00	9.00	4.00
85 Mathewson-NY	22.50	15.00	6.00
86 McGraw-NY	15.00	10.00	4.00
87 Merkle-NY	10.00	6.50	3.00
88 Meyers-NY	9.00	6.00	2.50
89 Murray-NY	9.00	6.00	2.50
90 Raymond-NY	9.00	6.00	2.50
91 Schlei-NY	9.00	6.00	2.50
92 Snodgrass-NY	10.00	6.50	3.00
93 Wiltse (2)-NY	9.00	6.00	2.50
94 Bates-Phil	9.00	6.00	2.50
95 Dooin-Phil	9.00	6.00	2.50
96 Doolan-Phil	9.00	6.00	2.50
97 Ewing-Phil	9.00	6.00	2.50
98 Lobert-Phil	9.00	6.00	2.50
99 Moran-Phil	9.00	6.00	2.50
100 Paskert-Phil	9.00	6.00	2.50
101 Rowan-Phil	9.00	6.00	2.50
102 Titus-Phil	9.00	6.00	2.50
103 Byrne-Pitts	9.00	6.00	2.50
104 Camnitz-Pitts	9.00	6.00	2.50
105 Clarke-Pitts	13.00	9.00	4.00
106 Flynn-Pitts	9.00	6.00	2.50
107 Gibson-Pitts	9.00	6.00	2.50
108 Leach-Pitts	9.00	6.00	2.50
109 Leifield-Pitts	9.00	6.00	2.50
110 Miller-Pitts	9.00	6.00	2.50
111 Phillippe-Pitts	10.00	6.50	3.00
112 White-Pitts	9.00	6.00	2.50
113 Wilson-Pitts	9.00	6.00	2.50
114 Bresnahan (2)-StL	13.00	9.00	4.00
115 Evans-StL	9.00	6.00	2.50
116 Hauser-StL	9.00	6.00	2.50
117 Huggins-StL	13.00	9.00	4.00
118 Konetchy-StL	9.00	6.00	2.50
119 Oakes-StL	9.00	6.00	2.50

S81 BASEBALL SILKS (25)

5" X 7"
7" X 9"

These large and attractive silks are found in two sizes—approximately 5" X 7" or 7" X 9". Unlike the smaller S74 Baseball Silks, these silks are numbered, beginning with number 86 and ending at number 110. The pose of the picture is the same as that of the T3 Turkey Red baseball cards. The silks were issued in 1911 and are frequently found grouped on pillow covers.

	MINT	VG-E	F-G
COMPLETE SET	4500.00	3000.00	1200.00
COMMON PLAYER	150.00	100.00	40.00
86 Marquard, NY NL	225.00	150.00	60.00
87 O'Toole, Pitt	150.00	100.00	40.00
88 Rube Benton, Cinn	150.00	100.00	40.00
89 Alexander, Phil NL	270.00	180.00	80.00
90 Ford, NY AL	150.00	100.00	40.00
91 McGraw, NY NL	270.00	180.00	80.00
92 Rucker, Brooklyn	150.00	100.00	40.00
93 Mitchell, Cinn	150.00	100.00	40.00
94 Bender, Phil AL	225.00	150.00	60.00
95 Baker, Phil AL	225.00	150.00	60.00
96 Lajoie, Cleve	270.00	180.00	80.00
97 Tinker, Chicago NL	225.00	150.00	60.00
98 Magee, Phila NL	150.00	100.00	40.00
99 Camnitz, Pitt	150.00	100.00	40.00
100 Collins, Phila AL	225.00	150.00	60.00
101 Dooin, Phila NL	150.00	100.00	40.00
102 Cobb, Detroit	600.00	400.00	150.00
103 Jennings, Detroit	225.00	150.00	60.00
104 Bresnahan, StL NL	225.00	150.00	60.00
105 Stahl, Boston AL	180.00	120.00	50.00
106 Speaker, Boston AL	270.00	180.00	80.00
107 Walsh, Chicago AL	225.00	150.00	60.00
108 Mathewson, NY NL	350.00	225.00	90.00
109 Evers, Chicago NL	225.00	150.00	60.00
110 Johnson, Washington	350.00	225.00	90.00

HARTLAND STATUES

During the years 1958 to 1963 the Hartland Plastics Company of Hartland, Wisconsin, produced a series of baseball, football and TV western star plastic statues which have, today, become some of the most sought after sports collectibles. The statues bear an excellent resemblance (particularly the facial features of the baseball and western characters) to the personalities portrayed. We shall concern ourselves here primarily with the 20 baseball statues; however, mention will be made of the football and western statues as they too are quite popular.

Of the 20 baseball Hartland statues, 18 are full-sized (8") replicas of popular major league baseball players. Each is posed in a stance for which he is well known. In addition to the standard-sized baseball statues, two others were produced— the Little Leaguer and the 4" batter. The 6" Little Leaguer, sometimes called the "batboy", was produced for a short period of time by the Hartland Company until legal problems with Little League, Inc., of Williamsport, PA, over the use of the name Little League curtailed production. The 4" batter, occasionally called the "Minor Leaguer", rounds out the set of baseball Hartlands. The 4" batter, which is supposedly part of a miniature set including a golfer, a bowler, and a tennis player, is a nameless replica of a batter attached to a black base. It is quite inferior aesthetically to the larger statues; however, because of its relative scarcity and the fact that it is a Hartland statue portraying a baseball player, it has merited collector attention.

Originally, the statues could be purchased at department stores, 5 and 10 cent stores and similar retail establishments for between $3.00 and $4.00 in a box with the picture of the player inside printed on the box. The boxes themselves have also become a sought after collectible (Why not? They're made of cardboard just like baseball cards). The statues were issued in the order listed in the checklist below. Many of the statues included a removeable piece (bat, mask) or a standing aide (toe plate, pitching rubber, base) in addition to the player himself. The bats came in a small and large size and the toe plate is either white or purple.

VARIATONS

At least three of the statues are known to exist in more than one form (variations). The Mays statue has either an orange or light brown glove. The Aparicio statue comes with or without a toe plate (to aid the figure in standing). The Aaron statue variations are the only one's known where there appears to be a definite change or alteration made to the statue mold. One style has the right foot flat on the surface on which it is stood. This style also has the hands configured in a manner to give the impression that the bat is tilted toward Aaron's head. The other style of Aaron statue has, in its most stable standing position, the toe of the right foot raised considerably from the surface and has the hands of Aaron configured so that the bat is parallel to Aaron's head. The facial color of this variation is noticeably lighter (more brown than black) than the first variation.

Additional variations of the Fox and Aparicio statues have been reported; however, the authors cannot confirm or deny the reports at this time. Supposedly, the red border around the word "Sox" was omitted to save painting time for a "hurry-up" promotional event at a Chicago ball park.

SCARCENESS

Unlike baseball cards, whose price structure is based more on the popularity of the player on the card than the scarceness of the card, Hartland statues are priced, in general, according to scarcities. For years, The Groat statue was considered the most scarce Hartland and the prize of the set; however, there is a growing group of collectors, including one of the authors, who believe the Colavito statue is in fact the most scarce one of the set. Other statues that exhibit some measure of scarcity are Killebrew, Drysdale, Maris, Snider, Aparicio and Banks.

CONDITION GRADING

Condition grades for Hartland statues are somewhat different from condition grades for cards. The prime determinants of a statue's condition are boldness and clarity of the painted parts, number and severity of scratches, yellowing, and the ability of the statue to stand by itself. All missing parts (bats, mask, toe plates, etc.) and broken parts (arms, hats, heads) should be described in addition to the condition grade. Repaired statues should be noted as such.

An EX-MT Hartland statue should have boldly painted markings which have shown little fading; very minor, if any, scratches; little or no yellowing; and the ability to stand by itself without the aid of bracing or adhesive additions. Collectible statues with noticeable wear, fading, yellowing, and scratching are graded G-VG. The value of statues below the G-VG condition grade drops significantly and such statues are normally held only as fillers until a better condition replacement can be found.

OTHER HARTLAND STATUES

Hartland issued four different types of football statues—a Johnny Unitas statue, a Jon Arnett statue, a running back statue and a lineman statue. The Unitas and Arnett statues have the names of these players on the base on which the players stand. The running backs and lineman were available for all teams in the NFL. A sheet of decal numbers was included with each nameless running back and lineman so the number of one's favorite lineman or back could be added to the statue.

The TV western star Hartland statues came in two varieties. The cowboy and horse (usually referred to as the Hartland western) and the standing cowboy (usually referred to as the gunfighter). These statues bear excellent resemblances to the character portrayed. The Hartland westerns are characterized by an abundance of paraphenalia to supplement the rider and horse—guns, hats, saddles, blankets, rifles, reins, to name a few. The standing figures or gunfighters have some moveable parts in addition to a few items of paraphenalia (guns, hats). While no proven scarcity of any of the TV westerns have been confirmed, the authors find the Roy Rodgers statue to be amongst the most plentiful and the Annie Oakley to be amongst the most difficult to obtain. Series of Hartland patriots and miniature western statues also exist.

HARTLAND NUMBER	DESCRIPTION	EX–MT	G–V
910	MICKEY MANTLE Large bat	80.00	45.00
911	BABE RUTH Large bat	80.00	45.00
912	HANK AARON Large bat	70.00	35.00
913	EDDIE MATHEWS	60.00	30.00
914	TED WILLIAMS Large bat, toe plate	80.00	45.00
915	STAN MUSIAL Large bat	70.00	35.00
916	WARREN SPAHN	60.00	30.00
917	YOGI BERRA Mask	85.00	50.00
918	WILLIE MAYS	70.00	35.00
919	NELLIE FOX	90.00	50.00
920	ERNIE BANKS Small bat	125.00	75.00
921	DUKE SNIDER Large bat	150.00	80.00
922	DON DRYSDALE Pitching rubber, toe plate	200.00	110.00
923	ROCKY COLAVITO Large bat, toe plate	325.00	150.00
924	LUIS APARICIO With or without toe plate	125.00	75.00
925	HARMON KILLEBREW Small bat, standing base	225.00	120.00
926	DICK GROAT Small bat	375.00	175.00
927	ROGER MARIS Small bat, standing base	150.00	80.00
	LITTLE LEAGUER (BAT BOY)	150.00	50.00
	4" BATTER (MINOR LEAGUER)	200.00	60.00

R332 SCHUTTER–JOHNSON (50?) 2 1/4" X 2 7/8"

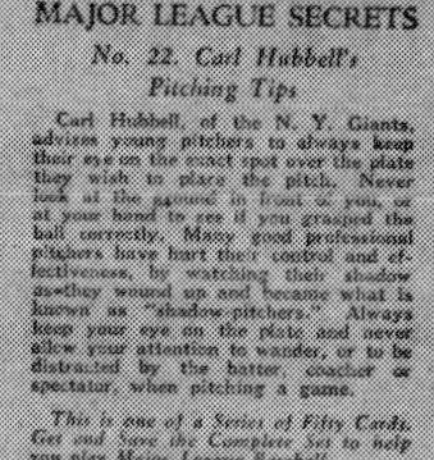

This set of 50 cards was issued by the Schutter–Johnson Candy Corporation around 1930. While each card in the series is numbered, the ones in the checklist below are the only ones known at the present time. These black line-drawing cards on a red field are entitled "Major League Secrets" and feature tips from major league players on the reverse.

	MINT	VG-E	F-G
COMPLETE SET	675.00	450.00	180.00
COMMON PLAYER	15.00	10.00	4.00
1 Al Simmons (Swing 3 or 4 bats)	21.00	14.00	6.00
7 How to Practice Control (Rogers Hornsby Pitching Tips)	27.00	18.00	8.00
8 Carl May's "Under-hand Ball"	15.00	10.00	4.00
9 Umpire Charles Wrigley (Pitcher's feet with no base runners)	15.00	10.00	4.00
10 Mathewson's Fade-Away Pitch	27.00	18.00	8.00
11 Bill Dickey (waste ball)	27.00	18.00	8.00
12 Walter Berger (don't step in the bucket	15.00	10.00	4.00
13 George Earnshaw's Curve	15.00	10.00	4.00
14 "Hack" Wilson (grip bat at extreme end)	21.00	14.00	6.00
15 Charley Grimm (testing pitcher at first)	15.00	10.00	4.00
16 Waner Brothers (word signs in out-field)	21.00	14.00	6.00
17 Chuck Klein (keep eye on ball)	21.00	14.00	6.00
18 Woody English (bunt flat-footed)	15.00	10.00	4.00
19 Alexander's side arm Fastball	21.00	14.00	6.00
20 Lou Gehrig (hit ball where pitched)	40.00	25.00	10.00
21 Wes Ferrell's Wind-up	15.00	10.00	4.00
22 Carl Hubbell (Wind-up Pitching Tips)	21.00	14.00	6.00
24 Gus Mancuso (getting under foul ball)	15.00	10.00	4.00
25 Ben Cantwell, Braves (curve ball grip)	15.00	10.00	4.00
27 "Goose" Goslin (throw from outfield)	21.00	14.00	6.00
29 Kiki Cuyler ('halfslide')	21.00	14.00	6.00
30 Jimmy Wilson (delayed steal)	15.00	10.00	4.00
31 Dizzy Dean (curve ball)	33.00	22.00	9.00
32 Mickey Cochrane (Mickey Coch-rane's signs)	27.00	18.00	8.00
34 Si Johnson's Slow Ball	15.00	10.00	4.00
36 Pepper Martin (bunting)	15.00	10.00	4.00
37 Joe Cronin (Battery Tips)	27.00	18.00	8.00
39 Oscar Melillo (play ball, don't let ball play you)	15.00	10.00	4.00
40 Ben Chapman (hook slide)	15.00	10.00	4.00
41 John McGraw's Coaching Signs	27.00	18.00	8.00
42 Babe Ruth (choke grip)	60.00	40.00	16.00
43 "Red" Lucas (illegal action)	15.00	10.00	4.00
44 Charley Root (Hold-ing Runners on First)	15.00	10.00	4.00
45 Dazzy Vance (drop pitch)	21.00	14.00	6.00
46 Hugh Critz (second baseman's throw)	15.00	10.00	4.00
47 Firpo Marberry (Raise Ball)	15.00	10.00	4.00
48 Grover Alexander (Full Windup)	21.00	14.00	6.00
49 Lefty Grove (fast ball grip)	21.00	14.00	6.00
50 Heine Meine (three types of curves)	15.00	10.00	4.00

R344 MARANVILLE'S SECRETS (20) OF BASEBALL

3 5/8" X 6"

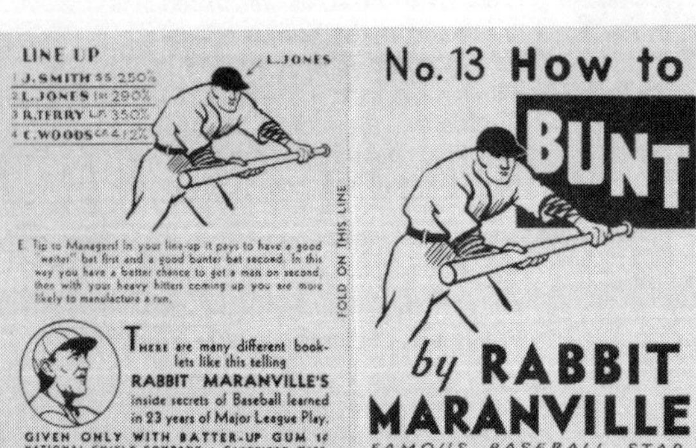

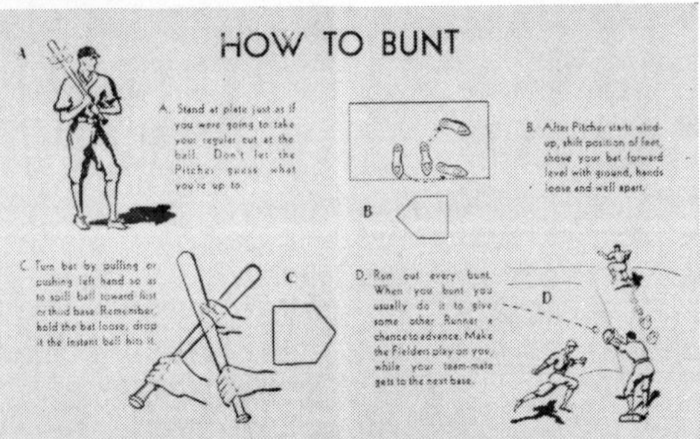

This paper set of 20 was issued in 1936 by the National Chicle Company. It carries the printing "Given Only With Batter-up Gum" on the back page. While the illustration shows the issue to be elongated, the papers were meant to be folded to create a four-page booklet. As the title implies, the set features instructional tips by Rabbit Maranville.

	MINT	VG-E	F-G
COMPLETE SET	300.00	200.00	80.00
COMMON CARD	15.00	10.00	4.00
1 How to Pitch (the Out Shoot)	15.00	10.00	4.00
2 How to Throw (the In Shoot)	15.00	10.00	4.00
3 How to Pitch (the Drop)	15.00	10.00	4.00
4 How to Pitch (the Floater)	15.00	10.00	4.00
5 How to Run Bases	15.00	10.00	4.00
6 How to Slide	15.00	10.00	4.00
7 How to Catch Flies	15.00	10.00	4.00
8 How to Field Grounders	15.00	10.00	4.00
9 How to Tag A Man Out	15.00	10.00	4.00
10 How to Cover A Base	15.00	10.00	4.00
11 How to Bat	15.00	10.00	4.00
12 How to Steal Bases	15.00	10.00	4.00
13 How to Bunt	15.00	10.00	4.00
14 How to Coach Base Runners	15.00	10.00	4.00
15 How to Catch Behind the Bat	15.00	10.00	4.00
16 How to Throw to Bases	15.00	10.00	4.00
17 How to Signal	15.00	10.00	4.00
18 How to Umpire Balls and Strikes	15.00	10.00	4.00
19 How to Umpire Bases	15.00	10.00	4.00
20 How to Lay Out a Ball Field	15.00	10.00	4.00

R714-26A HOCUS FOCUS (18)
R714-26B HOCUS FOCUS (23)

1" X 1 5/8"
7/8" X 1 3/8"

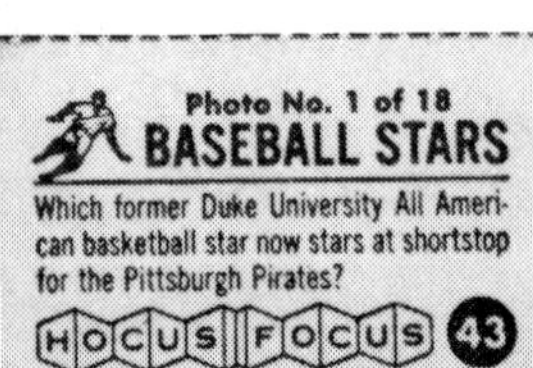

This 1956 Topps issue is often confused with the Magic Photos issue of 1950. The R714-26 set comes in two types, which we have arbitrarily labeled A and B. Style A, the larger size, contains 18 baseball subjects—the ones known are checklisted below. Type B, the smaller size, is reported to contain baseball subjects—those known are checklisted below. Like the Magic Photo set these cards were "developed" by sunlight. The baseball players in these sets are but a portion of the total cards in the set. Dogs, personalities, and other subjects were also featured.

	MINT	VG-E	F-G
COMPLETE SET	120.00	80.00	30.00
COMMON PLAYER	9.00	6.00	2.50
1 Dick Groat #43	9.00	6.00	2.50
3 Hank Sauer #30	9.00	6.00	2.50
4 Dusty Rhodes #86	9.00	6.00	2.50
6 Harvey Haddix #26	9.00	6.00	2.50
7 Ray Boone #31	9.00	6.00	2.50
8 Al Rosen #69	11.00	7.00	3.00
9 Mayo Smith #51	9.00	6.00	2.50
11 Jim Rivera #67	9.00	6.00	2.50
13 Gus Zernial #49	9.00	6.00	2.50
14 Jackie Robinson #13	21.00	14.00	6.00
15 Hal Smith #42	9.00	6.00	2.50
16 Johnny Schmitz #84	9.00	6.00	2.50
17 Spook Jacobs #60	9.00	6.00	2.50

	MINT	VG-E	F-G
COMPLETE SET	120.00	80.00	30.00
COMMON PLAYER	9.00	6.00	2.50
1 Babe Ruth #117	45.00	30.00	12.00
3 Dick Groat #43	9.00	6.00	2.50
8 Harvey Haddix #26	9.00	6.00	2.50
12 Warren Spahn #87	15.00	10.00	4.00
13 Jim Rivera #67	9.00	6.00	2.50
14 Ted Kluszewski #79	11.00	7.00	3.00
15 Gus Zernial #49	9.00	6.00	2.50
20 Karl Spooner #122	9.00	6.00	2.50
21 Ed Mathews #109	15.00	10.00	4.00

T209 CONTENTNEA (16)(220) 1 1/2" X 2 5/8"

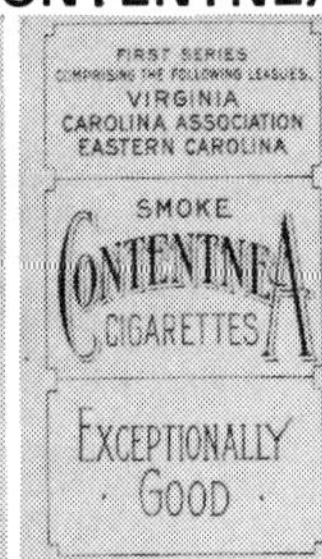

The baseball cards found as inserts in packs of Contentnea Cigarettes were released to the public in 1909 and 1910. Although both sets depict players from the "Virginia," "Carolina Association," and "Eastern Carolina" leagues, they are otherwise dissimilar. The 16-card color series—known as type one—was issued in 1909. The obverse captions are printed in blue and are located in the white border at the bottom. The reverse is marked "First Series," but no subsequent printings are known. There are 220 of the type two black & white "Photo Series" listed below, although more are believed to exist. The captions on this type are printed in black and are found within a white panel inside the picture area. Both types are considered to be scarce.

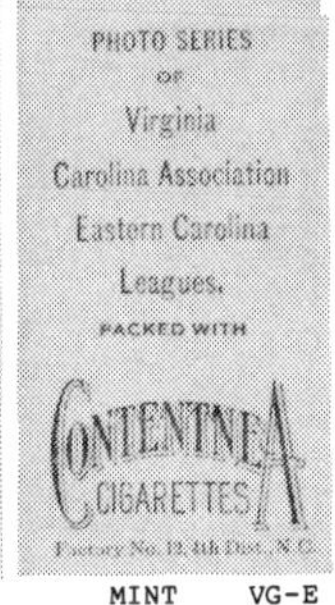

	MINT	VG-E	F-G
COMPLETE SET	2400.00	1600.00	650.00
COMMON PLAYER (1-16)	25.00	17.00	7.00
COMMON PLAYER (17-235)	10.00	6.50	3.00
1 Armstrong	25.00	17.00	7.00
2 Booles	25.00	17.00	7.00
3 Bourquise	25.00	17.00	7.00
4 Cooper	25.00	17.00	7.00
5 Cowell	25.00	17.00	7.00
6 Crockett	25.00	17.00	7.00
7 Fullenwider	25.00	17.00	7.00
8 Gilmore	25.00	17.00	7.00
9 Hoffman	25.00	17.00	7.00
10 Lane	25.00	17.00	7.00
11 Martin	25.00	17.00	7.00
12 McGeehan	25.00	17.00	7.00
13 Pope	25.00	17.00	7.00
14 Sisson	25.00	17.00	7.00
15 Stubbe	25.00	17.00	7.00
16 Walsh	25.00	17.00	7.00
Anderson			
17 Byrd	10.00	6.50	3.00
18 Corbett	10.00	6.50	3.00
19 Farmer	10.00	6.50	3.00
20 Gorham	10.00	6.50	3.00
21 Harley	10.00	6.50	3.00
22 Kelly	10.00	6.50	3.00
23 A. McCarthy	10.00	6.50	3.00
24 J. McCarthy	10.00	6.50	3.00
25 Peloguin	10.00	6.50	3.00
26 Roth	10.00	6.50	3.00
27 Wehrell	10.00	6.50	3.00
Charlotte			
28 Bausewein	10.00	6.50	3.00
29 Brazelle	10.00	6.50	3.00
30 Coutts	10.00	6.50	3.00
31 Cross	10.00	6.50	3.00
32 Dobard	10.00	6.50	3.00
33 Duvie	10.00	6.50	3.00
34 Francisco	10.00	6.50	3.00
35 Garman	10.00	6.50	3.00
36 Hargrave	10.00	6.50	3.00
37 Hemphrey	10.00	6.50	3.00
38 McHugh	10.00	6.50	3.00
39 Taxis	10.00	6.50	3.00
40 Williams	10.00	6.50	3.00
Danville			
41 Bussey	10.00	6.50	3.00
42 Callahan	10.00	6.50	3.00
43 Griffin	10.00	6.50	3.00
44 Hooker	10.00	6.50	3.00
45 Mayberry	10.00	6.50	3.00
46 Mullinix	10.00	6.50	3.00
47 Priest	10.00	6.50	3.00
48 Rickert	10.00	6.50	3.00
49 Schrader	10.00	6.50	3.00
50 Sullivan	10.00	6.50	3.00
Fayetteville			
51 Boyle	10.00	6.50	3.00
52 Dobson	10.00	6.50	3.00
53 Galvin	10.00	6.50	3.00
54 Lavoia	10.00	6.50	3.00
55 Luyster	10.00	6.50	3.00
56 Schumaker	10.00	6.50	3.00
57 Waters	10.00	6.50	3.00
58 Wamack	10.00	6.50	3.00
Goldsboro			
59 Dailey	10.00	6.50	3.00
60 Evans	10.00	6.50	3.00
61 Fulton	10.00	6.50	3.00
62 Gates	10.00	6.50	3.00
63 Gunderson	10.00	6.50	3.00
64 Handiboe	10.00	6.50	3.00
65 Kelly	10.00	6.50	3.00
66 Malcolm	10.00	6.50	3.00
67 Merchant	10.00	6.50	3.00
68 Morgan	10.00	6.50	3.00
69 Sharp	10.00	6.50	3.00
70 Stofhr	10.00	6.50	3.00
71 Webb	10.00	6.50	3.00
72 Wolf	10.00	6.50	3.00
Greensboro			
73 Bentley	10.00	6.50	3.00
74 Beusse	10.00	6.50	3.00
75 Doak	10.00	6.50	3.00
76 Eldridge	10.00	6.50	3.00
77 Hammersley	10.00	6.50	3.00
78 Hicks	10.00	6.50	3.00
79 Jackson	10.00	6.50	3.00
80 Martin	10.00	6.50	3.00
81 Pickard	10.00	6.50	3.00
82 Ridgeway	10.00	6.50	3.00
83 Springs	10.00	6.50	3.00
84 Walters	10.00	6.50	3.00
85 Weldon	10.00	6.50	3.00
Greenville			
86 Blackstone	10.00	6.50	3.00
87 F. Derrick	10.00	6.50	3.00
88 C. Derrick	10.00	6.50	3.00
89 Drumm	10.00	6.50	3.00
90 Flowers	10.00	6.50	3.00
91 Jenkins	10.00	6.50	3.00
92 McFarlin	10.00	6.50	3.00
93 Noojin	10.00	6.50	3.00
94 Ochs	10.00	6.50	3.00
95 Redfern	10.00	6.50	3.00
96 Stouch	10.00	6.50	3.00
97 Wingo	10.00	6.50	3.00
98 Workman	10.00	6.50	3.00
Lynchburg			
99 Brandon	10.00	6.50	3.00
100 Griffin	10.00	6.50	3.00
101 Hoffman	10.00	6.50	3.00
102 Howedel	10.00	6.50	3.00
103 Levy	10.00	6.50	3.00
104 Lloyd	10.00	6.50	3.00
105 Lucia	10.00	6.50	3.00
106 Rawe	10.00	6.50	3.00
107 Sexton	10.00	6.50	3.00
108 A. Smith	10.00	6.50	3.00
109 D. Smith	10.00	6.50	3.00
110 Woolums	10.00	6.50	3.00
Norfolk			
111 Armstrong	10.00	6.50	3.00
112 Banner	10.00	6.50	3.00
113 Busch	10.00	6.50	3.00
114 Chandler	10.00	6.50	3.00
115 Clark	10.00	6.50	3.00

T209 Contentnea Cigarettes

116 Johnson	10.00	6.50	3.00
117 Mullany	10.00	6.50	3.00
118 Munsen	10.00	6.50	3.00
119 Murdock	10.00	6.50	3.00
120 Reggy	10.00	6.50	3.00
121 Tiedmann	10.00	6.50	3.00
122 Walker	10.00	6.50	3.00
123 Walsh	10.00	6.50	3.00
Portsmouth			
124 Bowen	10.00	6.50	3.00
125 Clunk	10.00	6.50	3.00
126 Guiheen	10.00	6.50	3.00
127 Hamilton	10.00	6.50	3.00
128 Hannifen	10.00	6.50	3.00
129 Kunkle	10.00	6.50	3.00
130 McFarland	10.00	6.50	3.00
131 Smith	10.00	6.50	3.00
132 Toner	10.00	6.50	3.00
133 Vail	10.00	6.50	3.00
134 Welsher	10.00	6.50	3.00
Raleigh			
135 Beatty	10.00	6.50	3.00
136 Biel	10.00	6.50	3.00
137 Bigbie	10.00	6.50	3.00
138 Clemens	10.00	6.50	3.00
139 Hart	10.00	6.50	3.00
140 Hawkins	10.00	6.50	3.00
141 Hobbs	10.00	6.50	3.00
142 Jobson	10.00	6.50	3.00
143 Keating	10.00	6.50	3.00
144 "King" Kelly	10.00	6.50	3.00
145 Lathrop	10.00	6.50	3.00
146 McCormick	10.00	6.50	3.00
147 Mundell	10.00	6.50	3.00
148 Phoenix	10.00	6.50	3.00
149 Prim	10.00	6.50	3.00
150 Richardson	10.00	6.50	3.00
151 Simmons	10.00	6.50	3.00
152 Turner	10.00	6.50	3.00
153 Wright	10.00	6.50	3.00
Richmond			
154 Baker	10.00	6.50	3.00
155 Bigbie	10.00	6.50	3.00
156 Brown	10.00	6.50	3.00
157 Cowan	10.00	6.50	3.00
158 Hale	10.00	6.50	3.00
159 Irvine	10.00	6.50	3.00
160 Landgraff	10.00	6.50	3.00
161 Missitt	10.00	6.50	3.00
162 Morrissey	10.00	6.50	3.00
163 Salve	10.00	6.50	3.00
164 Shaw	10.00	6.50	3.00
165 Titman	10.00	6.50	3.00
166 Verbout	10.00	6.50	3.00
167 Wallace	10.00	6.50	3.00
Roanoake			
168 Andrada	10.00	6.50	3.00
169 Cafalu	10.00	6.50	3.00
170 Doyle	10.00	6.50	3.00
171 Fisher	10.00	6.50	3.00
172 Halland	10.00	6.50	3.00
173 Jenkins	10.00	6.50	3.00
174 Newton	10.00	6.50	3.00
175 Powell	10.00	6.50	3.00
176 Presley & Pritchard	10.00	6.50	3.00
177 Pritchard	10.00	6.50	3.00
178 Schmidt	10.00	6.50	3.00
179 Schaughnessy	10.00	6.50	3.00
180 Spratt	10.00	6.50	3.00
Rocky Mount			
181 Bonner	10.00	6.50	3.00
182 Creagan	10.00	6.50	3.00
183 Forque	10.00	6.50	3.00
184 Gatmeyer	10.00	6.50	3.00
185 Gillespie	10.00	6.50	3.00
186 Novak	10.00	6.50	3.00
187 Phealean	10.00	6.50	3.00
Spartanburg			
188 Abercrombie	10.00	6.50	3.00
189 Averett	10.00	6.50	3.00
190 Fairbanks	10.00	6.50	3.00
191 Gardin	10.00	6.50	3.00
192 Harrington	10.00	6.50	3.00
193 Harris	10.00	6.50	3.00
194 Jackson	10.00	6.50	3.00
195 Thompson	10.00	6.50	3.00
196 Vickery	10.00	6.50	3.00
197 Walker	10.00	6.50	3.00
198 Wood	10.00	6.50	3.00
199 Wynne	10.00	6.50	3.00
Wilmington			
200 Bourquin	10.00	6.50	3.00
201 Cooper	10.00	6.50	3.00
202 Doak	10.00	6.50	3.00
203 Ebinger	10.00	6.50	3.00
204 Foltz	10.00	6.50	3.00
205 Gehring	10.00	6.50	3.00
206 Howard	10.00	6.50	3.00
207 Hyames	10.00	6.50	3.00
208 Kelley	10.00	6.50	3.00
209 Kite	10.00	6.50	3.00
210 Tydeman	10.00	6.50	3.00
Wilson			
211 Clapp	10.00	6.50	3.00
212 Cowells	10.00	6.50	3.00
213 Foreman	10.00	6.50	3.00
214 Hearne	10.00	6.50	3.00
215 Hudson	10.00	6.50	3.00
216 Lane	10.00	6.50	3.00
217 C. McGeehan	10.00	6.50	3.00
218 D. McGeehan	10.00	6.50	3.00
219 Miller	10.00	6.50	3.00
220 Stewart	10.00	6.50	3.00
221 B.E. Thompson	10.00	6.50	3.00
222 Westlake	10.00	6.50	3.00
Winston-Salem			
223 Brent	10.00	6.50	3.00
224 Cote	10.00	6.50	3.00
225 Ferrell	10.00	6.50	3.00
226 Fogarty	10.00	6.50	3.00
227 King	10.00	6.50	3.00
228 Loval	10.00	6.50	3.00
229 MacConachie	10.00	6.50	3.00
230 McKeavitt	10.00	6.50	3.00
231 Midkiff	10.00	6.50	3.00
232 Painter	10.00	6.50	3.00
233 Swindell	10.00	6.50	3.00
234 Templin	10.00	6.50	3.00
235 Willis	10.00	6.50	3.00

T210 OLD MILL RED BORDERS (603) 1 1/2" X 2 5/8"

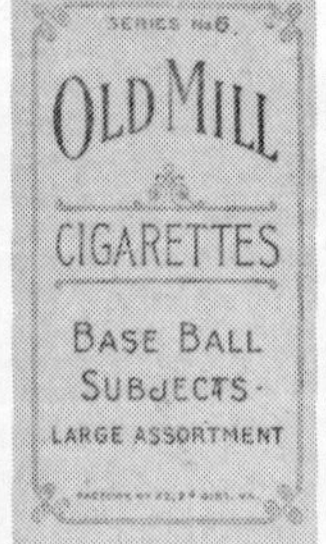

This is the largest 20th Century tobacco-issued baseball series, and it presents a formidable challenge to the collector. Eight minor leagues are each represented by a specific numbered series (indicated on the reverse of each card): South Atlantic (No. 1), Virginia (No. 2), Texas (No. 3), Virginia Valley (No. 4), Carolina Association (No. 5), Blue Grass (No. 6), Eastern Carolina (No. 7), and Southern (No. 8). Each player's name and team are printed in black within the bottom border. "Old Mill" was an American Tobacco Company brand, and all the cards of this series seem to have been distributed via a single Virginia factory. Some orange-bordered cards exist and are valued slightly higher than those with red borders.

	MINT	VG-E	F-G
COMPLETE SET	3000.00	2000.00	800.00
COMMON SERIES 2,3	5.00	3.50	1.40
COMMON SERIES 8	7.50	5.00	2.00
COMMON OTHER PLAYERS	6.00	4.00	1.60

T211 RED SUN GREEN BORDERS (75) 1 1/2" X 2 5/8"

The obverse design of the 1910 Red Sun Cigarette baseball series resembles that of set T210 except for the green borders surrounding the black & white picture area. There are a total of 75 Southern Association players depicted in the set. The reverse of each card contains a bright red-on-white advertisement and the line "First Series 1 to 75" (no subsequent series are known). The New Orleans factory which produced the Red Sun brand was a branch of the American Tobacco Company.

	MINT	VG-E	F-G
COMPLETE SET	1250.00	850.00	350.00
COMMON PLAYER	20.00	13.00	5.50
Atlanta			
1 Bartley	20.00	13.00	5.50
2 Bayless	20.00	13.00	5.50
3 Fisher	20.00	13.00	5.50
4 Griffin	20.00	13.00	5.50
5 Gornhorst	20.00	13.00	5.50
6 Hanks	20.00	13.00	5.50
7 Jordan	20.00	13.00	5.50
8 Moran	20.00	13.00	5.50
9 Rogers	20.00	13.00	5.50
10 Seitz	20.00	13.00	5.50
11 Sid Smith	20.00	13.00	5.50
12 Sweeney	20.00	13.00	5.50
13 Walker	20.00	13.00	5.50
Birmingham			
14 Gygli	20.00	13.00	5.50
15 Kane	20.00	13.00	5.50
16 Molesworth	20.00	13.00	5.50
Memphis			
17 Babb	20.00	13.00	5.50
18 Cross	20.00	13.00	5.50
19 Davis	20.00	13.00	5.50
20 Dick	20.00	13.00	5.50
21 Fritz	20.00	13.00	5.50
22 Steele	20.00	13.00	5.50
Mobile			
23 Allen	20.00	13.00	5.50
24 Berger	20.00	13.00	5.50
25 Bittroff	20.00	13.00	5.50
26 Chappelle	20.00	13.00	5.50
27 Dunn	20.00	13.00	5.50
28 Hickman	20.00	13.00	5.50
29 Huelsman	20.00	13.00	5.50
30 Kerwin	20.00	13.00	5.50
31 Rhoton	20.00	13.00	5.50
32 Swacina	20.00	13.00	5.50
33 Wagner	20.00	13.00	5.50
34 Wilder	20.00	13.00	5.50
Montgomery			
35 Jud Daly	20.00	13.00	5.50
36 Greminger	20.00	13.00	5.50
37 Gribbin	20.00	13.00	5.50
38 Hart	20.00	13.00	5.50
39 McCreary	20.00	13.00	5.50
40 Miller	20.00	13.00	5.50
41 Nolley	20.00	13.00	5.50
42 Pepe	20.00	13.00	5.50
43 Pratt	20.00	13.00	5.50
44 Smith	20.00	13.00	5.50
45 Thomas	20.00	13.00	5.50
Nashville			
46 Anderson	20.00	13.00	5.50
47 Bay	20.00	13.00	5.50
48 Bernard	20.00	13.00	5.50
49 Bronkie	20.00	13.00	5.50
50 Case	20.00	13.00	5.50
51 Cohen	20.00	13.00	5.50
52 Erloff	20.00	13.00	5.50
53 Flood	20.00	13.00	5.50
54 Kelly	20.00	13.00	5.50
55 Keupper	20.00	13.00	5.50
56 Lynch	20.00	13.00	5.50
57 Perdue	20.00	13.00	5.50
58 Seabrough	20.00	13.00	5.50
59 Siegel	20.00	13.00	5.50
60 Vinson	20.00	13.00	5.50
61 Wiseman	20.00	13.00	5.50
62 Wolf	20.00	13.00	5.50
New Orleans			
63 Breitenstein	20.00	13.00	5.50
64 Brooks	20.00	13.00	5.50
65 Cafalu	20.00	13.00	5.50
66 DeMontreville	20.00	13.00	5.50
67 E. DeMontreville	20.00	13.00	5.50
68 Foster	20.00	13.00	5.50
69 Hess	20.00	13.00	5.50
70 LaFitte	20.00	13.00	5.50
71 Lindsay	20.00	13.00	5.50
72 Manush	20.00	13.00	5.50
73 Paige	20.00	13.00	5.50
74 Robertson	20.00	13.00	5.50
75 Rohe	20.00	13.00	5.50

T212 OBAK BASE BALL SERIES (426) 1 7/16" X 2 5/8"

The ACC designation "T212" actually encompasses three separate minor league sets (listed in sequence in the checklist below). Set 1 (Nos. 1-75) features 75 colored, player cards representing six PCL teams and was issued in 1909. The obverse captions are stylized (slanted), and the word "Obak" on the reverse is inscribed in "Old English" letters. Set 2 contains 175 colored cards (Nos. 76-251) of players from six PCL and four NWL teams. The captions are not slanted, and "Obak" appears in large block letters on the back. Reverses advertise either "150" or "175" subjects, and some 35 different slogans exist. The backs of sets 1 and 2 are printed in blue. In contrast, the 1911 set of 175 colored cards has red-printed backs which contain a short biography and some statistics (Nos. 252-426). The PCL and NWL are each represented by six teams in this set (Note: there is a Portland club in each league). The Obak brand was produced and distributed in California by a branch of the American Tobacco Company.

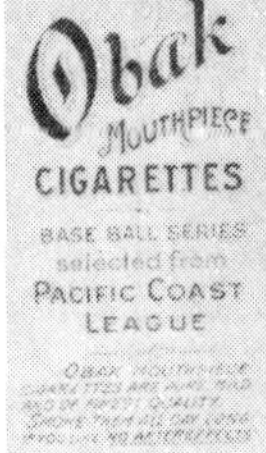

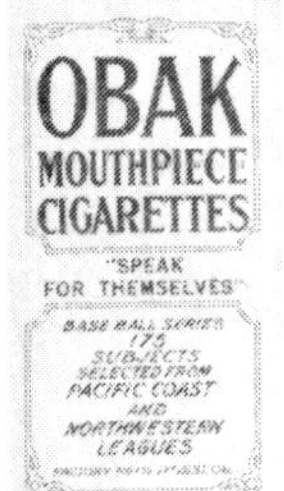

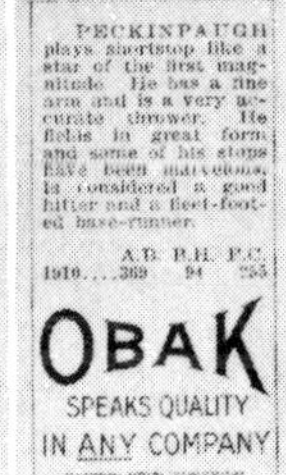

	MINT	VG-E	F-G
COMPLETE SET	1500.00	1000.00	400.00
COMMON PLAYER (1-76)	13.50	9.00	4.00
COMMON PLAYER (77-426)	3.75	2.50	1.00

T213 COUPON BASE BALL (64)(93) SERIES 1 1/2" X 2 5/8"

The ACC classification "T213"—like its predecessor T212—contains three separate sets, two of which are checklisted below. Set 1 was issued in 1909-1910 and consists of brown-captioned designs (64 known) taken directly from set T206 (to which many collectors feel it more properly belongs). Set 2 cards (93 known) are also T206 designs, but with pale blue captions. They were produced in 1914-1915 and contain many team changes and Federal League affiliations. Set 1 cards are printed on heavy paper; set 2 cards are printed on cardboard and have a glossy surface, which has resulted in a distinctive type of surface cracking. The "Coupon" brand of cigarettes was manufactured by a branch of the American Tobacco Company located in New Orleans.

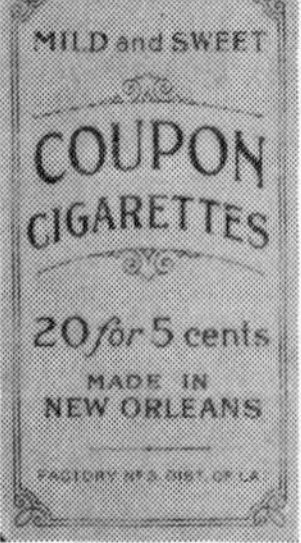

	MINT	VG-E	F-G
COMPLETE SET	1350.00	900.00	400.00
COMMON PLAYER	20.00	13.00	5.50
1 Bay, Nashville	30.00	20.00	8.00
2 Becker	20.00	13.00	5.50
3 Bender	30.00	20.00	8.00
4 Bernhard, Nashville	30.00	20.00	8.00
5 Breitenstein, N.O.	30.00	20.00	8.00
6 Byrne	20.00	13.00	5.50
7 Campbell	20.00	13.00	5.50
8 Carey, Memphis	30.00	20.00	8.00
9 Chance	50.00	35.00	14.00
10 Charles	20.00	13.00	5.50
11 Chase (2)	25.00	17.00	7.00
12 Cobb	165.00	110.00	45.00
13 Cree	20.00	13.00	5.50
14 Donovan	20.00	13.00	5.50
15 Doolan	20.00	13.00	5.50
16 Dubuc	20.00	13.00	5.50
17 Dunn	20.00	13.00	5.50
18 Ellam, Nashville	30.00	20.00	8.00
19 Engle	20.00	13.00	5.50
20 Evers	30.00	20.00	8.00
21 Fletcher	20.00	13.00	5.50
22 Fritz, New Orleans	30.00	20.00	8.00
23 Greminger, Montgomery	30.00	20.00	8.00
24 Hart (Little Rock)	30.00	20.00	8.00
25 Hart (Montgomery)	30.00	20.00	8.00
26 Hartsel	20.00	13.00	5.50
27 Hickman, Mobile	30.00	20.00	8.00
28 Hoffman	20.00	13.00	5.50
29 Howell	20.00	13.00	5.50
30 Huggins (2)	30.00	20.00	8.00
31 Hunter	20.00	13.00	5.50
32 A.O. Jordan, Atlanta	30.00	20.00	8.00
33 Killian	20.00	13.00	5.50
34 Knabe	20.00	13.00	5.50
35 Laporte	20.00	13.00	5.50
36 Lennox	20.00	13.00	5.50
37 Lentz, Little Rock	30.00	20.00	8.00
38 Marquard	30.00	20.00	8.00
39 Marshall	20.00	13.00	5.50
40 Mathewson	75.00	50.00	20.00
41 McBride	20.00	13.00	5.50
42 McElveen	20.00	13.00	5.50
43 McIntyre	20.00	13.00	5.50
44 Mitchell	20.00	13.00	5.50
45 Molesworth, Birmingham	30.00	20.00	8.00
46 Mowrey	20.00	13.00	5.50
47 Myers (2)	20.00	13.00	5.50
48 Paskert	20.00	13.00	5.50
49 Perdue, Nashville	30.00	20.00	8.00
50 Persons, Montgomery	30.00	20.00	8.00
51 Reagan, New Orleans	30.00	20.00	8.00
52 Rhoades	20.00	13.00	5.50
53 Rockenfeld, New Orleans	30.00	20.00	8.00
54 Rossman	20.00	13.00	5.50
55 Schmidt	20.00	13.00	5.50
56 Sid Smith, Atlanta	30.00	20.00	8.00
57 Starr	20.00	13.00	5.50
58 Street	20.00	13.00	5.50
59 Summers	20.00	13.00	5.50
60 Sweeney	20.00	13.00	5.50
61 Thomas	20.00	13.00	5.50
62 Thornton, Mobile	30.00	20.00	8.00
63 Willett	20.00	13.00	5.50
64 Wilson	20.00	13.00	5.50

	MINT	VG-E	F-G
COMPLETE SET	1200.00	800.00	350.00
COMMON PLAYER	12.00	8.00	3.50
1 Ames (2)	12.00	8.00	3.50
2 Baker (2)	22.50	15.00	6.50
3 Barger	12.00	8.00	3.50
4 Bender (6)	22.50	15.00	6.50
5 Bradley	12.00	8.00	3.50
6 Bresnahan (2)	22.50	15.00	6.50
7 Bridwell	12.00	8.00	3.50
8 Brown (2)	22.50	15.00	6.50
9 Byrne	12.00	8.00	3.50
10 Camnitz (2)	12.00	8.00	3.50
11 Campbell	12.00	8.00	3.50
12 Chance (2)	25.00	17.00	7.00
13 Chappelle	12.00	8.00	3.50
14 Chase (6)	15.00	10.00	4.00
15 Cobb (2)	110.00	70.00	30.00
16 Collins (2)	22.50	15.00	6.50
17 Crandall (2)	12.00	8.00	3.50
18 Crawford	22.50	15.00	6.50
19 Cree	12.00	8.00	3.50
20 Davis	12.00	8.00	3.50
21 Demmitt	12.00	8.00	3.50
22 Devore (2)	12.00	8.00	3.50
23A Donlin, N.Y. Nat.	15.00	10.00	4.00
23B Donlin, .300 Batter 7 Years	25.00	17.00	7.00
24 Donovan	12.00	8.00	3.50
25 Doolan (4)	12.00	8.00	3.50
26 Downey	12.00	8.00	3.50
27 Doyle (2)	15.00	10.00	4.00
28 Dubuc	12.00	8.00	3.50
29 Eiberfeld (2)	12.00	8.00	3.50
30 Evans	12.00	8.00	3.50
31 Evers	22.50	15.00	6.50
32 Ford	12.00	8.00	3.50
33 Fromme	12.00	8.00	3.50
34 Gandil	12.00	8.00	3.50
35 Geyer	12.00	8.00	3.50
36 Griffith	22.50	15.00	6.50
37 Groom	12.00	8.00	3.50
38 Herzog	12.00	8.00	3.50
39 Hofman	12.00	8.00	3.50
40 Huggins (2)	22.50	15.00	6.50
41 Hummel	12.00	8.00	3.50
42 Jennings (2)	22.50	15.00	6.50
43 Johnson	45.00	30.00	12.00
44 Jordan	12.00	8.00	3.50
45 Kelly (2)	12.00	8.00	3.50
46 Knabe	12.00	8.00	3.50
47 Konetchy (3)	12.00	8.00	3.50
48 Krause	12.00	8.00	3.50
49 Lajoie (3)	30.00	20.00	8.00
50 Leach (2)	12.00	8.00	3.50
51 Lennox	12.00	8.00	3.50
52 Magee (2)	12.00	8.00	3.50
53 Marquard (2)	22.50	15.00	6.50
54 Mathewson	45.00	30.00	12.00
55 McGraw (2)	25.00	17.00	7.00
56 McLean	12.00	8.00	3.50
57 McQuillan (2)	12.00	8.00	3.50
58 Merkle	15.00	10.00	4.00
59 Meyers (3)	12.00	8.00	3.50
60 Miller	12.00	8.00	3.50
61 Mitchell	12.00	8.00	3.50
62 Mowrey (2)	12.00	8.00	3.50
63 Mullin (2)	12.00	8.00	3.50
64 Murphy	12.00	8.00	3.50

T213 Coupon Base Ball Series

No.	Player	Price 1	Price 2	Price 3
65	Murray (3)	12.00	8.00	3.50
66	Needham	12.00	8.00	3.50
67	Oakes	12.00	8.00	3.50
68	Oldring	12.00	8.00	3.50
69	Paskert	12.00	8.00	3.50
70	Purtell	12.00	8.00	3.50
71	Quinn	12.00	8.00	3.50
72	Reulbach (2)	12.00	8.00	3.50
73	Rucker	12.00	8.00	3.50
74	Rudolph	12.00	8.00	3.50
75	Schaefer (3)	12.00	8.00	3.50
76	Schmidt	12.00	8.00	3.50
77	Schulte	12.00	8.00	3.50
78	Smith	12.00	8.00	3.50
79	Speaker	30.00	20.00	8.00
80	Stovall	12.00	8.00	3.50
81	Street	12.00	8.00	3.50
82	Summers	12.00	8.00	3.50
83A	Sweeney (2) (Little Rock)	15.00	10.00	4.00
83B	Sweeney (Montgomery)	15.00	10.00	4.00
84	Thomas (2)	12.00	8.00	3.50
85	Tinker (2)	22.50	15.00	6.50
86	Wagner	15.00	10.00	4.00
87	Warhop (2)	12.00	8.00	3.50
88	Wheat	22.50	15.00	6.50
89	Wilhelm	12.00	8.00	3.50
90	Willett	12.00	8.00	3.50
91	Wilson	12.00	8.00	3.50
92	Wiltse (4)	12.00	8.00	3.50
93	Zimmerman	12.00	8.00	3.50

W625-1 1952 STAR CAL DECALS (67) 4 1/8" X 6 1/8"

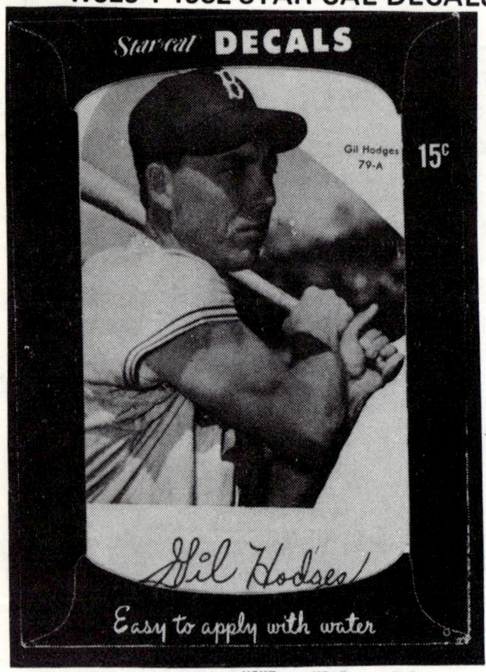

Type 1 of the Star-Cal Decal set, issued in 1952, contains (theoretically) the cards listed in the checklist below. Cards 73F, 80B, and 80D have not been verified although they are listed as being available on the cards themselves. Card 76C, Bobby Shantz, and card 77C, Kurt Simmons, were verified just before this issue went to press. A card numbered 71H featuring Hoot Evers with Boston also exists. The common card price can be used for these additions. When the decal is taken from the paper wrapper, a checklist of existing decals is revealed on the wrapper. The set was issued by the Meyercord Company of Chicago.

No.	Player	MINT	VG-E	F-G
	COMPLETE SET	1200.00	800.00	300.00
	COMMON PLAYER	9.00	6.00	2.50
70A	Allie Reynolds	10.00	6.50	3.00
70B	Ed Lopat	10.00	6.50	3.00
70C	Yogi Berra	30.00	20.00	8.00
70D	Vic Raschi	10.00	6.50	3.00
70E	Jerry Coleman	9.00	6.00	2.50
70F	Phil Rizzuto	15.00	10.00	4.00
70G	Mickey Mantle	300.00	200.00	80.00
71A	Mel Parnell	9.00	6.00	2.50
71B	Ted Williams	75.00	50.00	20.00
71C	Ted Williams	75.00	50.00	20.00
71D	Vern Stephens	9.00	6.00	2.50
71E	Billy Goodman	9.00	6.00	2.50
71F	Dom DiMaggio	12.50	8.50	3.50
71G	Dick Gernert	9.00	6.00	2.50
72A	George Kell	10.00	6.50	3.00
72B	Hal Newhouser	10.00	6.50	3.00
72C	Hoot Evers	9.00	6.00	2.50
72D	Vic Wertz	9.00	6.00	2.50
72E	Fred Hutchinson	10.00	6.50	3.00
72F	Bill Groth	9.00	6.00	2.50
73A	Al Zarilla	9.00	6.00	2.50
73B	Billy Pierce	10.00	6.50	3.00
73C	Eddie Robinson	9.00	6.00	2.50
73D	Chico Carrasguel	9.00	6.00	2.50
73E	Minnie Minoso	10.00	6.50	3.00
73F	Jim Busby	9.00	6.00	2.50
73G	Nellie Fox	10.00	6.50	3.00
73H	Sam Mele	9.00	6.00	2.50
74A	Larry Doby	10.00	6.50	3.00
74B	Al Rosen	12.50	8.50	3.50
74C	Bob Lemon	12.50	8.50	3.50
74D	Jim Hegan	9.00	6.00	2.50
74E	Bob Feller	21.00	14.00	6.00
74F	Dale Mitchell	9.00	6.00	2.50
75A	Ned Garver	9.00	6.00	2.50
76A	Gus Zernial	9.00	6.00	2.50
76B	Ferris Fain	9.00	6.00	2.50
77A	Richie Ashburn	12.50	8.50	3.50
77B	Ralph Kiner	15.00	10.00	4.00
78A	Bobby Thomson	10.00	6.50	3.00
78B	Alvin Dark	9.00	6.00	2.50
78C	Sal Maglie	9.00	6.00	2.50
78D	Larry Jansen	9.00	6.00	2.50
78E	Willie Mays	100.00	65.00	30.00
78F	Monte Irvin	15.00	10.00	4.00
78G	Whitey Lockman	9.00	6.00	2.50
79A	Gil Hodges	15.00	10.00	4.00
79B	Pee Wee Reese	15.00	10.00	4.00
79C	Roy Campanella	50.00	35.00	14.00
79D	Don Newcombe	10.00	6.50	3.00
79E	Duke Snider	30.00	20.00	8.00
79F	Preacher Roe	10.00	6.50	3.00
79G	Jackie Robinson	50.00	35.00	14.00
80A	Eddie Miksis	9.00	6.00	2.50
80B	Dutch Leonard	9.00	6.00	2.50
80C	Randy Jackson	9.00	6.00	2.50
80D	Bob Rush	9.00	6.00	2.50
80E	Hank Sauer	10.00	6.50	3.00
80F	Phil Cavarretta	10.00	6.50	3.00
80G	Warren Hacker	9.00	6.00	2.50
81A	Red Schoendienst	10.00	6.50	3.00
81B	Wally Westlake	9.00	6.00	2.50
81C	Cliff Chambers	9.00	6.00	2.50
81D	Enos Slaughter	12.50	8.50	3.50
81E	Stan Musial	50.00	35.00	14.00
81F	Stan Musial	50.00	35.00	14.00
81G	Jerry Staley	9.00	6.00	2.50

W625-2 1952 STAR CAL DECALS (64) 3 1/16" X 4 1/8"

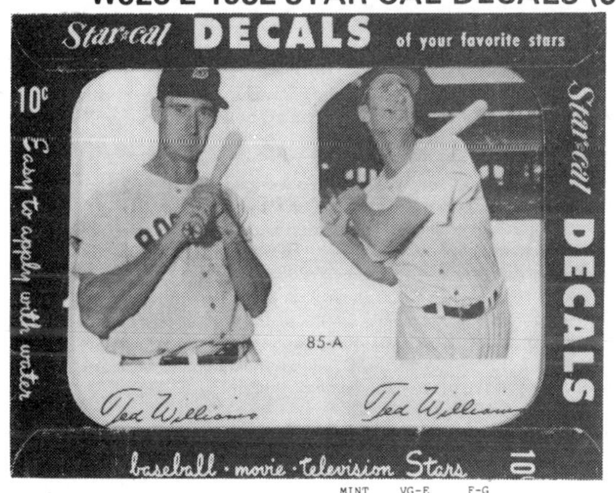

Type 2 of the Star-Cal Decal set features a decal package of the same size as the W625-1 set, but each sheet contains two decals, each of which is approximately half the size of the large decal found in the W625-1 set. This set was also issued by the Meyercord Company of Chicago. The checklist below features two players per "card."

	MINT	VG-E	F-G
COMPLETE SET	360.00	240.00	90.00
COMMON CARD	7.50	5.00	2.00
84A Allie Reynolds/Vic Raschi	8.50	6.00	2.50
84B Ed Lopat/Yogi Berra	13.50	9.00	4.00
84C Phil Rizzuto/Jerry Coleman	10.00	6.50	3.00
85A Ted Williams/Ted Williams	65.00	45.00	20.00
85B Dom DiMaggio/Mel Parnell	8.50	6.00	2.50
85C Vern Stephens/Billy Goodman	7.50	5.00	2.00
86A George Kell/Hal Newhouser	7.50	5.00	2.00
86B Hoot Evers/Vic Wertz	7.50	5.00	2.00
86C Bill Groth/Fred Hutchinson	7.50	5.00	2.00
87A Eddie Robinson/Eddie Robinson	7.50	5.00	2.00
87B Chico Carrasquel/Minnie Minoso	8.50	6.00	2.50
87C Billy Pierce/Nellie Fox	10.00	6.50	3.00
87D Al Zarilla/Jim Busby	7.50	5.00	2.00
88A Bob Lemon/Jim Hegan	8.50	6.00	2.50
88B Larry Doby/Bob Feller	10.00	6.50	3.00
88C Dale Mitchell/Al Rosen	8.50	6.00	2.50
89A Ned Garver/Ned Garver	7.50	5.00	2.00
89B Ferris Fain/Gus Zernial	7.50	5.00	2.00
89C Richie Ashburn/Richie Ashburn	13.50	9.00	4.00
89D Ralph Kiner/Ralph Kiner	16.50	11.00	4.50
90A Willie Mays/Monty Irvin	50.00	35.00	14.00
90B Larry Jansen/Sal Maglie	7.50	5.00	2.00
90C Bobby Thomson/Al Dark	8.50	6.00	2.50
91A Gil Hodges/Pee Wee Reese	16.50	11.00	4.50
91B Roy Campanella/Jackie Robinson	50.00	35.00	14.00
91C Duke Snider/Preacher Roe	16.50	11.00	4.50
92A Phil Cavarretta/Dutch Leonard	7.50	5.00	2.00
92B Randy Jackson/Eddie Miksis	7.50	5.00	2.00
92C Bob Rush/Hank Saver	7.50	5.00	2.00
93A Stan Musial/Stan Musial	50.00	35.00	14.00
93B Red Schoendienst/Enos Slaughter	13.50	9.00	4.00
93C Cliff Chambers/Wally Westlake	7.50	5.00	2.00

1949 & 1951 ROYAL (24) 2 1/2" X 3 1/2"

ROYAL STARS OF BASEBALL No. 2

"PEE WEE" REESE

Harold (also "Little Colonel") Reese has been a Brooklyn Dodger since 1940, excepting 3 years in the Navy. Born in Ekron, Ky., July 23, 1919. Pee Wee is 5' 10", weighs 168, hits and throws right-handed.

Pee Wee's 1949 fielding averaged .977, tops for National League shortstops. He scored 132 runs to lead the league. Reese has played in 3 World's Series and on 4 All-Star teams.

Send for a Plastic Album to Hold Your Royal Stars Collection!

Eight clear envelopes, bound with colorful cover, displays 16 photographs. Mail 15¢ and 3 Royal Desserts package fronts to Royal, Box 89, New York 46, N. Y.

This FREE Card Starts Your ROYAL STARS Collection!

Look on the other side of this card for a signed photo and short life story of "Pee Wee" Reese. You will find other photos and histories of many more famous Movie and Baseball Stars on the package backs of Royal Puddings and Royal Gelatin Desserts. Use this card to start your exciting collection of ROYAL STARS of Baseball and Movies!

This set of 24 black and white, numbered cards has a red band across the top which calls the set "Royal Stars of Baseball." These cards were issued on the backs of Royal Pudding packages in 1949 and 1951. The two years are distinguishable best by biography changes. Card nos. 6, 7, 8, 14, 19, and 21 all appear with team changes. The ACC designation is F219—1.

	MINT	VG-E	F-G
COMPLETE SET	300.00	200.00	80.00
COMMON PLAYER(1-24)	12.00	8.00	3.50
1 Musial,Stan	50.00	35.00	14.00
2 Reese,PeeWee	18.00	12.00	5.00
3 Kell,George	13.50	9.00	4.00
4 DiMaggio,Dom	15.00	10.00	4.00
5 Spahn,Warren	18.00	12.00	5.00
6 Pafko,Andy	12.00	8.00	3.50
7 Seminick,Andy	12.00	8.00	3.50
8 Brissie,Lou	12.00	8.00	3.50
9 Blackwell,Ewell	13.50	9.00	4.00
10 Thomson,Bobby	15.00	10.00	4.00
11 Rizzuto,Phil	18.00	12.00	5.00
12 Henrich,Tommy	15.00	10.00	4.00
13 Gordon,Joe	13.50	9.00	4.00
14 Scarborough,Ray	12.00	8.00	3.50
15 Rojek,Stan	12.00	8.00	3.50
16 Appling,Luke	18.00	12.00	5.00
17 Marshall,Willard	12.00	8.00	3.50
18 Dark,Alvin	13.50	9.00	4.00
19 Sisler,Dick	12.00	8.00	3.50
20 Ostrowski,Johnny	12.00	8.00	3.50
21 Trucks,Virgil	12.00	8.00	3.50
22 Robinson,Eddie	13.50	9.00	4.00
23 Fernandez,Nanny	13.00	8.00	3.50
24 Fain,Ferris	13.50	9.00	4.00

POSTCARDS

This section includes but one type of postcard—the baseball player postcard. We have not included here either stadium postcards or team-issued postcards. Both of these types are quite popular, however, the space allotted in this book is not sufficient to accurately describe the multitude of these issues. Popular, collected, and significant postcards of baseball players issued since the turn of the century are listed.

There are many similarities between postcards and baseball cards. Both are paper collectibles featuring a photo or drawing of a ballplayer. The market for baseball player postcards is not, however, as active or as structured as the market for baseball cards; consequently, there is a much greater variance in prices for postcards. Most baseball cards have now been catalogued and checklisted. On the other hand, new baseball player postcards are found frequently, and such discoveries will continue to occur in the near future. We should appreciate any assistance postcard collectors can provide us concerning the sources and checklist additions to the postcards included here. Sets herein have been numbered when the authors feel reasonably sure the checklists are complete at the number presented. Although a numbering system for postcards is in the American Card Catalogue (ACC), many older sets are not included and postcards issued since 1960 were not given a number in the ACC. These uncatalogued postcards are listed in this volume as PC plus some identifying feature of the set, usually the name of the printer or issuer.

Postcards are purchased to send through the mail. Given this purpose, several statements can be made concerning condition and value of postcards. A postcard is no longer mint when it has been sent or even prepared for sending. In other words, placing a stamp on a postcard, addressing it, or writing any notes or messages on the postcard, even though it is not sent, destroys the mint classification of this postcard. Because most postcards, particularly those issued before 1950, were purchased and sent through the mails, mint pre-1950 postcards are far from plentiful. As individual mint postcards are "scarce," mint sets are even more difficult to obtain; consequently, the mint set price for pre-World War II postcards is approximately 160% the sum of the individual postcards in the set. A set premium of about 140% has been placed on postcard sets in the very good to excellent condition grade, as the accumulation of complete sets, even in this mid-range condition, is somewhat difficult. Mint and very good to excellent set prices for postcards after 1950 do show a premium above the sum of the individual cost of the cards in the set, but not as much of a premium as pre-1950 issues. Backs are included in the illustrations when they provide some information as to the identification of the particular postcards; otherwise they are omitted.

PC741 BILL & BOB (19) 3 1/2" X 5 1/2"

The Bill and Bob postcards issued during the 1956-1958 time period feature Milwaukee Braves only. The cards are unnumbered, other than the K card number at the middle base on the reverse, and present some of the most attractive color postcards issued in the postwar period. Three poses of Adcock, and two poses each of Bruton and Crandall exist. The Torre card has been seen with a Pepsi Cola advertisement on the reverse.

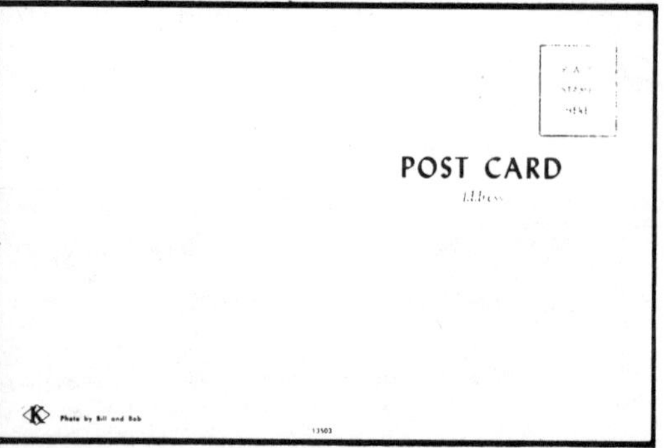

	MINT	VG–E	F–G
COMPLETE SET	300.00	180.00	70.00
COMMON PLAYER	12.50	7.00	2.00
1 Aaron, Hank	30.00	20.00	12.00
2 Adcock, Joe (3)	12.50	7.00	2.00
3 Bruton, Bill (2)	12.50	7.00	2.00
4 Buhl, Bob	12.50	7.00	2.00
5 Burdette, Lew	15.00	10.00	5.00
6 Conley, Gene	12.50	7.00	2.00
7 Covington, Wes	12.50	7.00	2.00
8 Crandall, Del (2)	12.50	7.00	2.00
9 Dressen, Chuck	12.50	7.00	2.00
10 Grimm, Charlie	12.50	7.00	2.00
11 Haney, Fred	12.50	7.00	2.00
12 Keely, Boby	12.50	7.00	2.00
13 Mathews, Ed	20.00	15.00	10.00
14 Spahn, Warren	20.00	15.00	10.00
15 Torre, Frank	15.00	10.00	5.00

PC742-1 BOSTON AMERICAN SERIES (6) 3 1/2" X 5 3/8"

This cream-colored card with sepia photo and printing was issued in 1912 by the Boston Amercan newspaper. The set features players from the 1912 World Champion Boston Red Sox only. It is reasonable to assume that additional cards in this set will be found in the future. Unlike the PC742-2 Boston Daily American Souvenir set, this set features excellent quality photos.

	MINT	VG–E	F–G
COMPLETE SET	175.00	90.00	25.00
COMMON PLAYER	15.00	9.00	3.00
Cady, Forrest	15.00	9.00	3.00
Perdue, Hub	15.00	9.00	3.00
Speaker, Tris	30.00	18.00	7.00
Stahl, Jake	15.00	9.00	3.00
Wagner, Heinie	15.00	9.00	3.00
Wood, Joe	20.00	12.00	5.00

PC742-2 BOSTON DAILY AMERICAN (3) 3 1/2" X 5 1/2" SOUVENIR

This black and white postcard set was issued in 1912 and features players from the World Champion Boston Red Sox of that year. The printing quality of the card is rather poor.

	MINT	VG–E	F–G
COMPLETE SET	40.00	20.00	7.50
COMMON PLAYER	8.00	5.00	2.00
Cady, Forrest	8.00	5.00	2.00
Collins, Ray	8.00	5.00	2.00
Wagner, Heinie	8.00	5.00	2.00

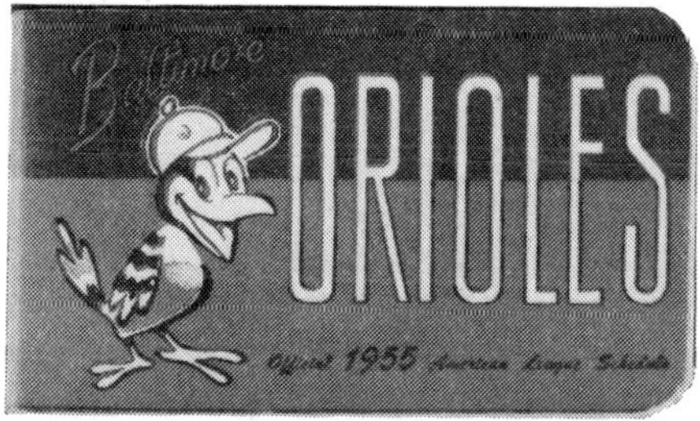

PC743 H. H. BREGSTONE (48?) 3 3/8" X 5 3/8"

The H. H. Bregstone postcards were issued during the 1909-1911 time period. They feature St. Louis Browns and St. Louis Cardinals only. The cards are sepia and black in appearance and are of consistent quality in the printing. Each card features the line "by H. H. Bregstone, St. Louis" at the bottom on the obverse. The player's last name, his position, and his team are enumerated. The reverses feature the letters AZO in the stamp area. B. Gregory of the Trolley League is probably Howie Gregory who played for the Browns that year.

DELAHANTY, l f
St. Louis National League Ball Club "CARDINALS"
by H.H. Bregstone, St. Louis

POST CARD
AZO PLACE STAMP HERE AZO
CORRESPONDENCE HERE
NAME AND ADDRESS HERE

	MINT	VG–E	F–G
COMPLETE SET	1500.00	950.00	350.00
COMMON PLAYER	20.00	15.00	7.00
CARDINALS			
Barry, rf	20.00	15.00	7.00
Beebe, p	20.00	15.00	7.00
Bliss	20.00	15.00	7.00
Bresnahan, c & mgr	30.00	18.00	9.00
Byrne, ss	20.00	15.00	7.00
Charles, 3b	20.00	15.00	7.00
Corridon	20.00	15.00	7.00
Delahanty, Joe	20.00	15.00	7.00
Evans	20.00	15.00	7.00
Geyer	20.00	15.00	7.00
Gilbert, 2b	20.00	15.00	7.00
Harmon	20.00	15.00	7.00
Higginbotham, p	20.00	15.00	7.00
Huggins, Miller	30.00	18.00	9.00
Hulswitt	20.00	15.00	7.00
Johnson	20.00	15.00	7.00
Konetchy	20.00	15.00	7.00
Lush	20.00	15.00	7.00
Magee	20.00	15.00	7.00
Oakes	20.00	15.00	7.00
Phelps	20.00	15.00	7.00
Reiger	20.00	15.00	7.00
Rhodes, p	20.00	15.00	7.00
Sallee, p	20.00	15.00	7.00
Willis, p	20.00	15.00	7.00
BROWNS			
Bailey	20.00	15.00	7.00
Criss, p	20.00	15.00	7.00
Criger	20.00	15.00	7.00
Dineen, p	20.00	15.00	7.00
Graham	20.00	15.00	7.00
Griggs	20.00	15.00	7.00
Hartzell	20.00	15.00	7.00
Hoffman	20.00	15.00	7.00
Howell	20.00	15.00	7.00
Jones, 1b	20.00	15.00	7.00
McAleer	20.00	15.00	7.00
Patterson	20.00	15.00	7.00
Pelty, p	20.00	15.00	7.00
Schweitzer	20.00	15.00	7.00
Smith	20.00	15.00	7.00
Stephens, c	20.00	15.00	7.00
Stone, lf	20.00	15.00	7.00
Waddell	30.00	18.00	9.00
Wallace, ss	20.00	15.00	7.00
Williams	20.00	15.00	7.00
MAPLEWOOD/TROLLEY LEAGUE			
Gregory, B.(probably Howie Gregory)	20.00	15.00	7.00

PC744 GEORGE BURKE (100's) 3 3/8" X 5 3/8"

The Burke postcards were issued by Chicago photographer George Burke during the period from 1948 through the 1950's. Because there are hundreds known and new ones are discovered frequently, a checklist has not been provided. The reverses feature the stamped name of "Geo. Burke, his address, and the city "Chicago."

	MINT	VG–E	F–G
COMMON PLAYER (1938-1948)	2.50	1.00	.50
COMMON PLAYER (1948 on)	1.00	.50	.25

PC748 LOUIS DORMAND (45) 3 1/2" X 5 1/2"

One of the most attractive and popular postcards ever issued are the full-color postcards of Louis Dormand, which were issued in the New York area as premiums by the Mason Candy Company. The cards are numbered on the reverse in the line which separates the address portion from the message portion of the postcard. Two variations of McDougald, Collins, and Sain exist. Rizzuto and Mantle also exist in a 6" X 9" postcard, and a 9" X 12" postcard of Mantle also exists. The Hodges card is quite scarce.

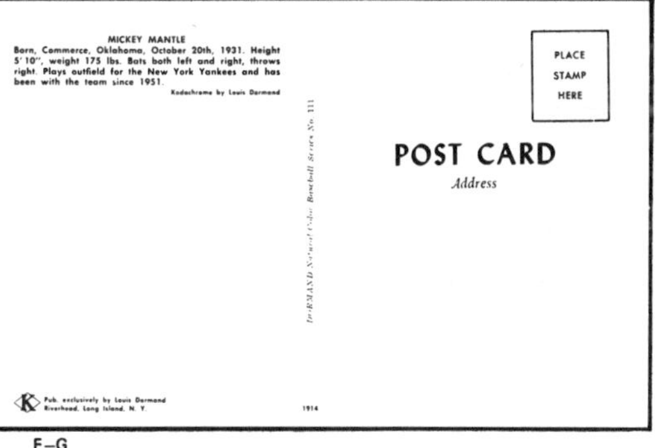

		MINT	VG–E	F–G
	COMPLETE SET	300.00	150.00	60.00
	COMMON PLAYER	4.00	1.00	.50
101	Rizzuto, Phil	6.00	3.00	1.00
101a	Rizzuto, Phil (Jumbo 6 X 9)	6.00	3.00	1.00
102	Berra, Yogi	7.00	4.00	1.50
103	Lopat, Ed	4.00	1.00	.50
104	Bauer, Hank	4.00	1.00	.50
105	Collins, Joe (with patch on sleeve)	4.00	1.00	.50
105a	Collins, Joe (w/o patch on sleeve)	4.00	1.00	.50
106	Houk, Ralph	4.00	1.00	.50
107	Miller, Bill	4.00	1.00	.50
108	Scarborough, Ray	4.00	1.00	.50
109	Reynolds, Allie	4.00	1.00	.50
110	McDougald, Gil	4.00	1.00	.50
110a	McDougald, Gil (signature variation)	4.00	1.00	.50
111	Mantle, Mickey (batting left)	10.00	7.00	4.00
111a	Mantle, Mickey (bat on shoulder)	25.00	15.00	7.00
111b	Mantle, Mickey (Jumbo 6 X 9)	30.00	18.00	9.00
111c	Mantle, Mickey (Jumbo 9 X 12)	75.00	50.00	20.00
112	Mize, Johnny	6.00	3.00	1.00
113	Stengel, Casey	7.00	4.00	1.50
114	Shantz, Bobby	4.00	1.00	.50
115	Ford, Whitey	7.00	4.00	1.50
116	Sain, Johnny	4.00	1.00	.50
116a	Sain, Johnny (pose variation)	4.00	1.00	.50
117	McDonald, Jim	4.00	1.00	.50
118	Woodling, Gene	4.00	1.00	.50
119	Silvera, Charlie	4.00	1.00	.50
120	Bollweg, Don	4.00	1.00	.50
121	Pierce, Billy	4.00	1.00	.50
122	Carrasquel, Chico	4.00	1.00	.50
123	Miranda, Willie	4.00	1.00	.50
124	Erskine, Carl	5.00	1.50	.75
125	Campanella, Roy	7.00	4.00	1.50
126	Coleman, Jerry	4.00	1.00	.50
127	Reese, Peewee	6.00	3.00	1.00
128	Furillo, Carl	4.00	1.00	.50
129	Hodges, Gil	100.00	75.00	30.00
130	Martin, Billy	6.00	3.00	1.00
131	Unknown	XXX	XXX	XXX
132	Noren, Irv	4.00	1.00	.50
133	Slaughter, Enos	5.00	1.50	.75
134	Gorman, Tom	4.00	1.00	.50
135	Robinson, Jackie	8.00	5.00	2.00
136	Crosetti, Frank	5.00	1.50	.75
137	Unknown	XXX	XXX	XXX
138	Konstanty, Jim	4.00	1.00	.50
139	Howard, Elston	5.00	1.50	.75
140	Skowron, Bill	4.00	1.00	.50

PC749 GRAPHIC ARTS SERVICE (17) 3 1/4" X 5 1/2"

The Graphic Art Service postcards were issued in the late 1950's and early 1960's in Cincinnati, Ohio. These black and white, unnumbered cards feature facsimile autographs on the front. Two poses of Reno Bertoia exist.

	MINT	VG–E	F–G
COMPLETE SET	65.00	40.00	20.00
COMMON PLAYER	3.00	2.00	1.00
1 Aber, Al	3.00	2.00	1.00
2 Aquirre, Hank	3.00	2.00	1.00
3 Bertoia, Reno (2)	3.00	2.00	1.00
4 Bolling, Frank	3.00	2.00	1.00
5 Bunning Jim	4.00	2.50	1.50
6 Foytack, Paul	3.00	2.00	1.00
7 Hegan, Jim	3.00	2.00	1.00
8 Henrich, Tom	4.00	2.50	1.50
9 Hoeft, Bill	3.00	2.00	1.00
10 House, Frank	3.00	2.00	1.00
11 Kuenn, Harvey	4.00	2.50	1.50
12 Martin, Billy	6.00	4.00	2.00
13 Morgan, Tom	3.00	2.00	1.00
14 Shaw, Bob	3.00	2.00	1.00
15 Slater, Lou	3.00	2.00	1.00
16 Thompson, Tim	3.00	2.00	1.00

PC750 HAYES COMPANY (1) 3 1/2" X 5 1/2"

The 1959 Hayes Company postcard consists of but one card. The Dexter Press printed Hank Bauer card is in full color and features a facsimile autograph of Bauer at the bottom of the card.

1 Bauer	4.00	2.00	1.00

PC751 HOWARD PHOTO SERVICE (2) 3 1/2" X 5 1/2"

The Howard Photo Service late 1950's postcard set was, until recently, thought to contain only the Bob Turley card. However, the recently discovered Willie Mays card makes one think that additional cards may be found in the future. These black and white postcards were issued in New York.

Mays, Willie	10.00	7.00	3.00
Turley, Bob	4.00	2.00	1.00

PC753 J. D. McCARTHY (1000's) 3 5/8" X 5 5/8"

One of the most prolific producers of postwar postcards was J. D. McCarthy of Michigan. During the 1950's and 1960's, thousands of these black and white postcards were issued. Most of the popular players of that era have been featured on the McCarthy postcards, and a checklist is not provided.

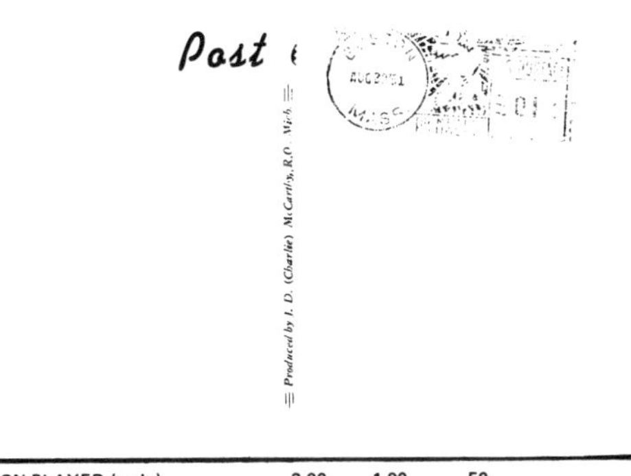

COMMON PLAYER (early)	3.00	1.00	.50
COMMON PLAYER (later)	1.00	.50	.20

PC754-2 ALBERTYPE HALL OF FAME (62) 3 1/2" X 5 1/2"

The Albertype Company issued postcards of Hall of Fame inductees during the period from 1936 through 1952. This black and white postcard set, the cards being called plaques as they feature the Hall of Fame plaque of the player, was addended to each year by new Hall of Fame inductees. Sixty-two Albertype postcards are known and are listed in the checklist below.

POST CARD

	MINT	VG–E	F–G
COMMON PLAYER	2.00	1.00	.50
Cobb, Ty	4.00	2.00	1.00
Johnson, Walter	3.00	1.50	.75
Mathewson, Christy	3.00	1.50	.75
Ruth, Babe	5.00	2.50	1.50
Wagner, Honus	3.00	1.50	.75
Bulkeley, Morgan	2.00	1.00	.50
Johnson, Ban	2.00	1.00	.50
Lajoie, Nap	2.00	1.00	.50
Mack, Connie	2.00	1.00	.50
McGraw, John	2.00	1.00	.50
Speaker, Tris	2.00	1.00	.50
Wright, George	2.00	1.00	.50
Young, Cy	2.00	1.00	.50
Alexander, Grover Cleveland	2.00	1.00	.50
Cartwright, Alexander	2.00	1.00	.50
Chadwick, Henry	2.00	1.00	.50
Anson, Cap	2.00	1.00	.50
Collins, Eddie	2.00	1.00	.50
Comiskey, Charlie	2.00	1.00	.50
Cummings, Candy	2.00	1.00	.50
Ewing, Buck	2.00	1.00	.50
Gehrig, Lou	4.00	2.00	1.00
Keeler, Willie	2.00	1.00	.50
Radbourne, Ole Hoss	2.00	1.00	.50
Sisler, George	2.00	1.00	.50
Spalding, Albert	2.00	1.00	.50
Hornsby, Rogers	2.00	1.00	.50
Landis, Kenesaw Mountain	2.00	1.00	.50

PC754-2 Albertype Hall of Fame Plaque postcards

Bresnahan, Roger	2.00	1.00	.50
Brouthers, Dan	2.00	1.00	.50
Clarke, Fred	2.00	1.00	.50
Collins, Jimmy	2.00	1.00	.50
Delahanty, Ed	2.00	1.00	.50
Duffy, Hugh	2.00	1.00	.50
Jennings, Hughie	2.00	1.00	.50
Kelly, King	2.00	1.00	.50
O'Rourke, Jimmy	2.00	1.00	.50
Robinson, Wilbert	2.00	1.00	.50
Burkett, Jesse	2.00	1.00	.50
Chance, Frank	2.00	1.00	.50
Chesbro, Jack	2.00	1.00	.50
Evers, Johnny	2.00	1.00	.50
Griffith, Clark	2.00	1.00	.50
McCarthy, Tom	2.00	1.00	.50
McGinnity, Joe	2.00	1.00	.50
Plank, Eddie	2.00	1.00	.50
Tinker, Joe	2.00	1.00	.50
Waddell, Rube	2.00	1.00	.50
Walsh, Ed	2.00	1.00	.50
Cochrane, Mickey	2.00	1.00	.50
Frisch, Frankie	2.00	1.00	.50
Grove, Lefty	2.00	1.00	.50
Hubbell, Carl	2.00	1.00	.50
Pennock, Herb	2.00	1.00	.50
Traynor, Pie	2.00	1.00	.50
Brown, Mordecai	2.00	1.00	.50
Gehringer, Charlie	2.00	1.00	.50
Nichols, Kid	2.00	1.00	.50
Foxx, Jimmy	3.00	1.50	.75
Ott, Mel	2.00	1.00	.50
Heilmann, Harry	2.00	1.00	.50
Waner, Paul	2.00	1.00	.50

PC754-3 ARTVUE HALL OF FAME (94) 3 1/2" X 5 1/2"

PC754-4 CURTEICH HALL (VARIABLE) OF FAME 3 1/2" X 5 1/2"

PC754-5 HALL OF FAME (20) VIEWCARDS 3 1/2" X 5 1/2"

The Artvue Company purchased the Albertype Company in 1953 and continued to issue Hall of Fame postcards in the same format as Albertype through 1963. A total of 94 Hall of Famers can be found on Artvue Hall of Fame plaques. Prices for the Artvue postcards are comparable to those of the Albertype style. Major Hall of Famers, e.g., DiMaggio, Jackie Robinson, etc. are valued in the $3.00-$4.00 range in mint condition. The Elmer Flick plaque, one of the last issued by the Artvue Company, is valued at $5.00 in mint condition. Beginning in 1964, the Curteich Hall of Fame postcards came into existence. These plaque postcards are of a yellow and brown color, giving a much better rendition of what the plaque actually looked like. All Hall of Famers are known in this set and they are still readily available for purchase; hence, a priced checklist on this set is meaningless. A set of Hall of Fame viewcards is also available picturing views of the Hall of Fame Museum and associated subjects. Unfortunately, a checklist and illustration are not available at this time.

PC756 SPIC & SPAN DRY CLEANERS (18) 4" X 5 7/8"
(18) 5" X 7"

This 1956 issue features oversized black and white photos with a Spic and Span logo and motto on the front of the postcard. The set features Milwaukee Brave players only and was issued in two sizes— 4" X 6" and 5" X 7". A facsimile autograph appears on the face of the card.

	MINT	VG–E	F–G
COMPLETE SET (large or small)	175.00	90.00	40.00
COMMON PLAYER (large or small)	8.00	4.00	2.00
1 Aaron, Henry	12.00	7.00	3.00
2 Bruton, Billy	8.00	4.00	2.00
3 Buhl, Bob	8.00	4.00	2.00
4 Burdette, Lou	8.00	4.00	2.00
5 Conley, Gene	8.00	4.00	2.00
6 Crandall, Del	8.00	4.00	2.00
7 Crone, Ray	8.00	4.00	2.00
8 Dittmer, Jack	8.00	4.00	2.00
9 Johnson, Ernie	8.00	4.00	2.00
10 Jolly, Dave	8.00	4.00	2.00
11 Mathews, Edwin L. Jr.	10.00	6.00	2.50
12 Nichols, Chet	8.00	4.00	2.00
13 O'Connell, Danny	8.00	4.00	2.00
14 Pafko, Andy	8.00	4.00	2.00
15 Thomson, Bob	8.00	4.00	2.00
16 Spahn, Warren	10.00	6.00	2.50
17 Adcock, Joe	8.00	4.00	2.00
18 Logan, Johnny	8.00	4.00	2.00

PC757 SPORTING NEWS (6) 3 3/8" X 5 1/2"

This 1915 postcard features color, a rare commodity in early baseball postcards. The inscription "published by the Sporting News" appears on the front of the card along with the player's name and his team. The postcards are believed to have been issued as premiums, and the set is believed to be complete at six cards.

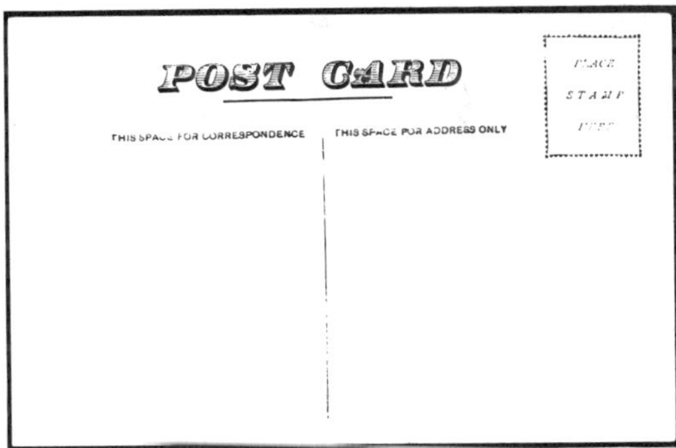

	MINT	VG–E	F–G
COMPLETE SET	600.00	340.00	130.00
1 Bresnahan, Roger–St. Louis N.L.	50.00	35.00	20.00
2 Cobb, Tyrus–Detroit A.L.	100.00	60.00	30.00
3 Collins, Eddie–Philadelphia Athletics	60.00	40.00	20.00
4 Gregg, Vean–Cleveland A.L.	35.00	20.00	10.00
5 Johnson, Walter–Street, Charles–Wash, A. L.	75.00	50.00	25.00
6 Marquard, Rube–New York Nationals	60.00	40.00	20.00

PC758 MAX STEIN/UNITED STATES (26) 3 1/2" X 5 1/2" PUBLISHING HOUSE

These sepia-colored postcards were issued from the 1909-1916 time period. The Marquard and Zimmerman cards have "United States Pub." marked on the back, leading to the theory that perhaps these two belong to another postcard set. The backs, incidentally, are quite attractive as one can see below.

	MINT	VG–E	F–G
COMMON PLAYER	15.00	8.00	4.00
Bodie	15.00	8.00	4.00
Chance	30.00	15.00	7.00
Cobb	75.00	50.00	25.00
Evers	30.00	15.00	7.00
Marquard	30.00	15.00	7.00
Mathewson	50.00	30.00	15.00
McGraw	30.00	15.00	7.00
Meyers	15.00	8.00	4.00
O'Toole	15.00	8.00	4.00
Schulte	15.00	8.00	4.00
Speaker	30.00	15.00	7.00
Stahl	15.00	8.00	4.00
Thorpe	30.00	15.00	7.00
Tinker	30.00	15.00	7.00
Wagner	50.00	30.00	15.00
Walsh	30.00	15.00	7.00
Weaver	15.00	8.00	4.00
Wood	30.00	15.00	7.00
Zimmerman	15.00	8.00	4.00
Five Cubs—Evers, Archer, Heckenger, Bresnahan, Needham	25.00	12.00	6.00
Five Cubs—Miller, Goode, Mitchell Clymer, Schulte	25.00	12.00	6.00
Boston American Team	40.00	20.00	10.00
Cubs—1916	40.00	20.00	10.00
Cincinnati Reds—1916	40.00	20.00	10.00
N.Y. National Team	40.00	20.00	10.00

PC759 SUNBEAM/PURETA (12) 3 1/4" X 5 1/2"

This 1949 set was co-issued by Sunbeam Bread and Pureta Sausage and features Sacramento Solon players only. The fronts feature the player and an insert of a microphone with station call letters printed on it. The backs feature ads for both Sunbeam Bread and Pureta Sausage.

	MINT	VG–E	F–G
COMPLETE SET	325.00	190.00	90.00
COMMON PLAYER	25.00	15.00	7.00
1 Baker, Del	25.00	15.00	7.00
2 Dasso, Frankie	25.00	15.00	7.00
3 Dropo, Walt	30.00	20.00	10.00
4 Grace, Joe	25.00	15.00	7.00
5 Gillespie, Bob	25.00	15.00	7.00
6 Hodgin, Ralph	25.00	15.00	7.00
7 Marsh, Freddie	25.00	15.00	7.00
8 Marty, Joe	25.00	15.00	7.00
9 Ratto, Len	25.00	15.00	7.00
10 Tabor, Jim	25.00	15.00	7.00
11 White, Al	25.00	15.00	7.00
12 Wilson, Bill	25.00	15.00	7.00

PC760 THE ROSE COMPANY (204?) 3 1/2" X 5 1/2"

One of the most attractive postcards ever issued, The Rose Company postcards were released during the 1908 and probably 1909 time period. The set features a black and white photo in a circle surrounded by a yellow and green baseball field, crossed bats and small figures. Imprints on the reverse contain the three letters TRC, with the loop around the bottom of the C possibly accounting for a lower case "o," giving Co. The Rose Co. baseball series is listed by teams in the checklist below—research indicates each of the 16 major league teams is represented by 12 Rose postcards (to date all have not been found). Seven Scranton players are known as are five postcards with no team identification whatsoever. The Scranton player postcards are somewhat more difficult to obtain.

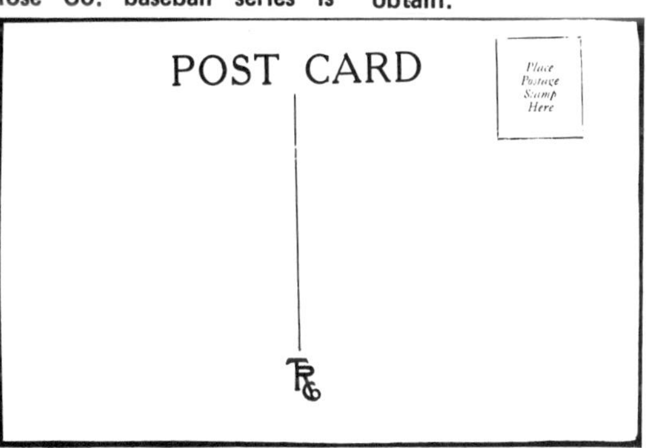

	MINT	VG–E	F–G
COMMON PLAYER	35.00	25.00	12.00
SCRANTON PLAYER	50.00	30.00	15.00
BOSTON RED SOX			
Glaze	35.00	25.00	12.00
Hale	35.00	25.00	12.00
LaPorte	35.00	25.00	12.00
Lord	35.00	25.00	12.00
Pruiett	35.00	25.00	12.00
Thoney	35.00	25.00	12.00
Unglaub	35.00	25.00	12.00
Wagner	35.00	25.00	12.00
Winter	35.00	25.00	12.00
Young, Cy	60.00	40.00	17.50
CHICAGO WHITE			
Altrock	35.00	25.00	12.00
Anderson	35.00	25.00	12.00
Donohue	35.00	25.00	12.00
Isbel	35.00	25.00	12.00
Jones	35.00	25.00	12.00
Parent	35.00	25.00	12.00
Smith	35.00	25.00	12.00
Sullivan	35.00	25.00	12.00
Tannehill	35.00	25.00	12.00
White	35.00	25.00	12.00
CLEVELAND INDIANS			
Bemis	35.00	25.00	12.00
Birmingham	35.00	25.00	12.00
Bradley	35.00	25.00	12.00
Clarke, J.	35.00	25.00	12.00
Hinchman	35.00	25.00	12.00
Joss, Addie	50.00	30.00	15.00
Lajoie, Nap	60.00	40.00	17.50
Leibhardt	35.00	25.00	12.00
Rhoades	35.00	25.00	12.00
Turner	35.00	25.00	12.00
DETROIT TIGERS			
Cobb, Ty	100.00	60.00	30.00
Coughlin	35.00	25.00	12.00
Crawford, Sam	50.00	30.00	15.00
Donovan	35.00	25.00	12.00
Killian	35.00	25.00	12.00
McIntyre	35.00	25.00	12.00
Mullin	35.00	25.00	12.00
O'Leary	35.00	25.00	12.00
Rossman	35.00	25.00	12.00
Schaefer	35.00	25.00	12.00
Schmidt	35.00	25.00	12.00
Summers	35.00	25.00	12.00

	MINT	VG–E	F–G
NEW YORK YANKEES			
Chase, Hal	40.00	27.50	13.00
Chesbro, Jack	50.00	30.00	15.00
Conroy	35.00	25.00	12.00
Elberfeld, Kid	40.00	27.50	13.00
Glade	35.00	25.00	12.00
Hemphill	35.00	25.00	12.00
Keeler, Willie	60.00	40.00	17.50
Kleinow	35.00	25.00	12.00
Newton	35.00	25.00	12.00
Niles	35.00	25.00	12.00
Orth	35.00	25.00	12.00
Stahl	35.00	25.00	12.00
PHILADELPHIA ATHLETICS			
Bender, Chief	50.00	30.00	15.00
Collins, Jimmy	50.00	30.00	15.00
Coombs	35.00	25.00	12.00
Davis	35.00	25.00	12.00
Dygert	35.00	25.00	12.00
Hartsel	35.00	25.00	12.00
Murphy, D.	35.00	25.00	12.00
Nichols (Nicholls)	35.00	25.00	12.00
Oldring	35.00	25.00	12.00
Plank	50.00	30.00	15.00
Schreck	35.00	25.00	12.00
Seybold	35.00	25.00	12.00
ST. LOUIS BROWNS			
Ferris	35.00	25.00	12.00
Hoffman	35.00	25.00	12.00
Howell	35.00	25.00	12.00
Jones, T.	35.00	25.00	12.00
Powell	35.00	25.00	12.00
Spencer	35.00	25.00	12.00
Stone	35.00	25.00	12.00
Waddell, Rube	50.00	30.00	15.00
Williams	35.00	25.00	12.00
WASHINGTON NATIONALS			
Clymer	35.00	25.00	12.00
Delahanty, Jim	35.00	25.00	12.00
Ganley	35.00	25.00	12.00
Freeman	35.00	25.00	12.00
Johnson, Walter	75.00	50.00	20.00
McBride	35.00	25.00	12.00
Patten	35.00	25.00	12.00
Milan	35.00	25.00	12.00
Shipke	35.00	25.00	12.00
Smith	35.00	25.00	12.00
Warner	35.00	25.00	12.00

WANTED

Postcards of Baseball players wanted for personal collection. Hundreds needed!!! These are needs for a serious collector. Should have POST CARD backs, but will make some exceptions. Will pay good prices for quality post cards, in Excellent condition. Especially pre-1940 cards.

Our greatest interests are in cards from a publisher, however, we will buy or trade for others.

Condition is of the greatest importance. The rule is half value for anything less than excellent-mint.

These are our main wants, but will consider any offerings of quality or bulk.

PC741 - Bill & Bob
PC742 - Boston American Series
PC743 - H. H. Bregstone
PC757 - Sporting News
PC758 - Max Stein
PC759 - Sunbeam - Pureta
PC760 - TR Company
PC761 - Van Patrick
PC762 - Don Wingfield
PC765 - A. C. Dietsche
PC770 - American League Pub. Co.
PC772 - L. L. Cook Co.
PC773 - Topping & Co.
PC773 - Wolverine News Co.
PC773 - H. M. Taylor
PC774 - Film Fotos, Inc.
PC775 - G. F. Grignon Co.
PC776 - Boston Dailey Souviner
PC778 - Morgan Stationary
PC782 - Rotograph Co.
PC783 - Sears-East St. Louis
PC787 - Souvenir PC Shop
PC786 - Obcajo Photo Art
PC787 - A. W. Spargo
PC797 - Gunther Beer
PC799 - Cinn. World Champs

+++++ PLEASE QUOTE OTHERS +++++ PLEASE QUOTE OTHERS +++++

Also want photographer cabinet (Usually 5x7) photos of Baseball players and teams. These usually have photo mounted on heavy cardboard. Please send on approval. Will likely take all.

Also want novelity or fold-out post cards of players, teams, stadiums and other unusal baseball cards.
Especially interested in post cards of negro players, teams, and stadiums. Federal League players, team and stadiums. Baseball post cards with advertising.

Also purchase large or small lots of Tobacco, candy, gum and meat cards with pictures of Baseball player shown.

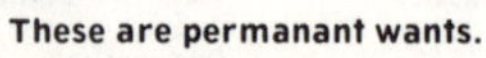

These are permanant wants.

Please send offers or approvals to:

TOM COLLIER
107 DELAWARE AVENUE
ELKTON, MARYLAND 21921
301-398-0722

BOSTON BRAVES			
Beaumont	35.00	25.00	12.00
Brown	35.00	25.00	12.00
Dahlen	35.00	25.00	12.00
Ferguson	35.00	25.00	12.00
Lindeman	35.00	25.00	12.00
Ritchey	35.00	25.00	12.00
BROOKLYN DODGERS			
Alperman	35.00	25.00	12.00
Hummel	35.00	25.00	12.00
Lumley	35.00	25.00	12.00
Maloney	35.00	25.00	12.00
McIntyre	35.00	25.00	12.00
Rucker	35.00	25.00	12.00
Sheehan	35.00	25.00	12.00
CHICAGO CUBS			
Brown, Mordecai	50.00	30.00	15.00
Chance, Frank	50.00	30.00	15.00
Evers, Johnny	50.00	30.00	15.00
Hofman	35.00	25.00	12.00
Kling	35.00	25.00	12.00
Overall	35.00	25.00	12.00
Reulbach	35.00	25.00	12.00
Schulte	35.00	25.00	12.00
Sheckard	35.00	25.00	12.00
Slagle	35.00	25.00	12.00
Steinfeldt	35.00	25.00	12.00
Tinker, Joe	50.00	30.00	15.00
CINCINNATI REDS			
Campbell	35.00	25.00	12.00
Coakley	35.00	25.00	12.00
Ewing, Bob	35.00	25.00	12.00
Ganzel	35.00	25.00	12.00
Huggins, Miller	50.00	30.00	15.00
Hulswitt	35.00	25.00	12.00
Lobert	35.00	25.00	12.00
McLean	35.00	25.00	12.00
Mitchell	35.00	25.00	12.00
Mowery	35.00	25.00	12.00
Paskert	35.00	25.00	12.00
Weimer	35.00	25.00	12.00
NEW YORK GIANTS			
Bresnahan, Roger	50.00	30.00	15.00
Devlin	35.00	25.00	12.00
Donlin	35.00	25.00	12.00
Doyle	35.00	25.00	12.00
Mathewson, Christy	75.00	50.00	20.00
McGinnity, Joe	50.00	30.00	15.00
Seymour	35.00	25.00	12.00
Shannon	35.00	25.00	12.00
Taylor	35.00	25.00	12.00
Tenney	35.00	25.00	12.00
Wiltse	35.00	25.00	12.00
PHILADELPHIA PHILS			
Bransfield	35.00	25.00	12.00
Brown, Buster	35.00	25.00	12.00
Corridon	35.00	25.00	12.00
Dooin	35.00	25.00	12.00
Doolan	35.00	25.00	12.00
Grant	35.00	25.00	12.00
Knabe	35.00	25.00	12.00
Magee	35.00	25.00	12.00
McQuillan	35.00	25.00	12.00
Osborne	35.00	25.00	12.00
Sparks	35.00	25.00	12.00
Titus	35.00	25.00	12.00
PITTSBURGH PIRATES			
Abbaticchio	35.00	25.00	12.00
Camnitz	35.00	25.00	12.00
Clarke, Fred	50.00	30.00	15.00
Gibson	35.00	25.00	12.00
Kane	35.00	25.00	12.00
Leach	35.00	25.00	12.00
Maddox	35.00	25.00	12.00
Philippe, Deacon	40.00	27.50	13.00
Thomas	35.00	25.00	12.00
Wagner, Honus	75.00	50.00	20.00
Wilson	35.00	25.00	12.00
Young	35.00	25.00	12.00
ST. LOUIS CARDINALS			
Barry	35.00	25.00	12.00
Beebe	35.00	25.00	12.00
Bryne	35.00	25.00	12.00
Delahanty, Joe	35.00	25.00	12.00
Gilbert	35.00	25.00	12.00
Hoesetter	35.00	25.00	12.00
Karger	35.00	25.00	12.00
Konetchy	35.00	25.00	12.00
Lush	35.00	25.00	12.00
McGlynn	35.00	25.00	12.00
Murray	35.00	25.00	12.00
O'Rourke, Patsy	35.00	25.00	12.00
SCRANTON			
Bills	50.00	30.00	15.00
Graham	50.00	30.00	15.00
Halligan	50.00	30.00	15.00
Houser	50.00	30.00	15.00
Moran	50.00	30.00	15.00
Schultz	50.00	30.00	15.00
Steele	50.00	30.00	15.00
NO TEAM NAMED			
Coakley	35.00	25.00	12.00
Knight	35.00	25.00	12.00
Schlei	35.00	25.00	12.00
Spade	35.00	25.00	12.00
Speaker, Tris	60.00	40.00	17.50

PC761 VAN PATRICK (24) 3 1/2" X 5 1/2"

This set of 24 black and white postcards was issued in 1949 and features Cleveland Indian players only. The cards were obtained by writing to Van Patrick, then the Cleveland announcer. The backs of the postcards featured the name of the player on the front in a short note from Van Patrick. Two cards of Feller exist.

Dear Fan:

Here's your autographed photo of **Bob Lemon.**

Cordially,

Van Patrick

	MINT	VG–E	F–G
COMPLETE SET	750.00	425.00	160.00
COMMON PLAYER	25.00	15.00	6.00
1 Black	25.00	15.00	6.00
2 Bockman	25.00	15.00	6.00
3 Boudreau	30.00	17.50	8.00
4 Conway	25.00	15.00	6.00
5 Edwards	25.00	15.00	6.00
6 Embree	25.00	15.00	6.00
7 Feller (2)	35.00	20.00	10.00
8 Fleming	25.00	15.00	6.00

PC761 Van Patrick-1949

9 Gettel	25.00	15.00	6.00
10 Gordon	25.00	15.00	6.00
11 Gromek	25.00	15.00	6.00
12 Harder	25.00	15.00	6.00
13 Hegan	25.00	15.00	6.00
14 Keltner	25.00	15.00	6.00
15 Klieman	25.00	15.00	6.00
16 Lemon	30.00	17.50	8.00
17 Lopez	30.00	17.50	8.00
18 Metkovich	25.00	15.00	6.00
19 Mitchell	25.00	15.00	6.00
20 Robinson, E.	25.00	15.00	6.00
21 Ruszowski	25.00	15.00	6.00
22 Seerey	25.00	15.00	6.00
23 Stephens, B.	25.00	15.00	6.00

PC762 DON WINGFIELD (7) (37) (1) 3 1/2" X 5 1/2"

This set of black & white and color postcards was issued in 1955 and consists of three definite types. Type I postcards consist of Washington Senator players only and feature the player's name – Washington Nationals, copyright 1955 – Don Wingfield, Griffith Stadium, Washington, D.C., at the base on the front. The Type II postcards feature players from many teams and present the player's name on the back down the center of the card. The Type III postcard is in color and consists of but one card (Killebrew). Multiple player poses of several of the Type II postcards exist.

	MINT	VG–E	F–G
COMPLETE SET	120.00	55.00	17.50
COMMON PLAYER (TYPE I)	3.00	1.50	.50
COMMON PLAYER (TYPE II)	1.50	.75	.25
TYPE I			
Dressen	3.00	1.50	.50
Fitzgerald	3.00	1.50	.50
Sievers	4.00	2.00	1.00
Stobbs	3.00	1.50	.50
Stone	3.00	1.50	.50
Vernon	3.00	1.50	.50
Yost	3.00	1.50	.50
TYPE II			
Allison (2)	1.50	.75	.25
Banks	3.00	1.50	.50
Battey (2)	1.50	.75	.25
Cash	1.50	.75	.25
Coates	1.50	.75	.25
Colavito	1.50	.75	.25
Cottier	1.50	.75	.25
Daniels	1.50	.75	.25
Dobbek	1.50	.75	.25
Fox, N.	2.00	1.00	.30
Gentile	1.50	.75	.25
Green, G.	1.50	.75	.25
Hamilton	1.50	.75	.25
Hamlin	1.50	.75	.25
Hernandez	1.50	.75	.25
Hobaugh	1.50	.75	.25
Howard, E.	2.00	1.00	.30
Johnson, G.	1.50	.75	.25
Kemmerer	1.50	.75	.25
Killebrew (3)	2.50	1.25	.40
Long, D.	1.50	.75	.25
Mantle	4.00	2.00	1.00
Maris	2.50	1.25	.40
Mays	4.00	2.00	1.00
Musial	3.50	1.75	.75
Osteen	1.50	.75	.25
Retzer	1.50	.75	.25
Robinson, B.	3.00	1.50	.50
Rudolph	1.50	.75	.25
Stenhouse	1.50	.75	.25
Valdivielso	1.50	.75	.25
Woodling	1.50	.75	.25
Zipfel	1.50	.75	.25
TYPE III			
Killebrew	4.00	2.00	1.00

PC765-1 A. C. DIETSCHE (16) (15) (3) 3 1/2" X 5 1/2"

This set of black and white postcards was issued during the 1907-1909 time period and features Detroit Tiger players only. The cards are listed by year of issue in the checklist below. The 1908 cards exist with the name on the front and without the name on the front. Those with the name on the front are asterisked in the checklist below.

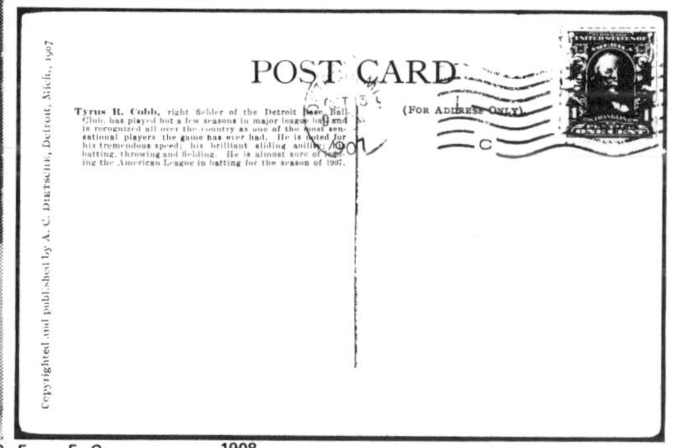

	MINT	VG–E	F–G
COMPLETE SET	500.00	225.00	85.00
COMMON PLAYER	8.00	4.00	2.00
1907			
Cobb, Tyrus (2)	20.00	14.00	10.00
Coughlin, William	8.00	4.00	2.00
Crawford, Samuel	12.00	6.00	3.00
Donovan, William	8.00	4.00	2.00
Downs, Jerome	8.00	4.00	2.00
Jennings, Hughie	12.00	6.00	3.00
Jones, David	8.00	4.00	2.00
Killian, Edward	8.00	4.00	2.00
Mullin, George	8.00	4.00	2.00
O'Leary, Charles	8.00	4.00	2.00
Payne, Fred	8.00	4.00	2.00
Rossman, Claud	8.00	4.00	2.00
Schaefer, Herman	8.00	4.00	2.00
Schmidt, Charles	8.00	4.00	2.00
Siever, Edward	8.00	4.00	2.00
1908			
*Beckendorf, Henry	8.00	4.00	2.00
Crawford, Samuel	12.00	6.00	3.00
Donovan, William	8.00	4.00	2.00
*Downs, Jerome	8.00	4.00	2.00
Jennings, Hughie	12.00	6.00	3.00
*Killian, Edward	8.00	4.00	2.00
*McIntyre, Matthew	8.00	4.00	2.00
*Moriarty, George	8.00	4.00	2.00
*Payne, Fred	8.00	4.00	2.00
*Schmidt, Charles	8.00	4.00	2.00
*Stanage, Oscar	8.00	4.00	2.00
*Summers, Oren Edgar	8.00	4.00	2.00
*Thomas, (Ira)	8.00	4.00	2.00
*Willett, Edgar	8.00	4.00	2.00
*Winter, (George)	8.00	4.00	2.00
1909			
Delahanty, James	8.00	4.00	2.00
Jones, Tom	8.00	4.00	2.00
Works, Ralph	8.00	4.00	2.00

PC 765-2 A. C. DIETSCHE (15) 3 3/8" X 5 3/8"

This second set of Dietsche postcards was issued in 1907 and features Chicago Cubs only. Cards have been seen with and without the player's name on the front.

	MINT	VG–E	F–G
COMPLETE SET	210.00	100.00	40.00
COMMON PLAYER	8.00	4.00	2.00
Brown, Mordecai	12.00	6.00	3.00
Chance, Frank	12.00	6.00	3.00
Evers, Johnny	12.00	6.00	3.00
Hoffman, Arthur	8.00	4.00	2.00
Kling, John	8.00	4.00	2.00
Lungren, Carl	8.00	4.00	2.00
Moran, Patrick	8.00	4.00	2.00
Overall, Orval	8.00	4.00	2.00

Pfeister, John	8.00	4.00	2.00
Reulbach, Edward	8.00	4.00	2.00
Schulte, Frank	8.00	4.00	2.00
Sheckard, James	8.00	4.00	2.00
Steinfeldt, Harry	8.00	4.00	2.00
Slagle, James	8.00	4.00	2.00
Tinker, Joseph	12.00	6.00	3.00

PC766 ROBERT ROBINSON SERIES (4) 3 1/2" X 5 1/2"

This set of four Robert Robinson paintings was copyrighted by the Edward Gross Company of New York. The set is rather attractive and interesting as it both features odd subjects and is multicolored.

	MINT	VG–E	F–G
COMPLETE SET	100.00	65.00	30.00
Batter	15.00	12.00	6.00
Catcher	15.00	12.00	6.00
Little Boy Pitcher	15.00	12.00	6.00
Group of Fans	15.00	12.00	6.00

PC767 REQUENA "K" (21?) 3 1/2" X 5 3/8"

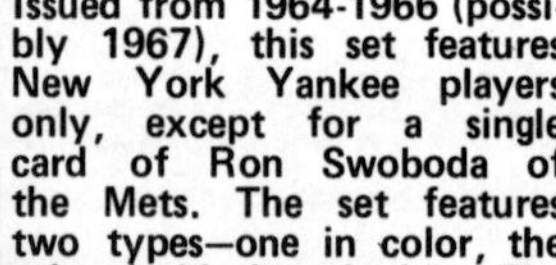

Issued from 1964-1966 (possibly 1967), this set features New York Yankee players only, except for a single card of Ron Swoboda of the Mets. The set features two types—one in color, the other in black and white. The number listed with the Type I color cards in the checklist below is that found at the middle base on the reverse. Like the Dormand and Bill and Bob postcards, Requena postcards feature a K on the lower left of the reverse.

YOGI BERRA
Catcher-Manager — New York Yankees

PLACE STAMP HERE

POST CARD
Address

Color Photo by Requena

69891

	MINT	VG–E	F–G
COMPLETE SET	100.00	46.00	23.00
COMMON PLAYER (B & W)	2.00	1.00	.50
COMMOM PLAYER (Color)	4.00	2.00	1.00
TYPE I COLOR			
Barber - 101461	2.00	1.00	.50
Berra - 69891	6.00	4.00	2.00
Blanchard - 74284	2.00	1.00	.50
Bouton - 66881	2.00	1.00	.50
Boyer - 66880	2.00	1.00	.50
Ford - 66888	6.00	4.00	2.00
Howard - 66885	5.00	3.00	1.50
Kubek - 66884	5.00	3.00	1.50
Linz - 66443	2.00	1.00	.50
Peterson	2.00	1.00	.50
Pepitone - 66883	2.00	1.00	.50
Ramos - 78909	2.00	1.00	.50
Richardson - 66889	2.00	1.00	.50
Stafford - 66887	2.00	1.00	.50
Stottlemyre - 78910	2.00	1.00	.50
Terry - 66886	2.00	1.00	.50
Tresh - 66882	2.00	1.00	.50
TYPE II B & W			
Bridges	2.00	1.00	.50
Ford	4.00	2.00	1.00
Tresh	2.00	1.00	.50
METS			
Swoboda	4.00	2.00	1.00

PC768 H. F. GARDNER SPORTS (5) STARS 3 1/2" X 5 5/8"

HANK AND TOMMY AARON
Both of the brothers were born and reared in Mobile, Alabama. Hank plays rightfield and is one of the top players in the National League. His batting average is usually among the best in the League, and has one of the best arms in the league, as well as being a good glove man. Tommy Aaron usually plays first base, but is such a good all-around player that he is moved to other positions when needed. Both are favorites with Milwaukee Braves fans.

C15066

Color by H. F. Gardner

This colorful 1960's set features black stars only. The reverses can be identified by the line "Color by H.F. Gardner" at the lower left. A short biography of the subject player(s) is present on the reverse.

	MINT	VG–E	F–G
COMPLETE SET	13.00	9.50	4.00
1 Hank & Tommy Aaron	4.00	3.00	1.50
2 Billy Burton	2.00	1.50	.50
3 Lee Maye	2.00	1.50	.50
4 Billy Williams	2.50	2.00	1.00
5 Jesse Owens	2.00	1.50	.50

PC770 AMERICAN LEAGUE (15) PUBLISHING CO. 3 3/8" X 5 1/2"

This 1908-issued set features a large action shot or pose of the player in uniform and also a small portrait of the player in street clothes in an oval at the top of the card. A short biography in a rectangular box is also featured at the base of the front, and the identifying line "American League Pub. Company, Cleveland, O." is located directly below the box.

	MINT	VG–E	F–G
COMPLETE SET	475.00	275.00	110.00
COMMON PLAYER	15.00	10.00	5.00
Bay, Harry E.	15.00	10.00	5.00
Berger, Charles	15.00	10.00	5.00
Birmingham, Joseph	15.00	10.00	5.00
Bradley, W. J.	15.00	10.00	5.00
Clarkson, Walter	15.00	10.00	5.00
Cobb, Tyrus R.	40.00	25.00	12.00
Flick, Elmer	25.00	15.00	8.00
Hickman, C. T.	15.00	10.00	5.00
Hichman, William	15.00	10.00	5.00
Joss, Adrain	25.00	15.00	8.00
Lajoie, Nap	30.00	20.00	10.00
Liebhardt, Glen	15.00	10.00	5.00
Nill, George	15.00	10.00	5.00
Perring, George	15.00	10.00	5.00
Wagner, Honus	35.00	22.50	11.00

PC F. J. OFFERMAN (19?) 3 1/2" X 5 1/2"

This set was issued in 1908 by F.J. Offerman and bears remarkable similarities to the PC770 American League Publishing set above. Like the PC770 set, this set features a large action shot of the player plus a smaller street clothes shot enclosed in an oval on the front of the card. The set features Buffalo players only.

	MINT	VG–E	F–G
COMPLETE SET	450.00	250.00	100.00
COMMON PLAYER	15.00	10.00	5.00
Archer, James	15.00	10.00	5.00
Cleary, James	15.00	10.00	5.00
Hestefer, Larry	15.00	10.00	5.00
Hill, Hunter	15.00	10.00	5.00
Kester, William H.	15.00	10.00	5.00
Kisinger, Charles	15.00	10.00	5.00
Knapp, Leri	15.00	10.00	5.00
McAllister, Lew	15.00	10.00	5.00
McConnell, George N.	15.00	10.00	5.00
Milligan, William J.	15.00	10.00	5.00
Murray, James	15.00	10.00	5.00
Nattress, William H.	15.00	10.00	5.00
Parrott, Ralph	15.00	10.00	5.00
Ryan, John B.	15.00	10.00	5.00
Schirm, George	15.00	10.00	5.00
Smith, George	15.00	10.00	5.00
Vowinkle, John H.	15.00	10.00	5.00
White, John	15.00	10.00	5.00
Whitney, Merton	15.00	10.00	5.00

PC773-1 TOPPING AND COMPANY (20) 3 1/2" X 5 3/8"

This set of Detroit Tiger stars is believed to have been issued in late 1909 and early 1910. This distinctive set features yellow bands at the top and bottom and a face shot of the player in the center of a six-pointed star, which also contains a yellow outline. The words "Tiger Stars" are printed in the upper yellow band whereas the player's name and position appears in the lower band. Topping and Publishers Company, Detroit, is identified on the reverse.

	MINT	VG–E	F–G
COMPLETE SET	1200.00	650.00	200.00
COMMON PLAYER	35.00	20.00	8.00
Beckendorf, Henry - Catcher	35.00	20.00	8.00
Bush, Donie - Shortstop	35.00	20.00	8.00
Cobb, Ty - Right Field	100.00	60.00	20.00
Crawford, Sam - Center Field	50.00	30.00	12.00
Delahanty, Jim - Second Base	35.00	20.00	8.00
Donovan, Bill - Pitcher	35.00	20.00	8.00
Jennings, Hughie - Manager	50.00	30.00	12.00
Jones, Davey - Utility	35.00	20.00	8.00
Jones, Tom - First Base	35.00	20.00	8.00
Killian, Ed - Pitcher	35.00	20.00	8.00
McIntyre, Matty - Left Field	35.00	20.00	8.00
Moriarty, George - Third Base	35.00	20.00	8.00
Mullin, George - Pitcher	35.00	20.00	8.00
O'Leary, Charlie - Utility	35.00	20.00	8.00
Schmidt, Charlie - Catcher	35.00	20.00	8.00
Speer, George - Pitcher	35.00	20.00	8.00
Stanage, Oscar - Catcher	35.00	20.00	8.00
Summers, Eddie - Pitcher	35.00	20.00	8.00
Willet, Edgar - Pitcher	35.00	20.00	8.00
Works, Ralph - Pitcher	35.00	20.00	8.00

PC773-2 H. M. TAYLOR (7) 3 1/2" X 5 1/2"

The H.M. Taylor postcard set was issued during the 1909-1911 time period and features Detroit Tiger players only. The cards are black and white with a rather large border around the card. The name of the player and the activity in the picture is listed on the front of the card. The H.M. Taylor identification is presented on the back of the card.

Post Card

Put a One Cent Stamp Here

Rights reserved by H. M. Tay'or, Detroit

	MINT	VG–E	F–G
COMPLETE SET	225.00	135.00	60.00
COMMON PLAYER	15.00	10.00	5.00
Tyrus Cobb at bat	35.00	20.00	10.00
Bill Coughlin batting	15.00	10.00	5.00
Sam Crawford - Ready for the ball	20.00	15.00	9.00
Detroit Team Card	15.00	10.00	5.00
Floral Horsehoe presented to "Wild" Bill Donovan at Philadelphia	15.00	10.00	5.00
"Wee Ah" - Yours truly Hughie Jennings	20.00	15.00	9.00
"Wild" Bill Donovan, Hughie Jennings, Frank Chance - In dugout	25.00	18.00	9.50

PC773-3 WOLVERINE NEWS CO. (20) 3 3/8" X 5 3/8"

The 1909 Wolverine News Company postcard issue features Detroit Tiger players only. Two poses each of Ty Cobb and Sam Crawford highlight this black and white set. The Wolverine News Company identification is printed on the back of the card.

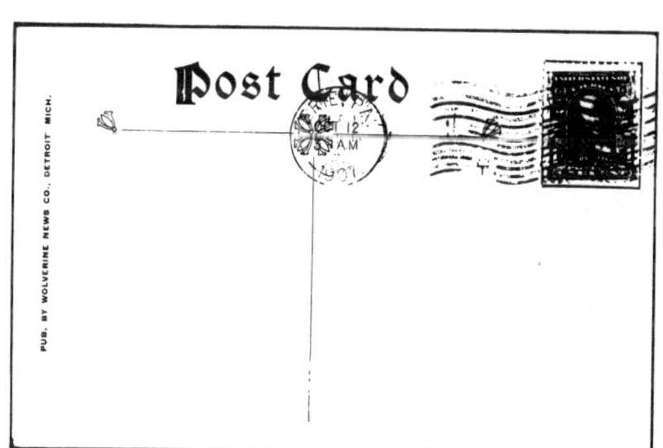

	MINT	VG–E	F–G
COMPLETE SET	525.00	300.00	125.00
COMMON PLAYER	12.00	8.00	4.00
Ty Cobb at bat	40.00	25.00	12.00
Cobb, Ty - Right Field	40.00	25.00	12.00
Coughlin, Bill - Capt. and 3rd Baseman	12.00	8.00	4.00
Crawford, Sam - Bunting	20.00	15.00	9.00
Crawford, Sam - Center Field	20.00	15.00	9.00
Donovan, "Wild Bill" - Pitcher	12.00	8.00	4.00
Downs, Jerry - Utility	12.00	8.00	4.00
Jennings, Hughie - Manager	20.00	15.00	9.00
Jennings on the coaching line	20.00	15.00	9.00
Jones, Davey	12.00	8.00	4.00
Killian, Ed - Pitcher	12.00	8.00	4.00
Mullin, George - Pitcher	12.00	8.00	4.00
O'Leary, Charlie	12.00	8.00	4.00
Payne, Fred - Catcher	12.00	8.00	4.00
Rossman, Claude - 1st Baseman	12.00	8.00	4.00
Schaefer, Herman	12.00	8.00	4.00
Schaefer & O'Leary working the double play	12.00	8.00	4.00
Schmidt, Charlie - Catcher	12.00	8.00	4.00
Siever, Eddie - Pitcher	12.00	8.00	4.00
"Wild" Bill at the water wagon	12.00	8.00	4.00

PC775 G. F. GRIGNON CO. (16) 3 1/2" X 5 1/2"

This rather intersting postcard set issued in 1907 features a Chicago Cub player in a circle in the upper right corner on the front of the card. In addition to the player, an animated teddy bear on a green field is presumably reciting an obnoxious punch line. While the cards are unnumbered, the set is believed to be complete at 16.

	MINT	VG–E	F–G
COMPLETE SET	550.00	350.00	150.00
COMMON PLAYER	20.00	15.00	8.00
1 Brown, Mordecai - Pitcher	25.00	18.00	10.00
2 Chance, Capt. Frank - First Base and Manager	25.00	18.00	10.00
3 Evers, John - Second Baseman	25.00	18.00	10.00
4 Hofman, Arthur - Utility player	20.00	15.00	8.00
5 Kling, John - Catcher	20.00	15.00	8.00
6 Lundgren, Carl - Pitcher	20.00	15.00	8.00
7 Moran, Pat - Catcher	20.00	15.00	8.00
8 Overall, Orvie - Pitcher	20.00	15.00	8.00
9 Pfiester, Jack - Pitcher	20.00	15.00	8.00
10 Ruehlback, Ed - Pitcher	20.00	15.00	8.00
11 Schulte, Frank - Right Field	20.00	15.00	8.00
12 Sheckard, James - Left Field	20.00	15.00	8.00
13 Slagle, James - Center Field	20.00	15.00	8.00
14 Steinfeldt, Harry - Third Base	20.00	15.00	8.00
15 Taylor, Jack - Pitcher	20.00	15.00	8.00
16 Tinker, Joe - Shortstop	25.00	18.00	10.00

PC778 MORGAN STATIONARY (10) 3 1/2" X 5 3/8"

This color set features Ohio baseball players in action, all photos of which were taken at the Palace of Stars Stadium in Cincinnati. All the players are shown wearing a red belt; consequently, this set has been called the Red Belt Set. The set is believed to be complete at 10 cards.

	MINT	VG–E	F–G
COMPLETE SET	120.00	60.00	15.00
COMMON PLAYER	6.00	3.00	1.00
1 A Home Run - Shows Toledo player rounding third.	6.00	3.00	1.00
2 After a High One - Shows player in uniform reaching for high ball.	6.00	3.00	1.00
3 Hit & Run - Shows player in white uniform bunting.	6.00	3.00	1.00
4 In Consultation - Shows three Toledo players in group.	6.00	3.00	1.00
5 Its All in the Game - "Noise" Shows player in dark uniform with hands cupped at mouth.	6.00	3.00	1.00
6 Miller Huggins - Second Baseman - Par Excellence.	20.00	15.00	5.00
7 Out to the Long Green - Shows player in white uniform hitting fungos.	6.00	3.00	1.00
8 Practice Makes Perfect - Shows pitcher (Leever) about to pitch. (Leever was from Goshen, Ohio)	6.00	3.00	1.00
9 Safe	6.00	3.00	1.00
10 Use Two If Necessary - Shows player in white uniform holding two bats on shoulder.	6.00	3.00	1.00

PC782 ROTOGRAPH CO. (10) 3 1/4" X 5 3/8"

This rather distinguished looking set was printed by the Rotograph Company of New York in 1905. Some of the cards are numbered while others are not. The Clark Griffith card was initially issued with the name misspelled and later reissued corrected. The Rotograph identification is printed on the back of the card. New York teams only are portrayed.

POST CARD

The Rotograph Co., N. Y. City.

This side for the Address.

	MINT	VG–E	F–G
COMPLETE SET	475.00	250.00	100.00
B319 Puttman, A.	35.00	20.00	10.00
B320 Chesbro, Jack (2)	45.00	30.00	15.00
B321 Brown, George	30.00	15.00	8.00
B322 Dahlen, Wm. F.	30.00	15.00	8.00
B323 McGraw, John J.	45.00	30.00	15.00
B324 Griffill (misspelled), Clark	60.00	40.00	20.00
B324 Griffith, Clark	45.00	30.00	15.00
– McGinnity, Joe	45.00	30.00	15.00
– Taylor, Luther	30.00	15.00	8.00

PC783 SEARS–EAST ST. LOUIS (61) 3 1/2" X 5 3/8"

This black and white set was issued in 1946 and given away by Sears at their East St. Louis location. The set features St. Louis Cardinals and St. Louis Browns only. The backs of the cards are blank. Two poses of John Miller of the Browns exist.

	MINT	VG–E	F–G
COMPLETE SET	850.00	450.00	190.00
COMMON PLAYER	10.00	6.00	3.00
CARDINALS			
Adams, Buster	10.00	6.00	3.00
Barrett, Red	10.00	6.00	3.00
Beazley, Johnny	10.00	6.00	3.00
Brazle, Al	10.00	6.00	3.00
Burkhart, Ken	10.00	6.00	3.00
Burmeister, Jerry	10.00	6.00	3.00
Cross, Joffre	10.00	6.00	3.00
Dickson, Murray	10.00	6.00	3.00
Dusak, Erv	10.00	6.00	3.00
Dyer, Eddie	10.00	6.00	3.00
Endicott, Bill	10.00	6.00	3.00
Gonzales, Mike	10.00	6.00	3.00
Klein, Lou	10.00	6.00	3.00
Klutz, Clyde	10.00	0.00	3.00
Krist, Howard	10.00	6.00	3.00
Marion, Marty	14.00	9.00	4.50
Martin, Fred	10.00	6.00	3.00
Moore, Terry	10.00	6.00	3.00
Musial, Stan	20.00	12.00	6.00
Pollet, Howard	10.00	6.00	3.00
Rice, Del	10.00	6.00	3.00
Schoendienst, Al	14.00	9.00	4.50
Sessi, Walt	10.00	6.00	3.00
Sisler, Dick	10.00	6.00	3.00
Slaughter, Enos	14.00	9.00	4.50
Surkont, Max	10.00	6.00	3.00
Walker, Harry	10.00	6.00	3.00
Wares, Buzzy	10.00	6.00	3.00
White, Ernie	10.00	6.00	3.00
Wilks, Ted	10.00	6.00	3.00

BROWNS

Berardino, John	12.00	8.00	4.00
Biscan, Frank	10.00	6.00	3.00
Christman, Mark	10.00	6.00	3.00
Dahlgren, Babe	10.00	6.00	3.00
Dillinger, Bob	10.00	6.00	3.00
Ferens, Stanley	10.00	6.00	3.00
Galehouse, Dennis	10.00	6.00	3.00
Grace, Joe	10.00	6.00	3.00
Heath, Jeff	10.00	6.00	3.00
Helf, Henry	10.00	6.00	3.00
Hoffman, Fred	10.00	6.00	3.00
Judnich, Walt	10.00	6.00	3.00
Kinder, Ellis	10.00	6.00	3.00
Kramer, Jack	10.00	6.00	3.00
Laabs, Chester	10.00	6.00	3.00
Lucadello, John	10.00	6.00	3.00
Manuso, Frank	10.00	6.00	3.00
McQuillen, Glenn	10.00	6.00	3.00
Miller, John (2)	10.00	6.00	3.00
Muncrief, Bob	10.00	6.00	3.00
Potter, Nelson	10.00	6.00	3.00
Sears, Ken	10.00	6.00	3.00
Sewell, Luke	10.00	6.00	3.00
Schultz, Joe	10.00	6.00	3.00
Shirley, Tex	10.00	6.00	3.00
Stephens, Vern	10.00	6.00	3.00
Stevens, Chuck	10.00	6.00	3.00
Taylor, Zack	10.00	6.00	3.00
Zarilla, Al	10.00	6.00	3.00
Zoldak, Sam	10.00	6.00	3.00

PC785 SOUVENIR POSTCARD SHOP (1) OF CLEVELAND 3 1/4" X 5 1/2"

This distinguished looking black and white set is similar to PC782 in appearance and it was also issued in 1905. The Souvenir Postcard Shop of Cleveland identification appears on the front of the card. The backs are devoid of company identification. While the set has been frequently reported to contain 17 Cleveland baseball players, no card other than the Lajoie card illustrated has been seen.

	MINT	VG–E	F–G
Lajoie	30.00	15.00	9.00

PC786 ORCAJO PHOTO ART (26)(5)(2) 3 1/2" X 5 1/2"

The postcards in this set come in three styles. The first contains an Orcajo Photo Art back. Type II is marked "Courtesy of Val Decker Packing Co., Piquality Brand Meats" on the front. Type III is marked "Metropolitan Clothing Co." on the front. The cards are listed in the checklist below by type. The set was issued in 1939 and features a card of Joe DiMaggio, the only apparent non-Cincinnati player. The cards are sepia in color and feature white borders.

PC786 - Orcajo Photo Art—Dayton, Ohio

	MINT	VG–E	F–G
COMPLETE SET	650.00	300.00	115.00
COMMON PLAYER (TYPE I)	12.00	6.00	3.00
COMMON PLAYER (TYPE II)	15.00	8.00	4.00
COMMON PLAYER (TYPE III)	15.00	8.00	4.00
TYPE I			
Berger, Wally	12.00	6.00	3.00
Bongiovanni, Nino	12.00	6.00	3.00
Bordagaray, Frenchy	12.00	6.00	3.00
Craft, Harry	12.00	6.00	3.00
Davis, Ray	12.00	6.00	3.00
Derringer, Paul	12.00	6.00	3.00
DiMaggio, Joe	20.00	10.00	5.00
Frey, Linus	12.00	6.00	3.00
Gamble, Lee	12.00	6.00	3.00
Goodman, Ivan	12.00	6.00	3.00
Gowdy, Hank	12.00	6.00	3.00
Grissom, Lee	12.00	6.00	3.00
Herschberger, William (name in white)	12.00	6.00	3.00
Joost, Edwin	12.00	6.00	3.00
McCormick, Frank	12.00	6.00	3.00
McKecknie, Bill - Manager	12.00	6.00	3.00
Meyers, Billy	12.00	6.00	3.00
Moore, Whitey	12.00	6.00	3.00
Riggs, Lew	12.00	6.00	3.00
Scarsella, Les	12.00	6.00	3.00
Shoffner, Milburn	12.00	6.00	3.00
Thompson, Junior	12.00	6.00	3.00
Walters, Bucky	12.00	6.00	3.00
Werber, Bill	12.00	6.00	3.00
West, Dick	12.00	6.00	3.00
Wilson, Jimmie	12.00	6.00	3.00
TYPE II			
Cooke, Alan	15.00	8.00	4.00
Frey, Linus (small projection)	15.00	8.00	4.00
Herschberger, Willard (name in black)	15.00	8.00	4.00
Lombardi, Ernie (name plain)	15.00	8.00	4.00
Vander Meer, Johnny	15.00	8.00	4.00
TYPE III			
Lombardi, Ernie (name fancy)	15.00	8.00	4.00
Vander Meer, Johnny	15.00	8.00	4.00

PC796 SEPIA ANON (25) 3 1/2" X 5 1/2"

This sepia with white border set issued circa 1910 features 25 cards of popular players of the era. No markings are found either on the fronts or on the backs of the cards to indicate a manufacturer or issuer. As can be noted from the illustration "Honus" is misspelled "Honas" on the Cobb—Wagner card in this set.

	MINT	VG–E	F–G
COMPLETE SET	1440.00	675.00	310.00
COMMON PLAYER	25.00	15.00	7.00
1 Bresnahan - Full catching pose	35.00	25.00	12.00
2 Bridwell - Stooped fielding (NY on sleeve)	25.00	15.00	7.00
3 Brown - Pitching - left leg up (Cubs)	35.00	25.00	12.00
4 Cobb - Batting to hips (Detroit)	75.00	50.00	20.00
5 Cobb, Ty and Wagner, Honus shaking hands	75.00	50.00	20.00
6 Mgr. Frank Chance - Throwing (Cubs)	35.00	25.00	12.00
7 Chase - Fielding at 1B (NY on sleeve)	25.00	15.00	7.00
8 Collins, Eddie - Batting (A's)	35.00	25.00	12.00
9 Crawford, Sam - Batting (Detroit)	35.00	25.00	12.00
10 Evers-Schaefer - Standing	35.00	25.00	12.00
11 Devlin - Glove outstretched	25.00	15.00	7.00
12 Dooin - Arms high - Ball in one hand, glove in other	25.00	15.00	7.00
13 Frock - Portrait	25.00	15.00	7.00
14 Gibson - Full catching position	25.00	15.00	7.00
15 Hoffman, Artie - Fielding for high one	25.00	15.00	7.00
16 Johnson, Walter - Pitching	60.00	40.00	18.00
17 Lajoie - Full batting pose	40.00	30.00	14.00
18 Lord, Harry, Throwing (Arms extended)	25.00	15.00	7.00
19 Mathewson - Pitching - right leg up (NY)	60.00	40.00	18.00
20 Overall - Pitching - left leg up (Cubs)	25.00	15.00	7.00
21 Plank - Portrait - arms over head	35.00	25.00	12.00
22 Speaker, Tris - Batting pose (Boston on shirt)	40.00	30.00	14.00
23 Street, Charley - Full catching about to throw	25.00	15.00	7.00
24 Wagner - Full batting pose	60.00	40.00	18.00
25 Walsh - Full bunting pose (C on shirt)	35.00	25.00	12.00

PC NOVELTY CUTLERY CO. (25) 3 1/2" X 5 1/2"

TY COBB AND HONAS WAGNER

The Novelty Cutlery Company of Canton, Ohio, postcard set of 1910 contains the same poses as the PC796 set above; however, the pictures have been reduced and enclosed in an ornate frame border. The backs of these postcards are blank. The checklist and prices listed for postcards in the PC796 set may also be used for this set, as values are comparable.

PC799 CINCINNATI REDS (24) CHAMPIONS 3 1/2" X 5 1/2"

PAT MORAN, Manager
Cincinnati "Reds" World's Champions 1919

This black and white set of Cincinnati players was issued in 1920 and appears with either of two captions in the border on the front of the card–World Champions 1919 or National League Champions 1919.

	MINT	VG–E	F–G
COMPLETE SET	575.00	275.00	80.00
COMMON PLAYER	15.00	8.00	3.00

	MINT	VG–E	F–G
1 Allen, Nick	15.00	8.00	3.00
2 Bressler, Rube	15.00	8.00	3.00
3 Daubert, Jake	15.00	8.00	3.00
4 Duncan, Pat	15.00	8.00	3.00
5 Eller, Hod	15.00	8.00	3.00
6 Fisher, Ray	15.00	8.00	3.00
7 Gerner, Eddie	15.00	8.00	3.00
8 Groh, Heinie	15.00	8.00	3.00
9 Kopf, Larry	15.00	8.00	3.00
10 Luque, Adolfo	15.00	8.00	3.00
11 Magee, Sherwood	15.00	8.00	3.00
12 Mitchell, Roy	15.00	8.00	3.00
13 Moran, Pat	15.00	8.00	3.00
14 Neale, Greasy	15.00	8.00	3.00
15 Rariden, Bill	15.00	8.00	3.00
16 Rath, Morris	15.00	8.00	3.00
17 Reuther, Walter	15.00	8.00	3.00
18 Ring, Jimmy	15.00	8.00	3.00
19 Roush, Edd	20.00	10.00	5.00
20 Sallee, Harry	15.00	8.00	3.00
21 Schreiber, Hank	15.00	8.00	3.00
22 See, Charles	15.00	8.00	3.00
23 Smith, Jimmy	15.00	8.00	3.00
24 Wingo, Ivy	15.00	8.00	3.00

PC A. J. BEGYN-SILVERCRAFT (3) 3 1/2" X 5 1/2"

This 1952-1953 set features three New York Yankee players. The reverse contains the A.J. Begyn identification vertically at the left and the Silvercraft—Dexter Press identification vertically at the center. The player's name and the New York Yankee team identification are also contained on the reverse.

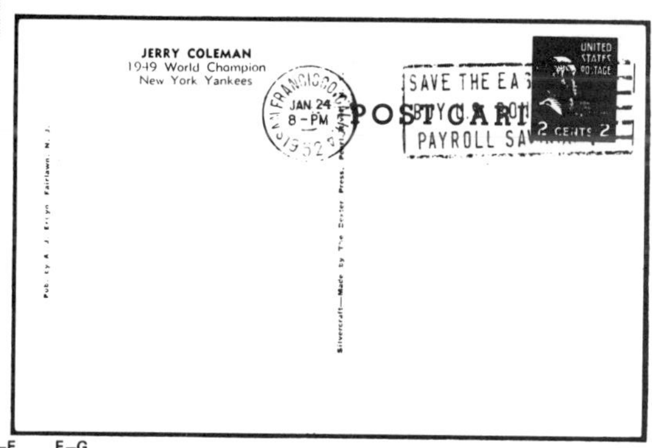

	MINT	VG–E	F–G
Coleman, Jerry	3.00	1.50	.50
Noren, Irv	3.00	1.50	.50
Woodling, Gene	3.00	1.50	.50

PC COLONIAL MEAT PRODUCTS (2) 3 1/2" X 5 3/8"

This 1954 black and white borderless postcard issue by Colonial Meat Products contains but two cards. Both of these cards feature Jimmy Piersall; however, the cropping and the color of the facsimile autograph on the front of the card are different. The backs of the cards contain a Colonial Meat advertisement and endorsement by Piersall.

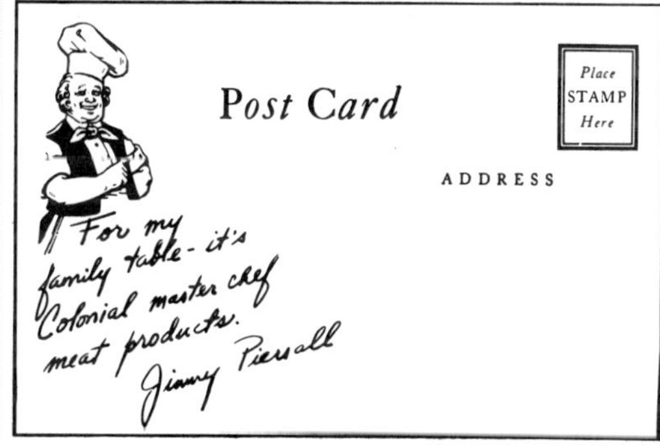

	MINT	VG–E	F–G
Jimmy Piersall - Name in black (facsimile autograph) - pictured to chest.	5.00	3.00	1.00
Jimmy Piersall - Name in blue (facsimile autograph) - pictured to hips.	5.00	3.00	1.00

PC J. J. K. COPYART (31) PHOTOGRAPHERS — 3 1/2" X 5 1/2"

This 1950 set features New York Giants, Boston Braves, Philadelphia Phillies, and a Brooklyn Dodger. The postcards are black and white glossy photos with no company identification on the back.

	MINT	VG–E	F–G
COMPLETE SET	135.00	60.00	25.00
COMMON PLAYER	3.00	1.50	.50
BOSTON BRAVES			
Crandall, Del	3.00	1.50	.50
Holmes, Tommy	4.00	2.00	1.00
Marshall, Willard	3.00	1.50	.50
Mathews, Eddie (2)	8.00	4.00	2.00
O'Connell, Danny	3.00	1.50	.50
Sisti, Sibby	3.00	1.50	.50
Stanky, Eddie	3.00	1.50	.50
BROOKLYN DODGERS			
Robinson, Jackie	10.00	5.00	2.50
PHILADELPHIA PHILLIES			
Ennis, Del	3.00	1.50	.50
Roberts, Robin	8.00	4.00	2.00
Simmons, Curt	3.00	1.50	.50
NEW YORK GIANTS			
Antonelli, Johnny (2)	3.00	1.50	.50
Calderone, Sam	3.00	1.50	.50
Hearn, Jim (2)	3.00	1.50	.50
Jansen, Larry	3.00	1.50	.50
Lockman, Whitey (2)	3.00	1.50	.50
Mueller, Don	3.00	1.50	.50
Rigney, Bill (2)	3.00	1.50	.50
Sauer, Hank	3.00	1.50	.50
Schoendienst, Red	3.00	1.50	.50
Stanky, Eddie	3.00	1.50	.50
Westrum, Wes (2)	3.00	1.50	.50
Wilheim, Hoyt	4.00	2.00	1.00
Worthington, Al	3.00	1.50	.50

PC OLMES STUDIOS (8) — 3 1/2" X 5 1/2"

The 1949 Olmes Studio set features Philadelphia players only. Two poses of Ferris Fain exist. The Olmes Studies identification is printed on the back of the postcard.

	MINT	VG–E	F–G
COMPLETE SET	35.00	15.00	5.00
COMMON PLAYER	3.00	1.50	.50
Chapman, Sam	3.00	1.50	.50
Fain, Ferris (2)	4.00	2.00	1.00
Fowler, Dick	3.00	1.50	.50
Hooper, Bob	3.00	1.50	.50
Roberts, Robin	6.00	3.00	1.50
Scheib, Carl	3.00	1.50	.50
Tipton, Joe	3.00	1.50	.50

PC GEORGE W. HULL (12) 3 1/2" X 5 1/2"

This 1907 black and white issue contains World Champion Chicago White Sox players only. Each postcard contains club president Chas. Comiskey's picture in a circle at the lower left on the front of the card; assorted White Sox players pictures in ovals on socks on a clothesline; and the subject player's picture on the right side of the card. The Geo. W. Hall identification is printed on the front of the card.

	MINT	VG–E	F–G
COMPLETE SET	400.00	250.00	140.00
COMMON PLAYER	20.00	15.00	10.00
Altrock, Nick - Pitcher	20.00	15.00	10.00
Davis, George - Shortstop	20.00	15.00	10.00
Donohue, Jiggs - 1st Baseman	20.00	15.00	10.00
Dougherty, Pat - Left Fielder	20.00	15.00	10.00
Isbell, Frank - 2nd Baseman	20.00	15.00	10.00
Jones, Capt. Fielder - Center Fielder	20.00	15.00	10.00
McFarland, Ed - Catcher	20.00	15.00	10.00
Owens, Frank - Pitcher	20.00	15.00	10.00
Patterson, Roy - Pitcher	20.00	15.00	10.00
Smith, Frank - Pitcher	20.00	15.00	10.00
Walsh, Eddie - Pitcher	30.00	20.00	15.00
White, Doc - Pitcher	20.00	15.00	10.00

PC A. W. SPARGO (12) 3 3/8" X 5 1/2"

This 1908 black and white issue features ballplayers in a large oval on the front of the card. The players featured are from the Hartford team of the Connecticut League. Four cards are known at this time. The A.W. Spargo identification is printed on the reverse vertically up the left side.

PUBLISHED BY A. W. SPARGO, HARTFORD, CONN.

Post Card

ONE CENT STAMP HERE

	MINT	VG–E	F–G
Arbogast, C. P.	15.00	10.00	5.00
Connery, Tom J.	15.00	10.00	5.00
Fisher, Ray L.	15.00	10.00	5.00
Wadleigh, C. A	15.00	10.00	5.00

W600 SPORTING LIFE CABINETS (100's) 5"X 7 1/2"

These large and attractive cabinet-type cards were issued by the Sporting Life Publishing Company around 1911. The exact number of cards in the set is not known but it is estimated to be about 450. The cards are not numbered and might appear to have a slight reddish or sepia tint. Many are found still in the glassine envelope in which they were issued. The backs are blank.

	MINT	VG-E	F-G
COMPLETE SET	16000.00	9500.00	4000.00
COMMON PLAYER	45.00	30.00	12.00

No.	Player	MINT	VG-E	F-G
1	W. Abstein	45.00	30.00	12.00
2	C. Adams	45.00	30.00	12.00
3	C. Alperman	45.00	30.00	12.00
4	N. Altrock	45.00	30.00	12.00
5	L. Ames	45.00	30.00	12.00
6	F. Arelanes	45.00	30.00	12.00
7	C. Armbruster	45.00	30.00	12.00
8	W. Armour	45.00	30.00	12.00
9	H. Arndt	45.00	30.00	12.00
10	J. Aubrey	45.00	30.00	12.00
11	J. Austin	45.00	30.00	12.00
12	C. Babb	45.00	30.00	12.00
13	Frank Baker	70.00	47.50	20.00
14	J. Barbeau	45.00	30.00	12.00
15	E. Barger	45.00	30.00	12.00
16	J. Barrett	45.00	30.00	12.00
17	J. (C.) Barry	45.00	30.00	12.00
18	J. (J.) Barry	45.00	30.00	12.00
19	H. Barton	45.00	30.00	12.00
20	H. Batch	45.00	30.00	12.00
21	J. Bates	45.00	30.00	12.00
22	H. Bay	45.00	30.00	12.00
23	C. Beaumont	45.00	30.00	12.00
24	F. Beck	45.00	30.00	12.00
25	H. Beckendorf	45.00	30.00	12.00
26	F. Beebe	45.00	30.00	12.00
27	G. Bell	45.00	30.00	12.00
28	H. Bemis	45.00	30.00	12.00
29	Chief Bender	70.00	47.50	20.00
30	J. Bennett	45.00	30.00	12.00
31	W. Bergen	45.00	30.00	12.00
32	C. Berger	45.00	30.00	12.00
33	W. Bernhardt	45.00	30.00	12.00
34	R. Bescher	45.00	30.00	12.00
35	W. Beville	45.00	30.00	12.00
36	R. Blackburne	45.00	30.00	12.00
37	E. Bliss	45.00	30.00	12.00
38	F. Bowerman	45.00	30.00	12.00
39	B. Bradley	45.00	30.00	12.00
40	W. Bradley	45.00	30.00	12.00
41	D. Brain	45.00	30.00	12.00
42	W. Bransfield	45.00	30.00	12.00
43	Roger Bresnahan	70.00	47.50	20.00
44	Al Bridwell	45.00	30.00	12.00
45	C. Brown	45.00	30.00	12.00
46	Mordecai Brown	70.00	47.50	20.00
47	S. Brown	45.00	30.00	12.00
48	G. Browne	45.00	30.00	12.00
49	J. Burke	45.00	30.00	12.00
50	J. Callahan	45.00	30.00	12.00
51	H. Camnitz	45.00	30.00	12.00
52	W. Cannell	45.00	30.00	12.00
53	J. Cantilon	45.00	30.00	12.00
54	P. Carney	45.00	30.00	12.00
55	C. Carr	45.00	30.00	12.00
56	W. Carrigan	45.00	30.00	12.00
57	J. Casey	45.00	30.00	12.00
58	Frank Chance	110.00	70.00	30.00
59	Hal Chase	50.00	35.00	15.00
60	Jack Chesbro	70.00	47.50	20.00
61	E. Cicotte	45.00	30.00	12.00
62	Fred Clarke	70.00	47.50	20.00
63	J. Clarke	45.00	30.00	12.00
64	T. Clarke	45.00	30.00	12.00
65	W. Clarkson	45.00	30.00	12.00
66	O. Clymer	45.00	30.00	12.00
67	A. Coakley	45.00	30.00	12.00
68	Ty Cobb	250.00	170.00	75.00
69	Eddie Collins	70.00	47.50	20.00
70	Jimmy Collins	70.00	47.50	20.00
71	W. Congalton	45.00	30.00	12.00
72	W. Conroy	45.00	30.00	12.00
73	R. Cooley	45.00	30.00	12.00
74	Jack Coombs	50.00	35.00	15.00
75	F. Corridon	45.00	30.00	12.00
76	W. Couglin	45.00	30.00	12.00
77	E. Courtney	45.00	30.00	12.00
78	O. Crandall	45.00	30.00	12.00
79	Sam Crawford	70.00	47.50	20.00
80	L. Criger	45.00	30.00	12.00
81	D. Criss	45.00	30.00	12.00
82	J. Cronin	45.00	30.00	12.00
83	L. Cross	45.00	30.00	12.00
84	M. Cross	45.00	30.00	12.00
85	C. Currie	45.00	30.00	12.00
86	W. Dahlen	45.00	30.00	12.00
87	G. Davis	45.00	30.00	12.00
88	H. Davis	45.00	30.00	12.00
89	J. Delehanty	45.00	30.00	12.00
90	A. Devlin	45.00	30.00	12.00
91	F. Dillon	45.00	30.00	12.00
92	W. Dineen	45.00	30.00	12.00

93 J. Dobbs	45.00	30.00	12.00
94 E. Doheny	45.00	30.00	12.00
95 C. Dolan	45.00	30.00	12.00
96 J. Donahue	45.00	30.00	12.00
97 M. Donlin	45.00	30.00	12.00
98 P. Donovan	45.00	30.00	12.00
99 W. Donovan	45.00	30.00	12.00
100 C. Dooin	45.00	30.00	12.00
101 M. Doolan	45.00	30.00	12.00
102 T. Doran	45.00	30.00	12.00
103 A. Dorner	45.00	30.00	12.00
104 P. Dougherty	45.00	30.00	12.00
105 T. Downey	45.00	30.00	12.00
106 J. Downs	45.00	30.00	12.00
107 James F. Doyle	45.00	30.00	12.00
108 Judd B. Doyle	45.00	30.00	12.00
109 Larry J. Doyle	45.00	30.00	12.00
110 Hugh Duffy	70.00	47.50	20.00
111 W. Duggleby	45.00	30.00	12.00
112 A. Dundon	45.00	30.00	12.00
113 J. Dunleavy	45.00	30.00	12.00
114 J. Dunn	45.00	30.00	12.00
115 J. Dygert	45.00	30.00	12.00
116 R. Egan	45.00	30.00	12.00
117 N. Elberfeld	45.00	30.00	12.00
118 C. Elliott	45.00	30.00	12.00
119 G. Ellis	45.00	30.00	12.00
120 Johnny Evers	70.00	47.50	20.00
121 R. Ewing	45.00	30.00	12.00
122 F. Falkenberg	45.00	30.00	12.00
123 J. Farrell	45.00	30.00	12.00
124 C. Ferguson	45.00	30.00	12.00
125 H. Ferris	45.00	30.00	12.00
126 T. Fisher	45.00	30.00	12.00
127 P. Flaherty	45.00	30.00	12.00
128 J. Flynn	45.00	30.00	12.00
129 W. Foxen	45.00	30.00	12.00
130 C. Fraser	45.00	30.00	12.00
131 W. Freil	45.00	30.00	12.00
132 A. Fromme	45.00	30.00	12.00
133 D. Fultz	45.00	30.00	12.00
134 R. Ganley	45.00	30.00	12.00
135 J. Ganzel	45.00	30.00	12.00
136 V. Garvin	45.00	30.00	12.00
137 H. Gasper	45.00	30.00	12.00
138 P. Geier	45.00	30.00	12.00
139 H. Gessler	45.00	30.00	12.00
140 G. Gibson	45.00	30.00	12.00
141 N. Gibson	45.00	30.00	12.00
142 W. Gilbert	45.00	30.00	12.00
143 F. Glade	45.00	30.00	12.00
144 H. Gleason	45.00	30.00	12.00
145 E. Grant	45.00	30.00	12.00
146 D. Green	45.00	30.00	12.00
147 E. Greminger	45.00	30.00	12.00
148 Clark Griffith	70.00	47.50	20.00
149 M. Grimshaw	45.00	30.00	12.00
150 H. Hackett	45.00	30.00	12.00
151 E. Hahn	45.00	30.00	12.00
152 F. Hahn	45.00	30.00	12.00
153 C. Hall	45.00	30.00	12.00
154 W. Hallman	45.00	30.00	12.00
155 E. Hanlon	45.00	30.00	12.00
156 R. Harmon	45.00	30.00	12.00
157 C. Harper	45.00	30.00	12.00
158 H. Hart	45.00	30.00	12.00
159 F. Hartsel	45.00	30.00	12.00
160 R. Hartzell	45.00	30.00	12.00
161 C. Hemphill	45.00	30.00	12.00
162 W. Henley	45.00	30.00	12.00
163 O. Hess	45.00	30.00	12.00
164 C. Hickman	45.00	30.00	12.00
165 H. Hill	45.00	30.00	12.00
166 H. Hillebrand	45.00	30.00	12.00
167 H. Hinchman	45.00	30.00	12.00
168 W. Hinchman	45.00	30.00	12.00
169 R. Hoblitzel	45.00	30.00	12.00
170 D. Hoffman	45.00	30.00	12.00
171 A. Hofman	45.00	30.00	12.00
172 W. Hogg	45.00	30.00	12.00
173 A. Holesketter	45.00	30.00	12.00
174 W. Holmes	45.00	30.00	12.00
175 G. Howard	45.00	30.00	12.00
176 H. Howell	45.00	30.00	12.00
177 J. Huelsman	45.00	30.00	12.00
178 Miller Huggins	70.00	47.50	20.00
179 J. Hughes	45.00	30.00	12.00
180 T. Hughes	45.00	30.00	12.00
181 R. Hulswitt	45.00	30.00	12.00
182 J. Hummell	45.00	30.00	12.00
183 H. Hyatt	45.00	30.00	12.00
184 F. Isbell	45.00	30.00	12.00
185 F. Jacklitsch	45.00	30.00	12.00
186 Joe Jackson	90.00	60.00	25.00
187 H. Jacobson	45.00	30.00	12.00
188 Hugh Jennings	70.00	47.50	20.00
189 C. Jones	45.00	30.00	12.00
190 D. Jones	45.00	30.00	12.00
191 O. Jones	45.00	30.00	12.00
192 T. Jones	45.00	30.00	12.00
193 O. Jordan	45.00	30.00	12.00
194 M. Kahoe	45.00	30.00	12.00
195 E. Karger	45.00	30.00	12.00
196 Robert F. Keefe	45.00	30.00	12.00
197 Willie Keeler	90.00	60.00	25.00
198 W. Keister	45.00	30.00	12.00
199 Joe Kelley	70.00	47.50	20.00
200 W. Kennedy	45.00	30.00	12.00
201 E. Killian	45.00	30.00	12.00
202 J. Kissinger	45.00	30.00	12.00
203 M. Kittridge	45.00	30.00	12.00
204 J. Kleinrow	45.00	30.00	12.00
205 Johnny Kling	50.00	35.00	15.00
206 B. Koehler	45.00	30.00	12.00
207 E. Konetchy	45.00	30.00	12.00
208 H. Krause	45.00	30.00	12.00
209 O. Krueger	45.00	30.00	12.00
210 G. LaChance	45.00	30.00	12.00
211 Napolean Lajoie	110.00	70.00	30.00
212 J. Lake	45.00	30.00	12.00
213 F. Laporte	45.00	30.00	12.00
214 L. Laroy	45.00	30.00	12.00
215 T. Leach	45.00	30.00	12.00
216 W. Lee	45.00	30.00	12.00
217 S. Leever	45.00	30.00	12.00
218 P. Lewis	45.00	30.00	12.00
219 V. Lindaman	45.00	30.00	12.00
220 P. Livingstone	45.00	30.00	12.00
221 J. Lobert	45.00	30.00	12.00
222 H. Long	45.00	30.00	12.00
223 B. Lord	45.00	30.00	12.00
224 H. Lord	45.00	30.00	12.00
225 H. Lumley	45.00	30.00	12.00
226 C. Lundgren	45.00	30.00	12.00
227 J. Lush	45.00	30.00	12.00
228 Connie Mack	90.00	60.00	25.00
229 N. Maddox	45.00	30.00	12.00
220 S. Magee	45.00	30.00	12.00
231 G. Magoon	45.00	30.00	12.00
232 J. Malarkey	45.00	30.00	12.00
233 W. Maloney	45.00	30.00	12.00
234 W. Marshall	45.00	30.00	12.00
235 Christy Mathewson	150.00	100.00	40.00
236 J. McAleer	45.00	30.00	12.00
237 L. McAlister	45.00	30.00	12.00
238 J. McCarthy	45.00	30.00	12.00
239 J. McCloskey	45.00	30.00	12.00
240 A. McConnell	45.00	30.00	12.00
241 H. McCormick	45.00	30.00	12.00
242 C. McFarland	45.00	30.00	12.00
243 H. McFarland	45.00	30.00	12.00
244 D.L. McGann	45.00	30.00	12.00
245 Joe McGinnity	70.00	47.50	20.00
246 John McGraw	90.00	60.00	25.00
247 H. McIntyre	45.00	30.00	12.00
248 M. McIntyre	45.00	30.00	12.00
249 J. McLean	45.00	30.00	12.00
250 Fred Merkle	50.00	35.00	15.00
251 S. Mertes	45.00	30.00	12.00
252 C. Milan	45.00	30.00	12.00
253 J. Miller	45.00	30.00	12.00
254 W. Milligan	45.00	30.00	12.00
255 F. Mitchell	45.00	30.00	12.00
256 M. Mitchell	45.00	30.00	12.00
257 E. Moore	45.00	30.00	12.00
258 P. Moran	45.00	30.00	12.00
259 L. Moren	45.00	30.00	12.00
260 H. Morgan	45.00	30.00	12.00
261 E. Moriarty	45.00	30.00	12.00
262 M. Mowery	45.00	30.00	12.00
263 G. Mullin	45.00	30.00	12.00
264 D. Murphy	45.00	30.00	12.00
265 J. Murray	45.00	30.00	12.00
266 W. Murray	45.00	30.00	12.00
267 D. Needham	45.00	30.00	12.00
268 E. Newton	45.00	30.00	12.00
269 H. Niles	45.00	30.00	12.00
270 G. Nill	45.00	30.00	12.00
271 P. Noonan	45.00	30.00	12.00
272 J. O'Brien	45.00	30.00	12.00
273 P. O'Brien	45.00	30.00	12.00
274 R. Oldring	45.00	30.00	12.00
275 C. O'Leary	45.00	30.00	12.00
276 J. O'Neil	45.00	30.00	12.00
277 M. O'Neil	45.00	30.00	12.00
278 A. Orth	45.00	30.00	12.00
279 O. Overall	45.00	30.00	12.00
280 F. Owens	45.00	30.00	12.00
281 F. Parent	45.00	30.00	12.00
282 G. Paskert	45.00	30.00	12.00
283 J. Pastorious	45.00	30.00	12.00
284 R. Paterson	45.00	30.00	12.00

285 F. Payne	45.00	30.00	12.00
286 B. Pelty	45.00	30.00	12.00
287 F. Pfeiffer	45.00	30.00	12.00
288 J. Pfiester	45.00	30.00	12.00
289 E. Phelps	45.00	30.00	12.00
290 C. Phillippe	50.00	35.00	15.00
291 W. Phillips	45.00	30.00	12.00
292 Eddie Plank	90.00	60.00	25.00
293 E. Poole	45.00	30.00	12.00
294 J. Powell	45.00	30.00	12.00
295 W. Purtell	45.00	30.00	12.00
296 A. Puttman	45.00	30.00	12.00
297 T. Raub	45.00	30.00	12.00
298 F. Raymer	45.00	30.00	12.00
299 W. Reidy	45.00	30.00	12.00
300 Ed Reulbach	50.00	35.00	15.00
301 R. Rhoades	45.00	30.00	12.00
302 D. Richie	45.00	30.00	12.00
303 C. Ritchey	45.00	30.00	12.00
304 L. Ritter	45.00	30.00	12.00
305 C. Robinson	45.00	30.00	12.00
306 G. Rohe	45.00	30.00	12.00
307 C. Rossman	45.00	30.00	12.00
308 F. Roth	45.00	30.00	12.00
309 J. Rowan	45.00	30.00	12.00
310 H. Sallee	45.00	30.00	12.00
311 H. Schaefer	45.00	30.00	12.00
312 G. Schiel	45.00	30.00	12.00
313 C. Schmidt	45.00	30.00	12.00
314 F. Schulte	45.00	30.00	12.00
315 A. Schweitzer	45.00	30.00	12.00
316 T. Sebring	45.00	30.00	12.00
317 A. Selbach	45.00	30.00	12.00
318 J. Seymour	45.00	30.00	12.00
319 W. Shannon	45.00	30.00	12.00
320 D. Shay	45.00	30.00	12.00
321 D. Shean	45.00	30.00	12.00
322 J. Sheckard	45.00	30.00	12.00
323 E. Siever	45.00	30.00	12.00
324 J. Slagle	45.00	30.00	12.00
325 J. Slattery	45.00	30.00	12.00
326 C. Smith	45.00	30.00	12.00
327 E. Smith	45.00	30.00	12.00
328 F. Smith	45.00	30.00	12.00
329 H. Smith	45.00	30.00	12.00
330 H. Smoot	45.00	30.00	12.00
331 F. Sparks	45.00	30.00	12.00
332 C. Stahl	45.00	30.00	12.00
333 Jake Stahl	50.00	35.00	15.00
334 J. Stanley	45.00	30.00	12.00
335 Harry Steinfeldt	50.00	35.00	15.00
336 G. Stone	45.00	30.00	12.00
337 G. Stovall	45.00	30.00	12.00
338 J. Stovall	45.00	30.00	12.00
339 S. Strang	45.00	30.00	12.00
340 E. Stricklett	45.00	30.00	12.00
341 W. Sudhoff	45.00	30.00	12.00
342 J. Sugden	45.00	30.00	12.00
343 W. Sullivan	45.00	30.00	12.00
344 E. Summers	45.00	30.00	12.00
345 W. Sweeney	45.00	30.00	12.00
346 L. Tannehill	45.00	30.00	12.00
347 J. Taylor	45.00	30.00	12.00
348 L. Taylor	45.00	30.00	12.00
349 F. Tenney	45.00	30.00	12.00
350 I. Thomas	45.00	30.00	12.00
351 J. Thoney	45.00	30.00	12.00
352 Joe Tinker	70.00	47.50	20.00
353 T. Turner	45.00	30.00	12.00
354 R. Unglaub	45.00	30.00	12.00
355 G. Van Haltren	45.00	30.00	12.00
356 F. Veil	45.00	30.00	12.00
357 G. "Rube" Waddell	70.00	47.50	20.00
358 C. Wagner	45.00	30.00	12.00
359 Honus Wagner	150.00	100.00	40.00
360 Bobby Wallace	70.00	47.50	20.00
361 Ed Walsh	70.00	47.50	20.00
362 J. Warner	45.00	30.00	12.00
363 A. Weaver	45.00	30.00	12.00
364 J. Weimer	45.00	30.00	12.00
365 O. White	45.00	30.00	12.00
366 R. Wicker	45.00	30.00	12.00
367 F. Wilhelm	45.00	30.00	12.00
368 E. Willett	45.00	30.00	12.00
369 J. Williams	45.00	30.00	12.00
370 O. Williams	45.00	30.00	12.00
371 G. Wiltse	45.00	30.00	12.00
372 G. Winter	45.00	30.00	12.00
373 W. Wolfe	45.00	30.00	12.00
374 H. Wolverton	45.00	30.00	12.00
375 J. Yeager	45.00	30.00	12.00
376 Denton "Cy" Young	110.00	70.00	30.00
377 I. Young	45.00	30.00	12.00
378 C. Zimmer	45.00	30.00	12.00
379 H. Zimmerman	45.00	30.00	12.00

R303-A 1939 DIAMOND STARS (48) 4" X 6 3/16"

GUM—BROWN

This series of 48 paper premiums were issued in 1939 by the Goudey Gum Company. This set carries the name Diamond Stars Gum on the reverse, although the National Chicle Company who produced the Diamond Stars baseball cards is in no way connected with this set. The backs contain instructions on various baseball disciplines. The color of the set is brown, not the more reddish color of sepia normally listed for this set.

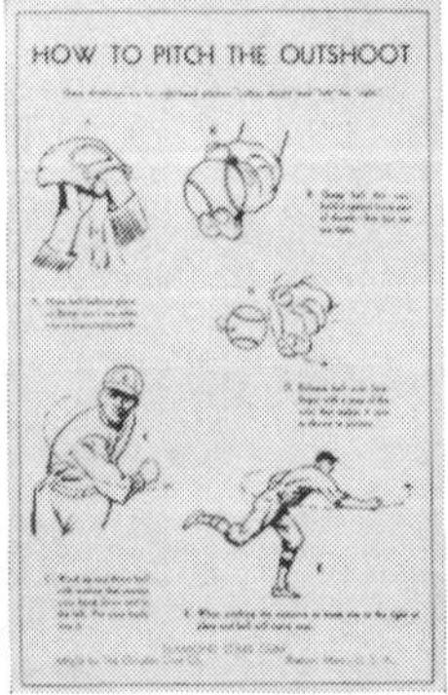

	MINT	VG-E	F-G
COMPLETE SET	500.00	350.00	150.00
COMMON PLAYER	8.50	6.00	2.50
1 Luke Appling	10.00	6.50	3.00
2 Earl Averill	10.00	6.50	3.00
3 Wally Berger	8.50	6.00	2.50
4 Darrell Blanton	8.50	6.00	2.50
5 Zeke Bonura	8.50	6.00	2.50
6 Mace Brown	8.50	6.00	2.50
7 George Case	8.50	6.00	2.50
8 Ben Chapman	8.50	6.00	2.50
9 Joe Cronin	11.00	7.25	3.25
10 Frank Crosetti	9.00	6.25	2.75
11 Paul Derringer	9.00	6.25	2.75
12 Bill Dickey	13.00	9.00	4.00
13 Joe DiMaggio	45.00	30.00	12.00
14 Bob Feller	18.00	12.00	5.00
15 Jimmy Foxx	18.00	12.00	5.00
16 Charlie Gehringer	11.00	7.25	3.25
17 Lefty Gomez	11.00	7.25	3.25
18 Ival Goodman	8.50	6.00	2.50
19 Joe Gordon	9.00	6.25	2.75
20 Hank Greenberg	11.00	7.25	3.25
21 Buddy Hassett	8.50	6.00	2.50
22 Jeff Heath	8.50	6.00	2.50
23 Tom Henrich	9.00	6.25	2.75
24 Billy Herman	10.00	6.50	3.00
25 Frank Higgins	8.50	6.00	2.50
26 Fred Hutchinson	9.00	6.25	2.75
27 Bob Johnson	8.50	6.00	2.50
28 Ken Keltner	8.50	6.00	2.50
29 Mike Kreevich	8.50	6.00	2.50
30 Ernie Lombardi	9.00	6.25	2.75
31 Gus Mancuso	8.50	6.00	2.50
32 Eric McNair	8.50	6.00	2.50

R303-A

		MINT	VG-E	F-G
33	Van Mungo	9.00	6.25	2.75
34	Buck Newsom	9.00	6.25	2.75
35	Mel Ott	13.00	9.00	4.00
36	Marvin Owen	8.50	6.00	2.50
37	Frankie Pytlak	8.50	6.00	2.50
38	Woody Rich	8.50	6.00	2.50
39	Charlie Root	8.50	6.00	2.50
40	Al Simmons	11.00	7.25	3.25
41	Jim Tabor	8.50	6.00	2.50
42	Cecil Travis	8.50	6.00	2.50
43	Hal Trosky	8.50	6.00	2.50
44	Arky Vaughn	9.00	6.25	2.75
45	Joe Vosmik	8.50	6.00	2.50
46	Lon Warneke	8.50	6.00	2.50
47	Ted Williams	30.00	20.00	8.00
48	Rudy York	9.00	6.25	2.75

R303-B 1939 DIAMOND STARS (24) 4 3/4" X 7 5/16"
GUM—BLACK & WHITE —SEPIA

This set of 24 paper photos is slightly larger than its counterpart R303-A. The photos of the R303-A series are the same ones depicted on these cards, and the reverses contain "How to" instructions and the Diamond Stars Gum name. While the photos, the checklists, and the values are the same, this set comes in two distinct colors—black and sepia.

		MINT	VG-E	F-G
COMPLETE SET		250.00	170.00	70.00
COMMON PLAYER		8.50	6.00	2.50
1	Luke Appling	10.00	6.50	3.00
2	George Case	8.50	6.00	2.50
3	Ben Chapman	8.50	6.00	2.50
4	Joe Cronin	11.00	7.25	3.25
5	Bill Dickey	13.00	9.00	4.00
6	Joe DiMaggio	45.00	30.00	12.00
7	Bob Feller	18.00	12.00	5.00
8	Jimmy Foxx	18.00	12.00	5.00
9	Lefty Gomez	11.00	7.25	3.25
10	Ival Goodman	8.50	6.00	2.50
11	Joe Gordon	9.00	6.25	2.75
12	Hank Greenberg	11.00	7.25	3.25
13	Jeff Heath	8.50	6.00	2.50
14	Billy Herman	10.00	6.50	3.00
15	Frank Higgins	8.50	6.00	2.50
16	Ken Keltner	8.50	6.00	2.50
17	Mike Kreevich	8.50	6.00	2.50
18	Ernie Lombardi	9.00	6.25	2.75
19	Gus Mancuso	8.50	6.00	2.50
20	Mel Ott	13.00	9.00	4.00
21	Al Simmons	11.00	7.25	3.25
22	Arky Vaughn	9.00	6.25	2.75
23	Joe Vosmik	8.50	6.00	2.50
24	Rudy York	9.00	6.25	2.75

HOW TO CATCH FLIES

1933 R309-1 GOUDEY PREMIUM (4) 5 1/2" X 8 15/16"

The most ambitious premium issue of the Goudey Gum Company was the R309–1 set of 1933. Printed on heavy cardboard, the black & white picture was embellished with a gold, frame-like border and a back stand.

	MINT	VG-E	F-G
COMPLETE SET	450.00	300.00	125.00
COMMON PLAYER(1-4)	100.00	65.00	30.00
1 American League All-Stars of 1933	100.00	65.00	30.00
2 National League All-Stars of 1933	100.00	65.00	30.00
3 World's Champions of 1933	100.00	65.00	30.00
4 George Herman (Babe) Ruth	175.00	115.00	50.00

1933 R309-2 GOUDEY PREMIUM (18) 5 1/2" X 9"

The cards in the R309–2 Goudey premium set are unnumbered, glossy black & white photos on thin paper stock. The ballplayer is identified by his name rendered in longhand in the "wide pen" style of later Goudey issues. This written name is not a facsimile autograph.

	MINT	VG-E	F-G
COMPLETE SET	225.00	150.00	65.00
COMMON PLAYER(1-18)	10.00	6.50	3.00
1 Boston Red Sox	12.00	8.00	3.50
2 Cleveland Indians	12.00	8.00	3.50
3 Washington Senators	12.00	8.00	3.50
4 Auker,Elden	10.00	6.50	3.00
5 Babich,Johnny	10.00	6.50	3.00
6 Bartell,Dick	10.00	6.50	3.00
7 Bell,Lester R.	10.00	6.50	3.00
8 Berger,Wally	10.00	6.50	3.00
9 Cochrane,Mickey	20.00	13.00	5.50
10 Fox,Ervin	10.00	6.50	3.00
11 Gomez,Vernon	20.00	13.00	5.50
12 Goslin,Leon "Goose	16.50	11.00	4.50
13 Greenberg,Hank	20.00	13.00	5.50
14 Melillo,Oscar	10.00	6.50	3.00
15 Ott,Mel	20.00	13.00	5.50
16 Rowe,Schoolboy	12.00	8.00	3.50
17 Tamulis,Vito	10.00	6.50	3.00
18 Walker,Gerald	10.00	6.50	3.00

1934 R310 BUTTERFINGER (65)

7 3/4" X 9 1/2"
7 7/16" X 9 7/16"

This large-size premium set comes either in paper or on heavy cardboard stock with advertising for Butterfinger or other candy at the top. The cards are unnumbered and Foxx exists as Fox or Foxx. The ACC designation is R310.

	MINT	VG-E	F-G
COMPLETE SET	450.00	300.00	125.00
COMMON PLAYER(1-65)	6.00	4.00	1.50
1 Averill,Earl	10.00	6.50	3.00
2 Bartell,Richard	6.00	4.00	1.50
3 Benton,Lawrence	6.00	4.00	1.50
4 Berger,Walter	6.00	4.00	1.50
5 Bottomley,Jim	10.00	6.50	3.00
6 Boyle,Ralph	6.00	4.00	1.50
7 Carleton,Tex	6.00	4.00	1.50
8 Carroll,Owen T.	6.00	4.00	1.50
9 Chapman,Ben	6.00	4.00	1.50
10 Cochrane,Mickey	12.00	8.00	3.50
11 Collins,James	6.00	4.00	1.50
12 Cronin,Joe	12.00	8.00	3.50
13 Crowder,Alvin	6.00	4.00	1.50
14 Dean,"Dizzy"	20.00	13.00	5.50
15 Derringer,Paul	7.00	4.75	2.00
16 Dickey,William	14.00	10.00	4.00
17 Durocher,Leo	8.00	5.50	2.25
18 Earnshaw,George	6.00	4.00	1.50
19 Ferrell,Richard	6.00	4.00	1.50
20 Fonseca,Lew	6.00	4.00	1.50
21 Foxx,Jimmy(2)	20.00	13.00	5.50
22 Frey,Benny	6.00	4.00	1.50
23 Frisch,Frankie	12.00	8.00	3.50
24 Gehrig,Lou	30.00	20.00	8.00
25 Gehringer,Chas.	12.00	8.00	3.50
26 Gomez,Vernon	12.00	8.00	3.50
27 Grabowski,Ray	6.00	4.00	1.50
28 Grove,Robert	14.00	10.00	4.00
29 Haas,George (Mule)	6.00	4.00	1.50
30 Hafey,"Chick"	10.00	6.50	3.00
31 Harris,Stanley	10.00	6.50	3.00
32 Hogan,Francis J.	6.00	4.00	1.50
33 Holley,Ed	6.00	4.00	1.50
34 Hornsby,Rogers	16.50	11.00	4.50
35 Hoyt,Waite	10.00	6.50	3.00
36 Johnson,Walter	16.50	11.00	4.50
37 Jordan,Jim	6.00	4.00	1.50
38 Kuhel,Joe	6.00	4.00	1.50
39 Lee,Hal	6.00	4.00	1.50
40 Mancuso,Gus	6.00	4.00	1.50
41 Manush,Henry	10.00	6.50	3.00
42 Marberry,Fred	6.00	4.00	1.50
43 Martin,Pepper	7.00	4.75	2.00
44 Melillo,Oscar	6.00	4.00	1.50
45 Moore,Johnny	6.00	4.00	1.50
46 Morrisey,Joe	6.00	4.00	1.50
47 Mowrey,Joe	6.00	4.00	1.50
48 O'Farrell,Bob	6.00	4.00	1.50
49 Ott,Melvin	14.00	10.00	4.00
50 Pearson,Monte	6.00	4.00	1.50
51 Reynolds,Carl	6.00	4.00	1.50
52 Ruffing,Chas.	10.00	6.50	3.00
53 Ruth,"Babe"	45.00	30.00	12.00
54 Ryan,John "Blondy"	6.00	4.00	1.50
55 Simmons,Al	10.00	6.50	3.00
56 Spohrer,Al	6.00	4.00	1.50
57 Suhr,Gus	6.00	4.00	1.50
58 Swetonic,Steve	6.00	4.00	1.50
59 Vance,"Dazzy"	10.00	6.50	3.00
60 Vosmik,Joe	6.00	4.00	1.50
61 Waner,Lloyd	10.00	6.50	3.00
62 Waner,Paul	10.00	6.50	3.00
63 West,Sam	6.00	4.00	1.50
64 Whitehill,Earl	6.00	4.00	1.50
65 Wilson,Jimmy	6.00	4.00	1.50

ATTEND A SPORTS MEMORABILIA SHOW OR CONVENTION IN YOUR AREA SOMETIME THIS YEAR. THEY ARE BOTH INTERESTING AND ENJOYABLE TO ALL MEMBERS OF THE FAMILY.

1936 R311 LEATHER SURFACE (15) 6" X 8"

1936 R311 GLOSSY SURFACE (28) 6" X 8"

The 1936 R311 set of Portraits and Team Baseball Photos exist in two different forms. Fifteen leather-like or uneven surface cards comprise the first type. Twenty-eight glossy surface, sepia or black and white cards comprise the second type. The Boston Red Sox team exists with or without a sky above the building at the right of the card. Scarcities include Pepper Martin, Harder, Rowe, and the Dodgers, Pirates, Braves, and Columbus team cards.

	MINT	VG-E	F-G
COMPLETE SET	540.00	360.00	150.00
COMMON PLAYER(LEATHERY)	15.00	10.00	4.00
COMMON PLAYER(GLOSSY)	7.50	5.00	2.00
L 1 Paul Derringer	15.00	10.00	4.00
L 2 West Ferrell	15.00	10.00	4.00
L 3 Jimmy Foxx	36.00	24.00	10.00
L 4 Charlie Gehringer	24.00	16.00	7.00
L 5 Mel Harder	15.00	10.00	4.00
L 6 Gabby Hartnett	21.00	14.00	6.00
L 7 Rogers Hornsby	30.00	20.00	8.00
L 8 Connie Mack	30.00	20.00	8.00
L 9 Van Mungo	15.00	10.00	4.00
L10 Steve O'Neill	15.00	10.00	4.00
L11 Charles Ruffing	21.00	14.00	6.00
L12 DiMaggio-Crosetti-Lazzeri	45.00	30.00	12.00
L13 Arky Vaughn-Honus Wagner	30.00	20.00	8.00
L14 American League Pennant Winners -1935	15.00	10.00	4.00
L15 National League Pennant Winners -1935	15.00	10.00	4.00
G 1 Earl Averill	11.00	7.00	3.00
G 2 James L. "Jim" Bottomley	11.00	7.00	3.00
G 3 Gordon S. "Mickey" Cochrane	13.00	9.00	4.00
G 4 Joe Cronin	13.00	9.00	4.00
G 5 Jerome"Dizzy" Dean	20.00	13.00	5.50
G 6 Jimmy Dykes	7.50	5.00	2.00
G 7 Jimmy Foxx	16.50	11.00	4.50
G 8 Frankie Frisch	13.00	9.00	4.00
G 9 Henry "Hank" Greenberg	13.00	9.00	4.00
G10 Mel Harder	7.50	5.00	2.00
G11 Ken Keltner	7.50	5.00	2.00
G12 Pepper Martin	7.50	5.00	2.00
G13 Lynwood "Schoolboy" Rowe	7.50	5.00	2.00
G14 William "Bill" Terry	13.00	9.00	4.00
G15 Harold "Pie" Traynor	13.00	9.00	4.00
G16 American League All Stars-1935	7.50	5.00	2.00
G17 American League Pennant Winners -1934 (Detroit Tigers)	7.50	5.00	2.00
G18 Boston Braves-1935	13.00	9.00	4.00
G19 Boston Red Sox(2)	9.00	6.00	2.50
G20 Brooklyn Dodgers -1935	13.00	9.00	4.00
G21 Chicago White Sox-1935	9.00	6.00	2.50
G22 Columbus Red Birds-1934 Pennant Winners of American Assoc.	9.00	6.00	2.50
G23 National League All Stars-1934	7.50	5.00	2.00
G24 National League Champions-1935 (Chicago Cubs)	7.50	5.00	2.00
G25 New York Yankees -1935	9.00	6.00	2.50
G26 Pittsburgh Pirates-1935	9.00	6.00	2.50
G27 St. Louis Browns -1935	9.00	6.00	2.50
G28 The World Champions 1934 (St. Louis Cards)	9.00	6.00	2.50

1936 R312 (50) 4" X 5 1/2"

The 1936 R312 Baseball Photos set contains 25 color tinted, single player cards, listed with the letter A in the checklist; 14 multiple player cards, listed with the letter B in the checklist; 6 action cards with handwritten signatures, listed with the letter C in the checklist; and 5 action cards with printed titles, listed with the letter D in the checklist. The Allen card is reportedly more difficult to obtain than other cards in the set.

	MINT	VG-E	F-G
COMPLETE SET	450.00	300.00	120.00
COMMON CARDS	7.00	4.75	2.00
A 1 John Thomas Allen	9.00	6.00	2.50
A 2 Cy Blanton	7.00	4.75	2.00
A 3 Mace Brown	7.00	4.75	2.00
A 4 Dolph Camilli	7.00	4.75	2.00
A 5 Gordon Cochrane	11.00	7.00	3.00
A 6 "Rip" Collins	7.00	4.75	2.00
A 7 Ki Ki Cuyler	9.00	6.00	2.50
A 8 Bill Dickey	15.00	10.00	4.00
A 9 Joe DiMaggio	60.00	40.00	16.00
A10 "Chas." Dressen	8.00	5.50	2.25
A11 Benny Frey	7.00	4.75	2.00
A12 Hank Greenberg	11.00	7.00	3.00
A13 Mel Harder	7.00	4.75	2.00
A14 Rogers Hornsby	18.00	12.00	5.00
A15 Ernie Lombardi	8.00	5.50	2.25
A16 Pepper Martin	8.00	5.50	2.25
A17 "Johnny" Mize	9.00	6.00	2.50
A18 Van L. Mungo	7.00	4.75	2.00
A19 Bud Parmalee	7.00	4.75	2.00
A20 Chas. Ruffing	9.00	6.00	2.50
A21 Eugene Schott	7.00	4.75	2.00
A22 Casey Stengel	21.00	14.00	6.00
A23 Bill Sullivan	7.00	4.75	2.00
A24 Bill Swift	7.00	4.75	2.00
A25 Ralph Winegarner	7.00	4.75	2.00
B 1 Ollie Bejma-Rolly Hemsley	7.00	4.75	2.00
B 2 Cliff Bolton-Earl Whitehill	7.00	4.75	2.00
B 3 Bordagaray-Earnshaw	7.00	4.75	2.00
B 4 Cavaretta, Herman, Jurges, Hack	8.00	5.50	2.25
B 5 Pete Fox,"Jo Jo" White,Goslin	8.00	5.50	2.25
B 6 Galan, Herman, Lindstrom, Hartnett, 5 others	8.00	5.50	2.25
D 7 Harris-Cronin	9.00	6.00	2.50
B 8 Hartnett-Warnecke (sp.)	8.00	5.50	2.25
B 9 Hoag-Gomez	8.00	5.50	2.25
B10 Allen Lothoron-Rogers Hornsby	9.00	6.00	2.50
B11 Mack-Grove	18.00	12.00	5.00
B12 Taylor-Speaker-Cuyler	9.00	6.00	2.50
B13 Walker-Haas-Kreevich	7.00	4.75	2.00
B14 Paul and Lloyd Waner, and "Big Jim" Weaver	9.00	6.00	2.50
C 1 Altrock-Schacht, Clowning on the Diamond	8.00	5.50	2.25
C 2 Bell (St. Louis) Out At First "Zeke" Bonura first baseman	7.00	4.75	2.00
C 3 Jim Collins (Safe) and Stan Hack	7.00	4.75	2.00
C 4 Jimmie Foxx batting, Luke Sewell catching	9.00	6.00	2.50
C 5 Lopez Traps Two Cubs on Third Base	8.00	5.50	2.25
C 6 "Pie" Traynor-Augie Galan	8.00	5.50	2.25
D 1 Alvin Crowder, after victory in the World Series	7.00	4.75	2.00
D 2 Floyd Vaughn, present Pirate Short Stop, and Coach Hans Wagner	9.00	6.00	2.50
D 3 Gabby Hartnett crossing home plate after hitting homer...	8.00	5.50	2.25
D 4 Kids flock around Schoolboy Rowe, as he leaves Cubs park...	7.00	4.75	2.00
D 5 Van Atta, St. Louis pitcher, out at plate - Ferrell, Boston, catching	7.00	4.75	2.00

1936 R313 NATIONAL CHICLE (120) 3 1/4" X 5 3/8"
FINE PEN PREMIUMS

The 1936 Fine Pen premiums were issued anonymously by the National Chicle Company. The cards are blank backed, unnumbered and are among those premiums that could be obtained directly from a retail outlet rather than through the mail only. Four types of cards exist. Cards portraying but one player are listed with the letter A in the checklist; cards which portray several players are listed with a B in the checklist; cards which feature action poses are listed with a C in the checklist; and 1934 World Series cards featuring the Tigers and Cardinals are listed with a D in the checklist. The ACC designation is R313.

	MINT	VG-E	F-G
COMPLETE SET	675.00	450.00	180.00
COMMON CARDS (A)	2.25	1.50	.65
COMMON CARDS (B)	3.00	2.00	.80
COMMON CARDS (C)	3.75	2.50	1.00
COMMON CARDS (D)	10.00	6.50	3.00
A1 Melo Almada	2.25	1.50	.65
A2 Paul Andrews	2.25	1.50	.65
A3 Elden Auker	2.25	1.50	.65
A4 Earl Averill	3.75	2.50	1.00
A5 Jim Becher	2.25	1.50	.65
A6 Moe Berg	3.00	2.00	.80
A7 Walter Berger	2.25	1.50	.65
A8 Charles Berry	2.25	1.50	.65
A9 Ralph Birkhofer	2.25	1.50	.65
A10 "Cy" Blanton	2.25	1.50	.65
A11 O. Bluege	2.25	1.50	.65
A12 Cliff Bolton	2.25	1.50	.65
A13 Zeke Bonura	2.25	1.50	.65
A14 Thos. Bridges	2.25	1.50	.65
A15 Sam Byrd	2.25	1.50	.65
A16 Dolph Camilli	2.25	1.50	.65
A17 Bruce Campbell	2.25	1.50	.65
A18 Walter "Kit" Carson	2.25	1.50	.65
A19 Ben Chapman	2.25	1.50	.65
A20 "Rip" Collins	2.25	1.50	.65
A21 Joe Cronin	4.50	3.00	1.20
A22 Frank Crosetti	3.00	2.00	.80
A23 Paul Derringer	3.00	2.00	.80
A24 Bill Dietrich	2.25	1.50	.65
A25 Carl Doyle	2.25	1.50	.65
A26 Pete Fox	2.25	1.50	.65
A27 Frankie Frisch	4.50	3.00	1.20
A28 Martin Galatzer	2.25	1.50	.65
A29 Chas. Gehringer	4.50	3.00	1.20
A30 Charley Gelbert	2.25	1.50	.65
A31 Jose Gomez	2.25	1.50	.65
A32 Leon Goslin	3.75	2.50	1.00
A33 Hank Gowdy	2.25	1.50	.65
A34 "Hank" Greenberg	4.50	3.00	1.20
A35 "Lefty" Grove	6.00	4.00	1.60
A36 Stan Hack	2.25	1.50	.65
A37 Odell Hale	2.25	1.50	.65
A38 Wild Bill Hallahan	2.25	1.50	.65
A39 Mel Harder	2.25	1.50	.65
A40 Stanley Bucky Harris	3.75	2.50	1.00
A41 Frank Higgins	2.25	1.50	.65
A42 Oral C. Hildebrand	2.25	1.50	.65
A43 Myril Hoag	2.25	1.50	.65
A44 Rogers Hornsby	8.00	5.50	2.25
A45 Waite Hoyt	3.75	2.50	1.00
A46 Willis G. Hudlin(2)	2.25	1.50	.65
A47 "Woody" Jensen(2)	2.25	1.50	.65
A48 Wm. Knickerbocker	2.25	1.50	.65
A49 Joseph Kuhel	2.25	1.50	.65
A50 Cookie Lavagetto	2.25	1.50	.65
A51 Thornton Lee	2.25	1.50	.65
A52 Red Lucas	2.25	1.50	.65
A53 Pepper Martin	3.00	2.00	.80
A54 Joe Medwick	4.50	3.00	1.20
A55 Oscar Melillo	2.25	1.50	.65
A56 "Buddy" Meyer	2.25	1.50	.65
A57 Wallace Moses	2.25	1.50	.65
A58 V. Mungo	2.25	1.50	.65
A59 Lamar Newsom	2.25	1.50	.65
A60 Lewis "Buck" Newsom	2.25	1.50	.65
A61 Steve O'Neill	2.25	1.50	.65
A62 Tommie Paden	2.25	1.50	.65
A63 E. Babe Phillips	2.25	1.50	.65
A64 Bill Rogell	2.25	1.50	.65
A65 Lynn "Schoolboy" Rowe	3.00	2.00	.80
A66 Al Simmons	4.50	3.00	1.20
A67 Leon "Moose" Solters	2.25	1.50	.65
A68 Casey Stengel	8.00	5.50	2.25
A69 Bill Swift	2.25	1.50	.65
A70 Cecil Travis	2.25	1.50	.65
A71 "Pie" Traynor	4.50	3.00	1.20
A72 Wm. Urbansky	2.25	1.50	.65
A73 Arky Vaughn	3.00	2.00	.80
A74 Joe Vosmik	2.25	1.50	.65
A75 Honus Wagner	8.00	5.50	2.25
A76 Rube Walberg	2.25	1.50	.65
A77 Bill Walker	2.25	1.50	.65
A78 Gerald Walker	2.25	1.50	.65
A79 Bill Werber	2.25	1.50	.65
A80 Sam West	2.25	1.50	.65
A81 Pinkey Whitney	2.25	1.50	.65
A82 Vernon Whitshire	2.25	1.50	.65
A83 "Pep" Young	2.25	1.50	.65
B1 Babe and his babes	3.00	2.00	.80
B2 Stan Bordagaray-Geo. Earnshaw	3.00	2.00	.80
B3 James Bucher-John Babich	3.00	2.00	.80
B4 Ben Chapman-Bill Werber	3.00	2.00	.80
B5 Chicago White Sox 1936	3.75	2.50	1.00
B6 Fence Busters	3.00	2.00	.80
B7 Fox-Simmons-Cochrane	8.00	5.50	2.25
B8 "Gabby" and "KiKi"	6.00	4.00	1.60
B9 Gomez-Ruffing	6.00	4.00	1.60
B10 Hartnett-Warneke	3.75	2.50	1.00
B11 Diamond Daddies-Mack, McGraw	8.00	5.50	2.25
B12 Capt. Bill Myer-Mgr. Chas. Dressen	3.00	2.00	.80
B13 P & L Waner - Big Jim Weaver	6.00	4.00	1.60
B14 Wes-Rick (Ferrells)	3.00	2.00	.80
C1 Altrock-Schacht	3.75	2.50	1.00
C2 Big Bosses Clash-Dykes safe	3.75	2.50	1.00
C3 Bottomley tagging Gelbert	3.75	2.50	1.00
C4 Camilli catches Jurges off first	3.75	2.50	1.00

R313 (CONTINUED)

	MINT	VG-E	F-G
C5 CCS Radcliffe safe Harnett catching	3.75	2.50	1.00
C6 CCS Sewell blocks runner at plate	3.75	2.50	1.00
C7 CCS Washington safe	3.75	2.50	1.00
C8 Joe DiMaggio slams it, Erickson catching	18.00	12.00	5.00
C9 Double Play-McQuinn to Stine	3.75	2.50	1.00
C10 Dykes catches Crossetti between 2nd and 3rd	3.75	2.50	1.00
C11 Glenn uses football play at plate	3.75	2.50	1.00
C12 Greenberg doubles Dickey catching	6.00	4.00	1.60
C13 Hassett makes the out	3.75	2.50	1.00
C14 Lombardi says "Ugh"	3.75	2.50	1.00
C15 McQuinn gets his man	3.75	2.50	1.00
C16 Randy Moore hurt stealing second	3.75	2.50	1.00
C17 T. Moore out at plate - Wilson catching	3.75	2.50	1.00
C18 Sewell waits for ball while Clift scores	3.75	2.50	1.00
C19 Talking it over	3.75	2.50	1.00
C20 There she goes! CCS	3.75	2.50	1.00
C21 Ump says "No," Cleveland vs. Detroit	3.75	2.50	1.00
C22 L. Waner at bat, Gabby Hartnett behind plate	6.00	4.00	1.60
C23 World Series, 1935, Goslin out at first	6.00	4.00	1.60
D 1 Tommy Bridges	10.00	6.50	3.00
D 2 Mickey Cochrane	21.00	14.00	6.00
D 3 Dizzy Dean	36.00	24.00	9.00
D 4 Paul Dean	12.00	8.00	3.50
D 5 Frank Frisch	21.00	14.00	6.00
D 6 Goose Goslin	15.00	10.00	4.00
D 7 Bill Hallahan	10.00	6.50	3.00
D 8 Firpo Marberry	10.00	6.50	3.00
D 9 Pepper Martin	12.00	8.00	3.50
D10 Joe Medwick	15.00	10.00	4.00
D11 Bill Rogell	10.00	6.50	3.00
D12 "Jo-Jo" White	10.00	6.50	3.00

1936 GOUDEY WIDE PEN (137) PREMIUMS

3 1/4" X 5 1/2"

1936 GOUDEY WIDE PEN (41) CANADIAN PREMIUMS

3 1/4 X 5 1/2"

The 1936 Wide Pen Premiums were issued by the Goudey Gum Company. These black & white, unnumbered cards could be obtained directly from a retail outlet rather than through the mail only. Four types of this card exist. Type A contains cards, mainly individual players, with "Litho USA" in the bottom border. Type B does not have the "Litho USA" marking and comes both with and without a border. Type C cards are American players on creamy paper stock with medium thickness signatures and no "Litho USA" markings. Type D consists of Canadian players from Montreal (M) or Toronto (T) on creamy stock paper with non-glossy photos. The ACC designation is R314.

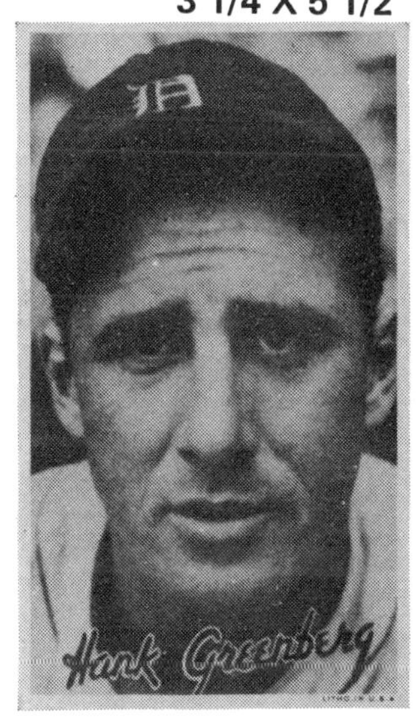

	MINT	VG-E	F-G
COMPLETE SET	900.00	600.00	250.00
COMMON CARD (A)	2.25	1.50	.65
COMMON CARD (B)	4.50	3.00	1.20
COMMON CARD (C)	4.50	3.00	1.20
COMMON CARD (D)	11.00	7.00	3.00
A1 Ethan Allen	2.25	1.50	.65
A2 Earl Averill	3.75	2.50	1.00
A3 Dick Bartell(hor)	2.25	1.50	.65
A4 Dick Bartell(port)	6.00	4.00	1.60
A5 Walter Berger	2.25	1.50	.65
A6 Geo. Blaeholder	2.25	1.50	.65
A7 "Cy" Blanton(port)	2.25	1.50	.65
A8 "Cliff" Bolton	2.25	1.50	.65
A9 Stan Bordagaray	2.25	1.50	.65
A10 Tommy Bridges (portrait)	2.25	1.50	.65
A11 Bill Brubaker	2.25	1.50	.65
A12 Sam Byrd	2.25	1.50	.65
A13 Dolph Camilli	2.25	1.50	.65
A14 Clydell Castleman (th)	2.25	1.50	.65
A15 Clydell Castleman (portrait)	2.25	1.50	.65
A16 Phil Cavaretta (hor)	2.25	1.50	.65
A17 "Mickey" Cochrane	4.50	3.00	1.20
A18 Earl Coombs(hor)	6.00	4.00	1.60
A19 Joe Coscarart	2.25	1.50	.65
A20 Joe Cronin	4.50	3.00	1.20
A21 Frank Crosetti	3.00	2.00	.80
A22 Tony Cuccinello	2.25	1.50	.65
A23 "KiKi" Cuyler	3.75	2.50	1.00
A24 Curt Davis	2.25	1.50	.65
A25 Virgil Davis(hor)	2.25	1.50	.65
A26 Paul Derringer	3.00	2.00	.80
A27 "Bill" Dickey	6.00	4.00	1.60
A28 Jimmy Dykes(kneel)	2.25	1.50	.65
A29 "Rick" Ferrell (horiz)	2.25	1.50	.65
A30 Wes Ferrell	2.25	1.50	.65
A31 Lou Finney	2.25	1.50	.65
A32 Ervin "Pete" Fox (port)	2.25	1.50	.65
A33 Tony Freitas	2.25	1.50	.65
A34 Lonnie Frey	2.25	1.50	.65
A35 Frankie Frisch	4.50	3.00	1.20
A36 "Augie" Galan (port)	2.25	1.50	.65
A37 Charles Gehringer	4.50	3.00	1.20
A38 Charlie Gelbert	2.25	1.50	.65
A39 "Lefty" Gomez	4.50	3.00	1.20
A40 "Goose" Goslin	3.75	2.50	1.00
A41 Earl Grace	2.25	1.50	.65
A42 Hank Greenberg (port)	4.50	3.00	1.20
A43 "Mule" Haas	2.25	1.50	.65
A44 Odell Hale	2.25	1.50	.65
A45 Bill Hallahan	2.25	1.50	.65

R314 (CONTINUED)

	MINT	VG-E	F-G
A46 "Mel" Harder	2.25	1.50	.65
A47 "Bucky" Harris	3.75	2.50	1.00
A48 "Gabby" Hartnett	18.00	12.00	5.00
A49 Ray Hayworth	2.25	1.50	.65
A50 Rolly Hemsley	2.25	1.50	.65
A51 Babe Herman	3.00	2.00	.80
A52 Frank Higgins (port)	2.25	1.50	.65
A53 Oral Hildebrand	2.25	1.50	.65
A54 Myril Hoag	2.25	1.50	.65
A55 Waite Hoyt	4.50	3.00	1.20
A56 Woody Jensen	2.25	1.50	.65
A57 Bob Johnson	2.25	1.50	.65
A58 "Buck" Jordan	2.25	1.50	.65
A59 Alex Kampouris	2.25	1.50	.65
A60 "Chuck" Klein	3.75	2.50	1.00
A61 Joe Kuhel	2.25	1.50	.65
A62 Lyn Lary	2.25	1.50	.65
A63 Harry Lavagetto	2.25	1.50	.65
A64 Sam Leslie	2.25	1.50	.65
A64 Freddie Lindstrom	3.75	2.50	1.00
A66 Lombardi (hor.)	3.00	2.00	.80
A67 "Al" Lopez (hor.)	4.50	3.00	1.20
A68 Dan MacFayden	2.25	1.50	.65
A69 John Marcum	2.25	1.50	.65
A70 "Pepper" Martin	3.00	2.00	.80
A71 Eric McNair	2.25	1.50	.65
A72 "Ducky" Medwick	3.75	2.50	1.00
A73 Gene Moore	2.25	1.50	.65
A74 Randy Moore	2.25	1.50	.65
A75 Terry Moore	2.25	1.50	.65
A76 Edward Moriarty	2.25	1.50	.65
A77 "Wally" Moses (port)	2.25	1.50	.65
A78 "Buddy" Myer	2.25	1.50	.65
A79 "Buck" Newsom	2.25	1.50	.65
A80 Fred Ostermueller	2.25	1.50	.65
A81 Marvin Owen	2.25	1.50	.65
A82 Tommy Padden	2.25	1.50	.65
A83 Ray Pepper	2.25	1.50	.65
A84 Tony Piet	2.25	1.50	.65
A85 "Rabbit" Pytlak (hor)	2.25	1.50	.65
A86 "Rip" Radcliff	2.25	1.50	.65
A87 Bobby Reis	2.25	1.50	.65
A88 "Lew" Riggs	2.25	1.50	.65
A89 Bill Rogell	2.25	1.50	.65
A90 "Red" Rolfe	2.25	1.50	.65
A91 "Schoolboy" Rowe (port)	3.00	2.00	.80
A92 Al Schacht	2.25	1.50	.65
A93 "Luke" Sewell	2.25	1.50	.65
A94 Al Simmons(port)	4.50	3.00	1.20
A95 John Stone	2.25	1.50	.65
A96 Gus Suhr	2.25	1.50	.65
A97 Joe Sullivan	2.25	1.50	.65
A98 Bill Swift	2.25	1.50	.65
A99 Vito Tamulis	2.25	1.50	.65
A100 Dan Taylor	2.25	1.50	.65
A101 Cecil Travis	2.25	1.50	.65
A102 Hal Troskey(port)	2.25	1.50	.65
A103 "Bill" Urbanski	2.25	1.50	.65
A104 Russ Van Atta	2.25	1.50	.65
A105 "Arky" Vaughn	3.00	2.00	.80
A106 Gerald Walker	2.25	1.50	.65
A107 "Buck" Walters	3.00	2.00	.80
A108 Lloyd Waner	3.75	2.50	1.00
A109 Paul Waner	3.75	2.50	1.00
A110 "Lon" Warneke	2.25	1.50	.65
A111 Warstler	2.25	1.50	.65
A112 Bill Werber	2.25	1.50	.65
A113 "Jo-Jo" White	2.25	1.50	.65
A114 Burgess Whitehead	2.25	1.50	.65
A115 John Whitehead (port)	2.25	1.50	.65
A116 Whitlow Wyatt	2.25	1.50	.65
A117 Ben Chapman.80			
A118 DiMaggio-McCarthy	24.00	16.00	7.00
A119 Wes & Rick Ferrell	3.75	2.50	1.00
A120 Frank Pytlak-Steve O'Neil	3.00	2.00	.80
B1 Mel Almada	4.50	3.00	1.20
B2 Lucius Appling (port)	4.50	3.00	1.20
B3 Henry Bonura(port)	4.50	3.00	1.20
B4 Bg (port)	4.50	3.00	1.20
B3 Henry Bonura(port)	4.50	3.00	1.20
B4 B4 Ben Chapman-Bill Werber	4.50	3.00	1.20
B5 Herman Clifton	4.50	3.00	1.20
B6 Roger "Doc" Cramer	4.50	3.00	1.20
B7 Joe Cronin	9.00	6.00	2.50
B8 Jimmy Dykes	4.50	3.00	1.20
B9 Ervin "Pete" Fox	4.50	3.00	1.20
B10 Jimmy Foxx	15.00	10.00	4.00
B11 Hank Greenberg	9.00	6.00	2.50
B12 Oral Hildebrand	4.50	3.00	1.20
B13 Alex Hooks(hor)	4.50	3.00	1.20
B14 Willis Hudlin	4.50	3.00	1.20
B15 Bill Knickerbocker	4.50	3.00	1.20
B16 Heinie Manush	7.50	5.00	2.00
B17 Steve O'Neill	4.50	3.00	1.20
B18 Marvin Owen	4.50	3.00	1.20
B19 Al Simmons	9.00	6.00	2.50
B20 Lem"Moose" Solters	4.50	3.00	1.20
B21 Hal Troskey	4.50	3.00	1.20
B22 Joe Vosmik(port)	4.50	3.00	1.20
B23 Joe Vosmik (batting)	4.50	3.00	1.20
B24 Earl Whitehill	4.50	3.00	1.20
C1 "Luke" Appling (batting)	7.50	5.00	2.00
C2 Earl Averill	7.50	5.00	2.00
C3 "Cy" Blanton	4.50	3.00	1.20
C4 "Zeke" Bonura (batting)	4.50	3.00	1.20
C5 Tom Bridges(port)	4.50	3.00	1.20
C6 "Joe" DiMaggio	45.00	30.00	12.00
C7 "Bobby" Doerr	4.50	3.00	1.20
C8 Jimmy Dykes(hor)	4.50	3.00	1.20
C9 "Bob" Feller	15.00	10.00	4.00
C10 "Elbie" Fletcher	4.50	3.00	1.20
C11 Pete Fox(batting)	4.50	3.00	1.20
C12 "Gus" Galan (batting)	4.50	3.00	1.20
C13 Charles Gehringer	9.00	6.00	2.50
C14 Hank Greenberg	9.00	6.00	2.50
C15 Mel Harder	4.50	3.00	1.20
C16 "Gabby" Hartnett	7.50	5.00	2.00
C17 "Pinky" Higgins	4.50	3.00	1.20
C18 Carl Hubbell	9.00	6.00	2.50
C19 "Wally" Moses (batting)	4.50	3.00	1.20
C20 Lou Newsom	4.50	3.00	1.20
C21 "Schoolboy" Rowe (throw)	4.50	3.00	1.20
C22 Julius Solters	4.50	3.00	1.20
C23 "Hal" Trosky	4.50	3.00	1.20
C24 Joe Vosmik(kneel)	4.50	3.00	1.20
C25 Johnnie Whitehead (throw)	4.50	3.00	1.20
D1 Buddy Bates(M)	11.00	7.00	3.00
D2 Del Bissonette(M)	11.00	7.00	3.00
D3 Lincoln Blakely(T)	11.00	7.00	3.00
D4 Isaac J. Boone(T)	11.00	7.00	3.00
D5 John H. Burnett(T)	11.00	7.00	3.00
D6 Leon Chagnon(M)	11.00	7.00	3.00
D7 Gus Dugas (M)	11.00	7.00	3.00
D8 Henry N. Erickson	11.00	7.00	3.00
D9 Art Funk (T)	11.00	7.00	3.00
D10 George Granger(M)	11.00	7.00	3.00
D11 Thomas G. Heath	11.00	7.00	3.00
D12 Phil Hensick(M)	11.00	7.00	3.00
D13 LeRoy Hermann(T)	11.00	7.00	3.00
D14 Henry Johnson(M)	11.00	7.00	3.00
D15 Hal King(M)	11.00	7.00	3.00
D16 Charles S. Lucas (T)	11.00	7.00	3.00
D17 Edward S. Miller (T)	11.00	7.00	3.00
D18 Jake F. Mooty(T)	11.00	7.00	3.00
D19 Guy Moreau	11.00	7.00	3.00
D20 George Murray(T)	11.00	7.00	3.00
D21 Glen Myatt(M)	11.00	7.00	3.00
D22 Lauri Myllykargos (M)	11.00	7.00	3.00
D23 Franci J. Nicholas (T)	11.00	7.00	3.00
D24 Bill O'Brien	11.00	7.00	3.00
D25 Thomas Oliver (T)	11.00	7.00	3.00
D26 James Pattison (T)	11.00	7.00	3.00
D27 Crip Polli (M)	11.00	7.00	3.00
D28 Harlin Pool (T)	11.00	7.00	3.00
D29 Walter Purcey (T)	11.00	7.00	3.00
D30 Bill Rhiel (M)	11.00	7.00	3.00
D31 Ben Sankey (M)	11.00	7.00	3.00
D32 Leslie Scarsella (T)	11.00	7.00	3.00
D33 Bob Seeds (M)	11.00	7.00	3.00
D34 Frank Shaughnessy (M)	11.00	7.00	3.00
D35 Harry Smythe (M)	11.00	7.00	3.00
D36 Ben Tate (M)	11.00	7.00	3.00
D37 Fresco Thompson (M)	11.00	7.00	3.00
D38 Charles Wilson (M)	11.00	7.00	3.00
D39 Francis Wistert (horiz)(T)	11.00	7.00	3.00

R315 PORTRAITS & ACTION (38) 3 5/16" X 5 1/4"

This 1928 issue contains 38 black & white or yellow and black cards. The player's name and the team name are located in a box within the frame line at the base of the card. The player's position and the team and league name are located in the border. The cards are blank backed.

	MINT	VG-E	F-G
COMPLETE SET	330.00	220.00	90.00
COMMON PLAYER	4.50	3.00	1.20
A1 Earl Averill	6.00	4.00	1.60
A2 "Benny" Bengough	4.50	3.00	1.20
A3 Laurence Benton	4.50	3.00	1.20
A4 "Max" Bishop	4.50	3.00	1.20
A5 "Sunny Jim" Bottomley	6.00	4.00	1.60
A6 "Freddy" Fitzsimmons	4.50	3.00	1.20
A7 "Jimmy" Foxx	15.00	10.00	4.00
A8 "Johnny" Fredericks	4.50	3.00	1.20
A9 "Lou" Gehrig	30.00	20.00	8.00
A10 "Goose" Goslin	6.00	4.00	1.60
A11 Burleigh Grimes	6.00	4.00	1.60
A12 "Lefty" Grove	11.00	7.00	3.00
A13 "Mule" Haas	4.50	3.00	1.20
A14 "Babe" Herman	5.25	3.50	1.40
A15 "Roger" Hornsby	15.00	10.00	4.00
A16 Carl Hubbell	7.50	5.00	2.00
A17 "Stonewall" Jackson	4.50	3.00	1.20
A18 "Chuck" Klein	6.00	4.00	1.60
A19 Mark Koenig	4.50	3.00	1.20
A20 "Tony" Lazzeri	5.25	3.50	1.40
A21 Fred Leach	4.50	3.00	1.20
A22 "Freddy" Lindstrom	6.00	4.00	1.60
A23 Fred Marberry	4.50	3.00	1.20
A24 "Bing" Miller	4.50	3.00	1.20
A25 Frank O'Doul	5.25	3.50	1.40
A26 "Bob" O'Farrell	4.50	3.00	1.20
A27 "Herbie" Pennock	6.00	4.00	1.60
A28 George Pipgras	4.50	3.00	1.20
A29 Andrew Reese	4.50	3.00	1.20
A30 "Babe" Ruth	45.00	30.00	12.00
A31 "Bob" Shawkey	4.50	3.00	1.20
A32 "Al" Simmons	7.50	5.00	2.00
A33 "Riggs" Stephenson	5.25	3.50	1.40
A34 "Bill" Terry	7.50	5.00	2.00
A35 "Dazzy" Vance	6.00	4.00	1.60
A36 Paul Waner	6.00	4.00	1.60
A37 "Hack" Wilson	6.00	4.00	1.60
A38 "Tom" Zachary	4.50	3.00	1.20
B1 "Max" Bishop	4.50	3.00	1.20
B2 "Sunny Jim" Bottomley	6.00	4.00	1.60
B3 "Freddy" Fitzsimmons	4.50	3.00	1.20
B4 "Mule" Haas	4.50	3.00	1.20
B5 "Babe" Herman	5.25	3.50	1.40
B6 Carl Hubbell	7.50	5.00	2.00
B7 "Stonewall" Jackson	4.50	3.00	1.20
B8 "Bing" Miller	4.50	3.00	1.20
B9 Andrew Reese	4.50	3.00	1.20
B10 Riggs Stephenson	5.25	3.50	1.40
B11 "Pie" Traynor	7.50	5.00	2.00
B12 "Dazzy" Vance	6.00	4.00	1.60
C1 Bill Cissell	4.50	3.00	1.20
C2 Harvey Hendricks	4.50	3.00	1.20
C3 Carl Reynolds	4.50	3.00	1.20
C4 Art Shires	4.50	3.00	1.20
D1 Bud Clancy	4.50	3.00	1.20

1929 R316 (101)

3 1/2" X 4 1/2"

The 1929 R316 Portraits and Action Baseball set features 101 unnumbered, blank backed, black and white cards. The name of the player is written in script at the bottom of the card. The Hadley, Haines, Siebold, and Todt cards are considered scarce.

	MINT	VG-E	F-G
COMPLETE SET	800.00	550.00	225.00
COMMON PLAYER(1-101)	5.00	3.50	1.50
1 Allen,Ethan N.	5.00	3.50	1.50
2 Alexander,Dale	5.00	3.50	1.50
3 Benton,Larry	5.00	3.50	1.50
4 Berg,Moe	5.00	3.50	1.50
5 Bishop,Max	5.00	3.50	1.50
6 Bissonette,Del	5.00	3.50	1.50
7 Blue,Lucerne A.	5.00	3.50	1.50
8 Bottomley,James	10.00	6.50	3.00
9 Bush,Guy T.	5.00	3.50	1.50
10 Carlson,Harold G.	5.00	3.50	1.50
11 Carroll,Owen	5.00	3.50	1.50
12 Cissell,Chalmers W	5.00	3.50	1.50
13 Combs,Earl	10.00	6.50	3.00
14 Critz,Hugh M.	5.00	3.50	1.50
15 DeBerry,H. J.	5.00	3.50	1.50
16 Donohue,Pete	5.00	3.50	1.50
17 Douthit,Taylor	5.00	3.50	1.50
18 Dressen,Chas W.	6.00	4.00	1.50
19 Dykes,Jimmy	6.00	4.00	1.50
20 Ehmke,Howard	6.00	4.00	1.50
21 English,Woody	5.00	3.50	1.50
22 Faber,Urban	10.00	6.50	3.00
23 Fitzsimmons,Fred	5.00	3.50	1.50

24	Fonseca,Lewis A.	6.00	4.00	1.50
25	Ford,Horace H.	5.00	3.50	1.50
26	Foxx,Jimmy	20.00	13.00	5.50
27	Frisch,Frank	15.00	10.00	4.50
28	Gehrig,Lou	40.00	26.00	10.00
29	Gehringer,Charles	12.00	8.00	3.50
30	Goslin,Leon	10.00	6.50	3.00
31	Grantham,George	5.00	3.50	1.50
32	Burleigh,Grimes	10.00	6.50	3.00
33	Grove,Robert	15.00	10.00	4.50
34	Hadley,Bump	60.00	40.00	15.00
35	Hafey,Charlie	10.00	6.50	3.00
36	Haines,Jesse J.	90.00	60.00	25.00
37	Hendrick,Harvey	5.00	3.50	1.50
38	Herman,Floyd C.	5.00	3.50	1.50
39	High,Andy	5.00	3.50	1.50
40	Hodapp,Urban J.	5.00	3.50	1.50
41	Hogan,Frank	5.00	3.50	1.50
42	Hornsby,Rogers	20.00	13.00	5.50
43	Hoyt,Waite	10.00	6.50	3.00
44	Hudlin,Willis	5.00	3.50	1.50
45	Hurst,Frank O.	5.00	3.50	1.50
46	Jamieson,Charlie	5.00	3.50	1.50
47	Johnson,Roy C.	5.00	3.50	1.50
48	Jones,Percy	5.00	3.50	1.50
49	Jones,Sam	5.00	3.50	1.50
50	Judge,Joseph	6.00	4.00	1.50
51	Kamm,Willie	5.00	3.50	1.50
52	Klein,Charles	10.00	6.50	3.00
53	Keonig,Mark	5.00	3.50	1.50
54	Kress,Ralph	5.00	3.50	1.50
55	Leach,Fred M.	5.00	3.50	1.50
56	Lindstrom,Fred	10.00	6.50	3.00
57	Liska,Ad	5.00	3.50	1.50
58	Lucas,Fred	5.00	3.50	1.50
59	Maguire,Fred	5.00	3.50	1.50
60	Malone,Perce L.	5.00	3.50	1.50
61	Manush,Harry	10.00	6.50	3.00
62	Maranville,Walter	10.00	6.50	3.00
63	McWeeney,Douglas	5.00	3.50	1.50
64	Melillo,Oscar	5.00	3.50	1.50
65	Miller,Ed "Bing"	5.00	3.50	1.50
66	O'Doul,Frank	7.50	5.00	2.00
67	Ott,Melvin	20.00	13.00	5.50
68	Pennock,Herbert	10.00	6.50	3.00
69	Regan,William,W.	5.00	3.50	1.50
70	Rice,Harry F.	5.00	3.50	1.50
71	Rice,Sam	10.00	6.50	3.00
72	Richbourg,Lance	5.00	3.50	1.50
73	Rommel,Eddie	6.00	4.00	1.50
74	Root,Chas. H.	5.00	3.50	1.50
75	Roush,Ed	10.00	6.50	3.00
76	Ruel,Harold	5.00	3.50	1.50
77	Ruffing,Charlie	10.00	6.50	3.00
78	Russell,Jack	5.00	3.50	1.50
79	Ruth,Babe	55.00	37.50	17.50
80	Schulte,Fred	5.00	3.50	1.50
81	Sewell,Joe	10.00	6.50	3.00
82	Sewell,Luke	6.00	4.00	1.50
83	Shires,Art	5.00	3.50	1.50
84	Seibold,Henry	60.00	40.00	15.00
85	Simmons,Al	12.00	8.00	3.50
86	Smith,Bob	5.00	3.50	1.50
87	Stephenson,Riggs	6.00	4.00	1.50
88	Terry,Wm. H.	15.00	10.00	4.50
89	Thomas,Alphonse	5.00	3.50	1.50
90	Thompson,Lafayette	5.00	3.50	1.50
91	Todt,Phil	60.00	40.00	15.00
92	Traynor,Harold J.	12.00	8.00	3.50
93	Vance,Dazzy	10.00	6.50	3.00
94	Waner,Lloyd	10.00	6.50	3.00
95	Waner,Paul	12.00	8.00	3.50
96	Welsh,Jimmy	5.00	3.50	1.50
97	Whitehill,Earl	5.00	3.50	1.50
98	Whitney,A. C.	5.00	3.50	1.50
99	Willoughby,Claude	5.00	3.50	1.50
100	Wilson,Hack	10.00	6.50	3.00
101	Zachary,Tom	5.00	3.50	1.50

1952 ROYAL (16) 5" X 7"

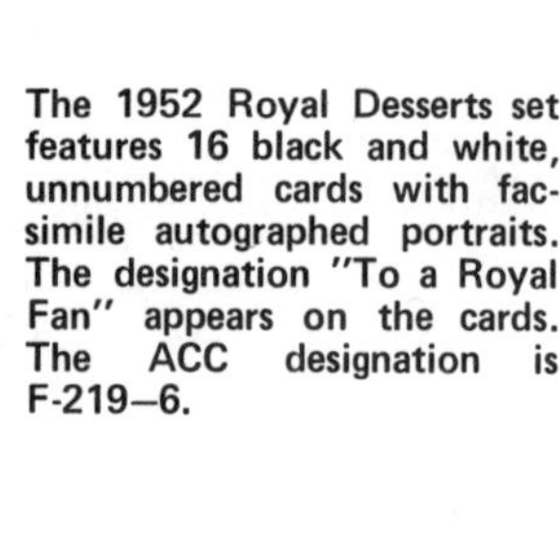

The 1952 Royal Desserts set features 16 black and white, unnumbered cards with facsimile autographed portraits. The designation "To a Royal Fan" appears on the cards. The ACC designation is F-219–6.

	MINT	VG-E	F-G
COMPLETE SET	180.00	120.00	50.00
COMMON PLAYER(1-16)	9.00	6.00	2.50
1 Blackwell,Ewell	10.00	6.50	3.00
2 Brissie,Jr,Leland	9.00	6.00	2.50
3 Dark,Alvin	12.00	8.00	3.50
4 DiMaggio,Dom	15.00	10.00	4.00
5 Fain,Ferris	10.00	6.50	3.00
6 Kell,George	12.00	8.00	3.50
7 Musial,Stan	50.00	35.00	14.00
8 Pafko,Andy	9.00	6.00	2.50
9 Reese,Pee Wee	18.00	12.00	5.00
10 Rizzuto,Phil	18.00	12.00	5.00
11 Robinson,Eddie	10.00	6.50	3.00
12 Scarborough,Ray	9.00	6.00	2.50
13 Seminick,Andy	9.00	6.00	2.50
14 Sisler,Dick	9.00	6.00	2.50
15 Spahn,Warren	18.00	12.00	5.00
16 Thomson,Bobby	15.00	10.00	4.00

One of the most common forms of baseball collectibles in existence today has been around since baseball began. Magazines extolling the virtues and detailing the statistics of baseball heroes have always been produced and sold in mass quantities. These publications may appear to have little value compared to baseball cards and other individual items of memorabilia; however, this apparent lack of relative value can be objectively explained. Generally, publications are (1) bulky, difficult to store, and difficult to carry around for sale; (2) mass produced and meant to be saved; (3) lacking in connection to one team (as opposed to yearbooks) or one player (other than the cover subject); (4) difficult to present in an aesthetically appealing display; and (5) up to this point in time (with the publication of this volume) difficult to evaluate as to current market price. All these factors have in some way contributed to the "reasonable" value of the publications listed below, in spite of a particular publication's beauty, newsworthiness or rarity.

The following listings give magazine per copy prices for regular and special issues. Special issues are defined to be those issued of the magazine which are in higher demand for any of the reasons given here: (1) major superstar on the cover, e.g., Mantle, Rose, Ruth, DiMaggio, Gehrig, Cobb, etc. (collectors should note that regional determinations of superstar status can inflate items to higher values in certain parts of the country because of local appeal); (2) issue containing content of lasting value or of special interest, e.g., World Series issue, baseball preview issue, college basketball (a baseball theme is not a necessity for the special issue designation) issue (SI); or (3) any Volume 1, Number 1 not otherwise indicated.

Cover subjects on annuals have not been indicated in the list below, although they may be in future editions. Several examples are pictured showing the covers used by Street & Smith, one of the most popular baseball annuals.

SIGNIFIES THE BEGINNING OF A PARTICULAR YEAR

```
*********************************************
** 1977 PUBLICATIONS, MAGAZINES, AND ANNUALS **
*********************************************
Baseball Digest
      regular issue                  .35/ .25
      special issue                  .75/ .50
Complete Sports
      Baseball Illustrated          3.00/2.00
Dell Baseball Annual                3.00/2.00
H & B Famous Slugger Yearbook       2.00/1.25
League Books
      Green Book - National         4.50/3.00
      Red Book - American           4.50/3.00
Sport Magazine
      regular issue                  .50/ .30
      special issue                 1.00/ .60
Sports Illustrated
      regular issue                  .15/ .10
      special issue                  .30/ .20
Sports Quarterly
      Baseball Annual               3.00/2.00
Street & Smith
      baseball annual               3.00/2.00
The Sporting News
      re[illegible]ar issue                  .25/ .15
      [illegible]pecial issue                .50/ .30
      Baseball Record Book          3.00/2.00
      Register                      5.00/3.00
      Guide                         4.00/[illegible]
      Dope Book                     2.[illegible].25
      Official Baseball Rules       2.[illegible]0/1.25
      W.S. Record Book              2.00/1.25
True Baseball Yearbook              2.00/1.25
Who's Who in Baseball
      (Baseball Magazine)           3.00/2.00
```

NAME OF PUBLICATION AND TYPE OF ISSUE

VALUE OF PUBLICATION IN EXCELLENT TO MINT AND VERY GOOD CONDITION CATEGORIES

PRE-1880 PUBLICATIONS, MAGAZINES, ANNUALS

1879 Beadle Guide	60.00/ 45.00
1879 DeWitt Guide	60.00/ 40.00
1879 Spaulding Guide	60.00/ 40.00
1878 Beadle Guide	60.00/ 40.00
1878 DeWitt Guide	60.00/ 40.00
1878 Spaulding Guide	60.00/ 40.00
1877 Beadle Guide	60.00/ 40.00
1877 DeWitt Guide	60.00/ 40.00
1877 Spaulding Guide	60.00/ 40.00
1876 Beadle Guide	60.00/ 40.00
1876 DeWitt Guide	60.00/ 40.00
1875 Beadle Guide	75.00/ 50.00
1875 DeWitt Guide	75.00/ 50.00
1875 Wright & Ditson Guide	75.00/ 50.00
1874 Beadle Guide	75.00/ 50.00
1874 DeWitt Guide	75.00/ 50.00
1874 Wright & Ditson Guide	75.00/ 50.00
1873 Beadle Guide	75.00/ 50.00
1873 DeWitt Guide	75.00/ 50.00
1872 Beadle Guide	75.00/ 50.00
1872 DeWitt Guide	75.00/ 50.00
1871 Beadle Guide	75.00/ 50.00
1871 DeWitt Guide	75.00/ 50.00
1870 Beadle Guide	75.00/ 50.00
1870 DeWitt Guide	75.00/ 50.00
1869 Beadle Guide	90.00/ 60.00
1869 DeWitt Guide	90.00/ 60.00
1868 Beadle Guide	90.00/ 60.00
1868 DeWitt Guide	90.00/ 60.00
1867 Beadle Guide	90.00/ 60.00
1866 Beadle Guide	100.00/ 65.00
1865 Beadle Guide	110.00/ 70.00
1864 Beadle Guide	120.00/ 80.00
1863 Beadle Guide	120.00/ 80.00
1862 Beadle Guide	120.00/ 80.00
1861 Beadle Guide	130.00/ 90.00
1860 Beadle Guide	150.00/100.00

1880 PUBLICATIONS, MAGAZINES, AND ANNUALS

Beadle Guide	60.00/40.00
DeWitt Guide	60.00/40.00
Spaulding Guide	60.00/40.00

1881 PUBLICATIONS, MAGAZINES, AND ANNUALS

Beadle Guide	60.00/40.00
DeWitt Guide	60.00/40.00
Spaulding Guide	60.00/40.00

1882 PUBLICATIONS, MAGAZINES, AND ANNUALS

DeWitt Guide	60.00/40.00
Spaulding Guide	60.00/40.00

1883 PUBLICATIONS, MAGAZINES, AND ANNUALS

DeWitt Guide	60.00/40.00
Reach Guide	60.00/40.00
Spaulding Guide	60.00/40.00
Sporting Life	30.00/20.00

1884 PUBLICATIONS, MAGAZINES, AND ANNUALS

DeWitt Guide	60.00/40.00
Reach Guide	60.00/40.00
Spaulding Guide	60.00/40.00
Sporting Life	30.00/20.00
Wright & Ditson Guide	50.00/30.00

1885 PUBLICATIONS, MAGAZINES, AND ANNUALS

DeWitt Guide	60.00/40.00
Reach Guide	60.00/40.00
Spaulding Guide	60.00/40.00
Sporting Life	30.00/20.00
The Sporting News	
regular issue	30.00/20.00
special issue	60.00/40.00
Wright & Ditson Guide	50.00/30.00

1886 PUBLICATIONS, MAGAZINES, AND ANNUALS

Reach Guide	50.00/30.00
Spaulding Guide	50.00/30.00
Sporting Life	30.00/20.00
The Sporting News	
regular issue	20.00/14.00
special issue	30.00/20.00
Wright & Ditson Guide	50.00/30.00

1887 PUBLICATIONS, MAGAZINES, AND ANNUALS

Reach Guide	50.00/30.00
Spaulding Guide	50.00/30.00
Sporting Life	30.00/20.00
The Sporting News	
regular issue	20.00/14.00
special issue	30.00/20.00

1888 PUBLICATIONS, MAGAZINES, AND ANNUALS

Reach Guide	45.00/30.00
Spaulding Guide	45.00/30.00
Sporting Life	30.00/20.00
The Sporting News	
regular issue	20.00/14.00
special issue	30.00/20.00

1889 PUBLICATIONS, MAGAZINES, AND ANNUALS

Reach Guide	15.00/10.00
Spaulding Guide	16.50/11.00
Sporting Life	27.00/18.00
The Sporting News	
regular issue	20.00/14.00
special issue	30.00/20.00

1890 PUBLICATIONS, MAGAZINES, AND ANNUALS

Reach Guide	45.00/30.00
Spaulding Guide	45.00/30.00
Sporting Life	27.00/18.00
The Sporting News	
regular issue	20.00/14.00
special issue	30.00/20.00
Universal Guide	75.00/50.00

1891 PUBLICATIONS, MAGAZINES, AND ANNUALS

Reach Guide	45.00/30.00
Spaulding Guide	45.00/30.00
Sporting Life	24.00/16.00
Sporting Life Guide	75.00/50.00
The Sporting News	
regular issue	20.00/14.00
special issue	30.00/20.00

1892 PUBLICATIONS, MAGAZINES, AND ANNUALS

Reach Guide	45.00/30.00
Spaulding Guide	45.00/30.00
Sporting Life	24.00/16.00
The Sporting News	
regular issue	16.00/11.00
special issue	24.00/16.00

1893 PUBLICATIONS, MAGAZINES, AND ANNUALS

Reach Guide	45.00/30.00
Spaulding Guide	45.00/30.00
Sporting Life	24.00/16.00
The Sporting News	
regular issue	16.00/11.00
special issue	24.00/16.00

****
** 1894 PUBLICATIONS, MAGAZINES, AND ANNUALS **
****

Reach Guide	45.00/30.00
Spaulding Guide	45.00/30.00
Sporting Life	24.00/16.00
The Sporting News	
regular issue	16.00/11.00
special issue	24.00/16.00

****
** 1895 PUBLICATIONS, MAGAZINES, AND ANNUALS **
****

Reach Guide	45.00/30.00
Spaulding Guide	45.00/30.00
Sporting Life	24.00/16.00
The Sporting News	
regular issue	16.00/11.00
special issue	24.00/16.00

****
** 1896 PUBLICATIONS, MAGAZINES, AND ANNUALS **
****

Reach Guide	45.00/30.00
Spaulding Guide	45.00/30.00
Sporting Life	21.00/14.00
The Sporting News	
regular issue	14.00/ 9.50
special issue	21.00/14.00
Victor Guide	75.00/50.00

****
** 1897 PUBLICATIONS, MAGAZINES, AND ANNUALS **
****

Reach Guide	45.00/30.00
Spaulding Guide	45.00/30.00
Sporting Life	21.00/14.00
The Sporting News	
regular issue	14.00/ 9.50
special issue	21.00/14.00
Victor Guide	75.00/50.00

****
** 1898 PUBLICATIONS, MAGAZINES, AND ANNUALS **
****

Reach Guide	45.00/30.00
Spaulding Guide	45.00/30.00
Sporting Life	21.00/14.00
The Sporting News	
regular issue	12.00/ 8.00
special issue	18.00/12.00

****
** 1899 PUBLICATIONS, MAGAZINES, AND ANNUALS **
****

Reach Guide	45.00/30.00
Spaulding Guide	45.00/30.00
Sporting Life	21.00/14.00
The Sporting News	
regular issue	12.00/ 8.00
special issue	18.00/12.00

****
** 1900 PUBLICATIONS, MAGAZINES, AND ANNUALS **
****

Reach Guide	40.00/25.00
Spaulding Guide	40.00/25.00
Sporting Life	15.00/10.00
The Sporting News	
regular issue	10.00/ 6.00
special issue	15.00/10.00

****
** 1901 PUBLICATIONS, MAGAZINES, AND ANNUALS **
****

Reach Guide	40.00/25.00
Spaulding Guide	40.00/25.00
Sporting Life	15.00/10.00
The Sporting News	
regular issue	10.00/ 6.00
special issue	15.00/10.00

****
** 1902 PUBLICATIONS, MAGAZINES, AND ANNUALS **
****

Reach Guide	40.00/25.00
Spaulding Guide	40.00/25.00
Sporting Life	15.00/10.00
The Sporting News	
regular issue	10.00/ 6.00
special issue	15.00/10.00

****
** 1903 PUBLICATIONS, MAGAZINES, AND ANNUALS **
****

Reach Guide	40.00/25.00
Spaulding Guide	40.00/25.00
Sporting Life	15.00/10.00
The Sporting News	
regular issue	10.00/ 6.00
special issue	15.00/10.00

****
** 1904 PUBLICATIONS, MAGAZINES, AND ANNUALS **
****

Reach Guide	36.00/24.00
Spaulding Guide	36.00/24.00
Sporting Life	15.00/10.00
The Sporting News	
regular issue	10.00/ 6.00
special issue	15.00/10.00

****
** 1905 PUBLICATIONS, MAGAZINES, AND ANNUALS **
****

Reach Guide	36.00/24.00
Spaulding Guide	36.00/24.00
Sporting Life	15.00/10.00
The Sporting News	
regular issue	10.00/ 6.00
special issue	15.00/10.00

****
** 1906 PUBLICATIONS, MAGAZINES, AND ANNUALS **
****

Lajoie Guide	45.00/30.00
Reach Guide	36.00/24.00
Spaulding Guide	36.00/24.00
Sporting Life	13.00/ 9.00
The Sporting News	
regular issue	10.00/ 6.00
special issue	15.00/10.00

****
** 1907 PUBLICATIONS, MAGAZINES, AND ANNUALS **
****

Lajoie Guide	45.00/30.00
Reach Guide	36.00/24.00
Spaulding Guide	36.00/24.00
Sporting Life	13.00/ 9.00
The Sporting News	
regular issue	10.00/ 6.00
special issue	15.00/10.00

****
** 1908 PUBLICATIONS, MAGAZINES, AND ANNUALS **
****

Baseball Magazine	
regular issue	20.00/12.00
special issue	50.00/30.00
Lajoie Guide	45.00/30.00
Reach Guide	33.00/22.00
Spaulding Guide	33.00/22.00
Sporting Life	13.00/ 9.00
The Sporting News	
regular issue	10.00/ 6.00
special issue	15.00/10.00
Record Book	11.00/ 7.00

****
** 1909 PUBLICATIONS, MAGAZINES, AND ANNUALS **
****

Baseball Magazine	
regular issue	15.00/10.00
special issue	30.00/20.00
Reach Guide	33.00/22.00
Spaulding Guide	33.00/22.00
Sporting Life	13.00/ 9.00
The Sporting News	
regular issue	10.00/ 6.00
special issue	15.00/10.00
Record Book	7.50/ 5.00

1910 PUBLICATIONS, MAGAZINES, AND ANNUALS

Item	Price
Baseball Magazine	
regular issue	15.00/10.00
special issue	30.00/20.00
Bull Durham Guide	35.00/25.00
Reach Guide	30.00/20.00
Spaulding Guide	30.00/20.00
Sporting Life	13.00/ 9.00
The Sporting News	
regular issue	9.00/ 6.00
special issue	13.00/ 9.00
Record Book	7.50/ 5.00
Wright & Ditson Guide	35.00/25.00

1911 PUBLICATIONS, MAGAZINES, AND ANNUALS

Item	Price
Baseball Magazine	
regular issue	15.00/10.00
special issue	30.00/20.00
Bull Durham Guide	35.00/25.00
Reach Guide	30.00/20.00
Spaulding Guide	30.00/20.00
Sporting Life	11.00/ 7.00
The Sporting News	
regular issue	9.00/ 6.00
special issue	13.00/ 9.00
Record Book	7.50/ 5.00

1912 PUBLICATIONS, MAGAZINES, AND ANNUALS

Item	Price
Baseball Magazine	
regular issue	11.00/ 7.00
special issue	22.00/15.00
Reach Guide	15.00/10.00
Spaulding Guide	16.50/11.00
Sporting Life	11.00/ 7.00
The Sporting News	
regular issue	9.00/ 6.00
special issue	13.00/ 9.00
Record Book	6.00/ 4.00
Who's Who in Baseball (Baseball Magazine)	75.00/50.00
Wright & Ditson Guide	35.00/25.00

1913 PUBLICATIONS, MAGAZINES, AND ANNUALS

Item	Price
Baseball Magazine	
regular issue	11.00/ 7.00
special issue	22.00/15.00
Reach Guide	30.00/20.00
Spaulding Guide	30.00/20.00
Sporting Life	11.00/ 7.00
The Sporting News	
regular issue	9.00/ 6.00
special issue	13.00/ 9.00
Record Book	6.00/ 4.00

1914 PUBLICATIONS, MAGAZINES, AND ANNUALS

Item	Price
Baseball Magazine	
regular issue	11.00/ 7.00
special issue	22.00/15.00
Reach Guide	30.00/20.00
Spaulding Guide	30.00/20.00
Sporting Life	9.00/ 6.00
The Sporting News	
regular issue	9.00/ 6.00
special issue	13.00/ 9.00
Record Book	6.00/ 4.00

1915 PUBLICATIONS, MAGAZINES, AND ANNUALS

Item	Price
Baseball Magazine	
regular issue	21.00/ 7.00
special issue	22.00/15.00
Reach Guide	30.00/20.00
Spaulding Guide	30.00/20.00
Sporting Life	9.00/ 6.00
The Sporting News	
regular issue	9.00/ 6.00
special issue	13.00/ 9.00
Record Book	6.00/ 4.00

1916 PUBLICATIONS, MAGAZINES, AND ANNUALS

Item	Price
Baseball Magazine	
regular issue	9.00/ 6.00
special issue	18.00/12.00
Reach Guide	27.00/18.00
Spaulding Guide	27.00/18.00
Sporting Life	9.00/ 6.00
The Sporting News	
regular issue	7.50/ 5.00
special issue	11.00/ 7.00
Record Book	6.00/ 4.00
Who's Who in Baseball (Baseball Magazine)	50.00/30.00

1917 PUBLICATIONS, MAGAZINES, AND ANNUALS

Item	Price
Baseball Magazine	
regular issue	9.00/ 6.00
special issue	18.00/12.00
Reach Guide	27.00/18.00
Spaulding Guide	27.00/18.00
Sporting Life	9.00/ 6.00
The Sporting News	
regular issue	7.50/ 5.00
special issue	11.00/ 7.00
Record Book	6.00/ 4.00
Who's Who in Baseball (Baseball Magazine)	30.00/20.00

1918 PUBLICATIONS, MAGAZINES, AND ANNUALS

Item	Price
Baseball Magazine	
regular issue	7.50/ 5.00
special issue	15.00/10.00
Reach Guide	24.00/16.00
Spaulding Guide	27.00/16.00
The Sporting News	
regular issue	7.50/ 5.00
special issue	11.00/ 7.00
Record Book	6.00/ 4.00
Who's Who in Baseball (Baseball Magazine)	24.00/16.00

1919 PUBLICATIONS, MAGAZINES, AND ANNUALS

Item	Price
Baseball Magazine	
regular issue	7.50/ 5.00
special issue	15.00/10.00
Reach Guide	24.00/16.00
Spaulding Guide	27.00/18.00
The Sporting News	
regular issue	6.00/ 4.00
special issue	9.00/ 6.00
Record Book	6.00/ 4.00
Who's Who in Baseball (Baseball Magazine)	24.00/16.00

1920 PUBLICATIONS, MAGAZINES, AND ANNUALS

Baseball Magazine	
regular issue	6.00/ 4.00
special issue	12.00/ 8.00
Reach Guide	22.00/15.00
Spaulding Guide	27.00/18.00
The Sporting News	
regular issue	6.00/ 4.00
special issue	9.00/ 6.00
Record Book	6.00/ 4.00
Who's Who in Baseball	
(Baseball Magazine)	24.00/16.00

1921 PUBLICATIONS, MAGAZINES, AND ANNUALS

Baseball Magazine	
regular issue	6.00/ 4.00
special issue	12.00/ 8.00
H & B Famous Slugger Yearbook	15.00/10.00
Reach Guide	22.00/15.00
Spaulding Guide	27.00/18.00
The Sporting News	
regular issue	6.00/ 4.00
special issue	9.00/ 6.00
Record Book	6.00/ 4.00
Who's Who in Baseball	
(Baseball Magazine)	24.00/16.00

1922 PUBLICATIONS, MAGAZINES, AND ANNUALS

Baseball Magazine	
regular issue	5.00/ 3.00
special issue	10.00/ 6.00
Reach Guide	22.00/15.00
Spaulding Guide	27.00/18.00
The Sporting News	
regular issue	6.00/ 4.00
special issue	9.00/ 6.00
Guide	3.50/ 2.50
Record Book	6.00/ 4.00
Who's Who in Baseball	
(Baseball Magazine)	21.00/14.00

1923 PUBLICATIONS, MAGAZINES, AND ANNUALS

Baseball Magazine	
regular issue	5.00/ 3.00
special issue	10.00/ 6.00
Reach Guide	22.00/15.00
Spaulding Guide	27.00/18.00
The Sporting News	
regular issue	6.00/ 4.00
special issue	9.00/ 6.00
Record Book	6.00/ 4.00
Who's Who in Baseball	
(Baseball Magazine)	21.00/14.00

1924 PUBLICATIONS, MAGAZINES, AND ANNUALS

Baseball Magazine	
regular issue	5.00/ 3.00
special issue	10.00/ 6.00
Reach Guide	20.00/13.00
Spaulding Guide	24.00/16.00
The Sporting News	
regular issue	6.00/ 4.00
special issue	9.00/ 6.00
Record Book	6.00/ 4.00
Who's Who in Baseball	
(Baseball Magazine)	21.00/14.00

1925 PUBLICATIONS, MAGAZINES, AND ANNUALS

Baseball Magazine	
regular issue	5.00/ 3.00
special issue	10.00/ 6.00
Reach Guide	20.00/13.00
Spaulding Guide	24.00/16.00
The Sporting News	
regular issue	4.50/ 3.00
special issue	7.50/ 5.00
Record Book	6.00/ 4.00
Who's Who in Baseball	
(Baseball Magazine)	21.00/14.00

1926 PUBLICATIONS, MAGAZINES, AND ANNUALS

Baseball Magazine	
regular issue	4.50/ 3.00
special issue	9.00/ 6.00
Reach Guide	20.00/13.00
Spaulding Guide	24.00/16.00
The Sporting News	
regular issue	4.50/ 3.00
special issue	7.50/ 5.00
Record Book	6.00/ 4.00
Who's Who in Baseball	
(Baseball Magazine)	20.00/13.00

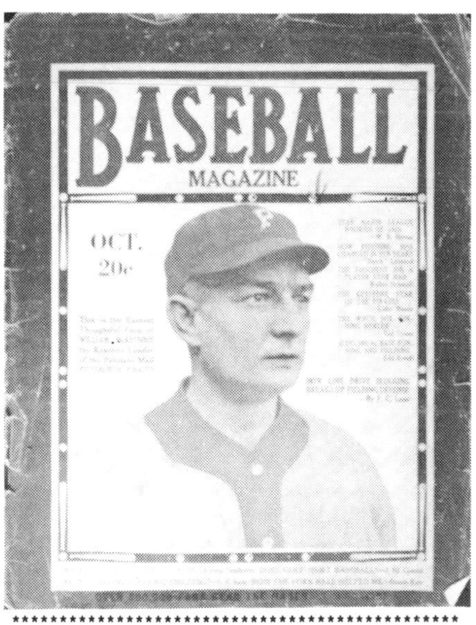

1927 PUBLICATIONS, MAGAZINES, AND ANNUALS

Baseball Magazine	
regular issue	4.50/ 3.00
special issue	9.00/ 6.00
H & B Famous Slugger Yearbook	11.00/13.00
Reach Guide	20.00/13.00
Spaulding Guide	24.00/16.00
The Sporting News	
regular issue	4.50/ 3.00
special issue	7.50/ 5.00
Record Book	6.00/ 4.00
Who's Who in Baseball	
(Baseball Magazine)	20.00/13.00

1928 PUBLICATIONS, MAGAZINES, AND ANNUALS

Baseball Magazine	
regular issue	4.50/ 3.00
special issue	9.00/ 6.00
H & B Famous Slugger Yearbook	9.00/ 6.00
Reach Guide	18.00/12.00
Spaulding Guide	21.00/14.00
The Sporting News	
regular issue	4.50/ 3.00
special issue	7.50/ 5.00
Record Book	6.00/ 4.00
Who's Who in Baseball	
(Baseball Magazine)	20.00/13.00

** 1929 PUBLICATIONS, MAGAZINES, AND ANNUALS **

Baseball Magazine	
regular issue	4.50/ 3.00
special issue	9.00/ 6.00
H & B Famous Slugger Yearbook	7.50/ 5.00
Reach Guide	18.00/12.00
Spaulding Guide	21.00/14.00
The Sporting News	
regular issue	4.50/ 3.00
special issue	7.50/ 5.00
Record Book	6.00/ 4.00
Who's Who in Baseball	
(Baseball Magazine)	20.00/13.00

** 1930 PUBLICATIONS, MAGAZINES, AND ANNUALS **

Baseball Magazine	
regular issue	4.50/ 3.00
special issue	9.00/ 6.00
H & B Famous Slugger Yearbook	7.50/ 5.00
Reach Guide	18.00/12.00
Spaulding Guide	21.00/14.00
The Sporting News	
regular issue	7.50/ 5.00
special issue	7.50/ 5.00
Record Book	6.00/ 4.00
Who's Who in Baseball	
(Baseball Magazine)	20.00/13.00

** 1931 PUBLICATIONS, MAGAZINES, AND ANNUALS **

Baseball Magazine	
regular issue	4.50/ 3.00
special issue	9.00/ 6.00
H & B Famous Slugger Yearbook	7.50/ 5.00
Reach Guide	18.00/12.00
Spaulding Guide	21.00/14.00
The Sporting News	
regular issue	4.50/ 3.00
special issue	7.50/ 5.00
Record Book	6.00/ 4.00
Who's Who in Baseball	
(Baseball Magazine)	19.00/13.00

** 1932 PUBLICATIONS, MAGAZINES, AND ANNUALS **

Baseball Magazine	
regular issue	4.50/ 3.00
special issue	9.00/ 6.00
H & B Famous Slugger Yearbook	6.00/ 4.00
Reach Guide	18.00/12.00
Spaulding Guide	21.00/14.00
The Sporting News	
regular issue	3.75/ 2.50
special issue	6.00/ 4.00
Record Book	6.00/ 4.00
Who's Who in Baseball	
(Baseball Magazine)	18.50/12.50

** 1933 PUBLICATIONS, MAGAZINES, AND ANNUALS **

Baseball Magazine	
regular issue	4.50/ 3.00
special issue	9.00/ 6.00
H & B Famous Slugger Yearbook	6.00/ 4.00
Reach Guide	18.00/12.00
Spaulding Guide	21.00/14.00
Speed Johnson Who's Who	135.00/90.00
The Sporting News	
regular issue	3.75/ 2.50
special issue	6.00/ 4.00
Record Book	6.00/ 4.00
Who's Who in Baseball	
(Baseball Magazine)	16.50/11.50

** 1934 PUBLICATIONS, MAGAZINES, AND ANNUALS **

Baseball Magazine	
regular issue	4.50/ 3.00
special issue	9.00/ 6.00
H & B Famous Slugger Yearbook	6.00/ 4.00
Little Red Book of Baseball	9.00/ 6.00
Reach Guide	16.50/11.00
Spaulding Guide	21.00/14.00
The Sporting News	
regular issue	3.75/ 2.50
special issue	6.00/ 4.00
Daguerreotypes	13.00/ 9.00
Record Book	6.00/ 4.00
Who's Who in Baseball	
(Baseball Magazine)	15.50/10.50

** 1935 PUBLICATIONS, MAGAZINES, AND ANNUALS **

Baseball Magazine	
regular issue	4.50/ 3.00
special issue	9.00/ 6.00
H & B Famous Slugger Yearbook	6.00/ 4.00
Little Red Book of Baseball	7.50/ 5.00
Reach Guide	16.50/11.00
Spaulding Guide	21.00/14.00
The Sporting News	
regular issue	3.75/ 2.50
special issue	6.50/ 4.00
Record Book	6.00/ 4.00
Who's Who in Baseball	
(Baseball Magazine)	14.50/10.00

** 1936 PUBLICATIONS, MAGAZINES, AND ANNUALS **

Baseball Magazine	
regular issue	3.75/ 2.50
special issue	7.50/ 5.00
H & B Famous Slugger Yearbook	6.00/ 4.00
Little Red Book of Baseball	6.00/ 4.00
Reach Guide	15.00/10.00
Spaulding Guide	21.00/14.00
The Sporting News	
regular issue	3.75/ 2.50
special issue	6.00/ 4.00
Record Book	6.00/ 4.00
Who's Who in Baseball	
(Baseball Magazine)	14.00/ 9.50

** 1937 PUBLICATIONS, MAGAZINES, AND ANNUALS **

Baseball Magazine	
regular issue	3.75/ 2.50
special issue	7.50/ 5.00
H & B Famous Slugger Yearbook	6.00/ 4.00
Little Red Book of Baseball	6.00/ 4.00
Reach Guide	15.00/10.00
Spaulding Guide	16.50/11.00
The Sporting News	
regular issue	3.75/ 2.50
special issue	6.00/ 4.00
Record Book	6.00/ 4.00
Who's Who in Baseball	
(Baseball Magazine)	14.00/ 9.50

** 1938 PUBLICATIONS, MAGAZINES, AND ANNUALS **

Baseball Magazine	
regular issue	3.75/ 2.50
special issue	7.50/ 5.00
H & B Famous Slugger Yearbook	6.00/ 4.00
Little Red Book of Baseball	6.00/ 4.00
Reach Guide	15.00/10.00
Spaulding Guide	16.50/11.00
The Sporting News	
regular issue	3.75/ 2.50
special issue	6.00/ 4.00
Record Book	6.00/ 4.00
Whitman Major League Baseball	10.00/ 6.50
Who's Who in Baseball	
(Baseball Magazine)	13.50/ 9.00

** 1939 PUBLICATIONS, MAGAZINES, AND ANNUALS **

Baseball Magazine	
regular issue	3.75/ 2.50
special issue	7.50/ 5.00
Carmichael Who's Who	16.00/10.50
H & B Famous Slugger Yearbook	6.00/ 4.00
Little Red Book of Baseball	6.00/ 4.00
Reach Guide	15.00/10.00
Spaulding Guide	16.50/11.00
The Sporting News	
regular issue	3.75/ 2.50
special issue	6.00/ 4.00
Record Book	6.00/ 4.00
Whitman Major League Baseball	9.00/ 6.50
Who's Who in Baseball	
(Baseball Magazine)	13.50/ 9.00

** 1940 PUBLICATIONS, MAGAZINES, AND ANNUALS **

Baseball Magazine	
regular issue	3.00/ 2.00
special issue	6.00/ 4.00
Carmichael Who's Who	15.00/ 9.50
H & B Famous Slugger Yearbook	6.00/ 4.00
Little Red Book of Baseball	6.00/ 4.00
Spalding/Reach Guide	20.00/13.00
The Sporting News	
regular issue	3.00/ 2.00
special issue	5.00/ 3.00
Register	30.00/20.00
Record Book	6.00/ 4.00
Whitman Major League Baseball	9.00/ 6.50
Who's Who in Baseball	
(Baseball Magazine)	12.50/ 8.50

** 1941 PUBLICATIONS, MAGAZINES, AND ANNUALS **

Baseball Magazine	
regular issue	3.00/ 2.00
special issue	6.00/ 4.00
Carmichael Who's Who	14.00/ 9.50
H & B Famous Slugger Yearbook	6.00/ 4.00
Little Red Book of Baseball	6.00/ 4.00
Spalding/Reach Guide	20.00/13.00
Street & Smith	
baseball annual	30.00/20.00
The Sporting News	
regular issue	3.00/ 2.00
special issue	5.00/ 3.00
Register	21.00/14.00
Record Book	6.00/ 4.00
Whitman Major League Baseball	9.00/ 6.50
Who's Who in Baseball	
(Baseball Magazine)	12.50/ 8.50

** 1942 PUBLICATIONS, MAGAZINES, AND ANNUALS **

Baseball Digest	
regular issue	7.50/ 5.00
special issue	15.00/10.00
Baseball Magazine	
regular issue	3.00/ 2.00
special issue	6.00/ 4.00
Carmichael Who's Who	13.00/ 9.00
H & B Famous Slugger Yearbook	4.50/ 3.00
Little Red Book of Baseball	6.00/ 4.00
Street & Smith	
baseball annual	25.00/16.50
The Sporting News	
regular issue	3.00/ 2.00
special issue	5.00/ 3.00
Register	18.00/12.00
Guide	18.00/12.00
Dope Book	2.00/ 1.25
Whitman Major League Baseball	8.00/ 5.50
Who's Who in Baseball	
(Baseball Magazine)	12.50/ 8.50

** 1943 PUBLICATIONS, MAGAZINES, AND ANNUALS **

Baseball Digest	
regular issue	5.00/ 3.00
special issue	7.50/ 5.00
Baseball Magazine	
regular issue	3.00/ 2.00
special issue	6.00/ 4.00
Carmichael Who's Who	12.00/ 8.00
Commissioner's Guide	30.00/20.00
H & B Famous Slugger Yearbook	4.50/ 3.00
Little Red Book of Baseball	6.00/ 4.00
Street & Smith	
baseball annual	21.00/14.00
The Sporting News	
regular issue	3.00/ 2.00
special issue	5.00/ 3.00
Register	18.00/12.00
Guide	15.00/10.00
Whitman Major League Baseball	8.00/ 5.50
Who's Who in Baseball	
(Baseball Magazine)	10.50/ 7.50

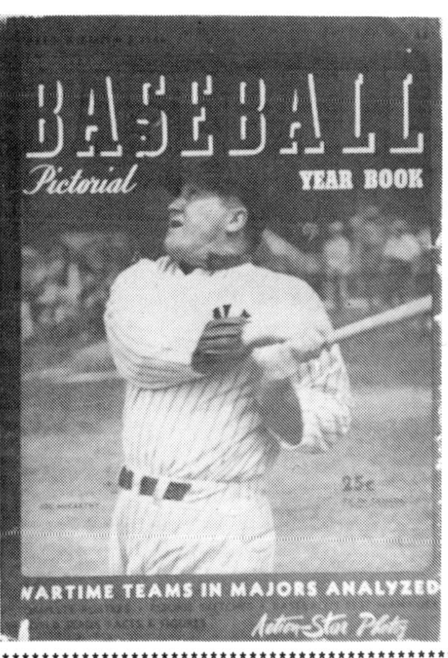

** 1944 PUBLICATIONS, MAGAZINES, AND ANNUALS **

Baseball Digest	
regular issue	5.00/ 3.00
special issue	7.50/ 5.00
Baseball Magazine	
regular issue	2.50/ 1.50
special issue	5.00/ 3.00
Carmichael Who's Who	11.00/ 7.00
H & B Famous Slugger Yearbook	4.50/ 3.00
Little Red Book of Baseball	6.00/ 4.00
Street & Smith	
baseball annual	20.00/13.00
The Sporting News	
regular issue	3.00/ 2.00
special issue	5.00/ 3.00
Register	16.50/11.00
Guide	13.00/ 9.00
Whitman Major League Baseball	7.00/ 5.00
Who's Who in Baseball	
(Baseball Magazine)	9.00/ 6.00

** 1945 PUBLICATIONS, MAGAZINES, AND ANNUALS **

Barnes Guide	9.00/ 6.00
Baseball Digest	
regular issue	4.00/ 2.50
special issue	6.00/ 4.00
Baseball Magazine	
regular issue	2.50/ 1.50
special issue	5.00/ 3.00
Carmichael Who's Who	11.00/ 7.00
H & B Famous Slugger Yearbook	4.50/ 3.00
Little Red Book of Baseball	6.00/ 4.00
Street & Smith	
baseball annual	20.00/13.00
The Sporting News	
regular issue	3.00/ 2.00
special issue	5.00/ 3.00
Register	16.50/11.00
Guide	13.00/ 9.00
Whitman Major League Baseball	7.00/ 5.00
Who's Who in Baseball	
(Baseball Magazine)	8.00/ 5.50

** 1946 PUBLICATIONS, MAGAZINES, AND ANNUALS **

Barnes Guide	9.00/ 6.00
Baseball Digest	
regular issue	3.05/ 2.00
special issue	5.00/ 3.00
Baseball Illustrated	13.00/ 9.00
Baseball Magazine	
regular issue	2.50/ 1.50
special issue	5.00/ 3.00
Carmichael Who's Who	11.00/ 7.00
H & B Famous Slugger Yearbook	4.50/ 3.00
Little Red Book of Baseball	6.00/ 4.00
Sport Magazine	
regular issue	10.00/ 6.00
special issue	20.00/12.00
Street & Smith	
baseball annual	18.00/12.00
The Sporting News	
regular issue	3.00/ 2.00
special issue	3.00/ 3.00
Register	16.50/11.00
Guide	13.50/ 9.00
Whitman Major League Baseball	7.00/ 5.00
Who's Who in Baseball	
(Baseball Magazine)	8.00/ 5.50

** 1947 PUBLICATIONS, MAGAZINES, AND ANNUALS **

Baseball Digest	
regular issue	3.00/ 2.00
special issue	5.00/ 3.00
Baseball Illustrated	13.00/ 9.00
Baseball Magazine	
regular issue	2.50/ 1.50
special issue	5.00/ 3.00
Carmichael Who's Who	11.00/ 7.00
H & B Famous Slugger Yearbook	4.50/ 3.00
League Books	
Green Book - National	13.00/ 9.00
Red Book - American	13.00/ 9.00
Little Red Book of Baseball	4.50/ 3.00
Sport Magazine	
regular issue	6.00/ 4.00
special issue	10.00/ 6.00
Street & Smith	
baseball annual	18.00/12.00
The Sporting News	
regular issue	3.00/ 2.00
special issue	5.00/ 3.00
Register	16.50/11.00
Guide	11.00/ 7.00
Whitman Major League Baseball	7.00/ 5.00
Who's Who in Baseball	
(Baseball Magazine)	7.00/ 5.00

** 1948 PUBLICATIONS, MAGAZINES, AND ANNUALS **

Baseball Digest	
regular issue	2.50/ 1.75
special issue	3.75/ 2.50
Baseball Illustrated	12.00/ 8.00
Baseball Magazine	
regular issue	2.50/ 1.50
special issue	5.00/ 3.00
Carmichael Who's Who	11.00/ 7.00
H & B Famous Slugger Yearbook	4.50/ 3.00
League Books	
Green Book - National	9.00/ 6.00
Red Book - American	9.00/ 6.00
Little Red Book of Baseball	4.50/ 3.00
Sport Life	5.00/ 3.00
Sport Magazine	
regular issue	4.50/ 3.00
special issue	9.00/ 6.00
Sports Album	7.00/ 5.00
Street & Smith	
baseball annual	18.00/12.00
The Sporting News	
regular issue	3.00/ 2.00
special issue	5.00/ 3.00
Register	16.50/11.00
Guide	11.00/ 7.00
Dope Book	7.50/ 5.00
Whitman Major League Baseball	7.00/ 5.00
Who's Who in Baseball	
(Baseball Magazine)	7.00/ 5.00

** 1949 PUBLICATIONS, MAGAZINES, AND ANNUALS **

Baseball Digest	
regular issue	2.50/ 1.75
special issue	3.75/ 2.50
Baseball Illustrated	11.00/ 7.00
Baseball Magazine	
regular issue	2.50/ 1.50
special issue	5.00/ 3.00
Carmichael Who's Who	11.00/ 7.00
Complete Baseball	7.50/ 5.00
Dell Baseball Stars	7.00/ 5.00
H & B Famous Slugger Yearbook	4.50/ 3.00
League Books	
Green Book - National	9.00/ 6.00
Red Book - American	6.00/ 6.00
Little Red Book of Baseball	4.50/ 3.00
Sport Life	5.00/ 3.00
Sport Magazine	
regular issue	4.50/ 3.00
special issue	9.00/ 6.00
Sports Album	6.00/ 4.00
Street & Smith	
baseball annual	16.00/ 9.75
The Sporting News	
regular issue	3.00/ 2.00
special issue	5.00/ 3.00
Register	15.00/10.00
Guide	11.00/ 7.00
Dope Book	6.00/ 4.00
One For The Book	7.50/ 5.00
Whitman Major League Baseball	7.00/ 5.00
Who's Who in Baseball	
(Baseball Magazine)	7.00/ 5.00

****
** 1950 PUBLICATIONS, MAGAZINES, AND ANNUALS **
****

Baseball Digest	
regular issue	2.00/1.25
special issue	3.00/2.00
Baseball Illustrated	11.00/7.00
Baseball Magazine	
regular issue	2.50/1.50
special issue	5.00/3.00
Carmichael Who's Who	11.00/7.00
Complete Baseball	5.00/3.00
Dell Baseball Stars	7.00/5.00
H & B Famous Slugger Yearbook	3.75/2.50
League Books	
Green Book - National	7.00/4.50
Red Book - American	7.00/4.50
Little Red Book of Baseball	4.50/3.00
Sport Life	5.00/3.00
Sport Magazine	
regular issue	4.50/3.00
special issue	9.00/6.00
Sports Album	6.00/4.00
Sports Review Baseball Yearly	4.50/3.00
Street & Smith	
baseball annual	14.00/9.00
The Sporting News	
regular issue	3.00/2.00
special issue	5.00/3.00
Register	15.00/9.00
Guide	11.00/7.00
Dope Book	4.50/3.00
Knotty Problems	3.00/2.00
One For The Book	6.00/4.00
True Baseball Yearbook	7.50/5.00
Whitman Major League Baseball	7.00/5.00
Who's Who in Baseball	
(Baseball Magazine)	7.00/5.00

****
** 1951 PUBLICATIONS, MAGAZINES, AND ANNUALS **
****

Baseball Digest	
regular issue	2.00/1.25
special issue	3.00/2.00
Baseball Illustrated	10.00/6.00
Baseball Magazine	
regular issue	2.50/1.50
special issue	5.00/3.00
Carmichael Who's Who	11.00/ 7.00
Complete Baseball	5.00/3.00
Dell Baseball Stars	6.00/4.00
H & B Famous Slugger Yearbook	3.75/2.50
League Books	
Green Book - National	7.00/4.50
Red Book - American	7.00/4.50
Little Red Book of Baseball	3.75/2.50
Official Baseball Annual	6.00/4.00
Sport Life	4.00/2.75
Sport Magazine	
regular issue	3.75/2.50
special issue	7.50/5.00
Sports Album	5.00/3.00
Sports Review Baseball Yearly	4.50/3.00
Street & Smith	
baseball annual	14.00/9.00
The Sporting News	
regular issue	3.00/2.00
special issue	5.00/3.00
Daguerreotypes	10.00/6.00
Register	15.00/9.00
Guide	11.00/7.00
Dope Book	4.50/3.00
Knotty Problems	3.00/2.00
One For The Book	4.50/3.00
True Baseball Yearbook	6.50/4.50
Whitman Major League Baseball	7.00/4.50
Who's Who in Baseball	
(Baseball Magazine)	7.00/5.00

****
** 1952 PUBLICATIONS, MAGAZINES, AND ANNUALS **
****

Baseball Digest	
regular issue	2.00/1.25
special issue	3.00/2.00
Baseball Illustrated	9.00/6.00
Baseball Magazine	
regular issue	2.50/1.50
special issue	5.00/3.00
Baseball's Best	7.00/5.00
Carmichael Who's Who	10.00/6.00
Complete Baseball	4.00/2.75
Dell Baseball Annual	8.00/5.50
Dell Baseball Stars	6.00/4.00
H & B Famous Slugger Yearbook	3.75/2.50
Inside Baseball	6.00/4.00

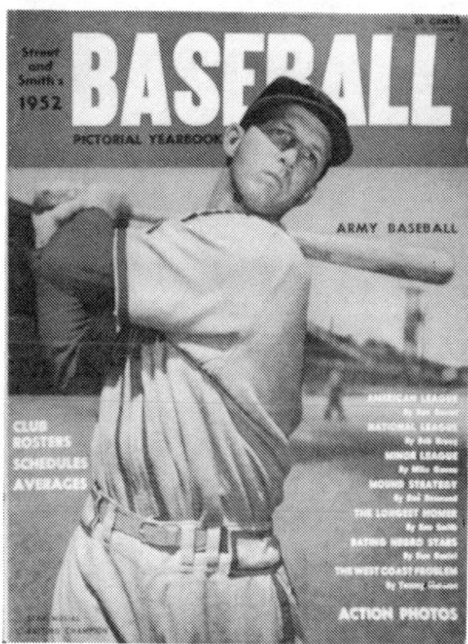

League Books	
Green Book - National	7.00/4.50
Red Book - American	7.00/4.50
Little Red Book of Baseball	3.75/2.50
Official Baseball Annual	6.00/4.00
Sport Life	4.00/2.75
Sport Magazine	
regular issue	3.75/2.50
special issue	7.50/5.00
Baseball's Best	11.00/7.00
Sports Album	5.00/3.00
Sports Review Baseball Yearly	3.75/2.50
Street & Smith	
baseball annual	14.00/9.00
The Sporting News	
regular issue	2.00/1.25
special issue	4.00/2.50
Register	15.00/9.00
Guide	11.00/7.00
Dope Book	4.50/3.00
Knotty Problems	3.00/2.00
One For The Book	4.50/3.00
True Baseball Yearbook	6.00/4.00
Whitman Major League Baseball	7.00/5.00
Who's Who in Baseball	
(Baseball Magazine)	7.00/5.00

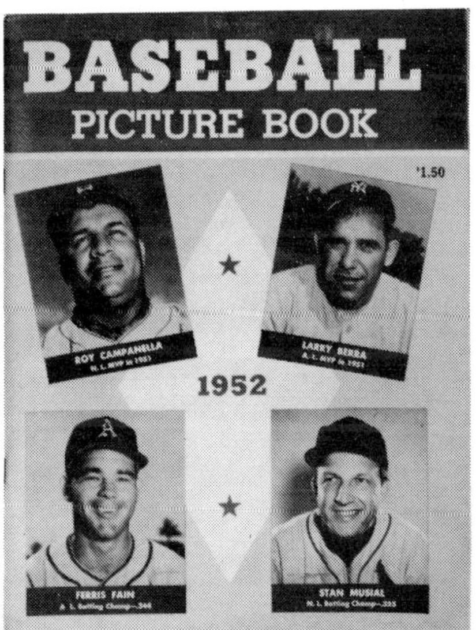

****
** 1953 PUBLICATIONS, MAGAZINES, AND ANNUALS **
****

Title	Price
Baseball Digest	
regular issue	2.00/1.25
special issue	3.00/2.00
Baseball Life	5.00/3.00
Baseball Magazine	
regular issue	2.50/1.50
special issue	5.00/3.00
Baseball's All-Stars (Maco)	8.00/5.50
Baseball's Best	6.00/4.00
Carmichael Who's Who	10.00/6.00
Complete Baseball	4.00/2.75
Dell Baseball Annual	7.00/5.00
Dell Baseball Stars	5.00/3.00
Dell Who's Who in Baseball	6.00/4.00
Dell Who's Who in Big Leagues (cover/Musial)	7.50/5.00
Gillette W.S. Record Book	5.00/3.00
H & B Famous Slugger Yearbook	3.75/2.50
Inside Baseball	5.00/3.00
League Books	
Green Book - National	7.00/4.50
Red Book - American	7.00/4.50
Little Red Book of Baseball	4.50/3.00
Official Baseball Annual	6.00/4.00
Sport Life	4.00/2.75
Sport Magazine	
regular issue	3.00/2.00
special issue	6.00/4.00
Baseball's Best	7.50/5.00
Sports Review Baseball Yearly	3.75/2.50
Street & Smith	
baseball annual	13.00/9.00
The Sporting News	
regular issue	2.00/1.25
special issue	4.00/2.50
Register	15.00/9.00
Guide	11.00/7.00
Dope Book	4.50/3.00
Knotty Problems	3.00/2.00
One For The Book	4.50/3.00
W.S. Record Book	5.00/3.00
True Baseball Yearbook	5.50/3.50
Whitman Major League Baseball	7.00/5.00
Who's Who in Baseball (Baseball Magazine)	7.00/5.00

****
** 1954 PUBLICATIONS, MAGAZINES, AND ANNUALS **
****

Title	Price
Baseball Digest	
regular issue	1.50/ 1.00
special issue	2.25/ 1.50
Baseball Life	5.00/ 3.00
Baseball Magazine	
regular issue	2.25/ 1.50
special issue	3.75/ 2.50
Baseball's All-Stars (Maco)	6.00/ 4.00
Complete Baseball	4.00/ 2.75
Dell Baseball Annual	6.00/ 4.00
Dell Baseball Stars	5.00/ 3.00
Dell Who's Who in Baseball	5.00/ 3.00
Dell Who's Who in Big Leagues	7.00/ 5.00
Gillette W.S. Record Book	4.50/ 3.00
H & B Famous Slugger Yearbook	3.75/ 2.50
Inside Baseball	5.00/ 3.00
League Books	
Green Book - National	7.00/ 4.50
Red Book - American	7.00/ 4.50
Little Red Book of Baseball	3.75/ 2.50
Official Baseball Annual	6.00/ 4.00
Sport Life	4.00/ 2.75
Sport Magazine	
regular issue	3.00/ 2.00
special issue	6.00/ 4.00
Baseball's Best	7.50/ 5.00
Sports Illustrated	
regular issue	1.00/ .60
special issue	4.50/ 3.00
Vol. 1, #1	22.50/15.00
Vol. 1, #2	15.00/10.00
Sports Review Baseball Yearly	3.75/ 2.50
Street & Smith	
baseball annual	12.00/ 8.00
The Sporting News	
regular issue	2.00/ 1.25
special issue	4.00/ 2.50
Register	13.00/ 9.00
Guide	11.00/ 7.50
Dope Book	4.50/ 3.00
Knotty Problems	3.00/ 2.00
One For The Book	4.50/ 3.00
W.S. Record Book	4.50/ 3.00
True Baseball Yearbook	5.50/ 3.50
Who's Who in Baseball (Baseball Magazine)	6.00/ 4.00

****
** 1955 PUBLICATIONS, MAGAZINES, AND ANNUALS **
****

Title	Price
Baseball Digest	
regular issue	1.50/1.00
special issue	2.25/1.50
Baseball Magazine	
regular issue	2.25/1.50
special issue	3.75/1.50
Baseball's All-Stars (Maco)	6.00/4.00
Dell Baseball Annual	6.00/4.00
Dell Baseball Stars	5.00/3.00
Dell Who's Who in Baseball	5.00/3.00
Dell Who's Who in Big Leagues	6.00/4.00
H & B Famous Slugger Yearbook	3.75/2.50
Inside Baseball	4.00/2.75
League Books	
Green Book - National	7.00/4.50
Red Book - American	7.00/4.50
Little Red Book of Baseball	3.75/2.50
Official Baseball Annual	6.00/4.00
Sport Magazine	
regular issue	3.00/2.00
special issue	6.00/4.00
Baseball's Best	7.50/5.00
Sports Illustrated	
regular issue	.60/ .40
special issue	2.50/1.50
Sports Review Baseball Yearly	3.75/2.50
Street & Smith	
baseball annual	12.00/8.00
The Sporting News	
regular issue	1.50/1.00
special issue	3.00/2.00
Register	13.00/9.00
Guide	9.00/6.00
Dope Book	4.50/3.00
Knotty Problems	3.00/2.00
One For The Book	4.50/3.00
W.S. Record Book	3.75/2.50
Who's Who in Baseball (Baseball Magazine)	6.00/4.00

****
** 1956 PUBLICATIONS, MAGAZINES, AND ANNUALS **
****

Title	Price
Baseball Digest	
regular issue	1.50/1.00
special issue	2.25/1.50
Baseball Magazine	
regular issue	2.00/1.25
special issue	3.00/2.00
Baseball's All-Stars (Maco)	4.50/3.00
Dell Baseball Annual	5.00/3.00
Dell Baseball Stars	4.00/2.75
Dell Who's Who in Baseball	5.00/3.00
Dell Who's Who in Big Leagues	5.00/3.00
H & B Famous Slugger Yearbook	3.75/2.50
Inside Baseball	4.00/2.75
League Books	
Green Book - National	7.50/5.00
Red Book - American	7.50/5.00

DEN'S COLLECTORS DEN

Plastic Card Protecting Pages
Largest Selection in Hobby!
16 Different Sizes

FINEST QUALITY PLASTIC SHEETS

FEATURING

- ✱ NON–MIGRATING PLASTIC IN ALL SHEETS
- ✱ PLASTIC THAT DOES NOT STICK TOGETHER
- ✱ STIFFNESS TO PREVENT CARD CURLING
- ✱ INTELLIGENT DESIGN
- ✱ RESISTANCE TO CRACKING
- ✱ FULL COVERAGE OF CARDS, PHOTOS & POSTCARDS

SEND $ 1.00 for DEN'S BIG 48-PAGE CATALOGUE

CATALOGUE WILL BE SENT FREE WITH ORDER

DEN'S COLLECTORS DEN

NO MIX & MATCH

STYLE	POCKETS / CAPACITY	RECOMMENDED FOR	PRICE EACH (DOES NOT INCLUDE P & H) 1-24	25-99	100-299	300-600
9	9 / 18	TOPPS (1957–PRESENT), FLEER (1959–63), LEAF (1960), KELLOGG, POST CEREAL, TOPPS CLOTH STICKER CARDS, SSPC (1976), RECENT NON–SPORTS	.25	.23.	.21	.19
8	8 / 16	TOPPS (1952–1956), BOWMAN (1953–55)	.25	.23	.21	.19
12	12 / 24	BOWMAN(1948–50), TOPPS (1951 RED AND BLUE BACKS), TICKET STUBS	.25	.23	.21	.19
1	1 / 2	PHOTOGRAPHS (8X10)	.25	.23	.21	.19
2	2 / 4	PHOTOGRAPHS (5X7)	.25	.23	.21	.19
4	4 / 8	POSTCARDS, TOPPS SUPER (1964, 1970, 1971), TOPPS BASKETBALL (1976), EXHIBITS	.25	.23	.21	.19
18	18 / 36	T CARDS, TOPPS COINS, BAZOOKA (1963–67 INDIVIDUAL CARDS)	.35	.35	.30	.27
9G	9 / 18	GOUDEY, DIAMOND STARS, LEAF (1948)	.35	.35	.30	.27
9PB	9 / 18	PLAYBALL, BOWMAN (1951–52), DOUBLE PLAY, 1975 TOPPS MINIS	.35	.35	.30	.27
1C	1 / 2	TURKEY REDS (T–3), 1977 PEPSI GLOVE AND DISC CARDS, PRESS GUIDES, POCKET SIZE 6"X9"	.35	.35	.30	.27
3	3 / 6	HOSTESS PANELS, HIRES ROOT BEER	.30	.25	.25	.20
6V	6 / 12	1955 TOPPS DOUBLE HEADERS, CONNIE MACKS, CURRENT STARS, TEAM CARDS, MECCA DOUBLE FOLDERS, HASSAN TRIPPLE FOLDERS, BAZOOKA PANELS (1963–67)	.35	.35	.30	.27
6D	6 / 12	RED MAN (WITH OR WITHOUT TABS), DISC, KAHN'S (1955–67)	.35	.35	.30	.27
1Y	1 / 1	YEARBOOKS, PROGRAMS, MAGAZINES, HOBBYPAPERS, TABLOIDS, POCKET SIZE 9"X12"	.35	.35	.30	.27
1S	1 / 2	ALL STAR GALLERY INDIVIDUAL PANELS, SMALL PROGRAMS AND OVERSIZED PHOTOS, POCKET SIZE 8½" X 11"	.30	.30	.25	.20
10	10 / 20	MATCHBOOK COVERS, POCKET SIZE 1 3/4" X 4 3/4"	.35	.35	.30	.27

POSTAGE & HANDLING SCHEDULE (P & H)
$ .01 to $ 20.00 add $ 2.00
$ 20.01 to $ 30.00 add $ 2.50
Over $ 30.00 add $ 3.00

MARYLAND RESIDENTS ADD 5% TAX
CANADIAN ORDERS – BOOKS ONLY
CANADIAN BOOK ORDERS ADD 25% postage
Orders outside contiguous U.S.A. add 25% more
U.S. FUNDS ONLY

TRY **DEN'S COLLECTORS DEN**
DEPT. MPG
P.O. BOX 606, LAUREL, MD 20707

DON'T SETTLE FOR LESS THAN THE BEST. BE SURE THAT THE STYLES 9,8,4,12,1 & 2 HAVE DEN'S COLLECTORS DEN EMBOSSED ON THE BORDER OF THE SHEET.

Little Red Book of Baseball	3.75/2.50
Official Baseball Annual	6.00/4.00
Sport Magazine	
regular issue	2.50/1.75
special issue	5.00/3.00
Baseball's Best	7.50/5.00
Sports Illustrated	
regular issue	.50/ .30
special issue	2.00/1.25
Sports Review Baseball Yearly	3.75/2.50
Street & Smith	
baseball annual	11.00/7.00
The Sporting News	
regular issue	1.50/1.00
special issue	3.00/2.00
Register	11.00/7.00
Guide	9.00/6.00
Dope Book	4.50/3.00
Knotty Problems	3.00/2.00
Official Baseball Rules	2.00/1.25
One For The Book	3.75/2.50
W.S. Record Book	3.75/2.50
True Baseball Yearbook	4.50/3.00
Who's Who in Baseball	
(Baseball Magazine)	6.00/4.00

****
** 1957 PUBLICATIONS, MAGAZINES, AND ANNUALS **
****

Baseball Digest	
regular issue	1.25/ .75
special issue	2.00/1.25
Baseball Magazine	
regular issue	2.00/1.25
special issue	3.00/2.00
Baseball's All-Stars (Maco)	4.50/3.00
Dell Baseball Annual	5.00/3.00
Dell Baseball Stars	4.50/3.00
Dell Who's Who in Baseball	4.50/3.00
Dell Who's Who in Big Leagues	5.00/3.00
H & B Famous Slugger Yearbook	3.75/2.50
Inside Baseball	4.00/2.75
League Books	
Green Book - National	7.50/5.00
Red Book - American	7.50/5.00
Little Red Book of Baseball	3.75/2.50
Sport Magazine	
regular issue	2.50/1.75
special issue	5.00/3.00
Baseball's Best	7.50/5.00
Sports Illustrated	
regular issue	.40/ .25
special issue	1.50/1.00
Sports Review Baseball Yearly	3.75/2.50
Street & Smith	
baseball annual	10.00/6.00
The Sporting News	
regular issue	1.50/1.00
special issue	3.00/2.00
Knotty Problems	3.00/2.00
Register	11.00/7.00
Guide	9.00/6.00
Dope Book	3.75/2.50
One For The Book	3.75/2.50
W.S. Record Book	3.75/2.50
True Baseball Yearbook	4.50/3.00
Who's Who in Baseball	
(Baseball Magazine)	6.00/4.00

****
** 1958 PUBLICATIONS, MAGAZINES, AND ANNUALS **
****

Baseball Digest	
regular issue	1.25/ .75
special issue	2.00/1.25
Baseball Heroes	4.00/2.75
Baseball's All-Stars (Maco)	4.50/3.00
Dell Baseball Annual	5.00/3.00
Dell Baseball Stars	4.00/2.75
Dell Who's Who in Baseball	4.00/2.75
Dell Who's Who in Big Leagues	5.00/3.00
H & B Famous Slugger Yearbook	3.75/2.50
Inside Baseball	3.00/2.00
League Books	
Green Book - National	7.50/5.00
Red Book - American	7.50/5.00
Little Red Book of Baseball	3.75/2.50
Sport Magazine	
regular issue	2.00/1.25
special issue	4.00/2.50
Baseball's Best	7.50/5.00
Sports Illustrated	
regular issue	.40/ .25
special issue	1.50/1.00
Sports Review Baseball Yearly	3.75/2.50
Street & Smith	
baseball annual	10.00/6.00
The Sporting News	
regular issue	1.50/1.00
special issue	3.00/2.00
Daguerreotypes	7.50/5.00
Knotty Problems	3.00/2.00
Register	11.00/7.00
Guide	9.00/6.00
Dope Book	3.75/2.50
Official Baseball Rules	2.00/1.25
One For The Book	3.75/2.50
W.S. Record Book	3.75/2.50
True Baseball Yearbook	4.50/3.00
Whitestone Baseball Heroes	6.00/4.00
Who's Who in Baseball	
(Baseball Magazine)	6.00/4.00

****
** 1959 PUBLICATIONS, MAGAZINES, AND ANNUALS **
****

Baseball Digest	
regular issue	1.25/ .75
special issue	2.00/1.25
Baseball Heroes	4.00/2.75
Baseball's All-Stars (Maco)	4.50/3.00
Dell Baseball Annual	5.00/3.00
Dell Baseball Stars	4.00/2.75
Dell Who's Who in Baseball	4.00/2.75
Dell Who's Who in Big Leagues	4.00/2.75
H & B Famous Slugger Yearbook	3.75/2.50
Inside Baseball	3.00/2.00
League Books	
Green Book - National	7.50/5.00
Red Book - American	7.50/5.00
Little Red Book of Baseball	3.75/2.50
Sport Magazine	
regular issue	2.00/1.25
special issue	4.00/2.50
Baseball's Best	7.50/5.00
Sports Forecast - Baseball	4.50/3.00
Sports Illustrated	
regular issue	.40/ .25
special issue	1.50/1.00
Sports Review Baseball Yearly	3.75/2.50
Street & Smith	
baseball annual	10.00/6.00
The Sporting News	
regular issue	1.50/1.00
special issue	3.00/2.00
Register	11.00/7.00
Guide	7.50/5.00
Dope Book	3.75/2.50
Knotty Problems	3.00/2.00
Official Baseball Rules	2.00/1.25
One For The Book	3.75/2.50
W.S. Record Book	3.75/2.50

True Baseball Yearbook	4.50/3.00
Whitestone Baseball Heroes	4.50/3.00
Who's Who in Baseball	
(Baseball Magazine)	5.00/3.00

** 1960 PUBLICATIONS, MAGAZINES, AND ANNUALS **

Baseball Digest	
regular issue	1.25/ .75
special issue	2.00/1.25
Baseball's All-Stars (Maco)	4.50/3.00
Dell Baseball Annual	4.50/3.00
Dell Baseball Stars	4.00/2.75
Dell Who's Who in Baseball	4.00/2.75
Dell Who's Who in Big Leagues	4.00/2.75
H & B Famous Slugger Yearbook	3.00/2.00
Inside Baseball	3.00/2.00
League Books	
Green Book - National	7.50/5.00
Red Book - American	7.50/5.00
Little Red Book of Baseball	3.75/2.50
Sport Magazine	
regular issue	2.00/1.25
special issue	4.00/2.50
Baseball's Best	7.50/5.00
Sports Forecast - Baseball	4.50/3.00
Sports Illustrated	
regular issue	.40/ .25
special issue	1.50/1.00
Sports Review Baseball Yearly	3.00/2.00
Street & Smith	
baseball annual	9.00/6.50
The Sporting News	
regular issue	1.50/1.00
special issue	3.00/2.00
Register	11.00/7.00
Guide	7.50/5.00
Dope Book	3.75/2.50
Official Baseball Rules	2.00/1.25
One For The Book	3.00/2.00
W.S. Record Book	3.00/2.00
True Baseball Yearbook	4.50/3.00
Whitestone Baseball Annual	4.50/3.00
Who's Who in Baseball	
(Baseball Magazine)	5.00/3.00

** 1961 PUBLICATIONS, MAGAZINES, AND ANNUALS **

Baseball Digest	
regular issue	1.25/ .75
special issue	2.00/1.25
Baseball's All-Stars (Maco)	4.50/3.00
Dell Baseball Annual	4.50/3.00
Dell Baseball Stars	3.75/2.50
Dell Who's Who in Baseball	3.75/2.50
H & B Famous Slugger Yearbook	3.00/2.00
Inside Baseball Annual	5.00/3.00
League Books	
Green Book - National	7.50/5.00
Red Book - American	7.50/5.00
Little Red Book of Baseball	3.00/2.00
Sport Magazine	
regular issue	2.00/1.25
special issue	4.00/2.50
Sports Illustrated	
regular issue	.30/ .20
special issue	1.00/ .60
Sports Review Baseball Yearly	3.00/2.00
Street & Smith	
baseball annual	8.00/5.50
The Sporting News	
regular issue	1.50/1.00
special issue	3.00/2.00
Daguerreotypes	7.50/5.00
Register	11.00/7.00
Guide	7.50/5.00
Dope Book	3.75/2.50
Official Baseball Rules	2.00/1.25
One For The Book	3.00/2.00
W.S. Record Book	3.00/2.00
True Baseball Yearbook	4.50/3.00
Whitestone Baseball Annual	3.75/2.50
Who's Who in Baseball	
(Baseball Magazine)	5.00/3.00

** 1962 PUBLICATIONS, MAGAZINES, AND ANNUALS **

Baseball Digest	
regular issue	1.25/ .75
special issue	2.00/1.25
Baseball Monthly	
Vol. 1, #1	9.00/6.00
other issues	3.00/2.00
Baseball's All-Stars (Maco)	3.75/2.50
Dell Baseball Annual	4.50/3.00
Dell Baseball Stars	3.00/2.00
Dell Who's Who in Baseball	3.75/2.50
H & B Famous Slugger Yearbook	3.00/2.00
League Books	
Green Book - National	7.50/5.00
Red Book - American	7.50/5.00
Little Red Book of Baseball	3.00/2.00
Sport Magazine	
regular issue	1.50/1.00
special issue	3.00/2.00
Sports Illustrated	
regular issue	.30/ .20
special issue	1.00/ .60
Sports Review Baseball Yearly	3.00/2.00
Street & Smith	
baseball annual	7.00/5.00
The Sporting News	
regular issue	1.50/1.00
special issue	3.00/2.00
Register	11.00/7.00
Guide	7.50/5.00
Dope Book	3.00/2.00
Official Baseball Rules	2.00/1.25
One For The Book	3.00/2.00
W.S. Record Book	3.00/2.00
True Baseball Yearbook	3.75/2.50
Whitestone Baseball Annual	3.75/2.50
Who's Who in Baseball	
(Baseball Magazine)	5.00/3.00

****

** 1963 PUBLICATIONS, MAGAZINES, AND ANNUALS **

****

Publication	Price
Baseball Digest	
regular issue	1.00/ .60
special issue	1.50/1.00
Baseball's All-Stars (Maco)	3.75/2.50
Dell Baseball Annual	4.50/3.00
Dell Baseball Stars	3.00/2.00
Dell Who's Who in Baseball	3.00/2.00
H & B Famous Slugger Yearbook	3.00/2.00
League Books	
Green Book - National	6.00/4.00
Red Book - American	6.00/4.00
Little Red Book of Baseball	3.00/2.00
Sport Magazine	
regular issue	1.50/1.00
special issue	3.00/2.00
Sports Illustrated	
regular issue	.30/ .20
special issue	1.00/ .60
Sports Review Baseball Yearly	3.00/2.00
Street & Smith	
baseball annual	7.00/5.00
The Sporting News	
regular issue	1.00/ .60
special issue	2.00/1.25
Register	11.00/7.00
Guide	7.50/5.00
Dope Book	3.00/2.00
Official Baseball Rules	2.00/1.25
One For The Book	3.00/2.00
W.S. Record Book	3.00/2.00
True Baseball Yearbook	3.75/2.50
Whitestone Baseball Annual	3.75/2.50
Who's Who in Baseball (Baseball Magazine)	5.00/3.00

****

** 1964 PUBLICATIONS, MAGAZINES, AND ANNUALS **

****

Publication	Price
Baseball Digest	
regular issue	1.00/ .60
special issue	1.50/1.00
Baseball's All-Stars (Maco)	3.75/2.50
Complete Sports	
Baseball Illustrated	4.50/3.00
Dell Baseball Annual	4.50/3.00
Dell Baseball Stars	3.00/2.00
Dell Who's Who in Baseball	3.00/2.00
H & B Famous Slugger Yearbook	3.00/2.00
League Books	
Green Book - National	6.00/4.00
Red Book - American	6.00/4.00
Little Red Book of Baseball	3.00/2.00
Sport Magazine	
regular issue	1.50/1.00
special issue	3.00/2.00
Sports Illustrated	
regular issue	.30/ .20
special issue	1.00/ .60
Sports Quarterly	
Baseball Annual	3.75/2.50
Sports Review Baseball Yearly	3.00/2.00
Sports Special - Baseball	3.75/2.50
Street & Smith	
baseball annual	7.00/5.00
The Sporting News	
regular issue	1.00/ .60
special issue	2.00/1.25
Register	9.00/6.00
Guide	6.00/4.00
Dope Book	3.00/2.00
Official Baseball Rules	2.00/1.25
One For The Book	3.00/2.00
W.S. Record Book	3.00/2.00
True Baseball Yearbook	3.75/2.50
Whitestone Baseball Annual	3.75/2.50
Who's Who in Baseball (Baseball Magazine)	4.50/3.00

****

** 1965 PUBLICATIONS, MAGAZINES, AND ANNUALS **

****

Publication	Price
Baseball Digest	
regular issue	1.00/ .60
special issue	1.50/1.00
Baseball's All-Stars (Maco)	3.00/2.00
Dell Baseball Annual	4.50/3.00
H & B Famous Slugger Yearbook	3.00/2.00
Hollander Baseball Yearbook	4.50/3.00
League Books	
Green Book - National	6.00/4.00
Red Book - American	6.00/4.00
Little Red Book of Baseball	3.00/2.00
Sport Magazine	
regular issue	1.50/1.00
special issue	3.00/2.00
Sports Illustrated	
regular issue	.30/ .20
special issue	1.00/ .60
Sports Quarterly	
Baseball Annual	3.75/2.50
Sports Review Baseball Yearly	3.00/2.00
Sports Special - Baseball	3.75/2.50
Street & Smith	
baseball annual	7.00/5.00
The Sporting News	
regular issue	1.00/ .60
special issue	2.00/1.25
Register	9.00/6.00
Guide	6.00/4.00
Dope Book	3.00/2.00
Official Baseball Rules	2.00/1.25
One For The Book	3.00/2.00
W.S. Record Book	3.00/2.00
True Baseball Yearbook	3.75/2.50
Whitestone Baseball Annual	3.75/2.50
Who's Who in Baseball (Baseball Magazine)	4.50/3.00

****

** 1966 PUBLICATIONS, MAGAZINES, AND ANNUALS **

****

Publication	Price
Baseball Digest	
regular issue	1.00/ .60
special issue	1.50/1.00
Baseball's All-Stars (Maco)	3.00/2.00
Complete Sports	
Baseball Illustrated	3.75/2.50
Dell Baseball Annual	4.50/3.00
H & B Famous Slugger Yearbook	3.00/2.00
Hollander Baseball Yearbook	3.75/2.50
League Books	
Green Book - National	6.00/4.00
Red Book - American	6.00/4.00
Little Red Book of Baseball	3.00/2.00
Sport Magazine	
regular issue	1.50/1.00
special issue	3.00/2.00
Sports Illustrated	
regular issue	.30/ .20
special issue	1.00/ .60
Sports Quarterly	
Baseball Annual	3.75/2.50
Sports Review Baseball Yearly	3.00/2.00
Sports Special - Baseball	3.75/2.50
Street & Smith	
baseball annual	6.00/4.00
The Sporting News	
regular issue	.75/ .50
special issue	1.50/1.00
Register	9.00/6.00
Guide	6.00/4.00
Dope Book	3.00/2.00
Official Baseball Rules	2.00/1.25
One For The Book	3.00/2.00
W.S. Record Book	3.00/2.00

True Baseball Yearbook 3.75/2.50
Whitestone Baseball Annual 3.75/2.50
Who's Who in Baseball
(Baseball Magazine) 4.50/3.00

****

** 1967 PUBLICATIONS, MAGAZINES, AND ANNUALS **

****

Baseball Digest	
regular issue	.75/ .50
special issue	1.25/ .75
Baseball's All-Stars (Maco)	3.00/2.00
Complete Sports	
Baseball Illustrated	3.75/2.50
Dell Baseball Annual	4.50/3.00
H & B Famous Slugger Yearbook	3.00/2.00
Hollander Baseball Yearbook	3.75/2.50
League Books	
Green Book - National	6.00/4.00
Red Book - American	6.00/4.00
Little Red Book of Baseball	3.00/2.00
Sport Magazine	
regular issue	1.25/ .75
special issue	2.25/1.50
Sports Illustrated	
regular issue	.30/ .20
special issue	1.00/ .60
Sports Quarterly	
Baseball Annual	3.00/2.50
Sports Review Baseball Yearly	3.00/2.00
Sports Special - Baseball	3.75/2.50
Street & Smith	
baseball annual	6.00/4.00
The Sporting News	
regular issue	.75/ .50
special issue	1.50/1.00
Register	9.00/6.00
Guide	6.00/4.00
Dope Book	3.00/2.00
Official Baseball Rules	2.00/1.25
One For The Book	3.00/2.00
W.S. Record Book	3.00/2.00
True Baseball Yearbook	3.75/2.50
Who's Who in Baseball	
(Baseball Magazine)	4.50/3.00

****

** 1968 PUBLICATIONS, MAGAZINES, AND ANNUALS **

****

Baseball Digest	
regular issue	.75/ .50
special issue	1.25/ .75
Baseball's All-Stars (Maco)	3.00/2.00
Complete Sports	
Baseball Illustrated	3.75/2.50
Dell Baseball Annual	4.50/3.00
H & B Famous Slugger Yearbook	3.00/2.00
Hollander Baseball Yearbook	3.75/2.50
League Books	
Green Book - National	6.00/4.00
Red Book - American	6.00/4.00
Little Red Book of Baseball	3.00/2.00
Sport Magazine	
regular issue	1.25/ .75
special issue	2.25/1.50
Sports Illustrated	
regular issue	.25/ .15
special issue	.75/ .50
Sports Quarterly	
Baseball Annual	3.00/2.00
Sports Review Baseball Yearly	3.00/2.00
Sports Special - Baseball	3.75/2.50
Street & Smith	
baseball annual	6.00/4.00
The Sporting News	
regular issue	.50/ .30
special issue	1.00/ .60
Daguerreotypes	9.00/5.00
Register	7.50/5.00
Guide	6.00/4.00
Dope Book	3.00/2.00
Official Baseball Rules	2.00/1.25
One For The Book	3.00/2.00
W.S. Record Book	2.00/1.25
True Baseball Yearbook	3.00/2.00
Who's Who in Baseball	
(Baseball Magazine)	4.00/2.75

****

** 1969 PUBLICATIONS, MAGAZINES, AND ANNUALS **

****

Baseball Digest	
regular issue	.75/ .50
special issue	1.25/ .75
Baseball's All-Stars (Maco)	3.00/2.00
Complete Sports	
Baseball Illustrated	3.75/2.50
Dell Baseball Annual	4.50/3.00
H & B Famous Slugger Yearbook	3.00/2.00
Hollander Baseball Yearbook	3.75/2.50
League Books	
Green Book - National	6.00/4.00
Red Book - American	6.00/4.00
Little Red Book of Baseball	3.00/2.00
Sport Magazine	
regular issue	1.00/ .60
special issue	2.00/1.25
Sports Illustrated	
regular issue	.25/ .15
special issue	.75/ .50
Sports Quarterly	
Baseball Annual	3.00/2.00
Sports Review Baseball Yearly	3.00/2.00
Sports Special - Baseball	3.75/2.50
Street & Smith	
baseball annual	5.50/3.75
The Sporting News	
regular issue	.50/ .30
special issue	1.00/ .60
Register	7.50/5.00
Guide	6.00/4.00
Dope Book	3.00/2.00
Official Baseball Rules	2.00/1.25
One For The Book	2.00/1.25
W.S. Record Book	2.00/1.25
True Baseball Yearbook	3.00/2.00
Who's Who in Baseball	
(Baseball Magazine)	4.00/2.75

****

** 1970 PUBLICATIONS, MAGAZINES, AND ANNUALS **

****

Baseball Digest	
regular issue	.75/ .50
special issue	1.25/ .75
Baseball's All-Stars (Maco)	3.00/2.00
Complete Sports	
Baseball Illustrated	3.75/2.50
Dell Baseball Annual	3.75/2.50
H & B Famous Slugger Yearbook	3.00/2.00
Hollander Baseball Yearbook	3.75/2.50
League Books	
Green Book - National	6.00/4.00
Red Book - American	6.00/4.00
Little Red Book of Baseball	3.00/2.00
Sport Magazine	
regular issue	1.00/ .60
special issue	2.00/1.25
Sports Illustrated	
regular issue	.25/ .15
special issue	.75/ .50
Sports Quarterly	
Baseball Annual	3.00/2.00
Sports Review Baseball Yearly	3.00/2.00
Sports Special - Baseball	3.75/2.50
Street & Smith	
baseball annual	5.00/3.00

The Sporting News	
regular issue	.35/ .25
special issue	1.00/ .60
Register	7.50/5.00
Guide	4.50/3.00
Dope Book	3.00/2.00
Official Baseball Rules	2.00/1.25
One For The Book	2.00/1.25
W.S. Record Book	2.00/1.25
True Baseball Yearbook	3.00/2.00
Who's Who in Baseball	
(Baseball Magazine)	3.50/2.50

****
** 1971 PUBLICATIONS, MAGAZINES, AND ANNUALS **
****

Baseball Digest	
regular issue	.75/ .50
special issue	1.25/ .75
Complete Sports	
Baseball Illustrated	3.00/2.50
Dell Baseball Annual	3.75/2.50
H & B Famous Slugger Yearbook	3.00/2.00
Hollander Baseball Yearbook	3.75/2.50
League Books	
Green Book - National	6.00/4.00
Red Book - American	6.00/4.00
Little Red Book of Baseball	3.00/2.00
Sport Magazine	
regular issue	1.00/ .60
special issue	2.00/1.25
Sports Illustrated	
regular issue	.75/ .15
special issue	.50/ .25
Sports Quarterly	
Baseball Annual	3.00/2.00
Sports Review Baseball Yearly	3.00/2.00
Sports Special - Baseball	3.75/2.50
Street & Smith	
baseball annual	4.50/3.00
The Sporting News	
regular issue	.35/ .25
special issue	.75/ .50
Daguerreotypes	6.00/4.00
Register	7.50/5.00
Guide	4.50/3.00
Dope Book	3.00/2.00
Official Baseball Rules	2.00/1.25
One For The Book	2.00/1.25
W.S. Record Book	2.00/1.25
True Baseball Yearbook	3.00/2.00
Who's Who in Baseball	
(Baseball Magazine)	3.50/2.50

****
** 1972 PUBLICATIONS, MAGAZINES, AND ANNUALS **
****

Baseball Digest	
regular issue	.50/ .30
special issue	1.00/ .60
Complete Sports	
Baseball Illustrated	3.00/2.00
Dell Baseball Annual	3.00/2.00
H & B Famous Slugger Yearbook	2.25/1.50
League Books	
Green Book - National	4.50/3.00
Red Book - American	4.50/3.00
Sport Magazine	
regular issue	.75/1.50
special issue	1.50/1.00
Sports Illustrated	
regular issue	.25/ .15
special issue	.50/ .35
Sports Quarterly	
Baseball Annual	3.00/2.00
Sports Special - Baseball	3.00/2.00
Street & Smith	
baseball annual	4.00/2.75
The Sporting News	
regular issue	.35/ .25
special issue	.75/ .50
Baseball Record Book	3.75/2.50
Register	7.50/5.00
Guide	4.50/3.00
Dope Book	3.00/2.00
Official Baseball Rules	2.00/1.25
W.S. Record Book	2.00/1.25
True Baseball Yearbook	3.00/2.00
Who's Who in Baseball	
(Baseball Magazine)	3.00/2.00

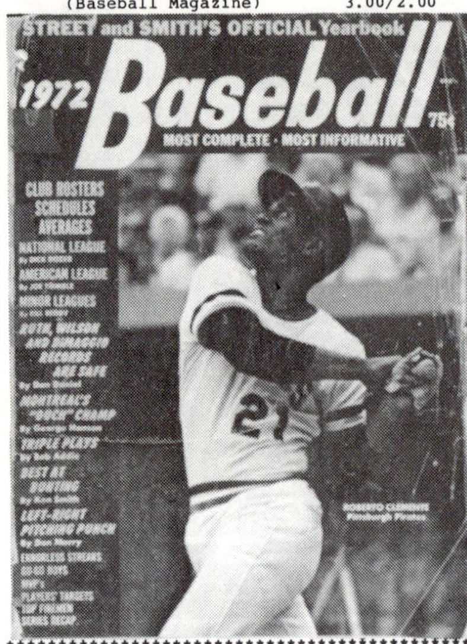

****
** 1973 PUBLICATIONS, MAGAZINES, AND ANNUALS **
****

Baseball Digest	
regular issue	.50/ .30
special issue	1.00/ .60
Complete Sports	
Baseball Illustrated	3.00/2.00
Dell Baseball Annual	3.00/2.00
H & B Famous Slugger Yearbook	2.25/1.50
League Books	
Green Book - National	4.50/3.00
Red Book - American	4.50/3.00
Sport Magazine	
regular issue	.75/ .50
special issue	1.50/1.00
Sports Illustrated	
regular issue	.25/ .15
special issue	.30/ .20
Sports Quarterly	
Baseball Annual	3.00/2.00
Sports Special - Baseball	3.00/2.00
Street & Smith	
baseball annual	3.50/2.50
The Sporting News	
regular issue	.35/ .25
special issue	.75/ .50
Baseball Record Book	3.00/2.00
Register	6.00/4.00
Guide	4.50/3.00
Dope Book	3.00/2.00
Official Baseball Rules	2.00/1.25
W.S. Record Book	2.00/1.25
True Baseball Yearbook	3.00/2.00
Who's Who in Baseball	
(Baseball Magazine)	3.00/2.00

1974 PUBLICATIONS, MAGAZINES, AND ANNUALS

Publication	Price
Baseball Digest	
regular issue	.50/ .30
special issue	1.00/ .60
Complete Sports	
Baseball Illustrated	3.00/2.00
Dell Baseball Annual	3.00/2.00
H & B Famous Slugger Yearbook	2.25/1.50
League Books	
Green Book - National	4.50/3.00
Red Book - American	4.50/3.00
Sport Magazine	
regular issue	.75/ .50
special issue	1.50/1.00
Sports Illustrated	
regular issue	.25/ .15
special issue	.50/ .30
Sports Quarterly	
Baseball Annual	3.00/2.00
Sports Special - Baseball	3.00/2.00
Street & Smith	
baseball annual	3.00/2.00
The Sporting News	
regular issue	.25/ .15
special issue	.50/ .30
Baseball Record Book	3.00/2.00
Register	6.00/4.00
Guide	4.50/3.00
Dope Book	2.00/1.25
Official Baseball Rules	2.00/1.25
W.S. Record Book	2.00/1.25
True Baseball Yearbook	3.00/2.00
Who's Who in Baseball	
(Baseball Magazine)	3.00/2.00

1975 PUBLICATIONS, MAGAZINES, AND ANNUALS

Publication	Price
Baseball Digest	
regular issue	.35/ .25
special issue	.75/ .50
Complete Sports	
Baseball Illustrated	3.00/2.00
Dell Baseball Annual	3.00/2.00
H & B Famous Slugger Yearbook	2.25/1.50
League Books	
Green Book - National	4.50/3.00
Red Book - American	4.50/3.00
Sport Magazine	
regular issue	.50/ .30
special issue	1.00/ .60
Sports Illustrated	
regular issue	.15/ .10
special issue	.30/ .20
Sports Quarterly	
Baseball Annual	3.00/2.00
Street & Smith	
baseball annual	3.00/2.00
The Sporting News	
regular issue	.25/ .15
special issue	.50/ .30
Baseball Record Book	3.00/2.00
Register	6.00/4.00
Guide	4.50/3.00
Dope Book	3.00/2.00
Official Baseball Rules	2.00/1.25
W.S. Record Book	2.00/1.25
True Baseball Yearbook	3.00/2.00
Who's Who in Baseball	
(Baseball Magazine)	3.00/2.00

1976 PUBLICATIONS, MAGAZINES, AND ANNUALS

Publication	Price
Baseball Digest	
regular issue	.35/ .25
special issue	.75/ .50
Complete Sports	
Baseball Illustrated	3.00/2.00
Dell Baseball Annual	3.00/2.00
H & B Famous Slugger Yearbook	2.00/1.25
League Books	
Green Book - National	4.50/3.00
Red Book - American	4.50/3.00
Sport Magazine	
regular issue	.50/ .30
special issue	1.00/ .60
Sports Illustrated	
regular issue	.15/ .10
special issue	.30/ .20
Sports Quarterly	
Baseball Annual	3.00/2.00
Street & Smith	
baseball annual	3.00/2.00
The Sporting News	
regular issue	.25/ .15
special issue	.50/ .30
Baseball Record Book	3.00/2.00
Register	5.00/3.00
Guide	4.00/2.75
Dope Book	2.00/1.25
Official Baseball Rules	2.00/1.25
W.S. Record Book	2.00/1.25
True Baseball Yearbook	3.00/2.00
Who's Who in Baseball	
(Baseball Magazine)	3.00/2.00

1977 PUBLICATIONS, MAGAZINES, AND ANNUALS

Publication	Price
Baseball Digest	
regular issue	.35/ .25
special issue	.75/ .50
Complete Sports	
Baseball Illustrated	3.00/2.00
Dell Baseball Annual	3.00/2.00
H & B Famous Slugger Yearbook	2.00/1.25
League Books	
Green Book - National	4.50/3.00
Red Book - American	4.50/3.00
Sport Magazine	
regular issue	.50/ .30
special issue	1.00/ .60
Sports Illustrated	
regular issue	.15/ .10
special issue	.30/ .20
Sports Quarterly	
Baseball Annual	3.00/2.00
Street & Smith	
baseball annual	3.00/2.00
The Sporting News	
regular issue	.25/ .15
special issue	.50/ .30
Baseball Record Book	3.00/2.00
Register	5.00/3.00
Guide	4.00/2.75
Dope Book	2.00/1.25
Official Baseball Rules	2.00/1.25
W.S. Record Book	2.00/1.25
True Baseball Yearbook	2.00/1.25
Who's Who in Baseball	
(Baseball Magazine)	3.00/2.00

1978 PUBLICATIONS, MAGAZINES, AND ANNUALS

Publication	Price
Baseball Digest	
regular issue	.35/ .25
special issue	.75/ .50
Complete Sports	
Baseball Illustrated	2.00/1.25
Dell Baseball Annual	3.00/2.00
H & B Famous Slugger Yearbook	2.00/1.25
League Books	
Green Book - National	4.50/3.00
Red Book - American	4.50/3.00

Sport Magazine	
regular issue	.35/ .25
special issue	.75/ .50
Sports Illustrated	
regular issue	.15/ .10
special issue	.30/ .20
Sports Quarterly	
Baseball Annual	2.00/1.25
Street & Smith	
baseball annual	3.00/2.00
The Sporting News	
regular issue	.25/ .15
special issue	.50/ .30
Baseball Record Book	3.00/2.00
Register	5.00/3.00
Guide	3.50/2.50
Dope Book	2.00/1.25
Official Baseball Rules	2.00/1.25
W.S. Record Book	2.00/1.25
True Baseball Yearbook	2.00/1.25
Who's Who in Baseball	
(Baseball Magazine)	2.50/1.50

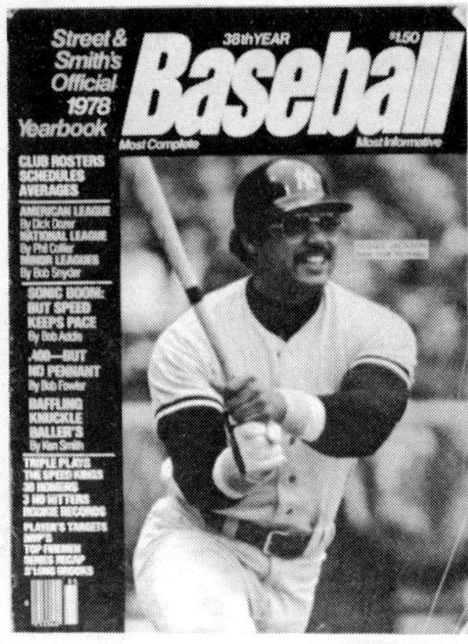

****

** 1979 PUBLICATIONS, MAGAZINES, AND ANNUALS **

****

Baseball Digest	
regular issue	.25/ .15
special issue	.50/ .30
Complete Sports	
Baseball Illustrated	2.00/1.25
Dell Baseball Annual	3.00/2.00
H & B Famous Slugger Yearbook	1.50/1.00
League Books	
Green Book - National	4.50/3.00
Red Book - American	4.50/3.00
Sport Magazine	
regular issue	.35/ .25
special issue	.75/ .50
Sports Illustrated	
regular issue	.15/ .10
special issue	.30/ .20
Sports Quarterly	
Baseball Annual	2.00/1.25
Street & Smith	
baseball annual	2.00/1.25
The Sporting News	
regular issue	.25/ .15
special issue	.50/ .30
Baseball Record Book	3.00/2.00
Register	5.00/3.00
Guide	3.50/2.50
Dope Book	2.00/1.25
Official Baseball Rules	2.00/1.25
One For The Book	2.00/1.25
W.S. Record Book	2.00/1.25
True Baseball Yearbook	2.00/1.25
Who's Who in Baseball	
(Baseball Magazine)	2.50/1.50

****

** 1980 PUBLICATIONS, MAGAZINES, AND ANNUALS **

****

Baseball Digest	
regular issue	.25/ .15
special issue	.50/ .30
Complete Sports	
Baseball Illustrated	2.00/1.25
Dell Baseball Annual	3.00/2.00
H & B Famous Slugger Yearbook	1.50/1.00
League Books	
Green Book - National	4.50/3.00
Red Book - American	4.50/3.00
Sport Magazine	
regular issue	.25/ .15
special issue	.50/ .30
Sports Illustrated	
regular issue	.15/ .10
special issue	.30/ .20
Sports Quarterly	
Baseball Annual	2.00/1.25
Street & Smith	
baseball annual	2.00/1.25
The Sporting News	
regular issue	.25/ .15
special issue	.50/ .30
Baseball Record Book	3.00/2.00
Register	5.00/3.00
Guide	3.50/2.50
Dope Book	2.00/1.25
Official Baseball Rules	2.00/1.25
W.S. Record Book	2.00/1.25
True Baseball Yearbook	2.00/1.25
Who's Who in Baseball	
(Baseball Magazine)	2.50/1.50

****

** 1981 PUBLICATIONS, MAGAZINES, AND ANNUALS **

****

Baseball Digest	
regular issue	.25/ .15
special issue	.50/ .30
Complete Sports	
Baseball Illustrated	2.00/1.25
Dell Baseball Annual	3.00/2.00
H & B Famous Slugger Yearbook	1.50/1.00
League Books	
Green Book - National	4.50/3.00
Red Book - American	4.50/3.00
Sport Magazine	
regular issue	.25/ .15
special issue	.50/ .30
Sports Illustrated	
regular issue	.15/ .10
special issue	.30/ .20
Sports Quarterly	
Baseball Annual	2.00/1.25
Street & Smith	
baseball annual	2.00/1.25
The Sporting News	
regular issue	.25/ .15
special issue	.50/ .30
Baseball Record Book	3.00/2.00
Daguerreotypes	8.00/5.50
Register	5.00/3.00
Guide	3.50/2.50
Dope Book	2.00/1.25
Official Baseball Rules	2.00/1.25
W.S. Record Book	2.00/1.25
True Baseball Yearbook	2.00/1.25
Who's Who in Baseball	
(Baseball Magazine)	2.50/1.50

SPAHN
MAYS
RUTH
MUSIAL
WILLIAMS
BERRA
APARACIO
GROAT
KILLEBREW
MARIS
SNIDER
DRYSDALE
COLAVITO
BANKS
MATTHEWS
MANTLE
AARON
FOX
BAT BOY
4" BATTER
WYATT EARP
FOOTBALL PLAYER
MATT DILLON
MAVERICK

WORLD SERIES PRESS PINS 1963-1980

63N L.A.

63A N.Y.

64N S.L.

64A N.Y.

65N L.A.

65A MINN

66N L.A.

66A BALT

67N S.L.

67A BOST

68A DET

68N S.L.

69N N.Y.

69A BALT

70N CINC

70A BALT

71N PITT

71A BALT

72N CINC

72A OAK1

73N N.Y.

73A OAK1

74N L.A.

74A OAK1

75N CINC

75A BOST

76N CINC

76A N.Y.

77N L.A.

77A N.Y.

78N L.A.

78A N.Y.

79N PITT

79A BALT

80N PHIL

80A K.C.

ALL-STAR GAME PRESS PINS
1941-1980

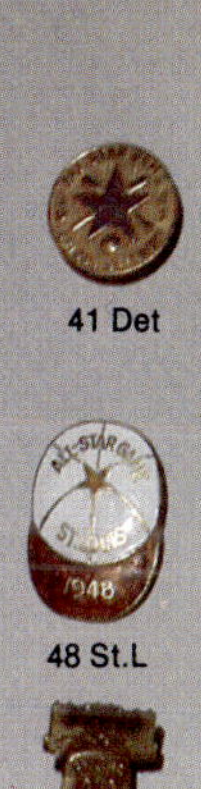

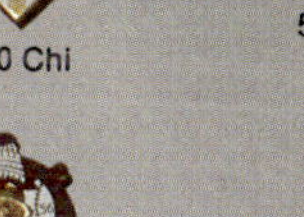

41 Det | 43 Phil | 46 Bost | 47 Chi

48 St.L | 49 Bkln | 46 Bost | 50 Chi | 51 Det

52 Phil | 54 Cleve | 55 Mil | 56 Wash | 57 St.L

58 Balt | 59 L.A. | 59 Pitt | 60 N.Y. | 60 K.C.

61 Bost | 61 S.F. | 62 Chi | 62 Wash | 63 Cleve | 64 N.Y.

65 Minn | 66 St.L | 67 Calif | 68 Hous | 69 Wash

70 Cinn | 71 Det | 72 Atl | 73 K.C. | 74 Pitt

75 Mil | 76 Phil | 77 N.Y. | 78 S.D. | 79 Seat | 80 L.A.

WRAPPERS 1933—1955

1933 GOUDEY

1934 GOUDEY

1936 GOUDEY

1938 GOUDEY

1941 GOUDEY

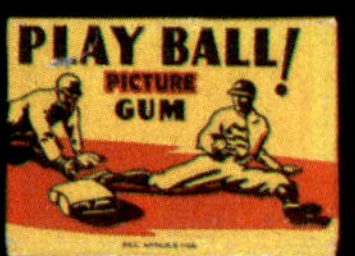

1933 DELONG

1933 SPORT KINGS

1934—36 DIAMOND STARS

1939 PLAY BALL

1940 PLAY BALL

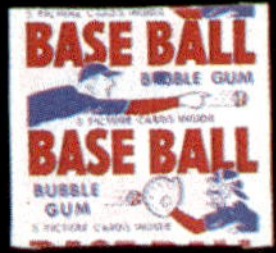

1949 BOWMAN

1951 BOWMAN

1952 BOWMAN

1953 BOWMAN B&W

1953 BOWMAN COLOR

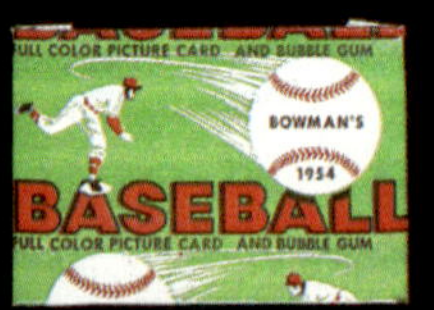

1954 BOWMAN

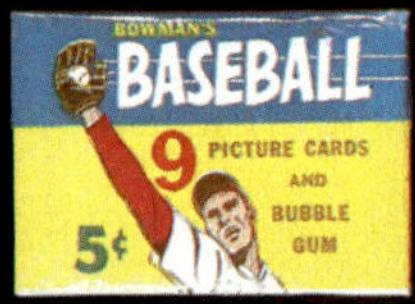

1955 BOWMAN

WRAPPERS
TOPPS 1951—1963
FLEER 1959-1963

1951 TOPPS REDBACK

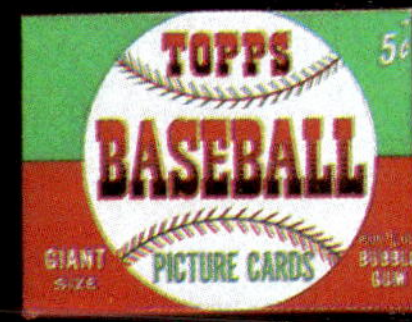

1952 TOPPS

1953 TOPPS

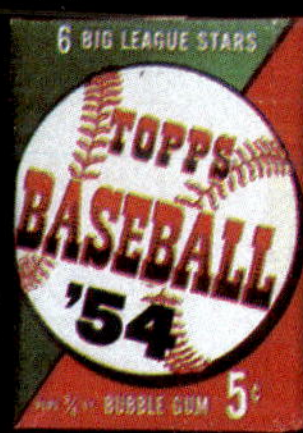

1954 TOPPS

1955 TOPPS

1955 TOPPS DOUBLEHEADER

1956 TOPPS

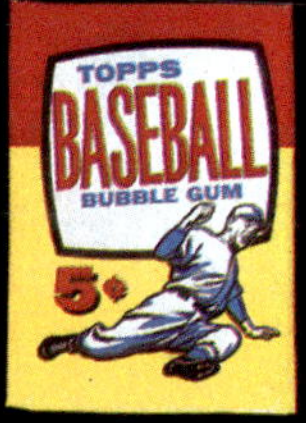

1957 TOPPS

1958 TOPPS—5¢

1958 TOPPS—1¢

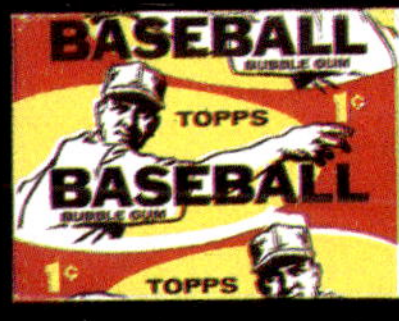

1959 TOPPS

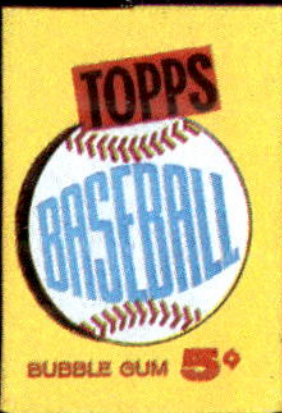

1960 TOPPS

1961 TOPPS

1962 TOPPS

1963 TOPPS

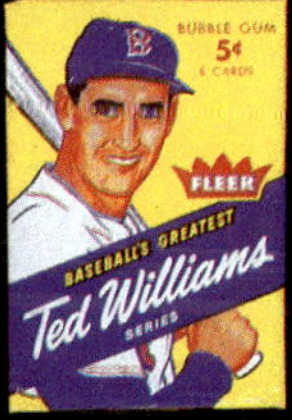

1959 FLEER

1960 FLEER

1961 FLEER

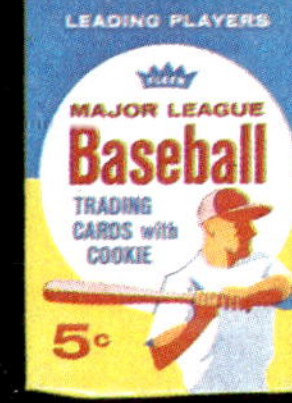

1963 FLEER

WRAPPERS
1964—1981 TOPPS
1981 DONRUSS & FLEER

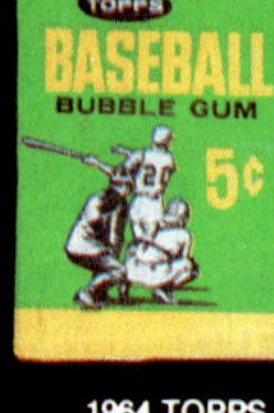

1964 TOPPS

1965 TOPPS

1966 TOPPS

1967 TOPPS

1968 TOPPS

1969 TOPPS

1970 TOPPS

1971 TOPPS

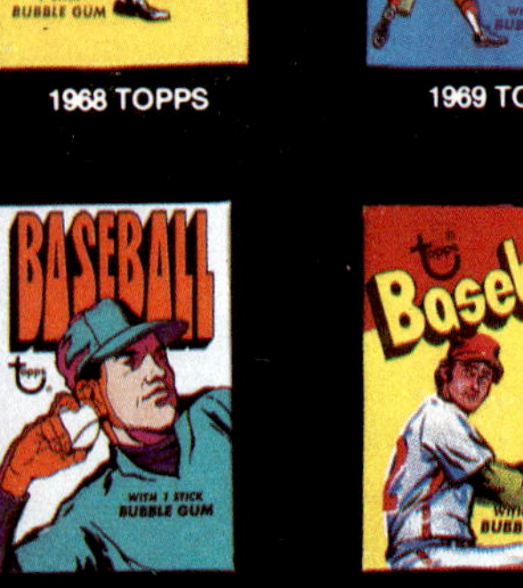

1972 TOPPS

1973 TOPPS

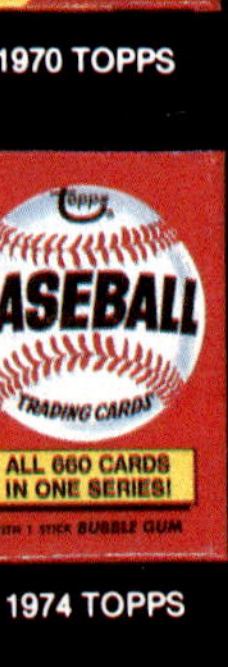

1974 TOPPS

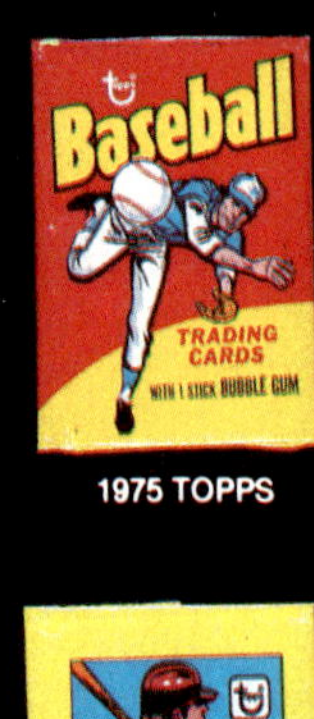

1975 TOPPS

1976 TOPPS

1977 TOPPS

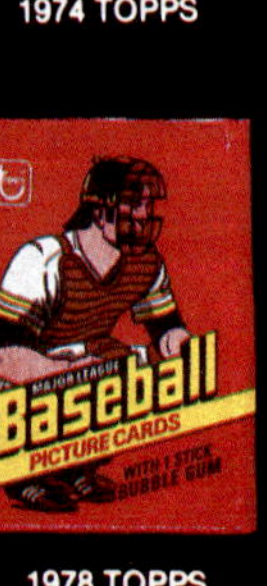

1978 TOPPS

1979 TOPPS

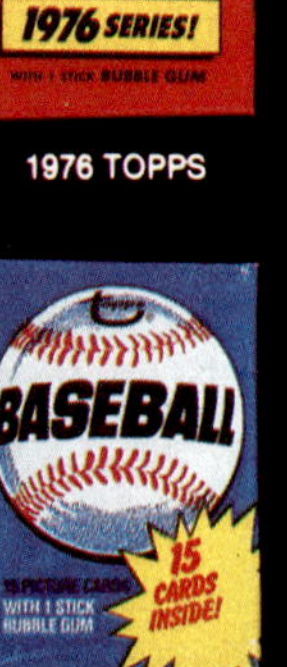

1980 TOPPS

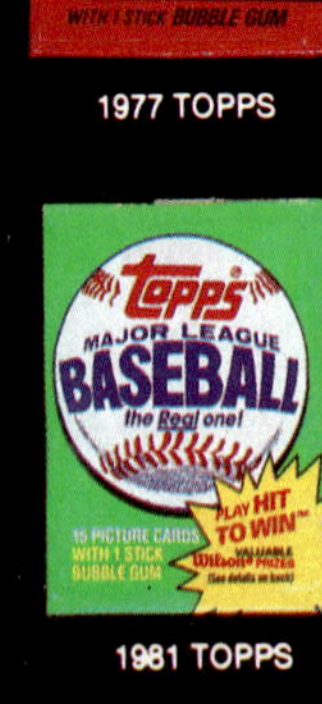

1981 TOPPS

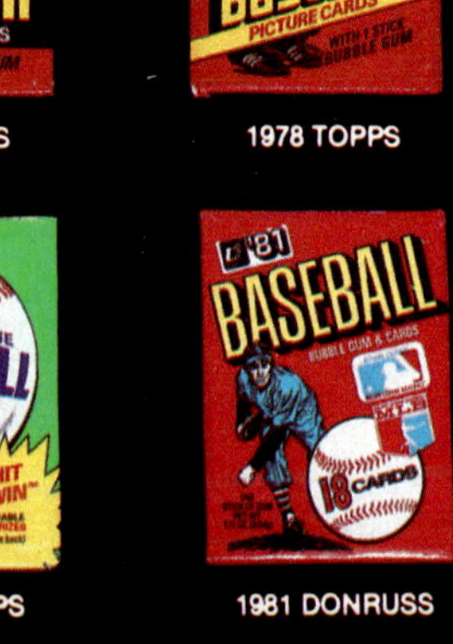

1981 DONRUSS

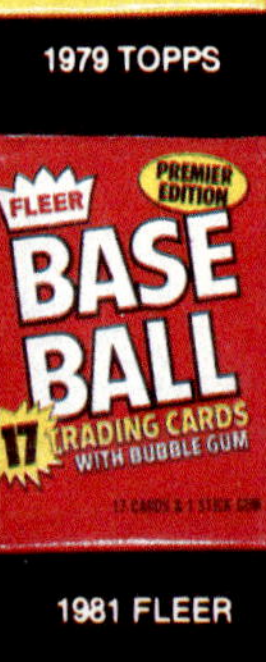

1981 FLEER

R316

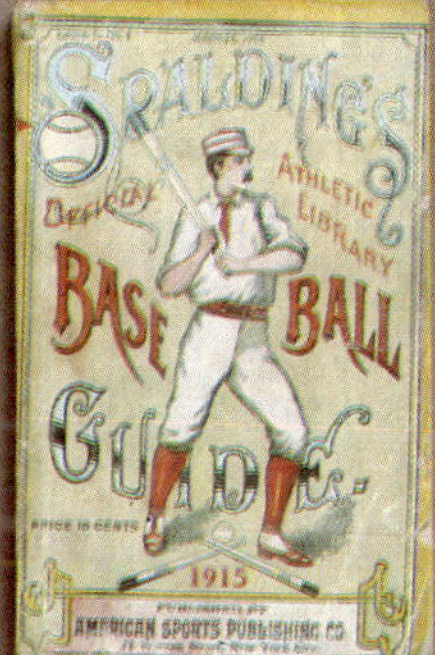

1915 SPALDING GUIDE

EXHIBIT CARD

STREET AND SMITH YEARBOOK

B18

WORLD SERIES PROGRAM

1961 TOPPS STAMPS

1969 TOPPS STAMPS

1962 TOPPS STAMPS

1961 TOPPS MAGIC RUB OFFS

1966 TOPPS RUB OFFS

1963 TOPPS STICK-ON INSERT

1969 TOPPS DECAL INSERT

1970 TOPPS STORY BOOKLET

1962 TOPPS BASEBALL BUCKS

1973 TOPPS CANDY LID

"1937" DIAMOND STAR ISSUED IN 1981

1970-71 TOPPS SCRATCH-OFF INSERT

DORMAND POSTCARD

BASEBALL COMMEMORATIVE ENVELOPE

PEREZ-STEELE

COINS & PINS

1956 TOPPS

1962 SALADA

1963 SALADA

1964 TOPPS

1964 TOPPS A/S

1964 TOPPS A/S

1971 TOPPS

ARMOUR

Baseball commemorative envelopes are not First Day Covers, which are very popular stamp collector items issued to mark the first day a new stamp is released to the public. There are many similarities, however, and the confusion between the two is understandable. A baseball commemorative envelope honors a significant baseball event, and has nothing whatsoever to do with the stamp placed on the envelope. A First Day Cover honors the issuance of the stamp on the envelope. After this distinction, most other aspects of the envelope can be similar. Both are neat, attractive (and in many cases artistic), usually devoid of an addressee, feature clear and legible cancellations, and are the type of item which exudes collectibility. The baseball commemorative envelope often contains an autograph in the place normally reserved for the addressee. An autograph on a First Day Cover, in most cases would be meaningless, although if the autographer had a direct connection with the stamp, such an autograph would seem quite appropriate and desirable.

Gateway Stamp Company, Inc., of Florrisant, Mo., issues full-color "silk" cachet (a picture, photo or other artwork on the face) envelopes which are postmarked on historic baseball occasions. The United States Postal Service will only date an item submitted prior to midnight of the date involved (except for First Day of Issue cancellations which are granted under special rules). Gateway's baseball (and other sports) commemoratives are not, as explained above, First Day Covers.

When a record of major importance is likely to occur, such as a player's 3,000th hit or his breaking an existing record, Gateway representatives follow that player to the city and date where the record is likely to occur. Upon the player's acquisition of the record, Gateway submits a determined number of envelopes with postage attached to the United States Postal Service in that city for hand-cancellation service. Hand-cancellation normally assures each envelope will be cleanly and deliberately dated. Additional charges are required by the Postal Service for hand-cancellation.

After dating, Gateway's commemorative envelopes undergo three printing processes. Separate companies print the gold borders, biographical copy, and the full-color silk cachets. The silks are one of Gateway's distinctive features and might include actual event photos (Brock's 3,000th hit), artists' renditions, or publicity photos as availability dictates at time of production.

A second distinctive Gateway feature is that most of the envelopes are personally autographed by the players commemorated. In the 113-year history of professional baseball, Gateway Stamp Company is the only company to create a product line in which every unit is designed to be personally autographed. Gateway's issues thereby are often limited in numbers to what players are able and willing to autograph. In its product line, Gateway has succeeded in acquiring for collectors autographs which have been considered "difficult" or "tough" on a very attractive, well-arranged item of historic significance.

The United States Postal Service has 302 post offices designated as philatelic stations, of which only a few have specially designed philatelic cancellations. Wherever possible, Gateway incorporates philatelic cancellations on its envelopes, especially where the design enhances the city's image. Philatelic cancellations used by Gateway include San Diego (Brock), Cincinnati (Rose & Seaver), Atlanta & New York (Rose), and Los Angeles (1978 World Series).

When unpredictable events such as no-hitters occur, Gateway is still under the midnight rule. The St. Louis based company must by whatever means possible submit envelopes to the Postal Service prior to midnight where the historic event occurs, or the postmarks are not granted. Nolan Ryan's fifth no-hitter in Houston and Len Barker's perfect game in Cleveland are examples of success in that regard.

Gateway officials stress a desire for uniformity; consequently, only five designated envelope variations have occurred from 1977-81. The handcrafted nature of each envelope might result in occasional erroneous placement of silks (50th All-Star player silk on logo envelope and vice versa). Use of different postage stamps of the same denomination exists, but should not be inordinately considered. Most Gateway envelopes bear commom postage stamps to avoid conflicting appearances with the sports theme of the envelope, and the existence of more than one type of stamp on the same envelope should not add to values in a true philatelic sense.

Cover condition entails cleanliness, envelope crispness and sharpness of corners (envelope manufacturers do not always fold envelopes with perfectly square corners), squaring of gold borders, centering of silks, positioning of title copy to the gold borders, clarity of postmarks, squareness of stamps to the upper right-hand corner, and quality of autographs (where a player's handwriting is consistent, readability of an autograph is not always a determinant of condition). Gateway makes every effort to provide "top notch" condition envelopes. As such, the authors feel justified in dispensing with condition as a prime determinant in the value of these envelopes. Future years might necessitate a change of philosophy in this regard, but at present, more value information can be presented in the available space by assuming (we think reasonably) that all envelopes are in "mint" condition.

Price information included with the descriptions can be interpreted as follows:

> The first price is the initial Gateway Stamp retail price at the time of issuance of the particular envelope. As many of the envelopes are issued and sold in sets of two or more, and in most cases, sets consist of both autographed and unautographed envelope components, autographed envelopes are arbitrarily valued at approximately twice the value of unautographed envelopes in the same set.
>
> The second price is the current or final (if out of stock) retail price as sold by Gateway; or the retail price as set by the marketplace when the item has had sufficient time at "out of stock" status to establish a new price, or when items which were not issued or released autographed by Gateway have been autographed subsequent to purchase.

There are many confirmed prices higher than those listed in the second price column; however, these confirmed prices might well be isolated cases, and the authors prefer to state prices for which sufficient sales have been made to justify such prices. As many of the envelopes listed now have a limited availability from Gateway, the number of out of stock items will no doubt increase as time goes by.

Several symbols have been used in the pricing data. These are:

NI - not issued by Gateway in the stated form
V - variation, not issued by Gateway without a special request from the purchaser
* - out of stock
Price + A - Add to this price the price listed in the player autographed section of this book for an autographed photo.

Other features which have a bearing on value which should be recognized are:

1. Gateway does not sell individual World Series Envelopes until all complete sets are sold.
2. Obtaining more than one autograph on an envelope, particularly if the autographs are those pictured on the cachet, would increase the value of that envelope.
3. Once an envelope reaches out of stock status, the differential in the value of a particular players autograph is expressed much more than in the initial price of an envelope, as Gateway does not usually differentiate player autographs (World Series or All-Star) by price.

Gateway Stamp Company was formed in 1977 to buy and sell stamps. In May of 1977, a number of large and small stamp companies throughout the United States issued their own designs of envelopes commemorating the 50th anniversary of the first solo flight across the Atlantic—the flight of Charles Lindbergh. Gateway entered into this market upon learning that a May 22nd cancellation would be issued by the United States Postal Service, but that no other company would be likely to acquire it. The Postal Service bulletins informing the public of special cancellations had accidentally omitted the May 22nd cancellation, so Gateway felt it had a significant opportunity to enter the cover market. In the process of selling the Lindbergh edition, someone mentioned to the president of Gateway, Mr. Tom Wiley, that someone should issue an envelope commemorating Lou Brock, another St. Louisan who would be making history of a different sort—baseball history—when he would tie and break the all-time stolen base record held by Ty Cobb. Mr. Wiley thought it was a great idea both from the standpoint of honoring Lou Brock and by his knowledge of covers in the philatelic world. A lack of existing sports covers might provide an excellent market for a Lou Brock commemorative. Wheras Lou Brock was Gateway's first baseball client, the Lindbergh predecessors deserve identification here to introduce Gateway's major product—baseball commemoratives and to provide consistency of the numbering system. No other publication has ever catalogued the Gateway issues, so here for the first time is a complete description and numbering of Gateway's baseball, football, and nonsport issues in chronological order.

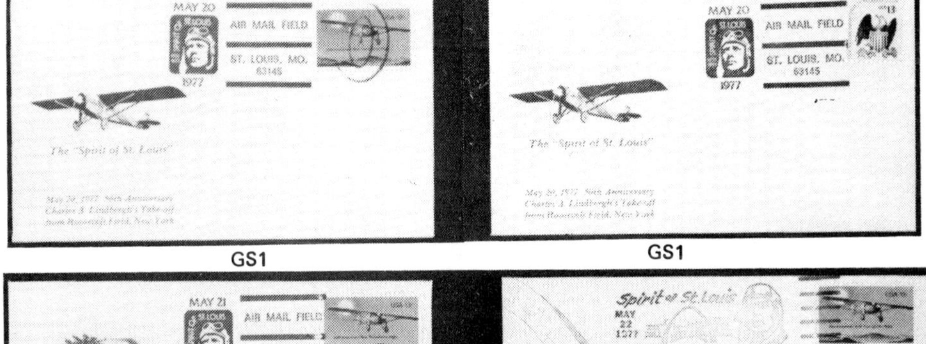

GS1 GS1

GS2 GS3

50th ANNIVERSARY OF THE FLIGHT OF CHARLES LINDBERGH
Set of Three

1977

GS1 CHARLES LINDBERGH. Postmarked May 20, 1977, St. Louis, with Air Mall Field Lindbergh Postmark. Envelope commemorates the 50th anniversary of Lindbergh's take-off from New York to Paris. Brown ink cachet design on plain white envelope. One thousand postmarks on 13 cent Lindbergh stamps issued that date in New York which were flown into St. Louis (first day of issue) and applied to envelopes for cancellation with 50th anniversary postmark. One thousand also issued with E. Pluribus Unum 13 cent stamp.

Envelopes postmarked on Lindbergh stamp	1.00	3.00
Envelopes postmarked on E. Pluribus Unum stamp	1.00	1.50

GS2 CHARLES LINDBERGH. Postmarked May 21, 1977, St. Louis, with Air Mail Field Lindbergh postmark. Envelope commemorates the 50th anniversary of Lindbergh's landing in Paris. Brown ink cachet design on plain white envelope. All postmarks on 13 cent Lindbergh commemorative stamp.

All envelopes	1.00	1.50

GS3 CHARLES LINDBERGH. Postmarked May 22, 1977,* St. Louis, with Spirit of St. Louis postmark. Envelope commemorates the Riverfront Celebration & Spirit of St. Louis replica flyby. Brown ink cachet design on plain white envelope. All postmarks on 13 cent Lindbergh commemorative stamp.

*Gateway was issued 2,000 May 22nd postmarks, and 500 were issued to John Zaso. Gateway, however, was the only company to gather all three postmarks on a commemorative issue.

All envelopes	1.00	2.00

GS4 GS5

LOU BROCK ALL–TIME STOLEN BASE RECORD
Set of Two

1977

GS4 STOLEN BASE 892. Postmarked August 29, 1977, San Diego, CA, on tying the all-time stolen base record of Ty Cobb. Artwork by Frank P. Zaso. Five thousand issued unautographed. One thousand Junipero Serra Museum cancellations used; 4,000 circle and bars used.

Autographed	NI	6.00
Unautographed	1.50	3.00

GS5 STOLEN BASE 893. Postmarked August 29, 1977, San Diego, CA, on breaking the all-time stolen base record. Steve Goldstein photo, 2,500 issued autographed; 2,500 unautographed. Three thousand Junipero Serra Museum cancellations used; 2,000 circle and bars used.

Autographed	3.50	*4.50
Unautographed	1.50	3.00

GS5a

GS5a STOLEN BASE 893. Fifty 892 silks attached to 893 envelopes. Autographed.

Autographed	V	10.00

BOB FORSCH NO–HITTER
Set of One

1978

GS6 BOB FORSCH NO–HITTER. One hundred five envelopes postmarked April 16, 1978, St. Louis, MO, on Bob Forsch's no-hitter against Philadelphia. To be released in 1982. Autographed. Sixty Independence Hall stamps used; 45 Indian Head Penny stamps used. Photo not available.

Autographed	NI	To be auctioned in 1982

GS7 GS8

PETE ROSE 3,000 HITS
Set of Two

1978

GS7 3.000 HITS. Postmarked May 5, 1978, Cincinnati, OH, on Pete Rose's 3,000th hit. Reds photo. Five thousand issued personally autographed. Round cancellation.

Autographed	3.50	7.50

GS8 PRIDE OF CINCINNATI. Postmarked May 5, 1978, Cincinnati, OH, with Fountain Square cancellations. Reds photo. Five thousand issued unautographed.

Autographed	NI	12.50
Unautographed	1.50	2.50

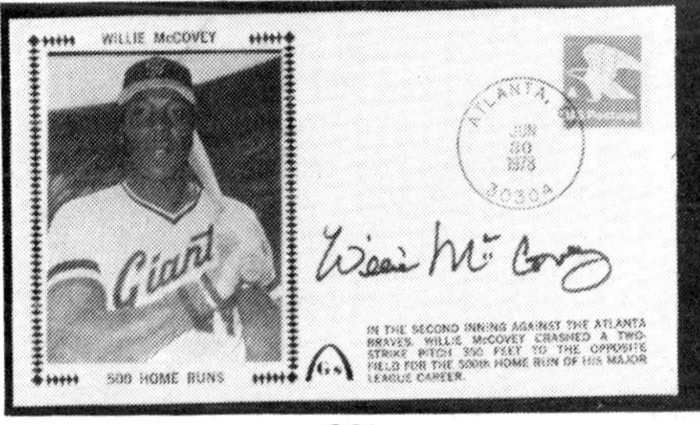

GS9 GS10

WILLIE McCOVEY 500 HOME RUNS
Set of Two

1978

GS9 500 HOME RUNS. Postmarked June 30, 1978, Atlanta, GA, on Willie McCovey's 500th home run. Giants photo. Two thousand issued autographed. All cancellations round.

Autographed	3.50	*7.50

GS10 PRIDE OF THE GIANTS. Postmarked June 30, 1978, San Francisco, CA, commemorating McCovey and San Francisco. Artwork by Marilyn Meystrick. Two thousand issued unautographed. All cancellations round.

Autographed	NI	9.50
Unautographed	1.50	*2.50

GS11 GS12

GS12a

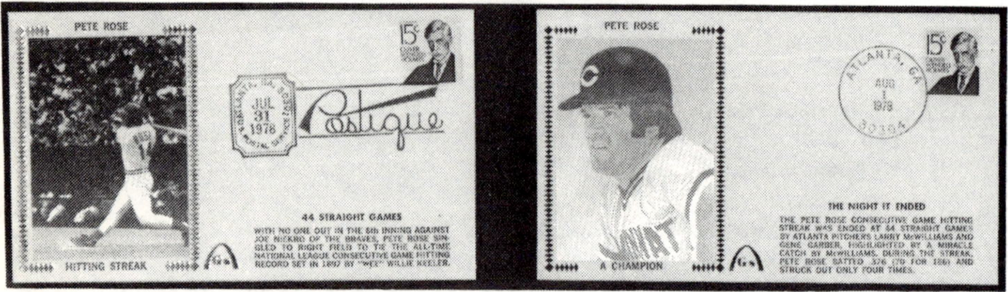

GS13 GS14

PETE ROSE'S 44 GAME HITTING STREAK
Set of Four

The Hitting Streak was designed to provide one envelope for each date and place where Pete Rose tied and broke the National League and all-time records up to Joe DiMaggio's 56 game streak. Two thousand envelopes each were postmarked the nights Pete tied and broke the modern National League record and the night he tied the all-time National League record. However, no plans had been made for an envelope for the night the streak would end. Following the drama of the McWilliams catch and the Garber strikeout to end the game, Gateway officials realized the ending of the streak was as much a part of the story as the records themselves, so at 11:55 PM they turned in 1,800 envelopes envelopes for cancellation. The Hitting Streak is thus 1,800 complete sets of four and 200 sets of three. The Game 38 variation is found only in complete sets, not as an additional envelope.

1978

GS11 GAME 37. Postmarked July 24, 1978, New York, NY, on Pete Rose's tying the modern National League consecutive game hitting streak of Tommy Holmes(1945). Reds photo. Two thousand issued unautographed with New York philatelic postmark.

Autographed	NI	7.50
Unautographed	2.50	2.50

GS12 GAME 38. Postmarked July 25, 1978, New York, NY, on Pete Rose's breaking the modern National League consecutive game hitting streak record. Reds photo. One thousand six hundred fifty issued unautographed with New York philatelic postmark.

Autographed	NI	7.50
Unautographed	2.50	2.50

GS12a GAME 38 VARIATION. Postmarked July 25, 1978, New York, NY, Bill Perry artwork and redesigned gold border to accomodate shifted New York postmark. Three hundred-fifty issued unautographed.

Autographed	NI	12.50
Unautographed	V	7.50

GS13 GAME 44. Postmarked July 31, 1978, Atlanta, GA, on Pete Rose's tying the all-time National League consecutive game hitting streak record. Reds photo. Two thousand issued unautographed with Atlanta philatelic postmark. Envelope incorrectly identifies opposing pitcher as Joe Niekro. Opposing pitcher was Phil Niekro.

Autographed	NI	7.50
Unautographed	2.50	2.50

GS14 THE NIGHT IT ENDED. Postmarked August 1, 1978, Atlanta, GA, ending the hitting streak of 44 games. Artwork by Bill Perry. One thousand eight hundred issued unautographed with Atlanta philatelic postmark.

Autographed	NI	10.00
Unautographed	2.50	*5.00

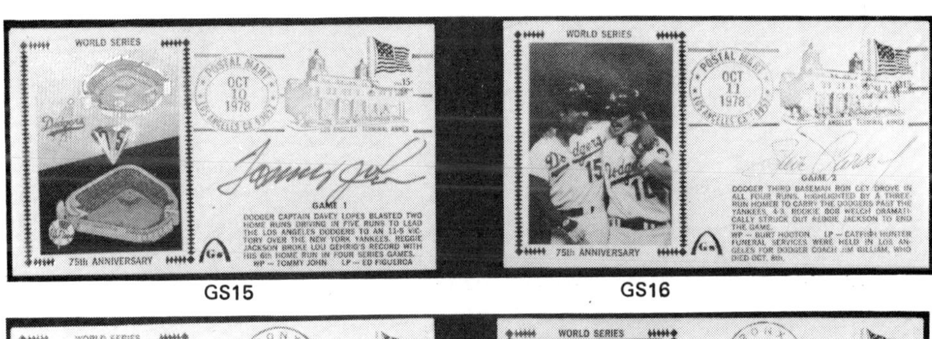

GS15 GS16

GS17 GS18a

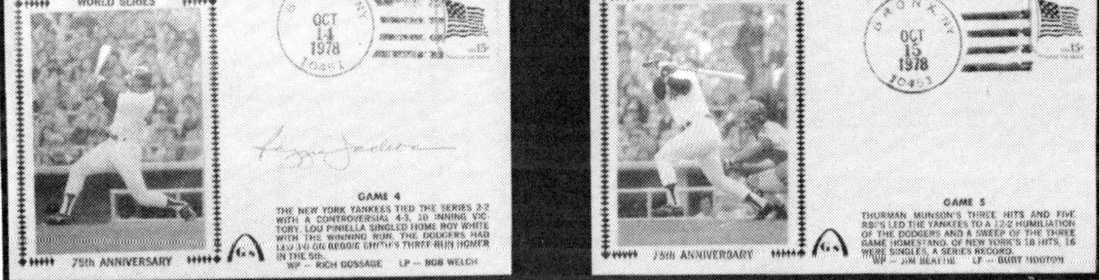

GS18b GS19a

GS19b GS20

75th ANNIVERSARY OF THE WORLD SERIES
Set of Six

Gateway's first World Series issue; 2,000 sets of six envelopes issued. Originally designed for the Jackson photo on Game 4 and Munson on Game 5, the availability of Tom Lasorda's argument (following the famous Jackson "bump") from Game 4 led to alternation of Jackson photo on Games 4 and 5. Autographs acquired by Gateway—Yogi Berra, Ron Cey, Bucky Dent, Steve Garvey, Ron Giudry, Catfish Hunter, Reggie Jackson, Tommy John, Tom Lasorda, Davy Lopes, Graig Nettles, Reggie Smith and Don Sutton.

1978

GS15 GAME 1. Postmarked October 10, 1978, Los Angeles, CA. Stadium artwork by Scott Forst. Two thousand issued with Los Angeles philatelic postmark. Unautographed or autographed (Lasorda, Lopes, Jackson or John).

Autographed		
Lasorda	3.00	*6.50
Lopes	3.00	*6.75
Jackson	3.00	*11.00
John	3.00	*6.75
Others	NI	6.00+A
Unautographed	1.00	*3.00

GS16 GAME 2. Postmarked October 11, 1978, Los Angeles, CA. Dodger photo of Cey and Lopes. Two thousand issued with Los Angeles philatelic postmark. Unautographed or autographed (Cey, Garvey or Sutton).

Autographed		
Cey	3.00	*6.50
Garvey	3.00	*7.00
Sutton	3.00	*6.50
Lopes	NI	6.75
Unautographed	1.00	*3.00

GS17 GAME 3. Postmarked October 13, 1978, Bronx, NY. Rich Pilling photo of Nettles. Two thousand issued, unautographed or autographed (Guidry or Nettles). Approximately 200 exist where Guidry signed inside the gold frame; autographs are visible beneath the silks along with second autograph.

Autographed		
Guidry	3.00	*6.00
Guidry (under silk)	3.00	*7.00
Nettles	3.00	*6.00
Unautographed	1.00	*3.00

GS18a GAME 4. Postmarked October 14, 1978, Bronx, NY. Dodger photo of Lasorda, Cey, and Garvey. One thousand eight hundred issued unautographed or autographed (Lasorda, Jackson or R. Smith).

Autographed		
Lasorda	3.00	*6.00
Jackson	3.00	*6.00
R. Smith	3.00	*6.00
Garvey	NI	7.00
Unautographed	1.00	*3.00

GS18b GAME 4. Rich Pilling photo of Reggie Jackson. Two hundred issued unautographed or autographed by Jackson.

Autographed (Jackson)	3.00	*9.00
Unautographed	1.00	*4.00

GS19a GAME 5. Postmarked October 15, 1978, Bronx, NY. Rich Pilling photo of Thurman Munson. One thousand issued unautographed. Only one Munson autograph known to exist on Game 5.

Autographed (Munson)	NI	Unique
Unautographed	1.00	5.00

GS19b GAME 5. Rich Pilling photo of Jackson. One thousand issued unautographed.

Autographed (Jackson)	NI	*9.00
Unautographed	1.00	4.00

GS20 GAME 6. Postmarked October 17, 1978, Los Angeles, CA. Tom Wiley photo of World Series trophy. Two thousand issued with Los Angeles philatelic postmark unautographed or autographed (Berra, Dent or Hunter).

Autographed		
Berra	3.00	*8.00
Dent	3.00	*6.50
Hunter	3.00	*7.00
Others	NI	6.00+A
Unautographed	1.00	*3.00

GS21 GS22

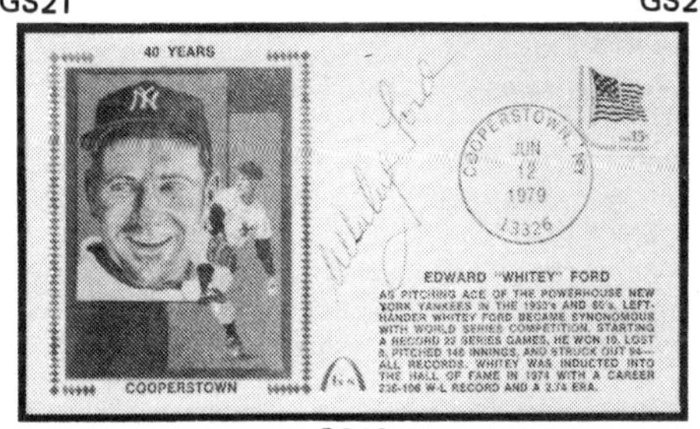

GS23

40th ANNIVERSARY OF THE HALL OF FAME

Set of Three

1979

GS21 MICKEY MANTLE. Postmarked June 12, 1979, Cooperstown, NY. Artwork by Phil Daigle. Two thousand issued, autographed.

Autographed	15.00	20.00

GS22 SATCHEL PAIGE. Postmarked June 12, 1979, Cooperstown, NY. Artwork by Phil Daigle. One thousand issued, autographed.

Autographed	10.00	10.00

GS23 WHITEY FORD. Postmarked June 12, 1979, Cooperstown, NY. Artwork by Bill Perry. One thousand issued, autographed.

Autographed	10.00	10.00

GS24 GS25

GS26

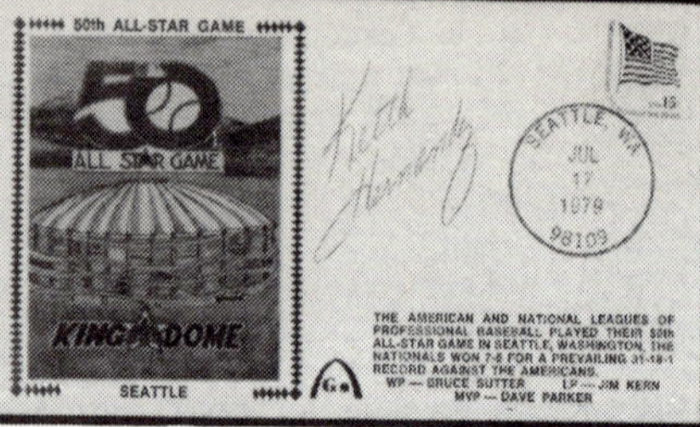

GS27

50th ALL–STAR GAME
Set of 16

Set of 16 postmarked July 17, 1979, Seattle, WA. Two thousand each of four different logo designs and 12 game photos were printed. Issued in sets of three, including a logo envelope, National League envelope and American League envelope. All logo envelopes were printed with the same game information; all National League envelopes record the N.L. players elected as starters and their starting substitutes; all American League envelopes record the A.L. players elected as starters and their starting substitutes. Only the art designs and photos are different. Twenty six thousand large round postmarks were used; 4,000 smaller "bullet" postmarks were used, but only on American League envelopes. Autographs acquired by Gateway: Juaquin Andujar, Don Baylor, Bruce Bochte, Larry Bowa, George Brett, Lou Brock, Rod Carew, Steve Carlton, Gary Carter, Ron Cey, George Foster, Steve Garvey, Ron Guidry, Keith Hernandez, Reggie, Jackson, Tommy John, Jim Kern, Dave Kingman, Tom Lasorda, Davey Lopes, Fred Lynn, Lee Mazzilli, Graig Nettles, Dave Parker, Gaylord Perry, Darrell Porter, Jim Rice, Pete Rose, Nolan Ryan, Mike Schmidt, Ted Simmons, Ken Singleton, Roy Smalley, Bruce Sutter, and Frank White. Any participating player's autographs can be found on a logo envelope. American Leaguers autographed on any of the six A.L. envelopes, and National Leaguers autographed on any of the six N.L. envelopes, thereby making available sets of three with three autographs. Very few envelopes were let out without autographs.

1979

GS24 50th ALL–STAR LOGO ON ANIMATED PLAYERS. Artwork by Scott Forst. Two thousand issued autographed or unautographed.

Autographed	6.00	6.00
Unautographed	3.00	3.00

GS25 50th ALL–STAR LOGO ON NORTHWEST TREES. Artwork by Scott Forst. Two thousand issued autographed or unautographed.

Autographed	6.00	6.00
Unautographed	3.00	3.00

GS26 50th ALL–STAR LOGO ON PLAYING FIELD. Artwork by Scott Forst. Two thousand issued autographed or unautographed.

Autographed	6.00	6.00
Unautographed	3.00	3.00

GS27 50th ALL–STAR LOGO ON KINGDOME. Artwork by Scott Forst. Two thousand issued autographed or unautographed.

Autographed	6.00	6.00
Unautographed	3.00	3.00

GS28

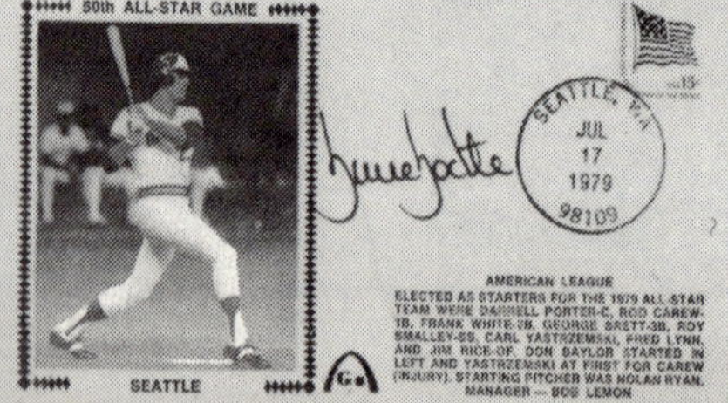

GS29

GS30 GS31

GS28 JUAQUIN ANDUJAR. Photo by Jeff Pruss. Two thousand issued, autographed or unautographed.

Autographed		
Andujar	6.00	6.75
Other National Leaguer	6.00	6.00
Unautographed	3.00	3.00

GS29 BRUCE BOCHTE. Photo by Jeff Pruss. Two thousand issued, autographed or unautographed.

Autographed		
Bochte	6.00	6.50
Other American Leaguer	6.00	6.00
Unautographed	3.00	3.00

GS30 STEVE CARLTON & SCHMIDT. Photo by Jeff Pruss. Two thousand issued, autographed or unautographed.

Autographed		
Carlton	6.00	7.50
Schmidt	6.00	7.50
Other National Leaguer	6.00	6.00
Unautographed	3.00	3.00

GS31 RON CEY. Photo by Jeff Pruss. Two thousand issued, autographed or unautographed.

Autographed		
Cey	6.00	6.50
Other National Leaguer	6.00	6.00
Unautographed	3.00	3.00

GS32 GS33

GS34 GS35

GS32 RON GUIDRY. Photo by Jeff Pruss. Two thousand issued, autographed or unautographed.

Autographed		
Guidry	6.00	7.50
Other American League	6.00	6.00
Unautographed	3.00	3.00

GS33 REGGIE JACKSON. Photo by Jeff Pruss. Two thousand issued, autographed or unautographed.

Autographed		
Jackson	6.00	7.50
Other American League	6.00	6.00
Unautographed	3.00	3.00

GS34 JIM KERN & GRAIG NETTLES. Photo by Jeff Pruss. Two thousand issued, autographed or unautographed.

Autographed		
Kern	6.00	6.50
Nettles	6.00	6.50
Other American League	6.00	6.00
Unautographed	3.00	3.00

GS35 FRED LYNN, CARL YASTRZEMSKI, DON BAYLOR. Photo by Jeff Pruss. Two thousand issued, autographed or unautographed.

Autographed		
Lynn	6.00	7.50
Yastrzemski (Full name)	NI	10.50
Baylor	6.00	6.75
Other American League	6.00	6.00
Unautographed	3.00	3.00

GS36 GS37

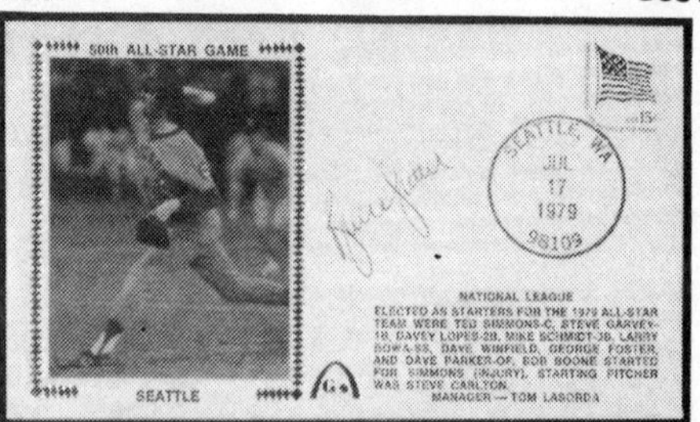

GS38

GS36 DAVE PARKER. Photo by Jeff Pruss. Two thousand issued, autographed or unautographed.

Autographed		
Parker	6.00	7.50
Other National League	6.00	6.00
Unautographed	3.00	3.00

GS37 DARRELL PORTER. Photo by Jeff Pruss. Two thousand issued, autographed or unautographed.

Autographed		
Porter	6.00	6.50
Other American League	6.00	6.00
Unautographed	3.00	3.00

GS38 BRUCE SUTTER. Photo by Jeff Pruss. Two thousand issued, autographed or unautographed.

Autographed		
Sutter	6.00	6.50
Other National League	6.00	6.00
Unautographed	3.00	3.00

GS39 NOT ISSUED.

GS40

WILLIE MAYS HALL OF FAME INDUCTION

Set of One

1979

GS40 WILLIE MAYS. Postmarked August 2, 1979, Cooperstown, NY. Artwork by Bill Perry. Two thousand issued, autographed.

Autographed	10.00	17.00

GS41 GS42

LOU BROCK 3,000 HITS & UNIFORM RETIREMENT

Set of Two

1979

GS41 LOU BROCK 3,000th HIT. Postmarked August 14, 1979, St. Louis, MO. Swing of the bat photo by Bob Merz. Five thousand issued, autographed, 1,000 unautographed.

Autographed	4.50	7.50
Unautographed	1.50	3.00

GS42 LOU BROCK DAY. Postmarked September 9, 1979, St. Louis, MO, on the retirement of Lou Brock's No. 20 by the St. Louis Cardinals. Photo by Bob Merz. Six thousand issued unautographed.

Autographed	NI	9.00
Unautographed	1.50	3.00

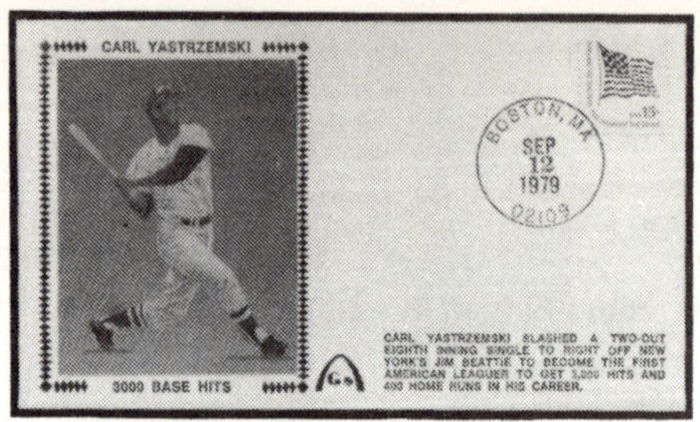

GS43
CARL YASTRZEMSKI 3,000 HITS
Set of One

1979

GS43 CARL YASTRZEMSKI. Postmarked September 12, 1979, Boston, MA, on Yastrzemski's 3,000th base hit. Artwork by Bill Perry. Three thousand issued unautographed.

Autographed	NI	12.00
Unautographed	3.50	4.75

GS44a GS44b

GS45a GS45b

1979 WORLD SERIES
Set of Seven

Gateway issued 2,000 sets of 1979 World Series envelopes postmarked in Baltimore and Pittsburgh each date the Series was played. The Game 1 logo artpiece was alternated with a Mike Flanagan photo. The Games 2 & 6 silks of Kent Tekulve and Jim Palmer were alternated equally to accommodate a wider distribution of autographs. Standard round cancellations were used in both cities. Autographs acquired by Gateway: Mark Belanger, Al Bumbry, John Candelaria, Rich Dauer, Rick Dempsey, Doug DeCinces, Mike Flanagan, Tim Foli, Kiko Garcia, Phil Garner, Grant Jackson, Scott McGregor, Bill Madlock, Omar Moreno, Eddie Murray, Jim Palmer, Dave Parker, Bill Robinson, Frank Robinson, Ken Singleton, Willie Stargell, Chuck Tanner, Kent Tekulve, and Earl Weaver.

1979

GS44a GAME 1. Postmarked October 10, 1979, Baltimore, MD. Stadium artwork by Scott Forst. One thousand five hundred issued, unautographed or autographed (Belanger, Dauer, DeCinces, Flanagan, Garner, Murray, F. Robinson, Singleton, or Tanner).

Autographed		
Belanger	2.00	5.00
Dauer	2.00	5.00
DeCinces	2.00	5.00
Flanagan	.2.00	5.00
Garner	2.00	5.00
Murray	2.00	5.00
F. Robinson	2.00	5.00
Singleton	2.00	5.00
Tanner	2.00	5.00
Other	NI	2.00+A
Unautographed	1.00	2.00

GS44b GAME 1. Mike Flanagan photo by Jerry Wachter. Five hundred issued, unautographed or autographed by Flanagan.

Autographed		
Flanagan	2.00	5.00
Unautographed	1.00	2.00

GS45a GAME 2. Postmarked October 11, 1979, Baltimore, MD. Jim Palmer photo by Jerry Wachter. One thousand issued, unautographed or autographed by Palmer.

Autographed		
Palmer	2.00	5.00
Unautographed	1.00	2.00

GS45b GAME 2. Kent Tekulve photo by Jerry Wachter. One thousand issued, unautographed or autographed by Tekulve, Garner or Tanner.

Autographed		
Tekulve	2.00	5.00
Garner	2.00	5.00
Tanner	2.00	5.00
Unautographed	1.00	2.00

GS46 GS47

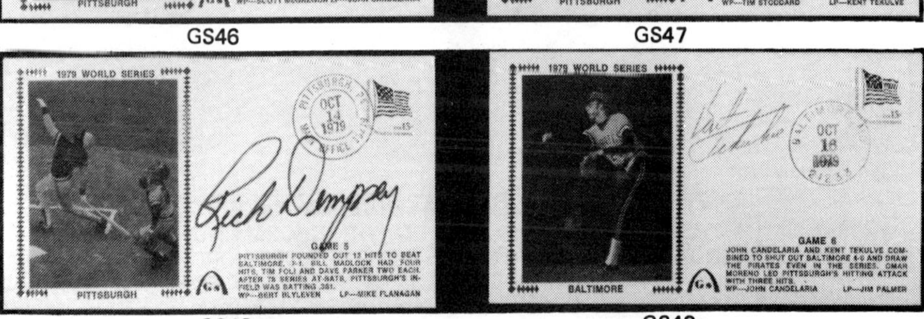

GS48 GS49a

GS46 GAME 3. Postmarked October 12, 1979, Pittsburgh, PA. Kiko Garcia photo by Jerry Wachter. Two thousand issued unautographed or autographed by Garcia, Belanger, Bumbry, Dauer, McGregor or Singleton.

Autographed		
Garcia	2.00	5.00
Belanger	2.00	5.00
Bumbry	2.00	5.00
Dauer	2.00	5.00
McGregor	2.00	5.00
Singleton	2.00	5.00
Unautographed	1.00	2.00

GS47 GAME 4. Postmarked October 13, 1979, Pittsburgh, PA. Earl Weaver photo by Jerry Wachter. Two thousand issued, unautographed or autographed by Weaver, Bumbry, Dauer, Garcia, F. Robinson or Singleton. Double autographs of Weaver and F. Robinson exist.

Autographed		
Weaver	2.00	5.00
Bumbry	2.00	5.00
Dauer	2.00	5.00
Garcia	2.00	5.00
F. Robinson	2.00	5.00
Singleton	2.00	5.00
Weaver and F. Robinson	NI	8.00
Unautographed	1.00	2.00

GS48 GAME 5. Postmarked October 14, 1979, Pittsburgh, PA. Dave Parker and Rick Dempsey photo by Jack Zapola. Two thousand issued, unautographed or autographed by Parker, Dempsey, Flanagan, Foli, Garner, Madlock or Tanner.

Autographed		
Parker	2.50	5.50
Dempsey	2.00	5.00
Flanagan	2.00	5.00
Foli	2.00	5.00
Garner	2.00	5.00
Madlock	2.00	5.00
Tanner	2.00	5.00
Unautographed	1.00	2.00

GS49a GAME 6. Postmarked Octaber 16, 1979, Baltimore, MD. Tekulve photo by Jerry Wachter. One thousand issued, unautographed or autographed by Tekulve, Candelaria, Garner, Moreno or Tanner. Double autographs of Candelaria and Moreno exist.

Autographed		
Tekulve	2.00	5.00
Candelaria	2.00	5.00
Garner	2.00	5.00
Moreno	2.00	5.00
Tanner	2.00	5.00
Candelaria and Moreno	NI	8.00
Unautographed	1.00	2.00

GS49b GS50

GS49b GAME 6. Palmer photo by Jerry Wachter. One thousand issued, unautographed or autographed by Palmer, Candelaria or Moreno. Double autographs of Candelaria and Moreno exist.

Autographed		
Palmer	2.00	5.00
Candelaria	2.00	5.00
Moreno	2.00	5.00
Candelaria and Moreno	NI	8.00
Unautographed	1.00	2.00

GS50 GAME 7. Postmarked October 17, 1979, Baltimore, MD. Willie Stargell/Bill Robinson photo by Jerry Wachter. Two thousand issued, unautographed or autographed by Willie Stargell, Bill Robinson, Grant Jackson or Chuck Tanner.

Autographed		
Stargell	2.50	5.50
Bill Robinson	2.00	5.00
Grant Jackson	2.00	5.00
Tanner	2.00	5.00
Unautographed	1.00	2.00

GS51 GS52

GS53

1980 SUPER BOWL

Set of Three

Gateway's first Super Bowl issue, the format was exactly the same as the All-Star sets—a neutral artpiece with game information recorded, a Ram envelope and a Steeler envelope, each listing the starting offensive and defensive players. Two postmarks were used to record the January 20th date, but it is uncertain as to how they are distributed throughout the sets. Autographs acquired by Gateway: Cullen Bryant, Vince Ferragamo, L. C. Greenwood, Franco Harris, Rich Saul, John Stallworth and Wendell Tyler.

1980

GS51 SUPER SUNDAY. Postmarked January 20, 1980, Pasadena, CA. Artwork by Scott Forst. Two thousand issued, unautographed or autographed by Bryant, Greenwood, Stallworth or Tyler.

Autographed	6.00	6.00
Unautographed	3.00	3.00

GS52 RAMS. Postmarked January 20, 1980, Pasadena, CA. Vince Ferragamo and Rich Saul photo by Rich Pilling. Two thousand issued, unautographed or autographed by Ferragamo, Saul, Bryant or Tyler.

Autographed	6.00	6.00
Unautographed	3.00	3.00

GS53 STEELERS. Postmarked January 20, 1980, Pasadena, CA. Franco Harris and Fred Dryer photo by Rich Pilling. Two thousand issued, unautographed or autographed by Harris, Greenwood or Stallworth.

Autographed	6.00	6.00
Unautographed	3.00	3.00

GS54 GS55

NOLAN RYAN 3,000 STRIKEOUTS
Set of Two

1980

GS54 3,000 STRIKEOUTS. Postmarked July 4, 1980, Cincinnati, OH, city of Nolan Ryan's 3,000th strikeout. Photo by Rich Pilling. Four thousand eight hundred issued autographed.

Autographed	5.00	7.00

GS54a 3,000 STRIKEOUTS. A variation of GS54. Copy rearranged (wording and placement) to accommodate placement of autographs. Two hundred issued autographed.

Autographed	V	7.50

GS55 3,000 STRIKEOUTS. Postmarked July 4, 1980, Houston, TX, Ryan's home city. Photo by Rich Pilling. Five thousand issued unautographed.

Autographed	NI	8.00
Unautographed	2.50	3.00

GS56

STEVE CARLTON ALL–TIME LEFT HANDED STRIKEOUT RECORD

Set of One

1980

GS56 LEFT HANDED STRIKEOUT RECORD. Postmarked July 6, 1980, St. Louis, MO., on Steve Carlton's passing Mickey Lolich as the all-time left handed strikeout leader. Artwork by Phil Daigle. One thousand issued autographed.

Autographed 7.50 9.00

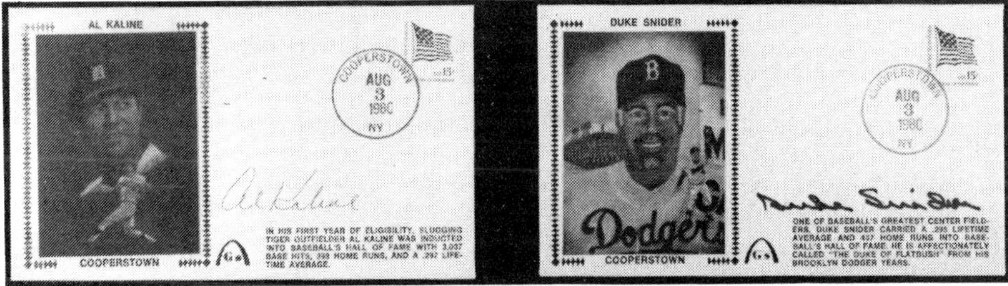

GS57 GS58

1980 HALL OF FAME INDUCTIONS

1980

GS57 AL KALINE. Set of One, postmarked August 3, 1980, Cooperstown, NY, on Al Kaline's induction into the Hall of Fame. Artwork by Phil Daigle. Three thousand issued autographed.

Autographed 10.00 10.00

GS58 DUKE SNIDER. Set of One, postmarked August 3, 1980, Cooperstown, NY, on Duke Snider's induction into the Hall of Fame. Artwork by Scott Forst. Three thousand issued autographed.

Autographed 10.00 10.00

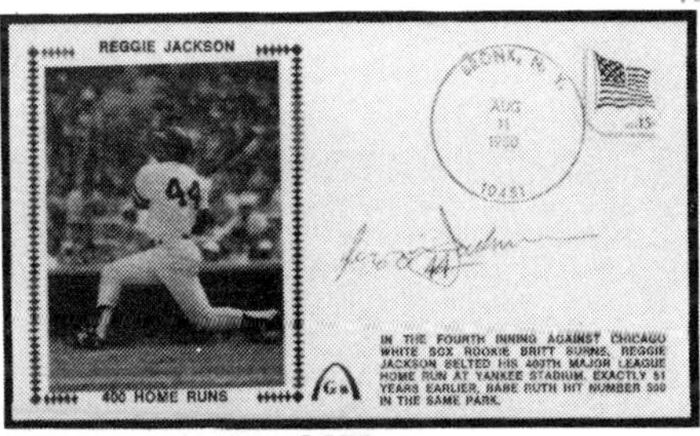

GS59

REGGIE JACKSON 400 HOME RUNS

Set of One

1980

GS59 400 HOME RUNS. Postmarked August 11, 1980, Bronx, NY, on Reggie Jackson's 400th home run. Photo by Rich Pilling. Two thousand issued autographed.

Autographed 7.50 9.00

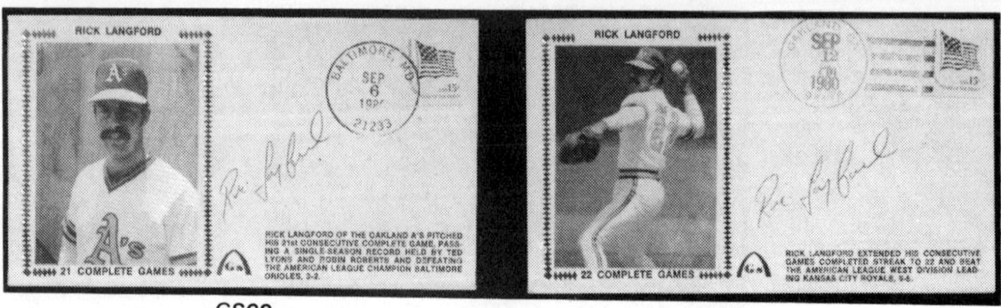

GS60 GS61

RICK LANGFORD CONSECUTIVE COMPLETED GAMES STREAK

Set of Two

1980

GS60 GAME 21. Postmarked September 6, 1980, Baltimore, MD, on Rick Langford's 21st consecutive nine inning game started and completed without relief help. Langford photo by Fred Kaplan. Five hundred issued, unautographed or autographed.

Autographed	6.50	*9.50
Unautographed	2.50	*4.00

GS61 GAME 22. Postmarked September 21, 1980, Oakland, CA on Langford's 22nd consecutive complete game. Photo by Fred Kaplan. One thousand issued, unautographed or autographed.

Autographed	6.50	9.00
Unautographed	2.50	*4.00

GS62

MINNIE MINOSO FIFTH DECADE

Set of One

1980

GS62 MINNIE MINOSO. Postmarked October 4, 1980, Chicago, IL, on Minnie Minoso's fifth decade of active major league play. White Sox photo. Five hundred issued autographed.

Autographed	6.50	*7.50

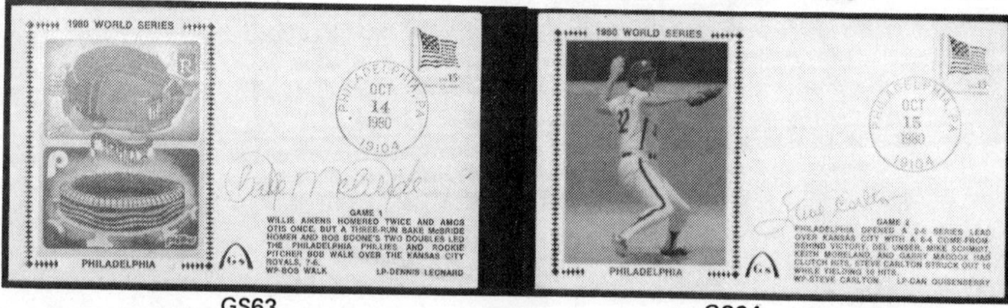

GS63 GS64

GS65 GS66

1980 WORLD SERIES
Set of Six

Set of six postmarked each date the Series was played in Philadelphia and Kansas City. Standard cancellations. Two thousand sets issued. No variations. Autographs acquired by Gateway: Willie Mays Aikens, Bob Boone, Larry Bowa, Steve Carlton, Larry Christenson, Dallas Green, Larry Gura, Greg Luzinski, Garry Maddox, Bake McBride, Tug McGraw, Hal McRae, Darrell Porter, Amos Otis, Dan Quisenberry, Pete Rose, Mike Schmidt, Manny Trillo, Del Unser, Frank White, and Willie Wilson, each on envelopes where they played a prominent part in the game.

1980

GS63 GAME 1. Postmarked October 14, 1980, Philadelphia, PA. Stadium artwork by Scott Forst. Two thousand issued unautographed and autographed by Boone, Bowa, Christenson, Green, Luzinski, Maddox, McBride, Otis, Porter, Rose, Trillo, Unser, White, or Wilson.

Autographed		
Boone	4.00	5.00
Bowa	4.00	5.00
Christenson	4.00	5.00
Green	4.00	5.00
Luzinski	4.00	5.00
Maddox	4.00	5.00
McBride	4.00	5.00
Otis	4.00	5.00
Porter	4.00	5.00
Rose	4.00	5.00
Trillo	4.00	5.00
Unser	4.00	5.00
White	4.00	5.00
Wilson	4.00	5.00
Other	NI	3.00+A
Unautographed	2.00	3.00

GS64 GAME 2. Postmarked October 15, 1980, Philadelphia, PA. Carlton photo by Rich Pilling. Two thousand issued unautographed or autographed by Carlton, Green, Gura, Maddox, Quisenberry, Trillo, or Unser.

Autographed		
Carlton	4.00	5.00
Green	4.00	5.00
Gura	4.00	5.00
Maddox	4.00	5.00
Quisenberry	4.00	5.00
Trillo	4.00	5.00
Unser	4.00	5.00
Unautographed	2.00	3.00

GS65 GAME 3. Postmarked October 17, 1980, Kansas City, KS. George Brett photo by Rich Pilling. Two thousand issued unautographed or autographed by Green, McGraw, Otis, Quisenberry, White, or Wilson.

Autographed		
Green	4.00	5.00
McGraw	4.00	5.00
Otis	4.00	5.00
Quisenberry	4.00	5.00
White	4.00	5.00
Wilson	4.00	5.00
Brett	NI	7.00
Unautographed	2.00	3.00

GS66 GAME 4. Postmarked October 18, 1980, Kansas City, KS. Willie Mays Aikens photo by Rich Pilling. Two thousand issued unautographed or autographed by Aikens, Christenson, Green, McRae, Otis, White, or Wilson.

Autographed		
Aikens	4.00	5.00
Christenson	4.00	5.00
Green	4.00	5.00
McRae	4.00	5.00
Otis	4.00	5.00
White	4.00	5.00
Wilson	4.00	5.00
Unautographed	2.00	3.00

GS67 GS68

GS67 GAME 5. Postmarked October 9, 1980, Kansas City, KS. Bob Boone and Darrell Porter photo by Rich Pilling. Two thousand issued unautographed or autographed by Boone, Porter, Green, Luzinski, Maddox, McGraw, Quisenberry, Trillo, or Unser. Double autographs of Boone and Porter or Boone and McGraw exist.

Autographed		
Boone	4.00	5.00
Porter	4.00	5.00
Green	4.00	5.00
Luzinski	4.00	5.00
Maddox	4.00	5.00
McGraw	4.00	5.00
Quisenberry	4.00	5.00
Trillo	4.00	5.00
Unser	4.00	5.00
Boone & Porter	NI	8.00
Boone & McGraw	NI	8.00
Unautographed	2.00	3.00

GS68 GAME 6. Postmarked October 21, 1980, Philadelphia, PA. Mike Schmidt photo by Rich Pilling. Two thousand issued unautographed or autographed by Schmidt, Bowa, Green, McGraw, or Rose.

Autographed		
Schmidt	4.00	5.00
Bowa	4.00	5.00
Green	4.00	5.00
McGraw	4.00	5.00
Rose	4.00	5.00
Unautographed	2.00	3.00

GS69 GS70

THE ELECTION AND INAUGURATION OF RONALD REAGAN
Set of Two

1980

GS69 ELECTION DAY. Postmarked November 4, 1980, Washington, DC, on Ronald Reagan's election as President of the United States. Wide World Photo. One thousand issued unautographed.

Unautographed	3.00	3.00

1981

GS70 INAUGURATION DAY. Postmarked January 20, 1981, Washington, DC, on Ronald Reagan's Inauguration as President. Wide World Photo. One thousand issued unautographed.

Unautographed	3.50	3.50

1981 SUPER BOWL
Set of Three

Two thousand sets of three commemorating the 1981 Super Bowl between the Philadelphia Eagles and the Oakland Raiders have been postmarked January 25, 1981, in New Orleans, LA, but have yet to be printed. As in 1980, the sets will consist of a neutral artpiece, an Eagle envelope, and a Raider envelope. Gateway catalog numbers of GS71-73 are reserved for this issue.

GS74 GS75

TOM SEAVER 3,000 STRIKEOUTS
Set of Two

1981

GS74 3,000 STRIKEOUTS. Postmarked April 18, 1981, Cincinnati, OH, city of Tom Seaver's 3,000th Strikeout. Photo by Malcolm Emmons. Five thousand issued autographed.

Autographed	5.00	7.00

GS75 3,000 STRIKEOUTS. Postmarked April 18, 1981, with Cincinnati philatelic postmark. Photo by Malcolm Emmons. Five thousand issued unautographed.

Autographed	NI	8.00
Unautographed	2.50	3.00

GS76 GS77

STEVE CARLTON 3,000 STRIKEOUTS

Set of Two

1981

GS76 3,000 STRIKEOUTS. Postmarked April 29, 1981, Philadelphia, PA, city of Steve Carlton's 3,000th Strikeout. Photo by Rich Pilling. Five thousand issued autographed.

Autographed	5.00	7.00

GS77 3,000 STRIKEOUTS. Postmarked April 29, 1981, Philadelphia, PA, Carlton's home city. Photo by Rich Pilling. Three thousand five hundred issued unautographed.

Autographed	NI	10.00
Unautographed	2.00	3.00

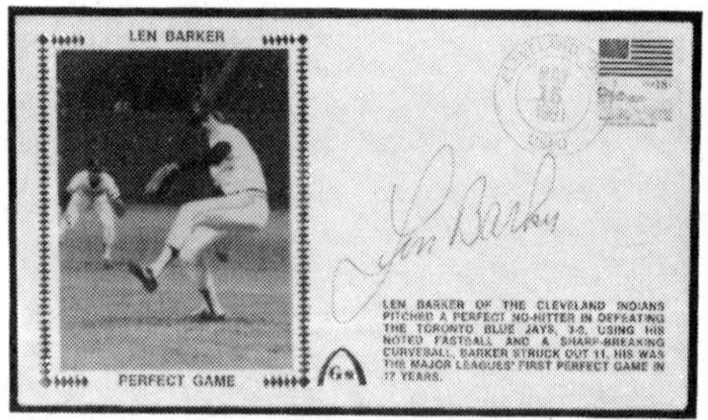

GS78

LEN BARKER PERFECT GAME

Set of One

1981

GS78 LEN BARKER PERFECT GAME. Postmarked May 15, 1981, Cleveland, OH. Photo by Jack Zapola. One thousand issued autographed. One hundred double autographs of Len Barker and Duane Kuiper issued. Five different stamps used - Amber Waves of Grain, Purple Mountains Majesty, Sea to Shining Sea, B Stamp, and Savings & Loan Commemorative.

Autographed		
Barker	7.50	9.00
Barker & Kuiper	11.50	13.00

GS79 GS83

PETE ROSE NATIONAL LEAGUE HIT RECORD
Set of Two

1981

GS79 HIT 3,630. Postmarked June 10, 1981, Philadelphia, PA, on Pete Rose's tying the all-time National League hit record (Stan Musial—1963). Swing of the bat photo by Rich Pilling. Five thousand issued unautographed and autographed. Date was last Phillies game prior to 1981 baseball players strike. Seven hundred issued with 18 cents Rose stamp, 4,300 with Amber Waves of Grain stamp.

Autographed	9.50	9.50
Unautographed	3.50	3.50

GS83 HIT 3,631. Postmarked August 10, 1981, Philadelphia, PA on Pete Rose's breaking the all-time National League record. Photo by Rich Pilling. Five thousand issued autographed. Date was Phillie's first game after the 1981 baseball strike. Seven hundred issued with 18 cents Rose stamp, 4,300 with 18 cents Amber Waves of Grain stamp.

Autographed	7.50	7.50

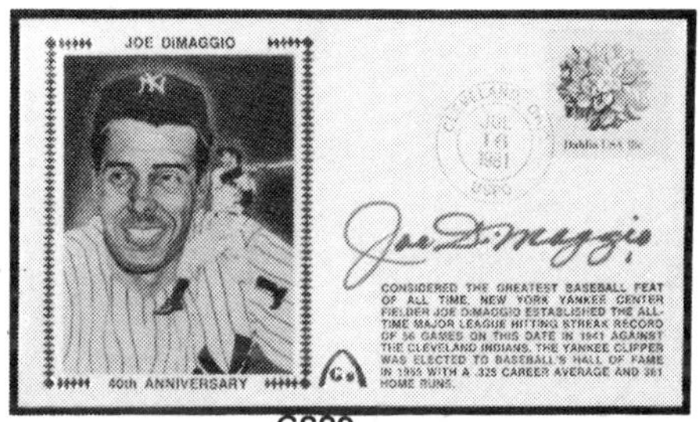

GS80

JOE DiMAGGIO 40TH ANNIVERSARY OF 56 GAME HITTING STREAK
Set of One

1981

GS80 JOE DiMAGGIO. Postmarked July 16, 1981, Cleveland, OH, on the 40th anniversary of the 56th game of DiMaggio's all-time record 56 game hitting streak. Artwork by Bill Perry. Two thousand issued autographed.

Autographed	20.00	25.00

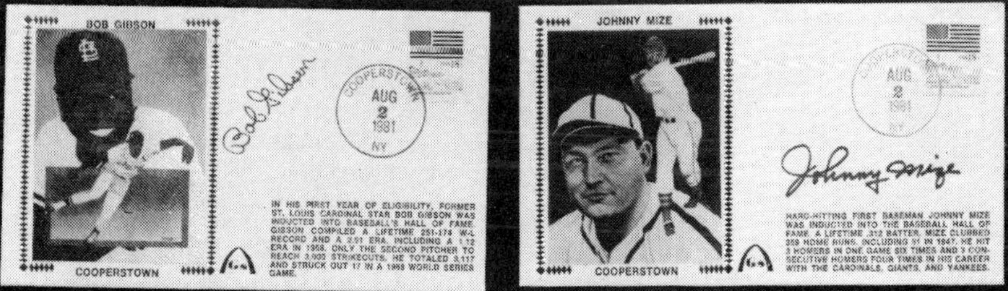

GS81 GS82

1981 HALL OF FAME INDUCTIONS
Set of Two

1981

GS81 BOB GIBSON. Postmarked August 2, 1981, Cooperstown, NY, on Bob Gibson's induction into the Hall of Fame. Artwork by Bill Perry. Three thousand issued autographed.

Autographed	10.00	12.00

GS82 JOHNNY MIZE. Postmarked August 2, 1981, Cooperstown, NY, on Johnny Mize's induction into the Hall of Fame. Artwork by Bill Perry. Two thousand issued autographed.

Autographed	10.00	10.00

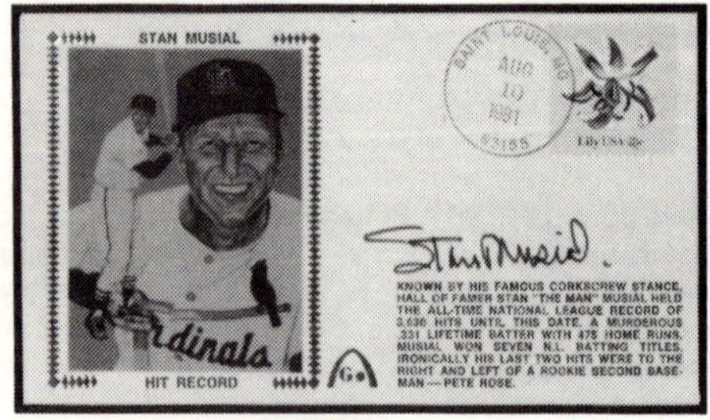

GS84
STAN MUSIAL HIT RECORD
Set of One

1981

GS84 STAN MUSIAL. Postmarked August 10, 1981, St. Louis, MO, the date Pete Rose broke Musial's all-time National League hit record. Envelope commemorates Musial's leadership through this date. Artwork by Bill Perry. Two thousand issued autographed.

Autographed	10.00	10.00

GS85
NOLAN RYAN FIFTH NO–HITTER
Set of One

1981

GS85 NOLAN RYAN FIFTH NO–HITTER. Postmarked September 26, 1981, Houston, TX, on Nolan Ryan's record fifth no-hitter. Photo by John Everett. One thousand issued autographed. Wide variety of stamps used.

Autographed	10.00	10.00

1981

GS86 RESERVED FOR ISSUE DATED SEPTEMBER 28, 1981

GS87	GS88
GS89	GS90
GS91	GS92

1981

GS87–GS92 RESERVED FOR 1981 WORLD SERIES

GS93

BEAR BRYANT ALL–TIME COLLEGE FOOTBALL COACHING RECORD

Set of One

1981

GS93 BEAR BRYANT. Postmarked November 28, 1981, Birmingham, AL, on Coach Bear Bryant's 315th career college football coaching victory. Photo by Malcolm Emmons. Two thousand issued autographed. Forty-eight issued with 1969 football stamps.

Autographed	12.00	15.00
Autographed w/football stamps	12.00	*15.00

PEREZ–STEELE HALL OF FAME POSTCARDS

In 1980, the Perez-Steele Galleries undertook an effort which was to result in the only Hall of Fame baseball art cards sanctioned by this hallowed organization since the Callahan cards of 1950-1956. This six-series postcard issue, three series of which where issued in 1980 and the remaining three in 1981, features water color renderings of all members of baseball's Hall of Fame through inductees of 1981. The set has been limited to 10,000 numbered prints with the individual numbers plainly visible on the postcard back side of the card. Each of the six series has been color coded — the color appearing on the box in which the cards are packaged and also as the color of the postcard back for each series. The box and back colors for each series are as follows: Series 1—brown, Series 2—green, Series 3—blue, Series 4—red, Series 5—yellow, and Series 6—orange.

The card fronts themselves are drawings by artist Dick Perez. Mr. Perez, born in Puerto Rico, raised in Spanish Harlem, and educated at the University of Pennsylvania and the Philadelphia College of Art, has become perhaps the most well-known portrair artist for sports related subjects in the country today. He was named official artist for the Philadelphia Eagles in 1970 and the Phildadelphia Phillies in 1971, and in 1976 placed first and second in the competition for developing the National League centennial logo—the logo which was adopted by the National League to commemorate their 100th year of existence. The Perez-Steele Galleries has been retained has consultant by the Donruss Corporation through 1984, and some of their work is presented in the 1982 Donruss Diamond Kings baseball cards, the first 26 cards of Donruss's 1982 edition (see Sport Americana Baseball Price Guide No. 4). The "Babe Ruth" Diamond King puzzle, distributed with Donruss baseball cards, is also a Perez-Steele creation.

The cards in this set are currently available from two sources, although when the set has been sold out it will be available only from collectors who have purchased these series. The Hall of Fame in Cooperstown, New York, and the Perez-Steele Galleries, Box 1776, Ft. Washinton, PA, 19034, are the two available sources of this set. The supply of Series 1 (cards 1-30) has diminished to a point where it can only be purchased in conjunction with the entire set.

While many organizations and collectors have in the past produced card sets featuring players inducted into the Hall of Fame, this particular set is, by far, aesthetically the best ever done. In fact, not since the gum cards of the 1930's has such exceptional artwork been featured on baseball card type media. A seventh series is scheduled for release in 1983, a series which will feature inductees through 1983 plus perhaps other interesting baseball related postcards to accommodate the print size of the sheet. It is expected that the series will contain from 10 to 16 cards depending upon the number of inductees.

The checklist for the set is presented below. Bear in mind that these series can still be purchased from the Hall of Fame or the Perez-Steele Galleries. The supply, however, is rapidly diminishing.

1980-81 PEREZ-STEELE HALL OF FAME POSTCARDS (180) 3 1/2" X 5 1/2"

	MINT	VG-E	F-G
COMPLETE SET	90.00	60.00	20.00
COMMON PLAYER	.50	.30	.10
First Series	30.00	20.00	8.00
1 Ty Cobb	2.00	1.25	.50
2 Walter Johnson	1.50	1.00	.40
3 Christy Mathewson	1.50	1.00	.40
4 Babe Ruth	3.00	2.00	.80
5 Honus Wagner	1.50	1.00	.40
6 Morgan Bulkeley	.50	.30	.10
7 Ban Johnson	.50	.30	.10
8 Nap Lajoie	1.00	.60	.20
9 Connie Mack	1.00	.60	.20
10 John McGraw	1.00	.60	.20
11 Tris Speaker	1.00	.60	.20
12 George Wright	.50	.30	.10
13 Cy Young	1.00	.60	.20
14 Grover Alexander	1.00	.60	.20
15 Alex. Cartwright	1.00	.60	.20
16 Henry Chadwick	.50	.30	.10
17 Cap Anson	1.50	1.00	.40
18 Eddie Collins	.75	.50	.20
19 Candy Cummings	.50	.30	.10
20 Charles Comiskey	.75	.50	.20
21 Buck Ewing	1.00	.60	.20
22 Lou Gehrig	2.00	1.25	.50
23 Willie Keeler	1.00	.60	.20
24 Hoss Radbourne	.75	.50	.20
25 George Sisler	.75	.50	.15
26 A.G. Spalding	1.00	.60	.20
27 Rogers Hornsby	1.00	.60	.20
28 Kenesaw Landis	.50	.30	.10
29 Roger Bresnahan	.50	.30	.10
30 Dan Brouthers	.75	.50	.20
Second Series	15.00	10.00	4.00
31 Fred Clarke	.50	.30	.10
32 Jimmy Collins	.50	.30	.10
33 Ed Delahanty	.50	.30	.10
34 Hugh Duffy	.50	.30	.10
35 Hughie Jennings	.50	.30	.10
36 King Kelly	.75	.50	.15
37 Jim O'Rourke	.50	.30	.10
38 Wilbert Robinson	.50	.30	.10
39 Jesse Burkett	.50	.30	.10
40 Frank Chance	.75	.50	.15
41 Jack Chesbro	.50	.30	.10
42 Johnny Evers	.50	.30	.10
43 Clark Griffith	.50	.30	.10
44 Thomas McCarthy	.50	.30	.10
45 Joe McGinnity	.50	.30	.10
46 Eddie Plank	.75	.50	.15
47 Joe Tinker	.75	.50	.15
48 Rube Waddell	.50	.30	.10
49 Ed Walsh	.50	.30	.10
50 Mickey Cochrane	.75	.50	.15
51 Frankie Frisch	.75	.50	.15
52 Lefty Grove	.75	.50	.15
53 Carl Hubbell	.75	.50	.15
54 Herb Pennock	.50	.30	.10
55 Pie Traynor	.75	.50	.15
56 Mordecai Brown	.50	.30	.10
57 Charlie Gehringer	.75	.50	.15
58 Kid Nichols	.50	.30	.10
59 Jimmy Foxx	.75	.50	.15
60 Mel Ott	.75	.50	.15
Third Series	15.00	10.00	4.00
61 Harry Heilmann	.75	.50	.15
62 Paul Waner	.50	.30	.10
63 Edward Barrow	.50	.30	.10
64 Chief Bender	.50	.30	.10
65 Tom Connolly	.50	.30	.10
66 Dizzy Dean	.90	.60	.20
67 Bill Klem	.50	.30	.10
68 Al Simmons	.75	.50	.15
69 Bobby Wallace	.50	.30	.10
70 Harry Wright	.50	.30	.10
71 Bill Dickey	.75	.50	.15
72 Rabbit Maranville	.50	.30	.10
73 Bill Terry	.75	.50	.15
74 Frank Baker	.50	.30	.10
75 Joe DiMaggio	1.25	.75	.25
76 Gabby Hartnett	.50	.30	.10
77 Ted Lyons	.50	.30	.10
78 Ray Schalk	.50	.30	.10
79 Dazzy Vance	.50	.30	.10
80 Joe Cronin	.75	.50	.15
81 Hank Greenberg	.75	.50	.15
82 Sam Crawford	.50	.30	.10
83 Joe McCarthy	.50	.30	.10
84 Zack Wheat	.50	.30	.10
85 Max Carey	.50	.30	.10
86 Billy Hamilton	.50	.30	.10
87 Bob Feller	.75	.50	.15
88 Bill McKechnie	.50	.30	.10
89 Jackie Robinson	.75	.50	.15
90 Edd Roush	.50	.30	.10
Fourth Series	15.00	10.00	4.00
91 John Clarkson	.50	.30	.10
92 Elmer Flick	.50	.30	.10
93 Sam Rice	.50	.30	.10
94 Eppa Rixey	.50	.30	.10
95 Luke Appling	.50	.30	.10
96 Red Faber	.50	.30	.10
97 Burleigh Grimes	.50	.30	.10
98 Miller Huggins	.50	.30	.10
99 Tim Keefe	.50	.30	.10
100 Heinie Manush	.50	.30	.10
101 John Ward	.50	.30	.10
102 Pud Galvin	.50	.30	.10
103 Casey Stengel	.75	.50	.15
104 Ted Williams	.90	.60	.20
105 Branch Rickey	.50	.30	.10
106 Red Ruffing	.50	.30	.10
107 Lloyd Waner	.50	.30	.10
108 Kiki Cuyler	.50	.30	.10

109 Goose Goslin	.50	.30	.10
110 Joe Medwick	.50	.30	.10
111 Roy Campanella	.75	.50	.15
112 Stan Coveleski	.50	.30	.10
113 Waite Hoyt	.50	.30	.10
114 Stan Musial	.75	.50	.15
115 Lou Boudreau	.50	.30	.10
116 Earl Combs	.50	.30	.10
117 Ford Frick	.50	.30	.10
118 Jesse Haines	.50	.30	.10
119 David Bancroft	.50	.30	.10
120 Jake Beckley	.50	.30	.10
Fifth Series	15.00	10.00	4.00
121 Chick Hafey	.50	.30	.10
122 Harry Hooper	.50	.30	.10
123 Joe Kelley	.50	.30	.10
124 Rube Marquard	.50	.30	.10
125 Satchel Paige	.75	.50	.15
126 George Weiss	.50	.30	.10
127 Yogi Berra	.75	.50	.15
128 Josh Gibson	.75	.50	.15
129 Lefty Gomez	.75	.50	.15
130 William Harridge	.50	.30	.10
131 Sandy Koufax	.75	.50	.15
132 Buck Leonard	.50	.30	.10
133 Early Wynn	.50	.30	.10
134 Ross Youngs	.50	.30	.10
135 Roberto Clemente	.75	.50	.15
136 Billy Evans	.50	.30	.10
137 Monte Irvin	.50	.30	.10
138 George Kelly	.50	.30	.10
139 Warren Spahn	.50	.30	.10
140 Mickey Welch	.50	.30	.10
141 Cool Papa Bell	.50	.30	.10
142 Jim Bottomley	.50	.30	.10
143 Jocko Conlan	.50	.30	.10
144 Whitey Ford	.75	.50	.15
145 Mickey Mantle	1.25	.75	.25
146 Sam Thompson	.50	.30	.10
147 Earl Averill	.50	.30	.10
148 Bucky Harris	.50	.30	.10
149 Billy Herman	.50	.30	.10
150 Judy Johnson	.50	.30	.10
Sixth Series	15.00	10.00	4.00
151 Ralph Kiner	.50	.30	.10
152 Oscar Charleston	.50	.30	.10
153 Roger Connor	.50	.30	.10
154 Cal Hubbard	.50	.30	.10
155 Bob Lemon	.50	.30	.10
156 Fred Lindstrom	.50	.30	.10
157 Robin Roberts	.50	.30	.10
158 Ernie Banks	.75	.50	.15
159 Martin Dihigo	.50	.30	.10
160 John Lloyd	.50	.30	.10
161 Al Lopez	.50	.30	.10
162 Amos Rusie	.50	.30	.10
163 Joe Sewell	.50	.30	.10
164 Addie Joss	.50	.30	.10
165 Larry MacPhail	.50	.30	.10
166 Eddie Mathews	.50	.30	.10
167 Warren Giles	.50	.30	.10
168 Willie Mays	.90	.60	.20
169 Hack Wilson	.50	.30	.10
170 Al Kaline	.75	.50	.15
171 Chuck Klein	.50	.30	.10
172 Duke Snider	.75	.50	.15
173 Tom Yawkey	.50	.30	.10
174 Rube Foster	.50	.30	.10
175 Bob Gibson	.75	.50	.15
176 Johnny Mize	.50	.30	.10
A Abner Doubleday	.75	.50	.15
B Stephen C. Clark	.50	.30	.10
C Paul S. Kerr	.50	.30	.10
D Edward W. Stack	.50	.30	.10

1981 SPORT AMERICANA "1937 (12) DIAMOND STARS" 2 3/8" X 2 7/8"

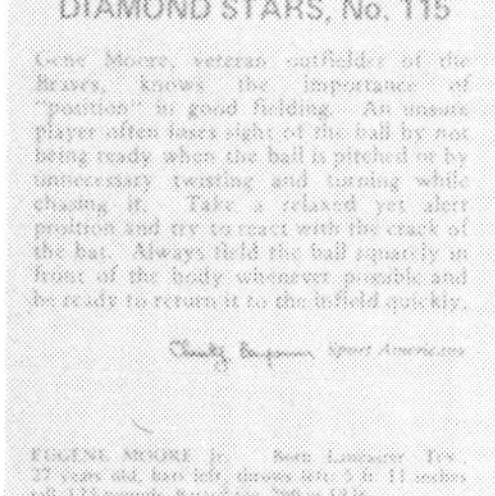

In early 1981, an uncut proof sheet of 12 cards resembling the 1930's National Chicle Diamond Star cards was discovered. The cards in this set are those found on this proof sheet. The backs were created to resemble the original Diamond Star backs, and a thick card stock comparable to the 1930's issues was used. Research of the players and their teams on the proof sheet suggests that the cards were scheduled for release in 1937; hence, the set was named accordingly.

	MINT	VG–E	F–G
COMPLETE SET	3.00	1.00	.00
COMMON PLAYER	.25	.10	.00
109 Frey, Benny	.25	.10	.00
110 Fox, Pete	.25	.10	.00
111 Cavaretta, Phil	.25	.10	.00
112 Goslin, Goose	.35	.15	.00
113 Harder, Mel	.25	.10	.00
114 Cramer, Roger	.25	.10	.00
115 Moore Gene	.25	.10	.00
116 Collins, Rip	.25	.10	.00
117 Frey Linus	.25	.10	.00
118 Gomez, Lefty	.35	.15	.00
119 Bottomley, Jim	.35	.15	.00
Hornsby, Rogers			
120 Warneke, Lon	.25	.10	.00

1982 "BOWMAN 1952" EXTENSION (15) 2 1/8" X 3 1/8"

CHRIS VAN CUYK

Pitcher—Brooklyn Dodgers
Born: Kimberly, Wis., March 1, 1927
Height: 6-6 Weight: 215
Bats: Left Throws: Left

One of the most promising young pitchers in Dodger organization. Spent most of last season in minors. Pitched in 9 games for Dodgers and posted 1-2 mark with 5.52 ERA in 29⅓ innings. Made major league debut in 1950. Had 1-3 record with 4.86 ERA. Older brother, John, was formerly in Dodger organization.

No. 255 in the 1952 SERIES
BASEBALL PICTURE CARDS
©1982 TCMA Ltd. Peekskill, N.Y.

In 1980, 15 unissued pieces of artwork initially intended to be used by Bowman Gum in their 1952 baseball card set were discovered. This set consists of 15 cards made from this original artwork. The backs have been created to resemble the original 1952 series, and the set has been numbered 253-267 (the next 15 cards in the 1952 Bowman sequence). The facsimile autograph on the original 1952 Bowman's has been omitted from cards in this set.

1981 Bowman—1952 Extension

	MINT	VG—E	F—G
COMPLETE SET	3.00	.50	.00
COMMON PLAYER	.20	.05	.00
253 Addis, Bob	.20	.05	.00
254 Kennedy, Bob	.20	.05	.00
255 Van Cuyk, Chris	.20	.05	.00
256 Trucks, Virgil	.20	.05	.00
257 Hopp, Johnny	.20	.05	.00
258 Lavagetto, Cookie	.20	.05	.00
259 McCosky, Barney	.20	.05	.00
260 Moore, Terry	.20	.05	.00
261 Thorpe, Bob	.20	.05	.00
262 Wilson, Jim	.20	.05	.00
263 Martin, Maury	.20	.05	.00
264 Henry, Bill	.20	.05	.00
265 Shuba, George	.20	.05	.00
266 Merson, John	.20	.05	.00
267 Dobson, Joe	.20	.05	.00

1981 TCMA—The 1960'S (189) SECOND SERIES

2 1/2" X 3 1/2"

The 1960's

HODGES, BERRA, YOST
WALKER, PIGNATANO
New York Mets

This continuation of the TCMA Stars of the 1960's set includes 189 additional cards for which the numbering sequence begins at number 294. They are similar in format and design to the first series, however, new and many different players are featured. The set was produced in 1981.

	MINT	VG-E	F-G
COMPLETE SET	10.00	6.50	2.50
COMMON PLAYER	.04	.02	.01
294 Fritzie Brickell	.04	.02	.01
295 Craig Anderson	.04	.02	.01
296 Cliff Cook	.04	.02	.01
297 Pumpsie Green	.04	.02	.01
298 Choo Choo Coleman	.04	.02	.01
299 Don Buford	.04	.02	.01
300 Sparkey Anderson	.08	.05	.02
301 John Anderson	.04	.02	.01
302 Ted Beard	.04	.02	.01
303 Mantle and Maris	.50	.35	.15
304 Gene Freese	.04	.02	.01
305 Don Wilkinson	.04	.02	.01
306 Walter Alston	.08	.05	.02
307 George Bamberger	.04	.02	.01
308 Nelson Briles	.04	.02	.01
309 Dave Baldwin	.04	.02	.01
310 Bob Bailey	.04	.02	.01
311 Paul Blair	.04	.02	.01
312 Ken Boswell	.04	.02	.01
313 Sam Bowens	.04	.02	.01
314 Ray Barker	.04	.02	.01
315 Hodges and Agee	.15	.10	.04
316 Elmer Valo	.04	.02	.01
317 Ken Walters	.04	.02	.01
318 Joel Horlen	.04	.02	.01
320 Charlie Maxwell	.04	.02	.01
321 Joe Foy	.04	.02	.01
322 Cleon Jones, Tommie Agee, Ron Swoboda	.04	.02	.01
323 Paul Foytack	.04	.02	.01
324 Ron Fairly	.04	.02	.01
325 Wilbur Wood	.04	.02	.01
326 Don Wilson	.04	.02	.01
327 Felix Mantilla	.04	.02	.01
328 Ed Bouchee	.04	.02	.01
329 Sandy Valdespino	.04	.02	.01
330 Al Ferrara	.04	.02	.01
331 Jose Tartabull	.04	.02	.01
332 Dick Kenworthy	.04	.02	.01
333 Don Pavletich	.04	.02	.01
334 Jim Fairey	.04	.02	.01
335 Rico Petrocelli	.04	.02	.01
336 Garry Roggenburk	.04	.02	.01
337 Rick Reichardt	.04	.02	.01
338 Ken McMullen	.04	.02	.01
339 Dooley Womack	.04	.02	.01
340 Joe Moock	.04	.02	.01
341 Lou Brock	.40	.25	.10
342 Hector Torres	.04	.02	.01
343 Ted Savage	.04	.02	.01
344 Hobie Landrith	.04	.02	.01
345 Ed Lopat	.08	.05	.02
346 Mel Nelson	.04	.02	.01
347 Mickey Lolich	.15	.10	.04
348 Al Lopez	.15	.10	.04
349 Frederico "Chi Chi" Olivo	.04	.02	.01
350 Bob Moose	.04	.02	.01
351 Bill McCool	.04	.02	.01
352 Ernie Bowman	.04	.02	.01
353 Tommy McCraw	.04	.02	.01
354 Sam Mele	.04	.02	.01
355 Len Boehmer	.04	.02	.01
356 Hank Aaron	.50	.35	.15
357 Ron Hunt	.04	.02	.01
358 Luis Aparicio	.15	.10	.04
359 Gene Mauch	.08	.05	.02
360 Barry Moore	.04	.02	.01
361 John Buzhardt	.04	.02	.01
362 St. Louis Cardinals, Spring Training	.04	.02	.01
363 Duke Snider	.30	.20	.08
364 Billy Martin	.20	.13	.05
365 Wes Parker	.08	.05	.02
366 Dick Stuart	.08	.05	.02
367 Glenn Beckert	.04	.02	.01
368 Ollie Brown	.04	.02	.01
369 Stan Bahnsen	.04	.02	.01
370 Wesley "Lee" Bales	.04	.02	.01
371 Johnny Keane	.04	.02	.01
372 Wally Moon	.08	.05	.02
373 Larry Miller	.04	.02	.01
374 Fred Newman	.04	.02	.01
375 John Orsino	.04	.02	.01
376 Joe Pactwa	.04	.02	.01
377 John O'Donoghue	.04	.02	.01
378 Jim Ollom	.04	.02	.01
379 Ray Oyler	.04	.02	.01
380 Ron Nischwitz	.04	.02	.01
381 Ron Paul	.04	.02	.01
382 Maris homers on May 24, 1961, and is greeted by Yogi Berra and Johnny Blanchard	.30	.20	.08
383 Jim McKnight	.04	.02	.01
384 Gene Michael	.08	.05	.02
385 Dave May	.04	.02	.01
386 Tim McCarver	.08	.05	.02
387 Larry Mason	.04	.02	.01
388 Don Hoak	.04	.02	.01
389 Nate Oliver	.04	.02	.01
390 Phil Ortega	.04	.02	.01
391 Billy Madden	.04	.02	.01
392 John Miller	.04	.02	.01
393 Danny Murtaugh	.08	.05	.02

394	Nelson Mathews	.04	.02	.01
395	Red Schoendienst	.08	.05	.02
396	Roger Nelson	.04	.02	.01
397	Tom Matchick	.04	.02	.01
398	Dennis Musgraves	.04	.02	.01
399	Tommy Harper	.08	.05	.02
399	Chet Trail	.04	.02	.01
400	Francis Peters	.04	.02	.01
401	Tony Pierce	.04	.02	.01
402	Billy Williams	.15	.10	.04
403	Dave Boswell	.04	.02	.01
404	Ray Washburn	.04	.02	.01
405	Al Worthington	.04	.02	.01
406	Jesus Alou	.04	.02	.01
407	Hodges, Berra, Yost, Walker, Pignatano	.08	.05	.02
408	Wally Bunker	.04	.02	.01
409	Jim Brenneman	.04	.02	.01
410	Bobby Bragan	.04	.02	.01
411	Cal McLish	.04	.02	.01
412	Curt Blefary	.04	.02	.01
413	Jim Bethke	.04	.02	.01
414	The St. Louis Cardinals' Infield	.08	.05	.02
415	Richie Allen	.08	.05	.02
416	Larry Brown	.04	.02	.01
417	Mike Andrews	.04	.02	.01
418	Don Mossi	.04	.02	.01
419	J.C. Martin	.04	.02	.01
420	Dick Rusteck	.04	.02	.01
421	Elly Rodriguez	.04	.02	.01
422	Casey Stengel	.30	.20	.08
423	Hodges and Ed Vargo Argue Over Call	.08	.05	.02
424	Johnny Briggs	.04	.02	.01
425	Bud Harrelson and Al Weis of Mets Turn A Double Play	.04	.02	.01
426	Doc Edwards	.04	.02	.01
427	Joe Hague	.04	.02	.01
428	Lee Elia	.04	.02	.01
429	Billy Moran	.04	.02	.01
430	Al Moran	.04	.02	.01
431	Pete Mikkelsen	.04	.02	.01
432	Aurelio Monteagudo	.04	.02	.01
433	Ken Mackenzie	.04	.02	.01
434	Dick Egan	.04	.02	.01
435	Al McBean	.04	.02	.01
436	Mike Ferraro	.04	.02	.01
437	Gary Wagner	.04	.02	.01
438	Jerry Grote and J.C. Martin	.04	.02	.01
439	Ted Kluszewski	.15	.10	.04
440	Jerry Johnson	.04	.02	.01
441	Ross Moschitto	.04	.02	.01
442	Zoilo Versalles	.04	.02	.01
443	Dennis Ribant	.04	.02	.01
444	Ted Williams	.50	.35	.15
445	Steve Whitaker	.04	.02	.01
446	Frank Bertaina	.04	.02	.01
447	Bo Belinsky	.08	.05	.02
448	Joe Moeller	.04	.02	.01
449	Ron Taylor and Don Shaw	.04	.02	.01
450	Al Downing, Mel Stottlemyre and Fritz Peterson with coach Whitey Ford	.08	.05	.02
451	Jack Tracy	.04	.02	.01
452	Tony Curry	.04	.02	.01
453	Roy White	.08	.05	.02
454	Jim Bunning	.08	.05	.02
455	Ralph Houk	.08	.05	.02
456	Bobby Shantz	.08	.05	.02
457	Bill Rigney	.04	.02	.01
458	Roger Repoz	.04	.02	.01
459	Bob Turley and Robin Roberts	.08	.05	.02
460	Gordon Richardson	.04	.02	.01
461	Dick Tracewski	.04	.02	.01
462	Thad Tillotson	.04	.02	.01
463	Larry "Bobo" Osborne	.04	.02	.01
464	Larry Burright	.04	.02	.01
465	Alan Foster	.04	.02	.01
466	Ron Taylor	.04	.02	.01
467	Fred Talbot	.04	.02	.01
468	Bob Miller	.04	.02	.01
469	Frank Tepedino	.04	.02	.01
470	Danny Frisella	.04	.02	.01
471	Cecil Perkins	.04	.02	.01
472	Danny Napoleon	.04	.02	.01
473	John Upham	.04	.02	.01
474	Maris, Berra, Mantle, Howard, Skowron, Blanchard	.30	.20	.08
475	Al Weis	.04	.02	.01
476	Rich Beck	.04	.02	.01
477	Boyer, Kubek, Richardson, Pepitone	.15	.10	.04
478	Jack Fisher	.04	.02	.01
479	Archie Moore	.04	.02	.01
480	Ralph Terry	.04	.02	.01
481	Hegan, Moses, Houk, Crosetti, Sain	.08	.05	.02
482	Hodges, Labine, Lavagetto, Craig, Zimmer, Neal, Stengel	.15	.10	.04

Many factors affect the value of team autographed balls. The values given here represent the value of a ball in very good condition with the signatures of at least a specified number of players who played on that team that year. A rough guideline for the number of players required to qualify the ball as a legitimate team autographed ball varies with the date of the ball, as there have been an increasing number of players per team over the years. These guidelines are: 1901-1920 at least 12 signatures on the ball; 1921-1940 at least 15 signatures on the ball; 1941-1960 at least 18 signatures on the ball; 1961-present at least 20 signatures on the ball. Naturally, balls with significantly more signatures would be worth more, especially when every player who played that year is included. The listing below gives a base price for the given ball with the required number of signatures without, in most cases, the key players or key signatures. Key player signature incremental prices are stated separately from the base price. These key players add the stated increment if they are present on the ball (and legible). This should not be interpreted as meaning that the additional key player's autograph is worth the given amount, but more properly, should be interpreted indirectly as the amount that the ball would drop in value if the key player were not on the ball. For example, Stan Musial is a superstar but not a difficult or valuable autograph (See individual autograph section for complete listing.); nevertheless, because he virtually personified the Cardinal teams of the late 40's and 50's, any Cardinal ball of that vintage would be greatly devalued, i.e., incomplete, without Musial's signature. Naturally, the same could be said for a Yankee ball without Ruth, Gehrig, DiMaggio, or Mantle, a Pirate ball without Wagner or Clemente, a Red Sox ball without Williams or Yastrzemski, a Cub ball without Ernie Banks, an Oriole ball without Brooks Robinson, a Tiger ball without Kaline, or a Giants ball without Willie Mays, etc. Other great players with clear identity with one specific team would affect the value of their team's ball more than these same players would affect some other team's ball and more than they would affect an all-star ball. For example, although Al Kaline would be essential on a Tiger ball, he is only one of the several American League stars who would appear on an all-star ball. Thus, his signature would add a lesser value to an autographed all-star team ball than to a Tiger autographed team ball. The absence of any of these name players from their respective team's ball would greatly reduce collector interest in the ball and would lower the value of that ball. This incremental approach to values should help potential buyers understand some of the variation in prices offered for balls of the same team and year but with slightly different players signing. Also, the incremental value for a given player will often change according to team and year. Thus, it would not be appropriate to extrapolate values for other balls listed herein except in a very conservative vain. As one can see from the listings below, the presence or absence of even one player on the ball can have quite an effect on the value of the ball.

Although they are the primary determinants, "which players?" and "how many players?" are not the only determinants of value. Some other factors influencing values are (with no order implied): (1) regulation American League or National League ball (if the ball which has been signed is not a regulation ball its value is reduced from that listed by as much as one-half); (2) faded signatures or a faded or scuffed ball can reduce the value of the ball by a factor of one-half or more, especially when the fading encompasses some of the key signatures; (3) shellacked balls do not have reduced value unless the shellack has darkened as to obscure the signatures; (4) it is beneficial to have the key player's signature clear and bold and to have the key player signed in an area of the ball suitable for display of that signature; (5) players who played only part of a season with a certain team because of injury or trade are noted in the listing below; these players often have "extra value" for that year (only) because of the limited opportunity for a collector to obtain his signature that year; (6) it would lower the value of the ball if the signatures were signed in a variety of contrasting inks; (7) any significant coaches (especially deceased Hall of Famers) also signing their team's ball would increase the value of the ball generally by the value of that coach's signature; (8) over the past 20 years or so, stamped (mechanically imprinted) balls have been mass produced and sold at ballpark souvenir stands; these facsimile autographed balls are usually detected by the ink similarity of the signatures and the equal solid pen pressure for each signature. They are worth between $4.00 (recent) and $10.00 (older) each; (9) non-team balls are not included herein as there are an infinite number of possibilities of combinations; they are generally not nearly as valuable as team balls unless the signatures are closely connected to some event of historical significance (e.g., Maris/Stallard, Ruth/Zachary, Dean/Averill, Gehrig/Pipp, Roseboro/Marichal, Vince/Dom/ Joe DiMaggio and, of course, Ruth/Gehrig) or have a "theme" (e.g., Hall of Fame inductees for a given year, no-hit pitchers, batting champions); (10) extra (non-team) players on the ball generally detract from the value of the ball; (11) personalized balls have less value except to persons with the same name; that is, a "To George" ball would be worth less than stated values herein, except to the original George and other Georges. Salutations (Yours truly) or indefinite personalizations (To a friend) do not affect value one way or the other.

The many balls listed below are not intended to be an exhaustive list (due to space limitations) of all possible team autographed balls; nevertheless, we feel that most of the more commonly seen balls have been included.

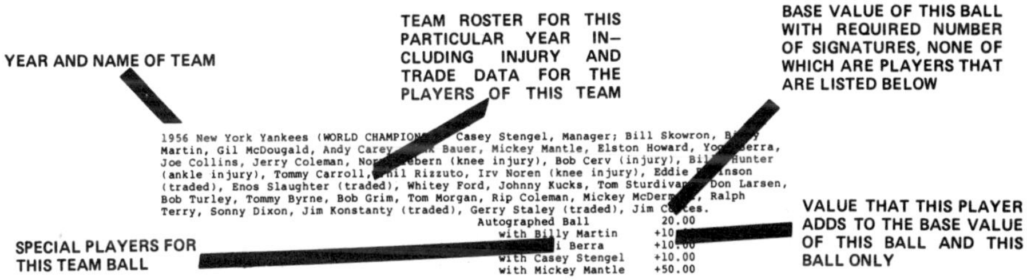

YEAR AND NAME OF TEAM

TEAM ROSTER FOR THIS PARTICULAR YEAR INCLUDING INJURY AND TRADE DATA FOR THE PLAYERS OF THIS TEAM

BASE VALUE OF THIS BALL WITH REQUIRED NUMBER OF SIGNATURES, NONE OF WHICH ARE PLAYERS THAT ARE LISTED BELOW

1956 New York Yankees (WORLD CHAMPION[illegible] Casey Stengel, Manager; Bill Skowron, B[illegible]y Martin, Gil McDougald, Andy Carey[illegible] Bauer, Mickey Mantle, Elston Howard, Yo[illegible]erra, Joe Collins, Jerry Coleman, No[illegible]ebern (knee injury), Bob Cerv (injury), Bi[illegible] Hunter (ankle injury), Tommy Carroll,[illegible]hil Rizzuto, Irv Noren (knee injury), Eddie [illegible]inson (traded), Enos Slaughter (traded), Whitey Ford, Johnny Kucks, Tom Sturdiva[illegible] Don Larsen, Bob Turley, Tommy Byrne, Bob Grim, Tom Morgan, Rip Coleman, Mickey McDer[illegible], Ralph Terry, Sonny Dixon, Jim Konstanty (traded), Gerry Staley (traded), Jim C[illegible]es.

Autographed Ball	20.00
with Billy Martin	+10[illegible]
[illegible]i Berra	+10[illegible]
with Casey Stengel	+10.00
with Mickey Mantle	+50.00

SPECIAL PLAYERS FOR THIS TEAM BALL

VALUE THAT THIS PLAYER ADDS TO THE BASE VALUE OF THIS BALL AND THIS BALL ONLY

THE INCREMENTAL VALUE OF THE AUTOGRAPH OF A PARTICULAR PLAYER TO A PARTICULAR BALL IS UNIQUE TO THAT BALL. IT IS NOT THE EXOGENOUS VALUE OF THAT PLAYER'S AUTOGRAPH. SEE THE INTRODUCTION TO TEAM AUTOGRAPHED BALLS.

1901 Chicago White Sox (American League Champs): Clark Griffith, Manager; Frank Isbell, Sam Mertes, Frank Shugart, Fred Hartman, Fielder Jones, Dummy Hoy, Herm McFarland, Billy Sullivan, Joe Sugden, Nixey Callahan (broken arm), Jimmy Burke (traded), Pop Foster (traded), Dave Brain, Roy Patterson, Jack Katoll, John Skopec, Wiley Piatt (traded), Zaza Harvey (traded), Frank Dupee, John McAleese.

Autographed Ball	300.00
with Clark Griffith	+200.00

1901 Pittsburgh Pirates (National League Champs): Fred Clarke, Manager; Kitty Bransfield, Claude Ritchey, Bones Ely (traded), Tommy Leach, Lefty Davis (traded), Ginger Beaumont, Chief Zimmer, Honus Wagner, Jack O'Connor, George Yeager (traded), Ed Poole, Jimmy Burke (traded), Lew Carr, Jud Smith, Truck Eagan (traded), Elmer Smith (traded), Jiggs Donahue (traded), Terry Turner, Deacon Phillippe, Jack Chesbro, Jesse Tannehill, Sam Leever (sore arm), Ed Doheny (traded), George Merritt, Snake Wiltse (traded), Rube Waddell.

Autographed Ball	200.00
with Honus Wagner	+250.00
with Rube Waddell	+100.00

1902 Philadelphia Athletics (American League Champs): Connie Mack, Manager; Harry Davis, Danny Murphy, Monte Cross, Lave Cross, Socks Seybold, Dave Fultz, Topsy Hartsel, Ossie Schreckengost (traded), Mike Powers, Louis Castro, Frank Bonner (traded), Elmer Flick (traded), Farmer Steelman, Nap Lajoie (holdout)(traded), Rube Waddell (jumped team), Eddie Plank, Bert Husting (traded), Snake Wiltse (traded), Highball Wilson, Fred Mitchell (traded), Andy Coakley, Bill Bernhard (holdout) (traded), Bill Duggleby (traded), Ed Kenna, Odie Porter, Clarence Quinn, Tom Walker.

Autographed Ball	250.00
with Connie Mack	+50.00
with Nap Lajoie	+100.00
with Eddie Plank	+100.00
with Rube Waddell	+100.00

1902 Pittsburgh Pirates (National League Champs): Fred Clarke, Manager; Kitty Bransfield (knee injury), Claude Ritchey, Wid Conroy, Tommy Leach, Lefty Davis (broken ankle), Ginger Beaumont, Harry Smith, Honus Wagner, Jimmy Burke, Jack O'Connor, Chief Zimmer, Jimmy Sebring, Eddie Phelps, Fred Crolius, George Merritt, Lee Fohl, Mike Hopkins, Bill Miller, Jack Chesbro, Jesse Tannehill, Deacon Phillippe, Ed Doheny (illness), Sam Leever (sore arm), Warry McLaughlin, Harv Cushman, Ed Poose (traded).

Autographed Ball	200.00
with Honus Wagner	+200.00
with Jack Chesbro	+150.00

1903 Boston Red Sox (WORLD CHAMPIONS): Jimmy Collins, Manager; Candy LaChance, Hobe Ferris, Freddy Parent, Buck Freeman, Chick Stahl (injury), Patsy Dougherty, Lou Criger, Jack O'Brien, Jake Stahl, Duke Farrell (broken leg), Broadway Aleck Smith, George Stone, Harry Gleason, Cy Young, Long Tom Hughes, Bill Dinneen, Norwood Gibson, George Winter, Nick Altrock (illness)(traded).

Autographed Ball	300.00
with Cy Young	+50.00
with Jimmy Collins	+200.00

1903 Pittsburgh Pirates (National League Champs): Fred Clarke, Manager; Kitty Bransfield, Claude Ritchey, Honus Wagner, Tommy Leach, Jimmy Sebring, Ginger Beaumont, Eddie Phelps, Otto Krueger, Harry Smith (injury), Art Weaver (traded), Joe Marshall, George Merritt (broken ankle), Fred Carisch, Eude Curtis, Hans Lobert, Solly Hofman, Bill Gray, Ernie Diehl, Lou Gertenrich, Sam Leever, Deacon Phillippe, Ed Doheny (illness), Brickyard Kennedy (injury), Bucky Veil, Kaiser Wilhelm, Lafe Winham, Gus Thompson, Cy Falkenberg, Lew Moren, Doc Scanlan, Jack Pfiester.

Autographed Ball	200.00
with Honus Wagner	+250.00

1904 Boston Red Sox (American League Champs): Jimmy Collins, Manager; Candy LaChance, Hobe Ferris, Freddy Parent, Buck Freeman, Chick Stahl, Kip Selbach (traded), Lou Criger, Duke Farrell, Patsy Dougherty (traded), Bill O'Neil (traded), Bob Unglaub (traded), Tom Doran, Cy Young, Bill Binnen, Jesse Tannehill, Norwood Gibson, George Winter.

Autographed Ball	250.00
with Cy Young	+50.00
with Jimmy Collins	+200.00

1904 New York Giants (National League Champs): John McGraw, Manager; Dan McGann, Billy Gilbert, Bill Dahlen, Art Devlin, George Browne, Roger Bresnahan, Sam Mertes, John Warner, Frank Bowerman, Jack Dunn, Moose McCormick (traded), Mike Donlin (traded), Doc Marshall (traded), Dan Brouthers, Jim O'Rourke, Joe McGinnity, Christy Mathewson, Dummy Taylor, Hooks Wiltse, Red Ames, Jack Dunn, Billy Milligan, Claude Elliot (traded).

Autographed Ball	75.00
with John McGraw	+75.00
with C. Mathewson	+100.00
with Rog Bresnahan	+100.00
with Dan Brouthers	+100.00
with Jim O'Rourke	+100.00
with Joe McGinnity	+100.00

1905 Phildelphia Athletics (American League Champs): Connie Mack, Manager; Harry Davis, Danny Murphy, Jack Knight, Lave Cross, Socks Seybold, Danny Offman, Topsy Hartsel, Ossee Schreckengost, Monte Cross, Bris Lord, Mike Powers (traded), Harry Barton, Rube Waddell, Eddie Plank, Andy Coakley, Chief Bender, Weldon Henley, Jimmy Dygert, Joe Myers.

Autographed Ball	100.00
with Connie Mack	+50.00
with Chief Bender	+50.00
with Eddie Plank	+100.00
with Rube Waddell	+150.00

1905 New York Giants (WORLD CHAMPIONS): John McGraw, Manager; Dan McGann, Billy Gilbert, Bill Dahlen, Art Devlin, George Browne, Mike Donlin, Sam Mertes, Roger Bresnahan, Sammy Strang, Frank Bowerman, Boileryard Clarke, Offa Neal, Moonlight Graham, Bob Hall (traded), Christy Mathewson, Joe McGinnity, Red Ames, Dummy Taylor, Hooks Wiltse, Claude Elliott.

Autographed Ball	75.00
with John McGraw	+75.00
with C. Mathewson	+100.00
with Rog Bresnahan	+100.00
with Joe McGinnity	+150.00

1906 Chicago White Sox (WORLD CHAMPIONS): Fielder Jones, Manager; Jiggs Donahue, Frank Isbell, George Davis, Lee Tannehill, Bill O'Neill, Eddie Hahn (traded), Billy Sullivan, Patsy Dougherty (traded), George Rohe, Gus Dundon, Hub Hart, Frank Roth, Frank Hemphill, Babe Towne, Ed McFarland, Rube Vinson, Lee Quillin, Frank Owen, Nick Altrock, Doc White, Ed Walsh, Roy Patterson, Frank Smith, Lou Fiene.

Autographed Ball	350.00
with Ed Walsh	+50.00

1906 Chicago Cubs (National League Champs): Frank Chance, Manager; Johnny Evers, Joe Tinker, Harry Steinfeldt, Wildfire Schulte, Jimmy Slagle, Jimmy Sheckard, Johnny Kling, Pat Moran, Solly Hofman, Doc Gessler (traded), Tom Walsh, Pete Noonan (traded), Bull Smith, Three Finger Brown, Jack Pfiester, Ed Reulbach, Carl Lundgren, Orvie Overall (traded), Jack Taylor (traded), Fred Beebe (traded), Bob Wicker (traded), Jack Harper (traded).

Autographed Ball	100.00
with Mordecai Brown	+50.00
with Johnny Evers	+75.00
with Joe Tinker	+75.00
with Frank Chance	+100.00

1907 Detroit Tigers (American League Champs): Hughie Jennings, Manager; Claude Rossman, Red Downs, Charley O'Leary, Bill Coughlin, Ty Cobb, Sam Crawford, Davy Jones, Boss Schmidt, G. Schaefer, George Mullin, Freddie Payne, Ed Killian, Matty McIntyre, Jimmy Archer, Bobby Lowe, Tex Erwin, Red Killefer, Wild Bill Donovan, Ed Siever, John Eubank, Ed Willett, Herm Malloy, Elijah Jones.

Autographed Ball	150.00
with Hugh Jennings	+100.00
with Ty Cobb	+150.00

1907 Chicago Cubs (WORLD CHAMPIONS): Frank Chance, Manager; Johnny Evers, Joe Tinker, Harry Steinfeldt, Wildfire Schulte (injury), Jimmy Slagle, Jimmy Sheckard, Johnny Kling, Solly Hofman, Pat Moran, Del Howard (traded), Newt Randall (traded), Kid Durbin, Mike Kahoe (traded), Bill Sweeney (traded), Heinie Zimmerman, Jack Hardy, Orvie Overall, Three Finger Brown, Carl Lundgren, Ed Reulbach, Jack Pfiester, Chick Fraser, Jack Taylor, Kid Durbin.

Autographed Ball	100.00
with Mordecai Brown	+50.00
with Johnny Evers	+75.00
with Joe Tinker	+75.00
with Frank Chance	+100.00

1908 Detroit Tigers (American League Champs): Hughie Jennings, Manager; Claude Rossman, Red Downs, Germany Schaefer, Bill Coughlin, Ty Cobb, Sam Crawford, Matty McIntyre, Boss Schmidt, Charley O'Leary (illness), Davy Jones, Ira Thomas, Red Killefer, Donie Bush, Freddie Payne (broken finger), Clay Perry, Ed Summers, Wild Bill Donovan, George Mullin, Ed Willett (injury), Ed Killian, George Winter (traded), Ed Siever, George Suggs, Herm Malloy.

Autographed Ball	150.00
with Ty Cobb	+150.00
with Hugh Jennings	+100.00

1908 Chicago Cubs (WORLD CHAMPIONS): Frank Chance, Manager; Johnny Evers, Joe Tinker, Harry Steinfeldt, Wildfire Schulte, Jimmy Slagle, Jimmy Sheckard, Johnny Kling, Solly Hofman, Del Howard, Pat Moran, Heinie Zimmerman, Kid Durbin, Doc Marshall (traded), Jack Hayden, Vin Campbell, Three Finger Brown, Ed Reulbach, Orvie Overall (injury), Jack Pfiester, Chick Fraser, Carl Lundgren, Andy Coakley (traded), Rube Kroh, Bill Mack, Carl Spongberg.

Autographed Ball	100.00
with Mordecai Brown	+50.00
with Johnny Evers	+75.00
with Joe Tinker	+75.00
with Frank Chance	+100.00

1909 Detroit Tigers (American League Champs): Hugh Jennings, Manager; Claude Rossman (traded), Germany Schaefer (traded), Donie Bush, George Moriarty, Ty Cobb, Sam Crawford, Matty McIntrye, Boss Schmidt, Oscar Stanage, Charles O'Leary, Davy Jones, Jim Delahanty (traded), Tom Jones (traded), Red Killefer (traded), Heinie Beckendorf, Joe Casey, Del Gainer, George Mullin, Ed Willett, Ed Summers, Ed Killian, Wild Bill Donovan, Ralph Works, Kid Speer, George Suggs, Elijah Jones.

Autographed Ball	150.00
with Ty Cobb	+150.00
with Hugh Jennings	+100.00

1909 Pittsburgh Pirates (WORLD CHAMPIONS): Fred Clarke, Manager; Bill Abstein, Dots Miller, Honus Wagner, Jap Barbeau (traded), Owen Wilson, Tommy Leach, George Gibson, Ham Hyatt, Bobby Byrne (traded), Alan Storke (traded), Ed Abbaticchio, Ward Miller (traded), Mike Simon, Paddy O'Connor, Kid Durbin (traded), Howie Camnitz, Vic Willis, Lefty Leifield, Nick Maddox, Babe Adams, Sam Leever, Deacon Phillippe, Sammy Frock, Chick Brandom, Bill Powell.

Autographed Ball	150.00
with Honus Wagner	+200.00

1910 Philadelphia Athletics (WORLD CHAMPIONS): Connie Mack, Manager; Harry Davis, Eddie Collins, Jack Barry, Frank Baker, Danny Murphy, Rube Oldring, Topsy Hartsel, Jack Lapp, Bris Lord (traded), Ira Thomas, Stuffy McInnis, Paddy Livingston, Ben Houser (shoulder injury), Heinie Heitmuller, Morrie Rath (traded), Amos Strunk, Pat Donahue (traded), Claude Derrick, Earle Mack, Jack Coombs, Chief Bender, Cy Morgan, Eddie Plank, Harry Krause, Jimmy Dygert, Tommy Atkins.

Autographed Ball	150.00
with Connie Mack	+50.00
with Chief Bender	+50.00
with Eddie Collins	+50.00
with Eddie Plank	+100.00

1910 Chicago Cubs (National League Champs): Frank Chance, Manager; Johnny Evers, Joe Tinker, Harry Steinfeldt, Wildfire Schulte, Solly Hofman, Jimmy Sheckard, Johnny Kling, H. Zimmerman, Jimmy Archer, Ginger Beaumont, John Kane, Tom Needham, Fred Luderus (traded), Doc Miller (traded), Three Finger Brown, King Cole, Harry McIntire, Orvie Overall (sore arm), Ed Reulbach (illness), Lew Richie (traded), Jack Pfiester, Rube Kroh (suspended by team), Big Jeff Pfeffer, Orlie Weaver.

Autographed Ball	100.00
with Mordecai Brown	+50.00
with Johnny Evers	+75.00
with Joe Tinker	+75.00
with Frank Chance	+100.00

1911 Philadelphia Athletics (WORLD CHAMPIONS): Connie Mack, Manager; Stuffy McInnis, Eddie Collins, Jack Barry, Frank Baker, Danny Murphy, Rube Oldring, Bris Lord, Ira Thomas, Amos Strunk, Jack Lapp, Harry Davis, Jack Coombs, Claude Derrick, Paddy Livingston (ankle injury), Topsy Hartsel, Chester Emerson, Willie Hogan (traded), Earle Mack, Eddie Plank, Chief Bender, Cy Morgan, Harry Krause, Dave Danforth, Elmer Leonard, Doc Martin, Boardwalk Brown.

Autographed Ball	150.00
with Connie Mack	+50.00
with Chief Bender	+50.00
with Eddie Collins	+50.00
with Eddie Plank	+100.00

1911 New York Giants (National League Champs): John McGraw, Manager; Fred Merkle, Larry Doyle, Al Bridwell (traded), Art Devlin, Red Murray, Fred Snodgrass, Josh Devore, Chief Meyers, Art Fletcher, Beals Becker, Buck Herzog (traded), Art Wilson, Doc Crandall, Mike Donlin (traded), Grover Hartley, Gene Paulette, George Burns, Hank Gowdy (traded), Admiral Schlei, Christy Mathewson, Rube Marquard, Doc Crandall, Hooks Wiltse, Red Ames, Bugs Raymond, Louis Drucke, Bert Maxwell.

Autographed Ball	100.00
with John McGraw	+75.00
with C. Mathewson	+125.00

1912 Boston Red Sox (WORLD CHAMPIONS): Jake Stahl, Manager; Steve Yerkes, Heinie Wagner, Larry Gardner, Harry Hooper, Tris Speaker, Duffy Lewis, Bill Carrigan, Clyde Engle, Hick Cady (ankle injury), Hugh Bradley, Olaf Henriksen, Les Nunamaker, Neal Ball (traded), Marty Krug, Pinch Thomas, Smokey Joe Wood, Hugh Bedient, Buck O'Brien, Charley Hall, Ray Collins (knee injury), Jack Bushelman, Larry Pape, Eddie Cicotte (traded), Ben Van Dyke, Casey Hageman, Doug Smith.

Autographed Ball	250.00
with Tris Speaker	+50.00

1912 New York Giants (National League Champs): John McGraw, Manager; Fred Merkle, Larry Doyle, Art Fletcher, Buck Herzog, Red Murray, Beals Becker, Fred Snodgrass, Chief Meyers, Josh Devore, Tillie Shafer, Art Wilson, Doc Crandall, Moose McCormick, George Burns, Heinie Groh (injury), Grover Hartley, Dave Robertson, Rube Marquard, Christy Mathewson, Jeff Tesreau, Doc Crandall, Red Ames, Hooks Wiltse, Lore Bader, LaRue Kirby, Al Demaree, Louis Drucks, Ted Goulait, Ernie Shore.

Autographed Ball	100.00
with John McGraw	+75.00
with C. Mathewson	+125.00

1913 Philadelphia Athletics (WORLD CHAMPIONS): Connie Mack, Manager; Stuffy McInnis, Eddie Collins, Jack Barry, Frank Baker, Eddie Murphy, Jimmy Walsh, Rube Oldring, Jack Lapp, Amos Strunk, Wally Schang, Tom Daley, Danny Murphy, Bill Orr, Ira Thomas, Harry Davis, George Brickley, Harry Fritz, Doc Lavan (traded), Chief Bender, Boardwalk Brown, Eddie Plank, Duke Houck, Bullet Joe Bush, Bob Shawkey, Herb Pennock, Weldon Wyckoff, Bill Taft, Jack Coombs (illness).

Autographed Ball	50.00
with Connie Mack	+50.00
with Chief Bender	+50.00
with Eddie Collins	+50.00
with Herb Pennock	+50.00
with Eddie Plank	+100.00

1913 New York Giants (National League Champs): John McGraw, Manager; Fred Merkle, Larry Doyle, Art Fletcher, Buck Herzog, Red Murray, Fred Snodgrass, George Burns, Chief Meyers, Tillie Shafer, Moose McCormick, Art Wilson, Doc Crandall (traded), Larry McLean (traded), Claude Cooper, Eddie Grant (traded), Grover Hartley, Jim Thorpe, Josh Devore (traded), Milt Stock, Heinie Groh (traded), Joe Evers, Howard Merritt, Christy Mathewson, Rube Marquard, Jeff Tesreau, Al Demaree, Art Fromme (traded), Red Ames (traded), Bunny Hearn, Rube Schauer, Hooks Wiltse, Ferdie Schupp.

Autographed Ball 75.00
with John McGraw +75.00
with C. Mathewson +100.00
with Jim Thorpe +100.00

1914 Philadelphia Athletics (American League Champs): Connie Mack, Manager; Stuffy McInnis, Eddie Collins, Jack Barry, Frank Baker, Eddie Murphy, Amos Strunk, Rube Oldring, Wally Schang, Jack Lapp, Jimmy Walsh (traded), Larry Kopf, Tom Daley (traded), Chick Davies, Shag Thompson, Bill Orr, Wickey McAvoy, Harry Davis, Press Cruthers, Dean Sturgis, Sam Crane, Earle Mack, Ferdie Moore, Chief Bender, Bullet Joe Bush, Bob Shawkey, Eddie Plank, Herb Pennock, Weldon Wyckoff, Rube Bressler, Chick Davies, Boardwalk Brown (traded), Jack Coombs.

Autographed Ball 50.00
with Connie Mack +50.00
with Chief Bender +50.00
with Eddie Collins +50.00
with Herb Pennock +50.00
with Eddie Plank +100.00

1914 Boston Bees (Braves) (WORLD CHAMPIONS): George Stallings, Manager; Butch Schmidt, Johnny Evers, Rabbit Maranville, Charlie Deal, Larry Gilbert, Les Mann, Joe Connolly, Hank Gowdy, P. Whitted (traded), Red Smith (traded), Bert Whaling, Oscar Dugey, Josh Devore (traded), Ted Cather (traded), Herbie Moran (traded), Jim Murray, Jack Martin (traded), Otto Hess, Wilson Collins, Tommy Griffith, Clancy Tyler, Clarence Kraft, Billy Martin, Dick Rudolph, Bill James, Lefty Tyler, Paul Strand (sore arm), Dick Crutcher, Otto Hess, George Davis, Gene Cocreham, Hub Perdue (traded).

Autographed Ball 225.00
with R. Maranville +50.00
with Johnny Evers +75.00

1914 Indianapolis (FEDERAL LEAGUE CHAMPS): Bill Phillips, Manager; Charlie Carr, Frank LaPorte, Jimmy Esmond, Bill McKechnie, Benny Kauff, Vin Campbell, Al Scheer, Bill Rariden, Edd Roush, Al Kaiser (illness), Carl Vandagrift, Biddy Dolan, Bill Warren, George Textor, Everett Booe (traded), Frank Rooney, Cy Falkenberg, Earl Moseley, George Kaiserling, George Mullin, Harry Billiard, Charlie Whitehouse, Ed Henderson (traded), Katsey Keifer, Frank Harter, Ralph McConnaughey.

Autographed Ball 400.00
with Bill McKechnie +50.00
with Eddie Roush +50.00

1914 Chicago (FEDERAL LEAGUE): Joe Tinker, Manager; Fred Beck, Jack Farrell, Rollie Zeider, Al Wickland, Dutch Zwilling, Max Flack, Art Wilson, Harry Fritz, Austin Walsh, Jim Stanley, Bruno Block, Bill Jackson, Count Clemens, Leq Kavanagh, Skipper Roberts (traded), Claude Hendrix, Erv Lange, Max Fiske, Rankin Johnson (traded), Doc Watson (traded), Ad Brennan, Tom McGuire, Mike Predergast, Dave Black.

Autographed Ball 200.00
with Joe Tinker +150.00

1915 Chicago (FEDERAL LEAGUE CHAMPS): Joe Tinker, Manager; Fred Beck, Rollie Zeider, Harry Fritz, Jimmy Smith (traded), Max Flack, Dutch Zwilling, Les Mann, Art Wilson, Bill Fischer, Charlie Hanford, Jack Farrell, Bill Jackson, Tex Westerzil (traded), Al Wickland (traded), Joe Weiss, Mickey Doolan (traded), Arnold Hauser (illness), Charlie Pechous, Count Clemens, George McConnell, Three Finger Brown, Claude Hendrix, Mike Predergast, Dave Black (traded), Bill Bailey (traded), Ad Brennan, Rankin Johnson (traded), Henry Rasmussen.

Autographed Ball 200.00
with Mordecai Brown +75.00
with Joe Tinker +75.00

1915 St. Louis (FEDERAL LEAGUE): Fielder Jones, Manager; Babe Borton, Bobby Vaughn, Ernie Johnson, Charlie Deal, Jack Tobin, Delos Drake, Ward Miller, Grove Hartley, Doc Crandall, Al Bridwell, Harry Chapman, LaRue Kirby, Art Kores, Armando Marsans, Jimmy Walsh (traded), Tex Westerzil (traded), Hughie Miller, Pete Compton (traded), Dave Davenport, Eddie Plank, Doc Crandall, Bob Groom, Doc Watson, Ed Willett, Ernie Herbert, LaRue Kirby.

Autographed Ball 200.00
with Eddie Plank +150.00

1915 Boston Red Sox (WORLD CHAMPIONS): Bill Carrigan, Manager; Dick Hoblitzell, Heinie Wagner, Everett Scott, Larry Gardner (injury), Harry Hooper, Tris Speaker, Duffy Lewis, Pinch Thomas, Hal Janvrin, Del Gainer, Jack Barry (traded), Hick Cady, Olaf Henriksen, Babe Ruth, Rube Foster, Mike McNally, Bill Rodgers (traded), Chick Shorten, Rube Foster, Ernie Shore, Smokey Joe Wood, Dutch Leonard, Vean Gregg (sore arm), Ray Collins, Carl Mays, Ralph Comstock (traded), Herb Pennock (traded).

Autographed Ball 50.00
with Tris Speaker +50.00
with Herb Pennock +50.00
with Babe Ruth +250.00

1915 Philadelphia Phillies (National League Champs): Pat Moran, Manager; Fred Luderus, Bert Niehoff, Dave Bancroft, Bobby Byrne, Gavy Cravath, Dode Paskert, Possum Whitted, Bill Killefer, Beals Becker, Milt Stock, Ed Burns, Oscar Dugey, Bud Weiser, Jack Adams, G.C. Pete Alexander, Erskine Mayer, Al Demaree, Eppa Rixey, George Chalmers, George McQuillan (traded), Joe Oeschger, Stan Baumgartner.

Autographed Ball 150.00
with G.C. Alexander +150.00

1916 Boston Red Sox (WORLD CHAMPIONS): Bill Carrigan, Manager; Dick Hoblitzell, Jack Barry, Everett Scott, Larry Gardner, Harry Hooper, Tilly Walker, Duffy Lewis, Pinch Thomas, Hal Janvrin, Mike McNally, Hick Cady, Olaf Henriksen, Babe Ruth, Del Gainer, Chick Shorten, Sam Agnew, Jimmy Walsh (traded), Heinie Wagner, Dutch Leonard, Carl Mays, Ernie Shore, Rube Foster, Vean Gregg, Sad Sam Jones, Marty McHale (traded), Herb Pennock, Weldon Wyckoff (sore arm) (traded).

Autographed Ball	100.00
with Herb Pennock	+50.00
with Babe Ruth	+250.00

1916 Brooklyn Dodgers (National League Champs): Wilbert Robinson, Manager; Jake Daubert, George Cutshaw, Ivy Olson, Mike Mowrey, Jimmy Johnston, Hy Myers, Zack Wheat, Chief Meyers, Casey Stengel, Otto Miller, Ollie O'Mara, Lew McCarty (traded), Jeff Pfeffer, Gus Getz, Fred Merkle (traded), Dave Hickman, Hack Miller, Bunny Fabrique, Jeff Pfeffer, Larry Cheney, Sherry Smith, Rube Marquard, Jack Coombs, Wheezer Dell, Nap Rucker, Ed Appleton, Duster Mails, Leon Cadore.

Autographed Ball	125.00
with Casey Stengel	+75.00
with Wil. Robinson	+100.00

1917 Chicago White Sox (WORLD CHAMPIONS): Pants Rowland, Manager; Chick Gandil, Eddie Collins, Swede Risberg, Buck Weaver, Nemo Leibold, Happy Felsch, Joe Jackson, Ray Schalk, Shano Collins, Fred McMullin, Eddie Murphy, Byrd Lynn, Ted Jourdan, Joe Jenkins, Ziggy Hasbrouck, Zeb Terry, Bobby Byrne (traded), Jack Fournier, Eddie Cicotte, Lefty Williams, Red Faber, Reb Russell, Dave Danforth, Joe Benz, Jim Scott (military service), Mellie Wolfgang (injury).

Autographed Ball	150.00
with Eddie Collins	+50.00
with Joe Jackson	+100.00

1917 New York Giants (National League Champs): John McGraw, Manager; Walter Holke, Buck Herzog, Art Fletcher, Heinie Zimmerman, Dave Robertson, Benny Kauff, George Burns, Bill Rariden, Lew McCarty, Hans Lobert, Jimmy Smith, George Gibson, Joe Wilhoit, Pete Kilduff (traded), Jim Thorpe (traded), Red Murray, Al Baird, Jack Onslow, Ernie Krueger (traded), Ross Youngs, Ferdie Schupp, Slim Sallee, Pol Perritt, Rube Benton, Jeff Tesreau, Fred Anderson, Al Demaree (traded), George Kelly (traded), Jim Middleton, Ad Swigler, George Smith.

Autographed Ball	75.00
with John McGraw	+75.00
with Ross Youngs	+75.00
with Jim Thorpe	+100.00

1918 Boston Red Sox (WORLD CHAMPIONS): Ed Barrow, Manager; Stuffy McInnis (military service), Dave Shean, Everett Scott, Fred Thomas (military service), Harry Hooper, Amos Strunk, Babe Ruth, Sam Agnew, Wally Schang, George Whiteman, Wally Mayer (military service), George Cochran, Dick Hoblitzell (military service), Jack Stansbury, Jack Coffey (traded), Frank Truesdale, Walter Barbare, Hack Miller, Carl Mays, Sad Sam Jones, Bullet Joe Bush, Dutch Leonard (military service), Vince Molyneaux, Lore Bader, Dick McCabe, Jean Dubuc, Walt Kinney, Bill Pertica, Weldon Wyckoff.

Autographed Ball	50.00
with Ed Barrow	+50.00
with Babe Ruth	+250.00

1918 Chicago Cubs (National League Champs): Fred Mitchell, Manager; Fred Merkle, Rollie Zeider, Charlie Hollocher, Charlie Deal, Max Flack, Dode Paskert, Les Mann, Bill Killefer, Turner Barber, Bob O'Farrell, Pete Kilduff (military service), Charlie Pick, Bill McCabe, Chuck Wortman, Rowdy Elliott (military service), Fred Lear, Tommy Clarke, Tom Daly, Hippo Vaughn, Claude Hendrix, Lefty Tyler, Phil Douglas, Speed Martin, Paul Carter, G.C. Pete Alexander (military service), Harry Weaver (military service), Roy Walker, Vic Aldridge (military service).

Autographed Ball	150.00
with G.C. Alexander	+100.00

1919 Chicago White Sox (BLACK SOX) (American League Champs): Kid Gleason, Manager; Chick Gandil, Eddie Collins, Swede Risberg, Buck Weaver, Nemo Leibold, Happy Felsch, Joe Jackson, Ray Schalk, Shano Collins, Fred McMullin, Eddie Murphy, Byrd Lynn, Joe Jenkins, Hervey McClellan, Eddie Cicotte, Lefty Williams, Dickie Kerr, Red Faber, Grover Lowdermilk (traded), Bill James (traded), Roy Wilkinson, Dave Danforth, Frank Shellenback, Erskine Mayer (traded), John Sullivan, Charlie Robertson, Joe Benz, Tom McGuire, Win Noyes (traded), Pat Ragan (traded), Reb Russell (sore arm).

Autographed Ball	250.00
with Eddie Collins	+50.00
with Red Faber	+50.00
with Ray Schalk	+50.00
with Joe Jackson	+100.00

1919 Cincinnati Reds (WORLD CHAMPIONS): Pat Moran, Manager; Jake Daubert, Morrie Rath, Larry Kopf, Heinie Groh, Greasy Neale, Edd Roush, Rube Bressler, Ivy Wingo, Bill Rariden, Sherry Magee, Hod Eller, Pat Duncan (military service), Manuel Cueto, Jimmy Smith, Hank Schreiber, Nick Allen, Charlie See, Wally Rehg, Slim Sallee, Hod Eller, Dutch Ruether, Ray Fisher, Jimmy Ring, Dolf Luque.

Autographed Ball	200.00
with Edd Roush	+50.00

1920 Cleveland Indians (WORLD CHAMPIONS): Tris Speaker, Manager; Doc Johnston, Bill Wambsganss, Ray Chapman (killed during a game by a pitch), Larry Gardner, Elmer Smith, Charlie Jamieson, Steve O'Neill, Jack Graney, Joe Evans, George Burns (traded), Les Nunamaker, Harry Lunte, Joe Sewell, Pinch Thomas, Jim Bagby, Stan Coveleski, Ray Caldwell, Guy Morton, Duster Mails, George Uhle, Elmer Myers (traded), Dick Niehaus, Bob Clark, Joe Boehling, Tony Faeth, Smokey Joe Wood.

Autographed Ball	150.00
with Tris Speaker	+50.00
with Ray Chapman	+75.00

Stan Coveleski P

World Series Foes
Wilbert Robinson & Tris Speaker

Ray Chapman SS

Bill Wambsganss 2B

Joe Sewell 2B

1920 Brooklyn Dodgers (National League Champs): Wilbert Robinson, Manager; Ed Konetchy, Pete Kilduff, Ivy Olson, Jimmy Johnston, Tommy Griffith, Hy Myers, Zack Wheat, Otto Miller, Bernie Neis, Clarence Mitchell, Ernie Krueger, Rowdy Elliott, Bill McCabe (traded), Ray Schmandt, Bill Lamar, Chuck Ward (illness), Wally Hood (traded), Doug Baird (traded), Zack Taylor, Burleigh Grimes, Jeff Pfeffer, Leon Cadore, Al Mamaux, Sherry Smith, Rube Marquard, Johnny Miljust, George Mohart.

Autographed Ball 100.00
with Wil. Robinson +100.00

1921 New York Yankees (American League Champs): Miller Huggins, Manager; Wally Pipp, Aaron Ward, Roger Peckinpaugh, Frank Baker, Bob Meusel, Elmer Miller, Babe Ruth, Wally Schang, Mike McNally, Chick Fewster, Braggo Roth, Chicken Hawks, Ping Bodie, Fred Hofmann, Al DeVormer, Johnny Mitchell, Tom Connelly, Carl Mays, Waite Hoyt, Bob Shawkey (injury), Rip Collins, Jack Quinn, Bill Piercy, Harry Harper (injury), Alex Ferguson, Tom Sheehan, Tom Rogers.

Autographed Ball 100.00
with Miller Huggins +100.00
with Babe Ruth +200.00

1921 New York Giants (WORLD CHAMPIONS): John McGraw, Manager; George Kelly, Johnny Rawlings (traded), Dave Bancroft, Frankie Frisch, Ross Youngs, George Burns, Irish Meusel (traded), Frank Snyder, Earl Smith, Eddie Brown, Curt Walker (traded), Goldie Rapp (traded), Bill Cunningham, Lee King (traded), Bill Patterson, Alex Gaston, John Monroe (traded), Casey Stengel (traded), Mike Gonzalez, Howard Berry, Hank Schreiber, Joe Connolly, Wally Kopf, Bud Heine, Butch Henline (traded), Jim Mahady, Art Nehf, Fred Toney, Jesse Barnes, Phil Douglas, Rosy Ryan, Slim Sallee, Rube Benton (declared ineligible), Red Shea, Pol Perritt (traded), Red Causey (traded).

Autographed Ball 50.00
with Casey Stengel +50.00
with John McGraw +75.00
with Ross Youngs +75.00

1922 New York Yankees (American League Champs): Miller Huggins, Manager; Wally Pipp, Aaron Ward, Everett Scott, Joe Dugan (traded), Bob Meusel (suspended), Whitey Witt, Babe Ruth (suspended), Wally Schang, Frank Baker (injury), Mike McNally, Elmer Miller (traded), Chick Fewster (traded), Fred Hofmann, Norm McMillan, Camp Skinner, Al DeVormer, Elmer Smith (traded), Bullet Joe Bush (injury), Bob Shawkey, Waite Hoyt, Sad Sam Jones, Carl Mays, George Murray, Lefty O'Doul.

Autographed Ball 100.00
with Miller Huggins +100.00
with Babe Ruth +200.00

1922 New York Giants (WORLD CHAMPIONS): John McGraw, Manager; George Kelly, Frankie Frisch, Dave Bancroft, Heinie Groh, Ross Youngs, Casey Stengel, Irish Meusel, Frank Snyder, Earl Smith, Johnny Rawlings, Bill Cunningham, Ralph Shinners, Dave Robertson, Lee King (traded), Alex Gaston, Howard Berry, Freddie Maguire, Mahlon Higbee, Travis Jackson, Waddy MacPhee, Art Nehf, Rosy Ryan, Jesse Barnes, Phil Douglas (declared ineligible), Jack Scott (traded), Claude Jonnard, Hugh McQuillan (traded), Fred Toney (holdout), Red Causey, Carmen Hill, Virgil Barnes, Red Shea.

Autographed Ball 50.00
with Casey Stengel +50.00
with John McGraw +75.00
with Ross Youngs +75.00

1923 New York Yankees (WORLD CHAMPIONS): Miller Huggins, Manager; Wally Pipp, Aaron Ward, Everett Scott, Joe Dugan, Babe Ruth, Whitey Witt, Bob Meusel, Wally Schang (injury), Fred Hofmann, Elmer Smith, Harvey Hendrick, Mike McNally, Hinkey Haines, Benny Bengough, Ernie Johnson (traded), Lou Gehrig, Mike Gazella, Sad Sam Jones, Herb Pennock, Bullett Joe Bush, Waite Hoyt, Bob Shawkey, Carl Mays, George Pipgras, Oscar Roettger.

Autographed Ball 25.00
with Herb Pennock +25.00
with Miller Huggins +100.00
with Lou Gehrig +150.00
with Babe Ruth +200.00

1923 New York Giants (National League Champs): John McGraw, Manager; George Kelly, Frankie Frisch, Dave Bancroft (illness), Heinie Groh, Ross Youngs, Jimmy O'Connell, Irish Meusel, Frank Snyder, Travis Jackson, Bill Cunningham, Casey Stengel, Hank Gowdy, Jack Bentley, Freddie Maguire, Jack Scott (injury), Ralph Shinners, Earl Smith (traded), Alex Gaston, Bill Terry, Hack Wilson, Moe Solomon, Rosy Ryan, Jack Scott (injury), Hugh McQuillan, Jack Bentley, Art Nehf, Mule Watson (traded), Claude Jonnard, Jesse Barnes (traded), Clint Blume, Fred Johnson, Virgil Barnes, Dinty Gearin, Walter Huntzinger, Red Lucas, Rube Walberg (traded).

Autographed Ball 25.00
with Casey Stengel +25.00
with Hack Wilson +25.00
with John McGraw +75.00
with Ross Youngs +75.00

1924 Washington Senators (WORLD CHAMPIONS): Bucky Harris, Manager; Joe Judge, Roger Peckinpaugh, Ossie Bluege, Sam Rice, Nemo Liebold, Goose Goslin, Muddy Ruel, Wid Matthews, Doc Prothro, Earl McNeely, Tom Zachary, Mule Shirley, Tommy Taylor, Pinky Hargrave, Bennie Tate, Showboat Fisher, Lance Richbourg, Ralph Miller, Bert Griffith, Carr Smith, Wade Lefler (traded), Walter Johnson, George Mogridge, Tom Zachary, Firpo Marberry, Curly Ogden (traded), Joe Martina, Allen Russell, Paul Zahniser, By Speece, Slim McGrew, Ted Wingfield (traded), Nick Altrock.

Autographed Ball 100.00
with Walter Johnson +100.00

1924 New York Giants (National League Champs): John McGraw, Manager; George Kelly, Frankie Frisch, Travis Jackson, Heinie Groh, Ross Youngs, Hack Wilson, Irish Meusel, Frank Snyder, Billy Southworth, Hank Gowdy, Bill Terry, Fred Lindstrom, Jimmy O'Connell (declared ineligible), Eddie Ainsmith, Grover Hartley, Buddy Crump, Jack Bentley, Virgil Barnes, Art Nehf, Hugh McQuillan, Rosy Rayn, Mule Watson, Wayland Dean, Claude Jonnard, Harry Baldwin, Joe Oeschger (traded), Walter Huntzinger, Ernie Maun, Dinty Gearin (traded), Leon Cadore, Kent Greenfield.

Autographed Ball 25.00
with Hack Wilson +25.00
with John McGraw +75.00
with Ross Youngs +75.00

1925 Washington Senators (American League Champs): Bucky Harris, Manager; Joe Judge, Roger Peckinpaugh, Ossie Bluege, Sam Rice, Earl McNeely, Goose Goslin, Muddy Ruel, Joe Harris (traded), Nemo Leibold, Hank Severeid (traded), Spencer Adams, Everett Scott (traded), Bobby Veach (traded), Bennie Tate, Tex Jeanes, Mule Shirley, Mike McNally, Stan Coveleski, Walter Johnson, Dutch Ruether, Tom Zachary, Firpo Marberry, Alex Ferguson (traded), George Mogridge (traded), Curly Ogden, Vean Gregg, Allen Russell, Win Ballou, Harry Kelley, Jim Lyle, Spence Pumpelly, Lefty Thomas.

Autographed Ball 75.00
with Walter Johnson +100.00

1925 Pittsburgh Pirates (WORLD CHAMPIONS): Bill McKechnie, Manager; George Grantham, Eddie Moore, Glenn Wright, Pie Traynor, Kiki Cuyler, Max Carey, Clyde Barnhart, Earl Smith, Johnny Gooch, Carson Bigbee, Stuffy McInnis, Johnny Rawlings, Al Niehaus (traded), Roy Spencer, Fresco Thompson, Mule Haas, Jewel Ens, Lee Meadows, Ray Kremer, Johnny Morrison, Emil Yde, Vic Aldridge, Babe Adams, Red Oldham, Tom Sheehan (traded), Bud Culloton, Lou Koupal, Don Songer.

Autographed Ball	100.00
with Bill McKechnie	+50.00
with Kiki Cuyler	+50.00

1926 New York Yankees (American League Champs): Miller Huggins, Manager; Lou Gehrig, Tony Lazzeri, Mark Koenig, Joe Dugan, Babe Ruth, Earle Combs, Bob Meusel (injury), Pat Collins, Ben Paschal, Mike Gazella, Hank Severeid (traded), Benny Bengough (shoulder injury), Roy Carlyle (traded), Spencer Adams, Aaron Ward, Dutch Ruether (traded), Bill Skiff, Nick Cullop, Honey Barnes, Kiddo Davis, Fred Merkle, Herb Pennock, Urban Shocker, Waite Hoyt, Sad Sam Jones, Bob Shawkey (injury), Myles Thomas, Garland Braxton, Walter Beall, Dutch Ruether (traded), Herb McQuaid, Hank Johnson.

Autographed Ball	25.00
with Herb Pennock	+25.00
with Miller Huggins	+100.00
with Lou Gehrig	+150.00
with Babe Ruth	+200.00

1926 St. Louis Cardinals (WORLD CHAMPIONS): Rogers Hornsby, Manager; Jim Bottomley, Tommy Thevenow, Les Bell, Billy Southworth (traded), Taylor Douthit, Ray Blades (injury), Bob O'Farrell, Chick Hafey, Specs Toporcer, Wattie Holm, Heinie Mueller (traded), Jake Flowers, Art Reinhart, Ernie Vick, Bill Warwick, Jack Smith (traded), Flint Rhem, Bill Sherdel, Jesse Haines, Vic Koen, Art Reinhart, G.C. Pete Alexander (injured and suspended) (traded), Hi Bell, Allan Sothoron, Eddie Dyer, Wild Bill Hallahan, Ed Clough, Walter Huntzinger (traded), Syl Johnson.

Autographed Ball	75.00
with Rogers Hornsby	+50.00
with Jim Bottomley	+50.00
with G.C. Alexander	+50.00

1927 New York Yankees (WORLD CHAMPIONS): Miller Huggins, Manager; Lou Gehrig, Tony Lazzeri, Mark Koenig, Joe Dugan, Babe Ruth, Earle Combs, Bob Meusel, Pat Collins, Ray Morehart, Johnny Grabowski, Cedric Durst, Mike Gazella, Ben Paschal, Julie Wera, Benny Bengough, Waite Hoyt, Wilcy Moore, Herb Pennock, Urban Shocker, Dutch Ruether, George Pipgras, Myles Thomas, Bob Shawkey, Joe Giard.

Autographed Ball	25.00
with Herb Pennock	+25.00
with Miller Huggins	+100.00
with Lou Gehrig	+150.00
with Babe Ruth	+200.00

1927 Pittsburgh Pirates (National League Champs): Donie Bush, Manager; Joe Harris, George Grantham, Glenn Wright, Pie Traynor, Paul Waner, Lloyd Waner, Clyde Barnhart, Johnny Gooch, Kiki Cuyler, Earl Smith (suspended), Hal Ryhne (illness), Roy Spencer, Fred Brickell, Adam Comorosky, Heinie Groh, Joe Cronin, Herman Layne, Eddie Sicking, Dick Bartell, Carmen Hill, Ray Kremer, Lee Meadows, Vic Aldridge, Johnny Miljus, Johnny Morrison (suspended), Joe Dawson, Mike Cvengros, Roy Mahaffey, Bullet Joe Bush (traded), Emil Yde, Chet Nichols, Don Songer (traded), Red Peery.

Autographed Ball	75.00
with Paul Waner	+50.00
with Kiki Cuyler	+50.00

1928 New York Yankees (WORLD CHAMPIONS): Miller Huggins, Manager; Lou Gehrig, Tony Lazzeri (shoulder injury), Mark Koenig, Joe Dugan, Babe Ruth, Earle Combs, Bob Meusel (injury), Johnny Grabowski, Leo Durocher, Gene Robertson, Cedric Durst, Pat Collins, Ben Paschal, Benny Bengough (injury), Mike Gazella, Bill Dickey, George Burns (traded), George Pipgras, Waite Hoyt, Herb Pennock (illness), Hank Johnson, Al Shealy, Stan Coveleski, Wilcy Moore, Tom Zachary (traded), Fred Heimach, Myles Thomas, Archie Campbell, Rosy Ryan, Urban Shocker (died).

Autographed Ball	25.00
with Urban Shocker	+25.00
with Herb Pennock	+25.00
with Miller Huggins	+100.00
with Lou Gehrig	+150.00
with Babe Ruth	+200.00

1928 St. Louis Cardinals (National League Champs): Bill McKechnie, Manager; Jim Bottomley, Frankie Frisch, Rabbit Maranville, Wattie Holm, George Harper (traded), Taylor Douthit, Chick Hafey, Jimmie Wilson (traded), Andy High, Tommy Thevenow, Wally Roettger (broken leg), Ray Blades, Pepper Martin, Ernie Orsatti, Earl Smith (traded), Bob O'Farrell (traded), Gus Mancuso, Howie Williamson, Specs Toporcer, Bill Sherdel, Jesse Haines, Pete Alexander, Flint Rhem, Syl Johnson, Clarence Mitchell (traded), Art Reinhart, Fred Frankhouse, Hal Haid, Carlisle Littlejohn.

Autographed Ball	50.00
with Bill McKechnie	+25.00
with Jim Bottomley	+25.00
with R. Maranville	+25.00
with G.C. Alexander	+25.00

1929 Philadelphia Athletics (WORLD CHAMPIONS): Connie Mack, Manager; Jimmie Foxx, Max Bishop, Sammy Hale, Bing Miller, Mule Haas, Al Simmons, Mickey Cochrane, Jimmy Dykes, Walt French, Cy Perkins, Homer Summa, Ossie Orwoll, George Burns (traded), Jim Cronin, Bevo LeBourveau, Eddie Collins, Bud Morse, Joe Hassler, Eric McNair, Cloy Mattox, Doc Cramer, Rudy Miller, George Earnshaw, Lefty Grove, Rube Walberg, Eddie Rommel, Jack Quinn, Bill Shores, Howard Ehmke, Carroll Yerkes.

Autographed Ball	100.00
with M. Cochrane	+25.00
with Connie Mack	+25.00
with Jimmie Foxx	+25.00
with Al Simmons	+25.00

THE INCREMENTAL VALUE OF THE AUTOGRAPH OF A PARTICULAR PLAYER TO A PARTICULAR BALL IS UNIQUE TO THAT BALL. IT IS NOT THE EXOGENOUS VALUE OF THAT PLAYER'S AUTOGRAPH. SEE THE INTRODUCTION TO TEAM AUTOGRAPHED BALLS.

1929 Chicago Cubs (National League Champs): Joe McCarthy, Manager; Charlie Grimm (injury), Rogers Hornsby, Woody English, Norm McMillan, Kiki Cuyler, Hack Wilson, Riggs Stephenson, Zack Taylor (traded), Cliff Heathcote, Mike Gonzalez, Clyde Beck, Johnny Moore, Chuck Tolson, Johnny Schulte, Earl Grace, Footsie Blair, Gabby Harnett (sore arm), Tom Angley, Danny Taylor, Pat Malone, Charlie Root, Guy Bush, Sheriff Blake, Hal Carlson, Art Nehf, Mike Cvengros, Trader Horne, Claude Jonnard.

Autographed Ball	50.00
with Joe McCarthy	+25.00
with Rogers Hornsby	+25.00
with Kiki Cuyler	+25.00
with Hack Wilson	+75.00

1930 Philadelphia Athletics (WORLD CHAMPIONS): Connie Mack, Manager; Jimmie Foxx, Max Bishop, Joe Boley, Jimmy Dykes, Bing Miller, Mule Haas, Al Simmons, Mickey Cochrane, Eric McNair, Dib Williams, Wally Schang, Doc Cramer, Homer Summa, Spence Harris, Cy Perkins, Jim Moore (traded), Pinky Higgins, Jim Keesey, Eddie Collins, Lefty Grove, George Earnshaw, Rube Walberg, Bill Shores, Eddie Rommel, Roy Mahaffey, Jack Quinn, Glen Liebhardt, Howard Ehmke, Charlie Perkins, Al Mahon.

Autographed Ball	100.00
with M. Cochrane	+25.00
with Connie Mack	+25.00
with Al Simmons	+25.00
with Jimmie Foxx	+25.00

1930 St. Louis Cardinals (National League Champs): Gabby Street, Manager; Jim Bottomley, Frankie Frisch, Charlie Gelbert, Sparky Adams, George Watkins, Taylor Douthit, Chick Hafey, Jimmie Wilson, Showboat Fisher, Gus Mancuso, Andy High, Ernie Orsatti, Ray Blades, Homer Peel, Doc Farrell (traded), George Puccinelli, Earl Smith, Pepper Martin, Wild Bill Hallahan, Burleigh Grimes (traded), Jesse Haines, Flint Rhem, Syl Johnson, Jim Lindsey, Al Grabowski, Hi Bell, Hal Haid, Bill Sherdel (traded), Fred Frankhouse (traded), Dizzy Dean.

Autographed Ball	75.00
with Dizzy Dean	+50.00
with Jim Bottomley	+50.00

1931 Philadelphia Athletics (American League Champs): Connie Mack, Manager; Jimmie Foxx, Max Bishop, Dib Williams, Jimmy Dykes, Bing Miller, Mule Haas (injury), Al Simmons, Mickey Cochrane, Eric McNair, Joe Boley, Doc Cramer (injury), Phil Todt, Jim Moore, Johnnie Heving, Joe Palmisano, Lou Finney, Lefty Grove, George Earnshaw, Rube Walberg, Roy Mafaffey, Waite Hoyt (traded), Eddie Rommel, Hank McDonald, Lew Krause, Jim Peterson, Bill Shores, Sol Carter.

Autographed Ball	75.00
with Jimmie Foxx	+25.00
with M. Cochrane	+25.00
with Connie Mack	+25.00
with Al Simmons	+25.00

1931 St. Louis Cardinals (WORLD CHAMPIONS): Gabby Street, Manager; Jim Bottomley, Frankie Frisch, Charlie Gelbert, Sparky Adams, George Watkins, Pepper Martin, Chick Hafey, Jimmie Wilson, Ripper Collins, Ernie Orsatti, Gus Mancuso, Andy High, Jake Flowers (traded), Wally Roettger (traded), Taylor Douthit (traded), Ray Blades, Mike Gonzalez, Joe Benes, Wild Bill Hallahan, Paul Derringer, Burleigh Grimes, Jesse Haines, Syl Johnson, Flint Rhem, Jim Lindsey, Allyn Stout, Tony Kaufman.

Autographed Ball	100.00
with Jim Bottomley	+50.00

1932 New York Yankees (WORLD CHAMPIONS): Joe McCarthy, Manager; Lou Gehrig, Tony Lazzeri, Frankie Crosetti, Joe Sewell, Babe Ruth, Earle Combs, Ben Chapman, Bill Dickey (suspended), Sammy Byrd, Lyn Lary, Art Jorgens, Myril Hoag, Doc Farrell, Jack Saltzgaver, Eddie Phillips, Joe Glenn, Dusty Cooke (broken leg), Roy Schalk, Lefty Gomez, Red Ruffing, Johnny Allen, George Pipgras, Herb Pennock, Danny MacFayden (traded), Jumbo Brown, Ed Wells, Wilcy Moore (traded), Ivy Andrews (traded), Hank Johnson (voluntarily retired), Gordon Rhodes (traded), Johnny Murphy.

Autographed Ball	25.00
with Herb Pennock	+25.00
with Lou Gehrig	+150.00
with Babe Ruth	+200.00

1932 Chicago Cubs (National League Champs): Rogers Hornsby, Charlie Grimm, Managers; Bill Herman, Billy Jurges, Woody English, Kiki Cuyler (injury), Johnny Moore, Riggs Stephenson, Gabby Hartnett, Stan Hack, Rollie Hemsley, Marv Gudat, Lance Richbourg, Vince Barton, Mark Koenig, Frank Demaree, Zack Taylor, Harry Taylor, Danny Taylor (traded), Lon Warneke, Guy Bush, Charlie Root, Pat Malone, Burleigh Grimes, Bud Tinning, Bob Smith, Leroy Herrmann, Jakie May, Bobo Newsom.

Autographed Ball	50.00
with Rogers Hornsby	+50.00
with Kiki Cuyler	+50.00

1933 AMERICAN LEAGUE ALL-STAR TEAM - Connie Mack (manager); Edward Collins and Arthur Fletcher (coaches); Richard Ferrell, James Dykes, Al Simmons, Earl Averill, Wes Ferrell, Oral Hildebrand, Charles Gehringer, Ben Chapman, William Dickey, Lou Gehrig, Vernon Gomez, Anthony Lazzeri, George H. (Babe) Ruth, James Foxx, Robert (Lefty) Grove, Samuel West, Joseph Cronin, Alvin Crowder.

Autographed Ball	25.00
with Connie Mack	+25.00
with Jimmie Foxx	+25.00
with Al Simmons	+25.00
with Lou Gehrig	+100.00
with Babe Ruth	+150.00

1933 NATIONAL LEAGUE ALL-STAR TEAM - John McGraw (manager); William McKechnie and Max Carey (coaches); Walter Berger, Anthony Cuccinello, Elwood English, Charles (Gabby) Hartnett, Lonnie Warneke, Charles (Chick) Hafey, Carl Hubbell, Frank O'Doul, Harold Schumacher, William Terry, Richard Bartell, Charles Klein, Harold (Pie) Traynor, Paul Waner, Frank Frisch, William Hallahan, John (Pepper) Martin, James Wilson.

Autographed Ball 100.00
with Bill McKechnie +25.00
with Chuck Klein +25.00
with John McGraw +75.00

1933 Washington Senators (American League Champs): Joe Cronin, Manager; Joe Kuhel, Buddy Myer, Ossie Bluege, Goose Goslin, Fred Schulte, Heinie Manush, Luke Sewell, Dave Harris, Sam Rice, Bob Boken, Moe Berg, Cliff Bolton, John Kerr, Cecil Travis, Nick Altrock, General Crowder, Earl Whitehill, Lefty Stewart, Jack Russell, Monty Weaver, Tommy Thomas, Bobby Burke, Bill McAfee, Ed Chapman.

Autographed Ball 75.00
with Joe Cronin +50.00

1933 New York Yankees: Joe McCarthy, Manager; Lou Gehrig, Tony Lazzeri, Frankie Crosetti, Joe Sewell, Babe Ruth, Earle Combs, Ben Chapman, Bill Dickey, Dixie Walker, Sammy Byrd, Lyn Lary, Doc Farrell, Art Jorgens, Tony Rensa, Joe Glenn, Bill Werber (traded), Lefty Gomez, Johnny Allen, Russ Van Atta, Red Ruffing, Jumbo Brown, Herb Pennock, George Uhle (traded), Don Brennan, Wilcy Moore, Danny MacFayden, Charlie Devens, George Pipgras (traded), Pete Appleton.

Autographed Ball 25.00
with Herb Pennock +25.00
with Lou Gehrig +150.00
with Babe Ruth +200.00

1933 New York Giants (WORLD CHAMPIONS): Bill Terry, Manager; Hughie Critz, Blondy Ryan, Johnny Vergez, Mel Ott, Kiddo Davis, Jo Jo Moore, Gus Mancuso, Homer Peel, Lefty O'Doul (traded), Bernie James, Travis Jackson, Paul Richards, Sam Leslie (traded), Chuck Dressen, Joe Malay, Phil Weintraub, Hank Leiber, Carl Hubbell, Hal Schumacher, Freddie Fritzsimmons, Roy Parmelee, Dolf Luque, Hi Bell, Watty Clark (traded), Bill Shores, George Uhle (traded), Glenn Spencer, Jack Salveson.

Autographed Ball 75.00
with Mel Ott +50.00

1933 Pittsburgh Pirates: George Gibson, Manager; Gus Suhr, Tony Piet, Arky Vaughan, Pie Traynor, Paul Waner, Fred Lindstrom, Lloyd Waner, Earl Grace, Tommy Thevenow, Woody Jensen, Adam Comorosky, Hal Finney, Tom Padden, Pep Young, Val Picinich (traded), Larry French, Heinie Meine, Bill Swift, Steve Swetonic, Hal Smith, Leon Chagnon, Waite Hoyt, Bill Harris, Ralph Birkofer, Ray Kremer.

Autographed Ball 50.00
with Pie Traynor +25.00
with Paul Waner +25.00

1934 AMERICAN LEAGUE ALL-STAR TEAM - Joseph Cronin (manager); Walter Johnson and Al Schacht (coaches); Richard Ferrell, James Dykes, Al Simmons, Earl Averill, Mel Harder, Thomas Bridges, Mickey Cochrane, Charles Gehringer, Ben Chapman, Bill Dickey, Lou Gehrig, Vernon Gomez, Charles Ruffing, Babe Ruth, James Foxx, Michael Higgins, Samuel West, Joe Cronin, Henry Manush, Jack Russell.

Autographed Ball 25.00
with M. Cochrane +25.00
with Walter Johnson +50.00
with Lou Gehrig +100.00
with Babe Ruth +100.00

1934 NATIONAL LEAGUE ALL-STAR TEAM - Bill Terry (manager); Charles (Casey) Stengel and Bill McKechnie (coaches); Walter Berger, Fred Frankhouse, Al Lopez, Van Mungo, Gabby Hartnett, Carl Hubbell, Travis Jackson, Joseph Moore (replaced by Kiki Cuyler), Mel Ott, Pie Traynor, Arky Vaughan, Paul Waner, Dizzy Dean, Frank Frisch, John (Pepper) Martin, Joe Medwick.

Autographed Ball 25.00
with Casey Stengel +25.00
with Bill McKechnie +25.00
with Dizzy Dean +25.00
with Mel Ott +25.00
with Kiki Cuyler +25.00

1934 Detroit Tigers (American League Champs): Mickey Cochrane, Manager; Hank Greenberg, Charlie Gehringer, Billy Rogell, Marv Owen, Pete Fox, Jo Jo White, Goose Goslin, Gee Walker, Frank Doljack, Ray Hayworth, Flea Clifton, Heinie Schuble, Rudy York, Frank Reiber, Cy Perkins, Icehouse Wilson, Schoolboy Rowe, Tommy Bridges, Firpo Marberry, Eldon Auker, Vic Sorrell, Carl Fischer, General Crowder (traded), Chief Hogsett, Luke Hamlin, Red Phillips, Vic Frasier, Steve Larkin.

Autographed Ball 50.00
with Hank Greenberg +25.00
with M. Cochrane +25.00

1934 New York Yankees: Joe McCarthy, Manager; Lou Gehrig, Tony Lazzeri, Frankie Crosetti, Jack Saltzgaver, Babe Ruth, Ben Chapman, Myril Hoag, Bill Dickey (injury), Sammy Byrd, Red Rolfe, Don Heffner, Earle Combs (injury), Art Jorgens, George Selkirk, Dixie Walker, Zack Taylor, Lyn Lary (traded), Lefty Gomez, Red Ruffing, Johnny Murphy, Johnny Broaca, Jimmie DeShong, Johnny Allen (sore arm), Danny MacFayden, Russ Van Atta, George Uhle, Burleigh Grimes (traded), Harry Smythe (traded).

Autographed Ball 50.00
with Lou Gehrig +150.00
with Babe Ruth +200.00

1934 St. Louis Cardinals (WORLD CHAMPIONS): Frankie Frisch, Manager; Rip Collins, Leo Durocher, Pepper Martin, Jack Rothrock, Ernie Orsatti, Joe Medwick, Spud Davis, Burgess Whitehead, Bill DeLancey, Chick Fullis (traded), Pat Crawford, Buster Mills, Kiddo Davis (traded), Francis Healy, Gene Moore, Lew Riggs, Red Worthington (traded), Dizzy Dean, Paul Dean, Tex Carleton, Bill Walker, Wild Bill Hallahan, Jesse Haines, Jim Mooney, Burleigh Grimes (traded), Flint Rhem (traded), Dazzy Vance (traded), Jim Winford, Jim Lindsey (traded), Clarence Heise.

Autographed Ball 50.00
with Dazzy Vance +25.00
with Frank Frisch +25.00
with Dizzy Dean +25.00

1934 New York Giants: Bill Terry, Manager; Hugh Critz, Travis Jackson, Johnny Vergez, Mel Ott, George Watkins, Jo Jo Moore, Gus Mancuso, Blondy Ryan, Lefty O'Doul, Hank Leiber, Harry Danning, Paul Richards, Phil Weintraub, George Grantham, Homer Peel, Fresco Thompson, Hal Schumacher, Carl Hubbell, Freddie Fitzsimmons, Roy Parmelee (illness), Joe Bowman, Hi Bell, Dolf Luque, Al Smith, Jack Salveson, Slick Castleman, Watty Clark (traded).

Autographed Ball 50.00
with Mel Ott +25.00

1935 AMERICAN LEAGUE ALL-STAR TEAM - Mickey Cochrane (playing manager); Del Baker and Rogers Hornsby (coaches); Joe Cronin, Richard Ferrell, Lefty Grove, Al Simmons, Earl Averill (replaced by Roger Cramer), Mel Harder, Joe Vosmik, Thomas Bridges, Charles Gehringer, Lynwood Rowe, W. Ben Chapman, Lou Gehrig, Vernon Gomez, James Foxx, Robert Johnson, Ralston Hemsley, Sam West, Oswald Bluege, Charles Myer.

Autographed Ball 25.00
with M. Cochrane +25.00
with Rogers Hornsby +25.00
with Jimmie Foxx +25.00
with Lou Gehrig +100.00

1935 NATIONAL LEAGUE ALL-STAR TEAM - Frank Frisch (manager); Charles Grimm and Charles Dressen (coaches); Walter Berger, Gabby Hartnett, Billy Herman, Paul Derringer, Carl Hubbell, Gus Mancuso, Joseph Moore, Mel Ott, Harold Schumacher, Bill Terry, James Wilson, Arky Vaughan, Paul Waner, James Collins, Jerome (Dizzy) Dean, John (Pepper) Martin, Joe Medwick, William Walker, Burgess Whitehead.

Autographed Ball 25.00
with Frank Frisch +25.00
with Dizzy Dean +50.00
with Mel Ott +50.00

1935 Detroit Tigers (WORLD CHAMPIONS): Mickey Cochrane, Manager; Hank Greenberg, Charlie Gehringer, Billy Rogell, Marv Owen, Pete Fox, Jo Jo White, Goose Goslin, Gee Walker, Ray Hayworth, Flea Clifton, Chet Morgan, Heinie Schuble, Hub Walker, Frank Reiber, Hugh Shelley, Tommy Bridges, Schoolboy Rowe, Eldon Auker, General Crowder, Chief Hogsett, Joe Sullivan, Vic Sorrell, Roxie Lawson, Clyde Hatter, Firpo Marberry, Carl Fischer (traded).

Autographed Ball 75.00
with Hank Greenberg +25.00
with M. Cochrane +25.00

1935 New York Yankees: Joe McCarthy, Manager; Lou Gehrig, Tony Lazzeri, Frankie Crosetti, Red Rolfe, George Selkirk, Ben Chapman, Jesse Hill, Bill Dickey, Earle Combs (collarbone), Jack Saltzgaver, Myril Hoag, Art Jorgens, Blondy Ryan (traded), Joe Glenn, Nolen Richardson, Don Heffner, Dixie Walker (shoulder injury), Red Ruffing, Johnny Broaca, Johnny Allen, Lefty Gomez, Vito Tamulis, Johnny Murphy, Jumbo Brown, Jimmie DeShong, Pat Malone, Russ Van Atta (traded).

Autographed Ball 50.00
with Lou Gehrig +150.00

1935 Chicago Cubs (National League Champs): Charlie Grimm, Manager; Phil Cavarretta, Billy Herman, Billy Jurges, Stan Hack, Chuck Klein, Frank Demaree, Augie Galan, Gabby Hartnett, Fred Lindstrom, Ken O'Dea, Tuck Stainback, Kiki Cuyler (traded), Woody English, Walter Stephenson, Bill Lee, Lon Warneke, Larry French, Charlie Root, Roy Henshaw, Tex Carleton, Fabian Kowalik, Clay Bryant, Hugh Casey.

Autographed Ball 50.00
with Kiki Cuyler +25.00
with Chuck Klein +25.00

1935 St. Louis Cardinals: Frankie Frisch, Manager; Rip Collins, Leo Durocher, Pepper Martin, Jack Rothrock, Terry Moore, Joe Medwick, Bill DeLancey, Burgess Whitehead, Spud Davis, Ernie Orsatti, Charlie Gelbert, Charlie Wilson, Bob O'Farrell, Lynn King, Lyle Judy, Tom Winsett, Dizzy Dean, Paul Dean, Wild Bill Hallahan, Bill Walker, Phil Collins (traded), Jesse Haines, Ed Heusser, Ray Harrell.

Autographed Ball 50.00
with Frank Frisch +25.00
with Dizzy Dean +25.00

1936 NATIONAL LEAGUE ALL-STAR TEAM - Charles Grimm (manager); Pie Traynor and William McKechnie (coaches); Walter Berger, Van Mungo, Curtis Davis, Frank Demaree, August Galan, Gabby Hartnett, Billy0Herman, Lon Warneke, Ernie Lombardi, Lewis Riggs, Carl Hubbell, Joseph Moore, Mel Ott, Arthur Whitney, Gus Suhr, J. Floyd Vaughan, James (Rip) Collins, Dizzy Dean, Leo Durocher, Stuart Martin, Joe Medwick.

Autographed Ball 25.00
with Bill McKechnie +25.00
with Dizzy Dean +25.00
with Mel Ott +25.00

1936 AMERICAN LEAGUE ALL-STAR TEAM - Joseph McCarthy (manager), Joseph Cronin and Arthur Fletcher (coaches); Richard Ferrell, James Foxx, Lefty Grove, Lucius Appling, Ray Radcliff, Earl Averill, Mel Harder, Thomas Bridges (replaced by Vern Kennedy), Charles Gehringer, Goose Goslin, Lynwood Rowe, Frank Crosetti, Bill Dickey, Joe DiMaggio, Lou Gehrig, Vernon Gomez, Monte Pearson, George Selkirk, Michael Higgins, Ralston Hemsley, Ben Chapman.

Autographed Ball 25.00
with Jimmie Foxx +25.00
with Joe DiMaggio +50.00
with Lou Gehrig +100.00

1936 New York Yankees (WORLD CHAMPIONS): Joe McCarthy, Manager; Lou Gehrig, Tony Lazzeri, Frankie Crosetti, Red Rolfe, George Selkirk, Jake Powell (traded), Joe DiMaggio, Bill Dickey, Roy Johnson, Myril Hoag (injury), Joe Glenn, Ben Chapman (traded), Jack Saltzgaver, Art Jorgens, Don Heffner, Bob Seeds, Dixie Walker (traded), Red Ruffing, Monte Pearson, Bump Hadley, Lefty Gomez, Johnny Broaca, Pat Malone, Johnny Murphy (injury), Jumbo Brown, Ted Kleinhans, Kemp Wicker.

Autographed Ball 50.00
with Joe DiMaggio +50.00
with Lou Gehrig +150.00

1936 Detroit Tigers: Mickey Cochrane, Manager; Jack Burns (traded), Charlie Gehringer, Billy Rogell, Marv Owen, Gee Walker, Al Simmons, Goose Goslin, Ray Hayworth, Pete Fox, Jo Jo White, Eldon Auker, Glenn Myatt, Frank Reiber, Flea Clifton, Hank Greenberg (broken wrist), Salty Parker, Birdie Tebbetts, Gil English, Tommy Bridges, Schoolboy Rowe, Eldon Auker, Roxie Lawson, Vic Sorrell, General Crowder, Jake Wade, Chad Kimsey, Red Phillips, Joe Sullivan, Chief Hogsett (traded).

Autographed Ball 25.00
with M. Cochrane +25.00
with Hank Greenberg +25.00
with Al Simmons +25.00

1936 New York Giants (National League Champs): Bill Terry, Manager; Sam Leslie, Burgess Whitehead, Dick Bartell, Travis Jackson, Mel Ott, Hank Leiber, Jo Jo Moore, Gus Mancuso, Jimmy Ripple, Kiddo Davis, Eddie Mayo, Mark Koenig, Harry Danning, Roy Spencer, Joe Martin, Charlie English, Johnny McCarthy, Jim Sheehan, Babe Young, Carl Hubbell, Al Smith, Harry Gumbert, Hal Schumacher, Freddie Fitzsimmons, Frank Gabler, Dick Coffman, Slick Castleman, Firpo Marberry (traded).

Autographed Ball	50.00
with Mel Ott	+25.00

1936 Chicago Cubs: Charlie Grimm, Manager; Phil Cavarretta, Billy Herman, Billy Jurges, Stan Hack, Frank Demaree, Augie Galan, Ethan Allen (traded), Gabby Hartnett, Ken O'Dea, Johnny Gill, Woody English, Tuck Stainback, Chuck Klein (traded), Gene Lillard, Walter Stephenson, Larry French, Bill Lee, Lon Warneke, Tex Carleton, Curt Davis (traded), Roy Henshaw, Charlie Root, Clay Bryant.

Autographed Ball	25.00
with Gabby Hartnett	+25.00
with Chuck Klein	+25.00

1937 AMERICAN LEAGUE ALL-STAR TEAM - Joseph McCarthy (manager), Del Baker and Arthur Fletcher (coaches); Roger Cramer, Joe Cronin, James Foxx, Lefty Grove, Luke Sewell, Monty Stratton (replaced by John Murphy), Earl Averill, Mel Harder, Thomas Bridges, Charles Gehringer, Henry Greenberg, Gerald Walker (replaced by Sam West), William Dickey, Joseph DiMaggio, Lou Gehrig, Roy Bell, Harlond Clift, Richard Ferrell, Wes Ferrell, Charles Myer.

Autographed Ball	50.00
with Joe DiMaggio	+50.00
with Lou Gehrig	+100.00

1937 NATIONAL LEAGUE ALL-STAR TEAM - William Terry (manager); Charles Dressen, Frank Frisch and Jesse Haines (coaches); Eugene Moore, Van Mungo, James (Rip) Collins, Frank Demaree, Charles (Gabby) Hartnett, William Herman, Billy Jurges, Lee Grissom, Ernie Lombardi, Dick Bartell, Carl Hubbell, Gus Mancuso, Joseph Moore, Melvin Ott, Burgess Whitehead, William (Bucky) Walters, Darrell (Cy) Blanton, J. Floyd Vaughan, Paul Waner, Dizzy Dean, Pepper Martin, Joe Medwick, John Mize.

Autographed Ball	25.00
with Frank Frisch	+25.00
with Dizzy Dean	+50.00
with Mel Ott	+50.00

1937 New York Yankees (WORLD CHAMPIONS): Joe McCarthy, Manager; Lou Gehrig, Tony Lazzeri, Frankie Crosetti, Red Rolfe, Myril Hoag, Joe DiMaggio, Jake Powell (illness), Bill Dickey, George Selkirk (injury), Tommy Henrich (injury), Don Heffner, Joe Glenn, Jack Saltzgaver, Art Jorgens, Roy Johnson (traded), Lefty Gomez, Red Ruffing, Johnny Murphy, Bump Hadley, Monte Pearson, Kemp Wicker, Spud Chandler, Frank Makosky, Pat Malone, Ivy Andrews (traded), Johnny Broaca (jumped team).

Autographed Ball	50.00
with Joe DiMaggio	+50.00
with Lou Gehrig	+150.00

1937 Detroit Tigers: Mickey Cochrane, Manager; Hank Greenberg, Charlie Gehringer, Billy Rogell, Marv Owen, Pete Fox, Jo Jo White, Gee Walker, Rudy York, Goose Goslin, Chet Laabs, Birdie Tebbetts, Ray Hayworth, Cliff Bolton, Charlie Gelbert (traded), Gil English (traded), Babe Herman, Flea Clifton, Roxie Lawson, Eldon Auker, Tommy Bridges, George Gill, Boots Poffenberger, Slick Coffman, Jake Wade, Jack Russell, Clyde Hatter, Schoolboy Rowe (arm injury), Pat McLaughlin.

Autographed Ball	25.00
with Hank Greenberg	+25.00
with M. Cochrane	+25.00

1937 New York Giants (National League Champs): Bill Terry, Manager; Johnny McCarthy, Burgess Whitehead, Dick Bartell, Lou Chiozza, Mel Ott, Jimmy Ripple, Jo Jo Moore, Harry Danning, Gus Mancuso (injury), Sam Leslie, Wally Berger (traded), Kiddo Davis (traded), Hank Leiber (injury), Mickey Haslin, Blondy Ryan, Phil Weintraub (traded), Ed Madjeski, Carl Hubbell, Cliff Melton, Hal Schumacher, Slick Castleman (arm injury), Harry Gumbert, Dick Coffman, Al Smith, Freddie Fitzsimmons (traded), Tom Baker (traded), Don Brennan (traded), Jumbo Brown (traded), Frank Gabler (traded).

Autographed Ball	25.00
with Bill Terry	+25.00
with Mel Ott	+50.00

1937 Chicago Cubs: Charlie Grimm, Manager; Rip Collins (injury), Billy Herman, Billy Jurges, Stan Hack, Frank Demaree, Joe Marty, Augie Galan, Gabby Hartnett, Phil Cavarretta, Ken O'Dea, Lonny Frey, Tuck Stainback, John Bottarini, Carl Reynolds, Bob Barbark, Dutch Meyer, Tex Carleton, Larry French, Bill Lee, Charlie Root, Curt Davis (illness), Clay Bryant, Clyde Shoun, Roy Parmelee.

Autographed Ball	50.00
with Gabby Hartnett	+25.00

1938 NATIONAL LEAGUE ALL-STAR TEAM - William Terry (manager); William McKechnie and Frank Frisch (coaches); Tony Cuccinello, James Turner, Leo Durocher, Harry Lavagetto, E. Gordon Phelps (replaced by Harry Danning), Stan Hack, Charles Hartnett, William Herman, William Lee, Paul Derringer, Ival Goodman, Ernie Lombardi, Frank McCormick, John VanderMeer, Carl Hubbell, Henry Leiber, Joseph Moore, Mel Ott, Hershel Martin, Mace Brown, Floyd (Arky) Vaughan, Lloyd Waner, Joe Medwick.

Autographed Ball	25.00
with Frank Frisch	+25.00
with Bill McKechnie	+25.00
with Mel Ott	+25.00

1938 AMERICAN LEAGUE ALL-STAR TEAM - Joseph McCarthy (manager); Delmer Baker and Arthur Fletcher (coaches); Roger Cramer, Joseph Cronin, James Foxx, Robert (Lefty) Grove, Michael Kreevich, John Allen, Robert Feller, Earl Averill, Charles Gehringer, Henry Greenberg (replaced by John Murphy), L. Vernon Kennedy, Rudy York, Bill Dickey, Joe DiMaggio, Lou Gehrig, Vernon Gomez, Red Rolfe, Red Ruffing, Robert Johnson, Louis Newsom, Richard Ferrell, John Lewis, Cecil Travis.

Autographed Ball	50.00
with Joe DiMaggio	+50.00
with Lou Gehrig	+150.00

1938 New York Yankees (WORLD CHAMPIONS): Joe McCarthy, Manager; Lou Gehrig, Joe Gordon, Frankie Crosetti, Red Rolfe, Tommy Henrich, Joe DiMaggio, George Selkirk, Bill Dickey, Myril Hoag, Bill Knickerbocker, Jake Powell, Joe Glenn, Babe Dahlgren, Art Jorgens, Red Ruffing, Lefty Gomez, Monte Pearson, Spud Chandler, Bump Hadley, Johnny Murphy, Steve Sundra, Joe Beggs, Wes Ferrell (traded), Ivy Andrews.

Autographed Ball	50.00
with Joe DiMaggio	+50.00
with Lou Gehrig	+150.00

THE INCREMENTAL VALUE OF THE AUTOGRAPH OF A PARTICULAR PLAYER TO A PARTICULAR BALL IS UNIQUE TO THAT BALL. IT IS NOT THE EXOGENOUS VALUE OF THAT PLAYER'S AUTOGRAPH. SEE THE INTRODUCTION TO TEAM AUTOGRAPHED BALLS.

1938 Boston Red Sox: Joe Cronin, Manager; Jimmie Foxx, Bobby Doerr, Pinky Higgins, Ben Chapman, Doc Cramer, Joe Vosmik, Gene Desautels, Red Nonnenkamp, Johnny Peacock, Eric McNair, Jim Tabor, Fabian Gaffke, Moe Berg, Jim Bagby, Jack Wilson, Lefty Grove (sore arm), Fritz Ostermueller, Joe Heving (traded), Archie McKain, Emerson Dickman, Bill Harris, Johnny Marcum, Dick Midkiff, Lee Rogers (traded), Charlie Wagner, Al Baker, Bill Humphrey, Bill LeFebvre, Ted Olson.

Autographed Ball	25.00
with Lefty Grove	+25.00
with Jimmie Foxx	+25.00

1938 Chicago Cubs (National League Champs): Charlie Grimm, Gabby Hartnett, Managers; Rip Collins, Billy Herman, Billy Jurges, Stan Hack, Frank Demaree, Carl Reynolds, Augie Galan, Phil Cavarretta, Ken O'Dea, Joe Marty, Tony Lazzeri, Bob Garbark, Jim Asbell, Coaker Triplett, Bill Lee, Clay Bryant, Tex Carleton, Larry French, Charlie Root, Dizzy Dean (arm injury), Jack Russell, Vance Page, Al Epperly, Bob Logan.

Autographed Ball	25.00
with Gabby Hartnett	+25.00
with Dizzy Dean	+50.00

1938 Pittsburgh Pirates: Pie Traynor, Manager; Gus Suhr, Pep Young, Arky Vaughan, Lee Handley, Paul Waner, Lloyd Waner, Johnny Rizzo, Al Todd, Woody Jensen, Bill Brubaker, Ray Berres, Red Lucas, Johnny Dickshot, Heinie Manush (traded), Tommy Thevenow, Mace Brown, Jim Tobin, Russ Bauers, Bob Klinger, Cy Blanton, Bill Swift, Red Lucas, Ed Brandt, Joe Bowman (sore arm), Rip Sewell.

Autographed Ball	25.00
with Paul Waner	+25.00
with Pie Traynor	+25.00

1939 AMERICAN LEAGUE ALL-STAR TEAM - Joseph McCarthy (manager); Arthur Fletcher and Russell Blackburne (coaches); Roger Cramer, Joseph Cronin, James Foxx, Lefty Grove, Lucius Appling, Thomas Bridges, Henry Greenberg, Louis (Bobo) Newsom, Frank Crosetti, William Dickey, Joe DiMaggio, Vernon Gomez, Joseph Gordon, John Murphy, Robert Rolfe, Charles Ruffing, George Selkirk, Frank Hayes, Robert Johnson, Myril Hoag, George McQuinn, George Case, Lou Gehrig (honorary).

Autographed Ball	50.00
with Joe DiMaggio	+50.00
with Lou Gehrig	+150.00

1939 NATIONAL LEAGUE ALL-STAR TEAM - Charles Hartnett (manager); John Corriden and William Terry (coaches); Lou Fette, Adolph Camilli, Harry (Cookie) Lavagetto, Ernest Phelps, Whit Wyatt, Stan Hack, Billy Herman, William Lee, Paul Derringer, Linus Frey, Ival Goodman, Ernie Lombardi, Frank McCormick, John VanderMeer, William (Bucky) Walters, Harry Danning, William Jurges, Mel Ott, Morris Arnovich, Arky Vaughan, Curtis Davis, Joe Medwick, John Mize, Terry Moore, Lon Warneke.

Autographed Ball	50.00
with Gabby Hartnett	+25.00
with Mel Ott	+25.00

1939 New York Yankees (WORLD CHAMPIONS): Joe McCarthy, Manager; Babe Dahlgren, Joe Gordon, Frankie Crosetti, Red Rolfe, Charlie Keller, Joe DiMaggio, George Selkirk, Bill Dickey, Tommy Henrich, Buddy Rosar, Jake Powell, Joe Gallagher (traded), Lou Gehrig (illness), Bill Knickerbocker, Art Jorgens, Red Ruffing, Atley Donald, Lefty Gomez, Bump Hadley, Monte Pearson, Steve Sundra, Oral Hildebrand, Marius Russo, Spud Chandler (broken leg), Johnny Murphy, Wes Ferrell, Marv Breuer.

Autographed Ball	50.00
with Joe DiMaggio	+50.00
with Lou Gehrig	+150.00

1939 Boston Red Sox: Joe Cronin, Manager; Jimmie Foxx, Bobby Doerr, Joe Cronin, Jim Tabor, Ted Williams, Doc Cramer, Joe Vosmik, Johnny Peacock, Lou Finney (traded), Gene Desautels, Red Nonnenkamp, Tom Carey, Boze Berger, Moe Berg, Fabian Gaffke, Lefty Grove, Joe Heving, Fritz Ostermueller, Jack Wilson, Eldon Auker, Denny Galehouse, Emerson Dickman, Jim Bagby, Woody Rich (sore arm), Charlie Wagner, Bill LeFebvre, Jake Wade (traded), Monty Weaver, Bill Sayles.

Autographed Ball	25.00
with Lefty Grove	+25.00
with Jimmie Foxx	+25.00
with Ted Williams	+50.00

1939 Cincinnati Reds (National League Champs): Bill McKechnie, Manager; Frank McCormick, Lonny Frey, Billy Myers, Bill Werber, Ival Goodman, Harry Craft, Wally Berger, Ernie Lombardi, Lee Gamble, Nino Bongiovanni, Willard Hershberger, Frenchy Bordagary, Eddie Joost, Lew Riggs, Les Scarsella (knee injury), Al Simmons, Vince DiMaggio, Dick West, Bud Hafey (traded), Jimmie Wilson, Milt Galatzer, Nolen Richardson, Bucky Walters, Paul Derringer, Whitey Moore, Junior Thompson, Lee Grissom, Johnny VanderMeer, Johnny Niggerling, Milt Shoffner (traded), Peaches Davis, Hank Johnson.

Autographed Ball	25.00
with W. Hershberger	+25.00
with Bill McKechnie	+25.00
with Al Simmons	+25.00

1939 St. Louis Cardinals: Ray Blades, Manager; Johnny Mize, Stu Martin, Jimmy Brown, Don Gutteridge, Enos Slaughter, Terry Moore, Joe Medwick, Mickey Owen, Don Padgett, Lynn King, Pepper Martin, Lynn Myers, Lyn Lary (traded), Herman Franks, Creepy Crespi, Herb Bremer, Joe Orengo, Johnny Hopp, Curt Davis, Bob Bowman, Lon Warneke, Mort Cooper, Bill McGee, Bob Weiland, Tom Sunkel, Clyde Shoun, Max Lanier, Nate Andrews, Paul Dean, Murry Dickson, Ken Raffensberger.

Autographed Ball	50.00
with Johnny Mize	+10.00
with Joe Medwick	+15.00

1940 NATIONAL LEAGUE ALL-STAR TEAM - Bill McKechnie (manager); Charles (Casey) Stengel and James Prothro (coaches); Max West, Pete Coscarart, Leo Durocher, Harry Lavagetto, Joseph Medwick, Ernest Phelps, Whit Wyatt, Lawrence French, Billy Herman, Henry Leiber (replaced by William Nicholson), Paul Derringer, Ernest Lombardi, Frank McCormick, William (Bucky) Walters, Harry Danning, Carl Hubbell, William Jurges (replaced by Edward Miller), Joseph Moore, Melvin Ott, W. Kirby Higbe, Merrill May, Hugh Mulcahy, Arky Vaughan, John Mize, Terry Moore.

Autographed Ball	25.00
with Bill McKechnie	+25.00
with Casey Stengel	+25.00
with Mel Ott	+25.00

1940 AMERICAN LEAGUE ALL-STAR TEAM - Joe Cronin (manager); Thomas Daly and Del Baker (coaches); Roger Cramer, Lou Finney, James Foxx, Ted Williams, Luke Appling, Ray Mack, Al Milnar, Tom Bridges, Henry Greenberg, Louis Newsom, Bill Dickey, Joe DiMaggio, Joe Gordon, Charles Keller, M. Monte Pearson, Robert Rolfe (replaced by Cecil Travis), Red Ruffing, Frank Hayes, Robert Johnson, George McQuinn, Emil (Dutch) Leonard.

Autographed Ball 25.00
with Ted Williams +50.00
with Joe DiMaggio +50.00

1940 Detroit Tigers (American League Champs): Del Baker, Manager; Rudy York, Charlie Gehringer, Dick Bartell, Pinky Higgins, Pete Fox, Barney McCosky, Hank Greenberg, Birdie Tebbetts, Bruce Campbell, Billy Sullivan, Earl Averill, Frank Croucher, Red Kress, Scat Metha, Dutch Meyer, Tuck Stainback, Pat Mullin, Frank Secory, Bobo Newsom, Schoolboy Rowe, Tommy Bridges, Hal Newhouser, Johnny Gorsica, Al Benton, Archie McKain, Dizzy Trout, Fred Hutchinson, Tom Seats, Floyd Giebell, Clay Smith, Cotton Pippen, Lynn Nelson.

Autographed Ball 50.00
with Hank Greenberg +10.00
with C. Gehringer +10.00

1940 Cleveland Indians: Ossie Vitt, Manager; Hal Trosky, Ray Mack, Lou Boudreau, Ken Keltner, Beau Bell, Roy Weatherly, Ben Chapman, Rollie Hemsley, Jeff Heath, Frankie Pytlak (illness), Odell Hale, Soup Campbell, Rusty Peters, Oscar Grimes (injury), Hank Helf, Bob Feller, Al Milnar, Al Smith, Mel Harder, Johnny Allen, Joe Dobson, Willie Hudlin (traded), Harry Eisenstat, Mike Naymick, Bill Zuber, John Hemphries, Nate Andrews, Dixie Howell.

Autographed Ball 50.00
with Bob Feller +10.00
with Lou Boudreau +10.00

1940 Cincinnati Reds (WORLD CHAMPIONS): Bill McKechnie, Manager; Frank McCormick, Lonny Frey, Billy Myers, Bill Werber, Ival Goodman, Harry Craft, Mike McCormick, Ernie Lombardi, Eddie Joost, Morrie Arnovich (traded), Willard Hershberger (deceased during season), Lew Riggs, Lew Gamble, Jimmy Ripple (traded), Johnny Rizzo (traded), Bill Baker, Jimmie Wilson, Mike Dejan, Dick West, Wally Berger (traded), Vince DiMaggio (traded), Bucky Walters, Paul Derringer, Junior Thompson, Jim Turner, Joe Beggs, Whitey Moore, Johnny Vander Meer, Johnny Hutchings, Milt Shoffner, Elmer Riddle.

Autographed Ball 50.00
with Bill McKechnie +25.00
with W. Hershberger +50.00

1940 Brooklyn Dodgers: Leo Durocher, Manager; Dolph Camilli, Pete Coscarart, Pee Wee Reese (injury), Cookie Lavagetto (illness), Joe Vosmik, Dixie Walker, Joe Medwick (traded), Babe Phelps, Johnny Hudson, Jimmy Wasdell (traded), Herman Franks, Gus Mancuso, Pete Reiser, Charlie Gilbert, Joe Gallagher (traded), Ernie Koy (traded), Roy Cullenbine (traded), Don Ross, Gene Moore (traded), Jimmy Ripple (traded), Freddie Fitzsimmons, Whit Wyatt, Hugh Casey, Luke Hamlin, Vito Tamulis, Curt Davis (traded), Tex Carleton, Tot Pressnell, Newt Kimball (traded), Lee Grissom (traded), Ed Head, Van Mungo (arm injury), Wes Flowers, Max Macon, Wes Ferrell.

Autographed Ball 50.00
with Leo Durocher +10.00
with Pee Wee Reese +10.00
with Joe Medwick +15.00

1941 AMERICAN LEAGUE ALL-STAR TEAM - Del Baker (manager); Mervyn Shea and Arthur Fletcher (coaches); Joe Cronin, Dom DiMaggio, Robert Doerr, James Foxx, Ted Williams, Lucius Appling, Thornton Lee, Edgar Smith, Lou Boudreau, Rob Feller, J. Geoffrey Heath, Kenneth Keltner, J. Alton Benton, Birdie Tebbetts, Rudolph York, Will Dickey, Joe DiMaggio, Joe Gordon, Charles Keller, Charles Ruffing, Marius Russo, Frank Hayes, Roy Cullenbine, Sid Hudson, Cecil Travis.

Autographed Ball 25.00
with Ted Williams +50.00
with Joe DiMaggio +50.00

1941 NATIONAL LEAGUE ALL-STAR TEAM - Bill McKechnie (manager); Leo Durocher and James Wilson (coaches); Edward Miller, Adolph Camilli (replaced by Frank McCormick), William Herman, Harry Lavagetto, Mickey Owen, Pete Reiser, Whit Wyatt, Stan Hack, Henry Leiber (replaced by Joe Medwick), William Nicholson, Claude Passeau, Paul Derringer, Linus Frey, Bucky Walters, Harry Danning, Carl Hubbell, Mel Ott, Darrell (Cy) Blanton, Robert Elliott, Al Lopez, J. Floyd Vaughan, John Mize, Terry Moore, Enos Slaughter, Lonnie Warneke.

Autographed Ball 50.00
with Bill McKechnie +25.00
with Mel Ott +25.00

1941 New York Yankees (WORLD CHAMPIONS): Joe McCarthy, Manager; Johnny Sturm, Joe Gordon, Phil Rizzuto, Red Rolfe, Tommy Henrich, Joe DiMaggio, Charlie Keller, Bill Dickey, George Selkirk, Buddy Rosar, Jerry Priddy, Frankie Crosetti, Frenchy Bordagaray, Ken Silvestri (illness), Johnny Lindell, Lefty Gomez, Red Ruffing, Marius Russo, Spud Chandler, Atley Donald, Ernie Bonham, Marv Breuer, Johnny Murphy, Norm Branch, Steve Peek, Charley Stanceu, George Washburn.

Autographed Ball 50.00
with Joe McCarthy +10.00
with Joe DiMaggio +75.00

1941 Boston Red Sox: Joe Cronin, Manager; Jimmie Foxx, Bobby Doerr, Jim Tabor, Lou Finney, Dom DiMaggio, Ted Williams, Frankie Pytlak, Skeeter Newsome, Stan Spence, Johnny Peacock, Pete Fox, Tom Carey, Odell Hale (traded), Al Flair, Dick Newsome, Joe Dobson, Charlie Wagner, Mickey Harris, Mike Ryba, Lefty Grove, Tex Hughson, Earl Johnson, Jack Wilson, Nels Potter (traded), Herb Hash, Bill Fleming, Emerson Dickman (military service), Oscar Judd.

Autographed Ball 25.00
with Lefty Grove +10.00
with Jimmie Foxx +15.00
with Ted Williams +50.00

1941 Brooklyn Dodgers (National League Champs): Leo Durocher, Manager; Dolph Camilli, Billy Herman (traded), Pee Wee Reese, Cookie Lavagetto, Dixie Walker, Pete Reiser, Joe Medwick, Mickey Owen, Jimmy Wasdell, Lew Riggs, Herman Franks, Pete Coscarart, Joe Vosmik, Augie Galan (traded), Alex Kampouris (back injury), Babe Phelps (suspended), Paul Waner (traded), Tommy Tatum, Kirby Higbe, Whit Wyatt, Hugh Casey, Curt Davis, Luke Hamlin, F. Fitzsimmons (arm injury), Johnny Allen (traded), Bill Swift, Newt Kimball, Mace Brown (injury)(traded), Bob Chipman, Tom Drake, Kemp Wicker, Vito Tamulis (traded), Larry French (traded), Van Mungo.

Autographed Ball 25.00
with Leo Durocher +10.00
with Billy Herman +10.00
with Pee Wee Reese +10.00
with Joe Medwick +10.00
with Paul Waner +10.00

1941 St. Louis Cardinals: Billy Southworth, Manager; Johnny Mize, Creepy Crespi, Marty Marion, Jimmy Brown, Enos Slaughter (collarbone), Terry Moore, Johnny Hopp, Gus Mancuso, Don Padgett, Estel Crabtree, Coaker Triplett, Walker Cooper (injury), Eddie Lake, Steve Mesner, Ernie Koy (traded), Stan Musial, Harry Walker, Erv Dusak, Whitey Kurowski, Ernie White, Lon Warneke, Mort Cooper (elbow injury), Harry Gumbert (traded), Howie Krist, Max Lanier, Sam Nahem, Howie Pollet, Clyde Shoun, Johnny Grodzicki, Hank Gornicki (traded), Bill Crouch (traded), Ira Hutchinson.

Autographed Ball	25.00
with Stan Musial	+50.00

1942 AMERICAN LEAGUE ALL-STAR TEAM - Joseph McCarthy (manager); Arthur Fletcher and Stanley Harris (coaches); Dominic DiMaggio, Robert Doerr, Cecil Hughson, Ted Williams, Edgar Smith, Jim Bagby, Lou Boudreau, Ken Keltner, J. Alton Benton, Harold Newhouser, George Tebbetts, Rudolph York, Ernest Bonham, Spud Chandler, Will Dickey, Joe DiMaggio, Joe Gordon, Thomas Henrich, Phil Rizzuto, Warren Rosar, Robert Johnson, George McQuinn, Sid Hudson, Stanley Spence.

Autographed Ball	25.00
with Joe McCarthy	+10.00
with Ted Williams	+50.00
with Joe DiMaggio	+50.00

1942 NATIONAL LEAGUE ALL-STAR TEAM - Leo Durocher (manager); Bill McKechnie and Frank Frisch (coaches); Ernie Lombardi, Edward Miller, Billy Herman, Joe Medwick, Mickey Owen, Pee Wee Reese, Pete Reiser, Arky Vaughan, Whit Wyatt, Claude Passeau, Paul Derringer (replaced by Ray Starr), Frank McCormick, John VanderMeer, Bucky Walters, Carl Hubbell, Willard Marshall, Cliff Melton, John Mize, Mel Ott, Dan Litwhiler, Bob Elliott, James Brown, Mort Cooper, Walker Cooper, Terry Moore, Enos Slaughter.

Autographed Ball	50.00
with Frank Frisch	+15.00
with Bill McKechnie	+15.00
with Mel Ott	+25.00

1942 New York Yankees (American League Champs): Joe McCarthy, Manager; Buddy Hassett, Joe Gordon, Phil Rizzuto, Frankie Crosetti, Tommy Henrich (military service), Joe DiMaggio, Charlie Keller, Bill Dickey (shoulder injury), Red Rolfe, Buddy Rosar, Jerry Priddy, George Selkirk, Rollie Hemsley (traded), Roy Cullenbine (traded), Tuck Stainback, Ed Levy, Ed Kearse, Ernie Bonham, Spud Chandler, Hank Borowy, Red Ruffing, Atley Donald, Marv Breuer, Lefty Gomez, Marius Russo (sore arm), Johnny Murphy, Johnny Lindell, Mel Queen, Jim Turner (traded), Norm Branch (military service).

Autographed Ball	30.00
with Bill Dickey	+10.00
with Joe McCarthy	+10.00
with Joe DiMaggio	+50.00

1942 Boston Red Sox: Joe Cronin, Manager; Tony Lupien, Bobby Doerr, Johnny Pesky, Jim Tabor, Lou Finney, Dom DiMaggio, Ted Williams, Bill Conroy, Johnny Peacock, Pete Fox, Jimmie Foxx (traded), Skeeter Newsome, Paul Campbell, Andy Gilbert, Tex Hughson, Charlie Wagner, Joe Dobson, Mace Brown, Oscar Judd, Dick Newsome, Bill Butland, Yank Terry, Ken Chase, Mike Ryba.

Autographed Ball	25.00
with Jimmie Foxx	+25.00
with Ted Williams	+50.00

1942 St. Louis Cardinals (WORLD CHAMPIONS): Billy Southworth, Manager; Johnny Hopp, Creepy Crespi, Marty Marion, Whitey Kurowski, Enos Slaughter, Terry Moore, Stan Musial, Walker Cooper, Jimmy Brown, Ray Sanders, Harry Walker, Coaker Triplett, Ken O'Dea, Buddy Blattner, Erv Dusak, Sam Narron, Estel Crabtree, Gus Mancuso (traded), Jeff Cross, Mort Cooper, Johnny Beazley, Howie Krist, Max Lanier, Harry Gumbert, Howie Pollet, Ernie White (sore arm), Murry Dickson, Lon Warneke (traded), Bill Beckmann (traded), Bill Lohrman (traded), Whitey Moore (traded)

Autographed Ball	25.00
with Stan Musial	+50.00

1942 Brooklyn Dodgers: Leo Durocher, Manager; Dolph Camilli, Billy Herman, Pee Wee Reese, Arky Vaughan, Dixie Walker, Pete Reiser (injury), Joe Medwick, Mickey Owen, Johnny Rizzo, Lew Riggs, Augie Galan, Frenchy Bordagaray, Billy Sullivan, Babe Dahlgren (traded), Alex Kampouris, Cliff Dapper, Stan Rojek, Whit Wyatt, Kirby Higbe, Larry French, Curt Davis, Ed Head, Johnny Allen, Hugh Casey, Max Macon, Les Webber, Newt Kimball, Bobo Newsom (traded), Schoolboy Rowe (traded).

Autographed Ball	50.00
with Leo Durocher	+10.00
with Joe Medwick	+10.00

1943 AMERICAN LEAGUE ALL-STAR TEAM - Joe McCarthy (manager); Arthur Fletcher and Russell Blackburne (coaches); Bobby Doerr, Cecil Hughson, Oscar Judd, Luke Appling, Jim Bagby, Lou Boudreau, Jeff Heath, Ken Keltner, Warren Rosar, Alfred Smith, Hal Newhouser, Rudy York, Ernest Bonham, Spud Chandler, Bill Dickey, Joe Gordon, Charles Keller (replaced by Richard Wakefield), John Lindell, Richard Siebert, Chet Laabs, Vern Stephens, George Case, Jacob Early, Robert Johnson, Emil (Dutch) Leonard.

Autographed Ball	60.00
with Joe McCarthy	+15.00
with Bill Dickey	+15.00

1943 NATIONAL LEAGUE ALL-STAR TEAM - William Southworth (manager); Frank Frisch and Miguel Gonzalez (coaches); Alva Javery, August Galan, William Herman, Arnold (Mickey) Owen, Fred Walker, Stan Hack, William Nicholson, Claude Passeau, Linus Frey, Frank McCormick (replaced by Elburt Fletcher), Edward Miller, John VanderMeer, Ernie Lombardi, Mel Ott, Ellsworth (Babe) Dahlgren, Vince DiMaggio, Rip Sewell, Mort Cooper, Walker Cooper, George (Whitey) Kurowski, Max Lanier, Martin Marion, Stan Musial, Howard Pollet (replaced by Ace Adams), Harry Walker.

Autographed Ball	25.00
with Frank Frisch	+10.00
with Mel Ott	+25.00
with Stan Musial	+30.00

1943 New York Yankees (WORLD CHAMPIONS): Joe McCarthy, Manager; Nick Etten, Joe Gordon, Frankie Crosetti (suspended by umpires), Billy Johnson, Bud Metheny, Johnny Lindell, Charlie Keller, Bill Dickey, Snuffy Stirnweiss, Roy Weatherly, Tuck Stainback, Ken Sears, Rollie Hemsley, Oscar Grimes, Spud Chandler, Ernie Bonham, Hank Borowy, Butch Wensloff, Johnny Murphy, Bill Zuber, Atley Donald, Marius Russo, Jim Turner, Tommy Byrne, Marv Breuer.

Autographed Ball	60.00
with Joe McCarthy	+10.00
with Bill Dickey	+10.00

1943 Washington Senators: Ossie Bluege, Manager; Mickey Vernon, Jerry Priddy, John Sullivan, Ellis Clary (traded), George Case, Stan Spence, Bob Johnson, Jake Early, Gene Moore, Sherry Robertson, Alex Kampouris (traded), Tony Giuliani, George Myatt, Jake Powell, Red Marion, Red Roberts, Harlond Clift (traded), Early Wynn, Dutch Leonard, Alex Carrasquel, Milo Candini, Mickey Haefner, Jim Mertz, Johnny Niggeling (traded), Ray Scarborough (military service), Ewald Pyle, Bobo Newsom (traded), Bill LeFebvre, Lefty Gomez, Dewey Adkins, Owen Scheetz.

Autographed Ball	30.00
with Early Wynn	+20.00
with Lefty Gomez	+20.00

1943 St. Louis Cardinals (National League Champs): Billy Southworth, Manager; Ray Sanders, Lou Klein, Marty Marion, Whitey Kurowski, Stan Musial, Harry Walker, Danny Litwhiler (traded), Walker Cooper, Johnny Hopp, Debs Garms, Ken O'Dea, Frank Demaree, George Fallon, Jimmy Brown, Sam Narron, Coaker Triplett (traded), Buster Adams (traded), Mort Cooper, Max Lanier, Howie Krist, Harry Gumbert, George Munger, Harry Brecheen, Murry Dickson, Al Brazle, Howie Pollet, Ernie White (sore arm).

Autographed Ball	25.00
with Stan Musial	+50.00

1943 Cincinnati Reds: Bill McKechnie, Manager; Frank McCormick, Lonny Frey, Eddie Miller, Steve Mesner, Max Marshall, Gee Walker, Eric Tipton, Ray Mueller, Bert Haas, Estel Crabtree, Dain Clay, Tony DePhillips, Woody Williams, Al Lakeman, Frankie Kelleher, Elmer Riddle, Bucky Walters, Johnny Vander Meer, Clyde Shoun, Ray Starr, Joe Beggs, Ed Heusser, Rocky Stone.

Autographed Ball	50.00
with Bill McKechnie	+25.00

1944 NATIONAL LEAGUE ALL-STAR TEAM - William Southworth (manager); Fred Fitzsimmons, John (Honus) Wagner, and Miguel Gonzalez (coaches); Nathan Andrews, Alva Javery, Cornelius Ryan, August Galan, Arnold Owen, Fred Walker, Phil Cavarretta, Don Johnson, William Nicholson, Frank McCormick, Edward Miller (replaced by Frank Zak), Ray Mueller, Bucky Walters, Joe Medwick, Mel Ott, Ken Raffensberger, Vince DiMaggio, Robert Elliott, Truett (Rip) Sewell, Walker Cooper, George Kurowski, Max Lanier, Martin Marion, George Munger, Stan Musial, Lanier and Munger replaced by James Tobin, William Voiselle.

Autographed Ball	25.00
with Mel Ott	+25.00
with Honus Wagner	+25.00
with Stan Musial	+25.00

1944 AMERICAN LEAGUE ALL-STAR TEAM - Joe McCarthy (manager); Joe Cronin and Arthur Fletcher (coaches); Rob Doerr, Cecil Hughson, Bob Johnson, Orval Grove, Thurman Tucker, Lou Boudreau, Roy Cullenbine, Oris Hockett, Kenneth Keltner, Michael Higgins, Hal Newhouser, Paul Trout, Rudy York, Henry Borowy, Ralston Hemsley, Joe Page, Frank Hayes, Louis Newsom, George McQuinn, Bob Muncrief, Vern Stephens, George Case (replaced by Ervin Fox), Rick Ferrell, Emil (Dutch) Leonard, Stanley Spence.

Autographed Ball	50.00
with Joe McCarthy	+10.00
with Lou Boudreau	+10.00

1944 St. Louis Browns (American League Champs): Luke Sewell, Manager; George McQuinn, Don Gutteridge, Vern Stephens, Mark Christman, Gene Moore, Milt Byrnes, Mike Kreevich, Red Hayworth, Al Zarilla, Frank Mancuso, Chet Laabs, Floyd Baker, Mick Chartak, Ellis Clary, Hal Epps (traded), Frank Demaree, Tom Turner (traded), Tom Hafey, Nels Potter, Jack Kramer, Bob Muncrief, Sig Jakucki, Denny Galehouse, George Caster, Tex Shirley, Al Hollingsworth, Sam Zoldak, Lefty West.

Autographed Ball	100.00

1944 Detroit Tigers: Steve O'Neill, Manager; Rudy York, Eddie Mayo, Joe Hoover, Pinky Higgins, Jimmy Outlaw, Doc Cramer, Dick Wakefield (military service), Paul Richards, Chuck Hostetler, Bob Swift, Don Ross, Dizzy Trout, Joe Orengo, Charlie Metro (traded), Al Unser, Red Borom, Don Heffner, Hack Miller, Hal Newhouser, Dizzy Trout, Rufe Gentry, Stubby Overmire, Johnny Gorsica, Joe Orrell, Boom Boom Beck, Bob Gillespie, Jake Mooty, Roy Henshaw, Zeb Eaton.

Autographed Ball	50.00

1944 St. Louis Cardinals (WORLD CHAMPIONS): Billy Southworth, Manager; Ray Sanders, Emil Verban, Marty Marion, Whitey Kurowski, Stan Musial, Johnny Hopp, Danny Litwhiler, Walker Cooper, Ken O'Dea, Augie Bergamo, Debs Garms, George Fallon, Pepper Martin, John Antonelli, Bob Keely, Mort Cooper, Ted Wilks, Max Lanier, Harry Brecheen, George Munger, Freddy Schmidt, Al Jurisich, Harry Gumbert (traded), Blix Donnelly, Bud Byerly.

Autographed Ball	50.00
with Stan Musial	+50.00

1944 Pittsburgh Pirates: Frankie Frisch, Manager; Babe Dahlgren, Pete Coscarart, Frankie Gustine, Bob Elliott, Johnny Barrett, Vince DiMaggio, Jim Russell, Al Lopez, Frank Colman, Al Rubeling, Frankie Zak, Tommy O'Brien, Hank Camelli, Spud Davis, Lee Handley, Lloyd Waner (traded), Al Gionfriddo, Bill Rodgers, Rip Sewell, Nick Strincevich, Preacher Roe, Max Butcher, Fritz Ostermueller (traded), Xavier Rescigno, Ray Starr, Cookie Cuccurullo.

Autographed Ball	40.00
with Frank Frisch	+10.00
with Lloyd Waner	+10.00

1945 - NO ALL-STAR GAME

1945 Detroit Tigers (WORLD CHAMPIONS): Steve O'Neill, Manager; Rudy York, Eddie Mayo, Skeeter Webb, Bob Maier, Roy Cullenbine (traded), Doc Cramer, Jimmy Outlaw, Bob Swift, Paul Richards, Hank Greenberg (military service), Joe Hoover, Red Borum, Chuck Hostetler, Hub Walker, John McHale, Ed Mierkowica, Don Ross (traded), Hack Miller, Russ Kerns, Carl McNabb, Milt Welch, Hal Newhouser, Dizzy Trout, Al Benton (broken ankle), Stubby Overmire, Les Mueller, George Caster (traded), Zeb Eaton, Jim Tobin (traded), Joe Orrell, Tommy Bridges (military service), Walter Wilson, Art Houtteman, Billy Pierce, Prince Oana, Virgil Trucks (military service).

Autographed Ball	50.00
with Hank Greenberg	+25.00

1945 Washington Senators: Ossie Bluege, Manager; Joe Kuhel, George Myatt, Gil Torres, Harlond Clift, Buddy Lewis (military service), George Binks, George Case, Rick Ferrell, Fred Vaughn, Hilly Layne, Mike Guerra, Jose Zardon, Al Evans, Mike Kreevich (traded), Jake Powell (traded), Dick Kimble, Vince Ventura, Walt Chipple, Cecil Travis (military service), Howie McFarland, Roger Wolff, Dutch Leonard, Mickey Haefner, Marino Pieretti, Alex Carrasquel, Johnny Niggeling, Sandy Ullrich, Pete Appleton (traded), Walt Holborow, Walt Masterson (military service).

Autographed Ball	60.00

THE INCREMENTAL VALUE OF THE AUTOGRAPH OF A PARTICULAR PLAYER TO A PARTICULAR BALL IS UNIQUE TO THAT BALL. IT IS NOT THE EXOGENOUS VALUE OF THAT PLAYER'S AUTOGRAPH. SEE THE INTRODUCTION TO TEAM AUTOGRAPHED BALLS.

1945 Chicago Cubs (National League Champs): Charlie Grimm, Manager; Phil Cavarretta, Don Johnson, Lennie Merullo. Stan Hack, Bill Nicholson, Andy Pafko, Peanuts Lowrey, Mickey Livingston, Paul Gillespie, Roy Hughes (knee injury), Heinz Becker, Dewey Williams, Ed Sauer, Bill Schuster, Frank Secory, Len Rice (injury), Reggie Otero, Johnny Moore, Hank Wyse, Claude Passeau, Paul Derringer, Ray Prim, Hank Borowy (traded), Hy Vandenberg, Paul Erickson, Bob Chipman, Ray Starr (traded), Mack Stewart, Lon Warneke, Jorge Comellas, Walter Signer.

Autographed Ball 60.00

1945 St. Louis Cardinals: Billy Southworth, Manager; Ray Sanders, Emil Verban, Marty Marion, Whitey Kurowski, Johnny Hopp, Buster Adams (traded), Red Schoendienst, Ken O'Dea, Augie Bergamo, Del Rice, Debs Garms, Pep Young, Art Rebel, Dave Bartosch, George Fallon, Lou Klein (military service), Jim Mallory (traded), Gene Crumling, Red Barrett (traded), Ken Burkhart, Harry Brecheen, George Dockins, Blix Donnelly, Jack Creel, Bud Byerly, Ted Wilks (sore arm), Glen Gardner, Al Jurisich, Mort Cooper (elbow injury) (traded), Max Lanier (military service), Bill Crouch.

Autographed Ball 50.00

1946 AMERICAN LEAGUE ALL-STAR TEAM - Stephen O'Neill (manager); Arthur Mills and Luke Sewell (coaches); Dom DiMaggio, Robert Doerr, David Ferriss, Maurice Harris, John Pesky, Harold Wagner, Ted Williams, Rudolph York, Lucius Appling, Robert Feller, Frank Hayes, Ken Keltner, Hal Newhouser, Spud Chandler, William Dickey, Joseph DiMaggio, Joseph Gordon, Charles Keller, George Stirnweiss, Samuel Chapman, Warren Rosar, John Kramer, Vernon Stephens, Stanley Spence, Mickey Vernon.

Autographed Ball 25.00
with Ted Williams +50.00
with Joe DiMaggio +50.00

1946 NATIONAL LEAGUE ALL-STAR TEAM - Charles Grimm (manager); William Southworth and Bill McKechnie (coaches); Mort Cooper, John Hopp, Phil Masi, W. Kirby Higbe, Pee Wee Reese (replaced by Frank McCormick), Pete Reiser, Fred Walker, Phil Cavarretta, Harry (Peanuts) Lowrey, Claude Passeau, John Schmitz, Ewell Blackwell, Ray Lamanno, Edward Miller (replaced by Emil Verban), Walker Cooper, John Mize, Del Ennis, Frank Gustine, Truett (Rip) Sewell, George (Whitey) Kurowski, Martin Marion, Stan Musial, Howard Pollet, Albert (Red) Schoendienst, Enos Slaughter.

Autographed Ball 30.00
with Bill McKechnie +15.00
with Stan Musial +30.00

1946 Boston Red Sox (American League Champs): Joe Cronin, Manager; Rudy York, Bobby Doerr, Johnny Pesky, Rip Russell, Catfish Metkovich, Dom DiMaggio, Ted Williams, Hal Wagner, Pinky Higgins (traded), Tom McBride, Leon Culberson, Wally Moses (traded), Roy Partee, Boo Ferriss, Tex Hughson, Mickey Harris, Joe Dobson, Jim Bagby, Bill Zuber (traded), Earl Johnson, Clem Dreisewerd, Mace Brown, Bob Klinger.

Autographed Ball 15.00
with Joe Cronin +10.00
with Ted Williams +50.00

Dom DiMaggio OF
1946 BOSTON RED SOX

Joe Cronin Mgr.
1946 BOSTON RED SOX

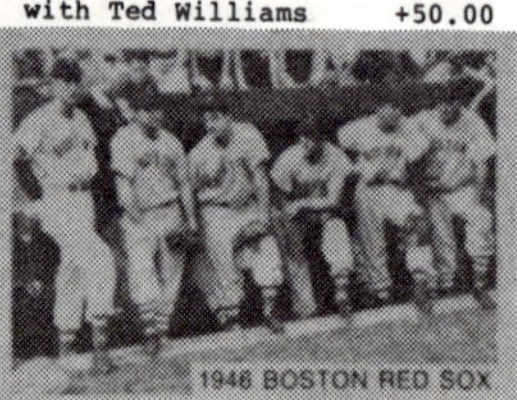
1946 BOSTON RED SOX

Ted Williams OF
1946 BOSTON RED SOX

1946 Detroit Tigers: Steve O'Neill, Manager; Hank Greenberg, Jimmy Bloodworth (military service), Eddie Lake, George Kell (traded), Roy Cullenbine, Hoot Evers (injured), Dick Wakefield, Birdie Tebbetts, Pat Mullin, Jimmy Outlaw, Doc Cramer, Skeeter Webb, Paul Richards, Eddie Mayo (injury), Anse Moore, Bob Swift, Barney McCosky (traded), Pinky Higgins (traded), Hal Newhouser, Dizzy Trout, Virgil Trucks, Fred Hutchinson, Al Benton, Stubby Overmire, George Caster.

Autographed Ball 50.00
with Hank Greenberg +10.00

1946 St. Louis Cardinals (WORLD CHAMPIONS): Eddie Dyer, Manager; Stan Musial, Red Schoendienst, Marty Marion, Whitey Kurowski, Enos Slaughter, Terry Moore (injury), Harry Walker, Joe Garagiola, Erv Dusak, Dick Sisler, Buster Adams, Del Rice, Clyde Kluttz (traded), Jeff Cross, Howie Pollet, Murray Dickson, Harry Brecheen, Al Brazle, Ted Wilks, Johnny Beazley, Max Lanier (suspended for playing in the Mexican League), Ken Burkhart, Red Barrett.

Autographed Ball 25.00
with Joe Garagiola +10.00
with Stan Musial +50.00

1942 St. Louis Cardinals

Leo Durocher & Eddie Dyer
1946 National League Playoff

Joe Garagiola Catcher
1942-1946 St. Louis Cardinals

Stan Musial Outfield
1942-1946 St. Louis Cardinals

1946 Brooklyn Dodgers: Leo Durocher, Manager; Ed Stevens, Eddie Stanky, Pee Wee Reese, Cookie Lavagetto, Dixie Walker, Carl Furillo, Pete Reiser (injury), Bruce Edwards, Dick Whitman, Augie Galan, Howie Schultz, Ferrell Anderson, Gene Hermanski, Bob Ramazotti, Billy Herman (traded), Stan Rojek, Joe Medwick, Kirby Higbe, Joe Hatten, Vic Lombardi, Hank Behrman, Hugh Casey, Art Herring, Rube Melton (military service), Hal Gregg, Ralph Branca.

Autographed Ball 30.00
with Leo Durocher +10.00
with Joe Medwick +10.00
with Billy Herman +10.00

1947 AMERICAN LEAGUE ALL-STAR TEAM - Joe Cronin (manager); Del Baker and Stephen O'Neill (coaches); Robert Doerr, Ted Williams*, Lucius Appling, Rudolph York, Louis Boudreau*, Joe Gordon*, Robert Feller (replaced by Early Wynn), James Hegan, George Kell*, Pat Mullin, Harold Newhouser, Dizzy Trout, Spurgeon (Spud) Chandler, Joe DiMaggio*, Charles Keller (replaced by Tommy Henrich), William Johnson, George McQuinn*, Joe Page, Aaron Robinson, Francis Shea, Warren Rosar, John Kramer, John Lewis*, Walter Masterson, Stanley Spence. Starters designated with an "*".

Autographed Ball	25.00
with Joe Cronin	+10.00
with Ted Williams	+40.00
with Joe DiMaggio	+40.00

1947 NATIONAL LEAGUE ALL-STAR TEAM - Edwin Dyer (manager); Mel Ott and Ben Chapman (coaches); Bob Elliott* (replaced by Whitey Kurowski), Phil Masi, John Sain, Warren Spahn, Ralph Branca, Bruce Edwards, Ed Stanky, Fred Walker*, Phil Cavarretta, Andy Pafko, Ewell Blackwell, Berthold Haas, Edward Miller (replaced by Harold Reese), Walker Cooper*, Willard Marshall, John Mize*, Lynwood Rowe, Emil Verban*, Harry Walker*, Frank Gustine, Harry Brecheen, Martin Marion, George Munger, Stan Musial, Enos Slaughter*. Starters designated with an "*".

Autographed Ball	40.00
with Mel Ott	+15.00
with Stan Musial	+25.00

1947 New York Yankees (WORLD CHAMPIONS): Bucky Harris, Manager; George McQuinn, Snuffy Stirnweiss, Phil Rizzuto, Billy Johnson, Tommy Henrich, Joe DiMaggio, Johnny Lindell, Aaron Robinson, Yogi Berra, Bobby Brown, Charlie Keller (injury), Ralph Houk, Allie Reymolds, Spec Shea, Joe Page, Spud Chandler, Vic Raschi, Bobo Newsom (traded), Bill Bevens, Karl Drews, Randy Gumpert.

Autographed Ball	30.00
with Bucky Harris	+10.00
with Yogi Berra	+10.00
with Joe DiMaggio	+50.00

1947 Detroit Tigers: Steve O'Neill, Manager; Roy Cullenbine, Eddie Mayo, Eddie Lake, George Kell, Pat Mullin, Hoot Evers, Dick Wakefield, Bob Swift, Vic Wertz, Doc Cramer, Hal Wagner (traded), Jimmy Outlaw, Skeeter Webb, John McHale, Fred Hutchinson, Hal Newhouser, Stubby Overmire, Dizzy Trout, Virgil Trucks, Art Houtteman, Al Benton, Hal White, Johnny Gorsica.

Autographed Ball	50.00

1947 Brooklyn Dodgers (National League Champs): Clyde Sukeforth, Burt Shotton, Manager; Jackie Robinson, Eddie Stanky, Pee Wee Reese, Spider Jorgensen, Dixie Walker, Carl Furillo, Pete Reiser (injury), Bruce Edwards, Gene Hermanski, Arky Vaughan, Eddie Miksis, Cookie Lavagetto, Duke Snider, Al Gionfriddo (traded), Stan Rojek, Gil Hodges, Bobby Bragan, Ralph Branca, Joe Hatten, Vic Lombardi, Hugh Casey, Harry Taylor, Clyde King, Rex Barney, Hank Behrman (traded), Hal Gregg.

Autographed Ball	40.00
with Gil Hodges	+10.00
with J. Robinson	+25.00

1947 St. Louis Cardinals: Eddie Dyer, Manager; Stan Musial, Red Schoendienst, Marty Marion, Whitey Kurowski, Erv Dusak, Terry Moore, Enos Slaughter, Del Rice, Ron Northey (traded), Chuck Diering, Joe Garagiola, Joe Medwick, Del Wilber, Jeff Cross, Dick Sisler, George Munger, Harry Brecheen, Al Brazle, Murry Dickson, Jim Hearn, Howie Pollet, Ted Wilks, Ken Burkhart.

Autographed Ball	15.00
with Joe Medwick	+10.00
with Joe Garagiola	+10.00
with Stan Musial	+40.00

1948 AMERICAN LEAGUE ALL-STAR TEAM - Stanley (Bucky) Harris (manager); John Corriden and Charles Dressen (coaches); Robert Doerr, Vernon Stephens, George Tebbetts, Ted Williams*, Joe Haynes, Lou Boudreau*, Bob Feller (replaced by Joe Dobson), Joe Gordon*, Ken Keltner, Bob Lemon, Walter Evers, George Kell*, Pat Mullin*, Hal Newhouser, Yogi Berra, Joe DiMaggio*, Thomas Henrich, George McQuinn*, Joseph Page, Vic Raschi, Joe Coleman, Warren Rosar*, Al Zarilla, Walter Masterson, Mickey Vernon. Starters designated with an "*".

Autographed Ball	25.00
with Bucky Harris	+10.00
with Ted Williams	+40.00
with Joe DiMaggio	+40.00

1948 NATIONAL LEAGUE ALL-STAR TEAM - Leo Durocher (manager); Mel Ott and Edwin Dyer (coaches); Bob Elliott, Thomas Holmes, Phil Masi, John Sain, Ed Stanky* (replaced by Bill Rigney), Ralph Branca, PeeWee Reese*, Clyde McCullough, Andy Pafko*, John Schmitz, Ed Waitkus, Ewell Blackwell, Walker Cooper*, Sid Gordon, John Mize*, Robert Thomson, Richie Ashburn*, Frank Gustine, Ralph Kiner, Elmer Riddle, Harry Brecheen, Martin Marion (replaced by John Kerr), Stan Musial*, Red Schoendienst, Enos Slaughter*. Starters designated with an "*".

Autographed Ball	40.00
with Mel Ott	+20.00
with Stan Musial	+20.00

1948 Cleveland Indians (WORLD CHAMPIONS): Lou Boudreau, Playing Manager; Eddie Robinson, Joe Gordon, Ken Keltner, Larry Doby, Thurman Tucker, Dale Mitchell, Jim Hegan, Allie Clark, Walt Judnich, John Berardino, Bob Kennedy (traded), Hank Edwards (injury), Joe Tipton, Hal Peck, Gene Bearden, Bob Lemon, Bob Feller, Steve Gromek, Sam Zoldak (traded), Satchel Paige, Bob Muncrief, Russ Christopher, Eddie Klieman.

Autographed Ball	25.00
with Lou Boudreau	+10.00
with Bob Lemon	+10.00
with Bob Feller	+10.00
with Satchel Paige	+20.00

1948 Boston Red Sox: Joe McCarthy, Manager; Billy Goodman, Bobby Doerr, Vern Stephens, Johnny Pesky, Stan Spence, Dom DiMaggio, Ted Williams, Birdie Tebbetts, Wally Moses, Sam Mele, Billy Hitchcock, Matt Batts, Jake Jones, Jack Kramer, Joe Dobson, Mel Parnell, Earl Johnson, Ellis Kinder, Denny Galehouse, Boo Ferriss, Mickey Harris, Tex Hughson (sore arm).

Autographed Ball	15.00
with Joe McCarthy	+10.00
with Ted Williams	+50.00

1948 Boston Braves (National League Champs): Billy Southworth, Manager; Earl Torgeson, Eddie Stanky (broken ankle), Al Dark, Bob Elliott, Tommy Holmes, Mike McCormick, Jeff Heath (broken ankle), Phil Masi, Clint Conatser, Jim Russell (illness), Sibby Sisti, Bill Salkeld, Frank McCormick, Connie Ryan, Johnny Sain, Warren Spahn, Bill Voiselle, Vern Bickford, Bobby Hogue, Red Barrett, Clyde Shoun, Nels Potter (traded).

Autographed Ball	30.00
with Warren Spahn	+20.00

1948 St. Louis Cardinals: Eddie Dyer, Manager; Nippy Jones, Red Schoendienst, Marty Marion, Don Lang, Enos Slaughter, Terry Moore, Stan Musial, Del Rice, Erv Dusak, Ron Northey, Ralph LaPointe, Whitey Kurowski (arm injury), Bill Baker, Murry Dickson, Babe Young (traded), Del Wilber, Joe Garagiola, Joe Medwick, Harry Brecheen, Howie Pollet, Murry Dickson, Al Brazle, George Munger, Jim Hearn, Ted Wilks, Gerry Staley, Ken Johnson, Al Papai, Ken Burkhart (traded).

Autographed Ball	20.00
with Joe Medwick	+10.00
with Joe Garagiola	+10.00
with Stan Musial	+35.00

1949 AMERICAN LEAGUE ALL-STAR TEAM - Lou Boudreau (manager); Will McKechnie and Herold Ruel (coaches); Dom DiMaggio*, Bill Goodman, Mel Parnell, Vern Stephens, George Tebbetts*, Ted Williams*, Cass Michaels*, Larry Doby, Joe Gordon, Jim Hegan, Rob Lemon, Dale Mitchell, George Kell*, Virgil Trucks, Vic Wertz, Yogi Berra, Joe DiMaggio, Thomas Henrich*, Vic Raschi, Allie Reynolds, Leland Brissie, Ed Joost*, Alex Kellner, Robert Dillinger, W. Edward Robinson*. Starters designated with an "*".

Autographed Ball	25.00
with Bill McKechnie	+10.00
with Ted Williams	+40.00
with Joe DiMaggio	+40.00

1949 NATIONAL LEAGUE ALL-STAR TEAM - Bill Southworth (manager); Burt Shotton and Bucky Walters (coaches); Vern Bickford, Warren Spahn, Ralph Branca, Roy Campanella, Gil Hodges, Don Newcombe, Harold Reese*, Jackie Robinson*, Preacher Roe, Andy Pafko, Ewell Blackwell, Walker Cooper, Sid Gordon, Willard Marshall*, John Mize*, Robert Thomson, Andy Seminick*, Ralph Kiner*, Ed Kazak*, Martin Marion, George Munger, Stan Musial*, Howard Pollett, Red Schoendienst, Enos Slaughter, Edward Waitkus (honorary). Starters designated with an "*".

Autographed Ball	20.00
with Eddie Waitkus	+10.00
with Gil Hodges	+10.00
with J. Robinson	+15.00
with Stan Musial	+15.00
with Roy Campanella	+30.00

1949 New York Yankees (WORLD CHAMPIONS): Casey Stengel, Manager; Tommy Henrich, Jerry Coleman, Phil Rizzuto, Bobby Brown, Hank Bauer, Cliff Mapes, Gene Woodling, Yogi Berra (injury), Billy Johnson, Johnny Lindell, Joe DiMaggio (injury), Snuffy Stirnweiss, Charlie Keller, Charlie Silvera, Dick Kryhoski, Jack Phillips (traded), Gus Niarhos, Johnny Mize (traded), Vic Raschi, Allie Reynolds, Tommy Byrne, Ed Lopat, Joe Page, Fred Sanford, Cuddles Marshall, Duane Pillette, Bob Porterfield (arm injury), Hugh Casey (traded), Spec Shea.

Autographed Ball	15.00
with Yogi Berra	+10.00
with Johnny Mize	+10.00
with Casey Stengel	+15.00
with Joe DiMaggio	+50.00

1949 Boston Red Sox: Joe McCarthy, Manager; Billy Goodman, Bobby Doerr, Vern Stephens, Johnny Pesky, Al Zarilla (traded), Dom DiMaggio, Ted Williams, Birdie Tebbetts, Matt Batts, Billy Hitchcock, Tommy O'Brien, Lou Stringer, Mel Parnell, Ellis Kinder, Joe Dobson, Chuck Stobbs, Jack Kramer, Mickey McDermott, Tex Hughson, Walt Masterson (traded), Earl Johnson.

Autographed Ball	15.00
with Joe McCarthy	+10.00
with Ted Williams	+50.00

1949 Brooklyn Dodgers (National League Champs): Burt Shotton, Manager; Gil Hodges, Jackie Robinson, Pee Wee Reese, Billy Cox, Carl Furillo, Duke Snider, Gene Hermanski, Roy Campanella, Bruce Edwards, Marv Rackley (traded), Mike McCormick, Spider Jorgensen, Eddie Miksis, Tommy Brown, Chuck Connors, Don Newcombe, Preacher Roe, Ralph Branca, Joe Hatten, Jack Banta, Rex Barney, Carl Erskine, Erv Palica, Paul Minner.

Autographed Ball	25.00
with Gil Hodges	+10.00
with Chuck Conners	+20.00
with J. Robinson	+20.00
with Roy Campanella	35.00

1949 St. Louis Cardinals: Eddie Dyer, Manager; Nippy Jones, Red Schoendienst, Marty Marion, Eddie Kazak (injury), Stan Musial, Chuck Diering, Enos Slaughter, Del Rice, Ron Northey, Tommy Glaviano, Rocky Nelson, Joe Garagiola, Lou Klein (suspended), Hal Rice, Howie Pollet, George Munger, Al Brazle, Harry Brecheen, Ted Wilks, Gerry Staley, Freddie Martin (suspended), Max Lanier (suspended), Bill Reeder, Jim Hearn, Ken Johnson.

Autographed Ball	20.00
with Joe Garagiola	+10.00
with Stan Musial	+35.00

1950 AMERICAN LEAGUE ALL-STAR TEAM - Casey Stengel (manager); Frank Crosetti and William Dickey (coaches); Dom DiMaggio, Robert Doerr*, Walter Dropo*, Vern Stephens, Ted Williams*, Ray Scarborough, Larry Doby*, Rob Feller, Jim Hegan, Rob Lemon, Walter Evers*, Ted Gray, Art Houtteman, George Kell*, Lawrence (Yogi) Berra*, Thomas Byrne, Gerald Coleman, Joe DiMaggio, Thomas Henrich, Vic Raschi, Allie Reynolds, Phil Rizzuto*, Ferris Fain, Sherm Lollar, Casimer Michaels. Starters designated with an "*".

Autographed Ball	20.00
with Casey Stengel	+10.00
with Ted Williams	+40.00
with Joe DiMaggio	+40.00

1950 NATIONAL LEAGUE ALL-STAR TEAM - Burt Shotton (mgr.); Jake Pitler and Milt Stock (coaches); Walker Cooper, Warren Spahn, Roy Campanella*, Gil Hodges, Don Newcombe, Harold Reese, Jackie Robinson*, Elwin Roe, Duke Snider, Andy Pafko, Bob Rush, Hank Sauer*, Ewell Blackwell, John Wyrostek, Larry Jansen, Ed Stanky, Willie Jones*, Jim Konstanty, Robin Roberts, Dick Sisler, Ralph Kiner*, Marty Marion, Stan Musial*, Red Schoendienst, Enos Slaughter*. Starters designated with an "*".

Autographed Ball	25.00
with Gil Hodges	+10.00
with Stan Musial	+15.00
with J. Robinson	+20.00
with Roy Campanella	+30.00

1950 New York Yankees (WORLD CHAMPIONS): Casey Stengel, Manager; Johnny Mize, Jerry Coleman, Phil Rizzuto, Billy Johnson, Hank Bauer, Joe DiMaggio, Gene Woodling, Yogi Berra, Cliff Mapes, Joe Collins, Bobby Brown, Tommy Henrich (knee injury), Jackie Jensen, Bill Martin, Johnny Hopp (traded), Charlie Silvera, Jim Delsing (traded), Ralph Houk, Vic Raschi, Ed Lopat, Allie Reynolds, Tommy Byrne, Whitey Ford, Tom Ferrick (traded), Fred Sanford, Joe Page, Joe Ostrowski (traded).

Autographed Ball	30.00
with Billy Martin	+10.00
with Casey Stengel	+10.00
with Joe DiMaggio	+50.00

1950 Detroit Tigers: Red Rolfe, Manager; Don Kolloway, Jerry Priddy, Johnny Lipon, George Kell, Vic Wertz, Johnny Groth, Hoot Evers, Aaron Robinson, Pat Mullin, Bob Swift, Dick Kryhoski, Charlie Keller, Neil Berry, Joe Ginsberg, Art Houtteman, Fred Hutchinson, Hal Newhouser, Dizzy Trout, Ted Gray (illness), Hal White, Marlin Stuart, Virgil Trucks (sore arm), Paul Calvert.

Autographed Ball 50.00

1950 Philadelphia Phillies (National League Champs): Eddie Sawyer, Manager; Eddie Waitkus, Mike Goliat, Granny Hamner, Willie Jones, Del Ennis, Richie Ashburn, Dick Sisler, Andy Seminick, Dick Whitman, Stan Lopata, Jimmy Bloodworth (traded), Putsy Caballero, Bill Nicholson, Robin Roberts, Curt Simmons, Jim Konstanty, Bob Miller, Russ Meyer, Bubba Church, Ken Johnson (traded), Ken Heintzelman, Blix Donnelly, Milo Candini.

Autographed Ball 50.00
with Jim Konstanty +10.00
with Robin Roberts +25.00

1950 Brooklyn Dodgers: Burt Shotton, Manager; Gil Hodges, Jackie Robinson, Pee Wee Reese, Billy Cox, Carl Furillo, Duke Snider, Gene Hermanski, Roy Campanella, Jim Russell, Bobby Morgan, Eddie Miksis, Bruce Edwards, Tommy Brown, Cal Abrams, George Shuba, Don Newcombe, Preacher Roe, Erv Palica, Dan Bankhead, Ralph Branca, Carl Erskine, Bud Podbielan, Jack Banta (sore arm), Joe Hatten, Rex Barney, Chris Van Cuyk.

Autographed Ball 35.00
with Gil Hodges +10.00
with J. Robinson +20.00
with Roy Campanella +35.00

1951 AMERICAN LEAGUE ALL-STAR TEAM - Casey Stengel (manager); Bill Dickey and Thomas Henrich (coaches); Dom DiMaggio*, Robert Doerr, Mel Parnell, Vern Stephens, Ted Williams*, Jim Busby, Chico Carrasquel*, Nellie Fox*, Randy Gumpert, Minnie Minoso, Eddie Robinson, Larry Doby, Jim Hegan, Bob Lemon, Fred Hutchinson, George Kell*, Vic Wertz*, Yogi Berra*, Joe DiMaggio, Ed Lopat, Phil Rizzuto, Ferris Fain*, Robert Shantz, Ned Garver, Conrado Marrero. Starters designated with an "*".

Autographed Ball 20.00
with Casey Stengel +10.00
with Ted Williams +40.00
with Joe DiMaggio +40.00

1951 NATIONAL LEAGUE ALL-STAR TEAM - Edwin Sawyer (manager); Bennie Bengough, Allen Cooke and Ralph Perkins (coaches); Bob Elliott*, Warren Spahn, Roy Campanella*, Gil Hodges*, Don Newcombe, Harold Reese, Jackie Robinson*, Preacher Roe, Duke Snider, Bruce Edwards, Dutch Leonard, Ewell Blackwell, John Wyrostek, Al Dark*, Larry Jansen, Sal Maglie, Richie Ashburn*, Del Ennis*, Willie Jones, Robin Roberts, Ralph Kiner, Stan Musial*, Red Schoendienst, Enos Slaughter, Wally Westlake. Starters designated with an "*".

Autographed Ball 25.00
with Gil Hodges +10.00
with Stan Musial +15.00
with J. Robinson +20.00
with Roy Campanella +35.00

1951 New York Yankees (WORLD CHAMPIONS): Casey Stengel, Manager; Johnny Mize, Jerry Coleman, Phil Rizzuto, Bobby Brown, Hank Bauer, Joe DiMaggio, Gene Woodling, Yogi Berra, Gil McDougald, Joe Collins, Mickey Mantle, Jackie Jensen, Billy Martin, Johnny Hopp, Cliff Mapes (traded), Ed Lopat, Vic Raschi, Allie Reynolds, Tom Morgan, Bob Kuzava (traded), Joe Ostrowski, Spec Shea, Art Schallock, Tommy Byrne (traded), Johnny Sain (traded), Bobby Hogue (traded), Tom Ferrick (traded), Stubby Overmire (traded), Jack Kramer (traded), Whitey Ford (military service).

Autographed Ball 10.00
with Whitey Ford +10.00
with Casey Stengel +10.00
with Mickey Mantle +40.00
with Joe DiMaggio +40.00

1951 Cleveland Indians: Al Lopez, Manager; Luke Easter, Bobby Avila, Ray Boone, Al Rosen, Bob Kennedy, Larry Doby, Dale Mitchell, Jim Hegan, Harry Simpson, Sam Chapman (traded), Birdie Tebbetts, Snuffy Stirnweiss, Barney McCosky (traded), Bob Feller, Mike Garcia, Early Wynn, Bob Lemon, Steve Gromek, Lou Brissie (traded), Bob Chakales, Sam Jones, Johnny VanderMeer, George Zuverink.

Autographed Ball 30.00
with Al Lopez +5.00
with Bob Feller +5.00
with Early Wynn +5.00
with Bob Lemon +5.00

1951 St. Louis Browns: Zack Taylor, Manager; Hank Arft, Bobby Young, Bill Jennings, Freddie Marsh, Ken Wood, Jim Delsing, Ray Coleman (traded), Sherm Lollar, Matt Batts (traded), Johnny Bero, Cliff Mapes (traded), Tom Upton, Jack Maguire (traded), Johnny Berardino, Dale Long (traded), Roy Sievers (shoulder injury), Don Lenhardt (traded), Bennie Taylor, Earl Rapp (traded), Paul Lehner (traded), Frank Saucier, Les Moss (traded), Bob Nieman, Ned Garver, Duane Pillette, Jim McDonald, Al Widmar, Tommy Byrne (traded), Satchel Paige, Fred Sanford (traded), Bob Mahoney (traded), Dick Starr (traded), Bobby Hogue (traded), Duke Markell, Bill Kennedy, Stubby Overmire (traded), Lou Sleater, Don Johnson (traded), Bob Turley, Cliff Fannin, Irv Medlinger, Sid Schacht (traded), Jim Suchecki, Tito Herrera, Eddie Gaedel.

Autographed Ball 30.00
with Bill Veeck +15.00
with Satchel Paige +20.00
with Eddie Gaedel +100.00

1951 New York Giants (National League Champs): Leo Durocher, Manager; Whitey Lockman, Eddie Stanky, Al Dark, Hank Thompson, Don Mueller, Willie Mays, Monte Irvin, Wes Westrum, Bobby Thomson, Ray Noble, Bill Rigney, Davey Williams, Spider Jorgensen, Sal Yvars, Lucky Lohrke, Clint Hartung, Sal Maglie, Larry Jansen, Jim Hearn, George Spencer, Dave Koslo, Sheldon Jones, Al Corwin, Roger Bowman, Al Gettel, Monte Kennedy.

Autographed Ball 10.00
with Monte Irvin +10.00
with Leo Durocher +10.00
with Willie Mays +50.00

Al Dark SS
1951 NEW YORK GIANTS

Bobby Thompson 3B-CF
1951 NEW YORK GIANTS

Jim Hearn P
1951 NEW YORK GIANTS

Sal Maglie P
1951 NEW YORK GIANTS

Monte Irvin LF
1951 NEW YORK GIANTS

1951 Brooklyn Dodgers: Chuck Dressen, Manager; Gil Hodges, Jackie Robinson, Pee Wee Reese, Billy Cox, Carl Furillo, Duke Snider, Andy Pafko (traded), Roy Campanella, Don Thompson, Cal Abrams, Rocky Bridges, Wayne Terwilliger (traded), Rube Walker (traded), Hank Edwards (traded), Gene Hermanski (traded), Dick Williams, Preacher Roe, Don Newcombe, Carl Erskine, Clyde King, Ralph Branca, Clem Labine, Bud Podbielan, Erv Palica, Joe Hatten (traded), Chris Van Cuyk, Johnny Schmitz (traded), Phil Haugstad.

Autographed Ball	25.00
with Chuck Dressen	+10.00
with Gil Hodges	+10.00
with J. Robinson	+20.00
with Roy Campanella	+35.00

1952 AMERICAN LEAGUE ALL-STAR TEAM - Casey Stengel (manager); Tony Cuccinello and Al Lopez (coaches); Dom DiMaggio*, George Kell (replaced by Gil McDougald), Nelson Fox, Orestes Minoso, Eddie Robinson*, Bob Avila*, Larry Doby, Mike Garcia, Jim Hegan, Bob Lemon, Dale Mitchell*, Al Rosen*, Vic Wertz, Hank Bauer*, Yogi Berra*, Mickey Mantle, Vic Raschi, Allie Reynolds, Phil Rizzuto*, Ferris Fain, Ed Joost, Bob Shantz, Leroy Paige, Jack Jensen, Ed Yost. Starters designated with an "*".

Autographed Ball	25.00
with Satchel Paige	+10.00
with Casey Stengel	+10.00
with Mickey Mantle	+50.00

1952 NATIONAL LEAGUE ALL-STAR TEAM - Leo Durocher (manager); Frank Shellenback and Edward Stanky (coaches); - Warren Spahn, Roy Campanella*, Carl Furillo, Gil Hodges, Pee Wee Reese, Jackie Robinson, Preacher Roe (replaced by Jim Hearn), Duke Snider, Toby Atwell, Bob Rush, Henry Sauer*, Grady Hatton, Al Dark, Monte Irvin, Granny Hamner*, Robin Roberts, Curt Simmons, Ralph Kiner, Stan Musial*, Red Schoendienst, Enos Slaughter*, Gerald Staley. Starters designated with an "*".

Autographed Ball	20.00
with Gil Hodges	+10.00
with J. Robinson	+20.00
with Stan Musial	+20.00
with Roy Campanella	+30.00

1952 New York Yankees (WORLD CHAMPIONS): Casey Stengel, Manager; Joe Collins, Billy Martin (broken ankle), Phil Rizzuto, Gil McDougald, Hank Bauer, Mickey Mantle, Gene Woodling, Yogi Berra, Irv Noren (traded), Johnny Mize, Jim Brideweser, Bob Cerv, Bobby Brown (military service), Charlie Silvera, Andy Carey, Johnny Hopp (traded), Allie Reynolds, Vic Raschi, Johnny Sain, Ed Lopat (injury), Bob Kuzava, Tom Gorman, Ray Scarborough (traded), Tom Morgan (military service), Bill Miller, Jim McDonald, Bobby Hogue (traded), Joe Ostrowski, Whitey Ford (military service).

Autographed Ball	20.00
with Whitey Ford	+10.00
with Billy Martin	+10.00
with Casey Stengel	+10.00
with Mickey Mantle	+50.00

1952 Cleveland Indians: Al Lopez, Manager; Luke Easter, Bobby Avila, Ray Boone, Al Rosen, Harry Simpson, Larry Doby, Dale Mitchell, Jim Hegan, Jim Fridley, Barney McCosky, Merrill Combs, Bill Glynn, Joe Tipton (traded), Birdie Tebbets, Hank Majeski (traded), Johnny Berardino (traded), Pete Reiser, George Strickland (traded), Wally Westlake (traded), Bob Kennedy (military service), Early Wynn, Mike Garcia, Bob Lemon, Bob Feller, Steve Gromek, Mickey Harris (traded), Lou Brissie, Sam Jones, Dick Rozek.

Autographed Ball	25.00
with Al Lopez	+5.00
with Bob Feller	+5.00
with Bob Lemon	+5.00
with Early Wynn	+5.00

1952 Brooklyn Dodgers (National League Champs): Chuck Dressen, Manager; Gil Hodges, Jackie Robinson, Pee Wee Reese, Billy Cox (elbow injury), Carl Furillo, Duke Snider, Andy Pafko, Roy Campanella, George Shuba, Bobby Morgan, Rocky Bridges, Rube Walker, Rocky Nelson, Dick Williams (injury), Tommy Holmes (traded), Joe Black, Carl Erskine, Billy Loes, Preacher Roe, Ben Wade, Clem Labine, Johnny Rutherford, Chris Van Cuyk, Ralph Branca (sore arm), Clyde King.

Autographed Ball	25.00
with Chuck Dressen	+10.00
with Gil Hodges	+10.00
with J. Robinson	+20.00
with Roy Campanella	+35.00

Duke

Jackie

Gil

Campy

1952 New York Giants: Leo Durocher, Manager; Whitey Lockman, Davey Williams, Al Dark, Bobby Thomson, Don Mueller, Hank Thompson, Bob Elliott, Wes Westrum, Dusty Rhodes, Sal Yvars, George Wilson (traded), Bill Rigney, Monte Irvin (broken ankle), Chuck Diering, Willie Mays (military service), Bobby Hofman, Clint Hartung, Sal Maglie, Hoyt Wilhelm, Jim Hearn, Larry Jansen (back injury), Dave Koslo, Max Lanier, Al Corwin, Bill Connelly, Monte Kennedy, George Spencer, Hal Gregg.

Autographed Ball	10.00
with Monte Irvin	+10.00
with Leo Durocher	+10.00
with Willie Mays	+50.00

1952 Boston Braves: Tommy Holmes, Charlie Grimm, Managers; Earl Torgeson, Jack Dittmer, Johnny Logan, Eddie Mathews, Bob Thorpe, Sam Jethroe, Sid Gordon, Walker Cooper, Jack Daniels, Sibby Sisti, George Crowe, Paul Burris, Jack Cusick, Ebba St. Claire, Roy Hartsfield, Pete Whisenant, Willard Marshall, Bill Reed, Warren Spahn, Max Surkont, Jim Wilson, Vern Bickford, Ernie Johnson, Lew Burdette, Virgil Jester, Bob Chipman, Dave Cole, Bert Thiel, Sheldon Jones, Dick Donovan, Gene Conley, Dick Hoover.

Autographed Ball	20.00
with Eddie Mathews	+15.00
with Warren Spahn	+15.00

THE INCREMENTAL VALUE OF THE AUTOGRAPH OF A PARTICULAR PLAYER TO A PARTICULAR BALL IS UNIQUE TO THAT BALL. IT IS NOT THE EXOGENOUS VALUE OF THAT PLAYER'S AUTOGRAPH. SEE THE INTRODUCTION TO TEAM AUTOGRAPHED BALLS.

1953 AMERICAN LEAGUE ALL-STAR TEAM - Casey Stengel (manager); Lou Boudreau and Jim Turner (coaches); William Goodman*, George Kell, Sammy White, Alfonso Carrasquel, Ferris Fain, Nelson Fox, Orestes Minoso, William Pierce, Lawrence Doby, Mike Garcia, Bob Lemon, Al Rosen*, Harvey Kuenn, Henry Bauer*, Yogi Berra*, Mickey Mantle*, John Mize, Allie Reynolds, Phil Rizzuto, John Sain, W. Edward Robinson, Gus Zernial*, G. William Hunter, Leroy (Satchel) Paige, James (Mickey) Vernon*, Ted Williams (honorary). Starters designated with an "*".

Autographed Ball	20.00
with Satchel Paige	+10.00
with Casey Stengel	+10.00
with Ted Williams	+30.00
with Mickey Mantle	+30.00

1953 NATIONAL LEAGUE ALL-STAR TEAM - Charles Dressen (manager); William Herman, Harry Lavagetto and Jacob Pitler (coaches); Roy Campanella*, Carl Furillo, Gil Hodges, Harold Reese*, Jackie Robinson, Duke Snider, Ralph Kiner, Gus Bell*, Ted Kluszewski*, Del Crandall (replaced by Clyde McCullough), Ed Mathews*, Warren Spahn, Granny Hamner, Robin Roberts, Curt Simmons, Murry Dickson, Harvey Haddix, Stan Musial*, Del Rice (replaced by Wes Westrum), Red Schoendienst*, Enos Slaughter*, Gerald Staley. Starters designated with an "*".

Autographed Ball	25.00
with Gil Hodges	+10.00
with Stan Musial	+15.00
with J. Robinson	+20.00
with Roy Campanella	+30.00

1953 New York Yankees (WORLD CHAMPIONS): Casey Stengel, Manager; Joe Collins, Billy Martin, Phil Rizzuto, Gil McDougald, Hank Bauer, Mickey Mantle, Gene Woodling, Yogi Berra, Irv Noren, Johnny Mize, Don Bollweg, Bill Renna, Andy Carey, Willie Miranda (traded), Charlie Silvera, Gus Triandos, Ralph Houk, Jerry Coleman (military service), Whitey Ford, Ed Lopat, Johnny Sain, Vic Raschi, Allie Reynolds, Jim McDonald, Bob Kuzava, Tom Gorman, Ewell Blackwell (sore arm), Bill Miller, Ray Scarborough (traded).

Autographed Ball	25.00
with Yogi Berra	+10.00
with Casey Stengel	+15.00
with Mickey Mantle	+50.00

1953 Cleveland Indians: Al Lopez, Manager; Bill Glynn, Bobby Avila, George Strickland, Al Rosen, Wally Westlake, Larry Doby, Dale Mitchell, Jim Hegan, Bob Kennedy, Harry Simpson, Luke Easter (injury), Hank Majeski, Al Smith, Joe Tipton, Joe Ginsberg (traded), Ray Boone (traded), Owen Friend (traded), Bob Lemon, Mike Garcia, Early Wynn, Bob Feller, Dave Hoskins, Art Houtteman (traded), Bob Hooper, Bill Wight (traded), Dick Tomanek, Al Aber (traded), Steve Gromek (traded), Bob Chakales, Lou Brissie.

Autographed Ball	25.00
with Al Lopez	+5.00
with Bob Feller	+5.00
with Bob Lemon	+5.00
with Early Wynn	+5.00

1953 St. Louis Browns: Marty Marion, Manager; Dick Kryhoski, Bobby Young, Billy Hunter, Jim Dyck, Vic Wertz, Johnny Groth, Dick Kokos, Clint Courtney, Don Lenhardt, Roy Sievers, Les Moss, Hank Edwards, Neil Berry (traded), Bob Elliott (traded), Vern Stephens (traded), Willie Miranda (traded), Dixie Upright, Johnny Lipon (traded), Marlin Stuart, Don Larsen, Dick Littlefield, Duane Pillette, Virgil Trucks (traded), Harry Brecheen, Bob Cain, Bobo Holloman, Satchel Paige, Mike Blyzka, Bob Turley (military service), Lou Kretlow (traded), Max Lanier (traded), Hal White (traded), Bob Habenicht.

Autographed Ball	35.00
with Marty Marion	+5.00
with Satchel Paige	+20.00

1953 Brooklyn Dodgers (National League Champs): Chuck Dressen, Manager; Gil Hodges, Jim Gilliam, Pee Wee Reese, Billy Cox, Carl Furillo, Duke Snider, Jackie Robinson, Roy Campanella, Don Thompson, George Shuba, Bobby Morgan, Wayne Belardi (arm injury), Rube Walker, Bill Antonello, Dick Williams, Carl Erskine, Russ Meyer, Billy Loes, Preacher Roe, Clem Labine, Johnny Podres, Bob Milliken, Ben Wade, Joe Black, Jim Hughes.

Autographed Ball	30.00
with Chuck Dressen	+10.00
with Gil Hodges	+10.00
with J. Robinson	+20.00
with Roy Campanella	+30.00

1953 Milwaukee Braves: Charlie Grimm, Manager; Joe Adcock, Jack Dittmer, Johnny Logan, Eddie Mathews, Andy Pafko, Bill Bruton, Sid Gordon, Del Crandall, Jim Pendleton, Walker Cooper, Harry Hanebrink, George Crowe, Sibby Sisti, Ebba St. Claire, Bob Thorpe, Warren Spahn, Lew Burdette, Bob Buhl, Johnny Antonelli, Max Surkont, Don Liddle, Ernie Johnson, Jim Wilson, Vern Bickford, Joey Jay, Dave Jolly, Dave Cole.

Autographed Ball	20.00
with Eddie Mathews	+15.00
with Warren Spahn	+15.00

1954 AMERICAN LEAGUE ALL-STAR TEAM - Casey Stengel (mgr.); Marty Marion and Fred Hutchinson (coaches); Bob Turley, Jim Piersall, Ted Williams, Chico Carrasquel*, Ferris Fain (replaced by Dean Stone), Nelson Fox, Bob Keegan, George Kell (replaced by Mickey Vernon), Sherm Lollar, Orestes Minoso*, Virgil Trucks, Bob Avila*, Larry Doby, Mike Garcia (replaced by Sandy Consuegra), Bob Lemon, Al Rosen*, Ray Boone*, Harvey Kuenn, Hank Bauer*, Yogi Berra*, Whitey Ford, Mickey Mantle*, Allie Reynolds (replaced by Irv Noren), Jim Finigan, Bob Porterfield. Starters designated with an "*".

Autographed Ball	10.00
with Casey Stengel	+10.00
with Mickey Mantle	+40.00
with Ted Williams	+40.00

1954 NATIONAL LEAGUE ALL-STAR TEAM - Walt Alston (manager); Charles Grimm and Leo Durocher (coaches); Roy Campanella*, Carl Erskine, Gil Hodges, Harold Reese, Jackie Robinson*, Duke Snider*, Ransom Jackson, David (Gus) Bell, Ted Kluszewski*, Del Crandall, Gene Conley, Warren Spahn, John Antonelli, Al Dark*, Marv Grissom, Willie Mays, Don Mueller, Forrest Burgess, Granville Hamner*, Robin Roberts, Frank Thomas, Harvey Haddix (replaced by Jim Wilson), Ray Jablonski*, Stan Musial*, Red Schoendienst. Starters designated with an "*".

Autographed Ball	15.00
with Gil Hodges	+10.00
with J. Robinson	+15.00
with Willie Mays	+15.00
with Stan Musial	+15.00
with Roy Campanella	+30.00

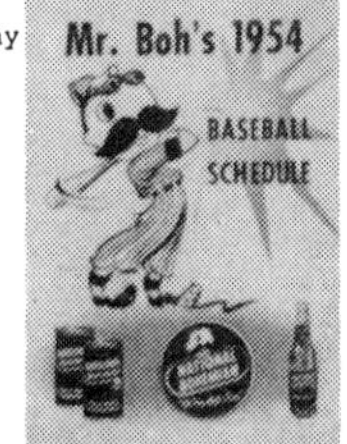

1954 Cleveland Indians (American League Champs): Al Lopez, Manager; Vic Wertz (traded), Bobby Avila, George Stickland (injury), Al Rosen, Dave Philley, Larry Doby, Al Smith, Jim Hegan, Billy Glynn, Wally Westlake, Sam Dente, Rudy Regalado, Dave Pope, Hank Majeski, Dale Mitchell, Hal Naragon, Bob Lemon, Early Wynn, Mike Garcia, Art Houtteman, Bob Feller, Hal Newhouser, Don Mossi, Ray Narleski, Bob Chakales (traded), Dave Hoskins, Bob Hooper.

Autographed Ball	30.00
with Al Lopez	+5.00
with Bob Feller	+5.00
with Bob Lemon	+5.00
with Early Wynn	+5.00

1954 New York Yankees: Casey Stengel, Manager; Joe Collins, Gil McDougald, Phil Rizzuto, Andy Carey, Hank Bauer, Mickey Mantle, Irv Noren, Yogi Berra, Jerry Coleman, Gene Woodling (injury), Willie Miranda, Bill Skowron, Eddie Robinson, Enos Slaughter (injury), Bob Cerv, Bobby Brown (military service), Charlie Silvera, Frank Leja, Bob Grim, Whitey Ford, Allie Reynolds, Ed Lopat, Tom Morgan, Harry Byrd, John Sain, Jim McDonald (injury), Marlin Stuart (traded), Bob Wiesler, Tommy Byrne, Ralph Branca (traded), Jim Konstanty (traded), Bob Kuzava (traded).

Autographed Ball	20.00
with Casey Stengel	+10.00
with Mickey Mantle	+50.00

1954 Baltimore Orioles: Jimmy Dykes, Manager; Eddie Waitkus, Bobby Young, Billy Hunter, Vern Stephens, Cal Abrams (traded), Chuck Diering, Gil Coan, Clint Courtney, Bob Kennedy (traded), Dick Kryhoski, Jim Fridley, Jim Brideweser, Sam Mele (traded), Les Moss, Chico Garcia, Vic Wertz, Ray Murray, Don Lenhardt (traded), Dick Kokos, Joe Durham, Frank Kellert, Bob Turley, Joe Coleman, Duane Pillette, Lou Kretlow, Bob Chakales (traded), Don Larsen, Billy O'Dell, Howie Fox, Marlin Stuart (traded), Bob Kuzava (traded), Mike Blyzka, Dave Koslo (traded), Vern Bickford, Dick Littlefield (traded), Jay Heard, Ryne Duren.

Autographed Ball	75.00

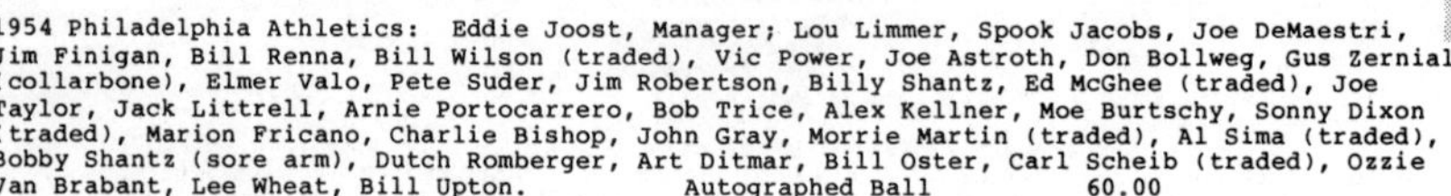

1954 Philadelphia Athletics: Eddie Joost, Manager; Lou Limmer, Spook Jacobs, Joe DeMaestri, Jim Finigan, Bill Renna, Bill Wilson (traded), Vic Power, Joe Astroth, Don Bollweg, Gus Zernial (collarbone), Elmer Valo, Pete Suder, Jim Robertson, Billy Shantz, Ed McGhee (traded), Joe Taylor, Jack Littrell, Arnie Portocarrero, Bob Trice, Alex Kellner, Moe Burtschy, Sonny Dixon (traded), Marion Fricano, Charlie Bishop, John Gray, Morrie Martin (traded), Al Sima (traded), Bobby Shantz (sore arm), Dutch Romberger, Art Ditmar, Bill Oster, Carl Scheib (traded), Ozzie Van Brabant, Lee Wheat, Bill Upton.

Autographed Ball	60.00

1954 New York Giants (WORLD CHAMPIONS): Leo Durocher, Manager; Whitey Lockman, Davey Williams, Al Dark, Hank Thompson, Don Mueller, Willie Mays, Monte Irvin, Wes Westrum, Ray Katt, Dusty Rhodes, Bobby Hofman, Billy Gardner, Bill Taylor, Ebba St. Claire, Foster Castleman, Hoot Evers (traded), Ron Samford, Joey Amalfitano, Joe Garagiola (traded), Johnny Antonelli, Ruben Gomez, Sal Maglie, Hoyt Wilhelm, Marv Grissom, Don Liddle, Jim Hearn, Larry Jansen, Windy McCall, George Spencer, Al Corwin, Al Worthington, Alex Konikowski, Paul Giel.

Autographed Ball	20.00
with Joe Garagiola	+10.00
with Leo Durocher	+10.00
with Willie Mays	+50.00

1954 Brooklyn Dodgers: Walt Alston, Manager; Gil Hodges, Jim Gilliam, Pee Wee Reese, Don Hoak, Carl Furillo, Duke Snider, Jackie Robinson, Roy Campanella (injury), Sandy Amoros, Billy Cox, Rube Walker, Walt Moryn, George Shuba, Don Thompson, Don Zimmer, Dick Williams, Carl Erskine, Billy Loes, Russ Meyer, Johnny Podres (illness), Don Newcombe, Jim Hughes, Clem Labine, Bob Milliken, Erv Palica, Preacher Roe, Karl Spooner, Ben Wade (traded).

Autographed Ball	35.00
with Gil Hodges	+10.00
with J. Robinson	+20.00
with Roy Campanella	+35.00

1955 AMERICAN LEAGUE ALL-STAR TEAM - Al Lopez (manager); Don Gutteridge and Anthony Cuccinello (coaches); James Wilson, Jack Jensen, Frank Sullivan, Ted Williams*, Alfonso Carrasquel, Nelson Fox*, Dick Donovan, Sherm Lollar, Bill Pierce, Bob Avila, Larry Doby, Al Rosen, Al Smith, Herb Score, Early Wynn, Bill Hoeft, Al Kaline*, Harvey Kuenn*, Jim Finigan*, Vic Power, Yogi Berra*, Edward (Whitey) Ford, Mickey Mantle*, Robert Turley, Mickey Vernon*. Starters designated with an "*".

Autographed Ball	20.00
with Mickey Mantle	+40.00
with Ted Williams	+40.00

1955 NATIONAL LEAGUE ALL-STAR TEAM - Leo Durocher (manager); Mayo Smith and Fred Haney (coaches); Roy Campanella* (replaced by Stan Lopata), Gil Hodges, Don Newcombe, Duke Snider*, Gene Baker, Ernie Banks*, Ransom Jackson, Sam Jones, Forrest Burgess, Ted Kluszewski*, Joe Nuxhall, Gene Conley, Del Crandall, John Logan, Ed Mathews*, Henry Aaron, Willie Mays, Don Mueller*, Del Ennis*, Robin Roberts, Frank Thomas, Luis Arroyo, Harvey Haddix, Stan Musial, Red Schoendienst. Starters designated with an "*".

Autographed Ball	15.00
with Gil Hodges	+10.00
with Hank Aaron	+15.00
with Willie Mays	+15.00
with Stan Musial	+15.00
with Roy Campanella	+30.00

1955 New York Yankees (American League Champs): Casey Stengel, Manager; Bill Skowron, Gil McDougald, Billy Hunter, Andy Carey, Hank Bauer, Mickey Mantle, Irv Noren, Yogi Berra, Joe Collins, Elston Howard, Eddie Robinson, Phil Rizzuto, Bob Cerv, Jerry Coleman (injury), Billy Martin (military service), Tommy Carroll, Whitey Ford, Bob Turley, Tommy Byrne, Don Larsen, Johnny Kucks, Jim Konstanty, Tom Morgan, Bob Grim (sore arm), Ed Lopat (traded), Rip Coleman, Tom Sturdivant, Bob Wiesler, Johnny Sain (traded).

Autographed Ball	10.00
with Yogi Berra	+10.00
with Billy Martin	+10.00
with Casey Stengel	+10.00
with Mickey Mantle	+50.00

1955 Cleveland Indians: Al Lopez, Manager; Vic Wertz (illness), Bobby Avila, George Strickland, Al Rosen, Al Smith, Larry Doby, Ralph Kiner, Jim Hegan, Gene Woodling (traded), Sam Dente, Hank Foiles, Dale Mitchell, Hal Naragon, Ferris Fain (traded), Dave Philley (traded), Joe Altobelli, Hoot Evers (traded), Hank Majeski (traded), Dave Pope (traded), Bob Lemon, Early Wynn, Herb Score, Mike Garcia, Art Houtteman, Ray Narleski, Don Mossi, Bob Feller, Jose Santiago, Hank Aguirre, Bud Daley, Sal Maglie (traded), Bill Wight (traded), Hal Newhouser.

Autographed Ball	30.00
with Early Wynn	+5.00
with Al Lopez	+5.00
with Bob Feller	+5.00

1955 Kansas City Athletics: Lou Boudreau, Manager; Vic Power, Jim Finigan, Joe DeMaestri, Hector Lopez, Bill Wilson, Harry Simpson (traded), Gus Zernial, Joe Astroth, Elmer Valo, Enos Slaughter (traded), Bill Renna, Billy Shantz, Clete Boyer, Jack Littrell (ankle injury), Dick Kryhoski, Pete Suder, Jerry Schypinski, Spook Jacobs, Art Ditmar, Alex Kellner, Tom Gorman, Cloyd Boyer, A. Portocarrero (shoulder injury), Bobby Shantz, Vic Raschi (traded), Art Ceccarelli, Bill Harrington (military service), Moe Burtschy, Johnny Sain (traded), Charlie Bishop, Lou Sleater, Ray Herbert, Gus Keriazakos, John Kume, Walt Craddock, John Gray.

Autographed Ball	40.00
with Lou Boudreau	+10.00
with Enos Slaughter	+10.00

1955 Brooklyn Dodgers (WORLD CHAMPIONS): Walt Alston, Manager; Gil Hodges, Jim Gilliam, Pee Wee Reese, Jackie Robinson, Carl Furillo, Duke Snider, Sandy Amoros, Roy Campanella, Don Hoak, Don Zimmer, Rube Walker, George Shuba, Frank Kellert, Dixie Howell, Walt Moryn, Bob Borkowski (traded), Don Newcombe, Clem Labine, Carl Erskine, Billy Loes, Johnny Podres, Don Bessent, Karl Spooner (sore arm), Russ Meyer (back injury), Joe Black (traded), Jim Hughes, Tom Lasorda.

Autographed Ball	40.00
with Tom Lasorda	+10.00
with Gil Hodges	+10.00
with J. Robinson	+20.00
with Roy Campanella	+35.00

1955 Milwaukee Braves: Charlie Grimm, Manager; George Crowe, Danny O'Connell, Johnny Logan, Eddie Mathews, Hank Aaron, Bill Bruton, Bobby Thomson, Del Crandall, Chuck Tanner, Andy Pafko, Joe Adcock (injury), Jack Dittmer, Del Rice (traded), Charlie White, Bennie Taylor, Warren Spahn, Lew Burdette, Bob Buhl, Gene Conley, Ray Crone, Chet Nichols, Ernie Johnson, Humberto Robinson, Phil Paine, Dave Jolly, Roberto Vargas, Joey Jay.

Autographed Ball	10.00
with Eddie Mathews	+10.00
with Warren Spahn	+10.00
with Hank Aaron	+40.00

1956 AMERICAN LEAGUE ALL-STAR TEAM - Charles Stengel (manager); James Turner and Charles Dressen (coaches); George Kell*, Thomas Brewer, James Piersall, James Vernon*, Frank Sullivan, Ted Williams*, Nelson Fox*, Sherm Lollar, William Pierce, James Wilson, Ray Narleski (replaced by Herb Score), Early Wynn, Ray Boone, Al Kaline*, Harvey Kuenn*, Charles Maxwell, Victor Power, Harry Simpson, Yogi Berra*, Whitey Ford, John Kucks, Mickey Mantle*, Billy Martin, Gil McDougald, Roy Sievers. Starters designated with an "*".

Autographed Ball	10.00
with Casey Stengel	+10.00
with Ted Williams	+40.00
with Mickey Mantle	+40.00

1956 NATIONAL LEAGUE ALL-STAR TEAM - Walt Alston (mgr.); George Tebbetts and Fred Hutchinson (coaches); Roy Campanella, Jim Gilliam, Clem Labine, Edwin Snider, Ernie Banks, Ed Bailey*, Gus Bell*, Ted Kluszewski, Brooks Lawrence, Roy McMillan*, Joe Nuxhall, Frank Robinson*, John Temple, Hank Aaron, Del Crandall (replaced by Stan Lopata), Ed Mathews, Warren Spahn, John Antonelli, Willie Mays, Robin Roberts, Bob Friend, Dale Long*, Ken Boyer*, Stan Musial*, Rip Repulski. Starters designated with an "*".

Autographed Ball	15.00
with Frank Robinson	+10.00
with Hank Aaron	+15.00
with Willie Mays	+15.00
with Stan Musial	+15.00
with Roy Campanella	+30.00

1956 New York Yankees (WORLD CHAMPIONS): Casey Stengel, Manager; Bill Skowron, Billy Martin, Gil McDougald, Andy Carey, Hank Bauer, Mickey Mantle, Elston Howard, Yogi Berra, Joe Collins, Jerry Coleman, Norm Siebern (knee injury), Bob Cerv (injury), Billy Hunter (ankle injury), Tommy Carroll, Phil Rizzuto, Irv Noren (knee injury), Eddie Robinson (traded), Enos Slaughter (traded), Whitey Ford, Johnny Kucks, Tom Sturdivant, Don Larsen, Bob Turley, Tommy Byrne, Bob Grim, Tom Morgan, Rip Coleman, Mickey McDermott, Ralph Terry, Jim Konstanty (traded).

Autographed Ball	20.00
with Billy Martin	+10.00
with Yogi Berra	+10.00
with Casey Stengel	+10.00
with Mickey Mantle	+50.00

1956 Cleveland Indians: Al Lopez, Manager; Vic Wertz, Bobby Avila, Chico Carrasquel, Al Rosen, Rocky Colavito, Jim Busby, Al Smith, Jim Hegan, Gene Woodling (illness), Preston Ward (traded), George Strickland, Sam Mele, Hal Naragon, Earl Averill, Dale Mitchell (traded), Dave Pope (traded), Early Wynn, Herb Score, Bob Lemon, Mike Garcia, Don Mossi, Ray Narleski (elbow injury), Hank Aguirre, Art Houtteman, Cal McLish, Bud Daley, Bob Feller, Sal Maglie (traded).

Autographed Ball	20.00
with Al Lopez	+5.00
with Bob Feller	+5.00
with Rocky Colavito	+5.00
with Early Wynn	+5.00

1956 Brooklyn Dodgers (National League Champs): Walt Alston, Manager; Gil Hodges, Jim Gilliam, Pee Wee Reese, Randy Jackson, Carl Furillo, Duke Snider, Sandy Amoros, Roy Campanella, Jackie Robinson, Gino Cimoli, Charlie Neal, Rube Walker, Chico Fernandez, Rocky Nelson (traded), Dale Mitchell (traded), Don Zimmer (injury), Don Newcombe, Sal Maglie (traded), Carl Erskine, Roger Craig, Clem Labine, Ed Roebuck, Don Drysdale, Don Bessent, Ken Lehman, Sandy Koufax.

Autographed Ball	10.00
with Sandy Koufax	+10.00
with Don Drysdale	+10.00
with Gil Hodges	+10.00
with J. Robinson	+20.00
with Roy Campanella	+35.00

1956 Milwaukee Braves: Charlie Grimm, Fred Haney, Managers; Joe Adcock, Danny O'Connell, Johnny Logan, Eddie Mathews, Hank Aaron, Bill Bruton, Bobby Thomson, Del Crandall, Frank Torre, Wes Covington, Del Rice, Chuck Tanner, Andy Pafko, Jack Dittmer, Felix Mantilla, Toby Atwell (traded), Jim Pendleton, Warren Spahn, Lew Burdette, Bob Buhl, Ray Crone, Gene Conley, Taylor Phillips, Ernie Johnson, Bob Trowbridge, Lou Sleater, Dave Jolly, Chet Nichols, Red Murff (back injury).

Autographed Ball	10.00
with Eddie Mathews	+10.00
with Warren Spahn	+10.00
with Hank Aaron	+35.00

1957 AMERICAN LEAGUE ALL-STAR TEAM - Charles Stengel (manager); Frank Crosetti and Jim Turner (coaches); George Kell*, Billy Loes, Gus Triandos, Frank Malzone, Ted Williams*, Nelson Fox*, Orestes Minoso, Bill Pierce, Don Mossi, Vic Wertz*, Early Wynn, Jim Bunning, Al Kaline*, Harvey Kuenn*, Charles Maxwell, Joseph DeMaestri, Yogi Berra*, Bob Grim, Elston Howard, Mickey Mantle*, Gil McDougald, Bobby Richardson, Bobby Shantz, Bill Skowron, Roy Sievers. Starters designated with an "*".

Autographed Ball	10.00
with Casey Stengel	+10.00
with Ted Williams	+35.00
with Mickey Mantle	+35.00

1957 NATIONAL LEAGUE ALL-STAR TEAM - Walt Alston (manager); Bob Scheffing and Robert Bragan (coaches); Gino Cimoli, Gil Hodges, Clem Labine, Ernie Banks, Ed Bailey, Gus Bell, Don Hoak*, Roy McMillan*, Frank Robinson*, John Temple*, Henry Aaron*, Lewis Burdette, John Logan, Edwin Mathews, Albert Schoendienst, Warren Spahn, John Antonelli, Willie Mays*, John Sanford, Curt Simmons, Henry Foiles, Larry Jackson, Wally Moon, Stan Musial*, Hal Smith. Starters designated with an "*".

Autographed Ball	10.00
with Gil Hodges	+10.00
with Hank Aaron	+20.00
with Willie Mays	+20.00
with Stan Musial	+20.00

1957 New York Yankees (American League Champs): Casey Stengel, Manager; Bill Skowron, Bobby Richardson, Gil McDougald, Andy Carey, Hank Bauer, Mickey Mantle, Enos Slaughter, Yogi Berra, Tony Kubek, Elston Howard, Joe Collins, Harry Simpson (traded), Jerry Coleman, Billy Martin (traded), Jerry Lumpe, Darrell Johnson, Bobby Del Greco (traded), Woodie Held (traded), Tom Sturdivant, Bob Turley, Bob Grim, Bobby Shantz, Whitey Ford (shoulder injury), Don Larsen, Art Ditmar, Johnny Kucks, Tommy Byrne, Sal Maglie (traded), Al Cicotte, Ralph Terry (traded).

Autographed Ball	10.00
with Whitey Ford	+10.00
with Billy Martin	+10.00
with Casey Stengel	+10.00
with Mickey Mantle	+40.00

1957 Chicago White Sox: Al Lopez, Manager; Earl Torgeson, Nellie Fox, Luis Aparicio, Bubba Phillips, Jim Rivera, Larry Doby, Minnie Minoso, Sherm Lollar (broken wrist), Jim Landis, Sammy Esposito, Walt Dropo, Fred Hatfield, Earl Battey, Les Moss, Ron Northey (traded), Ted Beard, Dave Philley (traded), Ron Jackson, Billy Pierce, Dick Donovan, Jim Wilson, Bob Keegan, Jack Harshman, Bill Fischer, Dixie Howell, Gerry Staley, Don Rudolph, Barry Latman, Paul LaPalme, Jim Derrington, Jim McDonald.

Autographed Ball	15.00
with Nellie Fox	+10.00
with Al Lopez	+10.00

1957 Milwaukee Braves (WORLD CHAMPIONS): Fred Haney, Manager; Frank Torre, Red Schoendienst (traded), Johnny Logan, Eddie Mathews, Hank Aaron, Bill Bruton (knee injury), Wes Covington, Del Crandall, Andy Pafko, Felix Mantilla, Joe Adcock (broken leg), Carl Sawatski, Del Rice (broken finger), Danny O'Connell (traded), Bob Hazle, Bobby Thomson, John DeMerit, Nippy Jones, Chuck Tanner (traded), Dick Cole, Bobby Malkmus, Warren Spahn, Bob Buhl, Lew Burdette, Gene Conley, Ernie Johnson, Bob Trowbridge, Juan Pizarro, Ray Crone (traded), Taylor Phillips, Red Murff, Don McMahon, Dave Jolly.

Autographed Ball	10.00
with Eddie Mathews	+10.00
with Warren Spahn	+10.00
with Hank Aaron	+40.00

1957 St. Louis Cardinals: Fred Hutchinson, Manager; Stan Musial, Don Blasingame, Al Dark, Eddie Kasko, Del Ennis, Ken Boyer, Wally Moon, Hal Smith, Joe Cunningham, Bobby Gene Smith, Hobie Landrith, Dick Schofield, Eddie Miksis (traded), Walker Cooper, Jim King, Irv Noren (traded), Chuck Harmon, Tom Alston (illness), Larry Jackson, Lindy McDaniel, Sam Jones, Willard Schmidt, Herm Wehmeier, Vinegar Bend Mizell, Von McDaniel, Murry Dickson, Billy Muffett, Lloyd Merritt, Hoyt Wilhelm (traded), Jim Davis (traded).

Autographed Ball	10.00
with Fred Hutchinson	+10.00
with Stan Musial	+35.00

1957 Brooklyn Dodgers: Walt Alston, Manager; Gil Hodges, Jim Gilliam, Charlie Neal, Pee Wee Reese, Carl Furillo, Duke Snider, Gino Cimoli, Roy Campanella, Sandy Amoros, Don Zimmer, Elmer Valo, Rube Walker, Randy Jackson (knee injury), Johnny Roseboro, Bob Kennedy (traded), Joe Pignatano, Jim Gentile, Don Drysdale, Johnny Podres, Don Newcombe, Ed Roebuck, Danny McDevitt, Sal Maglie (traded), Roger Craig, Carl Erskine (sore arm), Sandy Koufax, Clem Labine, Rene Valdes, Don Bessent.

Autographed Ball	20.00
with Sandy Koufax	+10.00
with Gil Hodges	+10.00
with Roy Campanella	+35.00

1957 New York Giants: Bill Rigney, Manager; Whitey Lockman, Danny O'Connell (traded), Daryl Spencer, Ray Jablonski, Don Mueller, Willie Mays, Hank Sauer, Valmy Thomas, Ozzie Virgil, Dusty Rhodes, Gail Harris, Bobby Thomson (traded), Ray Katt, Wes Westrum, Red Schoendienst (traded), Ed Bressoud, Andre Rodgers, Foster Castleman, Ruben Gomez, Johnny Antonelli, Curt Barclay, Al Worthington, Stu Miller, Marv Grissom, Ray Crone (traded), Mike McCormick, Ray Monzant, Jim Davis (traded), Jim Constable, Joe Margoneri, Pete Burnside, Gordon Jones, Steve Ridzik.

Autographed Ball	10.00
with Willie Mays	+40.00

1958 AMERICAN LEAGUE ALL-STAR TEAM - Casey Stengel (mgr.); Lum Harris and Jim Turner (coaches); Bill O'Dell, Gus Triandos, Jack Jensen*, Frank Malzone*, Ted Williams, Luis Aparicio*, Nelson Fox*, Sherm Lollar, Billy Pierce, Early Wynn, Ray Narleski, Mickey Vernon, Al Kaline, Harvey Kuenn, Bob Cerv*, Yogi Berra, Rinold Duren, Whitey Ford, Elston Howard, Tony Kubek, Mickey Mantle*, Gil McDougald, Bill Skowron*, Bob Turley, Rocky Bridges. Starters designated with an "*".

Autographed Ball	10.00
with Casey Stengel	+10.00
with Ted Williams	+35.00
with Mickey Mantle	+35.00

1958 NATIONAL LEAGUE ALL-STAR TEAM - Fred Haney (mgr.); Bill Rigney and Mayo Smith (coaches); Ernie Banks*, Walt Moryn, Lee Walls, George Crowe, Robert Purkey, John Podres, John Roseboro, Henry Aaron*, Del Crandall*, John Logan, Ed Mathews, Don McMahon, Warren Spahn, Richie Ashburn, Richard Farrell, Bob Friend, Bill Mazeroski*, Bob Skinner*, Frank Thomas*, Don Blasingame, Larry Jackson, Stan Musial*, John Antonelli, Willie Mays*, Bob Schmidt. Starters designated with an "*".

Autographed Ball	20.00
with Hank Aaron	+20.00
with Willie Mays	+20.00
with Stan Musial	+20.00

1958 New York Yankees (WORLD CHAMPIONS): Casey Stengel, Manager; Bill Skowron, Gil McDougald, Tony Kubek, Andy Carey, Hank Bauer, Mickey Mantle, Norm Siebern, Yogi Berra, Elston Howard, Jerry Lumpe, Enos Slaughter, Bobby Richardson, Marv Throneberry, Harry Simpson (traded), Bobby Del Greco, Bob Turley, Whitey Ford, Don Larsen (elbow injury), Art Ditmar, Johnny Kucks, Duke Maas (traded), Bobby Shantz, Ryne Duren, Zack Monroe, Tom Sturdivant (sore arm), Virgil Trucks (traded), Sal Maglie (traded), Murry Dickson (traded), Bob Grim (traded).

Autographed Ball	20.00
with Casey Stengel	+10.00
with Mickey Mantle	+50.00

1958 Chicago White Sox: Al Lopez, Manager; Ray Boone (traded), Nellie Fox, Luis Aparicio, Billy Goodman, Jim Rivera, Jim Landis, Al Smith, Sherm Lollar, Sammy Esposito, Earl Torgeson, Bubba Phillips (injury), Don Mueller, Earl Battey, Ron Jackson, Tito Francona (traded), Walt Dropo (traded), Ted Beard, Johnny Callison, Norm Cash, Jim McAnany, Billy Pierce, Dick Donovan, Early Wynn, Ray Moore, Jim Wilson, Bob Shaw (traded), Gerry Staley, Barry Latman, Turk Lown (traded), Bill Fischer (traded), Don Rudolph, Hal Trosky, Bob Keegan, Tom Qualters (traded).

Autographed Ball	15.00
with Al Lopez	+10.00
with Nellie Fox	+10.00

1958 Milwaukee Braves (National League Champs): Fred Haney, Manager; Frank Torre, Red Schoendienst (illness), Johnny Logan, Eddie Mathews, Hank Aaron, Bill Bruton (knee injury), Wes Covington, Del Crandall, Joe Adcock, Andy Pafko, Felix Mantilla, Harry Hanebrink, Mel Roach (knee injury), Del Rice, Casey Wise, Bob Hazle (traded), Joe Koppe, Warren Spahn, Lew Burdette, Bob Rush, Carl Willey, Don McMahon, Joey Jay, Juan Pizarro, Bob Buhl (sore arm), Ernie Johnson, Humberto Robinson, Bob Trowbridge, Dick Littlefield, Gene Conley (arm injury).

Autographed Ball	10.00
with Eddie Mathews	+10.00
with Warren Spahn	+10.00
with Hank Aaron	+30.00

1958 Pittsburgh Pirates: Danny Murtaugh, Manager; Ted Kluszewski, Bill Mazeroski, Dick Groat, Frank Thomas, Roberto Clemente, Bill Virdon, Bob Skinner, Hank Foiles, Roman Mejias, Dick Stuart, R.C. Stevens, Johnny Powers, Bill Hall, Danny Kravitz, Gene Baker (knee injury), Dick Schofield (traded), Gene Freese (traded), Harry Bright, Bob Friend, Vern Law, Ron Kline, George Witt, Curt Raydon, Roy Face, Don Gross, Bob Porterfield (traded), Ron Blackburn, Bob Smith.

Autographed Ball	10.00
with Danny Murtaugn	+10.00
with Rob Clemente	+30.00

1958 Los Angeles Dodgers: Walt Alston, Manager; Gil Hodges, Charlie Neal, Don Zimmer, Dick Gray, Carl Furillo, Duke Snider, Gino Cimoli, Johnny Roseboro, Jim Gilliam, Norm Larker, Elmer Valo, Joe Pignatano, Pee Wee Reese, Steve Bilko (traded), Don Demeter, Randy Jackson (traded), Rube Walker, Bob Lillis, Ron Fairly, Johnny Podres, Don Drysdale, Sandy Koufax, Stan Williams, Clem Labine, Fred Kipp, Carl Erskine, Johnny Klippstein, Roger Craig, Danny McDevitt, Don Bessent (sore arm), Ed Roebuck, Don Newcombe (traded), Babe Birrer, Larry Sherry.

Autographed Ball	20.00
with Don Drysdale	+10.00
with Duke Snider	+10.00
with Sandy Koufax	+10.00
with Gil Hodges	+10.00

1958 San Francisco Giants: Bill Rigney, Manager; Orlando Cepeda, Danny O'Connell, Daryl Spencer, Jim Davenport, Willie Kirkland, Willie Mays, Felipe Alou, Bob Schmidt, Whitey Lockman, Hank Sauer, Ray Jablonski, Leon Wagner, Ed Bressoud, Bob Speake, Valmy Thomas, Don Taussig, Jim King, Bill White (military service), Jim Finigan, Andre Rodgers, Jackie Brandt (military service), Johnny Antonelli, Al Worthington, Mike McCormick, Ruben Gomez, Ray Monzant, Marv Grissom, Stu Miller, Paul Giel, Gordon Jones, Jim Constable (traded), Curt Barclay, Ray Crone, Don Johnson.

Autographed Ball	20.00
with Orlando Cepeda	+10.00
with Willie Mays	+30.00

1959 AMERICAN LEAGUE ALL-STAR TEAM - Casay Stengel (mgr.); Tony Cuccinello and Harry Craft (coaches); Gus Triandos*, Hoyt Wilhelm, Frank Malzone, Pete Runnels, Ted Williams, Luis Aparicio*, Nelson Fox*, Sherm Lollar, Billy Pierce, Early Wynn, Rocco Colavito*, Orestes Minoso*, Vic Power, Jim Bunning, Al Kaline*, Harvey Kueen, Buddy Daley, Yogi Berra, Ryne Duren, Edward (Whitey) Ford, Mickey Mantle, Gil McDougald, Bill Skowron*, Harmon Killebrew*, Roy Sievers; Second Game - Bunning, Ford, Kuenn, McDougald, Pierce, Skowon (players replaced); Additions for Second Game - Frank Crosetti and Harry Lavagetto (coaches); William O'Dell, Jerry Walker, Eugene Woodling, Cal McLish, Roger Maris, Elston Howard, Tony Kubek, Robert Richardson, Camilo Pascual (replaced by Pedro Ramos), Bob Allison. Starters designated with an "*".

Autographed Ball	15.00
with Casey Stengel	+10.00
with Ted Williams	+35.00
with Mickey Mantle	+35.00

1959 NATIONAL LEAGUE ALL-STAR TEAM - Fred Haney (mgr.); Edwin Sawyer and Dan Murtaugh (coaches); Ernie Banks*, Vada Pinson, Frank Robinson, John Temple*, Don Drysdale, Wally Moon*, Henry Aaron*, Lew Burdette, Del Crandall*, Ed Mathews*, Warren Spahn, Gene Conley, Forrest Burgess, Roy Face, Dick Groat, Bill Mazeroski, Ken Boyer, Joe Cunningham, Wilmer Mizell (replaced by Don Elston), Stan Musial, Hal Smith, Bill White, John Antonelli, Orlando Cepeda*, Willie Mays*; Second Game - White (player replaced); Additions for Second Game - Billy Herman and John Fitzpatrick (coaches); Jim Gilliam, Charles Neal, John Logan, Sam Jones. Starters designated with an "*".

Autographed Ball	10.00
with Dan Murtaugh	+10.00
with Hank Aaron	+20.00
with Willie Mays	+20.00
with Stan Musial	+20.00

THE INCREMENTAL VALUE OF THE AUTOGRAPH OF A PARTICULAR PLAYER TO A PARTICULAR BALL IS UNIQUE TO THAT BALL. IT IS NOT THE EXOGENOUS VALUE OF THAT PLAYER'S AUTOGRAPH. SEE THE INTRODUCTION TO TEAM AUTOGRAPHED BALLS.

1959 Chicago White Sox (American League Champs): Al Lopez, Manager; Earl Torgeson, Nellie Fox, Luis Aparicio, Bubba Phillips, Jim McAnany, Jim Landis, Al Smith, Sherm Lollar, Billy Goodman, Jim Rivera, Sammy Esposito, Norm Cash, Johnny Romano, Johnny Callison, Harry Simpson (traded), Ted Kluszewski (traded), Del Ennis (traded), Earl Battey, Larry Doby (broken ankle)(traded), Ron Jackson, Early Wynn, Bob Shaw, Billy Pierce, Turk Lown, Dick Donovan, Gerry Staley, Barry Latman, Ray Moore, Rudy Arias, Joe Stanka, Ken McBride, Gary Peters.

Autographed Ball	20.00
with Al Lopez	+10.00
with Nellie Fox	+10.00
with Early Wynn	+10.00

LUIS APARICIO SS

AL LOPEZ Manager

NELLIE FOX 2nd

EARLY WYNN P.

1959 Cleveland Indians: Joe Gordon, Manager; Vic Power, Billy Martin (injury), Woodie Held, George Strickland, Rocky Colavito, Jimmy Piersall, Minnie Minoso, Russ Nixon, Tito Francona, Jim Baxes (traded), Ed Fitzgerald (injured)(traded), Dick Brown, Ray Webster, Elmer Valo, Carroll Hardy, Granny Hamner (traded), Hal Naragon (traded), Chuck Tanner, Gene Leek, Cal McLish, Gary Bell, Jim Perry, Mudcat Grant, Herb Score, Jack Harshman (traded), Don Ferrarese, Al Cicotte, Bobby Locke, Mike Garcia, Dick Brodowski, Riverboat Smith (traded).

Autographed Ball	20.00
with Dick Brown	+5.00
with Joe Gordon	+10.00
with Billy Martin	+10.00

1959 Los Angeles Dodgers (WORLD CHAMPIONS): Walt Alston, Manager; Gil Hodges, Charlie Neal, Don Zimmer, Jim Gilliam, Duke Snider, Don Demeter, Wally Moon, Johnny Roseboro, Ron Fairly, Norm Larker, Maury Wills, Rip Repulski, Joe Pignatano, Carl Furillo, Bob Lillis, Chuck Essegian (traded), Dick Gray (traded), Jim Baxes (traded), Frank Howard, Solly Drake (traded), Don Drysdale, Johnny Podres, Roger Craig, Danny McDevitt, Sandy Koufax, Larry Sherry, Stan Williams, Johnny Klippstein, Clem Labine, Chuck Churn, Art Fowler, Gene Snyder, Carl Erskine.

Autographed Ball	30.00
with Don Drysdale	+10.00
with Sandy Koufax	+10.00
with Gil Hodges	+10.00

WALTER ALSTON MGR

MAURY WILLS SS

DON DRYSDALE P

SANDY KOUFAX P

1959 Milwaukee Braves: Fred Haney, Manager; Joe Adcock, Felix Mantilla, Johnny Logan, Eddie Mathews, Hank Aaron, Bill Bruton, Wes Covington (knee injury), Del Crandall, Frank Torre, Mickey Vernon, Andy Pafko, Bobby Avila (traded), Lee Maye, Johnny O'Brien, Stan Lopata, Casey Wise, Enos Slaughter (traded), Lew Burdette, Warren Spahn, Bob Buhl (sore arm), Juan Pizarro, Joey Jay, Don McMahon, Bob Rush, Carl Willey, Bob Trowbridge, Bob Giggie.

Autographed Ball	10.00
with Eddie Mathews	+10.00
with Warren Spahn	+10.00
with Hank Aaron	+30.00

1960 AMERICAN LEAGUE ALL-STAR TEAM - Al Lopez (mgr.); Tony Cuccinello and Don Gutteridge (coaches); Chuck Estrada, Jim Gentile, Ron Hansen*, Brooks Robinson, Frank Malzone*, Bill Monbouquette, Pete Runnels*, Ted Williams, Luis Aparicio, Nelson Fox, Sherm Lollar, Orestes Minoso*, Al Smith, Gerald Staley, Early Wynn, Gary Bell, Harvey Kuenn, Vic Power, Dick Stigman, Al Kaline, Frank Lary, Buddy Daley, Lawrence Berra*, Jim Coates, Edward Ford, Elston Howard, Mickey Mantle*, Roger Maris*, Bill Skowron*, Camilo Pascual (replaced by Jim Lemon). Starters designated with an "*".

Autographed Ball	20.00
with Ted Williams	+30.00
with Mickey Mantle	+30.00

1960 NATIONAL LEAGUE ALL-STAR TEAM - Walt Alston (mgr.); Fred Hutchinson and Solly Hemus (coaches); Ernie Banks*, Ed Bailey, Bill Henry, Vada Pinson*, Norm Larker, Charles Neal, John Podres, Stan Williams, Hank Aaron*, Joe Adcock*, Bob Buhl, Del Crandall*, Ed Mathews*, Tony Taylor, Smokey Burgess, Roberto Clemente, Roy Face, Bob Friend, Richard Groat, Vern Law, Will Mazeroski*, Bob Skinner, Ken Boyer, Lawrence Jackson, Lyndall McDaniel, Stan Musial, William White, Orlando Cepeda, Willie Mays*, Mike McCormick. Starters designated with an "*".

Autographed Ball	10.00
with Fred Hutchinson	+10.00
with Hank Aaron	+15.00
with Willie Mays	+15.00
with Stan Musial	+15.00
with Rob Clemente	+20.00

1960 New York Yankees (American League Champs): Casey Stengel, Manager; Bill Skowron, Bobby Richardson, Tony Kubek, Clete Boyer, Roger Maris, Mickey Mantle, Hector Lopez, Elston Howard, Yogi Berra, Gil McDougald, Bob Cerv (traded), Kent Hadley, Johnny Blanchard (illness), Joe DeMaestri, Dale Long (traded), Ken Hunt, Jim Pisoni, Art Ditmar, Jim Coates, Whitey Ford, Ralph Terry, Bob Turley, Eli Grba, Duke Maas, Luis Arroyo, Johnny James, Bobby Shantz, Bill Stafford, John Gabler, Ryne Duren, Bill Short.

Autographed Ball	15.00
with Roger Maris	+10.00
with Casey Stengel	+10.00
with Mickey Mantle	+50.00

1960 Baltimore Orioles: Paul Richards, Manager; Jim Gentile, Marv Breeding, Ron Hansen, Brooks Robinson, Gene Stephens (traded), Jackie Brandt, Gene Woodling, Gus Triandos (hand injury), Al Pilarcik, Clint Courtney, Walt Dropo, Jim Busby (traded), Bob Boyd, Dave Nicholson, Albie Pearson, Billy Klaus, Willie Tasby (traded), Chuck Estrada, Milt Pappas, Hal Brown, Jack Fisher, Hoyt Wilhelm, Steve Barber, Arnie Portocarrero, Jerry Walker, Billy Hoeft, Wes Stock, Gordon Jones.
Autographed Ball 20.00
with Brooks Robinson +20.00

1960 Washington Senators: Cookie Lavagetto, Manager; Julio Becquer, Billy Gardner, Jose Valdivielso, Reno Bertoia, Bob Allison, Lenny Green, Jim Lemon, Earl Battey, Harmon Killebrew, Dan Dobbek, Billy Consolo, Faye Throneberry, Elmer Valo (traded), Pete Whisenant (traded), Hal Naragon, Don Mincher, Zoilo Versalles, Chuck Stobbs, Camilo Pascual, Pedro Ramos, Jack Kralick, Don Lee, Tex Clevenger, Rudy Hernandez, Hal Woodeshick, Ray Moore (traded), Bill Fischer (traded), Ted Sadowski, Tom Morgan (traded), Jim Kaat, Dick Hyde.
Autographed Ball 20.00
with Harm. Killebrew +20.00

1960 Pittsburgh Pirates (WORLD CHAMPIONS): Danny Murtaugh, Mgr.; Dick Stuart, Bill Mazeroski, Dick Groat, Don Hoak, Roberto Clemente, Bill Virdon, Bob Skinner, Smoky Burgess, Gino Cimoli, Rocky Nelson, Hal Smith, Dick Schofield, Joe Christopher, Gene Baker, Bob Oldis, Vern Law, Bob Friend, Wilmer Mizell (traded), Harvey Haddix, Roy Face, Fred Green, Joe Gibbon, Clem Labine (traded), Paul Giel, Tom Cheney, Earl Francis, Jim Umbricht, George Witt, Bennie Daniels, Don Gross, Diomedes Olivo.
Autographed Ball 10.00
with Danny Murtaugh +10.00
with Don Hoak +10.00
with Jim Umbricht +10.00
with Rob. Clemente +30.00

1960 MilwaukeeBraves: Chuck Dressen, Manager; Joe Adcock, Chuck Cottier, Johnny Logan, Eddie Mathews, Hank Aaron, Bill Bruton, Wes Covington, Del Crandall, Al Spangler, Red Schoendienst, Felix Mantilla, Al Dark (traded), Mel Roach, Lee Maye, Eddie Haas, Frank Torre, Charlie Lau, Ray Boone (traded), Warren Spahn, Lew Burdette, Bob Buhl, Joey Jay, Cal Willey, Juan Pizarro, Ron Piche, Don McMahon, George Brunet (traded), Bob Rush (traded), Don Nottebart, Ken MacKenzie.
Autographed Ball 5.00
with Chuck Dressen +10.00
with Eddie Mathews +10.00
with Warren Spahn +10.00
with Hank Aaron +20.00

1961 AMERICAN LEAGUE ALL-STAR TEAM - Paul Richards (mgr.); Frank Crosetti and James Vernon (coaches); John Brandt, Jim Gentile, Brooks Robinson*, Hoyt Wilhelm, Miguel Fornieles, Nelson Fox, Billy Pierce, Jim Perry, John Romano*, John Temple*, Norm Cash*, Rocco Colavito*, Al Kaline, Frank Lary, Jim Bunning, Dick Howser, Rinold Duren, Harmon Killebrew, Yogi Berra, Whitey Ford, Elston Howard, Tony Kubek*, Mickey Mantle*, Roger Maris*, Dick Donovan; 2nd Game - Duren, Fornieles, Lary, Perry, Pierce (players replaced); Additions 2nd Game - James Adair and Mike Higgins (coaches); Don Schwall, Roy Sievers, Luis Aparicio, Tito Francona, Barry Latman, Ken McBride, Camilo Pascual, Luis Arroyo, Bill Skowron. Starters designated with an "*".
Autographed Ball 35.00
with Mickey Mantle +40.00

1961 NATIONAL LEAGUE ALL-STAR TEAM - Dan Murtaugh (manager); Gene Mauch and Al Dark (coaches); George Altman, Don Zimmer, Joe Jay, Ed Kasko, Bob Purkey, Frank Robinson, Sandy Koufax, John Roseboro, Maury Wills*, Henry Aaron, Frank Bolling*, Ed Mathews*, Warren Spahn, Art Mahaffey, Forrest (Smokey) Burgess*, Roberto Clemente*, Roy Face, Dick Stuart, Ken Boyer, Stan Musial, Bill White*, Orlando Cepeda*, Willie Mays*, Mike McCormick, Stu Miller; Additions 2nd Game - El Tappe and Charles Dressen (coaches); Ernest Banks, Don Drysdale, Ed Bailey. Starters designated with an "*".
Autographed Ball 10.00
with Danny Murtaugh +5.00
with Willie Mays +15.00
with Stan Musial +15.00
with Hank Aaron +15.00
with Rob. Clemente +20.00

1961 New York Yankees (WORLD CHAMPIONS): Ralph Houk, Manager; Bill Skowron, Bobby Richardson, Tony Kubek, Clete Boyer, Roger Maris, Mickey Mantle, Yogi Berra, Elston Howard, Hector Lopez, Johnny Blanchard, Bob Cerv (traded), Billy Gardner, Joe DeMaestri, Jack Reed, Earl Torgeson (traded), Jesse Gonder, Deron Johnson (traded), Whitey Ford, Ralph Terry, Luis Arroyo, Bill Stafford, Jim Coates, Rollie Sheldon, Bud Daley (traded), Bob Turley (sore arm), Hal Reniff, Art Ditmar (traded), Tex Clevenger (traded), Danny McDevitt (traded), Al Downing, Ryne Duren (traded).
Autographed Ball 30.00
with Roger Maris +20.00
with Mickey Mantle +50.00

1961 Detroit Tigers: Bob Scheffing, Manager; Norm Cash, Jake Wood, Chico Fernandez, Steve Boros (injury), Al Kaline, Bill Bruton, Rocky Colavito, Dick Brown (injury), Mike Roarke, Dick McAuliffe, Charlie Maxwell, Bubba Morton, Bobo Osborne, Reno Bertoia (traded), Ozzie Virgil (traded), Frank House, George Thomas (traded), Chuck Cottier (traded), Frank Lary, Jim Bunning, Don Mossi, Paul Foytack, Phil Regan, Terry Fox, Ron Kline (traded), Hank Aguirre, Bill Fischer (traded), Howie Koplitz, Fred Gladding, Joe Grzenda, Jim Donohue (traded), Gerry Staley (traded), Hal Woodeshick (traded), Bob Bruce (eye injury), Manny Montejo.
Autographed Ball 20.00
with Al Kaline +25.00

1961 Minnesota Twins: Cookie Lavagetto, Sam Mele, Managers; Harmon Killebrew, Billy Martin (traded), Zoilo Versalles, Bill Tuttle (traded), Bob Allison, Lenny Green, Jim Lemon, Earl Battey, Jose Valdivielso, Dan Dobbek, Hal Naragon, Julio Becquer (traded), Ted Lepcio (traded), Billy Gardner (traded), Joe Altobelli, Reno Bertoia (traded), Don Mincher, Elmer Valo (traded), Camilo Pascual, Jack Kralick, Pedro Ramos, Jim Kaat, Bill Pleis, Ray Moore, Al Schroll, Don Lee, Chuck Stobbs, Danny McDevitt (traded), Paul Giel (traded), Lee Stange, Ed Palmquist (traded), Ted Sadowski.
Autographed Ball 20.00
with Billy Martin +10.00
with Harm. Killebrew +30.00

1961 Washington Senators: Mickey Vernon, Manager; Dale Long, Chuck Cottier (traded), Coot Veal, Danny O'Connell, Marty Keough, Willie Tasby, Chuck Hinton, Gene Green, Gene Woodling, Jim King, Billy Klaus, Pete Daley, Harry Bright, Bob Johnson, Bud Zipfel, Jim Mahoney, R.C. Stevens, Ken Retzer, Bennie Daniels, Dick Donovan, Joe McClain, Ed Hobaugh, Mary Kutyna, Pete Burnside, Hal Woodeshick (traded), John Gabler, Johnny Klippstein, Tom Sturdivant (traded), Dave Sisler, Claude Osteen (traded), Tom Cheney (sore arm) (traded), Mike Garcia.

Autographed Ball	45.00
with Danny O'Connell	+5.00

1961 Los Angeles Angels: Bill Rigney, Manager; Steve Bilko, Ken Aspromonte (traded), Joe Koppe (traded), Eddie Yost (injury), Albie Pearson, Ken Hunt, Leon Wagner, Earl Averill, Lee Thomas (traded), Ted Kluszewski, Rocky Bridges, George Thomas (traded), Eddie Sadowski, Gene Leek, Billy Moran, Del Rice, Ken Hamlin, Tom Satriano, Fritzie Brickell, Bob Cerv (traded), Bob Rodgers, Ken McBride, Ted Bowsfield, Eli Grba, Tom Morgan, Ryne Duren (traded), Art Fowler, Jim Donohue (traded), Ron Moeller, Jack Spring, Ron Kline (traded), Tex Clevenger (traded), Jerry Casale (traded), Johnny James (traded), Dean Chance, Ned Garver.

Autographed Ball	45.00
with Fritz Brickell	+5.00
with Steve Bilko	+5.00

1961 Cincinnati Reds (National League Champs): Fred Hutchinson, Manager; Gordy Coleman, Don Blasingame (traded), Eddie Kasko, Gene Freese, Frank Robinson, Vada Pinson, Wally Post, Jerry Zimmerman, Gus Bell, Jerry Lynch, Leo Cardenas, Elio Chacon, Johnny Edwards, Dick Gernert (traded), Bob Schmidt (traded), Pete Whisenant (traded), Darrell Johnson (traded), Ed Bailey (traded), Joey Jay, Jim O'Toole, Bob Purkey, Jim Brosnan, Ken Hunt, Ken Johnson (traded), Jim Maloney, Bill Henry, Howie Nunn (elbow injury), Sherman Jones, Jay Hook, Marshall Bridges.

Autographed Ball	15.00
with Gus Bell	+5.00
with Fred Hutchinson	+10.00
with Frank Robinson	+20.00

1961 Los Angeles Dodgers: Walt Alston, Manager; Norm Larker, Charlie Neal, Maury Wills, Jim Gilliam, Tommy Davis, Willie Davis, Wally Moon, Johnny Roseboro, Ron Fairly, Gil Hodges, Frank Howard, Duke Snider (injury), Daryl Spencer (traded), Norm Sherry, Bob Aspromonte, Gordie Windhorn, Carl Warwick (traded), Don Demeter (traded), Doug Camilli, Johnny Podres, Sandy Koufax, Stan Williams, Don Drysdale, Ron Perranoski, Dick Farrell (traded), Roger Craig, Larry Sherry, Ed Roebuck (shoulder injury), Jim Golden.

Autographed Ball	10.00
with Dick Farrell	+10.00
with Gil Hodges	+10.00
with Sandy Koufax	+10.00
with Duke Snider	+10.00

1962 AMERICAN LEAGUE ALL-STAR TEAM - Ralph Houk (mgr.); Billy Hitchcock and Mickey Vernon (coaches); Jim Gentile*, Brooks Robinson, Hoyt Wilhelm (replaced by Milt Pappas), Bill Monbouquette, Luis Aparicio*, Jim Landis, Dick Donovan, John Romano, Hank Aguirre, Jim Bunning, Rocco Colavito, Norm Siebern, Billy Moran*, LeRoy Thomas, Leon Wagner*, Earl Battey*, Camilo Pascual, Richard Rollins*, Elston Howard, Mickey Mantle*, Roger Maris*, Bobby Richardson, Ralph Terry, Tom Tresh, David Stenhouse; Second Game - Monbouquette, Landis (players replaced); Additions for Second Game - Henry Bauer and Bill Rigney (coaches); Pete Runnels, Al Kaline, Ken McBride (replaced by Ray Herbert), Jim Kaat, Yogi Berra. Starters designated with an "*".

Autographed Ball	40.00
with Mickey Mantle	+40.00

1962 NATIONAL LEAGUE ALL-STAR TEAM - Fred Hutchinson (mgr.); Casey Stengel and John Keane (coaches); Ernie Banks, Bob Purkey, Dick Farrell, Tommy Davis*, Don Drysdale, Sandy Koufax, John Roseboro, Maury Wills, Hank Aaron (replaced by Warren Spahn), Frank Bolling, Del Crandall*, Robert Shaw, Richie Ashburn, John Callison, Roberto Clemente*, Dick Groat*, Bill Mazeroski*, Ken Boyer*, Bob Gibson, Stan Musial, Felipe Alou, Orlando Cepeda*, Jim Davenport, Juan Marichal, Willie Mays*; 2nd Game - Koufax, Shaw, Drysdale, Alou (players replaced); Additions for 2nd Game - Harry Craft and George Tebbetts (coaches); Billy Williams, George Altman, Frank Robinson, John Podres, Hank Aaron, Ed Mathews, Art Mahaffey. Starters designated with an "*".

Autographed Ball	10.00
with Fred Hutchinson	+5.00
with Casey Stengel	+10.00
with Willie Mays	+15.00
with Stan Musial	+15.00
with Hank Aaron	+15.00
with Rob. Clemente	+20.00

1962 New York Yankees (WORLD CHAMPIONS): Ralph Houk, Manager; Bill Skowron, Bobby Richardson, Tom Tresh, Clete Boyer, Roger Maris, Mickey Mantle (knee injury), Hector Lopez, Elston Howard, Johnny Blanchard, Jack Reed, Yogi Berra, Phil Linz, Joe Pepitone, Tony Kubek (military service), Dale Long (traded), Bob Cerv (traded), Ralph Terry, Whitey Ford, Bill Stafford, Marshall Bridges, Bud Daley, Jim Coates, Jim Bouton, Rollie Sheldon, Bob Turley, Tex Clevenger, Luis Arroyo (sore arm).

Autographed Ball	25.00
with Yogi Berra	+10.00
with Mickey Mantle	+40.00

1962 Minnesota Twins: Sam Mele, Manager; Vic Power, Bernie Allen, Zoilo Versalles, Rich Rollins, Bob Allison, Lenny Green, Harmon Killebrew, Earl Battey, Bill Tuttle, Don Mincher, George Banks, Johnny Goryl, Marty Martinez, Jerry Zimmerman, Hal Naragon, Jim Lemon (injury), Tony Oliva, Camilo Pascual, Jim Kaat, Dick Stigman, Jack Kralick, Ray Moore, Joe Bonikowski, Frank Sullivan (traded), Lee Stange, Don Lee (traded), Bill Pleis, Ted Sadowski, Ruben Gomez (traded), George Maranda.

Autographed Ball	10.00
with Tony Oliva	+10.00
with Harm. Killebrew	+20.00

1962 San Francisco Giants (National League Champs): Al Dark, Manager; Orlando Cepeda, Chuck Hiller, Jose Pagan, Jim Davenport, Felipe Alou, Willie Mays, Harvey Kuenn, Tom Haller, Ed Bailey, Willie McCovey, Matty Alou, Manny Mota, Ernie Bowman, Bob Nieman (traded), Carl Boles, John Orsino, Jack Sanford, Billy O'Dell, Juan Marichal, Billy Pierce, Bobby Bolin, Don Larsen, Mike McCormick (sore arm), Stu Miller, Gaylord Perry, Jim Duffalo.

Autographed Ball 10.00
with Juan Marichal +10.00
with Willie McCovey +10.00
with Willie Mays +20.00

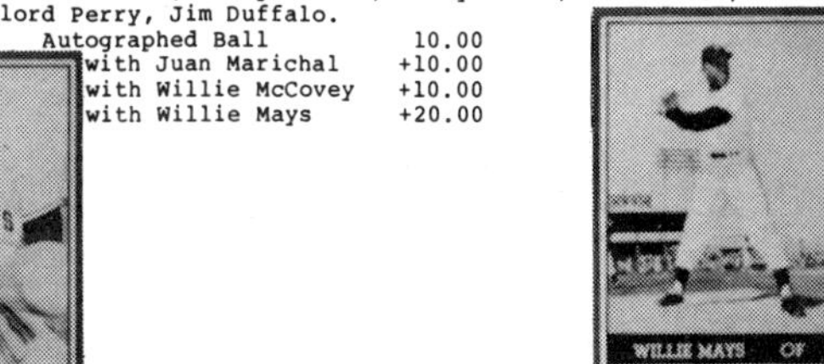

1962 Los Angeles Dodgers: Walt Alston, Manager; Ron Fairly, Jim Gilliam, Maury Wills, Daryl Spencer, Frank Howard, Willie Davis, Tommy Davis, Johnny Roseboro, Larry Burright, Wally Moon, Tim Harkness, Duke Snider, Lee Walls, Andy Carey, Doug Camilli, Norm Sherry, Dick Tracewski, Ken McMullen, Don Drysdale, Johnny Podres, Sandy Koufax (finger injury), Stan Williams, Ed Roebuck, Larry Sherry, Joe Moeller, Ron Perranoski, Pete Richert, Phil Ortega.

Autographed Ball 15.00
with Don Drysdale +10.00
with Sandy Koufax +10.00
with Maury Wills +10.00

1962 Houston Colts: Harry Craft, Manager; Norm Larker, Joey Amalfitano, Bob Lillis, Bob Aspromonte, Roman Mejias, Carl Warwick (traded), Al Spangler, Hal Smith, Jim Pendleton, Billy Goodman, Merritt Ranew, Pidge Browne, J.C. Hartman, Don Buddin (traded), Johnny Temple (traded), Jim Campbell, Al Heist, Bob Cerv (traded), Dave Roberts, Johnny Weekly, Bob Bruce, Dick Farrell, Jim Golden, Ken Johnson, Russ Kemmerer (traded), Don McMahon (traded), Hal Woodeshick, Jim Umbricht, Dean Stone (traded), Dave Giusti, Bobby Tiefenauer, George Brunet, Dick Drott (sore arm), Bobby Shantz (traded), George Witt (traded), John Anderson (traded).

Autographed Ball 20.00
with Johnny Weekly +10.00
with Dick Farrell +10.00
with Jim Umbricht +10.00

1962 New York Mets: Casey Stengel, Manager; Marv Throneberry (traded), Charlie Neal, Elio Chacon, Felix Mantilla, Richie Ashburn, Jim Hickman, Frank Thomas, Chris Cannizzaro, Rod Kanehl, Joe Christopher, Gene Woodling (traded), Sammy Taylor (injury) (traded), Choo Choo Coleman, Gil Hodges, Ed Bouchee, Cliff Cook (traded), Rick Herrscher, Gus Bell (traded), Joe Pignatano (traded), Sammy Drake, Hobie Landrith (traded), Jim Marshall (traded), Roger Craig, Jay Hook, Al Jackson, Ken MacKenzie, Craig Anderson, Bob Miller (traded), Galen Cisco (traded), Ray Daviault, Willard Hunter (traded), Bob Miller, Herb Moford, Larry Foss, Bob Moorhead, Vinegar Bend Mizell (traded), Sherman Jones, Dave Hillman, Clem Labine.

Autographed Ball 60.00
with Gus Bell +10.00
with Casey Stengel +10.00
with M. Throneberry +10.00
with Gil Hodges +10.00

1963 AMERICAN LEAGUE ALL-STAR TEAM - Ralph Houk (manager); John Pesky and Sam Mele (coaches); Luis Aparicio, Steve Barber (replaced by Bill Monbouquette), Brooks Robinson, Frank Malzone*, Dick Radatz, Carl Yastrzemski, Nelson Fox*, Juan Pizarro, Jim Grant, Jim Bunning, Al Kaline*, Norm Siebern, Ken McBride, Albert Pearson*, Leon Wagner*, Bob Allison, Earl Battey*, Harmon Killebrew, Zoilo Versalles*, Jim Bouton, Elston Howard, Mickey Mantle*, Joe Pepitone, Bob Richardson, Tom Tresh, Don Leppert. Mantle was sidelined with fracture of left foot when he was voted on team and was not included in squad. Starters designated with an "*".

Autographed Ball 30.00
with C. Yastrzemski +10.00
with Mickey Mantle +40.00

1963 NATIONAL LEAGUE ALL-STAR TEAM - Al Dark (manager); Bob Kennedy and Gene Mauch (coaches); Larry Jackson, Ron Santo, John Edwards, Jim O'Toole, Hal Woodeshick, Tommy Davis*, Don Drysdale, Sanford Koufax, Maury Wills, Henry Aaron*, Warren Spahn, Joe Torre, Edwin Snider, Ray Culp, Julian Javier, Ken Boyer*, Dick Groat*, Stan Musial, Bill White*, Ed Bailey*, Orlando Cepeda, Juan Marichal, Willie Mays*, Willie McCovey. Starters designated with an "*".

Autographed Ball 20.00
with Stan Musial +15.00
with Willie Mays +15.00
with Hank Aaron +15.00

1963 New York Yankees (American League Champs): Ralph Houk, Manager; Joe Pepitone, Bobby Richardson, Tony Kubek, Clete Boyer, Roger Maris, Tom Tresh, Hector Lopez, Elston Howard, Jack Reed, Johnny Blanchard, Phil Linz, Mickey Mantle (injured foot), Yogi Berra, Harry Bright (traded), Pedro Gonzalez, Dale Long, Jake Gibbs, Whitey Ford, Jim Bouton, Ralph Terry, Al Downing, Stan Williams, Steve Hamilton (traded), Hal Reniff, Bill Stafford, Bill Kunkel, Marshall Bridges, Luis Arroyo.

Autographed Ball 25.00
with Mickey Mantle +40.00

1963 Chicago White Sox: Al Lopez, Manager; Tommy McCraw, Nellie Fox, Ron Hansen, Pete Ward, Floyd Robinson, Jim Landis, Dave Nicholson, J.C. Martin, Mike Hershberger, Camilo Carreon, Al Weis, Charlie Maxwell, Joe Cunningham (collarbone), Jim Lemon (traded), Sherm Lollar, Deacon Jones, Don Buford, Gene Stephens, Ken Berry, Charley Smith, Gary Peters, Juan Pizarro, Ray Herbert, Joe Horlen, John Buzhardt (sore arm), Eddie Fisher, Hoyt Wilhelm, Dave DeBusschere, Jim Brosnan (traded), Frank Baumann (arm injury), Bruce Howard.

Autographed Ball 10.00
with Nellie Fox +10.00
with Al Lopez +10.00
with D. DeBusschere +10.00

1963 Los Angeles Dodgers (WORLD CHAMPIONS): Walt Alston, Manager; Ron Fairly, Jim Gilliam, Maury Wills, Ken McMullen, Frank Howard, Willie Davis, Tommy Davis, Johnny Roseboro, Wally Moon, Dick Tracewski, Bill Skowron, Nate Oliver, Lee Walls, Doug Camilli, Don Zimmer (traded), Al Ferrara, Marv Breeding (traded), Sandy Koufax, Don Drysdale, Ron Perranoski, Johnny Podres, Bob Miller, Pete Richert, Dick Calmus, Nick Wilhite, Ed Roebuck (traded), Larry Sherry, Ken Rowe.

Autographed Ball 30.00
with Sandy Koufax +10.00
with Don Drysdale +10.00

1963 St. Louis Cardinals: Johnny Keane, Manager; Bill White, Julian Javier, Dick Groat, Ken Boyer, George Altman, Curt Flood, Charlie James, Tim McCarver, Stan Musial, Gary Kolb, Duke Carmel (traded), Carl Sawatski, Dal Maxvill, Gene Oliver (traded), Mike Shannon, Leo Burke (traded), Phil Gagliano, Doug Clemens, Ernie Broglio, Bob Gibson, Curt Simmons, Ray Sadecki, Ron Taylor, Bobby Shantz, Ray Washburn, Ed Bauta (traded), Lew Burdette (traded), Barney Schultz (traded), Sam Jones, Harry Fanok, Bob Humphreys, Diomedes Olivo, Ken MacKenzie (traded).

Autographed Ball	10.00
with Johnny Keane	+10.00
with Bob Gibson	+15.00
with Stan Musial	+15.00

1964 AMERICAN LEAGUE ALL-STAR TEAM - Al Lopez (manager); Tony Cuccinello and Gil Hodges (coaches); Luis Aparicio (replaced by Ed Bressoud), Brooks Robinson*, Norman Siebern, Frank Malzone, Dick Radatz, Gary Peters, Juan Pizarro, John Kralick, William Freehan, Al Kaline (replaced by Rocky Colavito), Jerry Lumpe, Jonathan Wyatt, Dean Chance, Jim Fregosi*, W. Robert Allison*, Jimmie Hall, Harmon Killebrew*, Pedro (Tony) Oliva*, Camilo Pascual, Edward (Whitey) Ford, Elston Howard*, Mickey Mantle*, Joe Pepitone, Bobby Richardson*, Chuck Hinton. Starters designated with an "*".

Autographed Ball	20.00
with Gil Hodges	+10.00
with Mickey Mantle	+40.00

1964 NATIONAL LEAGUE ALL-STAR TEAM - Walt Alston (manager); Fred Hutchinson and Charles Stengel (coaches); Richard Ellsworth, Ron Santo, Billy Williams*, Chico Cardenas, Sandy Koufax, Henry Aaron, Joseph Torre*, Ron Hunt*, Jim Bunning, John Callison, Chris Short, Forrest Burgess, Roberto Clemente*, Bill Mazeroski, Wilver Stargell, Ken Boyer*, Curtis Flood, Dick Groat*, Bill White, Orlando Cepeda*, Juan Marichal, Willie Mays. Starters designated with an "*".

Autographed Ball	20.00
with Fred Hutchinson	+5.00
with Casey Stengel	+10.00
with Willie Mays	+15.00
with Hank Aaron	+15.00
with Rob. Clemente	+20.00

1964 New York Yankees (American League Champs): Yogi Berra, Manager; Joe Pepitone, Bobby Richardson, Tony Kubek (back injury), Clete Boyer, Roger Maris, Mickey Mantle, Tom Tresh, Elston Howard, Hector Lopez, Phil Linz, Pedro Gonzalez, Johnny Blanchard, Archie Moore, Jim Bouton, Whitey Ford, Al Downing, Mel Stottlemyre, Steve Hamilton, Pete Mikkelsen, Ralph Terry, Hal Reniff, Bill Stafford, Rollie Sheldon, Bud Daley (sore arm), Pedro Ramos (traded), Stan Williams.

Autographed Ball	20.00
with Yogi Berra	+10.00
with Mickey Mantle	+35.00

1964 Chicago White Sox: Al Lopez, Manager; Tommy McCraw, Al Weis, Ron Hansen, Pete Ward, Mike Hershberger, Jim Landis, Floyd Robinson, J.C. Martin, Don Buford, Dave Nicholson, Gene Stephens, Bill Skowron (traded), Jerry McNertney, Joe Cunningham, Cam Carreon (shoulder injury), Minnie Minoso, Jeoff Long (traded), Ken Berry, Smoky Burgess (traded), Gary Peters, Juan Pizarro, Joe Horlen, Hoyt Wilhelm, John Buzhardt, Eddie Fisher, Ray Herbert (elbow injury), Fred Talbot, Don Mossi, Frank Kreutzer (traded), Frank Baumann.

Autographed Ball	20.00
with Al Lopez	+5.00
with Minnie Minoso	+5.00

1964 St. Louis Cardinals (WORLD CHAMPIONS): Johnny Keane, Mgr.; Bill White, Julian Javier, Dick Groat, Ken Boyer, Mike Shannon, Curt Flood, Lou Brock (traded), Tim McCarver, Charlie James, Carl Warwick, Bob Skinner (traded), Bob Uecker, Johnny Lewis, Phil Gagliano, Dal Maxvill, Jerry Buchek, Doug Clemens (traded), Jeoff Long (traded), Ray Sadecki, Bob Gibson, Curt Simmons, Ron Taylor, Roger Craig, Mike Cuellar, Gordie Richardson, Ray Washburn (sore arm), Ernie Broglio (traded), Bob Humphreys, Lew Burdette (traded), Glen Hobbie (traded), Barney Schultz, Bob Shantz (traded).

Autographed Ball	15.00
with Lou Brock	+15.00
with Johnny Keane	+15.00
with Bob Gibson	+15.00

1964 Cincinnati Reds: Fred Hutchinson, Dick Sisler, Mgrs.; Deron Johnson, Pete Rose, Leo Cardenas, Steve Boros, Frank Robinson, Vada Pinson, Tommy Harper, Johnny Edwards, Marty Keough, Gordy Coleman, Chico Ruiz, Mel Queen, Bobby Klaus (traded), Don Pavletich, Hal Smith, Bob Skinner (traded), Tony Perez, Jimmie Coker, Jim O'Toole, Jim Maloney, Bob Purkey, Joey Jay, Sammy Ellis, Joe Nuxhall, John Tsitouris, Billy McCool, Bill Henry, Ryne Duren (traded).

Autographed Ball	10.00
with Fred Hutchinson	+10.00
with Pete Rose	+15.00
with Frank Robinson	+15.00

1964 Philadelphia Phillies: Gene Mauch, Manager; John Hernstein, Tony Taylor, Bobby Wine, Dick Allen, Johnny Callison, Tony Gonzalez, Wes Covington, Clay Dalrymple, Ruben Amaro, Cookie Rojas, Gus Triandos, Johnny Briggs, Danny Cater (broken arm), Roy Sievers (traded), Alex Johnson, Frank Thomas (injury) (traded), Vic Power (traded), Adolfo Phillips, Costen Shockley, Jim Bunning, Chris Short, Art Mahaffey, Dennis Bennett, Ray Culp (sore arm), Jack Baldschun, Ed Roebuck (traded), Rick Wise, John Boozer, Dallas Green, Johnny Klippstein (traded), Bobby Shantz (traded), Cal McLish (sore arm), Bobby Locke, Morrie Steevens, Ryne Duren (traded), Gary Kroll (traded), Dave Bennett.

Autographed Ball	30.00
with Dick Allen	+10.00

1965 AMERICAN LEAGUE ALL-STAR TEAM - Al Lopez (manager); Don Gutteridge and Sam Mele (coaches); Milt Pappas, Brooks Robinson*, Felix Mantilla*, Carl Yastrzemski (replaced by Will Freehan), Eddie Fisher, Bill Skowron* (replaced by Joe Pepitone), Max Alvis, Rocco Colavito*, Vic Davalillo*, Sam McDowell, Willie Horton*, Al Kaline, Dick McAuliffe*, John O'Donoghue, Bob Lee, Earl Battey*, Jim Grant, Jimmie Hall, Harmon Killebrew, Zoilo Versalles, Elston Howard, Mickey Mantle (replaced by Tony Oliva), Bobby Richardson, Mel Stottlemyre, Pete Richert. Starters designated with an "*".

Autographed Ball	40.00
with Mickey Mantle	+30.00

1965 NATIONAL LEAGUE ALL-STAR TEAM - Gene Mauch (mgr.); Dick Sisler and Bobby Bragan (coaches); Ernest Banks*, Ron Santo, Billy Williams, Leonardo Cardenas, John Edwards, Sam Ellis, Jim Maloney, Frank Robinson, Pete Rose*, Dick Farrell, Don Drysdale, Sandy Koufax, Maurice Wills*, Henry Aaron*, Joe Torre*, Ed Kranepool, Richie Allen*, John Callison, Cookie Rojas, Roberto Clemente, Wilver Stargell*, Bob Veale, Bob Gibson, Juan Marichal, Willie Mays*. Starters designated with an "*".

Autographed Ball	10.00
with Pete Rose	+15.00
with Willie Mays	+15.00
with Hank Aaron	+15.00
with Rob. Clemente	+20.00

1965 Minnesota Twins (American League Champs): Sam Mele, Manager; Don Mincher, Jerry Kindall, Zoilo Versalles, Rich Rollins, Tony Oliva, Jimmie Hall, Bob Allison, Earl Battey, Harmon Killebrew (elbow injury), Sandy Valdespino, Joe Nossek, Jerry Zimmerman, Frank Quilici, Andy Kosco, Frank Kostro, Bernie Allen (knee injury), Cesar Tovar, Rich Reese, Ted Uhlaender, John Sevcik, Mudcat Grant, Jim Kaat, Jim Perry, Al Worthington, Johnny Klippstein, Camilo Pascual (sore arm), Dave Boswell (illness), Jim Merritt, Dick Stigman, Bill Pleis, Jerry Fosnow, Garry Roggenburk, Mel Nelson.

Autographed Ball	25.00
with Harm. Killebrew	+20.00

1965 Chicago White Sox: Al Lopez, Manager; Bill Skowron, Don Buford, Ron Hansen, Pete Ward, Floyd Robinson, Ken Berry, Danny Cater, Johnny Romano, Tommy McCraw, J.C. Martin, Al Weis, Smoky Burgess, Dave Nicholson, Jimmie Schaffer (traded), Gene Freese (traded), Jim Hicks, Bill Voss, Tommie Agee (injured hand), Eddie Fisher, Tommy John, John Buzhardt, Joe Horlen, Gary Peters, Bruce Howard, Hoyt Wilhelm, Juan Pizarro (sore arm), Bob Locker, Ted Wills, Frank Lary (traded), Greg Bollo.

Autographed Ball	20.00
with Al Lopez	+5.00
with Tommy John	+5.00

1965 Los Angeles Dodgers (WORLD CHAMPIONS): Walt Alston, Manager; Wes Parker, Jim Lefebvre, Maury Wills, Jim Gilliam (retired to coach), Ron Fairly, Willie Davis, Lou Johnson, Johnny Roseboro, John Kennedy, Dick Tracewski, Jeff Torborg, Wally Moon, Willie Crawford, Al Ferrara, Don LeJohn, Derrell Griffith, Tommy Davis (broken ankle), Hec Valle, Sandy Koufax, Don Drysdale, Claude Osteen, Howie Reed, Johnny Podres, Ron Perranoski, Bob Miller, Jim Brewer (elbow injury), John Purdin, Nick Wilhite (traded), Mike Kekich, Bill Singer.

Autographed Ball	25.00
with Don Drysdale	+8.00
with Sandy Koufax	+12.00

1965 San Francisco Giants: Herman Franks, Mgr.; Willie McCovey, Hal Lanier, Dick Schofield (traded), Jim Ray Hart, Jesus Alou, Willie Mays, Matty Alou, Tom Haller, Jim Davenport, Len Gabrielson (traded), Cap Peterson, Ken Henderson, Jack Hiatt, Orlando Cepeda (injury), Bob Burda, Bob Schroder, Jose Pagan (traded), Tito Fuentes, Ed Bailey (traded), Harvey Kuenn (traded), Dick Bertell (traded), Juan Marichal, Bob Shaw, Bobby Bolin, Ron Herbel, Frank Linzy, Gaylord Perry, Masanori Murakami, Jack Sanford (traded), Warren Spahn (traded), Bill Henry (traded).

Autographed Ball	10.00
with Willie McCovey	+6.00
with Orlando Cepeda	+6.00
with Juan Marichal	+6.00
with M. Murakami	+20.00
with Willie Mays	+20.00

1965 Milwaukee Braves: Bobby Bragan, Manager; Gene Oliver, Frank Bolling, Woody Woodward, Eddie Mathews, Hank Aaron, Mack Jones, Felipe Alou, Joe Torre, Ty Cline, Rico Carty, Mike de la Hoz, Denis Menke (knee injury), Sandy Alomar, Lou Klimchock, Jesse Gonder (traded), Gary Kolb (traded), Don Dillard, Billy Cowan (traded), Lee Maye (traded), Frank Thomas (traded), Johnny Blanchard (traded), Tommie Aaron, Tony Cloninger, Wade Blasingame, Ken Johnson (traded), Billy O'Dell, Hank Fischer, Denny Lemaster (sore arm), Bob Sadowski, Phil Niekro, Dick Kelley, Clay Carroll, Dan Osinski.

Autographed Ball	20.00
with Eddie Mathews	+10.00
with Hank Aaron	+20.00

1966 AMERICAN LEAGUE ALL-STAR TEAM - Sam Mele (manager); Hank Bauer and Birdie Tebbetts (coaches); Stephen Barber, Andrew Etchebarren, Brooks Robinson*, Frank Robinson*, George Scott*, Carl Yastrzemski, James Fregosi, Robert Knoop*, Tommie Agee, Gary Bell, Rocco Colavito, Sam McDowell (replaced by Sonny Siebert), Norm Cash, William Freehan*, Al Kaline*, Richard McAuliffe*, Dennis McLain, James Hunter, Earl Battey, Jim Kaat, Harmon Killebrew, Tony Oliva*, Robert Richardson, Mel Stottlemyre, Pete Richert. Starters designated with an "*".

Autographed Ball	50.00
with C. Yastrzemski	+10.00

1966 NATIONAL LEAGUE ALL-STAR TEAM - Walt Alston (manager); Herman Franks and Harry Walker (coaches); Hank Aaron*, Felipe Alou, Joseph Torre*, Ron Santo, Leonardo Cardenas*, Bill McCool, Joe Morgan*, Claude Raymond, Sanford Koufax, James Lefebvre, Maurice Wills, Ron Hunt, Richard Allen, James Bunning, Roberto Clemente*, Wilver Stargell, Bob Veale, Curt Flood, Bob Gibson (replaced by Phil Regan), Tim McCarver, Thomas Haller, James Ray Hart, Juan Marichal, Willie Mays*, Willie McCovey*, Gaylord Perry. Morgan was sidelined with fractured kneecap after being named to starting lineup and was not included on squad. Starters designated with an "*".

Autographed Ball	15.00
with Sandy Koufax	+5.00
with Willie Mays	+15.00
with Hank Aaron	+15.00
with Rob. Clemente	+20.00

1966 Baltimore Orioles (WORLD CHAMPIONS): Hank Bauer, Manager; Boog Powell, Dave Johnson, Luis Aparicio, Brooks Robinson, Frank Robinson, Paul Blair, Russ Snyder, Andy Etchebarren, Curt Blefary, Sam Bowens, Bob Johnson, Woodie Held, Vic Roznovsky, Larry Haney, Charlie Lau (elbow injury), Jerry Adair (traded), Mark Belanger, Mike Epstein, Cam Carreon, Jim Palmer, Dave McNally, Steve Barber (arm injury), Wally Bunker, Stu Miller, Eddie Watt, Moe Drabowsky, Dick Hall, Eddie Fisher (traded), Gene Brabender, John Miller, Tom Phoebus, Bill Short (traded), Frank Bertaina.

Autographed Ball	30.00
with Jim Palmer	+5.00
with Brooks Robinson	+15.00
with Frank Robinson	+15.00

1966 Minnesota Twins: Sam Mele, Manager; Don Mincher, Bernie Allen, Zoilo Versalles, Harmon Killebrew, Tony Oliva, Ted Uhlaender, Jimmie Hall, Earl Battey, Cesar Tovar, Rich Rollins, Bob Allison, Jerry Zimmerman, Andy Kosco, Sandy Valdespino, Russ Nixon, George Mitterwald, Jim Kaat, Mudcat Grant, Dave Boswell, Jim Perry, Camilo Pascual (sore arm), Jim Merritt, Al Worthington, Dwight Siebler, Pete Cimino, Johnny Klippstein, Garry Roggenburk (traded).

Autographed Ball	20.00
with Harm. Killebrew	+20.00

1966 Los Angeles Dodgers (National League Champs): Walt Alston, Manager; Wes Parker, Jim Lefebvre, Maury Wills, John Kennedy, Ron Fairly, Willie Davis, Lou Johnson, Johnny Roseboro, Tommy Davis, Jim Gilliam, Nate Oliver, Al Ferrara, Jeff Torborg, Jim Barbieri, Dick Stuart (traded), Wes Covington (traded), Derrell Griffith, Dick Schofield (traded), Bart Shirley, Sandy Koufax, Claude Osteen, Phil Regan, Don Drysdale, Don Sutton, Ron Perranoski, Bob Miller, Joe Moeller, Jim Brewer (injury), Nick Willhite, Bill Singer, Johnny Podres (traded).

Autographed Ball	20.00
with Dick Stuart	+5.00
with Don Drysdale	+8.00
with Sandy Koufax	+12.00

1966 San Francisco Giants: Herman Franks, Manager; Willie McCovey, Hal Lanier, Tito Fuentes, Jim Ray Hart, Ollie Brown, Willie Mays, Jesus Alou, Tom Haller, Jim Davenport, Len Gabrielson, Cap Peterson, Don Landrum, Bob Barton, Ozzie Virgil, Don Mason, Bob Burda, Orlando Cepeda (traded), Jack Hiatt, Frank Johnson, Dick Dietz, Ken Henderson, Juan Marichal, Gaylord Perry, Bobby Bolin, Lindy McDaniel, Frank Linzy, Bob Priddy, Ron Herbel, Joe Gibbon, Ray Sadecki (traded), Bill Henry, Bob Shaw (traded), Masanori Murakami.

Autographed Ball	10.00
with Juan Marichal	+6.00
with Orlando Cepeda	+6.00
with Willie McCovey	+8.00
with M. Murakami	+20.00
with Willie Mays	+20.00

1966 Atlanta Braves: Bobby Bragan, Billy Hitchcock, Managers; Felipe Alou, Woody Woodward, Denis Menke, Eddie Mathews, Hank Aaron, Mack Jones (injury), Rico Carty, Joe Torre, Gary Geiger, Gene Oliver (anklè injury), Frank Bolling, Mike de la Hoz, Tony Cloninger, Ty Cline (traded), Lee Thomas (traded), Felix Millan, Sandy Alomar, John Herrnstein (traded), Marty Keough (traded), Lee Bales, Bill Robinson, Eddie Sadowski, Ken Johnson, Tony Cloninger, Denny Lemaster, Clay Carroll, Dick Kelley, Pat Jarvis, Chi Chi Olivo, Phil Niekro, Ted Abernathy (traded), Don Schwall (traded), Wade Blasingame (injury), Bill O'Dell (traded), Hank Fischer (traded), Charlie Vaughan, Ron Reed, Jay Ritchie, Herb Hippauf, Arnie Umbach, Joey Jay (traded), Dan Schneider.

Autographed Ball	20.00
with Eddie Mathews	+10.00
with Hank Aaron	+20.00

1967 AMERICAN LEAGUE ALL-STAR TEAM - Hank Bauer, Mgr.; Bill Rigney, Ed Stanky, Coaches; *Brooks Robinson, Andy Etchebarren, *Frank Robinson (replaced by Ken Berry), Tony Conigliaro, James Lonborg, *Rico Petrocelli, *Carl Yastrzemski, James Fregosi, James McGlothlin, Don Mincher, Tommie Agee, Joel Horlen, Garry Peters, Max Alvis, Steve Hargan, *William Freehan, *Al Kaline (replaced by Tony Oliva), Richard McAuliffe, James Hunter, *Rod Carew, Dean Chance, *Harmon Killebrew, Al Downing, Mickey Mantle, Paul Casanova. Starters designated with an "*".

Autographed Ball	20.00
with C. Yastrzemski	+10.00
with Jim McGlothlin	+10.00
with Mickey Mantle	+30.00

1967 NATIONAL LEAGUE ALL-STAR TEAM - Walter Alston, Mgr.; Herman Franks, Harry Walker, Coaches; *Hank Aaron, *Joe Torre, Denver Lemaster (replaced by Chris Short), Ernie Banks, Fergie Jenkins, Tommy Helms, Tony Perez, Pete Rose, Mike Cuellar, Rusty Staub, Jim Wynn, Don Drysdale, Claude Osteen, Tom Seaver, *Richie Allen, *Gene Alley, *Roberto Clemente, *Bill Mazeroski, *Lou Brock, *Orlando Cepeda, Bob Gibson, Tim McCarver, Tom Haller, Juan Marichal, Willie Mays. Starters designated with an "*".

Autographed Ball	10.00
with Pete Rose	+15.00
with Willie Mays	+15.00
with Hank Aaron	+15.00
with Rob. Clemente	+20.00

1967 Boston Red Sox (American League Champs): Dick Williams, Manager; George Scott, Mike Andrews, Rico Petrocelli, Joe Foy, Tony Conigliaro (eye injury), Reggie Smith, Carl Yastrzemski, Mike Ryan, Jose Tartabull, Jerry Adair (traded), Dalton Jones, George Thomas, Russ Gibson, Elston Howard (traded), Norm Siebern (traded), Bob Tillman (traded), Ken Harrelson (traded), Tony Horton (traded), Don Demeter (illness) (traded), Jim Lonborg, Jose Santiago, Gary Bell (traded), John Wyatt, Lee Stange, Dave Morehead, Darrell Brandon, Dennis Bennett (traded), Dan Osinski, Jerry Stephenson, Gary Waslewski, Billy Rohr, Bill Landis, Hank Fischer, Don McMahon (traded), Sparky Lyle, Galen Cisco, Ken Brett.

Autographed Ball	25.00
with Elston Howard	+5.00
with C. Yastrzemski	+25.00

1967 Detroit Tigers: Mayo Smith, Manager; Norm Cash, Dick McAuliffe, Ray Oyler, Don Wert, Al Kaline (broken arm), Jim Northrup, Willie Horton, Bill Freehan, Mickey Stanley, Jerry Lumpe, Dick Tracewski, Lenny Green, Earl Wilson, Gates Brown (injured wrist), Jim Price, Eddie Mathews (traded), Jim Landis (traded), Earl Wilson, Denny McLain, Joe Sparma, Mickey Lolich, Fred Gladding, John Hiller, Dave Wickersham, Johnny Podres, Fred Lasher, George Korince, Pat Dobson, Mike Marshall, Hank Aguirre, Larry Sherry (traded).

Autographed Ball	15.00
with Denny McLain	+5.00
with Eddie Mathews	+10.00
with Mike Marshall	+10.00
with Mayo Smith	+10.00
with Al Kaline	+20.00

1967 Kansas City A's: Al Dark, Luke Appling, Managers; Ramon Webster, John Donaldson, Bert Campaneris, Dick Green, Mike Hershberger, Rick Monday, Jim Gosger, Phil Roof, Danny Cater, Joe Nossek, Ken Harrelson (traded), Ted Kubiak, Sal Bando, Tim Talton, Roger Repoz (traded), Ken Suarez, Ossie Chavarria, Reggie Jackson, Dave Duncan, Ed Charles (traded), Joe Rudi, Catfish Hunter, Jim Nash, Chuck Dobson, Lew Krausse, Paul Lindblad, Tony Pierce, Diego Segui, Jack Aker, Blue Moon Odom, Bill Edgerton, Bobby Rodriguez, Jack Sanford (traded), Bill Stafford, Wes Stock.

Autographed Ball	20.00
with Luke Appling	+5.00
with Reggie Jackson	+20.00

1967 St. Louis Cardinals (WORLD CHAMPIONS): Red Schoendienst, Manager; Orlando Cepeda, Julian Javier, Dal Maxvill, Mike Shannon, Roger Maris, Curt Flood, Lou Brock, Tim McCarver, Bobby Tolan, Alex Johnson, Phil Gagliano, Ed Spiezio, Dave Ricketts, Ed Bressoud, Johnny Romano, Dick Hughes, Nelson Briles, Steve Carlton, Bob Gibson (broken leg), Ray Washburn, Al Jackson, Larry Jaster, Ron Willis, Joe Hoerner, Jack Lamabe (traded), Hal Woodeshick, Jim Cosman, Mike Torrez.

Autographed Ball	25.00
with Steve Carlton	+10.00
with Lou Brock	+10.00
with Bob Gibson	+10.00

1967 San Francisco Giants: Herman Franks, Manager; Willie McCovey, Tito Fuentes, Hal Lanier, Jim Ray Hart, Ollie Brown, Willie Mays, Jay Alou, Tom Haller, Jim Davenport, Jack Hiatt, Ken Henderson, Ty Cline (traded), Bob Schroder, Dick Dietz, Norm Siebern (traded), Bobby Etheridge, Dick Groat (traded), Cesar Gutierrez, Bill Sorrell, Mike McCormick, Gaylord Perry, Juan Marichal (leg injury), Ray Sadecki, Frank Linzy, Joe Gibbon, Bobby Bolin, Ron Herbel, Bill Henry, Lindy McDaniel.

Autographed Ball	10.00
with Juan Marichal	+6.00
with Willie McCovey	+8.00
with Willie Mays	+20.00

1968 AMERICAN LEAGUE ALL-STAR TEAM - Dick Williams, Manager; Cal Ermer, Mayo Smith, Coaches; Dave Johnson, Boog Powell, *Brooks Robinson, Ken Harrelson, Jose Santiago (replaced by Gary Bell), *Carl Yastrzemski, *Jim Fregosi, Tommy John, Duane Josephson, Jose Azcue, Samuel McDowell, Luis Tiant, *Will Freehan, *Willie Horton, Dennis McLain, Don Wert, *Rod Carew, *Harmon Killebrew, Tony Oliva, Mickey Mantle, Mel Stottlemyre, Bert Campaneris, Rick Monday, Johnny Odom, *Frank Howard. Starters designated with an "*".

Autographed Ball	30.00
with Mayo Smith	+5.00
with Mickey Mantle	+30.00

1968 NATIONAL LEAGUE ALL-STAR TEAM - Red Schoendienst, Manager; Dave Bristol, Herman Franks, Coaches; *Henry Aaron, Felipe Alou, Ron Reed, *Don Kessinger, *Ron Santo, Johnny Bench, *Tommy Helms, Atanasio (Tony) Perez, *Pete Rose (replaced by Billy Williams), Daniel (Rusty) Staub, Don Drysdale, Thomas Haller, *Gerald Grote, Jerry Koosman, Tom Seaver, Woodrow Fryman, Gene Alley (replaced by Chico Cardenas), Mateo Alou, Steven Carlton, *Curt Flood, Rob Gibson, Julian Javier, Juan Marichal, Willie Mays, *Willie McCovey. Starters designated with an "*".

Autographed Ball	25.00
with Pete Rose	+15.00
with Willie Mays	+15.00
with Hank Aaron	+15.00

1968 Detroit Tigers (WORLD CHAMPIONS): Mayo Smith, Manager; Norm Cash, Dick McAuliffe, Ray Oyler, Don Wert, Jim Northrup, Mickey Stanley, Willie Horton, Bill Freehan, Al Kaline, Dick Tracewski, Tom Matchick, Gates Brown, Jim Price, Wayne Comer, Earl Wilson, Eddie Mathews (back injury), Dave Campbell, Lenny Green, Bob Christian, Denny McLain, Mickey Lolich, Earl Wilson, Joe Sparma, John Hiller, Fred Lasher, Pat Dobson, Jon Warden, Don McMahon (traded), Dennis Ribant (traded), Daryl Patterson, Les Cain, John Wyatt (traded), Roy Face (traded), Jim Rooker.

Autographed Ball	15.00
with Mayo Smith	+10.00
with Denny McLain	+10.00
with Eddie Mathews	+10.00
with Al Kaline	+25.00

DETROIT TIGERS

1968 Baltimore Orioles: Hank Bauer, Earl Weaver, Managers; Boog Powell, Dave Johnson, Mark Belanger, Brooks Robinson, Frank Robinson, Paul Blair, Curt Blefary, Andy Etchebarren (broken finger), Don Buford, Dave May, Curt Motton, Ellie Hendricks, Fred Valentine (traded), Larry Haney, Merv Rettenmund, Chico Fernandez, Dave McNally, Jim Hardin, Tom Phoebus, Dave Leonhard, Pete Richert (military service), Gene Brabender, Eddie Watt, Roger Nelson, Moe Drabowsky, Wally Bunker, John Morris, Mike Adamson, Bruce Howard (traded), John O'Donoghue.

Autographed Ball	10.00
with Earl Weaver	+5.00
with Frank Robinson	+15.00
with Brooks Robinson	+15.00

1968 Oakland A's: Bob Kennedy, Manager; Danny Cater, John Donaldson, Bert Campaneris, Sal Bando, Reggie Jackson, Rick Monday, Mike Hershberger, Dave Duncan, Jim Gosger, Dick Green, Joe Rudi, Jim Pagliaroni (broken wrist), Ramon Webster, Floyd Robinson (traded), Ted Kubiak (military service), Joe Keough, Phil Roof (arm injury), Rene Lachemann, Blue Moon Odom, Catfish Hunter, Jim Nash, Chuck Dobson, Lew Krausse, Diego Segui, Paul Lindblad, Jack Aker, Ed Sprague, Tony Pierce, Ken Sanders, Warren Bogle, Rollie Fingers.

Autographed Ball	20.00
with Reggie Jackson	+20.00

1968 St. Louis Cardinals (National League Champs): Red Schoendienst, Manager; Orlando Cepeda, Julian Javier, Dal Maxvill, Mike Shannon, Roger Maris, Curt Flood, Lou Brock, Tim McCarver, Bobby Tolan, Johnny Edwards, Dick Schofield, Phil Gagliano, Ron Davis (traded), Ed Spiezio, Dick Simpson (traded), Dave Ricketts, Bob Gibson, Nelson Brilles, Ray Washburn, Steve Carlton, Larry Jaster, Joe Hoerner, Wayne Granger, Mel Nelson, Mike Torrez, Dick Hughes (sore arm), Ron Willis, Hal Gilson (traded).

Autographed Ball	20.00
with Orlando Cepeda	+5.00
with Lou Brock	+10.00
with Bob Gibson	+15.00

1968 San Francisco Giants: Herman Franks, Manager; Willie McCovey, Ron Hunt, Hal Lanier, Jim Davenport, Bobby Bonds, Willie Mays, Jesus Alou, Dick Dietz, Jim Ray Hart, Ty Cline, Jack Hiatt, Dave Marshall, Frank Johnson, Bob Barton, Ollie Brown, Nate Oliver (illness), Bob Schroder, Don Mason, Ken Henderson, Juan Marichal, Gaylord Perry, Mike McCormick, Ray Sadecki, Bob Bolin, Frank Linzy, Rich Robertson, Joe Gibbon, Ron Herbel, Lindy McDaniel (traded).

Autographed Ball	10.00
with Juan Marichal	+5.00
with Willie McCovey	+8.00
with Willie Mays	+20.00

1969 AMERICAN LEAGUE ALL-STAR TEAM - Mayo Smith, Manager; Al Dark, Earl Weaver, Theodore Williams, Coaches; Paul Blair, Dave Johnson (replaced by Mike Andrews), Dave McNally, *Boog Powell, Brooks Robinson, *Frank Robinson, Ray Culp, *Rico Petrocelli, Reggie Smith, Carl Yastrzemski, Jim Fregosi, Carlos May, Sam McDowell, *Bill Freehan, Mickey Lolich, Dennis McLain, Eliseo Rodriguez, *Rod Carew, Harmon Killebrew, Tony Oliva (replaced by Roy White), John Roseboro, Mel Stottlemyre, *Sal Bando, *Reggie Jackson, Johnny Odom, J. Michael Hegan, replaced by Don Mincher, *Frank Howard, Darold Knowles. Starters designated with an "*".

Autographed Ball	20.00
with Mayo Smith	+5.00
with Ted Williams	+15.00
with Reggie Jackson	+15.00

1969 NATIONAL LEAGUE ALL-STAR TEAM - Albert Schoendienst, Manager; Leo Durocher, David Bristol, Coaches; *Henry Aaron, *Felix Millan, Phil Niekro, Ernest Banks, Glen Beckert, Randy Hundley, *Don Kessinger, *Ron Santo, *Johnny Bench, Lee May, Tony Perez, Pete Rose, Lawrence Dierker, Denis Menke, Bill Singer, Rusty Staub, *Cleon Jones, Jerry Koosman, Tom Seaver, Grant Jackson, *Mateo Alou, Roberto Clemente, Steve Carlton, Bob Gibson, Chris Cannizzaro, Juan Marichal, Willie Mays, *Willie McCovey. Starters designated with an "*".

Autographed Ball	10.00
with Pete Rose	+15.00
with Willie Mays	+15.00
with Hank Aaron	+15.00
with Rob. Clemente	+20.00

1969 Baltimore Orioles (American League Champs): Earl Weaver, Manager; Boog Powell, Dave Johnson, Mark Belanger, Brooks Robinson, Frank Robinson, Paul Blair, Don Buford, Ellie Hendricks, Merv Rettenmund, Dave May, Andy Etchebarren, Curt Motton, Chico Salmon, Bobby Floyd, Clay Dalrymple, Terry Crowley, Mike Cuellar, Dave McNally, Jim Palmer (back injury), Tom Phoebus, Dave Leonhard, Pete Richert, Jim Hardin, Dick Hall, Eddie Watt, Marcelino Lopez, Al Severinsen, Mike Adamson.

Autographed Ball	10.00
with Jim Palmer	+5.00
with Frank Robinson	+15.00
with Brooks Robinson	+15.00

1969 Detroit Tigers: Mayo Smith, Manager; Norm Cash, Dick McAuliffe (knee injury), Tom Tresh (traded), Don Wert, Al Kaline, Jim Northrup, Willie Horton, Bill Freehan, Mickey Stanley, Tom Matchick, Jim Price, Ike Brown, Dick Tracewski, Gates Brown, Dave Campbell, Denny McLain, Mickey Lolich, Earl Wilson, Mike Kilkenny, Joe Sparma, Pat Dobson, Tom Timmerman, John Hiller, Don McMahon (traded), Fred Lasher, Dick Radatz (traded), Fred Scherman, Gary Taylor, Daryl Patterson (military service).

Autographed Ball	10.00
with Mayo Smith	+10.00
with Al Kaline	+20.00

1969 Minnesota Twins (Western Division Champs): Billy Martin, Manager; Rich Reese, Rod Carew, Leo Cardenas, Harmon Killebrew, Tony Oliva, Cesar Tovar, Ted Uhlaender, Johnny Roseboro, Frank Quilici, Graig Nettles, Chuck Manuel, Bob Allison, Rick Renick, George Mitterwald, Tom Tischinski, Jim Holt, Jim Perry, Dave Boswell, Jim Kaat, Ron Perranoski, Tom Hall, Dick Woodson, Dean Chance (sore arm), Bob Miller, Joe Grzenda, Al Worthington (voluntarily retired), Jerry Crider.

Autographed Ball	10.00
with Billy Martin	+5.00
with Rod Carew	+10.00
with Harm. Killebrew	+10.00

1969 Seattle Pilots: Joe Schultz, Manager; Don Mincher, John Donaldson (traded), Ray Oyler, Tommy Harper, Steve Hovley, Wayne Comer, Tommy Davis (traded), Jerry McNertney, Mike Hegan, Gus Gil, Steve Whitaker, John Kennedy (injury), Rich Rollins (knee injury), Ron Clark (traded), Merritt Ranew, Greg Goossen, Jim Gosger (traded), Danny Walton, Gene Brabender, Diego Segui, Marty Pattin, Fred Talbot (traded), Steve Barber (sore arm), Bob Locker (traded), John Gelnar, Mike Marshall, Jim Bouton (traded), Dooley Womack (traded), John O'Donoghue, Garry Roggenburk (traded), George Brunet (traded), Gary Bell (traded), Dick Baney, Mickey Fuentes, Darrell Brandon (traded), Skip Lockwood.

Autographed Ball	60.00
with Mike Marshall	+30.00

1969 Kansas City Royals: Joe Gordon, Manager; Mike Fiore, Jerry Adair, Jackie Hernandez, Joe Foy, Bob Oliver, Pat Kelly, Lou Piniella, Ellie Rodriguez, Ed Kirkpatrick, Juan Rios, Chuck Harrison, Buck Martinez (reported late), Joe Keough, Hawk Taylor, Paul Schaal, Jim Campanis, Luis Alcaraz, Wally Bunker, Moe Drabowsky, Dick Drago, Bill Butler, Roger Nelson, Jim Rooker, Tom Burgmeier, Mike Hedlund, Steve Jones, Dave Morehead, Dave Wickersham, Galen Cisco, Al Fitzmorris, Don O'Riley.

Autographed Ball	35.00
with Joe Gordon	+10.00

1969 New York Mets (WORLD CHAMPIONS): Gil Hodges, Manager; Ed Kranepool, Ken Boswell, Bud Harrelson, Wayne Garrett, Ron Swoboda, Tommie Agee, Cleon Jones, Jerry Grote, Rod Gaspar, Al Weis, Art Shamsky (back injury), Donn Clendenon (traded), J.C. Martin, Bobby Pfeil, Ed Charles, Amos Otis, Duffy Dyer, Tom Seaver, Jerry Koosman, Gary Gentry, Tug McGraw, Ron Taylor, Don Cardwell, Cal Koonce, Nolan Ryan (injury), Jim McAndrew, Jack DiLauro, Danny Frisella, Al Jackson (traded), Bob Johnson.

Autographed Ball	40.00
with Danny Frisella	+10.00
with Tom Seaver	+20.00
with Gil Hodges	+20.00

1969 Chicago Cubs: Leo Durocher, Manager; Ernie Banks, Glenn Beckert (broken finger), Don Kessinger, Ron Santo, Jim Hickman, Don Young, Billy Williams, Randy Hundley, Willie Smith, Al Spangler, Paul Popovich (traded), Nate Oliver (traded), Jim Qualls (shoulder injury), Adolpho Phillips, Bill Heath, Ken Rudolph, Oscar Gamble, Gene Oliver, Ferguson Jenkins, Bill Hands, Ken Holtzman, Phil Regan, Dick Selma (traded), Ted Abernathy, Rich Nye, Hank Aguirre, Jim Colborn, Joe Decker, Don Nottebart (traded), Ken Johnson (traded), Dave Lemonds, Joe Niekro (traded).

Autographed Ball	10.00
with Leo Durocher	+5.00
with Ernie Banks	+20.00

1969 Atlanta Braves (Western Division Champs): Lum Harris, Manager; Orlando Cepeda, Felix Millan, Sonny Jackson (injury), Clete Boyer, Hank Aaron, Felipe Alou, Tony Gonzalez (traded), Bob Didier, Mike Lum, Rico Carty, Gil Garrido, Bob Aspromonte, Bob Tillman, Tito Francona (traded), Tommie Aaron, Ralph Garr, Darrell Evans, Phil Niekro, Ron Reed, George Stone, Pat Jarvis, Jim Britton, Cecil Upshaw, Milt Pappas, Paul Doyle, Hoyt Wilhelm (traded), Claude Raymond (traded), Gary Neibauer, Ken Johnson (traded).

Autographed Ball	15.00
with Hank Aaron	+20.00

1969 Montreal Expos: Gene Mauch, Manager; Bob Bailey (injury), Gary Sutherland, Bobby Wine, Coco Laboy, Rusty Staub, Adolfo Phillips (illness) (traded), Mack Jones, Ron Brand, Ty Cline, John Bateman (injury), Ron Fairly (injury) (traded), Kevin Collins (traded), Don Bosch (knee injury), Maury Wills (traded), Joe Herrara, Floyd Wicker, John Boccabella, Donn Clendenon (traded), Manny Mota (traded), Angel Hermoso, Jim Fairey, Bill Stoneman, Dan McGinn, Howie Reed, Steve Renko, Mike Wegener, Jerry Robertson, Roy Face, Gary Waslewski (traded), Don Shaw, Claude Raymond (traded), Mudcat Grant (traded), Larry Jaster, Carroll Sembera, Carl Morton, Dick Radatz (traded), Steve Shea.

Autographed Ball	35.00
with Maury Wills	+5.00

1969 San Diego Padres: Preston Gomez, Manager; Nate Colbert, Jose Arcia, Tommy Dean, Ed Spiezio, Ollie Brown, Cito Gaston, Al Ferrara, Chris Cannizzaro, Roberto Pena, Ivan Murrell, Larry Stahl, Van Kelly, John Sipin (injury), Tony Gonzalez (traded), Walt Hriniak (traded), Bill Davis, Jerry DaVanon (traded), Jerry Morales, Sonny Ruberto, Ron Slocum, Jim Williams, Fred Kendall, Rafael Robles, Al Santorini, Joe Niekro (traded), Jack Baldschun, Clay Kirby, Johnny Podres, Dick Kelley, Billy McCool, Gary Ross (traded), Dick Selma (traded), Tommie Sisk, Tom Dukes, Frank Reberger, Mike Corkins, Al McBean (traded), Dave Roberts.

Autographed Ball	40.00

1970 AMERICAN LEAGUE ALL-STAR TEAM - Earl Weaver, Manager; Ralph Houk, Harold (Lefty) Phillips, Coaches; Mike Cuellar, Dave McNally, Jim Palmer, *Boog Powell, Brooks Robinson, *Frank Robinson, Gerry Moses, *Carl Yastrzemski, Sandy Alomar, Jim Fregosi, Alex Johnson, Clyde Wright, *Luis Aparicio, Ray Fosse, Sam McDowell, *Bill Freehan, Willie Horton, Amos Otis, Tommy Harper, *Rod Carew (replaced by Dave Johnson), *Harmon Killebrew, Tony Oliva, Jim Perry, Fred (Fritz) Peterson, Mel Stottlemyre, Roy White, Jim Hunter, *Frank Howard. Starters designated with an "*".

Autographed Ball	30.00
with C. Yastrzemski	+10.00

1970 NATIONAL LEAGUE ALL-STAR TEAM - Gil Hodges, Mgr.; Leo Durocher, Lum Harris, Coaches; *Henry Aaron, *Rico Carty, Felix Millan (replaced by Joe Morgan), Hoyt Wilhelm, *Glenn Beckert, James Hickman, *Don Kessinger, *Johnny Bench, Jim Merritt, *Tony Perez, Pete Rose, Wayne Simpson, Denis Menke, Billy Grabarkewitz, Claude Osteen, Rusty Staub, Bud Harrelson, Tom Seaver, Joe Hoerner, Roberto Clemente, *Richie Allen, Bob Gibson, Joe Torre, Clarence Gaston, Richard Dietz, *Willie Mays, Willie McCovey, Gaylord Perry. Starters designated with an "*".

Autographed Ball	10.00
with Pete Rose	+10.00
with Willie Mays	+10.00
with Hank Aaron	+10.00
with Gil Hodges	+10.00
with Rob. Clemente	+15.00

1970 Baltimore Orioles (WORLD CHAMPIONS): Earl Weaver, Manager; Boog Powell, Dave Johnson, Mark Belanger, Brooks Robinson, Frank Robinson, Paul Blair (collarbone), Don Buford, Ellie Hendricks, Merv Rettenmund, Terry Crowley, Andy Etchebarren, Chico Salmon, Curt Motton, Dave May (traded), Clay Dalrymple (broken ankle), Bobby Grich, Don Baylor, Johnny Oates, Bobby Floyd (traded), Roger Freed, Mike Cuellar, Dave McNally, Jim Palmer, Dick Hall, Pete Richert, Eddie Watt, Jim Hardin, Tom Phoebus, Moe Drabowsky (traded), Marcelino Lopez, Dave Leonhard.

Autographed Ball	10.00
with Jim Palmer	+5.00
with Brooks Robinson	+15.00
with Frank Robinson	+15.00

1970 New York Yankees: Ralph Houk, Manager; Danny Cater, Horace Clarke, Gene Michael, Jerry Kenney, Curt Blefary, Bobby Murcer, Roy White, Thurman Munson, Ron Woods, Jim Lyttle, Johnny Ellis, Pete Ward, Ron Hansen, Jake Gibbs, Frank Baker, Frank Tepedino, Bobby Mitchell, Fritz Peterson, Mel Stottlemyre, Stan Bahnsen, Lindy McDaniel, Mike Kekich (leg injury), Steve Kline, Ron Klimkowski, Jack Aker, Steve Hamilton (traded), John Cumberland (traded), Mike McCormick (traded), Gary Waslewski (traded).

Autographed Ball	20.00
with Thurman Munson	+20.00

1970 Minnesota Twins (Western Division Champs): Bill Rigney, Manager; Rich Reese, Danny Thompson, Leo Cardenas, Harmon Killebrew, Tony Oliva, Cesar Tovar, Jim Holt, George Mitterwald, Frank Quilici, Brant Alyea, Rick Renick, Paul Ratliff, Chuck Manuel, Rod Carew (knee injury), Bob Allison, Herm Hill, Tom Tischinski, Minnie Mendoza, Jim Nettles, Jim Perry, Jim Kaat, Tom Hall, Stan Williams, Bert Blyleven, Bill Zepp, Luis Tiant (injury), Ron Perranoski, Dave Boswell (back injury), Hal Haydel, Dick Woodson, Pete Hamm, Steve Barber.

Autographed Ball	10.00
with Danny Thompson	+5.00
with Rod Carew	+10.00
with Harm. Killebrew	+10.00

1970 Milwaukee Brewers: Dave Bristol, Manager; Mike Hegan, Ted Kubiak, Roberto Pena (traded), Tommy Harper, Russ Snyder, Dave May (traded), Danny Walton, Phil Roof, Ted Savage, Jerry McNertney, Bob Burda (traded), Gus Gil, Max Alvis, Tito Francona (traded), Mike Hershberger (shoulder injury), Bernie Smith, Steve Hovley (traded), Hank Allen (traded), John Kennedy (traded), Greg Goossen (traded), Floyd Wicker, Marty Pattin, Lew Krausse, Gene Brabender, Ken Sanders, Bob Bolin (traded), Skip Lockwood, John Gelnar, John Morris (illness), John O'Donoghue (traded), Dave Baldwin, Bob Humphreys (traded), Al Downing (traded), George Lauzerique, Bob Locker (traded), Bob Meyer, Dick Ellsworth (traded), Wayne Twitchell.

Autographed Ball	40.00

1970 Pittsburgh Pirates (Eastern Division Champs): Danny Murtaugh, Manager; Bob Robertson, Bill Mazeroski, Gene Alley, Richie Hebner, Roberto Clemente, Matty Alou, Willie Stargell, Manny Sanguillen, Al Oliver, Jose Pagan, Johnnie Jeter, Freddie Patek, Dave Cash, Jerry May, Gene Clines, Luke Walker, Dock Ellis, Bob Moose (sore arm), Steve Blass (elbow injury), Bob Veale, Dave Giusti, Bruce Dal Canton, Jim Nelson, Mudcat Grant (traded), Orlando Pena, Dick Colpaert, George Brunet (traded), Chuck Hartenstein (traded), Fred Cambria, Joe Gibbon.

Autographed Ball	10.00
with Danny Murtaugh	+5.00
with Bob Moose	+5.00
with Rob. Clemente	+25.00

1970 Chicago Cubs: Leo Durocher, Manager; Ernie Banks (knee injury), Glen Beckert, Don Kessinger, Ron Santo, Johnny Callison, Jim Hickman, Billy Williams, Randy Hundley (knee injury), Cleo James, Willie Smith, Paul Popovich, Jack Hiatt (traded), Joe Pepitone (traded), J. C. Martin, Jimmie Hall (traded), Phil Gagliano (traded), Al Spangler, Tommy Davis (traded), Ferguson Jenkins, Bill Hands, Ken Holtzman, Milt Pappas (traded), Phil Regan, Hank Aguirre, Jim Colborn, Roberto Rodriquez (traded), Joe Decker, Larry Gura, Steve Barber (traded), Hoyt Wilhelm (traded), Jimmy Dunegan, Archie Reynolds, Ted Abernathy (traded), Juan Pizzaro.

Autographed Ball	10.00
with Leo Durocher	+5.00
with Ernie Banks	+20.00

1970 Cincinnati Reds (National League Champs): Sparky Anderson, Manager; Lee May, Tommy Helms, Dave Concepcion, Tony Perez, Pete Rose, Bobby Tolan, Bernie Carbo, Johnny Bench, Jimmy Stewart, Woody Woodward, Hal McRae, Angel Bravo, Darrel Chaney, Ty Cline (illness) (traded), Pat Corrales, Frank Duffy, Jim Merritt (elbow injury), Gary Nolan, Wayne Simpson (shoulder injury), Jim McGlothlin, Clay Carroll, Tony Cloninger, Wayne Granger, Don Gullett, Ray Washburn, Milt Wilcox, Jim Maloney (injury), Mel Behney (military service), Pedro Borbon, Bo Belinsky.

Autographed Ball	10.00
with Johnny Bench	+10.00
with Pete Rose	+15.00

1971 AMERICAN LEAGUE ALL-STAR TEAM - Earl Weaver, Manager; G. William Hunter, Billy Martin, Coaches; Don Buford, Miguel Cuellar, James Palmer, *Boog Powell (replaced by Norm Cash), *Brooks Robinson, *Frank Robinson, Luis Aparicio, Sonny Siebert, *Carl Yastrzemski, Andy Messersmith, Bill Melton, *Ray Fosse (replaced by Dave Duncan), Sam McDowell (replaced by Wilbur Wood), Bill Freehan, Al Kaline, Michael Lolich, Amos Otis, Cookie Rojas, Marty Pattin, Leo Cardenas, *Rod Carew, Harmon Killebrew, *Tony Oliva (replaced by Reggie Jackson), James Perry, Thurman Munson, Bobby Murcer, Vida Blue, Frank Howard. Starters designated with an "*".

Autographed Ball	30.00
with Thurman Munson	+15.00

1971 NATIONAL LEAGUE ALL-STAR TEAM - Sparky Anderson, Manager; Walt Alston, Preston Gomez, Dan Murtaugh, Coaches; *Henry Aaron, Felix Millan, *Glenn Beckert, Ferguson Jenkins, Don Kessinger, Ron Santo, *Johnny Bench, Clay Carroll, Lee May, Pete Rose, Larry Dierker (replaced by Don Wilson), Willie Davis, Rusty Staub, *Bud Harrelson, Thomas Seaver, Rick Wise, Roberto Clemente, Dock Ellis, Manny Sanguillen, *Wilver Stargell, Lou Brock, Steve Carlton, *Joe Torre. Nate Colbert, Bobby Bonds, Juan Marichal, *Willie Mays, *Willie McCovey. Starters designated with an "*".

Autographed Ball	5.00
with Pete Rose	+10.00
with Willie Mays	+10.00
with Hank Aaron	+10.00
with Rob. Clemente	+15.00

1971 Baltimore Orioles (American League Champs): Earl Weaver, Manager; Boog Powell, Dave Johnson, Mark Belanger, Brooks Robinson, Merv Rettenmund, Paul Blair, Don Buford, Ellie Hendricks, Frank Robinson, Andy Etchebarren, Tom Shopay (ankle injury), Chico Salmon, Jerry DaVanon, Curt Motton, Clay Dalrymple, Terry Crowley, Bobby Grich, Don Baylor, Dave McNally (sore arm), Pat Dobson, Mike Cuellar, Jim Palmer, Dick Hall, Grant Jackson, Eddie Watt (injured hand), Pete Richert, Dave Leonhard, Dave Boswell (traded), Tom Dukes.

Autographed Ball	5.00
with Jim Palmer	+5.00
with Brooks Robinson	+15.00
with Frank Robinson	+15.00

1971 Detroit Tigers: Billy Martin, Manager; Norm Cash, Dick McAuliffe, Eddie Brinkman, Aurelio Rodriguez, Al Kaline, Mickey Stanley, Willie Horton (eye injury), Bill Freehan, Jim Northrup, Dalton Jones, Gates Brown, Ike Brown, Tony Taylor (traded), Cesar Gutierrez, Kevin Collins, Jim Price (leg injury), Marvin Lane, Mickey Lolich, Joe Coleman, Fred Scherman, Les Cain (shoulder injury), Tom Timmerman, Joe Niekro, Mike Kilkenny (illness), Dean Chance, Bill Gilbreth, Jim Hannan (traded), Bill Zepp, Daryl Patterson (traded), Ron Perranoski (traded), Bill Denehy.

Autographed Ball 10.00
with Billy Martin +5.00
with Al Kaline +15.00

1971 Oakland A's (Western Division Champs): Dick Williams, Manager; Mike Epstein (traded), Dick Green, Bert Campaneris, Sal Bando, Reggie Jackson, Rick Monday, Joe Rudi, Dave Duncan, Angel Mangual, Tommy Davis, Larry Brown (traded), Gene Tenace, Mike Hegan (traded), Curt Blefary (traded), George Hendrick, Catfish Hunter, Don Mincher (traded), Steve Hovley, Tony LaRussa (traded), Dwain Anderson, Adrian Garrett, Vida Blue, Catfish Hunter, Chuck Dobson (elbow injury), Diego Segui, Blue Moon Odom (elbow injury), Bob Locker, Darold Knowles (traded), Rollie Fingers, Ron Klimkowski, Mudcat Grant (traded), Paul Lindblad (traded), Jim Roland, Marcel Lachemann.

Autographed Ball 15.00
with Reggie Jackson +15.00

1971 Washington Senators: Ted Williams, Manager; Don Mincher (traded), Tim Cullen, Toby Harrah, Dave Nelson, Elliott Maddox, Del Unser, Frank Howard, Paul Casanova, Tommy McCraw, Dick Billings, Bernie Allen, Lenny Randle, Larry Biittner, Jeff Burroughs, Joe Foy, Richie Scheinblum, Mike Epstein (traded), Don Wert, Dick Bosman, Denny McLain, Paul Lindblad (traded), Bill Gogolewski, Joe Grzenda, Casey Cox, Pete Broberg, Denny Riddleberger, Jackie Brown, Jim Shellenback, Darold Knowles, Horacio Pina, Jerry Janeski, Mike Thompson.

Autographed Ball 10.00
with Denny McLain +5.00
with Ted Williams +15.00

1971 Pittsburgh Pirates (WORLD CHAMPIONS): Danny Murtaugh, Manager; Bob Robertson, Dave Cash, Gene Alley, Richie Hebner, Roberto Clemente, Al Oliver, Willie Stargell, Manny Sanguillen, Vic Davalillo, Gene Clines, Jackie Hernandez, Bill Mazeroski, Joes Pagan (injury), Rennie Stennett, Milt May, Charlie Sands, Dock Ellis, Steve Blass, Bob Moose, Luke Walker, Bob Johnson, Nelson Briles, Bob Veale, Bruce Kison, Mudcat Grant (traded), Dave Giusti, Jim Nelson, Bob Miller (traded), Ramon Hernandez.

Autographed Ball 20.00
with Bob Moose +5.00
with W. Stargell +5.00
with Danny Murtaugh +5.00
with Rob. Clemente +20.00

1971 St. Louis Cardinals: Red Schoendienst, Manager; Joe Hague, Ted Sizemore, Dal Maxvill, Joe Torre, Matty Alou, Jose Cruz, Lou Brock, Ted Simmons, Julian Javier, Jose Cardenal (traded), Luis Melendez, Jim Beauchamp, Bob Burda, Jerry McNertney (traded), Ted Kubiak (traded), Leron Lee (traded), Steve Carlton, Bob Gibson, Jerry Reuss, Reggie Cleveland, Don Shaw, Moe Drabowsky, Frank Linzy, Stan Williams (traded), Chuck Taylor, Chris Zachary, Denny Higgins, Mike Torrez (traded), Rudy Arroyo, Daryl Patterson (traded), Al Santorini (traded).

Autographed Ball 5.00
with Bob Gibson +10.00
with Steve Carlton +10.00
with Lou Brock +10.00

1971 San Francisco Giants (Western Division Champs): Charlie Fox, Manager; Willie McCovey (knee injury), Tito Fuentes, Chris Speier, Alan Gallagher, Bobby Bonds, Willie Mays, Ken Henderson, Dick Dietz, Hal Lanier, Jimmy Rosario, Fran Healy, Dave Kingman, George Foster (traded), Bernie Williams, Frank Johnson, Jim Ray Hart, Russ Gibson, Frank Duffy (traded), Ed Goodson, Bob Heise (traded), Juan Marichal, Gaylord Perry, Jerry Johnson, Don McMahon, John Cumberland, Ron Bryant (sore arm), Don Carrithers, Steve Stone, Frank Reberger (injury), Steve Hamilton, Rich Robertson, Jim Barr.

Autographed Ball 10.00
with Willie McCovey +7.00
with Willie Mays +15.00

1972 AMERICAN LEAGUE ALL-STAR TEAM - Earl Weaver, Mgr.; Bob Lemon, Dick Williams, Coaches; Pat Dobson, Dave McNally, Jim Palmer, *Brooks Robinson, *Luis Aparicio (replaced by Toby Harrah who was replaced by Bob Grich), Carlton Fisk, *Carl Yastrzemski, Nolan Ryan, *Richard Allen, Carlos May, Wilbur Wood, Gaylord Perry, Norm Cash, Joe Coleman (replaced by Ken Holtzman), *Bill Freehan, Mickey Lolich, Amos Otis (replaced by Reggie Smith), Freddie Patek (replaced by Bert Campaneris), Lou Pinella, Cookie Rojas, Richie Scheinblum, Eliseo Rodriquez, *Rod Carew, *Bobby Murcer, Sal Bando, James Hunter, *Reggie Jackson, Joe Rudi. Starters designated with an "*".

Autographed Ball 15.00
with Reggie Jackson +10.00
with C. Yastrzemski +10.00

1972 NATIONAL LEAGUE ALL-STAR TEAM - Danny Murtaugh, Manager; Charles Fox, Red Schoendienst, Coaches; *Henry Aaron, Glenn Beckert, *Don Kessinger, Ron Santo, Billy Williams, *Johnny Bench, Clay Carroll, *Joe Morgan, Gary Nolan (replaced by Ferguson Jenkins), Cesar Cedeno, *Lee May, Donald Sutton, Bill Stoneman, Willie Mays, Frank (Tug) McGraw, Thomas Seaver, Steve Carlton, Steve Blass, *Roberto Clemente, Al Oliver, Manuel Sanguillen, *Wilver Stargell, Lou Brock, Bob Gibson, Ted Simmons, *Joe Torre, Nate Colbert, Chris Speier. Starters designated with an "*".

Autographed Ball 10.00
with Danny Murtaugh +5.00
with Willie Mays +10.00
with Hank Aaron +10.00
with Rob. Clemente +20.00

1972 Detroit Tigers (Eastern Division Champs): Billy Martin, Manager; Norm Cash, Dick McAuliffe, Eddie Brinkman, Aurelio Rodriguez, Jim Northrup, Mickey Stanley, Willie Horton, Bill Freehan, Al Kaline (leg injury), Gates Brown, Tony Taylor, Tom Haller, Ike Brown, Duke Sims (traded), Paul Jata, Wayne Comer, Frank Howard (traded), John Knox, Mickey Lolich, Joe Coleman, Woody Fryman (traded), Chuck Seelbach, Tom Timmerman, Fred Scherman, Bill Slayback, Joe Niekro (injured hip), Jim Foor, Chris Zachary, John Hiller (illness), Lerrin LaGrow, Ron Perranoski (traded), Les Cain.

Autographed Ball 10.00
with Billy Martin +5.00
with Al Kaline +15.00

1972 Boston Red Sox: Eddie Kasko, Manager; Danny Cater, Doug Griffin, Luis Aparicio (broken finger), Rico Petrocelli, Reggie Smith, Tommy Harper, Carl Yastrzemski (knee injury), Carlton Fisk, Ben Oglivie, Rick Miller, John Kennedy, Phil Gagliano, Bob Burda, Juan Beniquez, Duane Josephson (illness), Bob Montgomery, Dwight Evans, Andy Kosco (traded), Marty Pattin, Luis Tiant, Sonny Siebert, John Curtis, Lynn McGlothen, Bill Lee, Ray Culp (shoulder injury), Don Newhouser, Gary Peters, Bob Veale (traded), Lew Krausse, Bob Bolin, Mike Garman, Ken Tatum (leg injury), Roger Moret.

Autographed Ball 15.00
with C. Yastrzemski +10.00

1972 Oakland A's (WORLD CHAMPIONS): Dick Williams, Manager; Mike Epstein, Tim Cullen, Bert Campaneris, Sal Bando, Angel Mangual, Reggie Jackson, Joe Rudi, Dave Duncan, Mike Hegan, Gene Tenace, George Hendrick, Ted Kubiak (traded), Larry Brown (back injury), Don Mincher (traded), Bill Voss (traded), Matty Alou (traded), Dal Maxwell (traded), Dick Green (back injury), Marty Martinez (traded), Gonzalo Marquez, Allen Lewis, Brant Alyea (traded), Ollie Brown (traded), Bobby Brooks, Catfish Hunter, Ken Holtzman, Blue Moon Odom, Rollie Fingers, Bob Locker, Dave Hamilton, Vida Blue (held out), Darold Knowles, Joe Horlen, Denny McLain (traded).

Autographed Ball	15.00
with Vida Blue	+5.00
with Denny McLain	+5.00
with Reggie Jackson	+10.00

1972 Texas Rangers: Ted Williams, Manager; Frank Howard (traded), Lenny Randle, Toby Harrah (illness), Dave Nelson, Ted Ford, Joe Lovitto, Elliott Maddox (injury), Dick Billings, Larry Biittner, Dalton Jones (traded), Tommy Grieve, Don Mincher (traded), Vic Harris, Hal King, Jim Mason, Ted Kubiak (traded), Bill Fahey, Marty Martinez (traded), Rich Hand, Mike Paul, Dick Bosman, Paul Lindblad, Jim Panther, Pete Broberg, Bill Gogolewski, Casey Cox (traded), Jim Shellenback, Horacio Pina, Don Stanhouse (elbow injury), Steve Lawson.

Autographed Ball	30.00
with Ted Williams	+10.00

1972 Pittsburgh Pirates (Eastern Division Champs): Bill Virdon, Manager; Willie Stargell, Dave Cash, Gene Alley, Richie Hebner, Roberto Clemente (ankle injury), Al Oliver, Vic Davalillo, Manny Sanguillen, Bob Robertson, Rennie Stennett, Gene Clines, Jackie Hernandez, Milt May, Jose Pagan, Bill Mazeroski (injury), Steve Blass, Dock Ellis, Nelson Briles, Bob Moose, Bruce Kison, Dave Giusti, Ramon Hernandez, Bob Miller, Bob Johnson, Luke Walker (back injury), Gene Garber, Bob Veale (traded).

Autographed Ball	20.00
with Rob. Clemente	+20.00

1972 Chicago Cubs: Leo Durocher, Whitey Lockman, Managers; Jim Hickman, Glenn Beckert, Don Kessinger, Ron Santo (broken wrist), Jose Cardenal, Rick Monday, Billy Williams, Randy Hundley, Carmen Fanzone, Joe Pepitone (voluntarily retired), Billy North, Paul Popovich (illness), Ken Rudolph, Gene Hiser, J.C. Martin (elbow injury), Ellie Hendricks (traded), Ferguson Jenkins, Milt Pappas, Bill Hands, Burt Hooton, Rick Reuschel, Jack Aker (traded), Juan Pizarro, Tom Phoebus (traded), Joe Decker, Steve Hamilton, Bill Bonham, Phil Regan (traded), Dan McGinn, Larry Gura.

Autographed Ball	18.00
with Leo Durocher	+5.00

1972 Cincinnati Reds (National League Champs): Sparky Anderson, Manager; Tony Perez, Joe Morgan, Dave Concepcion, Denis Menke, Cesar Geronimo, Bobby Tolan, Pete Rose, Johnny Bench, Darrel Chaney, Ted Uhlaender, Joe Hague (traded), Hal McRae, George Foster, Julian Javier, Bill Plummer (injury), Bernie Carbo (traded), Sonny Ruberto, Pat Corrales (traded), Gary Nolan, Ross Grimsley, Jack Billingham, Tom Hall, Jim McGlothlin, Don Gullett, Pedro Borbon, Wayne Simpson, Clay Carroll, Ed Sprague.

Autographed Ball	10.00
with Jim McGlothlin	+5.00
with Johnny Bench	+5.00
with Pete Rose	+10.00

1973 AMERICAN LEAGUE ALL-STAR TEAM - Dick Williams, Mgr.; Chuck Tanner, Whitey Herzog, Coaches; Paul Blair, *Brooks Robinson, *Carlton Fisk, Bill Lee, Carl Yastrzemski (replaced by Jim Spencer), Nolan Ryan, Bill Singer, *Richie Allen (replaced by Pat Kelly), Buddy Bell, Ed Brinkman, Bill Freehan, Willie Horton, John Mayberry, *Amos Otis, Cookie Rojas, Jim Colborn, Dave May, Bert Blyleven, *Rod Carew, Sparky Lyle, Thurman Munson, *Bobby Murcer, Sal Bando, *Bert Campaneris, Roland Fingers, Ken Holtzman, Jim Hunter, *Reggie Jackson, Dave Nelson. Starters designated with an "*".

Autographed Ball	20.00
with Thurman Munson	+10.00

1973 NATIONAL LEAGUE ALL-STAR TEAM - Sparky Anderson, Mgr.; Gene Mauch, Bill Virdon, Coaches; *Hank Aaron, Darrell Evans, Dave Johnson, *Ron Santo, *Billy Williams, *Johnny Bench, John Billingham, Dave Concepcion (replaced by Bill Russell), *Joe Morgan, *Pete Rose, *Cesar Cedeno, Bob Watson, Jim Brewer, Willie Davis, Manny Mota, Claude Osteen, Don Sutton, Ron Fairly, Willie Mays, Tom Seaver, Wayne Twitchell, Dave Giusti, Wilver Stargell, Ted Simmons, Joseph Torre, Richard Wise, Nathan Colbert, Bobby Bonds, *Chris Speier. Starters designated with an "*".

Autographed Ball	5.00
with Pete Rose	+10.00
with Willie Mays	+10.00
with Hank Aaron	+10.00

1973 Baltimore Orioles (Eastern Division Champs): Earl Weaver, Manager; Boog Powell, Bobby Grich, Mark Belanger, Brooks Robinson, Don Baylor, Paul Blair, Rich Coggins, Earl Williams, Tommy Davis, Al Bumbry, Merv Rettenmund, Andy Etchebarren, Terry Crowley, Frank Baker, Ellie Hendricks (injury), Enos Cabell, Larry Brown, Doug DeCinces, Jim Fuller, Sergio Robles, Curt Motton, Jim Palmer, Mike Cuellar, Dave McNally, Doyle Alexander (elbow injury), Grant Jackson, Bob Reynolds, Jesse Jefferson, Don Hood, Eddie Watt, Orlando Pena (traded), Wayne Garland.

Autographed Ball	15.00
with Jim Palmer	+5.00
with Brooks Robinson	+10.00

1973 Boston Red Sox: Eddie Kasko, Manager; Carl Yastrzemski, Doug Griffin (injured hand), Luis Aparicio, Rico Petrocelli (elbow injury), Reggie Smith, Tommy Harper, Rick Miller, Carlton Fisk, Orlando Cepeda, Dwight Evans, John Kennedy, Mike Guerrero, Danny Cater, Ben Oglivie, Bob Montgomery, Cecil Cooper, Buddy Hunter, Luis Tiant, Bill Lee, Marty Pattin, Roger Moret (knee injury), John Curtis, Dick Pole, Bob Bolin, Bob Veale, Ray Culp (injury), Lynn McGlothen (injury), Craig Skok, Sonny Siebert (traded), Mike Garman, Don Newhauser (back injury).

Autographed Ball	15.00
with C. Yastrzemski	+10.00

1973 Oakland A's (WORLD CHAMPIONS): Dick Williams, Manager; Gene Tenace, Dick Green, Bert Campaneris, Sal Bando, Reggie Jackson, Billy North, Joe Rudi, Ray Fosse, Deron Johnson (traded), Ted Kubiak, Mike Hegan (traded), Angel Mangual, Billy Conigliaro (knee injury), Rich McKinney, Vic Davalillo (traded), Jesus Alou (traded), Allen Lewis, Dal Maxvill (traded), Pat Bourque (traded), Jay Johnstone, Gonzalo Marquez (traded), Mike Andrews (traded), Manny Trillo, Tim Hosley, Phil Garner, Rico Carty (traded), Catfish Hunter (injury), Ken Holtzman, Vida Blue, Rollie Fingers, Horacio Pina, Dave Hamilton, Darold Knowles, Blue Moon Odom, Glenn Abbott, Paul Lindblad.

Autographed Ball	20.00
with Reggie Jackson	+10.00

1973 Kansas City Royals: Jack McKeon, Manager; John Mayberry, Cookie Rojas, Freddie Patek, Paul Schaal, Ed Kirkpatrick, Amos Otis, Lou Piniella, Fran Healy, Hal McRae, Steve Hovley, Kurt Bevacqua, Gail Hopkins, Carl Taylor, Frank White, Bobby Floyd, Jim Wohlford, Rick Reichardt (traded), Tom Poquette, Buck Martinez, George Brett, Jerry May (traded), Paul Splittorff, Steve Busby, Dick Drago, Gene Garber, Al Fitzmorris, Ken Wright, Bruce Dal Canton, Doug Bird, Steve Mingori (traded), Wayne Simpson, Joe Hoerner (traded), Mark Littell, Tom Burgmeier.

Autographed Ball	10.00
with George Brett	+10.00

THE INCREMENTAL VALUE OF THE AUTOGRAPH OF A PARTICULAR PLAYER TO A PARTICULAR BALL IS UNIQUE TO THAT BALL. IT IS NOT THE EXOGENOUS VALUE OF THAT PLAYER'S AUTOGRAPH. SEE THE INTRODUCTION TO TEAM AUTOGRAPHED BALLS.

1973 New York Mets (National League Champs): Yogi Berra, Manager; John Milner (leg injury), Felix Millan, Bud Harrelson (injured hand), Wayne Garrett, Rusty Staub, Don Hahn, Cleon Jones (injured wrist), Jerry Grote (broken arm), Ed Kranepool, Ted Martinez, Ken Boswell, Duffy Dyer, Willie Mays, Jim Beauchamp, Ron Hodges, Jim Fregosi (traded), George Theodore (injured hip), Jim Gosger, Tom Seaver, Jerry Koosman, Jon Matlack, George Stone, Harry Parker, Ray Sadecki, Tug McGraw, Jim McAndrew, Buzz Capra, Tommy Moore, Craig Swan, Phil Hennigan, Bob Apodaca.

Autographed Ball	20.00
with Yogi Berra	+10.00
with Tom Seaver	+10.00
with Willie Mays	+10.00

1973 St. Louis Cardinals: Red Schoendienst, Manager; Joe Torre, Ted Sizemore, Mike Tyson, Ken Reitz, Luis Melendez, Jose Cruz, Lou Brock, Ted Simmons, Tim McCarver, Bernie Carbo, Mick Kelleher, Bake McBride, Bill Stein, Jim Dwyer, Tommy Agee (traded), Ray Busse (traded), Rick Wise, Reggie Cleveland, Alan Foster, Bob Gibson (knee injury), Diego Segui, Orlando Pena (traded), Rich Folkers, Tom Murphy, Eddie Fisher (traded), Al Hrabosky, Wayne Granger (traded), John Andrews, Scipio Spinks (shoulder injury), Mike Nagy, Jim Bibby (traded).

Autographed Ball	10.00
with Lou Brock	+10.00
with Bob Gibson	+10.00

1973 Cincinnati (Western Division Champs): Sparky Anderson, Manager; Tony Perez, Joe Morgan, Dave Concepcion (broken ankle), Denis Menke, Bobby Tolan, Cesar Geronimo, Pete Rose, Johnny Bench, Darrel Chaney, Dan Driessen, Larry Stahl, Phil Gagliano, Bill Plummer, Andy Kosco, Ed Crosby (traded), Hal King, Gene Locklear (traded), Richie Scheinblum (traded), Ken Griffey, Joe Hague, Ed Armbrister, George Foster, Jack Billingham, Don Gullett, Ross Grimsley, Fred Norman (traded), Pedro Borbon, Tom Hall, Clay Carroll, Roger Nelson (injury), Jim McGlothin (traded), Dick Baney, Dave Tomlin, Ed Sprague (traded), Gary Nolan (sore arm).

Autographed Ball	10.00
with Johnny Bench	+5.00
with Jim McGlothin	+10.00
with Pete Rose	+10.00

1973 Los Angeles: Walt Alston, Manager; Bill Buckner, Dave Lopes, Bill Russell, Ron Cey, Willie Crawford, Willie Davis, Manny Mota, Joe Ferguson, Steve Garvey, Tom Paciorek, Von Joshua (broken wrist), Lee Lacy, Steve Yeager, Ken McMullen (injury), Chris Cannizzaro, Don Sutton, Tommy John, Claude Osteen, Andy Messersmith, Al Downing, Jim Brewer, Charlie Hough, Doug Rau, George Culver (traded), Pete Richert, Geoff Zahn.

Autographed Ball	15.00
with Steve Garvey	+5.00

1974 AMERICAN LEAGUE ALL-STAR TEAM - Dick Williams, manager; Earl Weaver, honorary manager; Whitey Herzog, Jack McKeon, coaches; Mike Cuellar, Bob Grich, *Brooks Robinson, *Carlton Fisk (replaced by Ed Herrmann who was replaced by Jim Sundberg), Luis Tiant, Carl Yastrzemski, Dave Chalk, Frank Robinson, *Richie Allen, Wilbur Wood, George Hendrick, Gaylord Perry, John Hiller, Al Kaline, Steve Busby, John Mayberry, Cookie Rojas, Darrell Porter, *Rod Carew, Thurman Munson, *Bobby Murcer, Sal Bando (replaced by Don Money), *Bert Campaneris, Roland Fingers, Jim Hunter, *Reggie Jackson, Joe Rudi, *Jeff Burroughs. Earl Weaver stepped down as manager of the A.L. in favor of Dick Williams. Starters designated with an "*".

Autographed Ball	15.00
with Dick Allen	+5.00
with C. Yastrzemski	+5.00
with Thurman Munson	+10.00

1974 NATIONAL LEAGUE ALL-STAR TEAM - Yogi Berra, Mgr.; Sparky Anderson, Red Schoendienst, Coaches; *Hank Aaron, Buzz Capra, Ralph Garr, Don Kessinger, *Johnny Bench, *Joe Morgan, Tony Perez, *Pete Rose, Cesar Cedeno, *Ron Cey, *Steve Garvey, Mike Marshall, Andy Messersmith, *Jim Wynn, Steve Rogers, Jerry Grote, Jon Matlack, *Larry Bowa, Steve Carlton, Dave Cash, Mike Schmidt, Ken Brett, Lou Brock, Lynn McGlothen, Ted Simmons, Reggie Smith, John Grubb, Chris Speier. Starters designated with an "*".

Autographed Ball	10.00
with Pete Rose	+10.00
with Hank Aaron	+10.00
with Mike Marshall	+10.00

1974 Baltimore Orioles (Eastern Division Champs): Earl Weaver, Manager; Boog Powell, Bobby Grich, Mark Belanger, Brooks Robinson, Rich Coggins, Paul Blair, Don Baylor, Earl Williams, Tommy Davis, Al Bumbry, Enos Cabell, Ellie Hendricks, Jim Fuller, Andy Etchebarren, Frank Baker, Jim Northrup (traded), Mike Cuellar, Ross Grimsley, Dave McNally, Bob Reynolds, Jim Palmer (sore arm), Grant Jackson, Doyle Alexander, Wayne Garland, Dave Johnson, Jesse Jefferson, Don Hood.

Autographed Ball	10.00
with Jim Palmer	+5.00
with Brooks Robinson	+10.00

1974 New York Yankees: Bill Virdon, Manager; Chris Chambliss (traded), Sandy Alomar (traded), Jim Mason, Graig Nettles, Bobby Murcer, Elliott Maddox, Lou Piniella, Thurman Munson, Ron Blomberg, Roy White, Bill Sudakis, Gene Michael, Fernando Gonzalez (traded), Rick Dempsey, Walt Williams, Fred Stanley, Otto Velez, Horace Clarke (traded), Mike Hegan (traded), Alex Johnson (traded), Pat Dobson, Doc Medich, Dick Tidrow (traded), Sparky Lyle, Rudy May (shoulder injury) (traded), Mike Wallace (traded), Mel Stottlemyre (shoulder injury), Larry Gura, Steve Kline (traded), Dick Woodson, Dave Pagan, Cecil Upshaw (traded), Sam McDowell (injury), Tippy Martinez, Fritz Peterson (traded).

Autographed Ball	15.00
with Thurman Munson	+10.00

1974 Oakland A's (American League Champs): Al Dark, Manager; Gene Tenace, Dick Green, Bert Campaneris, Sal Bando, Reggie Jackson, Billy North, Joe Rudi, Ray Fosse (back injury), Deron Johnson (traded), Angel Mangual, Ted Kubiak, Jesus Alou, Herb Washington, Larry Haney, Claudell Washington, Pat Bourque (traded), Dal Maxvill (traded), Jim Holt (traded), Phil Garner, Manny Trillo (injury), Catfish Hunter, Ken Holtzman, Vida Blue, Rollie Fingers, Dave Hamilton, Glen Abbott, Paul Lindblad, Darold Knowles, Blue Moon Odom, Leon Hooten.

Autographed Ball	15.00
with Reggie Jackson	+10.00

1974 Texas Rangers: Billy Martin, Manager; Mike Hargrove, Dave Nelson (injury), Toby Harrah, Lenny Randle, Cesar Tovar, Joe Lovitto, Jeff Burroughs, Jim Sundberg, Jim Spencer, Alex Johnson (traded), Tommy Grieve, Jim Fregosi, Larry Brown, Duke Sims (traded), Leo Cardenas, Ferguson Jenkins, Jim Bibby, Jackie Brown, Steve Hargan, Steve Foucault, David Clyde, Bill Hands (traded), Don Stanhouse, Jim Merritt (sore arm), Jim Shellenback, Stan Thomas, Lloyd Allen (traded), Pete Broberg.

Autographed Ball	15.00
with Billy Martin	+5.00

1974 Pittsburgh Pirates (Eastern Division Champs): Danny Murtaugh, Manager; Bob Robertson, Rennie Stennett, Frank Taveras, Richie Hebner, Richie Zisk, Al Oliver, Willie Stargell, Manny Sanguillen, Ed Kirkpatrick, Gene Clines, Mario Mendoza, Dave Parker (leg injury), Paul Popovich, Art Howe, Kurt Bevacqua (traded), Dave Augustine, Jerry Reuss, Jim Rooker, Ken Brett (elbow injury), Dock Ellis (injured hand), Bruce Kison, Dave Giusti, Larry Demery, Ramon Hernandez, Daryl Patterson, Juan Pizarro, Kent Tekulve, Bob Moose (illness), Steve Blass, John Morlan.

Autographed Ball 10.00
with Willie Stargell +5.00
with Bob Moose +5.00
with Dave Parker +5.00
with Danny Murtaugh +5.00

1974 St. Louis Cardinals: Red Schoendienst, Manager; Joe Torre, Ted Sizemore, Mike Tyson, Ken Reitz, Reggie Smith, Bake McBride, Lou Brock, Ted Simmons, Jose Cruz, Luis Melendez, Tim McCarver (traded), Jim Dwyer, Jim Hickman, Jack Heidemann (traded), Tom Heintzelman, Lynn McGlothen, Bob Gibson, John Curtis, Al Hrabosky, Sonny Siebert (elbow injury), Mike Garman, Bob Forsch, Alan Foster, Rich Folkers, Orlando Pena (traded), Ray Bare, Pete Richert (traded), John Denny, Claude Osteen (traded), Mike Thompson (traded).

Autographed Ball 10.00
with Lou Brock +5.00
with Bob Gibson +10.00

1974 Los Angeles Dodgers (WORLD CHAMPIONS): Walt Alston, Manager; Steve Garvey, Dave Lopes, Bill Russell, Ron Cey, Willie Crawford, Jim Wynn, Bill Buckner, Steve Yeager, Joe Ferguson, Tom Paciorek, Von Joshua, Manny Mota, Lee Lacy, Rick Auerbach, Ken McMullen (voluntarily retired), Gail Hopkins, Andy Messersmith, Don Sutton, Mike Marshall, Tommy John (elbow injury), Doug Rau, Charlie Hough, Al Downing, Jim Brewer (back injury), Geoff Zahn, Rick Rhoden.

Autographed Ball 15.00
with Steve Garvey +5.00
with Mike Marshall +15.00

1974 Cincinnati Reds: Sparky Anderson, Manager; Tony Perez, Joe Morgan, Dave Concepcion, Dan Driessen, George Foster, Cesar Geronimo, Pete Rose, Johnny Bench, Darrel Chaney, Ken Griffey, Terry Crowley, Merv Rettenmund, Bill Plummer, Phil Gagliano, Andy Kosco (injury), Junior Kennedy, Hal King, Ray Knight, Jack Billingham, Don Gullett, Fred Norman, Clay Carroll, Clay Kirby, Pedro Borbon, Tom Carroll, Roger Nelson (injury), Tom Hall, Will McEnaney, Dick Baney, Rawly Eastwick.

Autographed Ball 10.00
with Johnny Bench +5.00
with Pete Rose +10.00

1975 AMERICAN LEAGUE ALL-STAR TEAM - Al Dark, Manager; Del Crandall, Billy Martin, Coaches; James Palmer, Fred Lynn, Carl Yastrzemski, Dave Chalk, Nolan Ryan, Bucky Dent, Rich Gossage, Jim Kaat, Jorge Orta (replaced by Toby Harrah), George Hendrick, Bill Freehan, Steve Busby, Harold McRae, Henry Aaron, George Scott, *Rod Carew, *Bobby Bonds, Jim Hunter, *Thurman Munson, *Graig Nettles, Vida Blue, *Dagoberto Campaneris, Roland Fingers, *Reggie Jackson, *Joe Rudi, *Gene Tenace, Claudell Washington, Mike Hargrove. Starters designated with an "*".

Autographed Ball 20.00
with Hank Aaron +10.00
with Thurman Munson +15.00

1975 NATIONAL LEAGUE ALL-STAR TEAM - Walt Alston, Mgr; Dan Murtaugh, Red Schoendienst, Coaches; Phil Niekro, Bill Madlock, *Johnny Bench, *Dave Concepcion, *Joe Morgan, Tony Perez, *Pete Rose, Bob Watson, *Ron Cey, *Steve Garvey, Mike Marshall, Andy Messersmith, Don Sutton, *Jim Wynn, Gary Carter, Jon Matlack, Tom Seaver, Larry Bowa, Dave Cash, Greg Luzinski, Tug McGraw, Al Oliver, Jerry Reuss, Manny Sanguillen, *Lou Brock, Reggie Smith, Randy Jones, Bobby Murcer. Starters designated with "*".

Autographed Ball 20.00
with Pete Rose +10.00
with Mike Marshall +15.00

1975 Boston Red Sox (American League Champs): Darrell Johnson, Manager; Carl Yastrzemski, Denny Doyle (traded), Rick Burleson, Rico Petrocelli, Dwight Evans, Fred Lynn, Jim Rice, Carlton Fisk (broken arm), Cecil Cooper, Bernie Carbo, Doug Griffin, Juan Beniquez, Rick Miller, Bob Heise, Bob Montgomery, Tim Blackwell, Tony Conigliaro (injury), Tim McCarver (traded), Dick McAuliffe (voluntarily retired), Rick Wise, Luis Tiant, Bill Lee, Roger Moret, Reggie Cleveland, Jim Willoughby, Dick Pole (injury), Dick Drago, Diego Segui, Jim Burton.

Autographed Ball 20.00
with C. Yastrzemski +15.00

1975 Baltimore Orioles: Earl Weaver, Manager; Lee May, Bobby Grich, Mark Belanger, Brooks Robinson, Ken Singleton, Paul Blair, Don Baylor, Dave Duncan, Tommy Davis, Al Bumbry, Ellie Hendricks, Jim Northrup, Tony Muser (traded), Doug DeCinces, Tim Nordbrook, Tom Shopay, Andy Etchebarren (injury)(traded), Jim Palmer, Mike Torrez, Mike Cuellar, Ross Grimsley, Doyle Alexander, Dyar Miller, Grant Jackson, Paul Mitchell, Wayne Garland, Mike Flanagan.

Autographed Ball 10.00
with Jim Palmer +5.00
with Brooks Robinson +10.00

1975 Oakland A's (Western Division Champs): Al Dark, Manager; Joe Rudi (injury), Phil Garner, Bert Campaneris, Sal Bando, Reggie Jackson, Billy North, Claudell Washington, Gene Tenace, Billy Williams, Jim Holt, Ted Martinez (traded), Ray Fosse, Don Hopkins, Matt Alexander (injury), Angel Mangual, Larry Haney, Tommy Harper (traded), Ted Kubiak (traded), Cesar Tovar (traded), Vida Blue, Ken Holtzman, Dick Bosman (traded), Rollie Fingers, Paul Lindblad, Jim Todd, Stan Bahnsen, Glenn Abbott, Sonny Siebert (injury) (traded), Jim Perry (traded), Mike Norris (elbow injury), Dave Hamilton, Blue Moon Odom (traded).

Autographed Ball 15.00
with Reggie Jackson +10.00

1975 Kansas City Royals: Jack McKeon, Whitey Herzog, Manager; John Mayberry, Cookie Rojas, Freddie Patek, George Brett, Al Cowens, Amos Otis, Hal McRae, Buck Martinez, Harmon Killebrew, Jim Wohlford, Frank White, Vada Pinson, Tony Solaita, Bob Stinson, Fran Healy (injury), Rodney Scott, Jamie Quirk, Steve Busby, Al Fitzmorris, Dennis Leonard, Marty Pattin, Doug Bird, Paul Splittorff, Nelson Briles (injury), Lindy McDaniel (illness), Bob McClure, Ray Sadecki, Mark Littell, Steve Mingori (illness).

Autographed Ball 10.00
with H. Killebrew +5.00
with George Brett +10.00

1975 Pittsburgh Pirates (Eastern Division Champs): Danny Murtaugh, Manager; Willie Stargell (broken rib), Rennie Stennett, Frank Taveras, Richie Hebner, Dave Parker, Al Oliver, Richie Zisk, Manny Sanguillen, Bill Robinson, Ed Kirkpatrick, Bob Robertson, Art Howe, Mario Mendoza, Duffy Dyer, Craig Reynolds, Willie Randolph, Paul Popovich, Jerry Reuss, Jim Rooker, Bruce Kison, Ken Brett (elbow injury), John Candelaria, Dock Ellis, Ramon Hernandez, Larry Demery, Dave Giusti, Sam McDowell, Bob Moose (finger injury), Kent Tekulve, Odell Jones, Jim Minshall.

Autographed Ball	15.00
with Willie Stargell	+5.00
with Bob Moose	+5.00
with Danny Murtaugh	+5.00

1975 Philadelphia Phillies: Danny Ozark, Manager; Dick Allen (traded), Dave Cash, Larry Bowa (broken finger), Mike Schmidt, Jay Johnstone, Garry Maddox (injury)(traded), Greg Luzinski, Bob Boone, Mike Anderson, Tommy Hutton, Johnny Oates (traded), Ollie Brown, Tony Taylor, Jerry Martin, Terry Harmon, Tim McCarver (traded), Alan Bannister, Willie Montanez (traded), Steve Carlton, Tom Underwood, Larry Christenson, Gene Garber, Tug McGraw, Jim Lonborg (injury), Tom Hilgendorf, Wayne Twitchell, Ron Schueler, Dick Ruthven, Wayne Simpson, Joe Hoerner (injury).

Autographed Ball	10.00
with Mike Schmidt	+5.00
with Steve Carlton	+5.00
with Dick Allen	+10.00

1975 Cincinnati Reds (WORLD CHAMPIONS): Sparky Anderson, Manager; Tony Perez, Joe Morgan, Dave Concepcion, Pete Rose, Ken Griffey, Cesar Geronimo, George Foster, Johnny Bench, Merv Rettenmund, Doug Flynn, Dan Driessen, Darrel Chaney, Terry Crowley, Bill Plummer, Ed Armbrister, John Vukovich, Don Gullett (injury), Gary Nolan, Jack Billingham, Fred Norman, Pat Darcy, Clay Kirby, Pedro Borbon, Clay Carroll, Will McEnaney, Rawly Eastwick, Tom Carroll.

Autographed Ball	15.00
with Johnny Bench	+5.00
with Pete Rose	+10.00

1975 Los Angeles Dodgers: Walt Alston, Manager; Steve Garvey, Dave Lopes, Bill Russell (injury), Ron Cey, Willie Crawford, Jim Wynn, Bill Buckner (ankle injury), Steve Yeager, Lee Lacy, Rick Auerbach (ankle injury), John Hale, Joe Ferguson (broken wrist), Ivan DeJesus, Tom Paciorek, Henry Cruz, Manny Mota, Leron Lee (traded), Ken McMullen, Andy Messersmith, Burt Hooton (traded), Don Sutton, Doug Rau, Mike Marshall (injury), Jim Brewer (traded), Rick Rhoden, Charlie Hough, Al Downing, Stan Wall, Geoff Zahn (traded), Juan Marichal.

Autographed Ball	10.00
with Juan Marichal	+5.00
with Steve Garvey	+5.00
with Mike Marshall	+10.00

1976 AMERICAN LEAGUE ALL-STAR TEAM - Darrell Johnson, Manager; Gene Mauch, Frank Robinson, Coaches; Mark Belanger, *Bob Grich, Carlton Fisk, *Fred Lynn, Luis Tiant, Carl Yastrzemski, Frank Tanana, Rich Gossage, Dave LaRoche, Mark Fidrych, *Ron LeFlore, *Daniel (Rusty) Staub, *George Brett, Hal McRae, Amos Otis, Fred Patek, Don Money, Bill Travers, *Rod Carew, Harold Wynegar, Chris Chambliss, Jim Hunter, Sparky Lyle, *Thurman Munson, Willie Randolph (replaced by Phil Garner), Mickey Rivers, Roland Fingers, *Toby Harrah. Starters designated with an "*".

Autographed Ball	20.00
with Thurman Munson	+15.00

1976 NATIONAL LEAGUE ALL-STAR TEAM - Sparky Anderson, Manager; John McNamara, Dan Ozark, Coaches; Andy Messersmith (replaced by Dick Ruthven), Steve Swisher, *Johnny Bench, *Dave Concepcion, *George Foster, Ken Griffey, Joe Morgan, Tony Perez, Pete Rose, Cesar Cedeno, Ken Forsch, Ron Cey, *Steve Garvey, Rick Rhoden, Bill Russell, Woody Fryman, *Dave Kingman, Jon Matlack, Tom Seaver, Rob Boone, Larry Bowa, Dave Cash, *Greg Luzinski, Mike Schmidt, Al Oliver, Bake McBride, Randy Jones, John Montefusco. Starters designated with an "*".

Autographed Ball	20.00
with Pete Rose	+10.00

1976 New York Yankees (American League Champs): Billy Martin, Manager; Chris Chambliss, Willie Randolph, Fred Stanley, Graig Nettles, Oscar Gamble, Mickey Rivers, Roy White, Thurman Munson, Carlos May (traded), Lou Piniella, Jim Mason, Sandy Alomar, Otto Velez, Fran Healy (traded), Ellie Hendricks (traded), Rick Dempsey (traded), Elliott Maddox (knee injury), Ed Figueroa, Catfish Hunter, Dock Ellis, Doyle Alexander (traded), Ken Holtzman (traded), Sparky Lyle, Grant Jackson (traded), Rudy May (traded), Dick Tidrow, Tippy Martinez (traded), Ron Guidry, Ken Brett (traded).

Autographed Ball	15.00
with Thurman Munson	+20.00

1976 Baltimore Orioles: Earl Weaver, Manager; Tony Muser, Bobby Grich, Mark Belanger, Doug DeCinces, Reggie Jackson, Paul Blair, Ken Singleton, Dave Duncan, Lee May, Al Bumbry, Andres Mora, Brooks Robinson, Rick Dempsey (traded), Tommy Harper, Terry Crowley (traded), Ellie Hendricks (traded), Tim Nordbrook (traded), Royle Stillman, Tom Shopay, Jim Palmer, Wayne Garland, Rudy May (traded), Ross Grimsley, Ken Holtzman (traded), Fred Holdsworth, Mike Cuellar, Tippy Martinez (traded), Doyle Alexander (traded), Mike Flanagan, Dyar Miller, Grant Jackson (traded), Dennis Martinez, Dave Pagan (traded), Scott McGregor.

Autographed Ball	10.00
with Brooks Robinson	+10.00
with Reggie Jackson	+10.00

1976 Kansas City Royals (Western Division Champs): Whitey Herzog, Manager; John Mayberry, Frank White, Freddie Patek, George Brett, Al Cowens, Amos Otis, Tom Poquette, Buck Martinez, Hal McRae, Jim Wohlford, Bob Stinson, Dave Nelson, Jamie Quirk, Cookie Rojas, Tony Solaita (traded), Rupe Jones, John Wathan (injury), Willie Wilson, Tommy Davis (traded), Dennis Leonard, Al Fitzmorris, Doug Bird, Paul Splittorff (injury), Mark Littell, Marty Pattin, Steve Mingori, Andy Hassler (traded), Larry Gura (injury), Steve Busby (injury), Tom Bruno, Tom Hall (traded).

Autographed Ball	10.00
with Willie Wilson	+5.00
with George Brett	+10.00

1976 Oakland A's: Chuck Tanner, Manager; Gene Tenace (knee injury), Phil Garner, Bert Campaneris, Sal Bando, Claudell Washington, Billy North, Joe Rudi, Larry Haney, Billy Williams, Don Baylor, Ken McMullen, Larry Lintz, Matt Alexander, Jeff Newman, Tommy Sandt, Tim Hosley (traded), Cesar Tovar (broken wrist) (traded), Ron Fairly (traded), Vida Blue, Mike Torrez, Rollie Fingers, Paul Mitchell, Stan Bahnsen, Jim Todd, Paul Lindblad, Dick Bosman, Mike Norris, Glenn Abbott.

Autographed Ball	20.00

1976 Philadelphia Phillies (Eastern Division Champs): Danny Ozark, Manager; Dick Allen (shoulder injury), Dave Cash, Larry Bowa, Mike Schmidt, Jay Johnstone, Garry Maddox, Greg Luzinski, Bob Boone, Jerry Martin, Bobby Tolan, Tommy Hutton, Ollie Brown, Tim McCarver, Terry Harmon, Johnny Oates (injury), Tony Taylor (injury), Steve Carlton, Jim Lonborg, Larry Christenson, Jim Kaat, Tom Underwood, Gene Garber, Ron Reed, Tug McGraw, Wayne Twitchell, Ron Schueler.

Autographed Ball	15.00
with Steve Carlton	+5.00
with Dick Allen	+10.00

1976 Pittsburgh Pirates: Danny Murtaugh, Manager; Willie Stargell, Rennie Stennett, Frank Taveras, Richie Hebner, Dave Parker, Al Oliver, Richie Zisk, Manny Sanguillen, Bill Robinson, Ed Kirkpatrick, Duffy Dyer, Tommy Helms, Bob Robertson, Mario Mendoza, Omar Moreno, John Candelaria, Jim Rooker, Bruce Kison, Jerry Reuss, Larry Demery, Doc Medich, Kent Tekulve, Dave Giusti (injury), Bob Moose, Ramon Hernandez (traded), Rick Langford, Doug Bair.

Autographed Ball	10.00
with Willie Stargell	+5.00
with Bob Moose	+10.00
with Danny Murtaugh	+10.00

1976 Cincinnati Reds (WORLD CHAMPIONS): Sparky Anderson, Manager; Tony Perez, Joe Morgan, Dave Concepcion, Pete Rose, Ken Griffey, Cesar Geronimo, George Foster, Johnny Bench, Dan Driessen, Doug Flynn, Mike Lum, Ed Armbrister, Bob Bailey, Bill Plummer, Joe Youngblood, Don Werner, Gary Nolan, Pat Zachry, Fred Norman, Jack Billingham, Don Gullett (injury), Santo Alcala, Rawly Eastwick, Manny Sarmiento, Pedro Borbon, Joe Henderson, Pat Darcy, Will McEnaney, Rich Hinton.

Autographed Ball	10.00
with Johnny Bench	+5.00
with Pete Rose	+10.00

1976 Los Angeles Dodgers: Walt Alston, Manager; Steve Garvey, Dave Lopes, Bill Russell, Ron Cey, Reggie Smith (traded), Dusty Baker, Bill Buckner, Steve Yeager, Ted Sizemore, Ed Goodson, Joe Ferguson (traded), Lee Lacy (traded), Manny Mota, Henry Cruz, John Hale, Ellie Rodriguez, Rick Auerbach, Glenn Burke, Jim Lyttle (traded), Kevin Pasley, Leron Lee, Ivan DeJesus, Don Sutton, Doug Rau, Rick Rhoden, Charlie Hough, Burt Hooton, Tommy John, Mike Marshall (traded), Stan Wall, Elias Sosa (traded), Dennis Lewallyn, Al Downing, Rick Sutcliffe.

Autographed Ball	15.00
with Steve Garvey	+5.00
with Mike Marshall	+15.00

1977 AMERICAN LEAGUE ALL-STAR TEAM - Billy Martin, Mgr.; Alex Grammas, Bob Lemon, Coaches; Jim Palmer, Ken Singleton, *Rick Burleson, Bill Campbell, *Carlton Fisk, Fred Lynn, Jim Rice, George Scott, *Carl Yastrzemski, Frank Tanana (replaced by Nolan Ryan who was replaced by Dave LaRoche), *Rich Zisk, Dennis Eckersley, Mark Fidrych (replaced by Jim Kern), Jason Thompson, *George Brett, Don Money (replaced by Jim Slaton), *Rod Carew, Larry Hisle, Butch Wynegar, *Reggie Jackson, Sparky Lyle, Thurman Munson, Graig Nettles, *Willie Randolph, Vida Blue (replaced by Wayne Gross), Ruppert Jones, Bert Campaneris, Ron Fairly. Starters designated with "*".

Autographed Ball	20.00
with C. Yastrzemski	+5.00
with Thurman Munson	+15.00

1977 NATIONAL LEAGUE ALL-STAR TEAM - Sparky Anderson, Manager; Tom Lasorda, Danny Ozark, Coaches; Willie Montanez, Julio (Jerry) Morales, Rick Reuschel, Bruce Sutter (replaced by Rich Gossage), Manny Trillo, *Johnny Bench, *Dave Concepcion, *George Foster, Ken Griffey, *Joe Morgan, Pete Rose, Tom Seaver, Joaquin Andujar, *Ron Cey, *Steve Garvey, Reggie Smith, Don Sutton, Ellis Valentine, John Stearns, Steve Carlton, *Greg Luzinski, Mike Schmidt, John Candelaria, *Dave Parker, Ted Simmons, Garry Templeton, Dave Winfield, Gary Lavelle. Starters designated with "*".

Autographed Ball	20.00
with Pete Rose	+15.00

1977 New York Yankees (WORLD CHAMPIONS): Billy Martin, Manager; Chris Chambliss, Willie Randolph, Bucky Dent, Graig Nettles, Reggie Jackson, Mickey Rivers, Roy White, Thurman Munson, Carlos May (traded), Lou Piniella, Paul Blair, Cliff Johnson (traded), Fred Stanley, Jim Wynn (traded), Fran Healy, George Zeber, Dell Alston, Ellie Hendricks, Dave Kingman (traded), Ron Guidry, Ed Figueroa, Don Gullett (injury), Mike Torrez (traded), Sparky Lyle, Dick Tidrow, Catfish Hunter (injury), Ken Holtzman, Ken Clay, Dock Ellis (traded), Gil Patterson (injury).

Autographed Ball	10.00
with Dave Kingman	+10.00
with Reggie Jackson	+10.00
with Thurman Munson	+10.00

1977 Baltimore Orioles: Earl Weaver, Manager; Lee May, Billy Smith, Mark Belanger, Doug DeCinces, Ken Singleton, Al Bumbry (leg injury), Pat Kelly, Rick Dempsey (injured hand), Eddie Murray, Tony Muser, Rich Dauer, Dave Skaggs, Andres Mora, Tom Shopay, Kiko Garcia, Elliott Maddox (injury), Larry Harlow, Mike Dimmel, Brooks Robinson (vol. retired), Jim Palmer, Rudy May, Mike Flanagan, Dennis Martinez, Ross Grimsley, Dick Drago (traded), Tippy Martinez, Scott McGregor, Dyar Miller (traded), Ed Farmer, Fred Holdsworth (injury) (traded).

Autographed Ball	15.00
with Brooks Robinson	+10.00

1977 Toronto Blue Jays: Roy Hartsfield, Manager; Doug Ault, Steve Staggs, Hector Torres, Roy Howell (injury)(traded), Otto Velez, Bob Bailor (injury), Al Woods, Alan Ashby, Ron Fairly, Sam Ewing, Doug Rader (traded), Dave McKay, Steve Bowling, John Scott, Gary Woods, Pete Garcia, Rick Cerone (injury), Tim Nordbrook (traded), Ernie Whitt (injury), Jim Mason (traded), Dave Lemanczyk, Jerry Garvin, Jesse Jefferson, Pete Vuckovich, Jim Clancy, Tom Murphy (traded), Jerry Johnson, Mike Willis, Bill Singer (injury), Jeff Byrd, Steve Hargan (traded), Dennis DeBarr, Tom Bruno, Chuck Hartenstein (injury).

Autographed Ball	30.00

1977 Kansas City Royals (Western Division Champs): Whitey Herzog, Manager; John Mayberry, Frank White, Freddie Patek, George Brett, Al Cowens, Amos Otis, Tom Poquette, Darrell Porter, Hal McRae, Joe Zdeb, Pete LaCock, Cookie Rojas, John Wathan, Bob Heise, Joe Lahoud, Buck Martinez, Dave Nelson (injury), Willie Wilson, U.L. Washington, Clint Hurdle, Dennis Leonard, Jim Colborn, Paul Splittorff, Doug Bird, Marty Pattin, Andy Hassler (injury), Mark Littell, Larry Gura, Steve Mingori.

Autographed Ball	10.00
with Willie Wilson	+5.00
with George Brett	+10.00

1977 Texas Rangers: Frank Lucchesi, Eddie Stanky, Connie Ryan, Billy Hunter, Managers; Mike Hargrove, Bump Wills, Bert Campaneris, Toby Harrah, Dave May, Juan Beniquez, Claudell Washington, Jim Sundberg, Willie Horton (traded), Tommy Grieve (injury), Ken Henderson (injury), Sandy Alomar, Johnny Ellis, Kurt Bevacqua, Bill Fahey, Jim Mason (traded), Lou Beasley, Keith Smith, Ed Kirkpatrick (traded), Eddie Miller, Jim Fregosi (knee injury) (traded), Pat Putnam, Roy Howell (traded), Gary Gray, Doyle Alexander, Gaylord Perry, Bert Blyleven, Adrian Devine, Dock Ellis (traded), Nelson Briles (traded), Darold Knowles, Len Barker, Paul Lindblad, Roger Moret (injury), Mike Marshall (knee injury) (traded), Steve Hargan (traded), Tommy Boggs.

Autographed Ball	20.00
with Mike Marshall	+20.00

1977 Seattle Mariners: Darrell Johnson, Manager; Dan Meyer, Jose Baez, Craig Reynolds, Bill Stein, Lee Stanton, Ruppert Jones, Steve Braun, Bob Stinson, Juan Bernhardt (injury), Dave Collins, Carlos Lopez (broken wrist), Larry Milbourne, Julio Cruz, Skip Jutze, Larry Cox, Tommy Smith, Jimmy Sexton, Luis Delgado, Ray Fosse (traded), Joe Lis, Glenn Abbott, Enrique Romo, John Montague, Dick Pole (injury), Gary Wheelock (elbow injury), Mike Kekich (shoulder injury), Tom House (arm injury) (traded), Bill Laxton (sore arm) (traded), Paul Mitchell (traded), Doc Medich (traded), Tommy Moore, Stan Thomas (shoulder injury) (traded), Dave Pagan (traded), Rick Jones (elbow injury), Frank MacCormack, Byron McLaughlin, Rick Honeycutt, Bob Galasso, Diego Segui.

Autographed Ball	25.00

1977 Philadelphia Phillies (Eastern Division Champs): Danny Ozark, Manager; Richie Hebner, Ted Sizemore, Larry Bowa, Mike Schmidt, Jay Johnstone, Garry Maddox, Greg Luzinski, Bob Boone, Jerry Martin, Tommy Hutton, Tim McCarver, Bake McBride (traded), Dave Johnson, Ollie Brown, Terry Harmon, Barry Foote (traded), Bobby Tolan (traded), Dane Iorg (traded), Fred Andrews, Steve Carlton, Larry Christenson, Jim Lonborg (shoulder injury), Randy Lerch, Gene Garber, Warren Brusstar, Tug McGraw (elbow injury), Ron Reed, Jim Kaat, Tom Underwood (traded), Wayne Twitchell (traded).

Autographed Ball	15.00
with Steve Carlton	+5.00
with Mike Schmidt	+5.00

1977 Pittsburgh Pirates: Chuck Tanner, Manager; Willie Stargell (elbow injury), Rennie Stennett (leg injury), Frank Taveras, Phil Garner, Dave Parker, Omar Moreno, Al Oliver, Ed Ott, Bill Robinson, Duffy Dyer, Fernando Gonzalez, Mario Mendoza, Jerry Hairston (traded), Bobby Tolan (traded), Jim Fregosi (traded), Ken Macha, Miguel Dilone (finger injury), Ed Kirkpatrick (traded), Dale Berra, Tommy Helms (traded), Mike Easler, John Candelaria, Jim Rooker, Rich Gossage, Kent Tekulve, Jerry Reuss, Bruce Kison, Terry Forster, Larry Demery, Grant Jackson, Odell Jones, Eddie Whitson.

Autographed Ball	15.00
with W. Stargell	+5.00

1977 Los Angeles Dodgers (National League Champs): Tom Lasorda, Manager; Steve Garvey, Dave Lopes, Bill Russell, Ron Cey, Reggie Smith, Rick Monday, Dusty Baker, Steve Yeager, Glenn Burke, John Hale, Lee Lacy (injury), Ted Martinez (injury), Ed Goodson, Johnny Oates, Boog Powell, Manny Mota, Joe Simpson, Vic Davalillo, Jerry Grote (traded), Rafael Landestoy, Jeff Leonard, Ron Washington, Tommy John, Rick Rhoden, Don Sutton, Doug Rau, Burt Hooton, Charlie Hough, Lance Rautzhan, Mike Garman, Dennis Lewallyn, Elias Sosa, Stan Wall, Bobby Castillo, Al Downing (injury).

Autographed Ball	15.00
with Steve Garvey	+5.00

1977 Cincinnati Reds: Sparky Anderson, Manager; Dan Driessen, Joe Morgan, Jose Concepcion, Pete Rose, Ken Griffey, Cesar Geronimo, George Foster, Johnny Bench, Mike Lum, Ray Knight, Ed Armbrister, Champ Summers, Bill Plummer, Bob Bailey (traded), Doug Flynn (traded), Rick Auerbach, Tom Seaver (traded), Fred Norman, Pedro Borbon, Jack Billingham, Dale Murray, Doug Capilla (traded), Paul Moskau, Woody Fryman (vol. retired), Gary Nolan (traded), Tom Hume, Pat Zachry (traded), Rawly Eastwick (traded), Mario Soto, Santo Alcala (traded), Manny Sarmiento, Mike Caldwell (traded).

Autographed Ball	10.00
with Johnny Bench	+5.00
with Tom Seaver	+5.00
with Pete Rose	+10.00

1978 AMERICAN LEAGUE ALL-STAR TEAM - Billy Martin, Mgr.; Dorrel Herzog, Don Zimmer, Coaches; Mike Flanagan, Eddie Murray, Jim Palmer, Rick Burleson (replaced by Jerry Remy), *Carlton Fisk, Fred Lynn, *Jim Rice, Carl Yastrzemski (replaced by Dwight Evans), Frank Tanana, Chet Lemon, Jim Kern, Jason Thompson, *George Brett, *Freddie Patek, Frank White, *Don Money, Lary Sorensen, *Rod Carew, Rich Gossage, Ron Guidry, *Reginald Jackson (replaced by Graig Nettles who was replaced by Larry Hisle), Thurman Munson (replaced by Darrell Porter), Matt Keough, Craig Reynolds, James Sundberg, *Richard Zisk, Roy Howell. Starters designated with an "*".

Autographed Ball	30.00
with Thurman Munson	+20.00

1978 NATIONAL LEAGUE ALL-STAR TEAM - Thomas Lasorda, Manager; Charles Tanner, Daniel Ozark, Coaches; Jeff Burroughs, Phil Niekro, Bruce Sutter, *Johnny Bench (replaced by Biff Pocoroba), David Concepcion, *George Foster, *Joe Morgan, *Pete Rose, Tom Seaver, Terry Puhl, Ron Cey, *Steve Garvey, Thomas John, David Lopes, *Rick Monday, Reggie Smith, Ross Grimsley, Stephen Rogers, Pat Zachry, Bob Boone, *Lawrence Bowa, *Greg Luzinski, Wilver Stargell, Ted Simmons, Roland Fingers, David Winfield, Vida Blue, Jack Clark. Starters designated with an "*".

Autographed Ball	20.00
with Pete Rose	+10.00

1978 New York Yankees (WORLD CHAMPIONS): Billy Martin, Dick Howser, Bob Lemon, Managers; Chris Chambliss, Willie Randolph (knee injury), Bucky Dent (leg injury), Graig Nettles, Reggie Jackson, Mickey Rivers, Lou Piniella, Thurman Munson, Cliff Johnson, Roy White, Fred Stanley, Paul Blair, Jim Spencer, Gary Thomasson (traded), Brian Doyle, Jay Johnstone (traded), Mike Heath, Damaso Garcia, Ron Guidry, Ed Figueroa, Catfish Hunter (shoulder injury), Goose Gossage, Sparky Lyle, Dick Tidrow, Jim Beattie, Don Gullett (shoulder injury), Ken Clay (injury), Rawly Eastwick (traded), Ken Holtzman (traded), Paul Lindblad (traded), Dave Rajsich, Ron Davis, Andy Messersmith (injury).

Autographed Ball	10.00
with Reggie Jackson	+5.00
with Billy Martin	+5.00
with Thurman Munson	+15.00

1978 Boston Red Sox: Don Zimmer, Manager; George Scott (injury), Jerry Remy, Rick Burleson, Butch Hobson, Dwight Evans, Fred Lynn, Carl Yastrzemski, Carlton Fisk, Jim Rice, Jack Brohamer, Frank Duffy, Bob Bailey, Garry Hancock, Fred Kendall, Bernie Carbo (injury) (traded), Bob Montgomery, Dennis Eckersley, Mike Torrez, Bob Stanley, Luis Tiant, Bill Lee, Jim Wright, Bill Campbell (injury), Dick Drago, Tom Burgmeier, Andy Hassler (traded), Allen Ripley.

Autographed Ball	15.00
with C. Yastrzemski	+5.00

1978 Kansas City Royals (Western Division Champs): Whitey Herzog, Manager; Pete LaCock, Frank White, Freddie Patek, George Brett, Al Cowens (injury), Amos Otis, Clint Hurdle, Darrell Porter, Hal McRae, Willie Wilson, Tom Poquette, Jerry Terrell, U.L. Washington, John Wathan, Steve Braun (traded), Joe Zdeb, Jamie Quirk, Joe Lahoud, Dennis Leonard, Paul Splittorff, Larry Gura, Rich Gale, Al Hrabosky, Doug Bird, Marty Pattin, Steve Busby, Jim Colborn (traded), Steve Mingori, Andy Hassler (injury) (traded), Randy McGilberry.

Autographed Ball 10.00
with George Brett +10.00

1978 California Angels: Dave Garcia, Jim Fregosi, Managers; Ron Jackson (broken wrist), Bobby Grich, Dave Chalk, Carney Lansford (injury), Lyman Bostock (deceased), Rick Miller, Joe Rudi (injury), Brian Downing, Don Baylor, Ken Landreaux, Ron Fairly, Tony Solaita, Terry Humphrey, Rance Mulliniks, Merv Rettenmund, Jim Anderson, Danny Goodwin, Ike Hampton, Dave Machemer, Frank Tanana, Chris Knapp (injury), Don Aase, Dave LaRoche, Nolan Ryan (injury), Dyar Miller (injury), Paul Hartzell, Dave Frost, Tom Griffin, Ken Brett, Al Fitzmorris (traded).

Autographed Ball 15.00
with L. Bostock +20.00

1978 Philadelphia Phillies (Eastern Division Champs): Danny Ozark, Manager; Richie Hebner, Ted Sizemore (injured hand), Larry Bowa, Mike Schmidt, Bake McBride, Garry Maddox, Greg Luzinski, Bob Boone, Jerry Martin, Tim McCarver, Jose Cardenal, Bud Harrelson, Jim Morrison, Dave Johnson (traded), Barry Foote, Jay Johnstone (traded), Orlando Gonzalez, Lonnie Smith, Pete Mackanin, Kerry Dineen, Keith Moreland, Steve Carlton, Dick Ruthven (traded), Larry Christenson, Randy Lerch, Jim Kaat, Tug McGraw, Jim Lonborg, Warren Brusstar, Ron Reed, Rawly Eastwick (traded), Gene Garber (traded).

Autographed Ball 15.00
with Steve Carlton +5.00
with Mike Schmidt +5.00

1978 Pittsburgh Pirates: Chuck Tanner, Manager; Willie Stargell, Rennie Stennett (leg injury), Frank Taveras, Phil Garner, Dave Parker, Omar Moreno, Bill Robinson, Ed Ott, John Milner, Manny Sanguillen, Steve Brye, Duffy Dyer, Mario Mendoza, Dale Berra, Ken Macha, Jim Fregosi (retired to manage), Fernando Gonzalez (traded), Matt Alexander, Doe Boyland, Dave May (traded), Steve Nicosia, Don Robinson, Bert Blyleven, John Candelaria, Jim Rooker, Kent Tekulve, Jim Bibby, Grant Jackson, Bruce Kison (injury), Eddie Whitson, Jerry Reuss, Dave Hamilton (traded).

Autographed Ball 15.00
with W. Stargell +5.00

1978 Los Angeles Dodgers (National League Champs): Tom Lasorda, Manager; Steve Garvey, Dave Lopes, Bill Russell, Ron Cey, Reggie Smith, Billy North (traded), Dusty Baker, Steve Yeager (injury), Rick Monday, Lee Lacy, Vic Davalillo, Joe Ferguson (traded), Ted Martinez, Jerry Grote (broken wrist), Johnny Oates, Manny Mota, Glenn Burke (traded), Rudy Law, Joe Simpson, Myron White, Pedro Guerrero, Burt Hooton, Tommy John, Doug Rau, Don Sutton, Rick Rhoden, Bob Welch, Terry Forster, Charlie Hough, Lance Rautzhan, Rick Sutcliffe, Mike Garman (traded), Bobby Castillo.

Autographed Ball 15.00
with Steve Garvey +5.00

1978 Cincinnati Reds: Sparky Anderson, Manager; Dan Driessen, Joe Morgan, Dave Concepcion, Pete Rose, Ken Griffey, Cesar Geronimo, George Foster, Johnny Bench (injury), Dave Collins, Junior Kennedy, Mike Lum, Ray Knight, Ken Henderson (traded), Rick Auerbach, Vic Correll, Don Werner, Champ Summers, Arturo DeFreitas, Ron Oester, Mike Grace, Harry Spilman, Tom Seaver, Bill Bonham (injury), Fred Norman, Dave Tomlin, Manny Sarmiento, Pedro Borbon, Tom Hume, Doug Bair, Paul Moskau, Mike LaCoss, Mario Soto, Dale Murray (traded), Doug Capilla.

Autographed Ball 10.00
with Johnny Bench +5.00
with Pete Rose +10.00

1979 AMERICAN LEAGUE ALL-STAR TEAM - Bob Lemon, Manager; Pat Corrales, Roy Hartsfield, Darrell Johnson, Coaches; Ken Singleton, Don Stanhouse, Rick Burleson, *Fred Lynn, *James Rice, Rob Stanley, *Carl Yastrzemski, Don Baylor, *Rod Carew (replaced by Cecil Cooper), Mark Clear, Brian Downing, Bob Grich, Nolan Ryan, Chet Lemon, Sid Monge, Steve Kemp, *George Brett, *Darrell Porter, *Frank White, *Roy Smalley, Ron Guidry, Reggie Jackson, Tom John, Graig Nettles, Jeff Newman, Bruce Bochte, Jim Kern, Dave Lemanczyk. Starters designated with an "*".

Autographed Ball 25.00
with Reggie Jackson +5.00

1979 NATIONAL LEAGUE ALL-STAR TEAM - Tom Lasorda, Mgr.; Dan Ozark, Chuck Tanner, Coaches; Gary Matthews, Dave Kingman (replaced by Keith Hernandez), Bruce Sutter, Dave Concepcion (replaced by Larry Parrish), *George Foster, Mike LaCoss, Joe Morgan, Joaquin Andujar, Joe Niekro, Joe Sambito, Ron Cey, *Steve Garvey, *Dave Lopes, Gary Carter, Steve Rogers, Lee Mazzilli, Bob Boone, *Larry Bowa, Steve Carlton, Pete Rose, *Mike Schmidt, *Dave Parker, Lou Brock, *Ted Simmons (replaced by Johnny Bench who was replaced by John Stearns), Garry Templeton (replaced by Craig Reynolds), Gaylord Perry, *Dave Winfield, Jack Clark. Starters designated with "*".

Autographed Ball 20.00
with Pete Rose +10.00

1979 Baltimore Orioles (American League Champs): Earl Weaver, Manager; Eddie Murray, Rich Dauer, Kiko Garcia, Doug DeCinces (back injury), Ken Singleton, Al Bumbry, Gary Roenicke, Rick Dempsey, Lee May, Mark Belanger (broken finger), John Lowenstein (ankle injury), Pat Kelly, Billy Smith, Dave Skaggs, Terry Crowley, Benny Ayala, Larry Harlow (traded), Wayne Krenchicki, Mark Corey, Bob Molinaro, Tom Chism, Mike Flanagan, Dennis Martinez, Scott McGregor, Steve Stone, Tippy Martinez, Jim Palmer (elbow injury), Sammy Stewart, Don Stanhouse, Tim Stoddard (injury), Dave Ford.

Autographed Ball 15.00
with Jim Palmer +5.00

1979 Milwaukee Brewers: George Bamberger, Mgr; Cecil Cooper, Paul Molitor, Robin Yount, Sal Bando, Sixto Lezcano, Gorman Thomas, Ben Oglivie, Charlie Moore, Dick Davis, Don Money (injury), Jim Gantner, Buck Martinez, Jim Wohlford, Larry Hisle (injury), Ray Fosse, Lenn Sakata, Tim Nordbrook, Mike Caldwell, Jim Slaton, Lary Sorenson, Bill Travers, Moose Haas, Jerry Augustine, Bob McClure, Bill Castro, Bob Galasso, Paul Mitchell (traded), Reggie Cleveland.

Autographed Ball 15.00

1979 California Angels (Western Division Champs): Jim Fregosi, Manager; Rod Carew (injury), Bobby Grich (injury), Bert Campaneris (traded), Carney Lansford, Dan Ford, Rick Miller (injury), Joe Rudi (injury), Brian Downing, Don Baylor, Willie Aikens, Jim Anderson, Larry Harlow (traded), Willie Davis, Tom Donohue, Merv Rettenmund, Dickie Thon, Rance Mulliniks, Bobby Clark, Orlando Ramirez, Terry Humphrey (injury), Ralph Garr (traded), Dave Frost, Nolan Ryan, Mark Clear, Jim Barr, Don Aase, Frank Tanana (injury), Dave LaRoche, Chris Knapp (injury), John Montague (traded), Ralph Bottin, Mike Barlow (injury), Dyar Miller (traded).

Autographed Ball 10.00
with Rod Carew +5.00
with Nolan Ryan +5.00

1979 Kansas City Royals: Whitey Herzog, Manager; Pete LaCock, Frank White (injury), Freddie Patek (injury), George Brett, Al Cowens, Amos Otis, Willie Wilson, Darrell Porter, Hal McRae, U.L. Washington, John Wathan, Clint Hurdle, Steve Braun (injury), Todd Cruz, Jamie Quirk, George Scott (traded), Jerry Terrell (injury), Tom Poquette (traded), Joe Zdeb, Jim Nettles, German Barranca, Jim Gaudet, Paul Splittorff, Dennis Leonard (elbow injury), Larry Gura, Al Hrabosky, Rich Gale, Steve Busby, Marty Pattin (injury), Eduardo Rodriguez (injury), Craig Chamberlain, Dan Quisenberry, Steve Mingori (injury), Bill Paschall, Renie Martin.
Autographed Ball 10.00
with George Brett +10.00

1979 Texas Rangers: Pat Corrales, Manager; Pat Putnam, Bump Wills, Nelson Norman, Buddy Bell, Richie Zisk, Mickey Rivers (traded), Al Oliver, Jim Sundberg, Johnny Ellis, Bill Sample, Johnny Grubb (injury), Mike Jorgensen (injury), Larvell Blanks (injury), Oscar Gamble (injury) (traded), Eric Soderholm (traded), Dave Roberts (injury), Willie Montanez (traded), LaRue Washington, Gary Gray, Dave Chalk (traded), Bert Campaneris (traded), Steve Comer, Ferguson Jenkins, Jim Kern, Doc Medich, Jon Matlack (elbow injury), Doyle Alexander (injury), Sparky Lyle, Danny Darwin, Ed Farmer (traded), Johnny Johnson (traded), Dave Rajsich, Brian Allard, Dock Ellis (traded), Bob Babcock. Autographed Ball 15.00

1979 Pittsburgh Pirates (WORLD CHAMPIONS): Chuck Tanner, Mgr.; Willie Stargell, Rennie Stennett, Tim Foli (traded), Bill Madlock (traded), Dave Parker, Omar Moreno, Bill Robinson, Ed Ott, Phil Garner, John Milner, Lee Lacy, Steve Nicosia, Manny Sanguillen, Mike Easler, Dale Berra, Matt Alexander, Frank Taveras (traded), John Candelaria, Bruce Kison, Jim Bibby, Bert Blyleven, Enrique Romo, Kent Tekulve, Grant Jackson, Don Robinson, Dave Roberts (traded), Jim Rooker, Ed Whitson (traded), Joe Coleman (traded), Dock Ellis (traded), Rick Rhoden (injury).
Autographed Ball 15.00
with Dave Parker +5.00
with W. Stargell +10.00

1979 Montreal Expos: Dick Williams, Manager; Tony Perez, Rodney Scott, Chris Speier, Larry Parrish, Ellis Valentine, Andrew Dawson, Warren Cromartie, Gary Carter, Jerry White, Tommy Hutton, Dave Cash, Jim Mason, Rusty Staub (traded), Tony Solaita (traded), Duffy Dyer, Ken Macha, Tony Bernazard, John Tamargo (traded), Tim Raines, Bill Lee, Steve Rogers, Dave Palmer, Rudy May, Dan Schatzeder, Ross Grimsley, Scott Sanderson, Elias Sosa, Stan Bahnsen, Woody Fryman, Bill Atkinson, Dale Murray (traded), Bill Gullickson.
Autographed Ball 15.00
with Tim Raines +5.00

1979 Cincinnati Reds (Western Division Champs): John McNamara, Manager; Dan Driessen, Joe Morgan, Dave Concepcion, Ray Knight, Ken Griffey (injury), Cesar Geronimo, George Foster (injury), Johnny Bench, Dave Collins, Junior Kennedy, Paul Blair (traded), Heity Cruz (traded), Rick Auerbach, Vic Correll, Harry Spilman, Champ Summers (traded), Arturo DeFreitas, Ken Henderson (injury) (traded), Tom Seaver, Mike LaCoss, Doug Bair, Fred Norman, Tom Hume, Bill Bonham (injury), Frank Pastore, Paul Moskau, Mario Soto (injury), Dave Tomlin, Pedro Borbon (traded), Manny Sarmiento. Autographed Ball 10.00
with Johnny Bench +5.00
with Pete Rose +10.00

1979 Houston Astros: Bill Virdon, Manager; Cesar Cedeno, Art Howe (injury), Craig Reynolds, Enos Cabell, Jeff Leonard, Terry Puhl, Jose Cruz, Alan Ashby (injury), Rafael Landestoy, Denny Walling, Julio Gonzalez, Bruce Bochy, Jimmy Sexton, Bob Watson (traded), Jesus Alou, Luis Pujols, Danny Heep, Reggie Baldwin, Dave Bergman, Joe Niekro, J.R. Richard, Joaquin Andujar, Ken Forsch (injury), Joe Sambito, Rick Williams, Bert Roberge (injury), Randy Niemann, Frank Riccelli (injury), Vern Ruhle (injury), George Throop (traded), Pete Ladd, Tom Dixon (injury), Frank LaCorte (traded), Bob McLaughlin (traded).
Autographed Ball 15.00

1980 AMERICAN LEAGUE ALL-STAR TEAM - Earl Weaver, Manager; Frank Robinson, James Frey, Coaches; Al Bumbry, Steve Stone, Thomas Burgmeier, *Carlton Fisk, *Fred Lynn, *James Rice (replaced due to injury), *Rod Carew, Bob Grich, Ed Farmer, Jorge Orta, Lance Parrish, Alan Trammell, *George Brett (replaced due to injury), Larry Gura, Darrell Porter, Cecil Cooper, *Paul Molitor (replaced due to injury), Ben Oglivie, Robin Yount, Ken Landreaux, *Russel (Bucky) Dent, Rich Gossage, *Reggie Jackson, Thomas John, Graig Nettles, Willie Randolph, Rickey Henderson, Rick Honeycutt, David (Buddy) Bell, Al Oliver, David Stieb. Starters designated with an "*".
Autographed Ball 20.00
with Reggie Jackson +5.00

1980 NATIONAL LEAGUE ALL-STAR TEAM - Chuck Tanner, Manager; John McNamara, Bill Virdon, Coaches; Dale Murphy, *Dave Kingman, Bruce Sutter, *Johnny Bench, Dave Concepcion, Ken Griffey, Jose Cruz, J. Rodney Richard, *Steve Garvey, *Dave Lopes, Jerry Reuss, *Bill Russell, *Reggie Smith, Bob Welch, Gary Carter, John Stearns, Steve Carlton, Pete Rose, *Mike Schmidt (replaced by Ray Knight), Jim Bibby, Phil Garner, *Dave Parker, Kent Tekulve, George Hendrick, Keith Hernandez, Ken Reitz, Dave Winfield, Vida Blue (replaced by Ed Whitson). Starters designated with an "*". Autographed Ball 20.00
with Pete Rose +10.00

1980 New York Yankees (Eastern Division Champs): Dick Howser, Manager; Bob Watson, Willie Randolph, Bucky Dent, Graig Nettles (illness), Reggie Jackson, Ruppert Jones (injury), Lou Piniella, Rick Cerone, Eric Soderholm, Bobby Brown, Bobby Murcer, Jim Spencer, Oscar Gamble (injury), Joe Lefebvre, Aurelio Rodriguez (traded), Fred Stanley, Dennis Werth, John Oates, Brian Doyle, Paul Blair (retired - coach), Tommy John, Ron Guidry, Rudy May, Tom Underwood, Ron Davis, Luis Tiant (injury), Goose Gossage, Gaylord Perry, Doug Bird, Ed Figueroa, Mike Griffin, Tim Lollar, Jim Kaat (traded). Autographed Ball 15.00
with Reggie Jackson +5.00

1980 Baltimore Orioles: Earl Weaver, Manager; Eddie Murray, Rich Dauer, Mark Belanger, Doug DeCinces, Ken Singleton, Al Bumbry, Gary Roenicke (broken wrist), Rick Dempsey, Terry Crowley, Kiko Garcia, John Lowenstein (injury), Pat Kelly, Dan Graham, Lee May, Benny Ayala, Lenn Sakata, Mark Corey, Dave Skaggs (traded), Steve Stone, Scott McGregor, Jim Palmer, Mike Flanagan, Sammy Stewart, Dennis Martinez (injury), Tim Stoddard, Tippy Martinez, Dave Ford, Paul Hartzell. Autographed Ball 15.00

1980 Detroit Tigers: Sparky Anderson, Mgr; Richie Hebner (injury), Lou Whitaker, Alan Trammell, Tom Brookens, Al Cowens (traded), Kirk Gibson (injured wrist), Steve Kemp, Lance Parrish, Champ Summers, Rick Peters, John Wockenfuss, Tim Corcoran, Jim Lentine (traded), Dave Stegman, Duffy Dyer, Stan Papi (traded), Mark Wagner, Jason Thompson (traded), Lynn Jones (injury), Jack Morris, Aurelio Lopez, Milt Wilcox, Dan Schatzeder, Dan Petry, Dave Rozema, Bruce Robbins, Roger Weaver (injury), Pat Underwood, Mark Fidrych, Dave Tobik, John Hiller (vol. retired), Jerry Ujdur, Jack Billingham (traded).
Autographed Ball 10.00
with Kirk Gibson +:.00

1980 Cleveland Indians: Dave Garcia, Manager; Mike Hargrove, Duane Kuiper (knee injury), Tom Veryzer (shoulder injury), Toby Harrah, Jorge Orta, Rick Manning, Miguel Dilone, Ron Hassey, Joe Charboneau, Jerry Dybzinski, Alan Bannister (traded), Bo Diaz, Gary Alexander, Dave Rosello, Cliff Johnson (traded), Jack Brohamer (traded), Dell Alston, Gary Gray, Ron Pruitt (traded), Andres Mora, Len Barker, Dan Spillner, Rick Waits, John Denny (foot injury), Victor Cruz, Wayne Garland, Ross Grimsley (traded), Sid Monge, Bob Owchinko, Sandy Wihtol, Mike Stanton.

Autographed Ball	10.00
with Joe Charboreau	+3.00

THE INCREMENTAL VALUE OF THE AUTOGRAPH OF A PARTICULAR PLAYER TO A PARTICULAR BALL IS UNIQUE TO THAT BALL. IT IS NOT THE EXOGENOUS VALUE OF THAT PLAYER'S AUTOGRAPH. SEE THE INTRODUCTION TO TEAM AUTOGRAPHED BALLS.

CLEVELAND

1980 Toronto Blue Jays: Bobby Mattick, Manager; John Mayberry, Damaso Garcia, Alfredo Griffin, Roy Howell, Lloyd Moseby, Rick Bosetti (injury), Al Woods, Ernie Whitt, Otto Velez (injury), Barry Bonnell, Bob Bailor, Bob Davis, Garth lorg, Joe Cannon, Doug Ault, Danny Ainge (reported late), Steve Braun (traded), Willie Upshaw, Paul Hodgson, Jim Clancy, Dave Stieb, Joey McLaughlin, Jackson Todd, Paul Mirabella, Jerry Garvin, Jesse Jefferson (traded), Mike Barlow, Tom Buskey, Luis Leal, Jack Kucek, Mike Willis, Dave Lemanczyk, Den Schrom, Balor Moore.

Autographed Ball	10.00
Danny Ainge	+5.00

1980 Kansas City Royals (American League Champs): Jim Frey, Manager; Willie Aikens, Frank White, U.L. Washington, George Brett (foot injury), Clint Hurdle, Amos Otis (injury), Willie Wilson, Darrell Porter (illness), Hal McRae, John Wathan, Pete LaCock, Dave Chalk, Jamie Quirk, Rusty Torres, Rance Mulliniks, Jose Cardenal (traded), Jerry Terrell, Bobby Detherage, Steve Braun (traded), Onix Concepcion, Manny Castillo, German Barranca, Ken Phelps, Dennis Leonard, Larry Gura, Paul Splittorff, Rich Gale, Dan Quisenberry, Renie Martin, Marty Pattin, Gary Christenson, Jeff Twitty, Steve Busby, Ken Brett, Rawley Eastwick.

Autographed Ball	10.00
with George Brett	5.00

1980 Oakland A's: Billy Martin, Manager; Dave Revering, Dave McKay, Mario Guerrero, Wayne Gross, Tony Armas, Dwayne Murphy, Rickey Henderson, Jim Essian, Mitchell Page, Jeff Newman, Rob Picciolo, Mike Heath, Mickey Klutts (knee injury), Jeff Cox, Mike Davis, Mike Edwards, Orlando Gonzalez, Randy Elliott, Mike Norris, Rick Langford, Matt Keough, Steve McCatty, Brian Kingman, Bob Lacey, Jeff Jones, Dave Beard, Craig Minetto, Dave Hamilton.

Autographed Ball	10.00
with Billy Martin	+5.00

1980 Minnesota Twins: Gene Mauch, John Goryl, Mgrs.; Ron Jackson, Rob Wilfong, Roy Smalley, John Castino, Hosken Powell, Ken Landreaux, Rick Sofield, Butch Wynegar, Jose Morales, Pete Mackanin, Mike Cubbage, Glenn Adams, Dave Edwards, Danny Goodwin, Bombo Rivera (injury), Sal Butera, Willie Norwood, Greg Johnston, Gary Ward, Jesus Vega, Lenny Faedo, Bob Randall, Jerry Koosman, Geoff Zahn, Darrell Jackson, Doug Corbett, Pete Redfern (injury), Roger Erickson, Al Williams, Fernando Arroyo, John Verhoeven, Mike Marshall, Mike Kinnenun, Mike Bacsik.

Autographed Ball	10.00
with Mike Marshall	+10.00

1980 Texas Rangers: Pat Corrales, Mgr.; Pat Putnam, Bump Wills, Bud Harrelson (injury), Buddy Bell, Johnny Grubb, Mickey Rivers, Al Oliver, Jim Sundberg, Richie Zisk, Jim Norris, Pepe Frias (traded), Rusty Staub (broken finger), Dave Roberts, Bill Sample, Johnny Ellis, Mike Richardt, Nelson Norman, Odie Davis, Tucker Ashford, Danny Walton, Doc Medich, Danny Darwin, Ferguson Jenkins (suspended by court ruling), Jon Matlack, Gaylord Perry (traded), Sparky Lyle (traded), John Butcher, Jim Kern (injury), Dave Rajsich, Johnny Johnson, Charlie Hough (traded), Ken Clay, Steve Comer (injury), Adrian Devine (injury), Bob Babcock, Ed Figueroa (traded).

Autographed Ball	12.00

1980 Chicago White Sox: Tony LaRussa, Manager; Mike Squires, Jim Morrison, Todd Cruz (traded), Kevin Bell, Harold Baines, Chet Lemon, Wayne Nordhagen, Bruce Kimm, Lamar Johnson, Greg Pryor, Bob Molinaro, Thad Bosley (injured wrist), Marv Foley, Alan Bannister (traded), Junior Moore, Rusty Kuntz, Leo Sutherland, Ron Pruitt (traded), Claudell Washington, Glenn Borgmann, Harry Chappas, Fran Mullins, Ricky Seilheimer, Randy Johnson, Minnie Minoso, Britt Burns, Rich Dotson, Lamarr Hoyt, Steve Trout, Ed Farmer, Mike Proly, Rich Wortham, Ken Kravec, Ross Baumgarten (shoulder injury), Guy Hoffman, Dewey Robinson, Randy Scarberry, Nardi Contreras.

Autographed Ball	12.00

1980 California Angels: Jim Fregosi, Manager; Rod Carew, Bobby Grich, Freddie Patek, Carney Lansford, Dan Ford (injury), Rick Miller, Joe Rudi (injury), Brian Downing (broken ankle), Don Baylor (injury), Larry Harlow, Jason Thompson (traded), Tom Donohue, Dickie Thon, Bobby Clark, Bert Campaneris, Stan Cliburn, Dan Whitmer, Al Cowens (traded), Dave Skaggs (broken ankle)(traded), Gil Kubski, Ralph Garr, John Harris, Todd Cruz (traded), Mark Clear, Frank Tanana, Don Aase, Freddie Martinez, Andy Hassler (traded), John Montague, Dave Frost (injury), Ed Halicki (injury) (traded), Dave LaRoche, Bruce Kison (injury), Dave Lemanczyk (traded), Chris Knapp, Jim Dorsey, Jim Barr (injury), Dave Schuler, Bob Ferris, Ralph Botting.

Autographed Ball	13.00

1980 Seattle Mariners: Darrell Johnson, Maury Wills, Managers; Bruce Bochte, Julio Cruz, Mario Mendoza, Ted Cox, Leon Roberts, Juan Beniquez (shoulder injury), Dan Meyer, Larry Cox, Willie Horton (injury), Joe Simpson, Tom Paciorek, Jim Anderson, Larry Milbourne, Rodney Craig, Bill Stein (injury), Bob Stinson, Jerry Narron, Reggie Walton, Marc Hill (traded), Dave Edler, Kim Allen, Glenn Abbott, Rick Honeycutt, Floyd Bannister, Shane Rawley, Dave Heaverlo, Jim Beattie, Rob Dressler, Byron McLaughlin, Dave Roberts (traded), Mike Parrott (injury), Manny Sarmiento.

Autographed Ball	10.00
with Maury Wills	+5.00

1980 Philadelphia Phillies (WORLD CHAMPIONS): Dallas Green, Manager; Pete Rose, Manny Trillo, Larry Bowa, Mike Schmidt, Bake McBride, Garry Maddox, Greg Luzinski (knee injury), Bob Boone, Greg Gross, Lonnie Smith, Del Unser, George Vukovich, Keith Moreland, Ramon Aviles, John Vukovich, Luis Aguayo, Jay Loviglio, Bob Dernier, Tim McCarver, Steve Carlton, Dick Ruthven, Bob Walk, Ron Reed, Kevin Saucier (arm injury), Marty Bystrom, Larry Christenson (elbow injury), Tug McGraw, Randy Lerch, Nino Espinosa (shoulder injury), Warren Brusstar (shoulder injury), Dickie Noles, Sparky Lyle (traded), Lerrin LaGrow, Dan Larson.

Autographed Ball	10.00
with Steve Carlton	+5.00
with Pete Rose	+10.00

1980 Montreal Expos: Dick Williams, Mgr; Warren Cromartie, Rodney Scott, Chris Speier, Larry Parrish (injury), Ellis Valentine (injury), Andre Dawson, Ron LeFlore, Gary Carter, Rowland Office, Jerry White, Tony Bernazard, Tommy Hutton, Ken Macha, John Tamargo (injury), Bob Pate, Brad Mills, Bill Almon (traded), Tim Raines, Willie Montanez (traded), Bobby Ramos, Steve Rogers, Scott Sanderson, Bill Gullickson, Elias Sosa, Dave Palmer (injury), Woody Fryman, Charlie Lea, Stan Bahnsen, Fred Norman, Bill Lee (injury), Ross Grimsley (traded), Dale Murray, John D'Acquisto (traded). Autographed Ball 10.00
with Tim Raines +5.00

1980 Pittsburgh Pirates: Chuck Tanner, Manager; Willie Stargell (knee injury), Phil Garner, Tim Foli, Bill Madlock, Dave Parker, Omar Moreno, Mike Easler, Ed Ott, John Milner, Lee Lacy, Bill Robinson, Dale Berra, Steve Nicosia, Manny Sanguillen, Matt Alexander, Vance Law, Kurt Bevacqua (traded), Tony Pena, Bernie Carbo (traded), Jim Bibby, John Candelaria, Grant Jackson, Kent Tekulve, Bert Blyleven, Eddie Solomon, Rick Rhoden, Don Robinson, Enrique Romo, Jim Rooker (injury), Rod Scurry. Autographed Ball 10.00
with W. Stargell +3.00

1980 St. Louis Cardinals: Ken Boyer, Jack Krol, Whitey Herzog, Red Schoendienst, Managers; Keith Hernandez, Ken Oberkfell (injury), Garry Templeton (injury), Ken Reitz, George Hendrick, Tony Scott, Bobby Bonds, Ted Simmons, Dane Iorg, Leon Durham, Terry Kennedy, Tommy Herr, Mike Phillips, Mike Ramsey, Tito Landrum, Keith Smith, Steve Swisher, Bernie Carbo (traded), Pete Vuckovich, Bob Forsch, Jim Kaat (traded), Bob Sykes, John Littlefield, Silvio Martinez (injury), John Urrea, Don Hood, John Fulgham (injury), Andy Rincon, Kim Seaman, Roy Thomas, John Martin, Pedro Borbon, Donnie Moore, Jeff Little, Al Olmsted, George Frazier, Mark Littell (injury), Jim Otten. Autographed Ball 8.00
with G. Templeton +5.00

1980 New York Mets: Joe Torre, Manager; Lee Mazzilli, Doug Flynn (broken ankle), Frank Taveras, Elliott Maddox, Claudell Washington (traded), Joel Youngblood, Steve Henderson, John Stearns (injury), Mike Jorgensen, Alex Trevino, Jerry Morales, Dan Norman, Bill Almon (traded), Jose Moreno, Ron Hodges (injury), Mookie Wilson, Wally Backman, Jose Cardenal (traded), Hubie Brooks, Mario Ramirez, Butch Benton, Mark Bomback, Jeff Reardon, Neil Allen, Pete Falcone, Ray Burris (injury), Tom Hausman, Pat Zachry (injury), Craig Swan (injury), Ed Glynn, Johnny Pacella, Mike Scott, Ed Lynch, Dyar Miller, Kevin Kobel, Roy Jackson, Scott Holman, Juan Berenguer. Autographed Ball 12.00

1980 Chicago Cubs: Preston Gomez, Joey Amalfitano, Managers; Bill Buckner, Mike Tyson, Ivan DeJesus, Lenny Randle, Mike Vail, Jerry Martin, Dave Kingman (injury), Tim Blackwell, Larry Biittner, Jesus Figueroa, Mick Kelleher, Scot Thompson (injury), Steve Dillard, Cliff Johnson (traded), Barry Foote (injury), Ken Henderson (injury), Jim Tracy, Carlos Lezcano, Steve Ontiveros (went to Japanese League), Mike O'Berry, Steve Macko (injury), Lynn McGlothen, Rick Reuschel, Dennis Lamp, Mike Krukow, Dick Tidrow, Bruce Sutter, Bill Caudill, Lee Smith, Doug Capilla, Randy Martz, Willie Hernandez, George Riley.
Autographed Ball 8.00
with Dave Kingman +5.00

1980 Houston Astros (Western Division Champs): Bill Virdon, Manager; Art Howe, Joe Morgan, Craig Reynolds, Enos Cabell, Terry Puhl, Cesar Cedeno, Jose Cruz, Alan Ashby, Rafael Landestoy, Denny Walling, Dave Bergman, Jeff Leonard, Luis Pujols, Julio Gonzalez, Danny Heep, Bruce Bochy, Gary Woods, Joe Niekro, Vern Ruhle, Ken Forsch, Nolan Ryan, J.R. Richard (stroke), Joe Sambito, Frank LaCorte, Dave Smith, Joaquin Andujar, Bert Roberge, Randy Niemann, Gordy Pladson. Autographed Ball 10.00
with J.R. Richard +5.00

1980 Los Angeles Dodgers: Tom Lasorda, Manager; Steve Garvey, Dave Lopes, Bill Russell (injury), Ron Cey, Reggie Smith (shoulder injury), Rudy Law, Dusty Baker, Steve Yeager, Derrel Thomas, Jay Johnstone, Rick Monday, Gary Thomasson, Joe Ferguson (back injury), Pedro Guerrero (knee injury), Mickey Hatcher, Mike Scioscia, Jack Perconte, Pepe Frias (traded), Manny Mota (retired to coach), Vic Davalillo, Jerry Reuss, Burt Hooton, Bob Welch, Don Sutton, Bobby Castillo, Steve Howe, Dave Goltz, Joe Beckwith, Rick Sutcliffe, Fernando Valenzuela, Don Stanhouse (back injury), Terry Forster (elbow injury), Charlie Hough (traded).
Autographed Ball 10.00
with F. Valenzuela +10.00

1980 Cincinnati Reds: John McNamara, Manager; Dan Driessen, Junior Kennedy, Dave Concepcion, Ray Knight, Ken Griffey, Dave Collins, George Foster, Johnny Bench, Cesar Geronimo, Ron Oester, Sammy Mejias, Harry Spilman, Joe Nolan (traded), Heity Cruz, Don Werner, Rick Auerbach (traded), Paul Householder, Vic Correll (injury), Eddie Milner, Frank Pastore (injury), Mario Soto, Tom Seaver (shoulder injury), Charlie Leibrandt, Mike LaCoss, Paul Moskau, Tom Hume, Joe Price, Dave Tomlin, Doug Bair, Bill Bonham (shoulder injury), Bruce Berenyi.
Autographed Ball 10.00
with Johnny Bench +5.00

1980 Atlanta Braves: Bobby Cox, Manager; Chris Chambliss, Glenn Hubbard, Luis Gomez, Bob Horner, Gary Matthews, Dale Murphy, Jeff Burroughs, Bruce Benedict, Jerry Royster, Mike Lum, Larvell Blanks, Brian Asselstine (knee injury), Biff Pocoroba (arm injury), Bill Nahorodny, Rafael Ramirez, Charlie Spikes, Chico Ruiz, Terry Harper, Gary Cooper, Joe Nolan (traded), Eddie Miller, Phil Niekro, Doyle Alexander, Tommy Boggs, Rick Matula, Larry McWilliams, Rick Camp, Gene Garber, Al Hrabosky, Larry Bradford, Preston Hanna.
Autographed Ball 8.00
with Bob Horner +5.00

1980 San Francisco Giants: Dave Bristol, Manager; Mike Ivie (vol. retired), Rennie Stennett, Johnnie LeMaster, Darrell Evans, Jack Clark (injury), Billy North, Larry Herndon, Milt May, Terry Whitfield, Jim Wohlford, Joe Strain (injury), Mike Sadek, Max Venable, Joe Pettini, Rich Murray (injury), Willie McCovey (vol. retired), Roger Metzger, Guy Sularz, Marc Hill (traded), Dennis Littlejohn, Chris Bourjos, Vida Blue (injury), Eddie Whitson, Allen Ripley, Bob Knepper, Gary Lavelle, Tom Griffin, Al Holland, Greg Minton, Alan Hargesheimer, John Montefusco (injury), Bill Bordley, Mike Rowland, Randy Moffitt (illness), Ed Halicki (traded).
Autographed Ball 8.00
with Willie McCovey +5.00

1980 San Diego Padres: Jerry Coleman, Mgr.; Willie Montanez (traded), Dave Cash, Ozzie Smith, Aurelio Rodriguez (traded), Dave Winfield, Jerry Mumphrey, Gene Richards, Gene Tenace, Tim Flannery, Bill Fahey, Jerry Turner (injury), Barry Evans, Paul Dade, Kurt Bevacqua (traded), Von Joshua, Luis Salazar, Broderick Perkins, Craig Stimac, Randy Bass, Fred Kendall, Rollie Fingers, Bob Shirley, John Curtis, Steve Mura, Rick Wise (injury), Gary Lucas, Randy Jones (injury), Juan Eichelberger (illness), Dennis Kinney, Eric Rasmussen, Tom Tellmann, John D'Acquisto (traded), Mike Armstrong. Autographed Ball 8.00
with Dave Winfield +5.00

1960 TOPPS TATOOS (96) 1 9/16" X 3 1/2"

The 1960 Topps baseball tattoos are actually the reverses of the wrappers in which the product "Tattoo Bubble Gum" was packaged. The dimensions given are for the entire wrapper. The wrapper lists instructions on how to apply the tattoo. The tattoos are unnumbered and are colored. Additions to the checklist would be appreciated.

	MINT	VG-E	F-G
COMPLETE SET	40.00	26.00	11.00
COMMON PLAYER	.40	.25	.10
1 Aaron	2.50	1.70	.70
2 Allison	.40	.25	.10
3 Antonelli	.40	.25	.10
4 Ashburn	.75	.50	.20
5 Banks	1.75	1.15	.50
6 Berra	1.75	1.15	.50
7 Burdette	.60	.40	.15
8 Cepeda	.90	.60	.25
9 Colavito	.75	.50	.20
10 Cunningham	.40	.25	.10
11 Daley	.40	.25	.10
12 Drysdale	1.25	.85	.35
13 Face	.60	.40	.15
14 Ford	1.25	.85	.35
15 Fox	.75	.50	.20
16 Francona	.40	.25	.10
17 Freese	.40	.25	.10
18 Gilliam	.75	.50	.20
19 Groat	.60	.40	.15
20 Herbert	.40	.25	.10
21 Hobbie	.40	.25	.10
22 Jensen	.60	.40	.15
23 S. Jones	.40	.25	.10
24 Kaline	1.75	1.15	.50
25 Killebrew	1.25	.85	.35
26 Lary	.40	.25	.10
27 Law	.40	.25	.10
28 Malzone	.40	.25	.10
29 Maris	1.25	.85	.35
30 Mathews	1.25	.85	.35
31 Mays	2.50	1.70	.70
32 McLish	.40	.25	.10
33 Moon	.40	.25	.10
34 Moryn	.40	.25	.10
35 Mossi	.40	.25	.10
36 Neal	.40	.25	.10
37 Newcombe	.60	.40	.15
38 Pappas	.60	.40	.15
39 Pascual	.40	.25	.10
40 Pierce	.60	.40	.15
41 F. Robinson	1.75	1.15	.50
42 Roberts	1.25	.85	.35
43 Runnells	.40	.25	.10
44 Score	.60	.40	.15
45 Spahn	1.25	.85	.35
46 Temple	.40	.25	.10
47 Triandos	.60	.40	.15
48 Walker	.40	.25	.10
49 White	.60	.40	.15
50 Woodling	.40	.25	.10
51 E. Wynn	1.25	.85	.35
52 Cubs	.30	.20	.08
53 Reds	.30	.20	.08
54 Dodgers	.30	.20	.08
55 Braves	.30	.20	.08
56 Phillies	.30	.20	.08
57 Pirates	.30	.20	.08
58 Cardinals	.30	.20	.08
59 Giants	.30	.20	.08
60 Orioles	.30	.20	.08
61 Red Sox	.30	.20	.08
62 White Sox	.30	.20	.08
63 Indians	.30	.20	.08
64 Tigers	.30	.20	.08
65 Athletics	.30	.20	.08
66 Yankees	.40	.25	.10
67 Senators	.30	.20	.08

1961 TOPPS MAGIC RUB–OFFS (36) 2 1/16" X 3 1/16"

There are 36 "Magic Rub Offs" in this set of inserts also marketed in packages of 1961 Topps baseball cards. Of this number, 18 are team designs, while the remaining 18 depict players. The latter—one from each team—were apparently selected for their unusual nicknames. Note: The Duke Maas insert is misspelled "Mass."

	MINT	VG-E	F-G
COMPLETE SET	25.00	17.00	7.00
COMMON PLAYER	.75	.50	.20
1 Detroit Tigers	.75	.50	.20
2 N.Y. Yankees	1.00	.65	.30
3 Minn. Twins	.75	.50	.20
4 Wash. Senators	.75	.50	.20
5 Boston Red Sox	.75	.50	.20
6 L.A. Angels	.75	.50	.20
7 K.C. A's	.75	.50	.20
8 Balt. Orioles	.75	.50	.20
9 Chicago White Sox	.75	.50	.20
10 Cleveland Indians	.75	.50	.20
11 Pitt. Pirates	.75	.50	.20
12 S.F. Giants	.75	.50	.20
13 L.A. Dodgers	.75	.50	.20
14 Phila. Phillies	.75	.50	.20
15 Cinc. Red Legs	.75	.50	.20
16 St. Louis Cards	.75	.50	.20

1961 Topps Magic Rub Offs

17 Chicago Cubs	.75	.50	.20
18 Milwaukee Braves	.75	.50	.20
19 John Romano-Indians	.75	.50	.20
20 Ray Moore-Twins	.75	.50	.20
21 Ernie Banks-Cubs	2.25	1.50	.65
22 Charlie Maxwell-Tigers	.75	.50	.20
23 Yogi Berra-Yanks	2.25	1.50	.65
24 Henry Dotterer-Senators	.75	.50	.20
25 Jim Brosnan-Reds	.75	.50	.20
26 Billy Martin-Braves	1.50	1.00	.40
27 Jackie Brandt-Orioles	.75	.50	.20
28 Duke Maas-Angels	.75	.50	.20
29 Pete Runnels-Red Sox	.75	.50	.20
30 Joe Gordon-A's	.75	.50	.20
31 Sad Sam Jones-Giants	.75	.50	.20
32 Walt Moryn-Cards	.75	.50	.20
33 Harvey Haddix-Pirates	.75	.50	.20
34 Frank Howard-Dodgers	1.00	.65	.30
35 Turk Lown-White Sox	.75	.50	.20
36 Frank Hererra-Phillies	.75	.50	.20

1961 TOPPS STAMPS (207) 1 3/8" X 1 3/16"

There are 207 different baseball players depicted in this stamp series, which was issued as an insert in packages of the regular Topps cards of 1961. The set is actually comprised of 208 stamps: 104 players are pictured on brown stamps and 104 players appear on green stamps, with Kaline found in both colors. The stamps were issued in attached pairs and an album was sold separately (10 cents) at retail outlets.

	MINT	VG-E	F-G
COMPLETE SET	45.00	30.00	12.00
COMMON PLAYER	.18	.12	.05
1 Altman	.18	.12	.05
2 Anderson (brown)	.18	.12	.05
3 Ashburn	.25	.16	.06
4 Ernie Banks	1.00	.65	.25
5 Bouchee	.18	.12	.05
6 Brewer	.18	.12	.05
7 Ellsworth	.18	.12	.05
8 Elston	.18	.12	.05
9 Santo	.25	.16	.06
10 Taylor	.18	.12	.05
11 Will	.18	.12	.05
12 Williams	.25	.16	.06
13 Bailey	.18	.12	.05
14 Bell	.18	.12	.05
15 Brosnan (brown)	.18	.12	.05
16 Cardenas	.18	.12	.05
17 Freese	.18	.12	.05
18 Kasko	.18	.12	.05
19 Lynch	.18	.12	.05
20 B. Martin	.50	.35	.15
21 O'Toole	.18	.12	.05
22 Pinson	.25	.16	.06
23 Post	.18	.12	.05
24 F. Robinson	1.00	.65	.25
25 T. Davis	.25	.16	.06
26 Drysdale	.50	.35	.15
27 Howard (brown)	.25	.16	.06
28 Larker	.18	.12	.05
29 Moon	.18	.12	.05
30 Neal	.18	.12	.05
31 Podres	.18	.12	.05
32 Roebuck	.18	.12	.05
33 Roseboro	.18	.12	.05
34 Sherry	.18	.12	.05
35 Snider	1.00	.65	.25
36 S. Williams	.18	.12	.05
37 Aaron	2.00	1.30	.55
38 Adcock	.18	.12	.05
39 Bill Bruton	.18	.12	.05
40 Buhl	.18	.12	.05
41 Covington (brown)	.18	.12	.05
42 Crandall	.18	.12	.05
43 Jay	.18	.12	.05
44 Mantilla	.18	.12	.05
45 Mathews	.50	.35	.15
46 McMillan	.18	.12	.05
47 Spahn	.50	.35	.15
48 Willey	.18	.12	.05
49 Buzhardt	.18	.12	.05
50 Callison	.18	.12	.05
51 Curry	.18	.12	.05
52 Dalrymple (brown)	.18	.12	.05
53 Del Greco	.18	.12	.05
54 Farrell	.18	.12	.05
55 Gonzales	.18	.12	.05
56 Herrera	.18	.12	.05
57 Mahaffey	.18	.12	.05
58 Roberts	.50	.35	.15
59 Taylor	.18	.12	.05
60 Walls	.18	.12	.05
61 Burgess	.18	.12	.05
62 Face (brown)	.25	.16	.06
63 Friend	.18	.12	.05
64 Groat	.25	.16	.06
65 Hoak	.18	.12	.05
66 Law	.18	.12	.05
67 Mazeroski	.25	.16	.06
68 Nelson	.18	.12	.05
69 Skinner	.18	.12	.05
70 H. Smith	.18	.12	.05
71 Stuart	.18	.12	.05
72 Virdon	.25	.16	.06
73 Blasingame	.18	.12	.05
74 Bressoud (brown)	.18	.12	.05
75 Cepeda	.50	.35	.15
76 Davenport	.18	.12	.05
77 Kuenn	.25	.16	.06
78 Landrith	.18	.12	.05
79 Marichal	.50	.35	.15
80 Mays	2.00	1.30	.55
81 McCormick	.18	.12	.05
82 McCovey	1.00	.65	.25
83 O'Dell	.18	.12	.05
84 Sanford	.18	.12	.05
85 Boyer	.25	.16	.06
86 Flood	.25	.16	.06
87 Grammas (brown)	.18	.12	.05
88 L. Jackson	.18	.12	.05
89 Javier	.18	.12	.05
90 Kline	.18	.12	.05
91 L. McDaniel	.18	.12	.05
92 Musial	2.00	1.30	.55
93 Simmons	.18	.12	.05
94 H. Smith	.18	.12	.05
95 D. Spencer	.18	.12	.05
96 D. White	.18	.12	.05
97 Barber	.18	.12	.05
98 Brandt (brown)	.18	.12	.05
99 Breeding	.18	.12	.05
100 Estrada	.18	.12	.05
101 Gentile	.18	.12	.05
102 Hansen	.18	.12	.05
103 Pappas	.18	.12	.05
104 B. Robinson	1.00	.65	.25
105 Stephens	.18	.12	.05
106 Triandos	.18	.12	.05
107 Wilhelm	.25	.16	.06
108 Brewer	.18	.12	.05
109 Conley (brown)	.18	.12	.05
110 Delock	.18	.12	.05
111 Geiger	.18	.12	.05
112 Jensen	.25	.16	.06

1961 Topps Stamps

113 Malzone	.18	.12	.05
114 Monbouquette	.18	.12	.05
115 Nixon	.18	.12	.05
116 Runnels	.18	.12	.05
117 Tasby	.18	.12	.05
118 Wertz	.18	.12	.05
119 Yastrzemski	2.00	1.30	.55
120 Aparicio	.25	.16	.06
121 Kemmerer (brown)	.18	.12	.05
122 Landis	.18	.12	.05
123 Lollar	.18	.12	.05
124 J. C. Martin	.18	.12	.05
125 Minoso	.25	.16	.06
126 Pierce	.25	.16	.06
127 Shaw	.18	.12	.05
128 A. Smith	.18	.12	.05
129 Staley	.18	.12	.05
130 Wynn	.50	.35	.15
131 Antonelli (brown)	.18	.12	.05
132 Aspromonte	.18	.12	.05
133 Francona	.18	.12	.05
134 Grant	.18	.12	.05
135 Held	.18	.12	.05
136 Latman	.18	.12	.05
137 J. Perry	.18	.12	.05
138 Piersall	.25	.16	.06
139 Phillips	.18	.12	.05
140 Power	.18	.12	.05
141 Romano	.18	.12	.05
142 Temple	.18	.12	.05
143 Aguirre (brown)	.18	.12	.05
144 Bolling	.18	.12	.05
145 Boros	.18	.12	.05
146 Bunning	.25	.16	.06
147 Cash	.25	.16	.06
148 Chiti	.18	.12	.05
149 Fernandez	.18	.12	.05
150 Gernert	.18	.12	.05
151 Kaline (green)	1.00	.65	.25
152 Kaline (brown)	1.00	.65	.25
153 Lary	.18	.12	.05
154 Maxwell	.18	.12	.05
155 Sisler	.18	.12	.05
156 Bauer	.25	.16	.06
157 Boyd (brown)	.18	.12	.05
158 Carey	.18	.12	.05
159 Daley	.18	.12	.05
160 Hall	.18	.12	.05
161 Hartman	.18	.12	.05
162 Herbert	.18	.12	.05
163 Herzog	.25	.16	.06
164 Lumpe	.18	.12	.05
165 Siebern	.18	.12	.05
166 Throneberry	.25	.16	.06
167 Tuttle	.18	.12	.05
168 D. Williams	.25	.16	.06
169 Casale (brown)	.18	.12	.05
170 Cerv	.18	.12	.05
171 Garver	.18	.12	.05
172 Hunt	.18	.12	.05
173 Kluszewski	.25	.16	.06
174 Sadowski	.18	.12	.05
175 Yost	.18	.12	.05
176 Allison	.18	.12	.05
177 Battey (brown)	.18	.12	.05
178 Bertoia	.18	.12	.05
179 Gardner	.18	.12	.05
180 Kaat	.25	.16	.06
181 Killebrew	.50	.35	.15
182 Lemon	.18	.12	.05
183 Pascual	.18	.12	.05
184 Ramos	.18	.12	.05
185 Stobbs	.18	.12	.05
186 Versalles	.18	.12	.05
187 Whisenant	.18	.12	.05
188 Arroyo (brown)	.18	.12	.05
189 Berra	1.00	.65	.25
190 Blanchard	.18	.12	.05
191 Boyer	.18	.12	.05
192 Ditmar	.18	.12	.05
193 Ford	1.00	.65	.25
194 Howard	.25	.16	.06
195 Tony Kubek	.25	.16	.06
196 Mickey Mantle	2.50	1.70	.75
197 Roger Maris	2.00	1.30	.55
198 Shantz	.25	.16	.06
199 Stafford	.18	.12	.05
200 Bob Turley	.25	.16	.06
201 Daley (brown)	.18	.12	.05
202 Dick Donovan	.18	.12	.05
203 Klaus	.18	.12	.05
204 Klippstein	.18	.12	.05
205 Dale Long	.18	.12	.05
206 Semproch	.18	.12	.05
207 Gene Woodling	.18	.12	.05

1962 BASEBALL BUCKS (96)

1 3/4" X 4 1/8"

There are 96 "Baseball Bucks" in this unusual set released in its own one-cent package in 1962. Each depicts a player with accompanying biography and facsimile autograph to the left. To the right is found a drawing of the player's home stadium, and his team and position are listed under the ribbon design containing his name. The team affiliation and league are also indicated within circles on the reverse.

	MINT	VG-E	F-G
COMPLETE SET	200.00	130.00	55.00
COMMON PLAYER	1.00	.65	.30
1 Aaron (Braves)	11.00	7.00	3.00
2 Adcock (Braves)	1.00	.65	.30
3 Altman (Cubs)	1.00	.65	.30
4 Archer (Kansas City A's)	1.00	.65	.30
5 Ashburn (Mets)	1.75	1.15	.50
6 Banks (Cubs)	5.00	3.50	1.40
7 Battey (Twins)	1.00	.65	.30
8 Bell (Mets)	1.00	.65	.30
9 Berra (Yankees)	5.00	3.50	1.40
10 Boyer (Cardinals)	1.75	1.15	.50
11 Brandt (Orioles)	1.00	.65	.30
12 Bunning (Tigers)	1.25	.85	.35
13 Burdette (Braves)	1.25	.85	.35
14 Cardwell (Cubs)	1.00	.65	.30
15 Cash (Tigers)	1.25	.85	.35
16 Cepeda (Giants)	1.75	1.15	.50
17 Clemente (Pirates)	6.50	4.50	2.00
18 Colavito (Tigers)	1.75	1.15	.50
19 Cottier (Senators)	1.00	.65	.30
20 Craig (Mets)	1.00	.65	.30
21 Daniels (Senators)	1.00	.65	.30
22 Demeter (Phillies)	1.00	.65	.30
23 Drysdale (Dodgers)	2.50	1.70	.70
24 Estrada (Orioles)	1.00	.65	.30
25 Farrell (Colts)	1.00	.65	.30
26 Ford (Yankees)	2.50	1.70	.70
27 Fox (White Sox)	1.75	1.15	.50
28 Francona (Indians)	1.00	.65	.30
29 Friend (Pirates)	1.00	.65	.30
30 Gentile (Orioles)	1.00	.65	.30
31 Gernert (Colts)	1.00	.65	.30

32 Green (Twins)	1.00	.65	.30
33 Groat (Pirates)	1.25	.85	.35
34 Held (Indians)	1.00	.65	.30
35 Hoak (Pirates)	1.00	.65	.30
36 Hodges (Mets)	2.50	1.70	.70
37 Howard, E. (Yankees)	1.75	1.15	.50
38 Howard, F. (Dodgers)	1.75	1.15	.50
39 Howser (Kansas City A's)	1.75	1.15	.50
40 Hunt (Angels)	1.00	.65	.30
41 Jackson (Cardinals)	1.00	.65	.30
42 Jay (Reds)	1.00	.65	.30
43 Kaline (Tigers)	5.00	3.50	1.40
44 Killebrew (Twins)	2.50	1.70	.70
45 Koufax (Dodgers)	6.50	4.50	2.00
46 Kuenn (Giants)	1.25	.85	.35
47 Landis (White Sox)	1.00	.65	.30
48 Larker (Colts)	1.00	.65	.30
49 Lary (Tigers)	1.00	.65	.30
50 Lumpe (Kansas City A's)	1.00	.65	.30
51 Mahaffey (Phillies)	1.00	.65	.30
52 Malzone (Red Sox)	1.00	.65	.30
53 Mantilla (Mets)	1.00	.65	.30
54 Mantle (Yankees)	15.00	10.00	4.00
55 Maris (Yankees)	2.50	1.70	.70
56 Mathews (Braves)	2.50	1.70	.70
57 Mays (Giants)	11.00	7.00	3.00
58 McBride (Angels)	1.00	.65	.30
59 McCormick (Giants)	1.00	.65	.30
60 Miller (Giants)	1.00	.65	.30
61 Minoso (Cardinals)	1.75	1.15	.50
62 Moon (Dodgers)	1.25	.85	.35
63 Musial (Cardinals)	11.00	7.00	3.00
64 O'Connell (Senators)	1.00	.65	.30
65 O'Toole (Reds)	1.00	.65	.30
66 Pascual (Twins)	1.00	.65	.30
67 Perry (Indians)	1.25	.85	.35
68 Piersall (Senators)	1.25	.85	.35
69 Pinson (Reds)	1.25	.85	.35
70 Pizarro (White Sox)	1.00	.65	.30
71 Podres (White Sox)	1.25	.85	.35
72 Power (Indians)	1.00	.65	.30
73 Purkey (Reds)	1.75	1.15	.50
74 Ramos (Twins)	1.00	.65	.30
75 Robinson, Brooks (Orioles)	5.00	3.50	1.40
76 Robinson, Floyd (W.S.)	1.00	.65	.30
77 Robinson, Frank (Reds)	5.00.	3.50	1.40
78 Romano (Indians)	1.00	.65	.30
79 Runnels (Red Sox)	1.00	.65	.30
80 Schwall (Red Sox)	1.00	.65	.30
81 Shantz (Colts)	1.25	.85	.35
82 Siebern (Kansas City A's)	1.00	.65	.30
83 Sievers (Phillies)	1.25	.85	.35
84 Smith (Colts)	1.00	.65	.30
85 Spahn (Braves)	2.50	1.70	.70
86 Stuart (Pirates)	1.25	.85	.35
87 Taylor (Phillies)	1.00	.65	.30
88 Thomas (Angels)	1.00	.65	.30
89 Triandos (Orioles)	1.25	.85	.35
90 Wagner (Angels)	1.00	.65	.30
91 Walker (Kansas City A's)	1.00	.65	.30
92 White (Cardinals)	1.25	.85	.35
93 Williams (Cubs)	1.75	1.15	.50
94 Woodling (Senators)	1.00	.65	.30
95 Wynn (White Sox)	2.50	1.70	.70
96 Yastrzemski (Red Sox)	11.00	7.00	3.00

1962 TOPPS STAMPS (201) 1 3/8" X 1 7/8"

The 200 baseball player stamps inserted into the Topps regular issue of 1962 are color photos set upon red or yellow backgrounds (100 players for each color). They came in two-stamp panels with a small additional strip which contained advertising for an album. The illustration at left shows the Callison stamp, which is misspelled "Callizon." Sievers appears with Kansas City or Philadelphia.

	MINT	VG-E	F-G
COMPLETE SET	45.00	30.00	12.00
COMMON PLAYER	.18	.12	.05
1 Baltimore Emblom	.18	.12	.05
2 Adair	.18	.12	.05
3 Brandt	.18	.12	.05
4 Estrada	.18	.12	.05
5 Gentile	.18	.12	.05
6 Hansen	.18	.12	.05
7 Pappas	.18	.12	.05
8 B. Robinson	1.00	.65	.25
9 Triandos	.18	.12	.05
10 Wilhelm	.25	.16	.06
11 Boston Emblem	.18	.12	.05
12 Fornieles	.18	.12	.05
13 Gary Geiger	.18	.12	.05
14 Malzone	.18	.12	.05
15. Monbouquette	.18	.12	.05
16 Nixon	.18	.12	.05
17 Runnels	.18	.12	.05
18 Schilling	.18	.12	.05
19 Schwall	.18	.12	.05
20 Yastrzemski	2.00	1.30	.55
21 Chicago Emblem	.18	.12	.05
22 Aparicio	.25	.16	.06
23 Carreon	.18	.12	.05
24 Fox	.25	.16	.06
25 Herbert	.18	.12	.05
26 Landis	.18	.12	.05
27 J. C. Martin	.18	.12	.05
28 Pizzaro	.18	.12	.05
29 E. Robinson	.18	.12	.05
30 Wynn	.50	.35	.15
31 Cleveland Emblem	.18	.12	.05
32 Cline	.18	.12	.05
33 Donovan	.18	.12	.05
34 Francona	.18	.12	.05
35 Held	.18	.12	.05
36 Latman	.18	.12	.05
37 J. Perry	.18	.12	.05
38 J. Phillips	.18	.12	.05
39 Power	.18	.12	.05
40 Romano	.18	.12	.05
41 Detroit Emblem	.18	.12	.05
42 Boros	.18	.12	.05
43 Bruton	.18	.12	.05
44 Bunning	.25	.16	.06
45 Cash	.25	.16	.06
46 Colavito	.18	.12	.05
47 Kaline	.25	.16	.06
48 Lary	.18	.12	.05
49 Mossi	.18	.12	.05
50 Wood	.18	.12	.05
51 Kansas City Emblem	.18	.12	.05
52 Archer	.18	.12	.05
53 Howser	.18	.12	.05
54 Lumpe	.18	.12	.05
55 Posada	.18	.12	.05
56 Shaw	.18	.12	.05
57 Siebern	.18	.12	.05
58 Sievers	.18	.12	.05
59 Stephens	.18	.12	.05
60 Sullivan	.18	.12	.05
61 J. Walker	.18	.12	.05
62 Los Angeles Emblem	.18	.12	.05
63 Bilko	.18	.12	.05
64 Bowsfield	.18	.12	.05
65 Hunt	.18	.12	.05
66 McBride	.18	.12	.05

67	Pearson	.18	.12	.05
68	Rodgers	.18	.12	.05
69	G. Thomas	.18	.12	.05
70	L. Thomas	.18	.12	.05
71	Wagner	.18	.12	.05
72	Minnesota Emblem	.18	.12	.05
73	Allison	.18	.12	.05
74	Battey	.18	.12	.05
75	Green	.18	.12	.05
76	Killebrew	.50	.35	.15
77	Kralick	.18	.12	.05
78	Pascual	.18	.12	.05
79	Ramos	.18	.12	.05
80	Tuttle	.18	.12	.05
81	Versailles	.18	.12	.05
82	New York Emblem	.18	.12	.05
83	Berra	1.00	.65	.25
84	C. Boyer	.18	.12	.05
85	Ford	1.00	.65	.25
86	Howard	.25	.16	.06
87	Kubek	.25	.16	.06
88	Mantle	2.50	1.70	.75
89	Maris	.50	.35	.15
90	Richardson	.25	.16	.06
91	Skowron	.25	.16	.06
92	Washington Emblem	.18	.12	.05
93	Cottier	.18	.12	.05
94	Daley	.18	.12	.05
95	Daniels	.18	.12	.05
96	Hinton	.18	.12	.05
97	B. Johnson	.18	.12	.05
98	McClain	.18	.12	.05
99	O'Connell	.18	.12	.05
100	Piersall	.25	.16	.06
101	Woodling	.18	.12	.05
102	Chicago Emblem	.18	.12	.05
103	Altman	.18	.12	.05
104	Banks	1.00	.65	.25
105	Bertell	.18	.12	.05
106	Cardwell	.18	.12	.05
107	Ellsworth	.18	.12	.05
108	Hobbie	.18	.12	.05
109	Santo	.25	.16	.06
110	Schultz	.18	.12	.05
111	B. Williams	.25	.16	.06
112	Cincinnati Emblem	.18	.12	.05
113	G. Coleman	.18	.12	.05
114	J. Edwards	.18	.12	.05
115	Freese	.18	.12	.05
116	Jay	.18	.12	.05
117	Kasko	.18	.12	.05
118	O'Toole	.18	.12	.05
119	Pinson	.25	.16	.06
120	Purkey	.18	.12	.05
121	F. Robinson	1.00	.65	.25
122	Houston Emblem	.18	.12	.05
123	J. Amalfitano	.18	.12	.05
124	Aspromonte	.18	.12	.05
125	Farrell	.18	.12	.05
126	Heist	.18	.12	.05
127	S. Jones	.18	.12	.05
128	Shantz	.18	.12	.05
129	H. Smith	.18	.12	.05
130	Spangler	.18	.12	.05
131	Tiefenauer	.18	.12	.05
132	Los Angeles Emblem	.18	.12	.05
133	Drysdale	.50	.35	.15
134	Fairly	.18	.12	.05
135	F. Howard	.25	.16	.06
136	Koufax	1.00	.65	.25
137	Moon	.18	.12	.05
138	Podres	.18	.12	.05
139	Roseboro	.18	.12	.05
140	Snider	.50	.35	.15
141	D. Spencer	.18	.12	.05
142	Milwaukee Emblem	.18	.12	.05
143	Aaron	2.00	1.30	.55
144	Adcock	.18	.12	.05
145	F. Bolling	.18	.12	.05
146	Burdette	.25	.16	.06
147	Crandall	.18	.12	.05
148	Mathews	.50	.35	.15
149	McMillan	.18	.12	.05
150	Spahn	.50	.35	.15
151	Torre	.18	.12	.05
152	New York Emblem	.18	.12	.05
153	Bell	.18	.12	.05
154	Craig	.18	.12	.05
155	Hodges	.50	.35	.15
156	Hook	.18	.12	.05
157	Landrith	.18	.12	.05
158	Mantilla	.18	.12	.05
159	R. Miller	.18	.12	.05
160	Walls	.18	.12	.05
161	Zimmer	.25	.16	.06
162	Philadelphia Emblem	.18	.12	.05
163	Amaro	.18	.12	.05
164	Baldschun	.18	.12	.05
165	Callison	.18	.12	.05
166	Dalrymple	.18	.12	.05
167	Demeter	.18	.12	.05
168	Gonzalez	.18	.12	.05
169	Sievers	.18	.12	.05
170	Taylor	.18	.12	.05
171	Mahaffey	.18	.12	.05
172	Pittsburgh Emblem	.18	.12	.05
173	Burgess	.18	.12	.05
174	Clemente	2.00	1.30	.55
175	Face	.18	.12	.05
176	Friend	.18	.12	.05
177	Groat	.25	.16	.06
178	Hoak	.18	.12	.05
179	Mazeroski	.25	.16	.06
180	Stuart	.18	.12	.05
181	Virdon	.25	.16	.06
182	St. Louis Emblem	.18	.12	.05
183	K. Boyer	.25	.16	.06
184	L. Jackson	.18	.12	.05
185	Javier	.18	.12	.05
186	McCarver	.18	.12	.05
187	L. McDaniel	.18	.12	.05
188	Minoso	.25	.16	.06
189	Musial	2.00	1.30	.55
190	Sadecki	.18	.12	.05
191	B. White	.18	.12	.05
192	San Fran. Emblem	.18	.12	.05
193	F. Alou	.18	.12	.05
194	Bailey	.18	.12	.05
195	Orlando Cepeda	.50	.35	.15
196	Jim Davenport	.18	.12	.05
197	Harvey Kuenn	.18	.12	.05
198	Juan Marichal	.50	.35	.15
199	Willie Mays	2.00	1.30	.55
200	Mike McCormick	.18	.12	.05
201	Stu Miller	.18	.12	.05

1963 TOPPS STICK–ON INSERTS (46) 1 3/4" X 2 3/4"

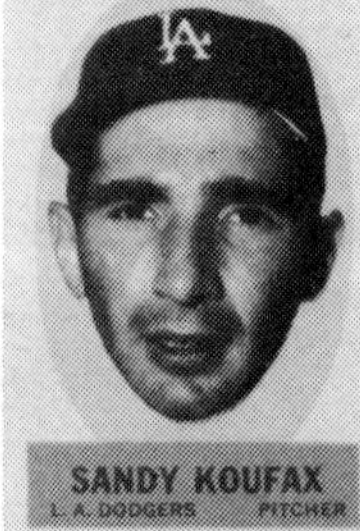

Stick-on inserts were found in several series of the 1963 Topps cards. They are found either with blank backs or with instructions on the reverse.

	MINT	VG-E	F-G
COMPLETE SET	45.00	32.00	13.00
COMMON PLAYER(1-46)	.45	.32	.13
1 Aaron,Hank	5.00	3.50	1.50
2 Aparicio,Luis	1.00	.70	.30
3 Ashburn,Richie	1.00	.70	.30
4 Aspromonte,Bob	.45	.32	.13
5 Banks,Ernie	2.50	1.75	.75
6 Boyer,Ken	.70	.50	.20
7 Bunning,Jim	.70	.50	.20
8 Callison,Johnny	.45	.32	.13

9 Clemente,Bob	3.50	2.50	1.00
10 Cepeda,Orlando	.70	.50	.20
11 Colavito,Rocky	1.00	.70	.30
12 Davis,Tommy	.70	.50	.20
13 Donovan,Dick	.45	.32	.13
14 Drysdale,Don	1.50	1.00	.45
15 Farrell,Dick	.45	.32	.13
16 Gentile,Jim	.45	.32	.13
17 Herbert,Ray	.45	.32	.13
18 Hinton,Chuck	.45	.32	.13
19 Hubbs,Ken	.70	.50	.20
20 Jackson,Al	.45	.32	.13
21 Kaline,Al	2.50	1.75	.75
22 Killebrew,Harmon	1.50	1.00	.45
23 Koufax,Sandy	3.50	2.50	1.00
24 Lumpe,Jerry	.45	.32	.13
25 Mahaffey,Art	.45	.32	.13
26 Mantle,Mickey	6.50	4.50	2.00
27 Mays,Willie	5.00	3.50	1.50
28 Mazeroski,Bill	.70	.50	.20
29 Monbouquette,Bill	.45	.32	.13
30 Musial,Stan	5.00	3.50	1.50
31 Pascual,Camilo	.45	.32	.13
32 Purkey,Bob	.45	.32	.13
33 Richardson,Bobby	.70	.50	.20
34 Robinson,Brooks	2.50	1.75	.75
35 Robinson,Floyd	.45	.32	.13
36 Robinson,Frank	2.50	1.75	.75
37 Rodgers,Bob	.45	.32	.13
38 Romano,Johnny	.45	.32	.13
39 Sanford,Jack	.45	.32	.13
40 Siebern,Norm	.45	.32	.13
41 Spahn,Warren	1.50	1.00	.45
42 Stenhouse,Dave	.45	.32	.13
43 Terry,Ralph	.45	.32	.13
44 Thomas,Lee	.45	.32	.13
45 White,Bill	.70	.50	.20
46 Yastrzemski,Carl	5.00	3.50	1.50

1964 TOPPS STAMPS (100) 1" X 1 1/2"

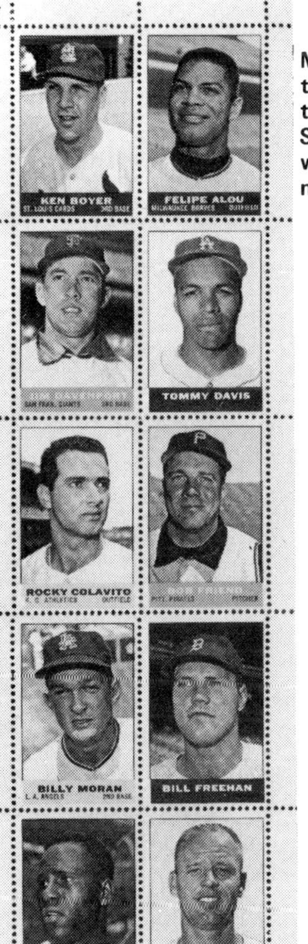

Many of the 100 color portraits of baseball players featured in this 1964 Topps Stamp series show players without caps. The subject's name, team and position are found in a colored rectangle beneath the picture area. The stamps were issued in sheets of 10, but an album to hold this particular set has not yet been seen.

	MINT	VG-E	F-G
COMPLETE SET	25.00	17.00	7.00
COMMON PLAYER	.18	.12	.05
1 Ed Charles-K.C.	.18	.12	.05
2 Vada Pinson-Reds	.25	.16	.06
3 Jimmy Hall-Twins	.18	.12	.05
4 Milt Pappas-Orioles	.18	.12	.05
5 Dick Ellsworth-Cubs	.18	.12	.05
6 Frank Malzone-R.Sox	.18	.12	.05
7 Max Alvis-Indians	.18	.12	.05
8 Pete Ward-White Sox	.18	.12	.05
9 Tony Taylor-Phils	.18	.12	.05
10 Bill White-Cards	.18	.12	.05
11 Don Zimmer-Senators	.25	.16	.06
12 B. Richardson-Yanks	.25	.16	.06
13 Larry Jackson-Cubs	.18	.12	.05
14 N. Siebern-Orioles	.18	.12	.05
15 Frank Robinson-Reds	1.00	.65	.25
16 B. Aspromonte-Colts	.18	.12	.05
17 Al McBean-Pirates	.18	.12	.05
18 Floyd Robinson-W.S.	.18	.12	.05
19 B.Monbouquette-R.S.	.18	.12	.05
20 Willie Mays-Giants	2.00	1.30	.55
21 B.Robinson-Orioles	1.00	.65	.25
22 J.Pepitone-Yankees	.18	.12	.05
23 C.Yastrzemski-R.Sox	2.00	1.30	.55
24 Don Lock-Senators	.18	.12	.05
25 Ernie Banks-Cubs	1.00	.65	.25
26 Dave Nicholson-W.S.	.18	.12	.05
27 B.Clemente-Pirates	2.00	1.30	.55
28 Curt Flood-Cards	.25	.16	.06
29 Woody Held-Indians	.18	.12	.05
30 Jesse Gonder-Mets	.18	.12	.05
31 Juan Pizarro-W.S.	.18	.12	.05
32 Jim Maloney-Reds	.18	.12	.05
33 Ron Santo-Cubs	.25	.16	.06
34 H.Killebrew-Twins	.50	.35	.15
35 Ed Roebuck-Seantors	.18	.12	.05
36 Boog Powell-Orioles	.25	.16	.06
37 Jim Grant-Indians	.18	.12	.05
38 Hank Aguirre-Tigers	.18	.12	.05
39 J.Marichal-Giants	.50	.35	.15
40 B.Mazeroski-Pirates	.25	.16	.06
41 Dick Radatz-Red Sox	.18	.12	.05
42 Alb. Pearson-Angels	.18	.12	.05
43 Tommy Harper-Reds	.18	.12	.05
44 Carl Willey-Mets	.18	.12	.05
45 Jim Bouton-Yanks	.25	.16	.06
46 R.Perranoski-Dodg.	.18	.12	.05
47 C.Hinton-Senators	.18	.12	.05
48 J.Romano-Indians	.18	.12	.05
49 Norm Cash-Tigers	.25	.16	.06
50 O.Cepeda-Giants	.50	.35	.15
51 Dick Stuart-Red Sox	.25	.16	.06
52 Rich Rollins-Twins	.18	.12	.05
53 M.Mantle-Yankees	2.50	1.70	.75
54 S.Barber-Orioles	.18	.12	.05
55 Jim O'Toole-Reds	.18	.12	.05
56 Gary Peters-W.Sox	.18	.12	.05
57 Warren Spahn-Braves	1.00	.65	.25
58 T.Gonzalez-Phillies	.18	.12	.05
59 Joe Torre-Braves	.25	.16	.06
60 Jim Fregosi-Angels	.25	.16	.06
61 Ken Boyer-Cards	.25	.16	.06
62 Felipe Alou-Braves	.25	.16	.06
63 J.Davenport-Giants	.18	.12	.05
64 Tommy Davis-Dodgers	.25	.16	.06
65 R.Colavito-Athlet.	.25	.16	.06
66 Bob Friend-Pirates	.18	.12	.05

67 Billy Morgan-Angels	.18	.12	.05
68 Bill Freehan-Tigers	.25	.16	.06
69 George Altman-Mets	.18	.12	.05
70 Ken Johnson-Colts	.18	.12	.05
71 Earl Battey-Twins	.18	.12	.05
72 Elston Howard-Yank.	.25	.16	.06
73 Billy Williams-Cubs	.25	.16	.06
74 Claude Osteen-Sen.	.18	.12	.05
75 Jim Gentile-Athlet.	.18	.12	.05
76 Donn Clendenon-Pir.	.18	.12	.05
77 Ernie Broglio-Cards	.18	.12	.05
78 H.Woodeshick-Colts	.18	.12	.05
79 D.Drysdale-Dodgers	.50	.35	.15
80 J.Callison-Phillies	.18	.12	.05
81 Dick Groat-Cards	.25	.16	.06
82 Moe Drabowsky-Athl.	.18	.12	.05
83 Frank Howard-Dodg.	.25	.16	.06
84 Hank Aaron-Braves	2.00	1.30	.55
85 Al Jackson-Mets	.18	.12	.05
86 Jerry Lumpe-Tigers	.18	.12	.05
87 Wayne Causey-Athl.	.18	.12	.05
88 Rusty Staub-Colts	.25	.16	.06
89 Ken McBride-Angels	.18	.12	.05
90 J.Baldschun-Phil.	.18	.12	.05
91 Sandy Koufax-Dodg.	1.00	.65	.25
92 C.Pascual-Twins	.18	.12	.05
93 Ron Hunt-Mets	.18	.12	.05
94 W.McCovey-Giants	1.00	.65	.25
95 Al Kaline-Tigers	1.00	.65	.25
96 Ray Culp-Phillies	.18	.12	.05
97 Ed Mathews-Braves	.50	.35	.15
98 Dick Farrell-Colts	.18	.12	.05
99 Lee Thomas-Angels	.18	.12	.05
100 V.Davalillo-Indians	.18	.12	.05

1965 TOPPS TRANSFERS (72) 2" X 3"

The 1965 Topps transfers were issued in series of 24 each as inserts in three of the regular1965 Topps cards series. Thirty-six of the transfers feature blue bands at the top and bottom while 36 feature red bands at the top and bottom. The team name and position are listed in the top band while the player's name is listed in the bottom band. Information on the 72nd transfer would be appreciated.

	MINT	VG-E	F-G
COMPLETE SET	60.00	40.00	15.00
COMMON PLAYER	.60	.40	.15
1 Allison	.60	.40	.15
2 Alvis	.60	.40	.15
3 Aparicio	1.00	.65	.30
4 Bond	.60	.40	.15
5 Bouton	.75	.50	.20
6 Bunning	.75	.50	.20
7 Carty	.75	.50	.20
8 Causey	.60	.40	.15
9 Cepeda	1.00	.65	.30
10 Chance	.60	.40	.15
11 Conigliaro	.75	.50	.20
12 Freehan	.75	.50	.20
13 Fregosi	.75	.50	.20
14 Gibson	2.25	1.50	.65
15 Groat	.75	.50	.20
16 Haller	.60	.40	.15
17 Jackson	.60	.40	.15
18 Knoop	.60	.40	.15
19 Maloney	.75	.50	.20
20 Marichal	1.50	1.00	.40
21 O'Toole	.60	.40	.15
22 Pascual	.60	.40	.15
23 Pinson	.75	.50	.20
24 Pizzaro	.60	.40	.15
25 Richardson	.75	.50	.20
26 Rogers	.60	.40	.15
27 Roseboro	.60	.40	.15
28 Stuart	.75	.50	.20
29 Tiant	.75	.50	.20
30 Torre	1.00	.65	.30
31 Veale	.60	.40	.15
32 Wagner	.60	.40	.15
33 Wickersham	.60	.40	.15
34 Williams	1.00	.65	.30
35 Yastrzemski	4.00	2.75	1.10
36 Aaron	4.00	2.75	1.10
37 Allen	1.00	.65	.30
38 Aspromonte	.60	.40	.15
39 Boyer	1.00	.65	.30
40 Callison	.60	.40	.15
41 B. Chance	.60	.40	.15
42 Christopher	.60	.40	.15
43 Clemente	3.00	2.00	.80
44 Colavito	1.00	.65	.30
45 Davis	.75	.50	.20
46 Drysdale	1.50	1.00	.40
47 Hinton	.60	.40	.15
48 Howard	1.00	.65	.30
49 Hunt	.60	.40	.15
50 Kaline	3.00	2.00	.80
51 Killebrew	1.50	1.00	.40
52 King	.60	.40	.15
53 Kline	.60	.40	.15
54 Koufax	3.00	2.00	.80
55 Kranepool	.60	.40	.15
56 Mantle	5.00	3.50	1.40
57 Mays	4.00	2.75	1.10
58 Mazeroski	.75	.50	.20
59 Oliva	1.00	.65	.30
60 Pappas	.75	.50	.20
61 Peters	.60	.40	.15
62 Powell	1.00	.65	.30
63 Radatz	.60	.40	.15
64 B. Robinson	2.25	1.50	.65
65 F. Robinson	2.25	1.50	.65
66 Santo	1.00	.65	.30
67 Segui	.60	.40	.15
68 Skowron	.75	.50	.20
69 Spangler	.60	.40	.15
70 Ward	.60	.40	.15
71 White	.75	.50	.20

1966 TOPPS RUB–OFFS (100)(20) 2 1/16" X 3"

There are 120 "rub-offs" in the Topps insert set of 1966, of which 100 depict players and the remaining 20 show team pennants. The color player photos are vertical while the team pennants are horizontal; both types of transfer have a large black printer's mark. These rub-offs were originally printed in rolls of 20 and are occasionally still found this way.

	MINT	VG-E	F-G
COMPLETE SET	65.00	45.00	20.00
COMMON PLAYER	.40	.25	.10

No.	Player	MINT	VG-E	F-G
1	White Sox	.40	.25	.10
2	Ward	.40	.25	.10
3	F. Robinson	.40	.25	.10
4	Skowron	.50	.35	.14
5	Horlen	.40	.25	.10
6	Fisher	.40	.25	.10
7	Astros	.40	.25	.10
8	Bruce	.40	.25	.10
9	Morgan	1.00	.65	.30
10	Farrell	.40	.25	.10
11	Wynn	.50	.35	.14
12	Aspromonte	.40	.25	.10
13	Dodgers	.50	.35	.14
14	Koufax	2.50	1.70	.70
15	Roseboro	.40	.25	.10
16	Drysdale	1.50	1.00	.40
17	W. Davis	.50	.35	.14
18	Fairly	.40	.25	.10
19	Mets	.50	.35	.14
20	Kranepool	.40	.25	.10
21	Kroll	.40	.25	.10
22	Fisher	.40	.25	.10
23	Swoboda	.40	.25	.10
24	Lewis	.40	.25	.10
25	Giants	.40	.25	.10
26	McCovey	1.50	1.00	.40
27	Mays	3.75	2.50	1.00
28	Hart	.40	.25	.10
29	Marichal	1.00	.65	.30
30	J. Alou	.40	.25	.10
31	Senators	.40	.25	.10
32	Ortega	.40	.25	.10
33	Howard	.75	.50	.20
34	Lock	.40	.25	.10
35	McMullen	.40	.25	.10
36	Richert	.40	.25	.10
37	Cards	.40	.25	.10
38	B. White	.50	.35	.14
39	Gibson	1.50	1.00	.40
40	McCarver	.40	.25	.10
41	K. Boyer	.75	.50	.20
42	Flood	.50	.35	.14
43	Pirates	.40	.25	.10
44	Stargell	1.50	1.00	.40
45	Mazeroski	.50	.35	.14
46	Veale	.40	.25	.10
47	Clemente	3.75	2.50	1.00
48	Law	.50	.35	.14
49	Twins	.40	.25	.10
50	Killebrew	1.50	1.00	.40
51	Hall	.40	.25	.10
52	Oliva	.75	.50	.20
53	Grant	.50	.35	.14
54	Battey	.50	.35	.14
55	Yankees	.50	.35	.14
56	Richardson	.50	.35	.14
57	Mantle	5.00	3.50	1.40
58	Stottlemyre	.40	.25	.10
59	Tresh	.40	.25	.10
60	Ford	1.50	1.00	.40
61	Tigers	.40	.25	.10
62	Horton	.50	.35	.14
63	Freehan	.50	.35	.14
64	McAuliffe	.40	.25	.10
65	Lolich	.50	.35	.14
66	Kaline	2.50	1.70	.70
67	Indians	.40	.25	.10
68	Alvis	.40	.25	.10
69	Terry	.40	.25	.10
70	Davalillo	.40	.25	.10
71	McDowell	.50	.35	.14
72	Colavito	.75	.50	.20
73	Phillies	.40	.25	.10
74	Allen	.75	.50	.20
75	Stuart	.50	.35	.14
76	Callison	.40	.25	.10
77	Rojas	.40	.25	.10
78	Bunning	.50	.35	.14
79	Angels	.40	.25	.10
80	Cardenal	.40	.25	.10
81	Knoop	.40	.25	.10
82	Newman	.40	.25	.10
83	Chance	.40	.25	.10
84	Fregosi	.50	.35	.14
85	Orioles	.40	.25	.10
86	Adair	.40	.25	.10
87	Blefary	.40	.25	.10
88	Pappas	.50	.35	.14
89	Orsino	.40	.25	.10
90	B. Robinson	2.50	1.70	.70
91	Reds	.40	.25	.10
92	Ellis	.40	.25	.10
93	Maloney	.50	.35	.14
94	F. Robinson	2.50	1.70	.70
95	Rose	5.00	3.50	1.40
96	Johnson	.40	.25	.10
97	Cubs	.40	.25	.10
98	Banks	2.50	1.70	.70
99	Landrum	.40	.25	.10
100	Ellsworth	.50	.35	.14
101	Williams	.75	.50	.20
102	Santo	.50	.35	.14
103	Athletics	.40	.25	.10
104	Talbot	.40	.25	.10
105	O'Donoghue	.40	.25	.10
106	Charles	.40	.25	.10
107	Harrelson	.50	.35	.14
108	Campaneris	.50	.35	.14
109	Red Sox	.50	.35	.14
110	Yastrzemski	3.75	2.50	1.00
111	Radatz	.40	.25	.10
112	Mantilla	.40	.25	.10
113	Conigliaro	.50	.35	.14
114	Monbouquette	.40	.25	.10
115	Braves	.40	.25	.10
116	Cloninger	.40	.25	.10
117	Aaron	3.75	2.50	1.00
118	Mathews	1.50	1.00	.40
119	Menke	.40	.25	.10
120	Torre	.75	.50	.20

1967 TOPPS PAPER INSERT (32) 5" X 7"

The wrappers of the 1967 Topps cards have the set advertised as follows: "Extra! All Star Pin-up inside." Printed on paper in full color, the "All Star" inserts have fold lines which are generally not noticeable when stored carefully. They are numbered and carry a facsimile autograph.

	MINT	VG-E	F-G
COMPLETE SET	14.00	10.00	4.00
COMMON PLAYER(1-32)	.24	.17	.07
1 Powell,Boog	.30	.20	.08
2 Campaneris,Bert	.24	.17	.07
3 Robinson,Brooks	1.10	.70	.30
4 Agee,Tommie	.24	.17	.07
5 Yastrzemski,Carl	1.50	1.00	.45
6 Mantle,Mickey	2.50	1.75	.75
7 Howard,Frank	.30	.20	.08
8 McDowell,Sam	.30	.20	.08
9 Cepeda,Orlando	.30	.20	.08
10 Cardenas,Chico	.24	.17	.07
11 Clemente,Bob	1.50	1.00	.45
12 Mays,Willie	1.50	1.00	.45
13 Jones,Cleon	.24	.17	.07
14 Callison,John	.24	.17	.07
15 Aaron,Hank	1.50	1.00	.45
16 Drysdale,Don	.80	.55	.20
17 Knoop,Bobby	.24	.17	.07
18 Oliva,Tony	.45	.30	.12
19 Robinson,Frank	1.10	.70	.30
20 McLain,Denny	.45	.30	.12
21 Kaline,Al	1.10	.70	.30
22 Pepitone,Joe	.30	.20	.08
23 Killibrew,Harmon	.80	.55	.20
24 Wagner,Leon	.24	.17	.07
25 Morgan,Joe	.60	.40	.15
26 Santo,Ron	.30	.20	.08
27 Torre,Joe	.45	.30	.12
28 Marichal,Juan	.60	.40	.15
29 Alou,Matty	.24	.17	.07
30 Alou,Felipe	.24	.17	.07
31 Hunt,Ron	.24	.17	.07
32 McCovey,Willie	.80	.55	.20

1968 TOPPS BASEBALL POSTERS (24) 9 3/4" X 18 1/8"

This 1968 color poster set is not an "insert" but was issued separately with a piece of gum and in its own wrapper (see IWC). The posters are numbered at the lower left and the player's name and team appear in a large star. The poster was folded six times to fit into the package, so fold lines are a factor in grading.

	MINT	VG-E	F-G
COMPLETE SET	45.00	32.00	13.00
COMMON PLAYER(1-24)	.75	.55	.20
1 Chance,Dean	.75	.55	.20
2 Alvis,Max	.75	.55	.20
3 Howard,Frank	1.00	.70	.30
4 Fregosi,Jim	1.00	.70	.30
5 Hunter,Jim	1.50	1.00	.45
6 Clemente,Bob	5.00	3.50	1.50
7 Drysdale,Don	2.00	1.40	.60
8 Wynn,Jim	.75	.55	.20
9 Kaline,Al	4.00	2.75	1.10
10 Killebrew,Harmon	2.00	1.40	.60
11 Lonborg,Jim	.75	.55	.20
12 Cepeda,Orlando	1.00	.70	.30
13 Peters,Gary	.75	.55	.20
14 Aaron,Hank	5.00	3.50	1.50
15 Allen,Richie	1.00	.70	.30
16 Yastrzemski,Carl	5.00	3.50	1.50
17 Swoboda,Ron	.75	.55	.20
18 Mantle,Mickey	7.50	5.50	2.20
19 McCarver,Tim	.75	.55	.20
20 Mays,Willie	5.00	3.50	1.50
21 Santo,Ron	1.00	.70	.30
22 Staub,Rusty	1.00	.70	.30
23 Rose,Pete	7.50	5.50	2.20
24 Robinson,Frank	3.00	2.00	.80

1969 TOPPS DECAL INSERTS (48) 1 1/2" X 1 1/2"

The 1969 Topps Decal Inserts are a set of 48 unnumbered decals issues as inserts in packages of 1969 Topps regular issue cards. The decals appear to be miniature versions of the Topps regular issue of that year. Most of the players on the decals are stars.

	MINT	VG-E	F-G
COMPLETE SET	90.00	65.00	25.00
COMMON PLAYER(1-48)	.90	.65	.25
1 Aaron,Hank	10.00	6.50	3.75
2 Allen,Richie	1.25	.90	.40
3 Alou,Felipe	.90	.65	.25
4 Alou,Matty	.90	.65	.25
5 Aparicio,Luis	1.25	.90	.40
6 Clemente,Bob	10.00	6.50	3.75
7 Clendenon,Donn	.90	.65	.25
8 Davis,Tommy	1.25	.90	.40
9 Drysdale,Don	4.00	2.75	1.00
10 Foy,Joe	.90	.65	.25
11 Fregosi,Jim	1.25	.90	.40
12 Gibson,Bob	4.00	2.75	1.00
13 Gonzalez,Tony	.90	.65	.25
14 Haller,Tom	.90	.65	.25
15 Harrelson,Ken	1.25	.90	.40
16 Helms,Tommy	.90	.65	.25
17 Horton,Willie	1.25	.90	.40
18 Howard,Frank	1.25	.90	.40
19 Jenkins,Fergie	1.75	1.25	.50
20 Killebrew,Harmon	4.00	2.75	1.00
21 Koosman,Jerry	1.25	.90	.40
22 McCarver,Tim	.90	.65	.25
23 McCovey,Willie	4.00	2.75	1.00
24 McDowell,Sam	1.25	.90	.40
25 McLain,Denny	1.25	.90	.40
26 McNally,Dave	1.25	.90	.40
27 Mantle,Mickey	15.00	10.00	4.50
28 Mays,Willie	10.00	6.50	3.75
29 Jackson,Reggie	10.00	6.50	3.75
30 Mincher,Don	.90	.65	.25
31 Monday,Rick	1.25	.90	.40
32 Oliva,Tony	1.75	1.25	.50
33 Pascual,Camilo	.90	.65	.25
34 Reichardt,Rick	.90	.65	.25
35 Rose,Pete	15.00	10.00	4.50
36 Robinson,Frank	4.00	2.75	1.00
37 Santo,Ron	1.25	.90	.40
38 Selma,Dick	.90	.65	.25
39 Seaver,Tom	6.00	4.00	1.50
40 Short,Chris	.90	.65	.25
41 Staub,Rusty	1.25	.90	.40
42 Stottlemyre,Mel	.90	.65	.25
43 Tiant,Luis	1.25	.90	.40
44 Ward,Pete	.90	.65	.25
45 Wilhelm,Hoyt	1.75	1.25	.50
46 Wills,Maury	1.75	1.25	.50
47 Wynn,Jim	.90	.65	.25
48 Yastrzemski,Carl	10.00	6.50	3.75

1969 TOPPS STAMPS (240) 1" X 1 7/16"

The 1969 Topps set of baseball player stamps contains 240 individual stamps and 24 separate albums—10 stamps and one album per major league team. The stamps were issued in strips of 12 and have gummed backs. The eight-page albums are bright orange and have an autograph feature on the back cover.

	MINT	VG-E	F-G
COMPLETE SET	40.00	26.00	10.00
COMMON PLAYER	.13	.09	.04
1 Hank Aaron	1.65	1.10	.50
2 F. Alou	.13	.09	.04
3 Clete Boyer	.13	.09	.04
4 Francona	.13	.09	.04
5 S. Jackson	.13	.09	.04
6 P. Jarvis	.13	.09	.04
7 Millan	.13	.09	.04
8 Pappas	.13	.09	.04
9 Ron Reed	.13	.09	.04
10 Joe Torre	.20	.13	.05
11 Abernathy	.13	.09	.04
12 Arrigo	.13	.09	.04
13 Johnny Bench	.80	.55	.22
14 Helms	.13	.09	.04
15 A. Johnson	.13	.09	.04
16 Maloney	.13	.09	.04
17 L. May	.13	.09	.04
18 Perez	.20	.13	.05
19 Pete Rose	2.25	1.50	.65
20 Tolan	.13	.09	.04
21 Banks	.80	.55	.22
22 Beckert	.13	.09	.04
23 Hands	.13	.09	.04
24 Hundley	.13	.09	.04
25 Jenkins	.20	.13	.05
26 Kessinger	.20	.13	.05

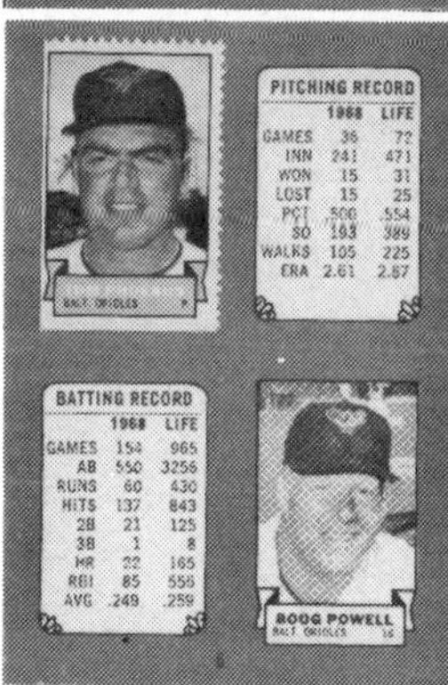

1969 Topps Stamps

27 A. Phillips	.13	.09	.04
28 Regan	.13	.09	.04
29 Santo	.20	.13	.05
30 Billy Williams	.20	.13	.05
31 B. Aspromonte	.13	.09	.04
32 Dierker	.13	.09	.04
33 Edwards	.13	.09	.04
34 Lemaster	.13	.09	.04
35 Menke	.13	.09	.04
36 Morgan	.20	.13	.05
37 Rader	.13	.09	.04
38 Staub	.20	.13	.05
39 D. Wilson	.13	.09	.04
40 Wynn	.20	.13	.05
41 W. Davis	.20	.13	.05
42 Don Drysdale	.40	.26	.10
43 Fairly	.13	.09	.04
44 Gabrielson	.13	.09	.04
45 Haller	.13	.09	.04
46 Lefebvre	.13	.09	.04
47 Osteen	.13	.09	.04
48 Popovich	.13	.09	.04
49 Singer	.13	.09	.04
50 Don Sutton	.20	.13	.05
51 J. Alou	.13	.09	.04
52 Bailey	.13	.09	.04
53 Bateman	.13	.09	.04
54 Clendenon	.13	.09	.04
55 Grant	.13	.09	.04
56 Jaster	.13	.09	.04
57 M. Jones	.13	.09	.04
58 Mota	.20	.13	.05
59 Sutherland	.13	.09	.04
60 Wills	.20	.13	.05
61 Agee	.13	.09	.04
62 Charles	.13	.09	.04
63 Grote	.13	.09	.04
64 Harrelson	.13	.09	.04
65 C. Jones	.13	.09	.04
66 Jerry Koosman	.20	.13	.05
67 Kranepool	.13	.09	.04
68 Seaver	.80	.55	.22
69 Shamsky	.13	.09	.04
70 Swoboda	.13	.09	.04
71 Allen	.20	.13	.05
72 Briggs	.13	.09	.04
73 Callison	.13	.09	.04
74 Clay Dalrymple	.13	.09	.04
75 Fryman	.13	.09	.04
76 Lock	.13	.09	.04
77 Rojas	.13	.09	.04
78 Short	.13	.09	.04
79 Taylor	.13	.09	.04
80 Wise	.13	.09	.04
81 Alley	.13	.09	.04
82 M. Alou	.13	.09	.04
83 Blass	.13	.09	.04
84 Bunning	.20	.13	.05
85 Clemente	1.35	.90	.40
86 Kune	.13	.09	.04
87 J. May	.13	.09	.04
88 Mazeroski	.20	.13	.05
89 Stargell	.80	.55	.22
90 Veale	.13	.09	.04
91 Arcia	.13	.09	.04
92 O. Brown	.13	.09	.04
93 Ferrara	.13	.09	.04
94 Gonzalez	.13	.09	.04
95 Giusti	.13	.09	.04
96 McBean	.13	.09	.04
97 Pena	.13	.09	.04
98 Selma	.13	.09	.04
99 Stahl	.13	.09	.04
100 Versalles	.13	.09	.04
101 Bolin	.13	.09	.04
102 Davenport	.13	.09	.04
103 Dietz	.13	.09	.04
104 Hart	.13	.09	.04
105 Hunt	.13	.09	.04
106 Lanier	.13	.09	.04
107 Marichal	.40	.26	.10
108 Mays	1.65	1.10	.50
109 McCovey	.80	.55	.22
110 G. Perry	.80	.55	.22
111 Briles	.13	.09	.04
112 Brock	.80	.55	.22
113 Cepeda	.40	.26	.10
114 Flood	.20	.13	.05
115 Gibson	.80	.55	.22
116 Javier	.13	.09	.04
117 Maxvill	.13	.09	.04
118 McCarver	.13	.09	.04
119 Pinson	.20	.13	.05
120 Shannon	.13	.09	.04
121 Belanger	.13	.09	.04
122 Blefary	.13	.09	.04
123 Buford	.13	.09	.04
124 Hardin	.13	.09	.04
125 D. Johnson	.13	.09	.04
126 McNally	.20	.13	.05
127 Phoebus	.13	.09	.04
128 Powell	.20	.13	.05
129 B. Robinson	.80	.55	.22
130 F. Robinson	.80	.55	.22
131 Andrews	.13	.09	.04
132 Culp	.13	.09	.04
133 Gibson	.13	.09	.04
134 Harrelson	.20	.13	.05
135 Lonborg	.20	.13	.05
136 Petrocelli	.20	.13	.05
137 Santiago	.13	.09	.04
138 Scott	.20	.13	.05
139 A. Smith	.13	.09	.04
140 Yastrzemski	1.65	1.10	.50
141 Brunet	.13	.09	.04
142 Davalillo	.13	.09	.04
143 Fisher	.13	.09	.04
144 Fregosi	.20	.13	.05
145 Knoop	.13	.09	.04
146 McGlothlin	.13	.09	.04
147 Reichardt	.13	.09	.04
148 Repoz	.13	.09	.04
149 Rodgers	.13	.09	.04
150 Satriano	.13	.09	.04
151 Alomar	.13	.09	.04
152 Aparicio	.20	.13	.05
153 Berry	.13	.09	.04
154 Horlen	.13	.09	.04
155 John	.40	.26	.10
156 Josephson	.13	.09	.04
157 Peters	.13	.09	.04
158 Wagner	.13	.09	.04
159 Ward	.13	.09	.04
160 Wood	.13	.09	.04
161 Alvis	.13	.09	.04
162 Azcue	.13	.09	.04
163 L. Brown	.13	.09	.04
164 Cardenal	.13	.09	.04
165 L. Maye	.13	.09	.04
166 McDowell	.20	.13	.05
167 Siebert	.13	.09	.04
168 Sims	.13	.09	.04
169 Tiant	.20	.13	.05
170 S. Williams	.13	.09	.04
171 Cash	.20	.13	.05
172 Freehan	.20	.13	.05
173 Horton	.20	.13	.05
174 Kaline	.80	.55	.22
175 Lolich	.20	.13	.05
176 McAuliffe	.13	.09	.04
177 McLain	.20	.13	.05
178 Northrup	.13	.09	.04
179 Stanley	.13	.09	.04
180 Wert	.13	.09	.04
181 Adair	.13	.09	.04
182 Bunker	.13	.09	.04
183 Drabowsky	.13	.09	.04
184 Fox	.13	.09	.04
185 Hernandez	.13	.09	.04
186 Nelson	.13	.09	.04
187 B. Oliver	.13	.09	.04
188 Schaal	.13	.09	.04
189 Whitaker	.13	.09	.04
190 Wilhelm	.20	.13	.05
191 Allison	.13	.09	.04
192 Carew	.80	.55	.22
193 Chance	.13	.09	.04
194 Kaat	.20	.13	.05
195 Killebrew	.40	.26	.10
196 Oliva	.20	.13	.05
197 Perranowski	.13	.09	.04
198 Roseboro	.13	.09	.04
199 Tovar	.13	.09	.04
200 Uhlaender	.13	.09	.04
201 Bahnsen	.13	.09	.04
202 Clarke	.13	.09	.04
203 Gibbs	.13	.09	.04
204 Kosko	.13	.09	.04
205 Mickey Mantle	2.25	1.50	.65
206 Pepitone	.20	.13	.05
207 W. Robinson	.13	.09	.04
208 Stottlemyre	.20	.13	.05
209 Tresh	.20	.13	.05
210 White	.20	.13	.05
211 Bando	.20	.13	.05
212 Campaneris	.20	.13	.05
213 Cater	.13	.09	.04
214 Duncan	.13	.09	.04
215 Green	.13	.09	.04
216 Hunter	.40	.26	.10
217 Krausse	.13	.09	.04
218 Rick Monday	.20	.13	.05

219 Nash	.13	.09	.04
220 Odom	.13	.09	.04
221 Aker	.20	.13	.05
222 Barber	.20	.13	.05
223 Bell	.20	.13	.05
224 Tommy Davis	.40	.26	.10
225 Harper	.20	.13	.05
226 McNertney	.20	.13	.05
227 Mincher	.20	.13	.05
228 Ray Oyler	.20	.13	.05
229 Rollins	.20	.13	.05
230 Salmon	.20	.13	.05
231 B. Allen	.13	.09	.04
232 Brinkman	.13	.09	.04
233 Casanova	.13	.09	.04
234 J. Coleman	.13	.09	.04
235 Mike Epstein	.13	.09	.04
236 Hannan	.13	.09	.04
237 Higgins	.13	.09	.04
238 Frank Howard	.20	.13	.05
239 McMullen	.13	.09	.04
240 Camilo Pascual	.13	.09	.04

1970 TOPPS PAPER INSERT (24) 8 11/16" X 9 5/8"

1970 marked the year that Topps raised its price per package of cards to ten cents, and a series of 24 color posters was included as a bonus to the collector. The thin-paper poster is numbered and features a large portrait and a smaller, black & white action pose. It was folded five times to fit the packaging.

	MINT	VG-E	F-G
COMPLETE SET	27.00	19.00	8.00
COMMON PLAYER(1-24)	.60	.40	.15
1 Horlen,Joe	.60	.40	.15
2 Niekro,Phil	1.00	.70	.30
3 Davis,Willie	.75	.55	.25
4 Brock,Lou	3.00	2.00	.80
5 Santo,Ron	.75	.55	.25
6 Harrelson,Ken	.75	.55	.25
7 McCovey,Willie	2.00	1.40	.60
8 Wise,Rick	.60	.40	.15
9 Messersmith,Andy	.75	.55	.25
10 Fairly,Ron	.75	.55	.25
11 Bench,Johnny	4.00	2.75	1.25
12 Robinson,Frank	2.00	1.40	.60
13 Agee,Tommie	.60	.40	.15
14 White,Roy	.60	.40	.15
15 Dierker,Larry	.60	.40	.15
16 Carew,Rod	3.00	2.00	.80
17 Mincher,Don	.60	.40	.15
18 Brown,Ollie	.60	.40	.15
19 Kirkpatrick,Ed	.60	.40	.15
20 Smith,Reggie	1.00	.70	.30
21 Clemente,Bob	4.00	2.75	1.25
22 Howard,Frank	1.00	.70	.30
23 Campaneris,Bert	.75	.55	.25
24 McLain,Denny	1.00	.70	.30

1970 TOPPS STORY BOOKLETS (24)

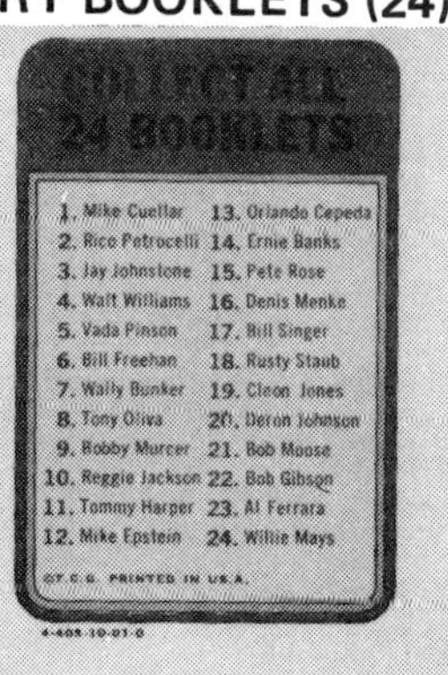

Inserted into packages of the 1970 Topps regular issue of cards, there are 24 miniature biographies of ballplayers in the set. Each numbered paper booklet contains 6 pages of comic-book-style story and a checklist of the booklet is available on the back page.

	MINT	VG-E	F-G
COMPLETE SET	12.00	8.00	3.00
COMMON PLAYER(1-24)	.30	.20	.08
1 Cuellar,Mike	.30	.20	.08
2 Petrocelli,Rico	.30	.20	.08
3 Johnstone,Jay	.30	.20	.08
4 Williams,Walt	.30	.20	.08
5 Pinson,Vada	.40	.27	.12
6 Freehan,Bill	.40	.27	.12
7 Bunker,Wally	.30	.20	.08
8 Oliva,Tony	.50	.35	.15
9 Murcer,Bobby	.40	.27	.12
10 Jackson,Reggie	1.50	1.00	.45
11 Harper,Tommy	.30	.20	.08
12 Epstein,Mike	.30	.20	.08
13 Cepeda,Orlando	.50	.35	.15
14 Banks,Ernie	1.50	1.00	.45
15 Rose,Pete	2.00	1.40	.60
16 Menke,Denis	.30	.20	.08
17 Singer,Bill	.30	.20	.08
18 Staub,Rusty	.50	.35	.15
19 Jones,Cleon	.30	.20	.08
20 Johnson,Deron	.30	.20	.08
21 Moose,Bob	.30	.20	.08
22 Gibson,Bob	1.00	.70	.30
23 Ferrara,Al	.30	.20	.08
24 Mays,Willie	2.00	1.40	.60

1970-71 TOPPS SCRATCH-OFF INSERTS (24) 3 3/8" X 5"

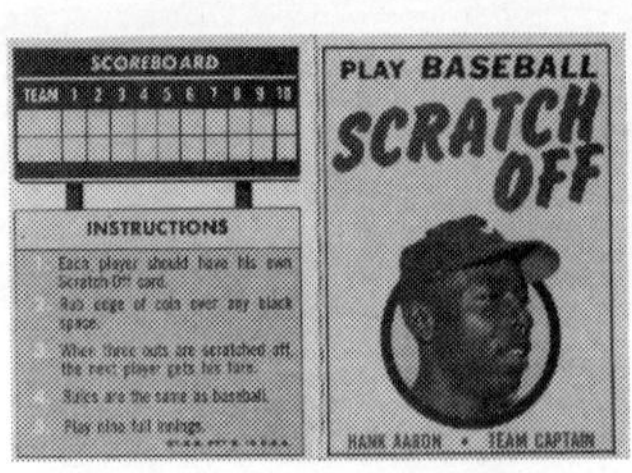

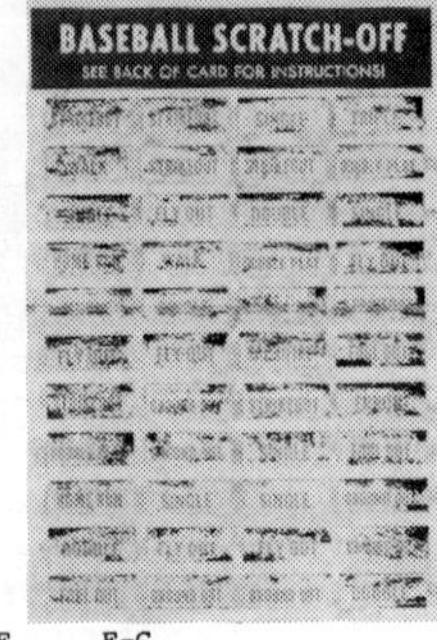

The 1970-71 Topps Scratch-off inserts are heavy cardboard, folded inserts issued with the regular card series of those years. Unfolded, they form a game board upon which a baseball game is played by means of rubbing off black ink from the playing squares to reveal moves. Inserts with white centers were issued in 1970 and inserts with red centers in 1971.

	MINT	VG-E	F-G
COMPLETE SET	15.00	10.00	4.00
COMMON PLAYER(1-24)	.30	.20	.08

	MINT	VG-E	F-G
1 Aaron,Hank	2.00	1.40	.55
2 Allen,Rich	.50	.35	.15
3 Aparicio,Luis	.50	.35	.15
4 Bando,Sal	.50	.35	.15
5 Beckert,Glenn	.30	.20	.08
6 Bosman,Dick	.30	.20	.08
7 Colbert,Nate	.30	.20	.08
8 Hegan,Mike	.30	.20	.08
9 Jones,Mack	.30	.20	.08
10 Kaline,Al	1.50	1.00	.40
11 Killebrew,Harmon	1.00	.70	.30
12 Marichal,Juan	1.00	.70	.30
13 McCarver,Tim	.30	.20	.08
14 McDowell,Sam	.40	.25	.10
15 Osteen,Claude	.30	.20	.08
16 Perez,Tony	.50	.35	.15
17 Piniella,Lou	.40	.25	.10
18 Powell,Boog	.40	.25	.10
19 Seaver,Tom	1.50	1.00	.40
20 Spencer,Jim	.30	.20	.08
21 Stargell,Willie	1.00	.70	.30
22 Stottlemyre,Mel	.30	.20	.08
23 Wynn,Jim	.30	.20	.08
24 Yastrzemski,Carl	2.25	1.50	.65

1971 TOPPS BASEBALL TATTOOS (16) 3 1/2" X 14 1/4" 1 3/4" X 2 3/8" 1 3/16" X 1 3/4"

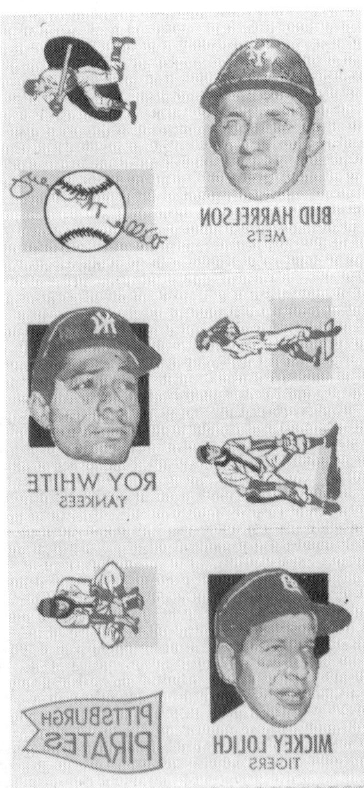

There are 16 different sheets of baseball tattoos issued by Topps in 1971. Each contains two distinct sizes of tattoos: those of players feature flesh-tone faces on red or yellow backgrounds; those of baseball figures, facsimile autographs and team pennants are one-half the player tattoo size. The "Baseball Tattoos" logo panel at the top of each sheet contains the sheet number. The small baseball figures are not priced in the checklist.

	MINT	VG-E	F-G
COMPLETE SET	30.00	20.00	8.00
COMMON PLAYER	.15	.10	.04
TATTOO SHEET ONE			
1 Sal Bando	.20	.13	.05
2 Dick Bosman	.15	.10	.04
3 Nate Colbert	.15	.10	.04
4 Cleon Jones	.15	.10	.04
5 Juan Marichal	.40	.25	.10
6 Brooks Robinson	.75	.50	.20
7 Brooks Robinson (autograph)	.25	.17	.07
8 Montreal Expos	.15	.10	.04
9 San Francisco Giants	.15	.10	.04
TATTOO SHEET TWO			
10 Glen Beckert	.15	.10	.04
11 Tommy Harper	.15	.10	.04
12 Ken Henderson	.15	.10	.04
13 Carl Yastrzemski	1.00	.60	.25
14 Carl Yastrzemski (autograph)	.25	.17	.07
15 Boston Red Sox	.20	.13	.05
16 New York Mets	.20	.13	.05

1971 Topps Baseball Tattoos

	TATTOO SHEET THREE			
17	Orlando Cepeda	.25	.17	.07
18	Jim Fregosi	.20	.13	.05
19	Fregosi (autograph)	.15	.10	.04
20	Randy Hundley	.15	.10	.04
21	Reggie Jackson	.75	.50	.20
22	Jerry Koosman	.20	.13	.05
23	Jim Palmer	.55	.35	.14
24	Philadephia Phillies	.15	.10	.04
25	New York Yankees	.20	.13	.05
	TATTOO SHEET FOUR			
26	Dick Dietz	.15	.10	.04
27	Clarence Gaston	.15	.10	.04
28	Dave Johnson	.15	.10	.04
29	Sam McDowell	.20	.13	.05
30	Sam McDowell (autograph)	.15	.10	.04
31	Gary Nolan	.15	.10	.04
32	Amos Otis	.20	.13	.05
33	Kansas City Royals	.15	.10	.04
34	Oakland A's	.15	.10	.04
	TATTOO SHEET FIVE			
35	Billy Grabarkewitz	.15	.10	.04
36	Al Kaline	.75	.50	.20
37	Kaline (autograph)	.25	.17	.07
38	Lee May	.20	.13	.05
39	Tom Murphy	.15	.10	.04
40	Vada Pinson	.20	.13	.05
41	Manny Sanguillen	.20	.13	.05
42	Atlanta Braves	.15	.10	.04
43	Los Angeles Dodgers	.20	.13	.05
	TATTOO SHEET SIX			
44	Luis Aparicio	.25	.17	.07
45	Paul Blair	.20	.13	.05
46	Chris Cannizzaro	.15	.10	.04
47	Donn Clendenon	.15	.10	.04
48	Larry Dierker	.15	.10	.04
49	Harmon Killebrew	.55	.35	.14
50	Harmon Killebrew (autograph)	.20	.13	.05
51	Chicago Cubs	.15	.10	.04
52	Cincinnati Reds	.15	.10	.04
	TATTOO SHEET SEVEN			
53	Rich Allen	.25	.17	.07
54	Bert Campaneris	.20	.13	.05
55	Don Money	.20	.13	.05
56	Boog Powell	.25	.17	.07
57	Powell (autograph)	.15	.10	.04
58	Ted Savage	.15	.10	.04
59	Rusty Staub	.25	.17	.07
60	Cleveland Indians	.15	.10	.04
61	Milwaukee Brewers	.15	.10	.04
	TATTOO SHEET EIGHT			
62	Leo Cardenas	.15	.10	.04
63	Bill Hands	.15	.10	.04
64	Frank Howard	.25	.17	.07
65	Howard (autograph)	.15	.10	.04
66	Wes Parker	.20	.13	.05
67	Reggie Smith	.25	.17	.07
68	Willie Stargell	.55	.35	.14
69	Chicago White Sox	.15	.10	.04
70	San Diego Padres	.15	.10	.04
	TATTOO SHEET NINE			
71	Hank Aaron	1.00	.60	.25
72	Aaron (autograph)	.25	.17	.07
73	Tommy Agee	.15	.10	.04
74	Jim Hunter	.40	.25	.10
75	Dick McAuliffe	.15	.10	.04
76	Tony Perez	.25	.17	.07
77	Lou Pinella	.20	.13	.05
78	Detroit Tigers	.20	.13	.05
	TATTOO SHEET TEN			
79	Roberto Clemente	1.00	.60	.25
80	Tony Conigliaro	.20	.13	.05
81	Fergie Jenkins	.25	.17	.07
82	Jenkins (autograph)	.15	.10	.04
83	Thurman Munson	.75	.50	.20
84	Gary Peters	.15	.10	.04
85	Joe Torre	.25	.17	.07
86	Baltimore Orioles	.20	.13	.05
	TATTOO SHEET ELEVEN			
87	Johnny Bench	.75	.50	.20
88	Bench (autograph)	.25	.17	.07
89	Rico Carty	.20	.13	.05
90	Bill Mazeroski	.20	.13	.05
91	Bob Oliver	.15	.10	.04
92	Rico Petrocelli	.20	.13	.05
93	Floyd Robinson	.15	.10	.04
94	Washington Senators	.15	.10	.04
	TATTOO SHEET TWELVE			
95	Bill Freehan	.20	.13	.05
96	Dave McNally	.20	.13	.05
97	Felix Millan	.15	.10	.04
98	Mel Stottlemyre	.15	.10	.04
99	Bob Tolan	.15	.10	.04
100	Billy Williams	.25	.17	.07
101	Billy Williams (autograph)	.15	.10	.04
102	Houston Astros	.15	.10	.04
	TATTOO SHEET THIRTEEN			
103	Ray Culp	.15	.10	.04
104	Bud Harrelson	.15	.10	.04
105	Mickey Lolich	.20	.13	.05
106	Willie McCovey	.55	.35	.14
107	McCovey (autograph)	.20	.13	.05
108	Ron Santo	.20	.13	.05
109	Roy White	.20	.13	.05
110	Pittsburgh Pirates	.15	.10	.04
	TATTOO SHEET FOURTEEN			
111	Bill Melton	.15	.10	.04
112	Jim Perry	.20	.13	.05
113	Pete Rose	1.25	.85	.35
114	Tom Seaver	.75	.50	.20
115	Seaver (autograph)	.25	.17	.07
116	Maury Wills	.25	.17	.07
117	Clyde Wright	.15	.10	.04
118	Minnesota Twins	.15	.10	.04
	TATTOO SHEET FIFTEEN			
119	Rod Carew	.75	.50	.20
120	Bob Gibson	.55	.35	.14
121	Gibson (autograph)	.20	.13	.05
122	Alex Johnson	.15	.10	.04
123	Don Kessinger	.20	.13	.05
124	Jim Merritt	.15	.10	.04
125	Rick Monday	.20	.13	.05
126	St. Louis Cards	.20	.13	.05
	TATTOO SHEET SIXTEEN			
127	Larry Bowa	.25	.17	.07
128	Mike Cuellar	.15	.10	.04
129	Ray Fosse	.15	.10	.04
130	Willie Mays	1.00	.60	.25
131	Mays (autograph)	.25	.17	.07
132	Carl Morton	.15	.10	.04
133	Tony Oliva	.25	.17	.07
134	California Angels	.15	.10	.04

1972 TOPPS BASEBALL POSTERS (24) 9 7/16" X 18"

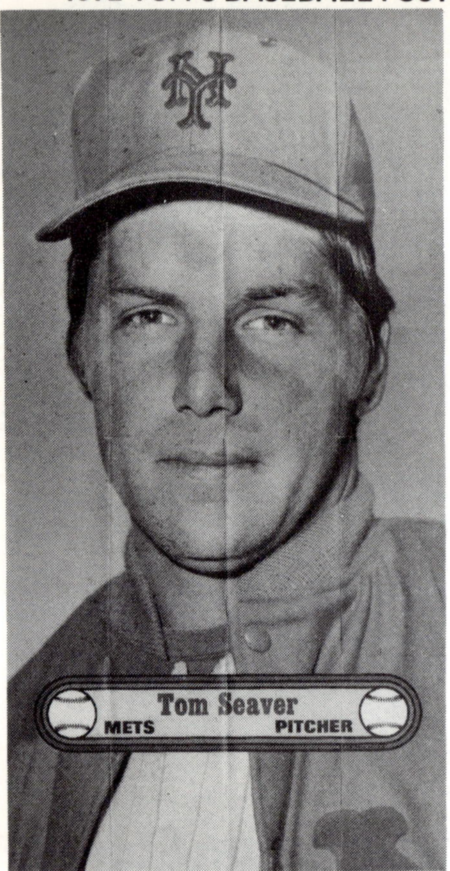

This giant, full-color series of 24 was issued as a separate set in 1972. The posters are individually numbered and, unlike other Topps posters described in this book, are borderless. They are printed on thin paper and were folded 5 times to facilitate packaging.

	MINT	VG-E	F-G
COMPLETE SET	40.00	26.00	10.00
COMMON PLAYER(1-24)	.70	.50	.20
1 McNally,Dave	.70	.50	.20
2 Yastrzemski,Carl	6.00	4.00	1.50
3 Melton,Bill	.70	.50	.20
4 Fosse,Ray	.70	.50	.20
5 Lolich,Mickey	.90	.65	.25
6 Otis,Amos	.90	.65	.25
7 Oliva,Tony	.90	.65	.25
8 Blue,Vida	1.25	.90	.40
9 Aaron,Hank	4.50	3.25	1.30
10 Jenkins,Fergie	1.25	.90	.40
11 Rose,Pete	6.00	4.00	1.50
12 Davis,Willie	.70	.50	.20
13 Seaver,Tom	3.50	2.50	1.00
14 Wise,Rick	.70	.50	.20
15 Stargell,Willie	1.75	1.25	.50
16 Torre,Joe	1.25	.90	.40
17 Mays,Willie	4.50	3.25	1.30
18 Messersmith,Andy	.90	.65	.25
19 Wood,Wilbur	.70	.50	.20
20 Killebrew,Harmon	1.75	1.25	.50
21 Williams,Billy	1.25	.90	.40
22 Harrelson,Bud	.70	.50	.20
23 Clemente,Roberto	3.50	2.50	1.00
24 McCovey,Willie	2.50	1.75	.75

1973 TOPPS CANDY LIDS (55) 1 7/8" D

One of Topps' most unusual test sets is this series of 55 color portraits of baseball players printed on the bottom of candy lids. The product was called "Baseball Stars Bubble Gum" and consisted of a small tub of candy-coated gum kernels. Issued in 1973, the lids are unnumbered and each has a small tab. Underneath the picture is a small ribbon design which contains the player's name, team and position.

	MINT	VG-E	F-G
COMPLETE SET	90.00	60.00	25.00
COMMON PLAYER	1.00	.65	.30
1 Hank Aaron	6.00	4.00	1.60
2 Dick Allen	1.50	1.00	.40
3 Dusty Baker	1.50	1.00	.40
4 Sal Bando	1.50	1.00	.40
5 Johnny Bench	4.00	2.75	1.10
6 Bobby Bonds	1.50	1.00	.40
7 Dick Bosman	1.00	.65	.30
8 Lou Brock	4.00	2.75	1.10
9 Rod Carew	4.00	2.75	1.10
10 Steve Carlton	4.00	2.75	1.10
11 Nate Colbert	1.00	.65	.30
12 Willie Davis	1.50	1.00	.40
13 Larry Dierker	1.00	.65	.30
14 Mike Epstein	1.00	.65	.30
15 Carlton Fisk	2.00	1.30	.55
16 Tim Foli	1.00	.65	.30
17 Ray Fosse	1.00	.65	.30
18 Bill Freehan	1.00	.65	.30
19 Bob Gibson	3.00	2.00	1.00
20 Bud Harrelson	1.00	.65	.30
21 Jim Hunter	2.00	1.30	.55

1973 Topps Candy Lids

22	Reggie Jackson	4.00	2.75	1.10
23	Fergie Jenkins	1.50	1.00	.40
24	Al Kaline	4.00	2.75	1.10
25	Harmon Killebrew	3.00	2.00	1.00
26	Clay Kirby	1.00	.65	.30
27	Mickey Lolich	1.50	1.00	.40
28	Greg Luzinski	1.50	1.00	.40
29	Willie McCovey	3.00	2.00	1.00
30	Mike Marshall	1.50	1.00	.40
31	Lee May	1.00	.65	.30
32	John Mayberry	1.00	.65	.30
33	Willie Mays	6.00	4.00	1.60
34	Thurman Munson	4.00	2.75	1.10
35	Bobby Murcer	1.50	1.00	.40
36	Gary Nolan	1.00	.65	.30
37	Amos Otis	1.50	1.00	.40
38	Jim Palmer	3.00	2.00	1.00
39	Gaylord Perry	3.00	2.00	1.00
40	Lou Piniella	1.50	1.00	.40
41	Brooks Robinson	4.00	2.75	1.10
42	Frank Robinson	4.00	2.75	1.10
43	Ellie Rodriguez	1.00	.65	.30
44	Pete Rose	8.00	5.50	2.25
45	Nolan Ryan	3.00	2.00	1.00
46	Manny Sanguillen	1.00	.65	.30
47	George Scott	1.50	1.00	.40
48	Tom Seaver	4.00	2.75	1.10
49	Chris Speier	1.00	.65	.30
50	Willie Stargell	3.00	2.00	1.00
51	Don Sutton	2.00	1.30	.55
52	Joe Torre	1.50	1.00	.40
53	Billy Williams	1.50	1.00	.40
54	Wilbur Wood	1.00	.65	.30
55	Carl Yastrzemski	6.00	4.00	1.60

1974 TOPPS TEST STAMPS (240) 1" X 1 1/2"

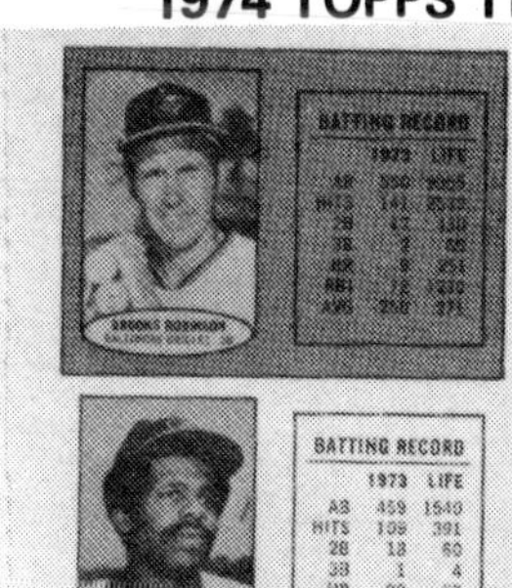

The 240 color portraits depicted on stamps in this 1974 Topps series have the player's name, team and position inside an oval below the picture area. The stamps were marketed in strips of six, along with an album, in their own wrapper (see wrapper section of this book). The booklets have eight pages and measure 2 1/2" X 3 7/8". There are 24 albums—one for each team—designed to hold 10 stamps apiece.

		MINT	VG-E	F-G
COMPLETE SET		85.00	60.00	25.00
COMMON PLAYER		.24	.16	.06
1	Hank Aaron	1.50	1.00	.40
2	Baker	.35	.22	.09
3	Evans	.24	.16	.06
4	Ralph Garr	.35	.22	.09
5	Harrison	.24	.16	.06
6	D. Johnson	.24	.16	.06
7	Lum	.24	.16	.06
8	Morton	.24	.16	.06
9	P. Niekro	.35	.22	.09
10	Oates	.24	.16	.06
11	Beckert	.24	.16	.06
12	Cardenal	.24	.16	.06
13	Harris	.24	.16	.06
14	Hooton	.35	.22	.09
15	Hundley	.24	.16	.06
16	Kessinger	.35	.22	.09
17	Monday	.35	.22	.09
18	R. Reuschel	.35	.22	.09
19	Santo	.35	.22	.09
20	Williams	.35	.22	.09
21	Johnny Bench	1.10	.70	.30
22	Billingham	.24	.16	.06
23	Borbon	.24	.16	.06
24	Concepcion	.35	.22	.09
25	Driessen	.24	.16	.06
26	Geronimo	.24	.16	.06
27	Gullett	.24	.16	.06
28	Morgan	.35	.22	.09
29	Perez	.35	.22	.09
30	Pete Rose	2.00	1.30	.55
31	Cedeno	.35	.22	.09
32	Helms	.24	.16	.06
33	L. May	.24	.16	.06
34	Metzger	.24	.16	.06
35	Rader	.24	.16	.06
36	Richard	.35	.22	.09
37	Roberts	.24	.16	.06
38	Reuss	.35	.22	.09
39	Watson	.35	.22	.09
40	Wynn	.35	.22	.09
41	Buckner	.35	.22	.09
42	Cey	.35	.22	.09
43	Crawford	.24	.16	.06
44	W. Davis	.35	.22	.09
45	Ferguson	.24	.16	.06
46	Lopes	.35	.22	.09
47	Messersmith	.35	.22	.09
48	Osteen	.24	.16	.06
49	Russell	.24	.16	.06
50	Sutton	.35	.22	.09
51	Bailey	.24	.16	.06
52	Boccabella	.24	.16	.06
53	Fairly	.24	.16	.06
54	Foli	.24	.16	.06
55	Hunt	.24	.16	.06
56	Jorgensen	.24	.16	.06
57	Marshall	.35	.22	.09
58	Renko	.24	.16	.06
59	Rogers	.35	.22	.09
60	Singleton	.35	.22	.09
61	Garrett	.24	.16	.06
62	Grote	.24	.16	.06
63	Harrelson	.24	.16	.06
64	C. Jones	.24	.16	.06
65	Koosman	.35	.22	.09
66	Matlack	.35	.22	.09
67	McGraw	.35	.22	.09
68	Millan	.24	.16	.06
69	Milner	.24	.16	.06
70	Tom Seaver	1.10	.70	.30
71	Boone	.35	.22	.09
72	Bowa	.35	.22	.09
73	Carlton	.60	.40	.15
74	Grabarkewitz	.24	.16	.06
75	Lonborg	.24	.16	.06
76	Luzinski	.35	.22	.09
77	Montanez	.24	.16	.06
78	W. Robinson	.24	.16	.06
79	Twitchell	.24	.16	.06
80	Unser	.24	.16	.06
81	Briles	.24	.16	.06
82	Ellis	.24	.16	.06
83	Giusti	.24	.16	.06
84	Hebner	.24	.16	.06
85	Oliver	.35	.22	.09
86	Parker	.60	.40	.15
87	Sanguillen	.24	.16	.06
88	Stargell	.60	.40	.15
89	Stennett	.24	.16	.06
90	Zisk	.35	.22	.09
91	Colbert	.24	.16	.06
92	Grief	.24	.16	.06
93	Grubb	.24	.16	.06
94	Jones	.35	.22	.09
95	Kendall	.24	.16	.06
96	Kirby	.24	.16	.06

1974 Topps Test Stamps

No.	Player			
97	McCovey	.60	.40	.15
98	Morales	.24	.16	.06
99	Roberts	.24	.16	.06
100	Winfield	1.10	.70	.30
101	Bonds	.35	.22	.09
102	Bradley	.24	.16	.06
103	Bryant	.24	.16	.06
104	Fuentes	.24	.16	.06
105	Goodson	.24	.16	.06
106	Kingman	.60	.40	.15
107	Maddox	.35	.22	.09
108	Rader	.24	.16	.06
109	Sosa	.24	.16	.06
110	Speier	.24	.16	.06
111	Brock	1.10	.70	.30
112	Cleveland	.24	.16	.06
113	J. Cruz	.35	.22	.09
114	Gibson	.60	.40	.15
115	McCarver	.24	.16	.06
116	Simmons	.35	.22	.09
117	Sizemore	.24	.16	.06
118	R. Smith	.35	.22	.09
119	Torre	.35	.22	.09
120	Tyson	.24	.16	.06
121	Baylor	.35	.22	.09
122	Belanger	.24	.16	.06
123	Blair	.24	.16	.06
124	T. Davis	.35	.22	.09
125	Grich	.35	.22	.09
126	G. Jackson	.24	.16	.06
127	McNally	.35	.22	.09
128	Palmer	1.10	.70	.30
129	B. Robinson	1.10	.70	.30
130	E. Williams	.24	.16	.06
131	Aparicio	.35	.22	.09
132	Cepeda	.60	.40	.15
133	Fisk	.60	.40	.15
134	Harper	.24	.16	.06
135	Lee	.24	.16	.06
136	Miller	.24	.16	.06
137	Moret	.24	.16	.06
138	Tiant	.35	.22	.09
139	Wise	.24	.16	.06
140	Carl Yastrzemski	1.50	1.00	.40
141	Alomar	.24	.16	.06
142	Epstein	.24	.16	.06
143	Oliver	.24	.16	.06
144	Pinson	.35	.22	.09
145	Frank Robinson	1.10	.70	.30
146	E. Rodriguez	.24	.16	.06
147	Nolan Ryan	.60	.40	.15
148	Scheinblum	.24	.16	.06
149	Singer	.24	.16	.06
150	Valentine	.24	.16	.06
151	Allen	.24	.16	.06
152	Bahnsen	.24	.16	.06
153	Forster	.24	.16	.06
154	Henderson	.24	.16	.06
155	Herrmann	.24	.16	.06
156	Kelly	.24	.16	.06
157	C. May	.24	.16	.06
158	Melton	.24	.16	.06
159	Orta	.24	.16	.06
160	Wood	.24	.16	.06
161	Buddy Bell	.35	.22	.09
162	Chambliss	.35	.22	.09
163	Duffy	.24	.16	.06
164	Duncan	.24	.16	.06
165	Ellis	.24	.16	.06
166	Gamble	.35	.22	.09
167	Hendrick	.35	.22	.09
168	Gaylord Perry	.60	.40	.15
169	Spikes	.24	.16	.06
170	Tidrow	.24	.16	.06
171	Brinkman	.24	.16	.06
172	Cash	.24	.16	.06
173	Coleman	.35	.22	.09
174	Freehan	.35	.22	.09
175	Hiller	.24	.16	.06
176	Horton	.35	.22	.09
177	Al Kaline	1.10	.70	.30
178	Lolich	.35	.22	.09
179	Rodriguez	.24	.16	.06
180	Stanley	.24	.16	.06
181	Busby	.24	.16	.06
182	Healy	.24	.16	.06
183	Kirkpatrick	.24	.16	.06
184	Mayberry	.35	.22	.09
185	Otis	.35	.22	.09
186	Patek	.24	.16	.06
187	Pattin	.24	.16	.06
188	Piniella	.35	.22	.09
189	Rojas	.24	.16	.06
190	Spittorff	.24	.16	.06
191	Jerry Bell	.24	.16	.06
192	Briggs	.24	.16	.06
193	Colborn	.24	.16	.06
194	Collucio	.24	.16	.06
195	Garcia	.24	.16	.06
196	Dave May	.24	.16	.06
197	Don Money	.35	.22	.09
198	Porter	.35	.22	.09
199	Scott	.24	.16	.06
200	Slaton	.24	.16	.06
201	Blyleven	.35	.22	.09
202	Braun	.24	.16	.06
203	Rod Carew	1.10	.70	.30
204	Corbin	.24	.16	.06
205	Darwin	.24	.16	.06
206	Decker	.24	.16	.06
207	Holt	.24	.16	.06
208	Killebrew	.60	.40	.15
209	Mitterwald	.24	.16	.06
210	Oliva	.35	.22	.09
211	Blomberg	.24	.16	.06
212	Lyle	.35	.22	.09
213	Medich	.35	.22	.09
214	Michaels	.35	.22	.09
215	Thurman Munson	1.10	.70	.30
216	Murcer	.35	.22	.09
217	Nettles	.35	.22	.09
218	Stottlemyre	.35	.22	.09
219	Velez	.24	.16	.06
220	White	.24	.16	.06
221	Bando	.35	.22	.09
222	Blue	.60	.40	.15
223	Campaneris	.35	.22	.09
224	Holtzman	.35	.22	.09
225	Jim Hunter	.60	.40	.15
226	Reggie Jackson	1.10	.70	.30
227	D. Johnson	.24	.16	.06
228	North	.24	.16	.06
229	Rudi	.35	.22	.09
230	Tenace	.35	.22	.09
231	Jim Bibby	.35	.22	.09
232	Burroughs	.35	.22	.09
233	Clyde	.24	.16	.06
234	Fregosi	.35	.22	.09
235	Harrah	.24	.16	.06
236	Jenkins	.35	.22	.09
237	Alex Johnson	.24	.16	.06
238	Dave Nelson	.24	.16	.06
239	Jim Spencer	.24	.16	.06
240	Sudakis	.24	.16	.06

BASEBALL WRAPPERS

Introduction and Pricing by Christopher Benjamin

The fantastic growth of baseball card collecting during the last five years has also resulted in an increased interest in wrappers. The astonishing aspect of this corollary to card collecting is that many wrappers—even from very obscure sets—have managed to survive the passage of time and have resurfaced into the collecting environment. This is amazing because these multi-colored cellophane packages were designed to attract our attention, much like a butterfly to a flower, leading us to spend our hard-earned childhood pennies on gum cards and candy. How many times did we, as children, sit under a tree or walk down the street during those carefree days of our youth, our mouths chock-full of bubble gum, our hands full of yesterday's heroes and also-rans, but leaving wadded-up wrappers discarded on the ground about us. Millions of baseball cards have survived as years passed by, but in contrast, perhaps only thousands or hundreds of wrappers, depending upon the specific set, have eluded destruction.

How did the old wrappers survive in the days before investment-minded collectors and dealers started "salting away" unopened boxes of baseball cards? Some were folded very carefully and stashed alongside that precious stack of cards in a shoe or cigar box; from time to time a collection is found containing a considerable number of wrappers stored in this manner. Sometimes they were simply dumped carelessly—wrappers and cards alike—into a container which was "discovered" many years later. Also, boxes and unopened packs of cards dating as far back as the 1930's have been unearthed during the past few years, some found gathering dust in the corner of a local wholesaler, some lying forgotten in the storage area of a retail store, while others have been brought to light by antique and collectibles dealers.

The most significant factor in wrapper survival, however, was the premium mechanism employed by the manufacturers of the early gum cards. Almost every 1930's or 1940's wrapper contains an advertisement offering additional baseball material as an inducement to buy the product. Goudey Gum would send a picture of Babe Ruth or the National or American League All-Star teams for only 50 wrappers apiece. National Chicle distributed pictures of baseball stars to its retailers with instructions to exchange them on the spot for specific amounts of wrappers. No money changed hands in these transactions, and they inspired major efforts by many young collectors to keep the neighborhood free from discarded wrappers. Many an accumulation of wrappers was undoubtedly halted by the interjection of new interests—girls and marbles being the principal distractions—and these "in limbo" piles are often discovered today. Wrappers from certain series of cards—neatly stapled together in stacks of 25—have even found their way into collectors' hands from the storerooms of long-departed gum card companies.

Whatever the reasons for their survival, baseball card wrappers exist in an amazing variety of designs and colors. Almost every popular set from 1948 to 1965 employed a one-cent and five-cent package, often with design variations. In some sets there are dated and undated versions. The packages may also vary in terms of layout: for example, every Bowman baseball card wrapper (1948-1955) is designed horizontally. In contrast, the Topps issues from 1951 to 1980, with few exceptions, are presented vertically. Wrappers have often varied according to the confection within: Bowman, the original manufacturer of gum for Gum Incorporated, always used chicle. Topps—daring to be different—advertised "baseball trading card candy" during its initial year of challenging Bowman, but encountered the "sticky-card" syndrome and joined the bubble gum crowd directly thereafter. Some companies, daring to be truly different, have marketed baseball cards with cookies and marbles inserted into the packages, but these ideas, brilliant as they may have seemed at their inception, soon joined caramel candy in the "impractical" classification. The 1982 baseball cards issued by Donruss and Fleer are being marketed without gum.

The basic attraction of baseball wrapper collecting is simple. Whereas a collector may require anywhere from 24 to 800-plus cards to complete a given set, he needs only one or two wrappers to represent a particular year and manufacturer. In addition, the most expensive wrapper in the hobby today cannot compare in cost to some of the superstar cards found in many sets. Wrappers are a unique art form which very often show more creativity in design and coloration than the cards found within (see color section). They add a special dimension to card collecting and often provide the collector with a pleasurable recollection of how wonderful it felt to be seven years old in some springtime long ago, with 10 cents in your pocket and the candy store just down the block.

The prices listed for wrappers in this section are based upon the condition grades of "excellent" and very good." A wrapper in "excellent" condition has no holes, tears, scuff marks, dirt or stains; it has no imperfections other than the natural fold lines found on all wrappers, and very little of the natural crumpling or wrinkles which often appear on wax paper and cellophane during the passage of time. "Very good" indicates that the wrapper is intact in shape and design, but has some or perhaps all of the imperfections listed above in minor degrees. A wrapper with parts missing, other than a minor tear or hole, cannot be considered to fall within either of these classifications, and is, accordingly, worth far less. There is no such condition as "excellent or very good for its age." This is a rationalization designed, by some, to justify a high price. Cards, wrappers and boxes have survived from the 1880's to the present in extremely nice condition; indeed, many of these older items were constructed of better materials than present-day collectibles and are capable of withstanding the "ravages of time" much more ably than their modern counterparts. Occasionally, a "mint" wrapper is offered for sale; most often this has been cut from a roll of wrappers (they are printed and rolled up like paper towels) which has been uncovered by a dealer or collector. Such wrappers command a premium price but the collector should beware for where there is one perfect wrapper there are probably many others, and such a "warehouse find" normally causes a dip in the price of that wrapper.

Wrappers vary greatly in terms of quality of construction and materials. Some 1930's wrappers like the 1933 and 1934 Goudey series, were printed on heavy waxed paper. The 1933 series, however, used a clear waxed paper, in contrast to the white waxed paper employed in 1934 (the latter seems to have survived in better condition because of thischange). Other Goudey issues of the 1930's and the Play Ball cards of 1939-1941 utilized cellophane, which allowed for a wider range of coloration and detail. Cellophane is now the most widely used material for wrappers, but it has one major defect as far as the collector is concerned: the wrapper often tears when the gum pack is opened. Wrappers from certain sets (1951, 1952 and 1956 Topps, for example) are notorious for having chunks of material missing from the margins and for tears which, once started, inevitably run across the surface and ruin the item. Several recent sets have been marketed in wrappers which have to be torn apart to get to the product within.

Wrapper values are susceptible to wild fluctuations depending upon a number of factors. There are far fewer wrapper collectors than card collectors, but as a group they are often very determined to add to their collections no matter the cost. Since wrappers seem to be fed into the supply side of the hobby in either of two extremes—one at a time or in bunches—there is a Jekyll-Hyde aspect to collecting them because the moderating effect of continuous supply is absent. Therefore, many wrappers are auctioned or sold at very high prices which constitute the "market value" for months or years to come. At any point in time, a hoard of heretofore "rare" wrappers might surface, with interested collectors demanding a lower price, but with the "finder" trying to keep prices high by releasing them one at a time. It is a "cat and mouse" game in which many a collector has become frustrated.

The best way to collect wrappers is to keep abreast of the latest news and prices by subscribing to the trade magazines and newspapers which service the collecting hobby. One of the best sources of information is THE WRAPPER, which has become a focal point for wrapper and non-sports card collectors during the past two years. Many hobbyists are now collecting unopened gum packs, and since these are subject to the same wild price fluctuations as the wrappers themselves, it is more important than ever to be well-informed as to what is going on within this sector of the hobby.

There are several ways to store your wrapper collection. Many collectors mount their wrappers with postage stamp hinges in permanent displays, and one need only see the color section on wrappers in this book to appreciate how beautiful such a display can be. One noted collector takes fresh bubble gum and some original cards and repacks the gum package to recapture the effect of days gone by. Others store their wrappers, folded or flattened out, in plastic sheets, while some reserve a space with each specific card set in which to place the wrapper. Collectors of unopened packs generally place their items side by side in display cases if they have the space to do so.

Whether you collect wrappers, unopened packs, or tobacco boxes (the "wrappers" of the tobacco era), your collection can be an interesting and valuable pastime. These pieces of packaging present a lively challenge and you shouldn't hesitate to inquire about them whether you are at a baseball card convention, an antique store, or the neighborhood flea market. Some of the best "finds" of recent years have been made in the most unexpected places. Happy collecting!

BASEBALL WRAPPERS

1948 BOWMAN
Price 50.00 35.00

1949 BOWMAN
Price 20.00 12.00

1950 BOWMAN
1 cent
Price 20.00 12.00

1951 BOWMAN
1 cent
Price 18.00 10.00

1951 BOWMAN
5 cents
Price 18.00 10.00

1952 BOWMAN
1 cent
Price 15.00 8.00

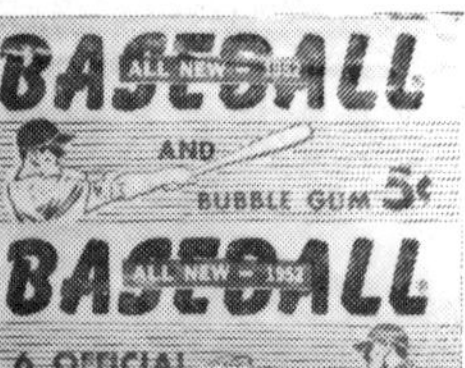

1952 BOWMAN
5 cents
Price 15.00 8.00

1953 BOWMAN
Color
Price 60.00 35.00

1953 BOWMAN
Black & White
Price 45.00 25.00

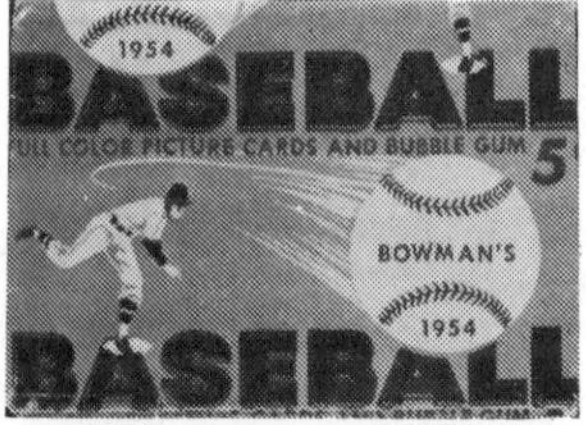

1954 BOWMAN
5 cents
Price 12.00 6.00

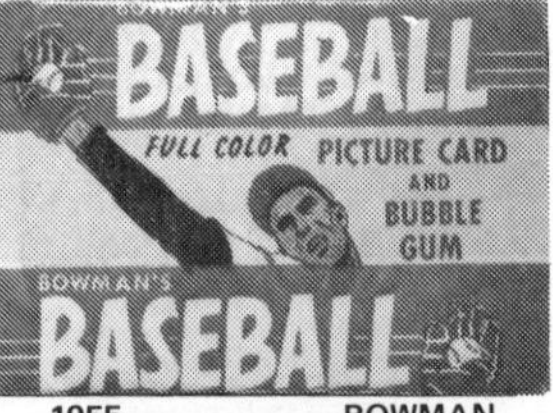

1955 BOWMAN
1 cent
Price 10.00 5.00

1955 BOWMAN
5 cents
Price 10.00 5.00

1933 DELONG
Price 125.00 90.00

1981 DONRUSS
Price .10 .05

1982 DONRUSS
Price .05 N/A

1959 FLEER
Price 20.00 10.00

1960 FLEER
Price 12.00 7.00

1961 FLEER
Price 10.00 4.00

1963 FLEER
Price 7.00 3.00

1981 FLEER
Price .10 N/A

1981 FLEER
Stickers
Price .10 N/A

1982 FLEER
Price .05 N/A

1933 GOUDEY
Six figures
Price 75.00 50.00

1933 GOUDEY
Three figures
Price 60.00 35.00

1933 GOUDEY
Four numbered corners
Price 45.00 25.00

1933 GOUDEY
Wrappers ad
Price 50.00 30.00

1933 GOUDEY
SPORT KINGS
Price 10.00 5.00

1934 GOUDEY
Price 60.00 40.00

1935 GOUDEY
Price 100.00 60.00

1936 GOUDEY
Price 90.00 50.00

1937 GOUDEY
SPORT KINGS GAME
Price 25.00 15.00

1938 GOUDEY
Price 125.00 85.00

1941 GOUDEY
Price 100.00 65.00

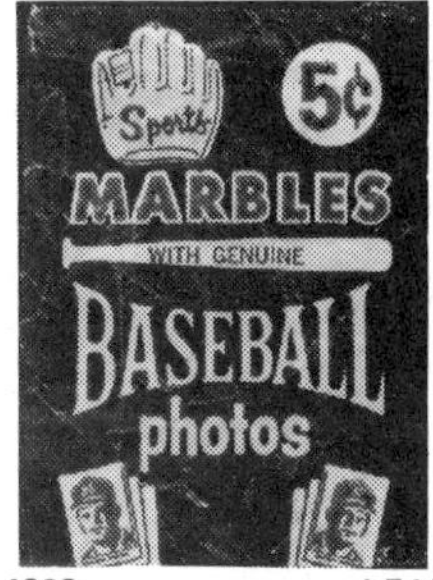

1960 LEAF
Price 5.00 2.00

1933 GEORGE C. MILLER
Price 350.00 250.00

1934? CANADIAN GOUDEY
DIAMOND STARS
Price 100.00 65.00

1934 NATIONAL CHICLE
DIAMOND STARS
Price(yellow) 60.00 35.00
Price(blue) 75.00 45.00

1934-35 NATIONAL CHICLE
BATTER–UP
Price 100.00 65.00

1936 NATIONAL CHICLE
BATTER–UP
Price 150.00 90.00

1961 NU–CARD
Price 6.00 3.00

1939 PLAY BALL
Price 50.00 30.00

1940 PLAY BALL
Price 100.00 60.00

1941 PLAY BALL
Price 200.00 100.00

1981 SPORT AMERICANA
1937 Diamond Stars
Price .10 N/A

1933 TATOO GUM
Price(blue) 25.00 15.00
Price(yellow) 25.00 15.00

1951 TOPPS
Blue Back
Price 25.00 15.00

1951 TOPPS
Large wrapper
Price 50.00 35.00

1951 TOPPS
Red Back
Price 5.00 2.00

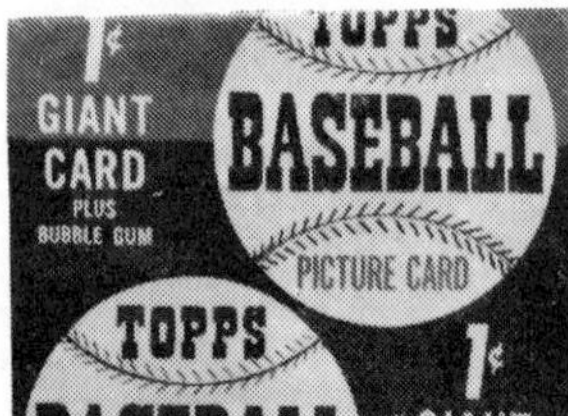

1952 TOPPS
1 cent
Price 15.00 8.00

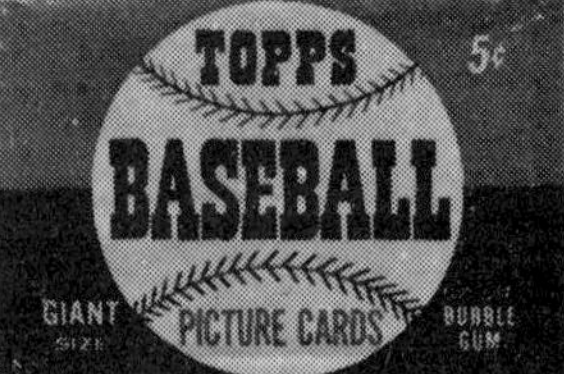

1952 TOPPS
5 cents
Price 15.00 8.00

1953 TOPPS
5 cents
Price 25.00 15.00

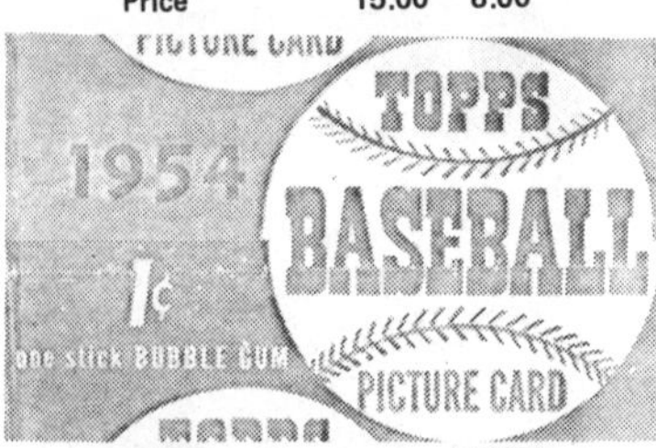

1954 TOPPS
1 cent
Price 35.00 20.00

1954 TOPPS
5 cents
Price 20.00 12.00

1955 TOPPS
5 cents
Price 20.00 12.00

1955 TOPPS
1 cent undated
Price 8.00 3.00

1955 TOPPS
1 cent dated
Price 12.00 7.00

1955 TOPPS
Double Header
Price 10.00 5.00

1956 TOPPS
1 cent
Price 12.00 8.00

1956 TOPPS
5 cents
Price 20.00 10.00

1957 TOPPS
1 cent
Price 12.00 8.00

1957 TOPPS
5 cents
Price 12.00 8.00

1958 TOPPS
1 cent
Price 5.00 2.00

1959 TOPPS
1 cent batter
Price 10.00 4.00

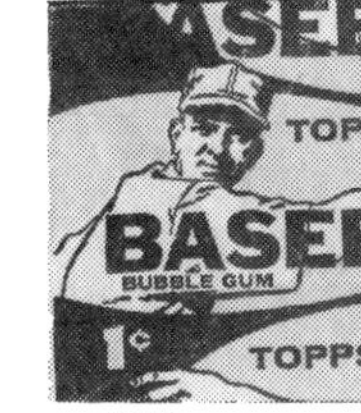

1959 TOPPS
1 cent pitcher
Price 10.00 4.00

1958 TOPPS
5 cents
Price 10.00 5.00

1959 TOPPS
5 cents
Price 6.00 3.00

1960 TOPPS
5 cents
Price 7.00 4.00

1960 TOPPS
Tatoo
Price 6.00 3.00

1961 TOPPS
1 cent
Price 8.00 4.00

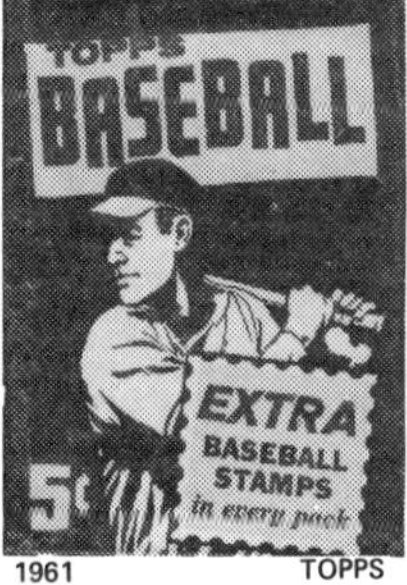

1961 TOPPS
5 cents
Price 5.00 2.50

1961 TOPPS
5 cents
Price 5.00 2.50

1962 TOPPS
5 cents
Price 5.00 2.00

1962 TOPPS
1 cent
Price 6.00 3.00

1962 TOPPS
Baseball Bucks
Price 15.00 10.00

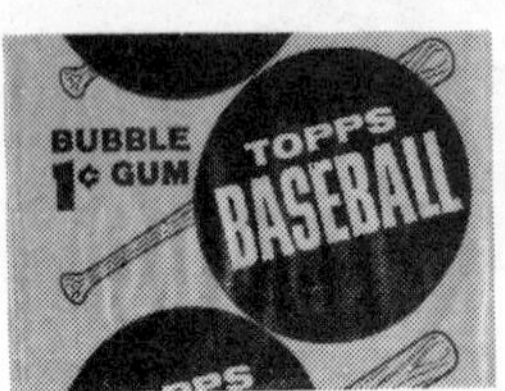

1963 TOPPS
1 cent
Price 6.00 3.00

1963 TOPPS
5 cents
Price 5.00 2.50

1964 TOPPS
5 cents
Price 5.00 2.50

1964 TOPPS
5 cents-Insert
Price 5.00 2.50

1964 TOPPS
Giants
Price 8.00 4.00

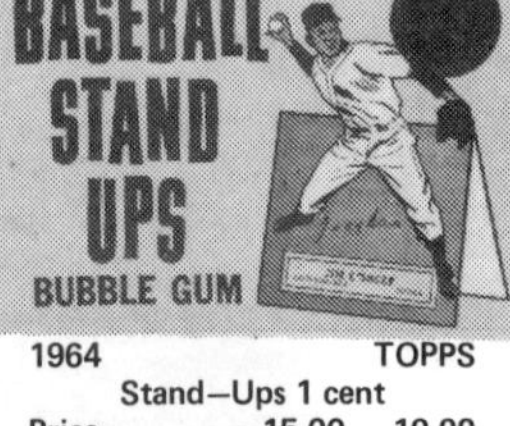

1964 TOPPS
Stand–Ups 1 cent
Price 15.00 10.00

1964 TOPPS
Stand–Ups 5 cents
Price 12.00 8.00

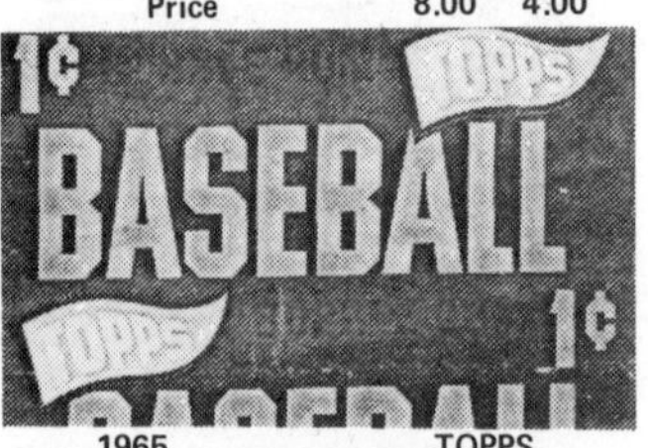

1965 TOPPS
1 cent
Price 6.00 3.00

1965 TOPPS
5 cents
Price 4.00 2.00

1966 TOPPS
5 cents
Price 2.00 .90

1967 TOPPS
5 cents
Price 4.00 2.00

1967 TOPPS
5 cents-Insert
Price 4.00. 2.00

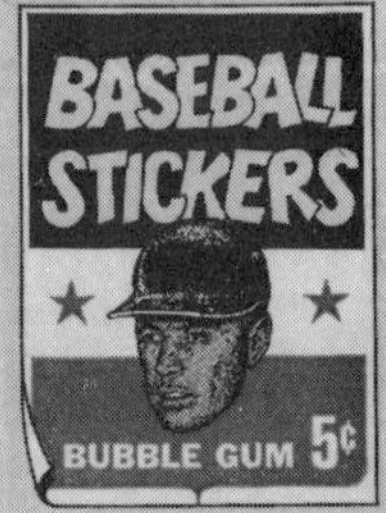

1967 TOPPS
Stickers Pirates & Boston
Price 35.00 25.00

1968 TOPPS
5 cents
Price 3.50 1.50

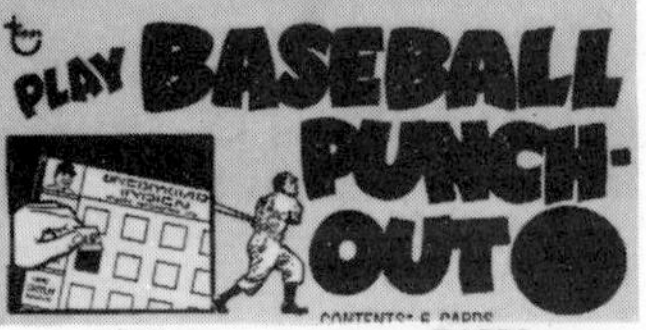

1967 TOPPS
Punch Out
Price 25.00 15.00

1968 TOPPS
5 cents-Insert
Price 4.00 2.00

1968 TOPPS
3–D
Price 75.00 50.00

1969 TOPPS
5 cents
Price 3.50 1.50

1969 TOPPS
Mini–Stickers
Price 35.00 25.00

1970 TOPPS
Super
Price 3.00 1.50

1968 TOPPS
Player Posters
Price 5.00 2.50

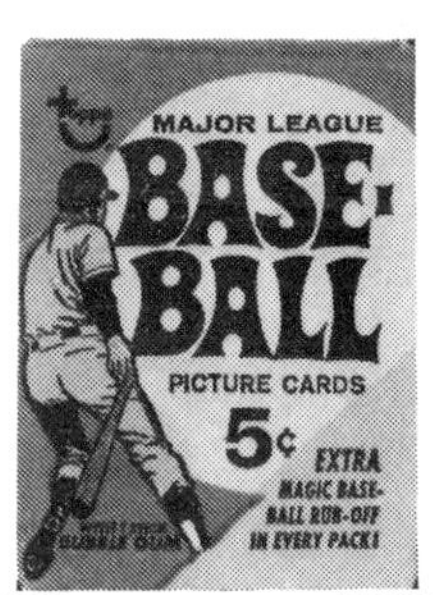

1969 TOPPS
5 cents-Insert
Price 4.00 2.00

1969 TOPPS
Stamps
Price 6.00 3.00

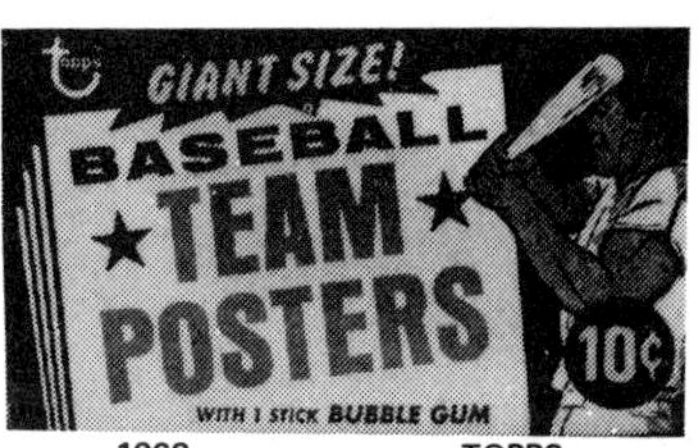

1968 TOPPS
Team Posters
Price 4.00 2.00

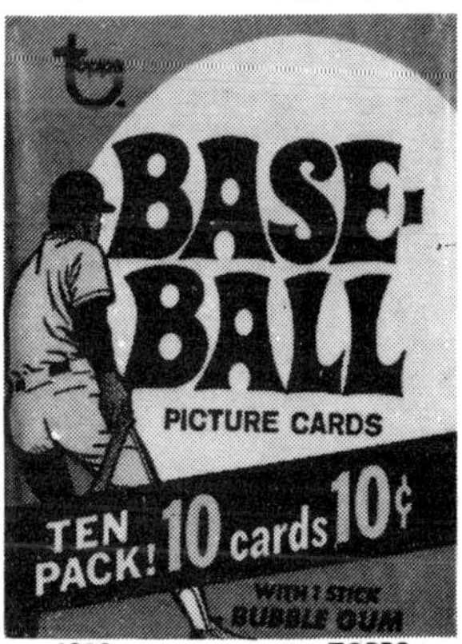

1969 TOPPS
10 cents
Price 5.00 2.50

1970 TOPPS
10 cents
Price 2.50 1.00

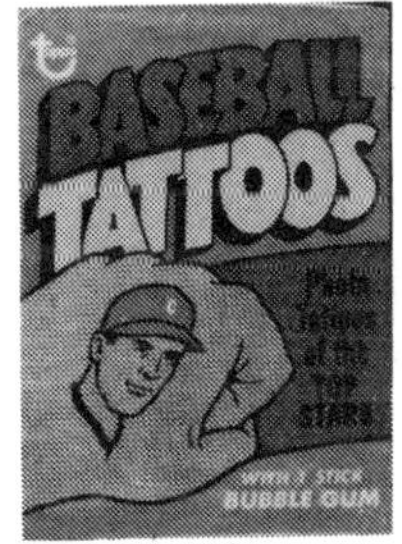

1970 TOPPS
Tatoos
Price 5.00 2.00

1971 TOPPS
Regular
Price 3.00 1.50

1971 TOPPS
Insert
Price 4.00 2.00

1972 TOPPS
Price 2.00 .90

1972 TOPPS
Posters
Price 3.50 1.50

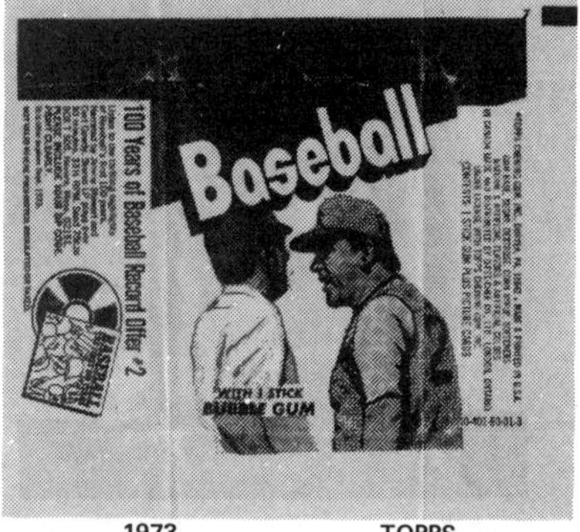

1973 TOPPS
Umpire
Price 2.00 .75

1973 TOPPS
Pitcher
Price 2.00 .75

1973 TOPPS
Batter
Price 2.00 .75

1973 TOPPS
Action Emblems
Price Not publicly issued

1973 TOPPS
Catcher
Price 2.00 .75

1973 TOPPS
Pin—Ups
Price Depends upon star

1974 TOPPS
Price 1.50 .50

1974 TOPPS
Deckle Edge
Price 8.00 4.00

1974 TOPPS
Jigsaw
Price 10.00 5.00

1974 TOPPS
Stamps & album
Price 25.00 15.00

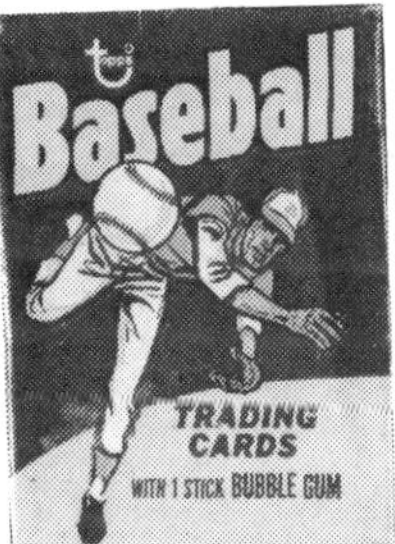

1975 TOPPS
Price 1.50 .50

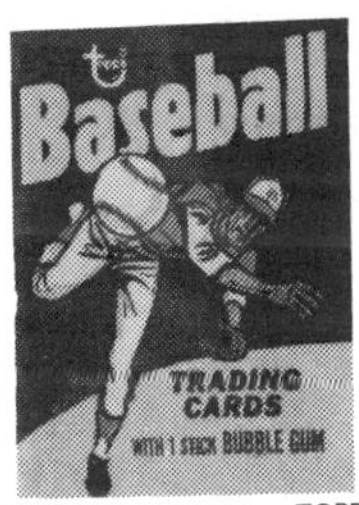

1975 TOPPS
Mini
Price 2.00 .90

1976 TOPPS
Price .75 .35

1977 TOPPS
Price .50 .20

1977 TOPPS
Cloth Stickers
Price 1.00 .45

1978 TOPPS
Price .35 .15

1979 TOPPS
Price .25 .10

1980 TOPPS
Price .15 N/A

1981 TOPPS
Home Team
Price .10 N/A

1981 TOPPS
Price .05 N/A

1981 TOPPS
Scratch–Offs
Price .05 N/A

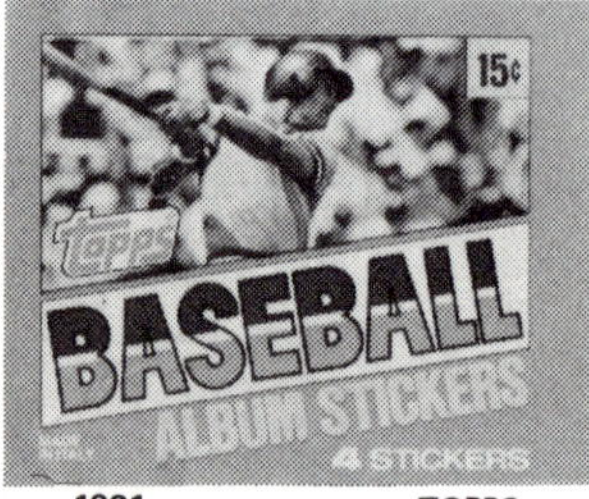

1981 TOPPS
Stickers
Price .05 N/A

1982 TOPPS
Price .03 N/A

The publications included in this section are among the most widely collected publications—from the team collector attempting to obtain all his team's programs and yearbooks to the more ambitious aficionado attempting to obtain all the World Series and All-star programs, ticket stubs, bats, etc. Yearbooks are priced back to 1933, and as one can see from the lists, not every team issued a yearbook every year. In fact, those yearbook prices which are asterisked refer to unofficial yearbooks (issued during a year when there was no official yearbook). An exhaustive list of yearbooks would also include any revised yearbooks or any unofficial yearbooks issued concurrent with an official yearbook; these yearbooks will have to wait for a second edition of this volume. The listing of yearbooks and programs also provides a list of major league teams that were in existence that year.

World Series memorabilia has been herein defined to be memorabilia involving the teams actually in the World Series that year. This means that "phantom" (involving teams who were "planning" to be in the World Series but met an unfortunate late season demise; the best recent example being the 1964 Phillies) World Series programs, full tickets, and press pins are not included in spite of their interest to a small group of collectors. Contrary to some recent advertising hype, "phantom" press pins and other non-successful ventures into "would be" memorabilia, are not "worth" any value near the value of the "real" thing nor are they sought after by a great number of collectors. Be careful when dealing with anyone attempting to perpetrate such a myth.

Autograph collectors are referred to the extensive autograph sections in this book for the additive value of autographs on items in this section, e.g., programs which have been personally autographed. For cross-reference, the autograph ball section of this volume serves as a series of team rosters, as every pennant winning team and every All-star team has been listed with each player on the team that year.

Ticket stubs to World Series and All-star games are beautiful items but are difficult to price and/or grade for condition. The prices given are for stubs, thus, mint condition can naturally only refer to the remaining half of the ticket. Full tickets would be valued and priced approximately 50% higher than the prices given for ticket stubs.

In addition to price information, this section includes data such as location of All-star games, winners and score of All-star games, games won by each World Series team, and divisional playoff teams and games won.

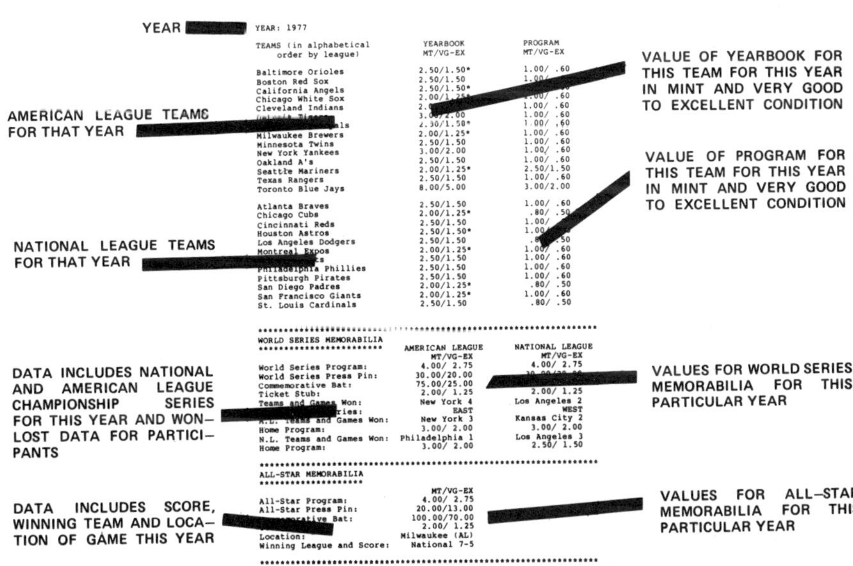

YEAR: 1977

TEAMS (in alphabetical order by league)	YEARBOOK MT/VG-EX	PROGRAM MT/VG-EX
Baltimore Orioles	2.50/1.50*	1.00/ .60
Boston Red Sox	2.50/1.50	1.00/ [illegible]
California Angels	2.50/1.50*	[illegible]
Chicago White Sox	2.00/1.25*	[illegible]/ .60
Cleveland Indians	2.[illegible]	1.00/ .60
[illegible]	3.[illegible]2.00	1.00/ .60
[illegible]ls	2.50/1.50*	1.00/ .60
Milwaukee Brewers	2.00/1.25*	1.00/ .60
Minnesota Twins	2.50/1.50	1.00/ .60
New York Yankees	3.00/2.00	1.00/ .60
Oakland A's	2.50/1.50	1.00/ .60
Seattle Mariners	2.00/1.25*	2.50/1.50
Texas Rangers	2.50/1.50	1.00/ .60
Toronto Blue Jays	8.00/5.00	3.00/2.00
Atlanta Braves	2.50/1.50	1.00/ .60
Chicago Cubs	2.00/1.25*	.80/ .50
Cincinnati Reds	2.50/1.50	1.00/ [illegible]
Houston Astros	2.50/1.50*	1.00[illegible]
Los Angeles Dodgers	2.50/1.50	.8[illegible] .50
Montreal Expos	2.00/1.25*	1.00/ .60
[illegible]s	2.50/1.50	1.00/ .60
Philadelphia Phillies	2.50/1.50	1.00/ .60
Pittsburgh Pirates	2.50/1.50	1.00/ .60
San Diego Padres	2.00/1.25*	.80/ .50
San Francisco Giants	2.00/1.25*	1.00/ .60
St. Louis Cardinals	2.50/1.50	.80/ .50

WORLD SERIES MEMORABILIA

	AMERICAN LEAGUE MT/VG-EX	NATIONAL LEAGUE MT/VG-EX
World Series Program:	4.00/ 2.75	4.00/ 2.75
World Series Press Pin:	30.00/20.00	[illegible]
Commemorative Bat:	75.00/25.00	[illegible]
Ticket Stub:	2.00/ 1.25	2.00/ 1.25
Teams and Games Won:	New York 4	Los Angeles 2
[illegible]ries:	EAST	WEST
A.L. Teams and Games Won:	New York 3	Kansas City 2
Home Program:	3.00/ 2.00	3.00/ 2.00
N.L. Teams and Games Won:	Philadelphia 1	Los Angeles 3
Home Program:	3.00/ 2.00	2.50/ 1.50

ALL-STAR MEMORABILIA

	MT/VG-EX
All-Star Program:	4.00/ 2.75
All-Star Press Pin:	20.00/13.00
[illegible]rative Bat:	100.00/70.00
[illegible]	2.00/ 1.25
Location:	Milwaukee (AL)
Winning League and Score:	National 7-5

YEAR: 1903

WORLD SERIES MEMORABILIA

	AMERICAN LEAGUE MT/VG-EX	NATIONAL LEAGUE MT/VG-EX
World Series Program:	1500.00/1000.00	1500.00/1000.00
World Series Press Pin:	1000.00/ 650.00	1000.00/ 650.00
Ticket Stub:	150.00/ 100.00	150.00/ 100.00
Teams and Games Won:	Boston 5	Pittsburgh 3

YEAR: 1904

WORLD SERIES MEMORABILIA - - - - - - - - NO SERIES PLAYED IN 1904

YEAR: 1905

WORLD SERIES MEMORABILIA

	AMERICAN LEAGUE MT/VG-EX	NATIONAL LEAGUE MT/VG-EX
World Series Program:	700.00/450.00	700.00/450.00
World Series Press Pin:	500.00/350.00	500.00/350.00
Ticket Stub:	70.00/ 45.00	70.00/ 45.00
Teams and Games Won:	Philadelphia 1	New York 4

YEAR: 1906

WORLD SERIES MEMORABILIA

	AMERICAN LEAGUE MT/VG-EX	NATIONAL LEAGUE MT/VG-EX
World Series Program:	600.00/400.00	600.00/400.00
World Series Press Pin:	500.00/350.00	500.00/350.00
Ticket Stub:	60.00/ 40.00	60.00/ 40.00
Teams and Games Won:	Chicago 4	Chicago 1

YEAR: 1907

WORLD SERIES MEMORABILIA

	AMERICAN LEAGUE MT/VG-EX	NATIONAL LEAGUE MT/VG-EX
World Series Program:	550.00/400.00	550.00/400.00
World Series Press Pin:	500.00/350.00	500.00/350.00
Ticket Stub:	55.00/ 40.00	55.00/ 40.00
Teams and Games Won:	Detroit 0	Chicago 4

YEAR: 1908

WORLD SERIES MEMORABILIA

	AMERICAN LEAGUE MT/VG-EX	NATIONAL LEAGUE MT/VG-EX
World Series Program:	500.00/350.00	500.00/350.00
World Series Press Pin:	450.00/300.00	450.00/300.00
Ticket Stub:	50.00/ 35.00	50.00/ 35.00
Teams and Games Won:	Detroit 1	Chicago 4

YEAR: 1909

WORLD SERIES MEMORABILIA

	AMERICAN LEAGUE MT/VG-EX	NATIONAL LEAGUE MT/VG-EX
World Series Program:	450.00/300.00	450.00/300.00
World Series Press Pin:	400.00/275.00	400.00/275.00
Ticket Stub:	45.00/ 30.00	45.00/ 30.00
Teams and Games Won:	Detroit 3	Pittsburgh 4

YEAR: 1910

WORLD SERIES MEMORABILIA

	AMERICAN LEAGUE MT/VG-EX	NATIONAL LEAGUE MT/VG-EX
World Series Program:	400.00/275.00	400.00/275.00
World Series Press Pin:	350.00/250.00	350.00/250.00
Ticket Stub:	40.00/ 25.00	40.00/ 25.00
Teams and Games Won:	Philadelphia 4	Chicago 1

YEAR: 1911

WORLD SERIES MEMORABILIA

	AMERICAN LEAGUE MT/VG-EX	NATIONAL LEAGUE MT/VG-EX
World Series Program:	400.00/275.00	400.00/275.00
World Series Press Pin:	350.00/250.00	350.00/250.00
Ticket Stub:	40.00/ 25.00	40.00/ 25.00
Teams and Games Won:	Philadelphia 4	New York 2

YEAR: 1912

WORLD SERIES MEMORABILIA

	AMERICAN LEAGUE MT/VG-EX	NATIONAL LEAGUE MT/VG-EX
World Series Program:	350.00/225.00	350.00/225.00
World Series Press Pin:	300.00/200.00	300.00/200.00
Ticket Stub:	40.00/ 25.00	40.00/ 25.00
Teams and Games Won:	Boston 4	New York 3

YEAR: 1913

WORLD SERIES MEMORABILIA

	AMERICAN LEAGUE MT/VG-EX	NATIONAL LEAGUE MT/VG-EX
World Series Program:	350.00/225.00	350.00/225.00
World Series Press Pin:	300.00/200.00	300.00/200.00
Ticket Stub:	40.00/ 25.00	40.00/ 25.00
Teams and Games Won:	Philadelphia 4	New York 1

YEAR: 1914

WORLD SERIES MEMORABILIA

	AMERICAN LEAGUE MT/VG-EX	NATIONAL LEAGUE MT/VG-EX
World Series Program:	350.00/225.00	350.00/225.00
World Series Press Pin:	300.00/200.00	300.00/200.00
Ticket Stub:	40.00/ 25.00	40.00/ 25.00
Teams and Games Won:	Philadelphia 0	Boston 4

YEAR: 1915

WORLD SERIES MEMORABILIA

	AMERICAN LEAGUE MT/VG-EX	NATIONAL LEAGUE MT/VG-EX
World Series Program:	300.00/200.00	300.00/200.00
World Series Press Pin:	250.00/150.00	250.00/150.00
Ticket Stub:	40.00/ 25.00	40.00/ 25.00
Teams and Games Won:	Boston 4	Philadelphia 1

YEAR: 1916

WORLD SERIES MEMORABILIA

	AMERICAN LEAGUE MT/VG-EX	NATIONAL LEAGUE MT/VG-EX
World Series Program:	275.00/175.00	275.00/175.00
World Series Press Pin:	225.00/150.00	225.00/150.00
Ticket Stub:	35.00/ 25.00	35.00/ 25.00
Teams and Games Won:	Boston 4	Brooklyn 1

YEAR: 1917

WORLD SERIES MEMORABILIA

	AMERICAN LEAGUE MT/VG-EX	NATIONAL LEAGUE MT/VG-EX
World Series Program:	250.00/150.00	250.00/150.00
World Series Press Pin:	210.00/140.00	210.00/140.00
Ticket Stub:	35.00/ 25.00	35.00/ 25.00
Teams and Games Won:	Chicago 4	New York 2

YEAR: 1918

WORLD SERIES MEMORABILIA

	AMERICAN LEAGUE MT/VG-EX	NATIONAL LEAGUE MT/VG-EX
World Series Program:	250.00/150.00	300.00/200.00
World Series Press Pin:	200.00/130.00	200.00/130.00
Ticket Stub:	35.00/ 25.00	35.00/ 25.00
Teams and Games Won:	Boston 4	Chicago 2

YEAR: 1919

WORLD SERIES MEMORABILIA

	AMERICAN LEAGUE MT/VG-EX	NATIONAL LEAGUE MT/VG-EX
World Series Program:	300.00/200.00	225.00/150.00
World Series Press Pin:	350.00/250.00	200.00/130.00
Ticket Stub:	50.00/ 35.00	40.00/ 25.00
Teams and Games Won:	Chicago 3	Cincinnati 5

YEAR: 1920

WORLD SERIES MEMORABILIA
****

	AMERICAN LEAGUE MT/VG-EX	NATIONAL LEAGUE MT/VG-EX
World Series Program:	200.00/130.00	200.00/130.00
World Series Press Pin:	190.00/125.00	190.00/125.00
Ticket Stub:	30.00/ 20.00	30.00/ 20.00
Teams and Games Won:	Cleveland 5	Brooklyn 2

****

YEAR: 1921

WORLD SERIES MEMORABILIA
****

	AMERICAN LEAGUE MT/VG-EX	NATIONAL LEAGUE MT/VG-EX
World Series Program:	210.00/135.00	200.00/130.00
World Series Press Pin:	200.00/130.00	175.00/115.00
Ticket Stub:	30.00/ 20.00	30.00/ 20.00
Teams and Games Won:	New York 3	New York 5

****

YEAR: 1922

WORLD SERIES MEMORABILIA
****

	AMERICAN LEAGUE MT/VG-EX	NATIONAL LEAGUE MT/VG-EX
World Series Program:	210.00/135.00	200.00/130.00
World Series Press Pin:	200.00/130.00	175.00/115.00
Ticket Stub:	30.00/ 20.00	30.00/ 20.00
Teams and Games Won:	New York 4	New York 0

****

YEAR: 1923

WORLD SERIES MEMORABILIA
****

	AMERICAN LEAGUE MT/VG-EX	NATIONAL LEAGUE MT/VG-EX
World Series Program:	185.00/125.00	175.00/115.00
World Series Press Pin:	200.00/130.00	175.00/115.00
Ticket Stub:	30.00/ 20.00	30.00/ 20.00
Teams and Games Won:	New York 4	New York 2

****

YEAR: 1924

WORLD SERIES MEMORABILIA
****

	AMERICAN LEAGUE MT/VG-EX	NATIONAL LEAGUE MT/VG-EX
World Series Program:	165.00/105.00	165.00/105.00
World Series Press Pin:	165.00/105.00	165.00/105.00
Ticket Stub:	30.00/ 20.00	30.00/ 20.00
Teams and Games Won:	Washington 4	New York 3

****

YEAR: 1925

WORLD SERIES MEMORABILIA
****

	AMERICAN LEAGUE MT/VG-EX	NATIONAL LEAGUE MT/VG-EX
World Series Program:	150.00/100.00	150.00/100.00
World Series Press Pin:	160.00/105.00	160.00/105.00
Ticket Stub:	30.00/ 20.00	30.00/ 20.00
Teams and Games Won:	Washington 3	Pittsburgh 4

****

YEAR: 1926

WORLD SERIES MEMORABILIA
****

	AMERICAN LEAGUE MT/VG-EX	NATIONAL LEAGUE MT/VG-EX
World Series Program:	160.00/105.00	150.00/100.00
World Series Press Pin:	175.00/115.00	150.00/100.00
Ticket Stub:	30.00/ 20.00	30.00/ 20.00
Teams and Games Won:	New York 3	St. Louis 4

****

YEAR: 1927

WORLD SERIES MEMORABILIA
****

	AMERICAN LEAGUE MT/VG-EX	NATIONAL LEAGUE MT/VG-EX
World Series Program:	175.00/125.00	125.00/ 80.00
World Series Press Pin:	250.00/150.00	150.00/100.00
Ticket Stub:	40.00/ 25.00	30.00/ 20.00
Teams and Games Won:	New York 4	Pittsburgh 0

****

YEAR: 1928

WORLD SERIES MEMORABILIA
****

	AMERICAN LEAGUE MT/VG-EX	NATIONAL LEAGUE MT/VG-EX
World Series Program:	135.00/ 90.00	125.00/80.00
World Series Press Pin:	150.00/100.00	125.00/80.00
Ticket Stub:	25.00/ 16.00	25.00/16.00
Teams and Games Won:	New York 4	St. Louis 0

****

YEAR: 1929

WORLD SERIES MEMORABILIA
****

	AMERICAN LEAGUE MT/VG-EX	NATIONAL LEAGUE MT/VG-EX
World Series Program:	130.00/90.00	120.00/80.00
World Series Press Pin:	125.00/85.00	125.00/85.00
Ticket Stub:	25.00/16.00	25.00/16.00
Teams and Games Won:	Philadelphia 4	Chicago 1

****

YEAR: 1930

WORLD SERIES MEMORABILIA
****

	AMERICAN LEAGUE MT/VG-EX	NATIONAL LEAGUE MTG/VG-EX
World Series Program:	125.00/80.00	115.00/75.00
World Series Press Pin:	115.00/75.00	115.00/75.00
Ticket Stub:	25.00/16.00	25.00/16.00
Teams and Games Won:	Philadelphia 4	Cardinals 2

****

YEAR: 1931

WORLD SERIES MEMORABILIA
****

	AMERICAN LEAGUE MT/VG-EX	NATIONAL LEAGUE MT/VG-EX
World Series Program:	110.00/70.00	110.00/70.00
World Series Press Pin:	115.00/75.00	115.00/80.00
Ticket Stub:	25.00/16.00	25.00/16.00
Teams and Games Won:	Philadelphia 3	Cardinals 4

****

YEAR: 1932

WORLD SERIES MEMORABILIA
****

	AMERICAN LEAGUE MT/VG-EX	NATIONAL LEAGUE MT/VG-EX
World Series Program:	100.00/65.00	100.00/65.00
World Series Press Pin:	120.00/80.00	110.00/70.00
Ticket Stub:	25.00/16.00	25.00/16.00
Teams and Games Won:	Yankees 4	Chicago 0

****

SPORT AMERICANA HOBBY REFERENCE MATERIAL IS THE RECOGNIZED STANDARD FOR INFORMATION AND PRICES OF SPORTS COLLECTIBLES. SEE INSIDE BACK COVER AND THE PAGE ADJACENT TO IT FOR DETAILS.

YEAR: 1933

TEAMS (in alphabetical order by league)	YEARBOOK MT/VG-EX	PROGRAM MT/VG-EX
Boston Red Sox	xx.xx/xxxxx	9.00/6.00
Chicago White Sox	xx.xx/xxxxx	8.00/5.00
Cleveland Indians	xx.xx/xxxxx	7.50/4.75
Detroit Tigers	xx.xx/xxxxx	10.00/6.50
New York Yankees	xx.xx/xxxxx	10.00/6.50
Philadelphia A's	xx.xx/xxxxx	8.00/5.00
St. Louis Browns	xx.xx/xxxxx	8.00/5.00
Washington Senators	xx.xx/xxxxx	10.00/6.50
Boston Braves	xx.xx/xxxxx	8.00/5.00
Brooklyn Dodgers	xx.xx/xxxxx	10.00/6.50
Chicago Cubs	xx.xx/xxxxx	8.00/5.00
Cincinnati Reds	xx.xx/xxxxx	8.00/5.00
New York Giants	xx.xx/xxxxx	10.00/6.50
Philadelphia Phillies	xx.xx/xxxxx	7.00/4.50
Pittsburgh Pirates	xx.xx/xxxxx	8.00/5.00
St. Louis Cardinals	xx.xx/xxxxx	7.00/4.50

WORLD SERIES MEMORABILIA

	AMERICAN LEAGUE MT/VG-EX	NATIONAL LEAGUE MT/VG-EX
World Series Program:	100.00/65.00	100.00/65.00
World Series Press Pin:	100.00/65.00	100.00/65.00
Ticket Stub:	20.00/13.00	20.00/13.00
Teams and Games Won:	Washington 1	New York 4

ALL-STAR MEMORABILIA

	MT/VG-EX
All-Star Program:	250.00/150.00
All-Star Press Pin:	250.00/150.00
Ticket Stub:	75.00/ 45.00
Location:	Chicago (AL)
Winning League and Score:	American 4-2

YEAR: 1934

TEAMS (in alphabetical order by league)	YEARBOOK MT/VG-EX	PROGRAM MT/VG-EX
Boston Red Sox	xx.xx/xxxxx	8.00/5.00
Chicago White Sox	xx.xx/xxxxx	8.00/5.00
Cleveland Indians	xx.xx/xxxxx	7.50/4.75
Detroit Tigers	50.00/35.00	10.00/6.50
New York Yankees	xx.xx/xxxxx	10.00/6.50
Philadelphia A's	xx.xx/xxxxx	8.00/5.00
St. Louis Browns	xx.xx/xxxxx	8.00/5.00
Washington Senators	xx.xx/xxxxx	8.00/5.00
Boston Braves	xx.xx/xxxxx	8.00/5.00
Brooklyn Dodgers	xx.xx/xxxxx	10.00/6.50
Chicago Cubs	50.00/35.00	7.00/4.50
Cincinnati Reds	xx.xx/xxxxx	8.00/5.00
New York Giants	xx.xx/xxxxx	8.00/5.00
Philadelphia Phillies	xx.xx/xxxxx	7.00/4.50
Pittsburgh Pirates	xx.xx/xxxxx	7.00/4.50
St. Louis Cardinals	xx.xx/xxxxx	6.00/4.00

WORLD SERIES MEMORABILIA

	AMERICAN LEAGUE MT/VG-EX	NATIONAL LEAGUE MT/VG-EX
World Series Program:	90.00/60.00	90.00/60.00
World Series Press Pin:	90.00/60.00	90.00/60.00
Ticket Stub:	20.00/13.00	20.00/13.00
Teams and Games Won:	Detroit 3	St. Louis 4

ALL-STAR MEMORABILIA

	MT/VG-EX
All-Star Program:	75.00/50.00
All-Star Press Pin:	75.00/50.00
Ticket Stub:	25.00/16.00
Location:	New York (NL)
Winning League and Score:	American 9-7

YEAR: 1935

TEAMS (in alphabetical order by league)	YEARBOOK MT/VG-EX	PROGRAM MT/VG-EX
Boston Red Sox	xx.xx/xxxxx	7.50/5.00
Chicago White Sox	xx.xx/xxxxx	7.00/4.50
Cleveland Indians	xx.xx/xxxxx	7.00/4.50
Detroit Tigers	xx.xx/xxxxx	9.00/6.00
New York Yankees	xx.xx/xxxxx	9.00/6.00
Philadelphia A's	xx.xx/xxxxx	7.00/4.50
St. Louis Browns	xx.xx/xxxxx	7.00/4.50
Washington Senators	xx.xx/xxxxx	7.00/4.50
Boston Braves	xx.xx/xxxxx	7.00/4.50
Brooklyn Dodgers	xx.xx/xxxxx	9.00/6.00
Chicago Cubs	xx.xx/xxxxx	8.00/5.00
Cincinnati Reds	xx.xx/xxxxx	7.00/4.50
New York Giants	xx.xx/xxxxx	7.00/4.50
Philadelphia Phillies	xx.xx/xxxxx	6.00/4.00
Pittsburgh Pirates	xx.xx/xxxxx	7.00/4.50
St. Louis Cardinals	xx.xx/xxxxx	6.00/4.00

WORLD SERIES MEMORABILIA

	AMERICAN LEAGUE MT/VG-EX	NATIONAL LEAGUE MT/VG-EX
World Series Program:	90.00/ 60.00	90.00/ 60.00
World Series Press Pin:	90.00/ 60.00	90.00/ 60.00
Commemorative Bat:	300.00/200.00	300.00/200.00
Ticket Stub:	20.00/ 13.00	20.00/ 13.00
Teams and Games Won:	Detroit 4	Chicago 2

ALL-STAR MEMORABILIA

	MT/VG-EX
All-Star Program:	70.00/45.00
All-Star Press Pin:	65.00/45.00
Ticket Stub:	20.00/13.00
Location:	Cleveland (AL)
Winning League and Score:	American 4-1

YEAR: 1936

TEAMS (in alphabetical order by league)	YEARBOOK MT/VG-EX	PROGRAM MT/VG-EX
Boston Red Sox	xx.xx/xxxxx	7.00/4.50
Chicago White Sox	xx.xx/xxxxx	7.00/4.50
Cleveland Indians	xx.xx/xxxxx	7.00/4.50
Detroit Tigers	xx.xx/xxxxx	7.00/4.50
New York Yankees	xx.xx/xxxxx	8.00/5.00
Philadelphia A's	xx.xx/xxxxx	7.00/4.50
St. Louis Browns	xx.xx/xxxxx	7.00/4.50
Washington Senators	xx.xx/xxxxx	7.00/4.50
Boston Braves	xx.xx/xxxxx	7.00/4.50
Brooklyn Dodgers	xx.xx/xxxxx	8.00/5.00
Chicago Cubs	xx.xx/xxxxx	7.00/4.50
Cincinnati Reds	xx.xx/xxxxx	7.00/4.50
New York Giants	xx.xx/xxxxx	8.00/5.00
Philadelphia Phillies	xx.xx/xxxxx	6.00/4.00
Pittsburgh Pirates	xx.xx/xxxxx	6.00/4.00
St. Louis Cardinals	xx.xx/xxxxx	6.00/4.00

WORLD SERIES MEMORABILIA

	AMERICAN LEAGUE MT/VG-EX	NATIONAL LEAGUE MT/VG-EX
World Series Program:	95.00/ 65.00	95.00/ 65.00
World Series Press Pin:	100.00/ 70.00	85.00/ 60.00
Commemorative Bat:	350.00/250.00	300.00/200.00
Ticket Stub:	20.00/ 13.00	20.00/ 13.00
Teams and Games Won:	New York 4	New York 2

ALL-STAR MEMORABILIA

	MT/VG-EX
All-Star Program:	65.00/45.00
All-Star Press Pin:	60.00/40.00
Ticket Stub:	20.00/13.00
Location:	Boston (NL)
Winning League and Score:	National 4-3

YEAR: 1937

TEAMS (in alphabetical order by league)	YEARBOOK MT/VG-EX	PROGRAM MT/VG-EX
Boston Red Sox	xx.xx/xxxxx	7.00/4.50
Chicago White Sox	xx.xx/xxxxx	7.00/4.50
Cleveland Indians	xx.xx/xxxxx	6.50/4.25
Detroit Tigers	xx.xx/xxxxx	7.00/4.50
New York Yankees	xx.xx/xxxxx	7.50/5.00
Philadelphia A's	xx.xx/xxxxx	7.00/4.50
St. Louis Browns	xx.xx/xxxxx	7.00/4.50
Washington Senators	xx.xx/xxxxx	7.00/4.50
Boston Braves	xx.xx/xxxxx	7.00/4.50
Brooklyn Dodgers	xx.xx/xxxxx	8.00/5.00
Chicago Cubs	xx.xx/xxxxx	7.00/4.50
Cincinnati Reds	xx.xx/xxxxx	7.00/4.50
New York Giants	xx.xx/xxxxx	8.00/5.00
Philadelphia Phillies	xx.xx/xxxxx	6.00/4.00
Pittsburgh Pirates	xx.xx/xxxxx	6.00/4.00
St. Louis Cardinals	xx.xx/xxxxx	5.00/3.50

WORLD SERIES MEMORABILIA

	AMERICAN LEAGUE MT/VG-EX	NATIONAL LEAGUE MT/VG-EX
World Series Program:	90.00/ 60.00	80.00/ 55.00
World Series Press Pin:	95.00/ 65.00	80.00/ 55.00
Commemorative Bat:	300.00/200.00	250.00/150.00
Ticket Stub:	18.00/ 12.00	18.00/ 12.00
Teams and Games Won:	New York 4	New York 1

ALL-STAR MEMORABILIA

	MT/VG-EX
All-Star Program:	60.00/40.00
All-Star Press Pin:	60.00/40.00
Ticket Stub:	16.00/10.50
Location:	Washington (AL)
Winning League and Score:	American 8-3

YEAR: 1938

TEAMS (in alphabetical order by league)	YEARBOOK MT/VG-EX	PROGRAM MT/VG-EX
Boston Red Sox	xx.xx/xxxxx	6.50/4.25
Chicago White Sox	xx.xx/xxxxx	6.00/4.00
Cleveland Indians	xx.xx/xxxxx	6.00/4.00
Detroit Tigers	xx.xx/xxxxx	6.00/4.00
New York Yankees	xx.xx/xxxxx	7.00/4.50
Philadelphia A's	xx.xx/xxxxx	6.00/4.00
St. Louis Browns	xx.xx/xxxxx	6.50/4.50
Washington Senators	xx.xx/xxxxx	6.00/4.00
Boston Braves	xx.xx/xxxxx	7.00/4.75
Brooklyn Dodgers	xx.xx/xxxxx	6.00/4.00
Chicago Cubs	xx.xx/xxxxx	6.00/4.00
Cincinnati Reds	xx.xx/xxxxx	6.00/4.00
New York Giants	xx.xx/xxxxx	6.00/4.00
Philadelphia Phillies	xx.xx/xxxxx	5.00/3.50
Pittsburgh Pirates	xx.xx/xxxxx	5.50/3.75
St. Louis Cardinals	xx.xx/xxxxx	5.00/3.50

WORLD SERIES MEMORABILIA

	AMERICAN LEAGUE MT/VG-EX	NATIONAL LEAGUE MT/VG-EX
World Series Program:	85.00/ 60.00	85.00/ 50.00
World Series Press Pin:	90.00/ 65.00	75.00/ 50.00
Commemorative Bat:	300.00/200.00	300.00/200.00
Ticket Stub:	17.00/ 11.00	17.00/ 11.00
Teams and Games Won:	New York 4	Chicago 0

ALL-STAR MEMORABILIA

	MT/VG-EX
All-Star Program:	45.00/30.00
All-Star Press Pin:	50.00/35.00
Ticket Stub:	15.00/10.00
Location:	Cincinnati (NL)
Winning League and Score:	National 4-1

YEAR: 1939

TEAMS (in alphabetical order by league)	YEARBOOK MT/VG-EX	PROGRAM MT/VG-EX
Boston Red Sox	xx.xx/xxxxx	6.00/4.00
Chicago White Sox	xx.xx/xxxxx	6.00/4.00
Cleveland Indians	xx.xx/xxxxx	5.50/3.75
Detroit Tigers	xx.xx/xxxxx	6.00/4.00
New York Yankees	xx.xx/xxxxx	7.00/4.50
Philadelphia A's	xx.xx/xxxxx	6.00/4.00
St. Louis Browns	xx.xx/xxxxx	6.50/4.50
Washington Senators	xx.xx/xxxxx	6.00/4.00
Boston Braves	xx.xx/xxxxx	7.00/4.75
Brooklyn Dodgers	xx.xx/xxxxx	6.00/4.00
Chicago Cubs	xx.xx/xxxxx	6.00/4.00
Cincinnati Reds	xx.xx/xxxxx	7.00/4.75
New York Giants	xx.xx/xxxxx	6.00/4.00
Philadelphia Phillies	xx.xx/xxxxx	5.00/3.50
Pittsburgh Pirates	xx.xx/xxxxx	5.00/3.50
St. Louis Cardinals	xx.xx/xxxxx	5.00/3.50

****

WORLD SERIES MEMORABILIA	AMERICAN LEAGUE MT/VG-EX	NATIONAL LEAGUE MT/VG-EX
World Series Program:	80.00/ 55.00	80.00/ 50.00
World Series Press Pin:	85.00/ 60.00	85.00/ 60.00
Commemorative Bat:	300.00/200.00	300.00/200.00
Ticket Stub:	15.00/ 10.00	15.00/ 10.00
Teams and Games Won:	New York 4	Cincinnati 0

ALL-STAR MEMORABILIA	MT/VG-EX
All-Star Program:	45.00/30.00
All-Star Press Pin:	50.00/35.00
Ticket Stub:	12.50/ 8.00
Location:	New York (AL)
Winning League and Score:	American 3-1

YEAR: 1940

TEAMS (in alphabetical order by league)	YEARBOOK MT/VG-EX	PROGRAM MT/VG-EX
Boston Red Sox	xx.xx/xxxxx	5.50/3.75
Chicago White Sox	xx.xx/xxxxx	5.50/3.75
Cleveland Indians	xx.xx/xxxxx	5.00/3.25
Detroit Tigers	xx.xx/xxxxx	6.50/4.50
New York Yankees	xx.xx/xxxxx	6.00/4.00
Philadelphia A's	xx.xx/xxxxx	5.00/3.25
St. Louis Browns	xx.xx/xxxxx	6.50/4.50
Washington Senators	xx.xx/xxxxx	5.00/3.25
Boston Braves	xx.xx/xxxxx	6.00/4.00
Brooklyn Dodgers	xx.xx/xxxxx	6.00/4.00
Chicago Cubs	xx.xx/xxxxx	5.00/3.25
Cincinnati Reds	xx.xx/xxxxx	7.00/4.50
New York Giants	xx.xx/xxxxx	6.00/4.00
Philadelphia Phillies	xx.xx/xxxxx	4.50/3.00
Pittsburgh Pirates	xx.xx/xxxxx	4.50/3.00
St. Louis Cardinals	xx.xx/xxxxx	4.50/3.00

WORLD SERIES MEMORABILIA	AMERICAN LEAGUE MT/VG-EX	NATIONAL LEAGUE MT/VG-EX
World Series Program:	75.00/ 50.00	75.00/ 50.00
World Series Press Pin:	75.00/ 50.00	75.00/ 50.00
Commemorative Bat:	250.00/150.00	250.00/150.00
Ticket Stub:	15.00/ 10.00	15.00/ 10.00
Teams and Games Won:	Detroit 3	Cincinnati 4

ALL-STAR MEMORABILIA	MT/VG-EX
All-Star Program:	40.00/ 28.00
All-Star Press Pin:	50.00/ 35.00
Commemorative Bat:	350.00/250.00
Ticket Stub:	12.50/ 8.00
Location:	St. Louis (NL)
Winning League and Score:	National 4-0

YEAR: 1941

TEAMS (in alphabetical order by league)	YEARBOOK MT/VG-EX	PROGRAM MT/VG-EX
Boston Red Sox	xx.xx/xxxxx	5.00/3.25
Chicago White Sox	xx.xx/xxxxx	5.00/3.25
Cleveland Indians	xx.xx/xxxxx	5.00/3.25
Detroit Tigers	xx.xx/xxxxx	5.00/3.25
New York Yankees	xx.xx/xxxxx	6.00/4.00
Philadelphia A's	xx.xx/xxxxx	5.00/3.25
St. Louis Browns	xx.xx/xxxxx	6.50/4.50
Washington Senators	xx.xx/xxxxx	5.00/3.25
Boston Braves	xx.xx/xxxxx	6.00/4.00
Brooklyn Dodgers	xx.xx/xxxxx	6.00/4.05
Chicago Cubs	xx.xx/xxxxx	5.00/3.25
Cincinnati Reds	xx.xx/xxxxx	5.00/3.25
New York Giants	xx.xx/xxxxx	5.00/3.25
Philadelphia Phillies	xx.xx/xxxxx	4.50/3.00
Pittsburgh Pirates	xx.xx/xxxxx	4.50/3.00
St. Louis Cardinals	xx.xx/xxxxx	4.00/2.75

WORLD SERIES MEMORABILIA	AMERICAN LEAGUE MT/VG-EX	NATIONAL LEAGUE MT/VG-EX
World Series Program:	75.00/ 50.00	70.00/ 45.00
World Series Press Pin:	75.00/ 50.00	70.00/ 45.00
Commemorative Bat:	250.00/150.00	250.00/150.00
Ticket Stub:	15.00/ 10.00	14.00/ 9.00
Teams and Games Won:	New York 4	Brooklyn 1

ALL-STAR MEMORABILIA	MT/VG-EX
All-Star Program:	39.00/ 27.00
All-Star Press Pin:	50.00/ 35.00
Commemorative Bat:	300.00/200.00
Ticket Stub:	12.00/ 8.00
Location:	Detroit (AL)
Winning League and Score:	American 7-5

YEAR: 1942

TEAMS (in alphabetical order by league)	YEARBOOK MT/VG-EX	PROGRAM MT/VG-EX
Boston Red Sox	xxx/xxxxx	5.00/3.50
Chicago White Sox	xxx/xxxxx	4.50/3.00
Cleveland Indians	xxx/xxxxx	4.50/3.00
Detroit Tigers	xxx/xxxxx	4.50/3.00
New York Yankees	xxx/xxxxx	5.50/3.75
Philadelphia A's	xxx/xxxxx	4.50/3.00
St. Louis Browns	xxx/xxxxx	6.00/4.00
Washington Senators	xxx/xxxxx	4.50/3.00
Boston Braves	xxx/xxxxx	5.00/3.50
Brooklyn Dodgers	xxx/xxxxx	5.00/3.50
Chicago Cubs	xxx/xxxxx	4.50/3.00
Cincinnati Reds	xxx/xxxxx	4.50/3.00
New York Giants	xxx/xxxxx	5.00/3.50
Philadelphia Phillies	xxx/xxxxx	4.50/3.00
Pittsburgh Pirates	xxx/xxxxx	4.50/3.00
St. Louis Cardinals	xxx/xxxxx	5.00/3.50

WORLD SERIES MEMORABILIA	AMERICAN LEAGUE MT/VG-EX	NATIONAL LEAGUE MT/VG-EX
World Series Program:	70.00/ 45.00	60.00/ 40.00
World Series Press Pin:	65.00/ 45.00	65.00/ 45.00
Commemorative Bat:	250.00/150.00	250.00/150.00
Ticket Stub:	13.00/ 9.00	13.00/ 9.00
Teams and Games Won:	New York 1	St. Louis 4

ALL-STAR MEMORABILIA	MT/VG-EX
All-Star Program:	38.00/ 26.00
All-Star Press Pin:	50.00/ 35.00
Commemorative Bat:	300.00/200.00
Ticket Stub:	10.00/ 6.50
Location:	New York (NL)
Winning League and Score:	American 3-1

YEAR: 1943

TEAMS (in alphabetical order by league)	YEARBOOK MT/VG-EX	PROGRAM MT/VG-EX
Boston Red Sox	xxx/xxxxx	4.50/3.00
Chicago White Sox	xxx/xxxxx	4.50/3.00
Cleveland Indians	xxx/xxxxx	4.50/3.00
Detroit Tigers	xxx/xxxxx	4.50/3.00
New York Yankees	xxx/xxxxx	5.50/3.75
Philadelphia A's	xxx/xxxxx	4.50/3.00
St. Louis Browns	xxx/xxxxx	6.00/4.00
Washington Senators	xxx/xxxxx	4.50/3.00
Boston Braves	xxx/xxxxx	4.50/3.00
Brooklyn Dodgers	xxx/xxxxx	4.50/3.00
Chicago Cubs	xxx/xxxxx	4.50/3.00
Cincinnati Reds	xxx/xxxxx	4.50/3.00
New York Giants	xxx/xxxxx	5.00/3.50
Philadelphia Phillies	xxx/xxxxx	4.50/3.00
Pittsburgh Pirates	xxx/xxxxx	4.00/2.75
St. Louis Cardinals	xxx/xxxxx	5.00/3.50

WORLD SERIES MEMORABILIA	AMERICAN LEAGUE MT/VG-EX	NATIONAL LEAGUE MT/VG-EX
World Series Program:	60.00/ 40.00	60.00/ 40.00
World Series Press Pin:	65.00/ 45.00	60.00/ 40.00
Commemorative Bat:	250.00/150.00	250.00/150.00
Ticket Stub:	12.50/ 8.00	12.50/ 8.00
Teams and Games Won:	New York 4	St. Louis 1

ALL-STAR MEMORABILIA	MT/VG-EX
All-Star Program:	37.00/ 25.00
All-Star Press Pin:	50.00/ 35.00
Commemorative Bat:	300.00/200.00
Ticket Stub:	10.00/ 6.50
Location:	Philadelphia (AL)
Winning League and Score:	American 5-3

YEAR: 1944

TEAMS (in alphabetical order by league)	YEARBOOK MT/VG-EX	PROGRAM MT/VG-EX
Boston Red Sox	xxx/xxxxx	4.50/3.00
Chicago White Sox	xxx/xxxxx	4.00/2.75
Cleveland Indians	xxx/xxxxx	4.00/2.75
Detroit Tigers	xxx/xxxxx	4.50/3.00
New York Yankees	xxx/xxxxx	5.00/3.50
Philadelphia A's	xxx/xxxxx	4.00/2.75
St. Louis Browns	xxx/xxxxx	6.50/4.50
Washington Senators	xxx/xxxxx	4.00/2.75
Boston Braves	xxx/xxxxx	4.50/3.00
Brooklyn Dodgers	xxx/xxxxx	4.50/3.00
Chicago Cubs	xxx/xxxxx	4.00/2.75
Cincinnati Reds	xxx/xxxxx	4.00/2.75
New York Giants	xxx/xxxxx	4.50/3.00
Philadelphia Phillies	xxx/xxxxx	4.00/2.75
Pittsburgh Pirates	xxx/xxxxx	4.00/2.75
St. Louis Cardinals	xxx/xxxxx	5.00/3.50

WORLD SERIES MEMORABILIA	AMERICAN LEAGUE MT/VG-EX	NATIONAL LEAGUE MT/VG-EX
World Series Program:	55.00/40.00	55.00/40.00
World Series Press Pin:	80.00/50.00	60.00/40.00
Commemorative Bat:	not issued	not issued
Ticket Stub:	16.00/10.00	12.00/ 8.00
Teams and Games Won:	St. Louis 2	St. Louis 4

ALL-STAR MEMORABILIA	MT/VG-EX
All-Star Program:	35.00/24.00
All-Star Press Pin:	50.00/35.00
Commemorative Bat:	not issued
Ticket Stub:	10.00/ 6.50
Location:	Pittsburgh (NL)
Winning League and Score:	National 7-1

YEAR: 1945

TEAMS (in alphabetical order by league)	YEARBOOK MT/VG-EX	PROGRAM MT/VG-EX
Boston Red Sox	xxx/xxxxx	4.50/3.00
Chicago White Sox	xxx/xxxxx	4.00/2.75
Cleveland Indians	xxx/xxxxx	4.00/2.75
Detroit Tigers	xxx/xxxxx	6.00/4.00
New York Yankees	xxx/xxxxx	5.00/3.50
Philadelphia A's	xxx/xxxxx	4.00/2.75
St. Louis Browns	xxx/xxxxx	5.00/3.50
Washington Senators	xxx/xxxxx	4.00/2.75
Boston Braves	xxx/xxxxx	4.50/3.50
Brooklyn Dodgers	xxx/xxxxx	4.00/2.75
Chicago Cubs	xxx/xxxxx	4.00/2.75
Cincinnati Reds	xxx/xxxxx	4.00/2.75
New York Giants	xxx/xxxxx	4.50/3.00
Philadelphia Phillies	xxx/xxxxx	4.00/2.75
Pittsburgh Pirates	xxx/xxxxx	4.00/2.75
St. Louis Cardinals	xxx/xxxxx	3.50/2.35

WORLD SERIES MEMORABILIA	AMERICAN LEAGUE MT/VG-EX	NATIONAL LEAGUE MT/VG-EX
World Series Program:	55.00/ 37.50	55.00/ 35.00
World Series Press Pin:	60.00/ 40.00	60.00/ 40.00
Commemorative Bat:	250.00/150.00	250.00/150.00
Ticket Stub:	11.00/ 7.00	11.00/ 7.00
Teams and Games Won:	Detroit 4	Chicago 3

ALL-STAR MEMORABILIA - - - - - - - - - - - - NO GAME PLAYED IN 1945

YEAR: 1946

TEAMS (in alphabetical order by league)	YEARBOOK MT/VG-EX	PROGRAM MT/VG-EX
Boston Red Sox	xx.xx/xx.xx	6.00/4.00
Chicago White Sox	xx.xx/xx.xx	3.75/2.50
Cleveland Indians	xx.xx/xx.xx	3.50/2.25
Detroit Tigers	xx.xx/xx.xx	3.75/2.50
New York Yankees	xx.xx/xx.xx	5.00/3.50
Philadelphia A's	xx.xx/xx.xx	3.75/2.50
St. Louis Browns	xx.xx/xx.xx	5.00/3.50
Washington Senators	xx.xx/xx.xx	3.75/2.50
Boston Braves	35.00/22.50	4.00/2.75
Brooklyn Dodgers	xx.xx/xx.xx	3.75/2.50
Chicago Cubs	xx.xx/xx.xx	3.50/2.35
Cincinnati Reds	20.00/13.00*	3.75/2.50
New York Giants	xx.xx/xx.xx	4.00/2.75
Philadelphia Phillies	xx.xx/xx.xx	3.75/2.50
Pittsburgh Pirates	xx.xx/xx.xx	3.75/2.50
St. Louis Cardinals	xx.xx/xx.xx	5.00/3.50

WORLD SERIES MEMORABILIA	AMERICAN LEAGUE MT/VG-EX	NATIONAL LEAGUE MT/VG-EX
World Series Program:	45.00/ 30.00	45.00/ 30.00
World Series Press Pin:	60.00/ 40.00	60.00/ 40.00
Commemorative Bat:	250.00/150.00	250.00/150.00
Ticket Stub:	11.00/ 7.50	11.00/ 7.50
Teams and Games Won:	Boston 3	St. Louis 4

ALL-STAR MEMORABILIA	MT/VG-EX
All-Star Program:	33.00/ 23.00
All-Star Press Pin:	40.00/ 25.00
Commemorative Bat:	250.00/150.00
Ticket Stub:	8.00/ 5.00
Location:	Boston (AL)
Winning League and Score:	American 12-0

YEAR: 1947

TEAMS (in alphabetical order by league)	YEARBOOK MT/VG-EX	PROGRAM MT/VG-EX
Boston Red Sox	xx.xx/xx.xx	4.50/3.00
Chicago White Sox	25.00/16.00*	3.75/2.50
Cleveland Indians	xx.xx/xx.xx	3.50/2.25
Detroit Tigers	xx.xx/xx.xx	3.50/2.25
New York Yankees	xx.xx/xx.xx	4.50/3.25
Philadelphia A's	xx.xx/xx.xx	3.75/2.50
St. Louis Browns	xx.xx/xx.xx	5.00/3.50
Washington Senators	40.00/25.00	3.75/2.50
Boston Braves	30.00/20.00	4.00/2.75
Brooklyn Dodgers	20.00/13.00*	3.75/2.50
Chicago Cubs	xx.xx/xx.xx	3.50/2.35
Cincinnati Reds	30.00/20.00	3.75/2.50
New York Giants	40.00/25.00	4.00/2.75
Philadelphia Phillies	xx.xx/xx.xx	3.75/2.50
Pittsburgh Pirates	xx.xx/xx.xx	3.75/2.50
St. Louis Cardinals	xx.xx/xx.xx	3.25/2.15

WORLD SERIES MEMORABILIA	AMERICAN LEAGUE MT/VG-EX	NATIONAL LEAGUE MT/VG-EX
World Series Program:	45.00/ 30.00	40.00/ 25.00
World Series Press Pin:	60.00/ 40.00	60.00/ 40.00
Commemorative Bat:	200.00/140.00	200.00/140.00
Ticket Stub:	10.00/ 6.50	10.00/ 3.50
Teams and Games Won:	New York 4	Brooklyn 3

ALL-STAR MEMORABILIA	MT/VG-EX
All-Star Program:	32.00/ 22.00
All-Star Press Pin:	35.00/ 25.00
Commemorative Bat:	250.00/150.00
Ticket Stub:	8.00/ 5.00
Location:	Chicago (NL)
Winning League and Score:	American 2-1

YEAR: 1948

TEAMS (in alphabetical order by league)	YEARBOOK MT/VG-EX	PROGRAM MT/VG-EX
Boston Red Sox	xx.xx/xx.xx	4.00/2.75
Chicago White Sox	20.00/13.00*	3.50/2.35
Cleveland Indians	27.50/19.00	5.00/3.50
Detroit Tigers	xx.xx/xx.xx	3.50/2.35
New York Yankees	xx.xx/xx.xx	4.00/2.75
Philadelphia A's	xx.xx/xx.xx	3.50/2.35
St. Louis Browns	xx.xx/xx.xx	5.00/3.50
Washington Senators	xx.xx/xx.xx	3.50/2.35
Boston Braves	xx.xx/xx.xx	5.00/3.50
Brooklyn Dodgers	xx.xx/xx.xx	3.75/2.50
Chicago Cubs	25.00/16.00	3.50/2.35
Cincinnati Reds	26.50/17.00	3.50/2.35
New York Giants	xx.xx/xx.xx	4.00/2.75
Philadelphia Phillies	xx.xx/xx.xx	3.50/2.35
Pittsburgh Pirates	xx.xx/xx.xx	3.50/2.35
St. Louis Cardinals	xx.xx/xx.xx	3.25/2.25

WORLD SERIES MEMORABILIA	AMERICAN LEAGUE MT/VG-EX	NATIONAL LEAGUE MT/VG-EX
World Series Program:	40.00/ 25.00	40.00/ 25.00
World Series Press Pin:	50.00/ 35.00	50.00/ 35.00
Commemorative Bat:	200.00/140.00	200.00/140.00
Ticket Stub:	10.00/ 6.50	10.00/ 6.50
Teams and Games Won:	Cleveland 4	Boston 2

ALL-STAR MEMORABILIA	MT/VG-EX
All-Star Program:	32.00/ 22.00
All-Star Press Pin:	35.00/ 25.00
Commemorative Bat:	250.00/150.00
Ticket Stub:	8.00/ 5.00
Location:	St. Louis (AL)
Winning League and Score:	American 5-2

YEAR: 1949

TEAMS (in alphabetical order by league)	YEARBOOK MT/VG-EX	PROGRAM MT/VG-EX
Boston Red Sox	xx.xx/xx.xx	4.00/2.75
Chicago White Sox	20.00/13.00*	3.50/2.35
Cleveland Indians	21.00/13.50	3.50/2.35
Detroit Tigers	xx.xx/xx.xx	3.50/2.35
New York Yankees	xx.xx/xx.xx	4.00/2.75
Philadelphia A's	25.00/16.00	3.50/2.35
St. Louis Browns	xx.xx/xx.xx	5.00/3.50
Washington Senators	xx.xx/xx.xx	3.50/2.35
Boston Braves	xx.xx/xx.xx	4.00/2.75
Brooklyn Dodgers	30.00/20.00	3.50/2.35
Chicago Cubs	20.00/13.00	3.00/2.00
Cincinnati Reds	25.00/16.00	3.50/2.35
New York Giants	xx.xx/xx.xx	4.00/2.75
Philadelphia Phillies	30.00/20.00	3.50/2.35
Pittsburgh Pirates	xx.xx/xx.xx	3.50/2.35
St. Louis Cardinals	xx.xx/xx.xx	3.00/2.00

WORLD SERIES MEMORABILIA	AMERICAN LEAGUE MT/VG-EX	NATIONAL LEAGUE MT/VG-EX
World Series Program:	40.00/ 25.00	40.00/ 25.00
World Series Press Pin:	60.00/ 40.00	60.00/ 40.00
Commemorative Bat:	200.00/140.00	200.00/140.00
Ticket Stub:	9.00/ 6.00	9.00/ 6.00
Teams and Games Won:	New York 4	Brooklyn 1

ALL-STAR MEMORABILIA	MT/VG-EX
All-Star Program:	31.00/ 21.00
All-Star Press Pin:	35.00/ 25.00
Commemorative Bat:	250.00/150.00
Ticket Stub:	7.50/ 5.00
Location:	Brooklyn (NL)
Winning League and Score:	American 11-7

YEAR: 1950

TEAMS (in alphabetical order by league)	YEARBOOK MT/VG-EX	PROGRAM MT/VG-EX
Boston Red Sox	xx.xx/xx.xx	4.00/2.75
Chicago White Sox	20.00/13.00*	3.25/2.25
Cleveland Indians	21.00/13.50	3.25/2.25
Detroit Tigers	xx.xx/xx.xx	3.50/2.50
New York Yankees	40.00/28.00	4.00/2.75
Philadelphia A's	23.00/16.00	3.25/2.25
St. Louis Browns	45.00/30.00	5.00/3.50
Washington Senators	25.00/16.00	3.25/2.25
Boston Braves	30.00/20.00	4.00/2.75
Brooklyn Dodgers	30.00/20.00	3.50/2.35
Chicago Cubs	20.00/13.00	3.00/2.00
Cincinnati Reds	xx.xx/xx.xx	3.25/2.25
New York Giants	xx.xx/xx.xx	3.25/2.25
Philadelphia Phillies	30.00/20.00	4.00/2.75
Pittsburgh Pirates	xx.xx/xx.xx	3.25/2.25
St. Louis Cardinals	15.00/10.00*	3.00/2.00

****

WORLD SERIES MEMORABILIA
****

	AMERICAN LEAGUE MT/VG-EX	NATIONAL LEAGUE MT/VG-EX
World Series Program:	40.00/ 25.00	40.00/ 25.00
World Series Press Pin:	60.00/ 40.00	60.00/ 40.00
Commemorative Bat:	200.00/140.00	200.00/140.00
Ticket Stub:	9.00/ 6.00	9.00/ 6.00
Teams and Games Won:	Yankees 4	Philadelphia 3

****

ALL-STAR MEMORABILIA
****

	MT/VG-EX
All-Star Program:	30.00/ 20.00
All-Star Press Pin:	35.00/ 25.00
Commemorative Bat:	250.00/150.00
Ticket Stub:	7.50/ 5.00
Location:	Chicago (AL)
Winning League and Score:	National 4-3

****

YEAR: 1951

TEAMS (in alphabetical order by league)	YEARBOOK MT/VG-EX	PROGRAM MT/VG-EX
Boston Red Sox	30.00/20.00	3.75/2.50
Chicago White Sox	28.00/19.00	3.25/2.25
Cleveland Indians	21.00/13.50	3.00/2.00
Detroit Tigers	xx.xx/xx.xx	3.25/2.25
New York Yankees	30.00/20.00	4.00/2.75
Philadelphia A's	23.00/16.00	3.25/2.25
St. Louis Browns	28.00/19.00	5.00/3.50
Washington Senators	21.00/13.50	3.25/2.25
Boston Braves	25.00/16.00	4.00/2.75
Brooklyn Dodgers	30.00/20.00	3.25/2.25
Chicago Cubs	20.00/13.00	3.00/2.00
Cincinnati Reds	20.00/13.00	3.25/2.25
New York Giants	30.00/20.00	4.00/2.75
Philadelphia Phillies	17.00/11.50	3.25/2.25
Pittsburgh Pirates	25.00/16.00	3.25/2.25
St. Louis Cardinals	30.00/20.00	3.00/2.00

****

WORLD SERIES MEMORABILIA
****

	AMERICAN LEAGUE MT/VG-EX	NATIONAL LEAGUE MT/VG-EX
World Series Program:	40.00/ 25.00	40.00/ 25.00
World Series Press Pin:	50.00/ 35.00	50.00/ 35.00
Commemorative Bat:	200.00/140.00	200.00/140.00
Ticket Stub:	8.00/ 5.00	8.00/ 5.00
Teams and Games Won:	New York 4	New York 2

****

ALL-STAR MEMORABILIA
****

	MT/VG-EX
All-Star Program:	35.00/ 24.00
All-Star Press Pin:	35.00/ 24.00
Commemorative Bat:	250.00/150.00
Ticket Stub:	7.00/ 4.50
Location:	Detroit (AL)
Winning League and Score:	National 8-3

****

YEAR: 1952

TEAMS (in alphabetical order by league)	YEARBOOK MT/VG-EX	PROGRAM MT/VG-EX
Boston Red Sox	22.50/15.00	3.50/2.50
Chicago White Sox	20.00/13.00	3.00/2.00
Cleveland Indians	19.00/12.00	3.00/2.00
Detroit Tigers	xx.xx/xx.xx	3.00/2.00
New York Yankees	28.00/18.00	3.50/2.50
Philadelphia A's	21.00/14.00	3.00/2.00
St. Louis Browns	24.00/16.00	5.00/3.50
Washington Senators	19.00/12.00	3.00/2.00
Boston Braves	25.00/16.00	4.00/2.75
Brooklyn Dodgers	25.00/16.00	3.00/2.00
Chicago Cubs	19.00/12.00	2.50/1.50
Cincinnati Reds	17.00/11.00	3.00/2.00
New York Giants	25.00/16.00	3.50/2.25
Philadelphia Phillies	16.00/10.00	3.00/2.00
Pittsburgh Pirates	18.00/12.00	3.00/2.00
St. Louis Cardinals	25.00/16.00	2.50/1.60

****

WORLD SERIES MEMORABILIA
****

	AMERICAN LEAGUE MT/VG-EX	NATIONAL LEAGUE MT/VG-EX
World Series Program:	40.00/ 25.00	40.00/ 25.00
World Series Press Pin:	50.00/ 35.00	50.00/ 35.00
Commemorative Bat:	200.00/140.00	200.00/140.00
Ticket Stub:	7.00/ 4.50	7.00/ 4.50
Teams and Games Won:	New York 4	Brooklyn 3

****

ALL-STAR MEMORABILIA
****

	MT/VG-EX
All-Star Program:	28.00/ 19.00
All-Star Press Pin:	35.00/ 25.00
Commemorative Bat:	250.00/150.00
Ticket Stub:	7.00/ 4.00
Location:	Philadelphia (NL)
Winning League and Score:	National 3-2

game called -- rain after five innings

****

NEWARK Eagles

PHILADELPHIA STARS

YEAR: 1953

TEAMS (in alphabetical order by league)	YEARBOOK MT/VG-EX	PROGRAM MT/VG-EX
Boston Red Sox	19.00/12.00	3.25/2.25
Chicago White Sox	18.00/11.50	2.50/1.60
Cleveland Indians	19.00/12.00	2.75/1.75
Detroit Tigers	xx.xx/xx.xx	2.75/1.75
New York Yankees	24.00/16.00	3.50/2.50
Philadelphia A's	6.00/ 4.00	3.00/2.00
St. Louis Browns	xx.xx/xx.xx	5.00/3.50
Washington Senators	6.00/ 4.00	3.00/2.00
Brooklyn Dodgers	22.50/16.00	3.00/2.00
Chicago Cubs	18.00/11.50	2.50/1.60
Cincinnati Reds	16.00/10.50	3.00/2.00
Milwaukee Braves	25.00/16.00	4.00/2.75
New York Giants	21.00/14.00	4.00/2.75
Philadelphia Phillies	7.50/ 5.00	2.50/1.60
Pittsburgh Pirates	17.00/12.00	3.00/2.00
St. Louis Cardinals	17.00/12.00	2.50/1.60

****

WORLD SERIES MEMORABILIA
****

	AMERICAN LEAGUE MT/VG-EX	NATIONAL LEAGUE MT/VG-EX
World Series Program:	35.00/ 24.00	35.00/ 20.00
World Series Press Pin:	50.00/ 35.00	50.00/ 35.00
Commemorative Bat:	200.00/140.00	200.00/140.00
Ticket Stub:	7.00/ 4.50	7.00/ 4.50
Teams and Games Won:	New York 4	Brooklyn 2

****

ALL-STAR MEMORABILIA
****

	MT/VG-EX
All-Star Program:	28.00/ 19.00
All-Star Press Pin:	35.00/ 25.00
Commemorative Bat:	250.00/150.00
Ticket Stub:	7.00/ 4.50
Location:	Cincinnati (NL)
Winning League and Score:	National 5-1

****

YEAR: 1954

TEAMS (in alphabetical order by league)	YEARBOOK MT/VG-EX	PROGRAM MT/VG-EX
Baltimore Orioles	25.00/16.00	5.00/3.50
Boston Red Sox	16.00/10.00	3.00/2.00
Chicago White Sox	16.00/10.00	2.50/1.60
Cleveland Indians	22.00/15.00	4.00/2.75
Detroit Tigers	xx.xx/xx.xx	2.75/1.75
New York Yankees	20.00/12.00	3.50/2.50
Philadelphia A's	22.00/15.00	3.50/2.50
Washington Senators	16.00/10.00	2.75/1.75
Brooklyn Dodgers	20.00/13.00	3.00/2.00
Chicago Cubs	16.00/10.00	2.50/1.50
Cincinnati Reds	16.00/10.00	2.75/1.75
Milwaukee Braves	20.00/13.00	3.00/2.00
New York Giants	25.00/16.00	4.00/2.75
Philadelphia Phillies	15.00/ 9.50	2.50/1.60
Pittsburgh Pirates	16.00/10.00	2.75/1.75
St. Louis Cardinals	16.00/10.00	2.50/1.60

****

WORLD SERIES MEMORABILIA
****

	AMERICAN LEAGUE MT/VG-EX	NATIONAL LEAGUE MT/VG-EX
World Series Program:	25.00/ 16.00	30.00/ 20.00
World Series Press Pin:	50.00/ 35.00	50.00/ 35.00
Commemorative Bat:	175.00/125.00	175.00/125.00
Ticket Stub:	6.00/ 4.00	6.00/ 4.00
Teams and Games Won:	Cleveland 0	New York 4

****

ALL-STAR MEMORABILIA
****

	MT/VG-EX
All-Star Program:	26.00/ 17.00
All-Star Press Pin:	35.00/ 25.00
Commemorative Bat:	250.00/150.00
Ticket Stub:	6.00/ 4.00
Location:	Cleveland (AL)
Winning League and Score:	American 11-9

****

YEAR: 1955

TEAMS (in alphabetical order by league)	YEARBOOK MT/VG-EX	PROGRAM MT/VG-EX
Baltimore Orioles	18.00/13.00	4.00/2.75
Boston Red Sox	16.00/10.00	2.75/1.75
Chicago White Sox	15.00/ 9.00	2.50/1.60
Cleveland Indians	17.00/11.00	2.50/1.60
Detroit Tigers	20.00/14.00	2.75/1.75
Kansas City A's	22.00/15.00	4.50/3.00
New York Yankees	18.00/13.00	3.50/2.50
Washington Senators	16.00/10.00	2.75/1.75
Brooklyn Dodgers	22.50/16.00	3.50/2.25
Chicago Cubs	16.00/10.00	2.25/1.50
Cincinnati Reds	15.00/ 9.50	2.50/1.60
Milwaukee Braves	16.00/10.00	3.00/2.00
New York Giants	18.00/12.00	3.00/2.00
Philadelphia Phillies	15.00/ 9.50	2.25/1.50
Pittsburgh Pirates	16.00/10.00	2.75/1.75
St. Louis Cardinals	15.00/ 9.50	2.50/1.60

****

WORLD SERIES MEMORABILIA
****

	AMERICAN LEAGUE MT/VG-EX	NATIONAL LEAGUE MT/VG-EX
World Series Program:	35.00/ 24.00	35.00/ 24.00
World Series Press Pin:	50.00/ 35.00	50.00/ 35.00
Commemorative Bat:	175.00/125.00	200.00/140.00
Ticket Stub:	6.00/ 4.00	6.00/ 4.00
Teams and Games Won:	New York 3	Brooklyn 4

****

ALL-STAR MEMORABILIA
****

	MT/VG-EX
All-Star Program:	25.00/ 16.00
All-Star Press Pin:	35.00/ 25.00
Commemorative Bat:	250.00/150.00
Ticket Stub:	6.00/ 4.00
Location:	Milwaukee (NL)
Winning League and Score:	National 6-5

****

YEAR: 1956

TEAMS (in alphabetical order by league)	YEARBOOK MT/VG-EX	PROGRAM MT/VG-EX
Baltimore Orioles	14.00/ 9.00	3.00/2.00
Boston Red Sox	14.00/ 9.00	2.75/1.75
Chicago White Sox	14.00/ 9.00	2.50/1.60
Cleveland Indians	16.00/10.50	2.50/1.60
Detroit Tigers	16.00/10.50	2.50/1.60
Kansas City A's	15.00/10.00	3.50/2.50
New York Yankees	18.00/13.00	3.25/2.25
Washington Senators	14.00/ 9.00	2.50/1.60
Brooklyn Dodgers	20.00/13.00	3.00/2.00
Chicago Cubs	14.00/ 9.00	2.00/1.25
Cincinnati Reds	14.00/ 9.00	2.25/1.50
Milwaukee Braves	15.00/10.00	2.50/1.60
New York Giants	16.00/10.50	3.00/2.00
Philadelphia Phillies	14.00/ 9.00	2.25/1.50
Pittsburgh Pirates	14.00/ 9.00	2.50/1.60
St. Louis Cardinals	14.00/ 9.00	2.25/1.50

****

WORLD SERIES MEMORABILIA
****

	AMERICAN LEAGUE MT/VG-EX	NATIONAL LEAGUE MT/VG-EX
World Series Program:	35.00/ 24.00	30.00/ 20.00
World Series Press Pin:	50.00/ 35.00	50.00/ 35.00
Commemorative Bat:	175.00/125.00	175.00/125.00
Ticket Stub:	6.00/ 4.00	6.00/ 4.00
Teams and Games Won:	New York 4	Brooklyn 3

****

ALL-STAR MEMORABILIA
****

	MT/VG-EX
All-Star Program:	25.00/ 16.00
All-Star Press Pin:	35.00/ 25.00
Commemorative Bat:	250.00/150.00
Ticket Stub:	6.00/ 4.00
Location:	Washington (AL)
Winning League and Score:	National 7-3

****

YEAR: 1957

TEAMS (in alphabetical order by league)	YEARBOOK MT/VG-EX	PROGRAM MT/VG-EX
Baltimore Orioles	14.00/ 9.00	2.75/1.75
Boston Red Sox	14.00/ 9.00	2.75/1.75
Chicago White Sox	13.00/ 8.50	2.25/1.50
Cleveland Indians	16.00/10.00	2.25/1.50
Detroit Tigers	16.00/10.00	2.50/1.60
Kansas City A's	14.00/ 9.00	3.00/2.00
New York Yankees	17.00/12.00	3.00/2.00
Washington Senators	14.00/ 9.00	2.50/1.60
Brooklyn Dodgers	20.00/13.00	3.00/2.00
Chicago Cubs	14.00/ 9.00	2.00/1.25
Cincinnati Reds	14.00/ 9.00	2.25/1.50
Milwaukee Braves	16.00/10.00	3.00/2.00
New York Giants	16.00/10.00	3.00/2.00
Philadelphia Phillies	14.00/ 9.00	2.25/1.50
Pittsburgh Pirates	14.00/ 9.00	2.25/1.50
St. Louis Cardinals	14.00/ 9.00	2.25/1.50

****

WORLD SERIES MEMORABILIA
****

	AMERICAN LEAGUE MT/VG-EX	NATIONAL LEAGUE MT/VG-EX
World Series Program:	30.00/ 20.00	25.00/ 16.00
World Series Press Pin:	50.00/ 35.00	50.00/ 35.00
Commemorative Bat:	150.00/100.00	150.00/100.00
Ticket Stub:	6.00/ 4.00	6.00/ 4.00
Teams and Games Won:	New York 3	Milwaukee 4

****

ALL-STAR MEMORABILIA
****

	MT/VG-EX
All-Star Program:	22.50/ 15.00
All-Star Press Pin:	35.00/ 25.00
Commemorative Bat:	250.00/150.00
Ticket Stub:	6.00/ 4.00
Location:	St. Louis (NL)
Winning League and Score:	American 6-5

****

YEAR: 1958

TEAMS (in alphabetical order by league)	YEARBOOK MT/VG-EX	PROGRAM MT/VG-EX
Baltimore Orioles	13.00/ 9.00	2.50/1.60
Boston Red Sox	11.50/ 7.50	2.50/1.60
Chicago White Sox	12.00/ 8.00	2.25/1.50
Cleveland Indians	14.00/ 9.00	2.25/1.50
Detroit Tigers	15.00/10.00	2.25/1.50
Kansas City A's	13.00/ 8.50	2.25/1.50
New York Yankees	16.00/10.50	2.75/1.75
Washington Senators	13.00/ 8.50	2.25/1.50
Chicago Cubs	7.00/ 4.50*	1.75/1.15
Cincinnati Reds	13.00/ 8.50	2.00/1.25
Los Angeles Dodgers	20.00/13.00	4.00/2.75
Milwaukee Braves	13.00/ 8.50	3.00/2.00
Philadelphia Phillies	11.50/ 7.50	2.25/1.50
Pittsburgh Pirates	13.00/ 8.50	2.25/1.50
San Francisco Giants	20.00/13.00	3.50/2.25
St. Louis Cardinals	13.00/ 8.50	2.25/1.50

****

WORLD SERIES MEMORABILIA
****

	AMERICAN LEAGUE MT/VG-EX	NATIONAL LEAGUE MT/VG-EX
World Series Program:	25.00/ 16.00	22.50/ 15.00
World Series Press Pin:	50.00/ 35.00	50.00/ 35.00
Commemorative Bat:	150.00/100.00	150.00/100.00
Ticket Stub:	6.00/ 4.00	5.00/ 3.50
Teams and Games Won:	New York 4	Milwaukee 3

****

ALL-STAR MEMORABILIA
****

	MT/VG-EX
All-Star Program:	22.50/ 15.00
All-Star Press Pin:	35.00/ 25.00
Commemorative Bat:	200.00/135.00
Ticket Stub:	6.00/ 4.00
Location:	Baltimore (AL)
Winning League and Score:	American 4-3

****

YEAR: 1959

TEAMS (in alphabetical order by league)	YEARBOOK MT/VG-EX	PROGRAM MT/VG-EX
Baltimore Orioles	11.50/ 7.50	2.25/1.50
Boston Red Sox	11.50/ 7.50	2.25/1.50
Chicago White Sox	15.00/10.00	3.00/2.00
Cleveland Indians	13.50/ 9.50	2.00/1.25
Detroit Tigers	11.50/ 7.50	2.25/1.50
Kansas City A's	12.00/ 8.00	2.25/1.50
New York Yankees	16.00/10.50	2.75/1.75
Washington Senators	11.50/ 7.50	2.25/1.50
Chicago Cubs	6.00/ 4.00*	1.75/1.15
Cincinnati Reds	11.50/ 7.50	2.00/1.25
Los Angeles Dodgers	12.50/ 8.50	3.00/2.00
Milwaukee Braves	11.00/ 7.00	2.25/1.50
Philadelphia Phillies	11.00/ 7.00	2.00/1.25
Pittsburgh Pirates	12.50/ 8.50	2.25/1.50
San Francisco Giants	12.50/ 8.50	2.50/1.60
St. Louis Cardinals	13.00/ 8.75	2.25/1.50

****

WORLD SERIES MEMORABILIA
****

	AMERICAN LEAGUE MT/VG-EX	NATIONAL LEAGUE MT/VG-EX
World Series Program:	24.00/ 16.00	10.00/ 6.50
World Series Press Pin:	50.00/ 35.00	50.00/ 35.00
Commemorative Bat:	150.00/100.00	150.00/100.00
Ticket Stub:	5.00/ 3.50	5.00/ 3.50
Teams and Games Won:	Chicago 2	Los Angeles 4

****

ALL-STAR MEMORABILIA
****

FIRST GAME	MT/VG-EX
All-Star Program:	20.00/ 14.00
All-Star Press Pin:	30.00/ 20.00
Commemorative Bat:	200.00/130.00
Ticket Stub:	6.00/ 4.00
Location:	Pittsburgh (NL)
Winning League and Score:	National 5-4
SECOND GAME	
All-Star Program:	20.00/ 14.00
All-Star Press Pin:	30.00/ 20.00
Commemorative Bat:	200.00/130.00
Ticket Stub:	6.00/ 4.00
Location:	Los Angeles (NL)
Winning League and Score:	American 5-3

****

YEAR: 1960

TEAMS (in alphabetical order by league)	YEARBOOK MT/VG-EX	PROGRAM MT/VG-EX
Baltimore Orioles	10.00/ 6.50	2.00/1.25
Boston Red Sox	10.00/ 6.50	2.25/1.50
Chicago White Sox	10.00/ 6.50	1.75/1.15
Cleveland Indians	12.00/ 8.00	2.00/1.25
Detroit Tigers	11.00/ 7.00	2.00/1.25
Kansas City A's	11.00/ 7.00	2.00/1.25
New York Yankees	15.00/10.00	2.50/1.50
Washington Senators	12.00/ 8.00	2.00/1.25
Chicago Cubs	6.00/ 4.00*	1.50/1.00
Cincinnati Reds	11.00/ 7.00	2.00/1.25
Los Angeles Dodgers	10.00/ 6.50	2.00/1.25
Milwaukee Braves	10.00/ 6.50	2.00/1.25
Philadelphia Phillies	10.00/ 6.50	2.00/1.25
Pittsburgh Pirates	15.00/10.00	3.50/2.35
San Francisco Giants	10.00/ 6.50	2.25/1.50
St. Louis Cardinals	11.00/ 7.00	2.00/1.25

WORLD SERIES MEMORABILIA

	AMERICAN LEAGUE MT/VG-EX	NATIONAL LEAGUE MT/VG-EX
World Series Program:	25.00/ 16.00	25.00/ 16.00
World Series Press Pin:	50.00/ 35.00	50.00/ 35.00
Commemorative Bat:	150.00/100.00	150.00/100.00
Ticket Stub:	5.00/ 3.50	5.00/ 3.50
Teams and Games Won:	New York 3	Pittsburgh 4

ALL-STAR MEMORABILIA

FIRST GAME	MT/VG-EX
All-Star Program:	20.00/ 14.00
All-Star Press Pin:	30.00/ 20.00
Commemorative Bat:	200.00/130.00
Ticket Stub:	6.00/ 4.00
Location:	Kansas City (AL)
Winning League and Score:	National 5-3
SECOND GAME	
All-Star Program:	20.00/ 14.00
All-Star Press Pin:	30.00/ 20.00
Commemorative Bat:	200.00/130.00
Ticket Stub:	6.00/ 4.00
Location:	New York (AL)
Winning League and Score:	National 6-0

YEAR: 1961

TEAMS (in alphabetical order by league)	YEARBOOK MT/VG-EX	PROGRAM MT/VG-EX
Baltimore Orioles	10.00/ 6.50	2.00/1.25
Boston Red Sox	10.00/ 6.50	2.25/1.50
Chicago White Sox	10.00/ 6.50	1.75/1.15
Cleveland Indians	15.00/10.00	2.00/1.25
Detroit Tigers	10.00/ 6.50	2.00/1.25
Kansas City A's	10.00/ 6.50	2.00/1.25
Los Angeles Angels	12.00/ 8.00*	5.00/3.50
Minnesota Twins	20.00/13.00	4.00/2.75
New York Yankees	14.00/ 9.50	2.50/1.50
Washington Senators	16.00/10.50	3.50/2.25
Chicago Cubs	6.00/ 4.00*	1.50/1.00
Cincinnati Reds	15.00/10.00	2.50/1.50
Los Angeles Dodgers	10.00/ 6.50	2.00/1.25
Milwaukee Braves	10.00/ 6.50	2.00/1.25
Philadelphia Phillies	10.00/ 6.50	2.00/1.25
Pittsburgh Pirates	10.00/ 6 50	2.00/1.25
San Francisco Giants	10.00/ 6.50	2.00/1.25
St. Louis Cardinals	10.00/ 6.50	2.00/1.25

WORLD SERIES MEMORABILIA

	AMERICAN LEAGUE MT/VG-EX	NATIONAL LEAGUE MT/VG-EX
World Series Program:	22.00/ 15.00	20.00/ 13.00
World Series Press Pin:	45.00/ 30.00	40.00/ 25.00
Commemorative Bat:	150.00/100.00	150.00/100.00
Ticket Stub:	5.00/ 3.50	5.00/ 3.50
Teams and Games Won:	New York 4	Cincinnati 1

ALL-STAR MEMORABILIA

FIRST GAME	MT/VG-EX
All-Star Program:	20.00/ 14.00
All-Star Press Pin:	30.00/ 20.00
Commemorative Bat:	200.00/130.00
Ticket Stub:	6.00/ 4.00
Location:	San Francisco (NL)
Winning League and Score:	National 5-4
SECOND GAME	
All-Star Program:	20.00/ 14.00
All-Star Press Pin:	30.00/ 20.00
Commemorative Bat:	200.00/130.00
Ticket Stub:	6.00/ 4.00
Location:	Boston (AL)
Winning League and Score:	Tie 1-1

game called -- rain after nine innings

YEAR: 1962

TEAMS (in alphabetical order by league)	YEARBOOK MT/VG-EX	PROGRAM MT/VG-EX
Baltimore Orioles	10.00/ 6.50	2.00/1.25
Boston Red Sox	10.00/ 6.50	2.00/1.25
Chicago White Sox	9.50/ 6.25	1.75/1.15
Cleveland Indians	11.00/ 7.00	2.00/1.25
Detroit Tigers	10.00/ 6.50	2.00/1.25
Kansas City A's	10.00/ 6.50	2.00/1.25
Los Angeles Angels	12.00/ 8.00	3.00/2.00
Minnesota Twins	12.00/ 8.00	3.00/2.00
New York Yankees	13.00/ 9.00	2.25/1.50
Washington Senators	10.00/ 6.50	2.00/1.25
Chicago Cubs	6.00/ 4.00*	1.50/1.00
Cincinnati Reds	11.00/ 7.00	1.50/1.00
Houston Colt 45's	40.00/25.00	4.50/3.00
Los Angeles Dodgers	10.00/ 6.50	2.00/1.25
Milwaukee Braves	10.00/ 6.50	2.00/1.25
New York Mets	75.00/50.00	6.00/4.00
Philadelphia Phillies	10.00/ 6.50	2.00/1.25
Pittsburgh Pirates	10.00/ 6.50	2.00/1.25
San Francisco Giants	12.50/ 8.00	3.00/2.00
St. Louis Cardinals	10.00/ 6.50	2.00/1.25

WORLD SERIES MEMORABILIA

	AMERICAN LEAGUE MT/VG-EX	NATIONAL LEAGUE MT/VG-EX
World Series Program:	20.00/ 3.00	23.00/ 15.00
World Series Press Pin:	40.00/ 25.00	40.00/ 25.00
Commemorative Bat:	150.00/100.00	150.00/100.00
Ticket Stub:	5.00/ 3.50	5.00/ 3.50
Teams and Games Won:	New York 4	San Francisco 3

ALL-STAR MEMORABILIA

FIRST GAME	MT/VG-EX
All-Star Program:	20.00/ 14.00
All-Star Press Pin:	30.00/ 20.00
Commemorative Bat:	250.00/130.00
Ticket Stub:	6.00/ 4.00
Location:	Washington (AL)
Winning League and Score:	National 3-1
SECOND GAME	
All-Star Program:	20.00/ 14.00
All-Star Press Pin:	30.00/ 20.00
Commemorative Bat:	200.00/130.00
Ticket Stub:	6.00/ 4.00
Location:	Chicago (NL)
Winning League and Score:	American 9-4

YEAR: 1963

TEAMS (in alphabetical order by league)	YEARBOOK MT/VG-EX	PROGRAM MT/VG-EX
Baltimore Orioles	9.00/ 6.00	2.00/1.25
Boston Red Sox	9.00/ 6.00	2.00/1.25
Chicago White Sox	8.50/ 5.75	1.75/1.15
Cleveland Indians	10.00/ 6.50	2.00/1.25
Detroit Tigers	9.00/ 6.00	2.00/1.25
Kansas City A's	9.00/ 6.00	2.00/1.25
Los Angeles Angels	11.00/ 8.50	3.00/2.00
Minnesota Twins	9.00/ 6.00	2.50/1.50
New York Yankees	12.00/ 8.50	2.00/1.25
Washington Senators	9.00/ 6.00	2.00/1.25
Chicago Cubs	6.00/ 4.00*	1.50/1.00
Cincinnati Reds	11.00/ 7.00	1.50/1.00
Houston Colt .45's	9.00/ 6.00*	3.00/2.00
Los Angeles Dodgers	11.00/ 7.00	2.00/1.25
Milwaukee Braves	9.00/ 6.00	3.00/2.00
New York Mets	20.00/13.00	2.00/1.25
Philadelphia Phillies	10.00/ 6.50	2.00/1.25
Pittsburgh Pirates	9.00/ 6.00	2.00/1.25
San Francisco Giants	9.00/ 6.00	2.00/1.25
St. Louis Cardinals	10.00/ 6.50	2.00/1.25

WORLD SERIES MEMORABILIA

	AMERICAN LEAGUE MT/VG-EX	NATIONAL LEAGUE MT/VG-EX
World Series Program:	20.00/13.00	18.00/12.00
World Series Press Pin:	40.00/25.00	40.00/25.00
Commemorative Bat:	125.00/75.00	125.00/75.00
Ticket Stub:	5.00/ 3.50	5.00/ 3.50
Teams and Games Won:	New York 0	Los Angeles 4

ALL-STAR MEMORABILIA

	MT/VG-EX
All-Star Program:	18.00/ 12.00
All-Star Press Pin:	30.00/ 20.00
Commemorative Bat:	200.00/130.00
Ticket Stub:	4.00/ 2.75
Location:	Cleveland (AL)
Winning League and Score:	National 5-3

YEAR: 1964

TEAMS (in alphabetical order by league)	YEARBOOK MT/VG-EX	PROGRAM MT/VG-EX
Baltimore Orioles	9.00/ 6.00	2.00/1.25
Boston Red Sox	9.00/ 6.00	2.00/1.25
California Angels	10.00/ 6.50	2.50/1.60
Chicago White Sox	8.00/ 5.00	1.75/1.15
Cleveland Indians	9.00/ 6.00	1.75/1.15
Detroit Tigers	9.00/ 6.00	2.00/1.25
Kansas City A's	9.00/ 6.00	2.00/1.25
Minnesota Twins	9.00/ 6.00	2.50/1.50
New York Yankees	11.00/ 7.50	2.00/1.25
Washington Senators	9.00/ 6.00	2.00/1.25
Chicago Cubs	6.00/ 4.00*	1.50/1.00
Cincinnati Reds	10.00/ 6.50	1.50/1.00
Houston Astros	15.00/10.00	3.00/2.00
Los Angeles Dodgers	9.00/ 6.00	2.00/1.25
Milwaukee Braves	9.00/ 6.00	2.00/1.25
New York Mets	16.00/10.00	2.50/1.60
Philadelphia Phillies	12.00/ 8.00	2.25/1.50
Pittsburgh Pirates	9.00/ 6.00	1.75/1.15
San Francisco Giants	9.00/ 6.00	2.00/1.25
St. Louis Cardinals	13.50/ 9.00	3.00/2.00

****

WORLD SERIES MEMORABILIA
****

	AMERICAN LEAGUE MT/VG-EX	NATIONAL LEAGUE MT/VG-EX
World Series Program:	20.00/13.00	17.00/11.00
World Series Press Pin:	40.00/25.00	40.00/25.00
Commemorative Bat:	125.00/75.00	125.00/75.00
Ticket Stub:	5.00/ 3.50	5.00/ 3.50
Teams and Games Won:	New York 3	St. Louis 4

****

ALL-STAR MEMORABILIA
****

	MT/VG-EX
All-Star Program:	17.00/ 11.00
All-Star Press Pin:	30.00/ 20.00
Commemorative Bat:	200.00/125.00
Ticket Stub:	4.00/ 2.75
Location:	New York (NL)
Winning League and Score:	National 7-4

****

YEAR: 1965

TEAMS (in alphabetical order by league)	YEARBOOK MT/VG-EX	PROGRAM MT/VG-EX
Baltimore Orioles	9.00/ 6.00	1.75/1.15
Boston Red Sox	8.00/ 5.00	2.00/1.25
California Angels	9.00/ 6.00	2.00/1.25
Chicago White Sox	7.00/ 4.50	1.75/1.15
Cleveland Indians	8.00/ 5.00	1.75/1.15
Detroit Tigers	9.00/ 6.00	1.75/1.15
Kansas City A's	9.00/ 6.00	1.75/1.15
Minnesota Twins	12.00/ 8.00	3.00/2.00
New York Yankees	10.00/ 6.50	2.00/1.25
Washington Senators	8.00/ 5.00	1.75/1.15
Chicago Cubs	5.50/ 3.75*	1.50/1.00
Cincinnati Reds	9.00/ 6.00	1.50/1.00
Houston Astros	15.00/10.00	3.00/2.00
Los Angeles Dodgers	8.00/ 5.00	1.75/1.15
Milwaukee Braves	6.00/ 4.00*	2.50/1.50
New York Mets	12.00/ 8.00	2.00/1.25
Philadelphia Phillies	9.00/ 6.00	1.75/1.15
Pittsburgh Pirates	8.00/ 5.00	1.75/1.15
San Francisco Giants	8.00/ 5.00	1.75/1.15
St. Louis Cardinals	9.00/ 6.00	1.75/1.15

****

WORLD SERIES MEMORABILIA
****

	AMERICAN LEAGUE MT/VG-EX	NATIONAL LEAGUE MT/VG-EX
World Series Program:	15.00/10.00	7.50/ 5.00
World Series Press Pin:	40.00/25.00	40.00/25.00
Commemorative Bat:	125.00/75.00	125.00/75.00
Ticket Stub:	4.00/ 2.75	4.00/ 2.75
Teams and Games Won:	Minnesota 3	Los Angeles 4

****

ALL-STAR MEMORABILIA
****

	MT/VG-EX
All-Star Program:	17.00/ 11.00
All-Star Press Pin:	30.00/ 20.00
Commemorative Bat:	200.00/125.00
Ticket Stub:	3.00/ 2.00
Location:	Minnesota (AL)
Winning League and Score:	National 6-5

****

YEAR: 1966

TEAMS (in alphabetical order by league)	YEARBOOK MT/VG-EX	PROGRAM MT/VG-EX
Baltimore Orioles	11.00/8.00	2.50/1.60
Boston Red Sox	8.00/5.00	1.75/1.15
California Angels	9.00/6.00	1.75/1.15
Chicago White Sox	7.00/4.50	1.75/1.15
Cleveland Indians	8.00/5.00	1.50/ .90
Detroit Tigers	9.00/6.00	1.75/1.15
Kansas City A's	9.00/6.00	1.75/1.15
Minnesota Twins	8.00/5.00	2.00/1.25
New York Yankees	9.00/6.00	1.75/1.15
Washington Senators	8.00/5.00	1.75/1.15
Atlanta Braves	12.00/8.00	2.50/1.50
Chicago Cubs	5.50/3.75	1.50/1.00
Cincinnati Reds	8.00/5.00	1.50/1.00
Houston Astros	12.00/8.00	2.00/1.25
Los Angeles Dodgers	6.00/4.00	1.75/1.15
New York Mets	11.00/7.00	1.75/1.15
Philadelphia Phillies	8.00/5.00	1.75/1.15
Pittsburgh Pirates	8.00/5.00	1.75/1.15
San Francisco Giants	7.00/4.50	1.75/1.15
St. Louis Cardinals	9.00/6.00	1.50/1.00

****

WORLD SERIES MEMORABILIA
****

	AMERICAN LEAGUE MT/VG-EX	NATIONAL LEAGUE MT/VG-EX
World Series Program:	13.00/ 9.00	7.50/ 5.00
World Series Press Pin:	40.00/25.00	40.00/25.00
Commemorative Bat:	125.00/75.00	125.00/75.00
Ticket Stub:	4.00/ 2.75	4.00/ 2.75
Teams and Games Won:	Baltimore 4	Los Angeles 0

****

ALL-STAR MEMORABILIA
****

	MT/VG-EX
All-Star Program:	16.00/ 11.00
All-Star Press Pin:	30.00/ 20.00
Commemorative Bat:	150.00/100.00
Ticket Stub:	3.00/ 2.00
Location:	St. Louis (NL)
Winning League and Score:	National 2-1

****

YEAR: 1967

TEAMS (in alphabetical order by league)	YEARBOOK MT/VG-EX	PROGRAM MT/VG-EX
Baltimore Orioles	7.00/4.50	1.50/ .90
Boston Red Sox	7.00/4.50	3.00/2.00
California Angels	8.00/5.50	1.75/1.25
Chicago White Sox	6.50/4.25	1.50/ .90
Cleveland Indians	7.00/4.50	1.50/ .90
Detroit Tigers	9.00/6.00	1.75/1.25
Kansas City A's	10.00/6.50	2.50/1.50
Minnesota Twins	7.00/4.50	1.75/1.25
New York Yankees	9.00/6.00	1.75/1.25
Washington Senators	7.00/4.50	1.50/ .90
Atlanta Braves	7.00/4.50	1.50/ .90
Chicago Cubs	5.00/3.50*	1.25/ .75
Cincinnati Reds	7.00/4.50	1.50/ .90
Houston Astros	5.00/3.50	1.75/1.15
Los Angeles Dodgers	5.00/3.50	1.50/ .90
New York Mets	10.00/6.50	1.75/1.15
Philadelphia Phillies	7.00/4.50	1.50/ .90
Pittsburgh Pirates	7.00/4.50	1.50/ .90
San Francisco Giants	6.50/4.25	1.50/ .90
St. Louis Cardinals	10.00/6.50	2.50/1.60

****

WORLD SERIES MEMORABILIA
****

	AMERICAN LEAGUE MT/VG-EX	NATIONAL LEAGUE MT/VG-EX
World Series Program:	17.00/11.00	15.00/10.00
World Series Press Pin:	45.00/30.00	40.00/25.00
Commemorative Bat:	125.00/75.00	125.00/75.00
Ticket Stub:	4.00/ 2.75	4.00/ 2.75
Teams and Games Won:	Boston 3	St. Louis 4

****

ALL-STAR MEMORABILIA
****

	MT/VG-EX
All-Star Program:	14.00/ 10.00
All-Star Press Pin:	25.00/ 16.00
Commemorative Bat:	150.00/100.00
Ticket Stub:	3.00/ 2.00
Location:	Anaheim (AL)
Winning League and Score:	National 2-1

****

YEAR: 1968

TEAMS (in alphabetical order by league)	YEARBOOK MT/VG-EX	PROGRAM MT/VG-EX
Baltimore Orioles	7.00/4.50	1.50/ .90
Boston Red Sox	7.00/4.50	1.75/1.25
California Angels	6.00/4.00*	1.50/ .90
Chicago White Sox	6.00/4.00	1.50/ .90
Cleveland Indians	7.00/4.50	1.50/ .90
Detroit Tigers	12.00/8.00	3.00/2.00
Minnesota Twins	7.00/4.50	1.50/ .90
New York Yankees	8.00/5.00	1.50/ .90
Oakland A's	13.00/9.00	2.50/1.50
Washington Senators	6.00/4.00	1.50/ .90
Atlanta Braves	6.50/4.25	1.50/ .90
Chicago Cubs	5.00/3.00*	1.25/ .75
Cincinnati Reds	7.00/4.50	1.50/ .90
Houston Astros	5.00/3.50*	1.50/ .90
Los Angeles Dodgers	4.50/3.00	1.50/ .90
New York Mets	9.00/6.00	1.50/ .90
Philadelphia Phillies	6.00/4.00	1.50/ .90
Pittsburgh Pirates	6.00/4.00	1.50/ .90
San Francisco Giants	6.00/4.00	1.50/ .90
St. Louis Cardinals	8.00/5.00	2.00/1.25

****

WORLD SERIES MEMORABILIA
****

	AMERICAN LEAGUE MT/VG-EX	NATIONAL LEAGUE MT/VG-EX
World Series Program:	16.00/10.00	14.00/ 9.00
World Series Press Pin:	35.00/25.00	35.00/25.00
Commemorative Bat:	125.00/75.00	125.00/75.00
Ticket Stub:	4.00/ 2.75	4.00/ 2.75
Teams and Games Won:	Detroit 4	St. Louis 3

****

ALL-STAR MEMORABILIA
****

	MT/VG-EX
All-Star Program:	12.00/ 8.00
All-Star Press Pin:	25.00/ 16.00
Commemorative Bat:	150.00/100.00
Ticket Stub:	3.00/ 2.00
Location:	Houston (NL)
Winning League and Score:	National 1-0

****

YEAR: 1969

TEAMS (in alphabetical order by league)	YEARBOOK MT/VG-EX	PROGRAM MT/VG-EX
Baltimore Orioles	8.50/ 6.00	2.50/1.25
Boston Red Sox	5.00/ 3.00	1.50/ .90
California Angels	5.00/ 3.00*	1.50/ .90
Chicago White Sox	5.00/ 3.00	1.50/ .90
Cleveland Indians	5.50/ 4.00	1.50/ .90
Detroit Tigers	5.00/ 3.00	1.50/ .90
Kansas City Royals	15.00/10.00	3.00/2.00
Minnesota Twins	6.00/ 4.00	1.50/ .90
New York Yankees	7.00/ 4.50	1.50/ .90
Oakland A's	6.00/ 4.00	1.50/ .90
Seattle Pilots	50.00/35.00	7.50/5.00
Washington Senators	5.00/ 3.00	1.50/ .90
Atlanta Braves	5.00/ 3.00	1.50/ .90
Chicago Cubs	4.00/ 2.75*	1.25/ .75
Cincinnati Reds	5.00/ 3.00	1.50/ .90
Houston Astros	4.00/ 2.75*	1.50/ .90
Los Angeles Dodgers	4.00/ 2.75	1.50/ .90
Montreal Expos	20.00/13.00	3.00/2.00
New York Mets	20.00/13.00	2.50/1.60
Philadelphia Phillies	4.50/ 3.00	1.50/ .90
Pittsburgh Pirates	5.00/ 3.00	1.50/ .90
San Diego Padres	25.00/16.00	3.00/2.00
San Francisco Giants	5.00/ 3.00	1.50/ .90
St. Louis Cardinals	5.50/ 3.75	1.25/ .75

****

WORLD SERIES MEMORABILIA
****

	AMERICAN LEAGUE MT/VG-EX	NATIONAL LEAGUE MT/VG-EX
World Series Program:	12.00/ 8.00	16.00/ 10.00
World Series Press Pin:	35.00/25.00	50.00/ 35.00
Commemorative Bat:	100.00/70.00	150.00/100.00
Ticket Stub:	3.00/ 2.00	5.00/ 3.50
Teams and Games Won:	Baltimore 1	New York 4
Championship Series:	EAST	WEST
A.L. Teams and Games Won:	Baltimore 3	Minnesota 0
Home Program:	6.50/ 4.50	8.00/ 5.50
N.L. Teams and Games Won:	New York 3	Atlanta 0
Home Program:	10.00/ 6.50	6.50/ 4.50

****

ALL-STAR MEMORABILIA
****

	MT/VG-EX
All-Star Program:	10.00/ 7.00
All-Star Press Pin:	25.00/ 16.00
Commemorative Bat:	150.00/100.00
Ticket Stub:	3.00/ 2.00
Location:	Washington (AL)
Winning League and Score:	National 9-3

****

YEAR: 1970

TEAMS (in alphabetical order by league)	YEARBOOK MT/VG-EX	PROGRAM MT/VG-EX
Baltimore Orioles	7.50/ 5.00	2.00/1.25
Boston Red Sox	5.00/ 3.00	1.50/ .90
California Angels	4.00/ 2.75*	1.50/ .90
Chicago White Sox	5.00/ 3.00	1.50/ .90
Cleveland Indians	5.00/ 3.00	1.50/ .90
Detroit Tigers	5.00/ 3.00	1.50/ .90
Kansas City Royals	6.50/ 4.50	2.00/1.25
Milwaukee Brewers	15.00/10.00	1.50/ .90
Minnesota Twins	5.00/ 3.00	1.50/ .90
New York Yankees	5.00/ 3.00	1.50/ .90
Oakland A's	5.00/ 3.00	1.50/ .90
Washington Senators	5.00/ 3.00*	1.50/ .90
Atlanta Braves	4.00/ 2.75	1.25/ .75
Chicago Cubs	4.00/ 2.75*	1.25/ .75
Cincinnati Reds	5.00/ 3.00	1.50/ .90
Houston Astros	4.00/ 2.75*	1.50/ .90
Los Angeles Dodgers	4.00/ 2.75	1.50/ .90
Montreal Expos	8.00/ 5.00	2.00/1.25
New York Mets	6.50/ 4.25	1.50/ .90
Philadelphia Phillies	4.00/ 2.75	1.50/ .90
Pittsburgh Pirates	5.00/ 3.00	1.50/ .90
San Diego Padres	3.50/ 2.35*	2.00/1.25
San Francisco Giants	5.00/ 3.00	1.25/ .75
St. Louis Cardinals	5.00/ 3.00	1.25/ .75

****

WORLD SERIES MEMORABILIA
****

	AMERICAN LEAGUE MT/VG-EX	NATIONAL LEAGUE MT/VG-EX
World Series Program:	10.00/ 6.50	12.00/ 8.50
World Series Press Pin:	25.00/25.00	25.00/25.00
Commemorative Bat:	100.00/70.00	100.00/70.00
Ticket Stub:	3.00/ 2.00	3.00/ 2.00
Teams and Games Won:	Baltimore 4	Cincinnati 1
Championship Series:	EAST	WEST
A.L. Teams and Games Won:	Baltimore 3	Minnesota 0
Home Program:	6.00/ 4.00	7.50/ 5.00
N.L. Teams and Games Won:	Pittsburgh 0	Cincinnati 3
Home Program:	6.00/ 4.00	6.00/ 4.00

****

ALL-STAR MEMORABILIA
****

	MT/VG-EX
All-Star Program:	9.00/ 6.00
All-Star Press Pin:	25.00/16.00
Commemorative Bat:	125.00/75.00
Ticket Stub:	3.00/ 2.00
Location:	Cincinnati (NL)
Winning League and Score:	National 5-4

****

YEAR: 1971

TEAMS (in alphabetical order by league)	YEARBOOK MT/VG-EX	PROGRAM MT/VG-EX
Baltimore Orioles	6.50/4.50	2.00/1.25
Boston Red Sox	3.50/2.25	1.25/ .75
California Angels	3.50/2.25*	1.50/1.00
Chicago White Sox	3.50/2.25*	1.25/ .75
Cleveland Indians	4.00/2.75	1.25/ .75
Detroit Tigers	4.00/2.75	1.25/ .75
Kansas City Royals	4.50/3.00	1.25/ .75
Milwaukee Brewers	3.50/2.25*	1.50/1.00
Minnesota Twins	3.50/2.25	1.25/ .75
New York Yankees	4.00/2.75	1.50/1.00
Oakland A's	4.00/2.75	1.75/1.25
Washington Senators	3.50/2.25*	1.50/1.00
Atlanta Braves	3.50/2.25	1.25/ .75
Chicago Cubs	3.50/2.25*	1.25/ .75
Cincinnati Reds	3.50/2.25	1.25/ .75
Houston Astros	3.50/2.25	1.25/ .75
Los Angeles Dodgers	3.50/2.25	1.25/ .75
Montreal Expos	5.50/3.75	1.50/1.00
New York Mets	4.00/2.75	1.50/1.00
Philadelphia Phillies	3.50/2.25	1.25/ .75
Pittsburgh Pirates	6.00/4.00	2.00/1.25
San Diego Padres	3.50/2.25*	1.50/1.00
San Francisco Giants	4.00/2.75	1.50/1.00
St. Louis Cardinals	3.50/2.25	1.25/ .75

****

WORLD SERIES MEMORABILIA
****

	AMERICAN LEAGUE MT/VG-EX	NATIONAL LEAGUE MT/VG-EX
World Series Program:	8.00/ 5.00	10.00/ 6.50
World Series Press Pin:	35.00/25.00	35.00/25.00
Commemorative Bat:	100.00/70.00	100.00/70.00
Ticket Stub:	3.00/ 2.00	3.00/ 2.00
Teams and Games Won:	Baltimore 3	Pittsburgh 4
Championship Series:	EAST	WEST
A.L. Teams and Games Won:	Baltimore 3	Oakland 0
Home Program:	5.00/ 3.50	5.00/ 3.50
N.L. Teams and Games Won:	Pittsburgh 3	San Francisco 1
Home Program:	5.00/ 3.50	6.00/ 4.00

****

ALL-STAR MEMORABILIA
****

	MT/VG-EX
All-Star Program:	9.00/ 6.00
All-Star Press Pin:	25.00/16.00
Commemorative Bat:	125.00/75.00
Ticket Stub:	3.00/ 2.00
Location:	Detroit (AL)
Winning League and Score:	American 6-4

****

YEAR: 1972

TEAMS (in alphabetical order by league)	YEARBOOK MT/VG-EX	PROGRAM MT/VG-EX
Baltimore Orioles	3.50/2.25	1.25/ .75
Boston Red Sox	3.50/2.25	1.25/ .75
California Angels	3.50/2.25*	1.25/ .75
Chicago White Sox	3.50/2.25*	1.25/ .75
Cleveland Indians	3.50/2.25	1.25/ .75
Detroit Tigers	5.00/3.50	1.75/1.25
Kansas City Royals	3.50/2.25	1.25/ .75
Milwaukee Brewers	3.50/2.25*	1.25/ .75
Minnesota Twins	3.50/2.25	1.25/ .75
New York Yankees	4.00/2.75	1.25/ .75
Oakland A's	5.00/5.50	1.50/1.00
Texas Rangers	4.00/2.75*	12.5/1.50
Atlanta Braves	3.50/2.25	1.25/ .75
Chicago Cubs	3.50/2.25*	1.00/ .60
Cincinnati Reds	3.50/2.25	1.25/ .75
Houston Astros	3.50/2.25	1.25/ .75
Los Angeles Dodgers	3.00/2.00	1.25/ .75
Montreal Expos	5.00/3.50	1.25/ .75
New York Mets	4.00/2.75	1.25/ .75
Philadelphia Phillies	3.50/2.25	1.25/ .75
Pittsburgh Pirates	3.50/2.25	1.25/ .75
San Diego Padres	3.50/2.25*	1.25/ .75
San Francisco Giants	3.50/2.25	1.25/ .75
St. Louis Cardinals	3.50/2.25	1.00/ .60

****

WORLD SERIES MEMORABILIA
****

	AMERICAN LEAGUE MT/VG-EX	NATIONAL LEAGUE MT/VG-EX
World Series Program:	9.00/ 6.00	7.50/ 5.00
World Series Press Pin:	30.00/20.00	30.00/20.00
Commemorative Bat:	100.00/70.00	100.00/70.00
Ticket Stub:	2.50/ 1.50	2.50/ 1.50
Teams and Games Won:	Oakland 4	Cincinnati 3
Championship Series:	EAST	WEST
A.L. Teams and Games Won:	Detroit 2	Oakland 3
Home Program:	6.00/ 4.00	5.00/ 3.50
N.L. Teams and Games Won:	Pittsburgh 2	Cincinnati 3
Home Program:	6.00/ 4.00	5.00/ 3.50

****

ALL-STAR MEMORABILIA
****

	MT/VG-EX
All-Star Program:	6.00/ 4.00
All-Star Press Pin:	25.00/16.00
Commemorative Bat:	125.00/75.00
Ticket Stub:	2.50/ 1.50
Location:	Atlanta (NL)
Winning League and Score:	National 4-3

****

YEAR: 1973

TEAMS (in alphabetical order by league)	YEARBOOK MT/VG-EX	PROGRAM MT/VG-EX
Baltimore Orioles	3.50/2.25	1.25/ .75
Boston Red Sox	3.50/2.25	1.25/ .75
California Angels	3.50/2.25*	1.25/ .75
Chicago White Sox	3.50/2.25*	1.00/ .60
Cleveland Indians	3.50/2.25*	1.00/ .60
Detroit Tigers	3.50/2.25	1.25/ .75
Kansas City Royals	3.50/2.25	1.25/ .75
Milwaukee Brewers	3.50/2.25*	1.25/ .75
Minnesota Twins	3.50/2.25	1.25/ .75
New York Yankees	4.00/2.75	1.25/ .75
Oakland A's	4.50/3.00	1.50/1.00
Texas Rangers	3.50/2.25*	1.50/1.00
Atlanta Braves	3.50/2.25	1.25/ .75
Chicago Cubs	3.00/2.00*	1.00/ .60
Cincinnati Reds	3.50/2.25	1.25/ .75
Houston Astros	3.00/2.00*	1.25/ .75
Los Angeles Dodgers	3.00/2.00	1.25/ .75
Montreal Expos	3.50/2.25*	1.25/ .75
New York Mets	5.00/3.50	1.50/1.00
Philadelphia Phillies	3.50/2.25	1.25/ .75
Pittsburgh Pirates	3.50/2.25	1.25/ .75
San Diego Padres	3.00/2.00*	1.25/ .75
San Francisco Giants	3.00/2.00	1.25/ .75
St. Louis Cardinals	3.00/2.00	1.00/ .60

****

WORLD SERIES MEMORABILIA
****

	AMERICAN LEAGUE MT/VG-EX	NATIONAL LEAGUE MT/VG-EX
World Series Program:	8.00/ 5.00	5.50/ 3.75
World Series Press Pin:	30.00/20.00	45.00/30.00
Commemorative Bat:	100.00/70.00	125.00/75.00
Ticket Stub:	2.50/ 1.50	3.00/ 2.00
Teams and Games Won:	Oakland 4	New York 3
Championship Series:	EAST	WEST
A.L. Teams and Games Won:	Baltimore 2	Oakland 3
Home Program:	4.50/ 3.25	4.50/ 3.25
N.L. Teams and Games Won:	New York 3	Cincinnati 2
Home Program:	5.50/ 4.00	4.50/ 3.25

****

ALL-STAR MEMORABILIA
****

	MT/VG-EX
All-Star Program:	6.00/ 4.00
All-Star Press Pin:	25.00/16.00
Commemorative Bat:	125.00/75.00
Ticket Stub:	2.50/ 1.50
Location:	Kansas City (AL)
Winning League and Score:	National 7-1

****

YEAR: 1974

TEAMS (in alphabetical order by league)	YEARBOOK MT/VG-EX	PROGRAM MT/VG-EX
Baltimore Orioles	3.50/2.25	1.25/ .75
Boston Red Sox	3.50/2.25	1.25/ .75
California Angels	3.50/2.25*	1.25/ .75
Chicago White Sox	3.50/2.25*	1.00/ .60
Cleveland Indians	3.50/2.25*	1.00/ .60
Detroit Tigers	3.50/2.25	1.25/ .75
Kansas City Royals	3.50/2.25	1.25/ .75
Milwaukee Brewers	3.50/2.25*	1.25/ .75
Minnesota Twins	3.00/2.00	1.25/ .75
New York Yankees	4.00/2.75	1.25/ .75
Oakland A's	4.00/2.75	1.50/1.00
Texas Rangers	3.50/2.25*	1.25/ .75
Atlanta Braves	3.50/2.25	1.25/ .75
Chicago Cubs	3.00/2.00*	1.00/ .60
Cincinnati Reds	3.50/2.25	1.25/ .75
Houston Astros	3.00/2.00*	1.25/ .75
Los Angeles Dodgers	3.50/2.25	1.25/ .75
Montreal Expos	3.50/2.25*	1.25/ .75
New York Mets	3.50/2.25	1.25/ .75
Philadelphia Phillies	3.50/2.25	1.25/ .75
Pittsburgh Pirates	3.50/2.25	1.25/ .75
San Diego Padres	3.00/2.00*	1.00/ .60
San Francisco Giants	3.00/2.00	1.25/ .75
St. Louis Cardinals	3.00/2.00	1.00/ .60

****

WORLD SERIES MEMORABILIA
****

	AMERICAN LEAGUE MT/VG-EX	NATIONAL LEAGUE MT/VG-EX
World Series Program:	4.50/ 3.25	4.50/ 3.25
World Series Press Pin:	30.00/20.00	30.00/20.00
Commemorative Bat:	100.00/70.00	100.00/70.00
Ticket Stub:	2.50/ 1.50	2.50/ 1.50
Teams and Games Won:	Oakland 4	Los Angeles 1
Championship Series:	EAST	WEST
A.L. Teams and Games Won:	Baltimore 1	Oakland 3
Home Program:	4.50/ 3.25	4.50/ 3.25
N.L. Teams and Games Won:	Pittsburgh 1	Los Angeles 3
Home Program:	4.50/ 3.25	4.50/ 3.25

****

ALL-STAR MEMORABILIA
****

	MT/VG-EX
All-Star Program:	6.00/ 4.00
All-Star Press Pin:	25.00/16.00
Commemorative Bat:	100.00/70.00
Ticket Stub:	2.50/ 1.50
Location:	Pittsburgh (NL)
Winning League and Score:	National 7-2

****

YEAR: 1975

TEAMS (in alphabetical order by league)	YEARBOOK MT/VG-EX	PROGRAM MT/VG-EX
Baltimore Orioles	3.00/2.00*	1.00/ .60
Boston Red Sox	3.00/2.00	1.50/1.00
California Angels	3.00/2.00*	1.00/ .60
Chicago White Sox	3.00/2.00*	1.00/ .60
Cleveland Indians	3.00/2.00*	1.00/ .60
Detroit Tigers	3.00/2.00	1.00/ .60
Kansas City Royals	3.00/2.00	1.00/ .60
Milwaukee Brewers	3.00/2.00*	1.00/ .60
Minnesota Twins	3.00/2.00	1.00/ .60
New York Yankees	3.50/2.25	1.00/ .60
Oakland A's	3.50/2.25	1.25/ .80
Texas Rangers	3.00/2.00*	1.00/ .60
Atlanta Braves	3.00/2.00	1.00/ .60
Chicago Cubs	3.00/2.00*	.80/ .50
Cincinnati Reds	3.50/2.25	1.00/ .60
Houston Astros	3.00/2.00*	1.00/ .60
Los Angeles Dodgers	2.50/1.50	1.00/ .60
Montreal Expos	3.00/2.00*	1.25/ .80
New York Mets	3.00/2.00	1.00/ .60
Philadelphia Phillies	3.00/2.00	1.00/ .60
Pittsburgh Pirates	3.00/2.00	1.00/ .60
San Diego Padres	3.00/2.00*	1.00/ .60
San Francisco Giants	3.00/2.00	1.00/ .60
St. Louis Cardinals	3.00/2.00	1.00/ .60

****

WORLD SERIES MEMORABILIA
****

	AMERICAN LEAGUE MT/VG-EX	NATIONAL LEAGUE MT/VG-EX
World Series Program:	4.00/ 2.75	4.00/ 2.75
World Series Press Pin:	35.00/25.00	30.00/20.00
Commemorative Bat:	100.00/70.00	80.00/55.00
Ticket Stub:	2.00/ 1.25	2.00/ 1.25
Teams and Games Won:	Boston 3	Cincinnati 4
Championship Series:	EAST	WEST
A.L. Teams and Games Won:	Boston 3	Oakland 0
Home Program:	4.00/ 2.75	4.00/ 2.75
N.L. Teams and Games Won:	Pittsburgh 0	Cincinnati 3
Home Program:	4.00/ 2.75	4.00/ 2.75

****

ALL-STAR MEMORABILIA
****

	MT/VG-EX
All-Star Program:	5.00/ 3.50
All-Star Press Pin:	25.00/16.00
Commemorative Bat:	100.00/70.00
Ticket Stub:	2.00/ 1.25
Location:	Milwaukee (AL)
Winning League and Score:	National 6-3

****

YEAR: 1976

TEAMS (in alphabetical order by league)	YEARBOOK MT/VG-EX	PROGRAM MT/VG-EX
Baltimore Orioles	3.00/2.00*	1.00/.60
Boston Red Sox	3.00/2.00	1.00/.60
California Angels	3.00/2.00*	1.00/.60
Chicago White Sox	3.00/2.00*	1.00/.60
Cleveland Indians	3.00/2.00*	1.00/.60
Detroit Tigers	3.00/2.00	1.00/.60
Kansas City Royals	3.00/2.00*	1.00/.60
Milwaukee Brewers	3.00/2.00*	1.00/.60
Minnesota Twins	3.00/2.00	1.00/.60
New York Yankees	3.50/2.50	1.00/.60
Oakland A's	3.50/2.00	1.00/.60
Texas Rangers	3.00/2.50	1.00/.60
Atlanta Braves	3.00/2.00	1.00/.60
Chicago Cubs	3.00/2.00*	.80/.50
Cincinnati Reds	3.50/2.25	1.00/.60
Houston Astros	3.00/2.00*	1.00/.60
Los Angeles Dodgers	2.50/1.50	1.00/.60
Montreal Expos	3.00/2.00*	1.00/.60
New York Mets	3.00/2.00	1.00/.60
Philadelphia Phillies	3.00/2.00	1.00/.60
Pittsburgh Pirates	3.00/2.00	1.00/.60
San Diego Padres	3.00/2.00*	1.00/.60
San Francisco Giants	2.50/1.60	1.00/.60
St. Louis Cardinals	2.50/1.60	.80/.50

****

WORLD SERIES MEMORABILIA
****

	AMERICAN LEAGUE MT/VG-EX	NATIONAL LEAGUE MT/VG-EX
World Series Program:	4.00/ 2.75	4.00/ 2.75
World Series Press Pin:	30.00/20.00	30.00/20.00
Commemorative Bat:	75.00/50.00	75.00/50.00
Ticket Stub:	2.00/ 1.25	2.00/ 1.25
Teams and Games Won:	New York 0	Cincinnati 4
Championship Series:	EAST	WEST
A.L. Teams and Games Won	New York 3	Kansas City 2
Home Program:	3.50/ 2.50	3.50/ 2.50
N.L. Teams and Games Won:	Philadelphia 0	Cincinnati 3
Home Program:	3.50/ 2.50	3.50/ 2.50

****

ALL-STAR MEMORABILIA
****

	MT/VG-EX
All-Star Program:	5.00/ 3.50
All-Star Press Pin:	25.00/16.00
Commemorative Bat:	100.00/70.00
Ticket Stub:	2.00/ 1.25
Location:	Philadelphia (NL)
Winning League and Score:	National 7-1

****

Hall's Nostalgia

If you're looking for those missing baseball cards in your collection, why not try buying them from Hall's Nostalgia? We have several hundred thousand cards from 1880 to date. If you can visit our store, you are welcome to browse around. However, we also serve over 10,000 mail order customers and would be happy to add your name to the growing list. Just send a stamped - self addressed - envelope, and 50¢ for handling, along with your want list, and we will promptly send out a price quote for your specific needs. We also carry thousands of sport publications so send $1.00 for our current publication list.

BASEBALL MEMORABILIA & CARDS WANTED

Paying 35% up to 100% of this guide.

Always check with us before you sell.

Call or Write

Hall's Nostalgia

21-25 Mystic Street
Dept. MPG , Box 408
Arlington, MA 02174

1- (617) 646-7757

NOW OPEN —
HALL'S NOSTALGIA #2
389 Chatham Street
Lynn, MA 01904
(617) 595-7757

CERTIFIED APPRAISERS
MID-AM ANTIQUE
APPRAISERS ASSOCIATION
REGISTERED MEMBER

YEAR: 1977

TEAMS (in alphabetical order by league)	YEARBOOK MT/VG-EX	PROGRAM MT/VG-EX
Baltimore Orioles	2.50/1.50*	1.00/ .60
Boston Red Sox	2.50/1.50	1.00/ .60
California Angels	2.50/1.50*	1.00/ .60
Chicago White Sox	2.00/1.25*	1.00/ .60
Cleveland Indians	2.00/1.25*	1.00/ .60
Detroit Tigers	3.00/2.00	1.00/ .60
Kansas City Royals	2.50/1.50*	1.00/ .60
Milwaukee Brewers	2.00/1.25*	1.00/ .60
Minnesota Twins	2.50/1.50	1.00/ .60
New York Yankees	3.00/2.00	1.00/ .60
Oakland A's	2.50/1.50	1.00/ .60
Seattle Mariners	2.00/1.25*	2.50/1.50
Texas Rangers	2.50/1.50	1.00/ .60
Toronto Blue Jays	8.00/5.00	3.00/2.00
Atlanta Braves	2.50/1.50	1.00/ .60
Chicago Cubs	2.00/1.25*	.80/ .50
Cincinnati Reds	2.50/1.50	1.00/ .60
Houston Astros	2.50/1.50*	1.00/ .60
Los Angeles Dodgers	2.50/1.50	.80/ .50
Montreal Expos	2.00/1.25*	1.00/ .60
New York Mets	2.50/1.50	1.00/ .60
Philadelphia Phillies	2.50/1.50	1.00/ .60
Pittsburgh Pirates	2.50/1.50	1.00/ .60
San Diego Padres	2.00/1.25*	.80/ .50
San Francisco Giants	2.00/1.25*	1.00/ .60
St. Louis Cardinals	2.50/1.50	.80/ .50

****

WORLD SERIES MEMORABILIA
****

	AMERICAN LEAGUE MT/VG-EX	NATIONAL LEAGUE MT/VG-EX
World Series Program:	4.00/ 2.75	4.00/ 2.75
World Series Press Pin:	30.00/20.00	30.00/20.00
Commemorative Bat:	75.00/25.00	75.00/25.00
Ticket Stub:	2.00/ 1.25	2.00/ 1.25
Teams and Games Won:	New York 4	Los Angeles 2
Championship Series:	EAST	WEST
A.L. Teams and Games Won:	New York 3	Kansas City 2
Home Program:	3.00/ 2.00	3.00/ 2.00
N.L. Teams and Games Won:	Philadelphia 1	Los Angeles 3
Home Program:	3.00/ 2.00	2.50/ 1.50

****

ALL-STAR MEMORABILIA
****

	MT/VG-EX
All-Star Program:	4.00/ 2.75
All-Star Press Pin:	20.00/13.00
Commemorative Bat:	100.00/70.00
Ticket Stub:	2.00/ 1.25
Location:	Milwaukee (AL)
Winning League and Score:	National 7-5

****

YEAR: 1978

TEAMS (in alphabetical order by league)	YEARBOOK MT/VG-EX	PROGRAM MT/VG-EX
Baltimore Orioles	2.50/1.50*	1.00/ .60
Boston Red Sox	2.50/1.50	1.00/ .60
California Angels	2.50/1.50*	1.00/ .60
Chicago White Sox	2.00/1.25*	1.00/ .60
Cleveland Indians	2.00/1.25*	1.00/ .60
Detroit Tigers	2.50/1.50	1.00/ .60
Kansas City Royals	2.50/1.50*	1.00/ .60
Milwaukee Brewers	2.00/1.25*	1.00/ .60
Minnesota Twins	3.00/2.00	1.00/ .60
New York Yankees	2.50/1.50	1.00/ .60
Oakland A's	2.00/1.25*	1.00/ .60
Seattle Mariners	2.00/1.25*	1.50/1.00
Texas Rangers	2.50/1.50	1.00/ .60
Toronto Blue Jays	2.00/1.25*	1.50/1.00
Atlanta Braves	2.50/1.50	1.00/ .60
Chicago Cubs	2.00/1.25*	.80/ .50
Cincinnati Reds	2.50/1.50	1.00/ .60
Houston Astros	2.50/1.50*	1.00/ .60
Los Angeles Dodgers	2.50/1.50	.80/ .50
Montreal Expos	2.00/1.25*	1.00/ .60
New York Mets	2.50/1.50	1.00/ .60
Philadelphia Phillies	2.50/1.50	1.00/ .60
Pittsburgh Pirates	2.50/1.50	1.00/ .60
San Diego Padres	2.00/1.25*	.80/ .50
San Francisco Giants	2.00/1.25*	.80/ .50
St. Louis Cardinals	2.00/1.25*	.80/ .50

****

WORLD SERIES MEMORABILIA
****

	AMERICAN LEAGUE MT/VG-EX	NATIONAL LEAGUE MT/VG-EX
World Series Program:	3.50/ 2.50	3.50/ 2.50
World Series Press Pin:	30.00/20.00	30.00/20.00
Commemorative Bat:	75.00/50.00	75.00/50.00
Ticket Stub:	2.00/ 1.25	2.00/ 1.25
Teams and Games Won:	New York 4	Los Angeles 2
Championship Series:	EAST	WEST
A.L. Teams and Games Won:	New York 3	Kansas City 1
Home Program:	2.50/ 1.50	2.50/ 1.50
N.L. Teams and Games Won:	Philadelphia 1	Los Angeles 3
Home Program:	2.50/ 1.50	2.50/ 1.50

****

ALL-STAR MEMORABILIA
****

	MT/VG-EX
All-Star Program:	3.50/ 2.35
All-Star Press Pin:	20.00/13.00
Commemorative Bat:	100.00/70.00
Ticket Stub:	2.00/ 1.25
Location:	San Diego (NL)
Winning League and Score:	National 7-3

****

YEAR: 1979

TEAMS (in alphabetical order by league)	YEARBOOK MT/VG-EX	PROGRAM MT/VG-EX
Baltimore Orioles	3.50/2.50*	1.50/1.00
Boston Red Sox	2.50/1.50	1.00/ .60
California Angels	2.00/1.25*	1.25/ .75
Chicago White Sox	2.00/1.25*	.80/ .50
Cleveland Indians	2.00/1.25*	1.00/ .60
Detroit Tigers	2.50/1.50	1.00/ .60
Kansas City Royals	2.00/1.25*	1.00/ .60
Milwaukee Brewers	2.00/1.25*	1.00/ .60
Minnesota Twins	2.50/1.50	1.00/ .60
New York Yankees	2.50/1.50	1.00/ .60
Oakland A's	2.00/1.25*	1.00/ .60
Seattle Mariners	2.00/1.25*	1.00/ .60
Texas Rangers	2.50/1.50	1.00/ .60
Toronto Blue Jays	3.00/2.00	1.00/ .60
Atlanta Braves	2.50/1.50	1.00/ .60
Chicago Cubs	2.00/1.25*	.80/ .50
Cincinnati Reds	2.50/1.50	1.00/ .60
Houston Astros	2.00/1.25*	1.00/ .60
Los Angeles Dodgers	2.50/1.50	.80/ .50
Montreal Expos	2.00/1.25*	1.00/ .60
New York Mets	2.50/1.50	1.00/ .60
Philadelphia Phillies	2.50/1.50	.80/ .50
Pittsburgh Pirates	3.00/2.00	1.00/ .60
San Diego Padres	2.50/1.50	.80/ .50
San Francisco Giants	2.50/1.50	.80/ .50
St. Louis Cardinals	2.00/1.25*	.80/ .50

WORLD SERIES MEMORABILIA

	AMERICAN LEAGUE MT/VG-EX	NATIONAL LEAGUE MT/VG-EX
World Series Program:	3.50/ 2.50	3.50/ 2.50
World Series Press Pin:	25.00/16.00	25.00/16.00
Commemorative Bat:	75.00/50.00	75.00/50.00
Ticket Stub:	2.00/ 1.25	2.00/ 1.25
Teams and Games Won:	Baltimore 3	Pittsburgh 4
Championship Series:	EAST	WEST
A.L. Teams and Games Won:	Baltimore 3	California 1
Home Program:	2.50/ 1.50	2.50/ 1.50
N.L. Teams and Games Won:	Pittsburgh 3	Cincinnati 0
Home Program:	2.50/ 1.50	2.50/ 1.50

ALL-STAR MEMORABILIA

	MT/VG-EX
All-Star Program:	3.00/ 2.00
All-Star Press Pin:	20.00/13.00
Commemorative Bat:	100.00/70.00
Ticket Stub:	2.00/ 1.25
Location:	Seattle (AL)
Winning League and Score:	National 7-6

YEAR: 1980

TEAMS (in alphabetical order by league)	YEARBOOK MT/VG-EX	PROGRAM MT/VG-EX
Baltimore Orioles	2.00/1.25*	1.00/.60
Boston Red Sox	2.50/1.50	1.00/.60
California Angels	2.00/1.25*	1.00/.60
Chicago White Sox	2.00/1.25*	.80/.50
Cleveland Indians	2.00/1.25*	.80/.50
Detroit Tigers	2.50/1.50	1.00/.60
Kansas City Royals	2.00/1.25*	1.25/.80
Milwaukee Brewers	2.00/1.25*	1.00/.60
Minnesota Twins	2.50/1.50	1.00/.60
New York Yankees	3.00/2.00	1.00/.60
Oakland A's	2.00/1.25*	1.00/.60
Seattle Mariners	2.00/1.25*	1.00/.60
Texas Rangers	2.50/1.50	.80/.50
Toronto Blue Jays	2.50/1.50	1.00/.60
Atlanta Braves	2.50/1.50	.80/.50
Chicago Cubs	2.00/1.25*	.80/.50
Cincinnati Reds	2.50/1.50	1.00/.60
Houston Astros	2.00/1.25*	1.00/.60
Los Angeles Dodgers	2.50/1.50	.80/.50
Montreal Expos	2.00/1.25*	1.00/.60
New York Mets	2.50/1.50	.80/.50
Philadelphia Phillies	3.00/2.00	1.00/.60
Pittsburgh Pirates	2.50/1.50	.80/.50
San Diego Padres	2.50/1.50	.80/.50
San Francisco Giants	2.50/1.50	.80/.50
St. Louis Cardinals	2.00/1.25*	.80/.50

WORLD SERIES MEMORABILIA

	AMERICAN LEAGUE MT/VG-EX	NATIONAL LEAGUE MT/VG-EX
World Series Program:	3.00/ 2.00	3.00/ 2.00
World Series Press Pin:	25.00/16.00	25.00/16.00
Commemorative Bat:	75.00/50.00	75.00/50.00
Ticket Stub:	2.00/ 1.25	2.00/ 1.25
Teams and Games Won:	Kansas City 2	Philadelphia 4
Championship Series:	EAST	WEST
A.L. Teams and Games Won:	New York 0	Kansas City 3
Home Program:	2.50/ 1.50	2.50/ 1.50
N.L. Teams and Games Won:	Philadelphia 3	Houston 2
Home Program:	2.50/ 1.50	2.50/ 1.50

ALL-STAR MEMORABILIA

	MT/VG-EX
All-Star Program:	3.00/ 2.00
All-Star Press Pin:	20.00/13.00
Commemorative Bat:	100.00/70.00
Ticket Stub:	2.00/ 1.25
Location:	Los Angeles (NL)
Winning League and Score:	National 4-2

YEAR: 1981

TEAMS (in alphabetical order by league)	YEARBOOK MT/VG-EX	PROGRAM MT/VG-EX
Baltimore Orioles	2.00/1.25*	1.00/.60
Boston Red Sox	2.50/1.50	1.00/.60
California Angels	2.00/1.25*	1.00/.60
Chicago White Sox	2.00/1.25*	.80/.50
Cleveland Indians	2.00/1.25*	.80/.50
Detroit Tigers	2.50/1.50	1.00/.60
Kansas City Royals	2.00/1.25*	1.00/.60
Milwaukee Brewers	2.00/1.25*	1.00/.60
Minnesota Twins	2.50/1.50	1.00/.60
New York Yankees	3.00/2.50	1.00/.60
Oakland A's	2.00/1.25*	1.00/.60
Seattle Mariners	2.00/1.25*	.80/.50
Texas Rangers	2.50/1.50	.80/.50
Toronto Blue Jays	2.50/1.50	1.00/.60
Atlanta Braves	2.50/1.50	.80/.50
Chicago Cubs	2.00/1.25*	.88/.50
Cincinnati Reds	2.50/1.50	1.00/.60
Houston Astros	2.00/1.25*	1.00/.60
Los Angeles Dodgers	2.50/1.50	.80/.50
Montreal Expos	2.00/1.25*	1.00/.60
New York Mets	2.50/1.50	.80/.50
Philadelphia Phillies	2.50/1.50	.80/.50
Pittsburgh Pirates	2.50/1.50	.80/.50
San Diego Padres	2.50/1.50	.80/.50
San Francisco Giants	2.50/1.50	.80/.50
St. Louis Cardinals	2.00/1.25*	.80/.50

WORLD SERIES MEMORABILIA

	AMERICAN LEAGUE MT/VG-EX	NATIONAL LEAGUE MT/VG-EX
World Series Program:	3.00/ 2.00	3.00/ 2.00
World Series Press Pin:	25.00/16.00	25.00/16.00
Commemorative Bat:	60.00/40.00	60.00/40.00
Ticket Stub:	2.00/ 1.25	2.00/ 1.25
Teams and Games Won:	New York 2	Los Angeles 4
Championship Series:	EAST	WEST
A.L. Home Program:	2.50/ 1.50	2.50/ 1.50
N.L. Home Program:	2.50/ 1.50	2.50/ 1.50

ALL-STAR MEMORABILIA

	MT/VG-EX
All-Star Program:	3.00/ 2.00
All-Star Press Pin:	20.00/13.00
Commemorative Bat:	100.00/70.00
Ticket Stub:	2.00/ 1.25
Location:	Cleveland (AL)